Sociology

Sociology

Experiencing Changing Societies

Fifth Edition

Economy Version

Kenneth C. W. Kammeyer
The University of Maryland

George Ritzer
The University of Maryland

Norman R. Yetman
The University of Kansas

ALLYN AND BACON

Boston London Toronto Sydney Tokyo Singapore

Previous editions were published under the title *Sociology: Experiencing a Changing
Society*, copyright 1987, 1982, 1979 by Allyn and Bacon.

Library of Congress Cataloging-in-Publication Data

Kammeyer, Kenneth C. W.
    Sociology, experiencing changing societies / Kenneth C. W. Kammeyer,
George Ritzer, Norman R. Yetman.—5th ed., economy version.
        p. cm.
    Includes bibliographical references and index.
    ISBN 0-205-13578-1
    1. Sociology.   2. Social change.   3. United States—Social
conditions.   I. Ritzer, George.   II. Yetman, Norman R.,
    III. Title.
    HM51.K27   1992
    301—dc20   91-33295
                                                            CIP

Series Editor: Karen Hanson
Series Editorial Assistant: Laura Lynch
Production Administrator: Marjorie Payne
Editorial-Production Service: Raeia Maes
Composition Buyer: Linda Cox
Manufacturing Buyer: Megan Cochran
Cover Administrator: Linda Dickinson
Cover Designer: Suzanne Harbison

A NOTE FROM THE PUBLISHER
This book is printed on recycled, acid-free paper.

Printed in the United States of America

10 9 8 7 6 5 4 3 2 1   97 96 95 94 93 92

CONTENTS

PREFACE

Since the publication of the fourth edition of this book, the onrush of world events has been breathtaking. The most monumental of these changes have been the end of the Cold War and the breakup of the Soviet Union, but there have been many others as well. The United States entered a war, Operation Desert Storm, in the Persian Gulf and achieved, with its allies, a smashing military victory only to learn once again that wars create as many problems as they solve. We have written this edition with our eye on these rapidly changing events because we believe sociology is at its best when it helps us to understand the continuing events in our society and in the world.

Many sociological lessons can be learned from events of the day. The Persian Gulf war introduced large numbers of American military personnel, and Americans generally, to Arab and Muslim cultures. Perhaps for the first time in their lives, military men and women who served in Saudi Arabia, Kuwait, and Iraq saw how important culture, a fundamental concern of sociology, is in shaping human behavior. American military personnel were surprised, for example, to learn that women in these cultures (and thus American women too) were not allowed to drive vehicles. The cultural lessons of the Persian Gulf war have been used as examples at several points in the book. Throughout the book we bring in a variety of news events whenever they illuminate or illustrate sociology.

To take full advantage of the learning potential of news events we are introducing a special feature in this edition: "Sociology in the News." In every chapter we present boxed inserts that feature an event that has been in the news and relate it to sociological principles or concepts found in that chapter. "Sociology in the News" is not limited to wars and political upheavals but also covers stories such as the fighting between street gangs in Los Angeles (Chapter 4), the signs of racism in "crack" cocaine laws (Chapter 9), Saturday morning children's television (Chapter 10), the Supreme Court ruling on pregnant women in the workplace (Chapter 13), and the use of power by presidential assistant John Sununu (Chapter 16).

An Annual Edition

In keeping with our view that sociology must both explain and use for illustrative purposes the events of the day, this edition is the first of what will be annual editions of our text. In each new edition we will use the year's major events (and other well-known news stories) to illustrate how sociology can provide insights into, and understanding of, contemporary events. Further, as with this edition, we will use current news items to illustrate sociological concepts and principles.

A further advantage of an annual edition is that we will be able to avoid the datedness that plagues textbooks. So often, only a year or two after publication, text materials are rendered obsolete by new circumstances and conditions. Descriptive data and statistics are also frequently old and out of date in texts that are only two or three years old. With an annual edition, we will be able to provide the most up-to-date statistical data from the United States and other countries, and we will be able to revise those data on a yearly basis.

Cross-national and Cross-cultural Studies

We have retained from the fourth edition our emphasis on cross-national and cross-cultural materials. Cross-national studies provide an important analytic strategy, which was articulated best by Melvin Kohn, former president of the American Sociological Association. Kohn had a particular vision of cross-national studies that specifically focused on testing theory in different societal contexts (see Chapter 2). While not disagreeing with Kohn's view, we are using the term *cross-national studies* more broadly to refer to any sociological studies conducted in contemporary countries other than the United States. Throughout the text we have cross-national boxes that report on sociological studies conducted in one or more contemporary nations other than the United States.

Some chapters have cross-cultural boxes, which follow more closely the anthropological tradition of describing other cultures, including those of small, nonliterate societies. As an example, the cross-cultural box in Chapter 11, The Family, describes polyandry (one woman married to two or more men), a marriage form found in only a few small societies of the world. Other cross-cultural materials are incorporated throughout the text, and especially in Chapter 3, Culture.

Our cross-national and cross-cultural focus does not mean, however, that we neglect the society and culture of the United States. We continue to give major attention to the society that is most familiar, and probably of most concern, to the majority of our readers. We offer a more balanced consideration, however—one that takes American society as a primary focus but also introduces data and analyses of other nations and societies, both contemporary and nonliterate.

Organization

The text is divided into four parts. Part One serves as an introduction to the fundamental ideas of sociology. In the first two chapters, we present key theories and research methods of sociology. The major sociological theories and classical theorists are introduced in Chapter 1 and then referred to when appropriate throughout the text. The chapters that follow introduce the concepts of *culture, interaction, groups, organizations, society, socialization,* and *deviance.* Chapter 4, "Forms of Social Life: Interaction, Groups, Organizations, and Societies," covers small and large units of society.

The final chapter of Part One—Chapter 7, "Sexual Behavior from a Sociological Perspective"—is a unique feature both to this book and to other introductory sociology texts. Here, we turn our attention to sexual behavior, a topic that is inherently interesting to most people. In this featured chapter we show how a sociological perspective can be usefully applied to this universal and fascinating human behavior. Our aim is to use the core sociological concepts presented in the first six chapters to illustrate how these basic sociological ideas can be applied to the study of sexual behavior and, by implication, to any other human behavior.

Part Two is concerned with the basic dimensions of inequality in societies. Again, whenever possible we introduce materials from other societies to supplement examples derived from the United States. Chapter 8 is concerned with socioeconomic stratification. Notable in this chapter is a discussion of the declining middle class, a relatively new social phenomenon not traditionally covered by introductory sociology texts. Chapter 9 explores race and ethnic inequality, and Chapter 10, gender and age stratification and inequality. In these chapters we discuss societal inequalities in Africa, Canada, China, India, and the Soviet Union, along with many other societies.

Part Three describes and analyzes in six chapters the basic institutions of societies—family, education, economy and work, health and medicine, religion, and politics. Once again the illustrative cases come from societies, both modern and preliterate, around the world. Part Four contains two chapters. One combines two societal features that have been especially important in the twentieth century: population growth and urbanization. This chapter presents succinctly an appropriate amount of introductory material on demography and urban sociology. The final chapter, Chapter 18, covers social change, collective behavior, and social movements.

"Connections"

The four "Connections" essays, which appear at the end of each part, are an integrative feature, one that illustrates key sociological concepts and theories within the context of real-world issues. In turn, they discuss the homeless, the fate of Mexicans who work along the United States–Mexico border, the phenomenon of working parents and "latchkey" children, and reproductive technologies such as surrogate parenthood and artificial insemination. After the social issue has been briefly described, the major theories (structural–functional, conflict, symbolic interaction, and social exchange) are applied to various aspects of the topic. How might structural functionalists view the issue of surrogate parenthood as compared to

the way in which symbolic interactionists view the issue? What might social exchange theorists see as the key to understanding the relationship
between the homeless and other members of society? How would conflict
theorists describe the plight of the Mexican *maquila* workers? Each
"Connections" essay closes with a section entitled "Looking at the Research," in which we discuss what sociological research has told us about
the issue, and, often, what additional research is needed. We believe this
innovative and important feature will provide a useful and interesting
break from the chapter-by-chapter pace that is so characteristic of introductory sociology classes.

Pedagogical Aids

At the end of each chapter, Critical Thinking questions challenge you to
probe more deeply into your sociological understanding. The questions
can serve as a springboard for classroom discussion or as home assignments. Each chapter has an introduction designed to draw you into the
subject of the chapter. At the end of each chapter, a summary allows you
to briefly review chapter content. Each major sociological concept is
printed in boldface. A complete glossary of all major terms appears at the
end of the book.

Study Guide.   A Study Guide is also available for this book, which contains: Learning Objectives, chapter outline, key terms and definitions,
key people, and self-tests (25 multiple choice, 20 true/false, 15 fill-in, 5
essay, glossary definitions, and answers to objective questions). Your
bookstore can assist you in ordering this, if your instructor has not done
so already. A computerized study guide is also available.

Acknowledgments

In the course of preparing this edition we have called on a number of
people to give us help, information, materials, and many other kinds of
information. We especially want to thank Bob Antonio, JoAnn DeFiore,
Jean Hendricks, Joan Hermsen, Gladys Martinez, Barbara Meeker,
Louis Mennerick, Mehrangiz Najafizadeh Mennerick, Jeremy Ritzer,
Morris Rosenberg, and Doug Yetman. Among the staff members in the
sociology department we have received help from Dorothy Bowers, Yo-
landa Hagler, Cass O'Toole, Gerry Todd, and Agnes Zane. We especially wish to thank Jeremy Ritzer for constructing the index.

We were encouraged to develop a fifth edition of this text by Karen
Hanson, our editor. She also receives credit for the idea to produce an
annual edition. We want to express our thanks to Karen. Marjorie Payne,
in the Allyn and Bacon offices, was once again a wonderful professional
with whom to work. Raeia Maes did a fine job of seeing the production
process through to the end.

Sociology

1 A Brief Introduction to Sociology

A Definition of Sociology

What is the subject matter of sociology? To put the question somewhat differently, What do sociologists study, analyze, and write about? The answer can be found simply by looking at the front page of any newspaper or by watching any television news broadcast. Newspaper and television stories are about what human beings are doing, sometimes as individuals, but often as groups, as members of organizations, or entire societies.

In the spring of 1991 the entire nation was shocked and disturbed when they saw an amateur videotape of Los Angeles police officers as they repeatedly beat and kicked a man lying on the ground. The tape showed three or four officers striking or kicking the apprehended African American male, even though he was offering no resistance. Other officers were shown watching the brutal attack and making no apparent effort to stop it. This film was shown countless times on television broadcasts and was described and analyzed in virtually every newspaper in the country.

This videotape of police mercilessly kicking and beating a man who was prone on the ground raised many questions about police behavior in particular and human behavior generally. Many of these questions reflect issues that are at the heart of sociology.

One fundamental question is how such a large number of police officers could engage in (or passively watch) such vicious and brutal behavior? If only one police officer (let us say it was a male) had committed such acts, we might explain his behavior on an individual or psychological level (he was a sadist, or he went berserk). But it is unlikely that all of these police officers were psychopaths, or that they all went "crazy" at the same moment. Somehow the explanation must be other than at the individual or psychological level.

Another set of questions relates to the races of those involved. Since the victim was an African American and the police appeared to be white, did race (or relations between the races) play a part in the actions of these police officers? Would these same police officers have used a similar level of violence if the person they apprehended had been white?

Was this an isolated incident of police using excessive violence or did the amateur video operator catch an example of more-or-less routine police behavior? If so, what would cause police to use violence routinely? Is it because people who choose to be police officers are drawn toward an occupation in which violence is likely to be part of the job or is violence something they learn to use after they become police officers?

In the aftermath of the incident, the Chief of Police of Los Angeles came under fire from critics who argued that police violence of this type could occur only if the entire organization was being run in such a way as to condone violence, especially against minority members of the community. That too raises a sociological question about how much an organization can influence the behavior of its members.

The Los Angeles incident also raises questions about the part that violence plays in American society generally. Is ours a society that favors action over inaction as a way of resolving problems, even if it means violence? Before the actual outbreak of the war against Iraq in 1991, one often heard Americans (both military and nonmilitary) voice the sentiment, "Let's go in and do what we have to do and get it over with." Action and war were thus seemingly preferred over the alternatives of inactivity, boredom, and not resolving the problem immediately. As we will see in chapter 3, Culture, there is some evidence that Americans value action over inaction, even if violence is involved.

This single incident of police violence in Los Angeles, and the questions it raises, reveal many of the interests and concerns of sociologists. Sociologists are interested in individual behavior, group behavior, the nature and influence of organizations, and of society. Most important, sociologists generally assume that there is some connection between human behavior and the groups, organizations, and societies of which people are a part. These concerns and assumptions are reflected in the following definition of sociology.

Sociology is the systematic study of:

A. the social behavior of individuals;
B. the workings of social groups, organizations, cultures, and societies; and
C. the influence of social groups, organizations, cultures, and societies on individual and group behavior.

Although some people believe that sociology is concerned only with social groups and societal behavior, the definition above calls attention to the fact that sociologists are also interested in the social behavior of individuals. By using the word *social* to modify behavior, we are simply signalling that sociologists have a special interest in the behavior of individuals as it is influenced by social groupings. The definition shows also that sociologists are interested in the way various kinds of social groupings work, and especially how their workings influence human behavior.

The Different Kinds of Sociologists

Sociology is a wide-ranging way of studying human behavior. While sociologists generally accept the definition offered above, there are many different kinds of sociologists, and their approaches to the field are often very different. From the beginning it is important to understand this feature of sociology. *There is no one sociology; there are many sociologies.* It is therefore fruitless to look for the *real* sociology; it is more realistic to look for the ways in which sociologists and sociologies differ. To show this clearly we will identify in this section some of the most important differences among sociologists, beginning with their specialties and subfields.

Subfield Interests

To illustrate the point that there are many different ways of doing sociology and different types of sociologists, we could reasonably ask of any sociologist, "What kind of sociologist are you?" A sociologist who is asked this question will probably respond by listing his or her specialties, or subfield interests. Specialties or subfields are either some part of human behavior (deviant behavior) or some aspect of social life (political sociology), or ways of studying these things. At leat 50 different speciali-

Table 1–1.   The Major Subfields and Specialties of Sociology

Aging, sociology of, or social gerontology	Mass communication and public opinion
Applied sociology and social policy	Medical sociology
Art and literature, sociology of	Mental health, sociology of
Collective behavior and social movements	Metatheory
	Methodology, qualitative approaches
Comparative or cross-national sociology	Methodology, statistics, and mathematical sociology
Computers and sociology	Military sociology and sociology of war
Criminology and criminal justice	
Cultural sociology	Occupations, work, and professions and industrial sociology
Demography or population studies	
Development or modernization, the sociology of	Political sociology
	Race and ethnicity, sociology of
Deviant behavior and social disorganization	Religion, sociology of
	Rural sociology
Economy and society	Science, sociology of
Education, sociology of	Small groups, sociology of
Emotions, sociology of	Social change
Environmental sociology	Social control
Ethnomethodology/phenomenology	Social psychology
Family and marriage, sociology of	Socialization
Gender, sociology of and women, sociology of	Sociological theory
	Sociology of knowledge
History of social thought	Stratification, mobility and social class
Human ecology	Urban sociology and community sociology
Language, sociology of, and social linguistics	
	World conflict and world systems, sociology of
Law and society	
Leisure, sports and recreation, sociology of	

zations or subfields exist in sociology. Just to give you a flavor of the different kinds of sociological interests, consider the following list: sociology of the elderly and aging, sociology of art and literature, criminology, demography (the study of population), sociology of emotions (a relatively new specialty), medical sociology, military sociology, the sociology of race and ethnic relations, sociology of religion, social psychology, social stratification, and urban sociology. (Table 1–1 provides a more extensive list of sociological specialties.) Obviously, not every subfield of sociology can be represented by a chapter in this book, although most will get some attention. But it will also be obvious that many chapters do represent major subfields of sociology, especially in parts 2, 3, and 4.

Most of these specialties can be further divided into subspecialties, which complicates the picture even more. All family sociologists, for example, study matters relating to marriage and the family, but any particular family sociologist will probably have special interests within this general area. Individual family sociologists can concentrate on the social history of marriage and the family, marriage and the family in different societies, the demography of marriage and the family, family problems (violence and divorce), sexual relations, childrearing, and so on.

Theoretical Preferences

It is possible that, when a sociologist is asked "What kind of sociologist are you?", the answer will reflect the person's theoretical orientation. Later in this chapter we will present four of the major theoretical approaches in sociology today. One is named *symbolic interactionism,* so some sociologists might answer by saying, "I'm a symbolic interactionist." Symbolic interaction theory is one of the basic theories associated with the subfield of social psychology (Rosenberg and Turner, 1990a). You will learn some key features of this theory later, but for now it is enough to know that when a sociologist claims to be a symbolic interactionist it means that he or she attaches a special importance to the words and symbols that people use when they interact with each other (Fine, 1990; Stryker, 1990).

Many sociologists do not limit themselves to one theory. They can see the usefulness and validity of different theoretical approaches, depending on what issue or problem is being studied. In this book we will not limit our discussions to one theoretical approach but will employ different theories as they reflect the field of sociology.

Research Preferences

Some sociologists have sociological identities that reflect their approaches to doing sociological research and scholarship. You have probably often read or heard about the results of surveys (e.g., surveys of how people feel about their work or about religion), so it would probably be fairly clear if a sociologist answered your question by saying, "I'm a survey researcher." It would mean that he or she does the research leading to survey results. In chapter 2 we will introduce major research methods used by sociologists, including a fuller description of what survey researchers do. We will also see that, in addition to surveys, sociologists use a variety of other research procedures to study human behavior.

With respect to research, sociologists can be classified according to whether they prefer quantitative research techniques or whether they favor a more qualitative approach. **Quantitative research** emphasizes numerical measurement and statistical analysis as a way of conducting sociological studies. **Qualitative research** relies more on verbal descriptions and analysis. Sociologists who prefer the quantitative approach often see the natural sciences as a model for sociology. Sociologists who prefer the qualitative approach emphasize that the subject matter of sociology cannot be easily reduced to mathematical formulae and statistical techniques. Although there are strong advocates of both the quantitative and qualitative approaches, many sociologists believe that both approaches are useful. Which approach is preferable at any given time is determined by the nature of the problem under study.

Microscopic Sociology and Macroscopic Sociology

There is another major way that sociologists are differentiated, but usually this distinction is not so much a matter of personal identity. Sociologists can be classified according to the level of analysis that they use in their sociological work (Ritzer, 1991; Wiley, 1988). In the above definition of sociology we mentioned individuals, groups, organizations, cultures, and societies. These are all points along a continuum that extends from the smallest units of sociological analysis, individuals, to the largest units, societies. The smallest units are at the microscopic end of the social continuum; the largest are at the macroscopic end.

The terms *microscopic* and *macroscopic* are borrowed from the physical world, where microscopic objects are the smaller units of nature, e.g., molecules, viruses, and so on. Macroscopic objects of the physical world are the large units such as continents, planets, and galaxies. **Microscopic sociology** refers to the study of the smallest social units, namely, individuals and their thoughts and actions. **Macroscopic sociology** focuses on larger social units such as groups, organizations, cultures, and societies.[1]

Between microscopic social units and macroscopic units there are many different social phenomena, such as families, small groups (bowling teams), large groups (religious congregations), and organizations (the United States Navy). For convenience we can divide the range of social phenomena into the microscopic and macroscopic realms, but we should

---

[1] Sociologists often use the shortened terms, *micro* and *macro,* to refer to these different levels of sociological analyses.

recognize that many social phenomena fall in the middle of the continuum and are difficult to categorize as strictly microscopic or macroscopic.

To sum up the differences among sociologists: first, differences are based on their specialties or subfields, but differences may also exist in their preferred theories or in their ways of doing sociological research and scholarship. Differences are also noticeable in the social levels in which they work. While it is true that differences exist among sociologists, it is necessary at the same time to note that sociologists generally agree about many aspects of their field. We will focus on these fundamental ideas of sociology in the next section.

All of this diversity in sociology may seem a bit overwhelming, but it is important to recognize this diversity at the beginning. Although it may make sociology seem more complex, there is a bright side to the picture, too. Since there are many different parts of sociology (specialties, theories, methods, and levels), a number of things will be especially interesting to you. The truth is that all sociologists have personal preferences. As individual sociologists, we think some specialties are more interesting than others, some theoretical approaches are more significant than others, and some kinds of research and scholarship are more important than others. Some of us prefer to work at the micro level of social life, while others of us prefer the macro level. Throughout this book we invite you to sample the range and diversity of sociology and to discover some, perhaps many, features of sociology that will interest and engage you.

Some Fundamental Ideas of Sociology

Since we have called attention to the variety and diversity of sociological views, it is important to emphasize the points on which almost all sociologists agree. Most agree that the actions and behaviors of humans create social settings and social rules, but that these same settings and rules, in turn, influence the way humans act. This idea is both simple and complex, and it is certainly important enough to consider more fully.

Societies and Other Social Settings Are Humanly Created

The social settings in which people live and the social rules by which they live have all been humanly created. We know, of course, that the customs and practices of our society today are not the same as those of the past. Changes have occurred; those changes have been the products of human actions.

Some examples taken from historical changes in U.S. society may help

Sociology in the News

When Sociologists Make News

Sociologists occasionally make news. They appear on television, are quoted in news stories, or sometimes have feature stories written about their research or writing.

Some sociologists tackle the society's biggest and most pressing problems, with the result that their research and writing deserve and receive national attention. Such is the case, for example, of William Julius Wilson, professor of sociology and public policy at the University of Chicago. Professor Wilson, who served as the president of the American Sociological Association in 1990 and 1991, has devoted much of his sociological career to the study of African Americans in the United States. When Wilson gave his presidential address to the American Sociological Association's annual meeting in 1990, he spoke about the research that needed to be done on the residents of America's inner-city ghettos (Wilson, 1991). Among other things, Wilson discussed the debate that has gone on in recent years, both in academic circles and in the mass media, about the use of the term *underclass* to describe the people who live in urban ghettos.

Sociologist Herbert Gans of Columbia University has argued that when the term *underclass* is applied to all types of poor people, it is little more than a negative stereotype (Gans, 1990). While Wilson had used this term in his earlier studies, he now acknowledges that the word *underclass* carries too much emotional baggage and he will henceforth use the concept *ghetto poor* (Wilson, 1990, p. 6). Reports of Wilson's speech appeared as prominent news, especially in the major newspapers of the country.

While the presidential address at the annual meeting of sociologists is very likely to be reported in the news, especially in the city where the meetings are being held, this is a time when other sociologists also receive media attention. Frequently at these annual August meetings of sociologists, some enterprising news and television reporters appear at the convention location, probably on instructions from their editors to "find an interesting story at the sociology meetings." There are many possibilities to choose from, since an average meeting has several thousand papers, reports, and discussions. Very often reporters under these circumstances seek out papers whose titles are unusual or titillating. Thus the report in the newspaper or on television news will often describe research on topics such as sex, violence, or deviance (e.g., "Is Alcohol Involved in Sexual Assaults?"), and so on. Reporters on such occasions may also seek out titles of papers filled with highly technical or jargonistic terms, terms that are no more than gibberish to a layperson and thus can be used to poke a little good-natured fun at academic types (e.g., "Toward a Postmodern, Postpositivist Model of Metatheory").

In another instance sociologists may be sought out by news reporters as experts on some topic that is in the news. The war against Iraq, for example, brought many U.S. military women into combatlike situations. Military sociologists, especially those who were experts on women in the military, were often interviewed for their knowledge of and views on women in combat.

Any new societal trend—decreasing divorce, increasing crime, more minorities going to college, increases in the number of immigrants—will have news reporters seeking out sociologists who can "explain" or interpret these trends. Sociologists in these instances usually give a spontaneous response, and reporters selectively use the statements that fit their story line.

Sometimes sociologists make news (or are well known), not because of their sociological research, but for some other reason. For example, many Americans know the name Andrew M. Greeley, but not as a sociologist. His name is familiar to the many millions who read his novels, such as *The Cardinal Sins*, *Lord of the Dance*, *Ascent into Hell*, *God Game*, *The Final Planet*, *Angel Fire*, and *Love Song*. Greeley's novels are usually associated in some way with the Roman Catholic Church and the clergy, for he is also an ordained Roman Catholic priest (Greeley, 1990). Although this prolific writer of fiction continues to do research and publish sociological books and articles, his fame (some would say his notoriety) is more likely to come from his novels and, if he achieves his ambition, movie screenplays (Greeley, 1990).

GANS, HERBERT J. "So Much for the 'Underclass'?" *The Washington Post*, Sept. 10, 1990.
GREELEY, ANDREW M. "The Crooked Lines of God." In Bennett M. Berger (ed.), *Authors of Their Own Lives*. Berkeley, CA: University of California Press, 1990.
WILSON, WILLIAM JULIUS. "Studying Inner-City Social Dislocations: The Challenge of Public Agenda Research." *American Sociological Review* 56, 1991.

us to see how, over time, social institutions can be changed by human actions. Women in the United States (as we will see more fully in chapter 10) were not considered qualified to vote by the men who wrote the Constitution. After more than a century of effort by many women and some men, women in the United States did achieve the right to vote. A parallel example is the case of African Americans, who were also not given voting rights by the white males who wrote the Constitution. Only after the great upheaval of the Civil War were African American males (at least in principle) given the right to vote.

The family in the United States also provides many examples of how our institutions have changed as the result of human actions. There was a time in the not too distant past when husbands were automatically assumed to be the heads of their households and, as such, controlled the economic resources of the family. Historically, under English common law, a husband acquired ownership and control of his wife's property at the time of marriage. When a woman was employed under these conditions, her husband was deemed to be in control of her wages (Weitzman, 1981). In the last few decades, largely through the efforts of feminists, these aspects of the family have changed.

Another example of changes in the family through human action comes in the case of child custody after divorce. In the first half of the nineteenth century in the United States, when a couple with children divorced, the custody of children was routinely given to the father. By the middle 1800s significant changes began to occur. For example, if a child at the time of a divorce was still nursing at its mother's breast, the court might allow the child to remain with the mother. Later, however, when the child was weaned, he or she was usually returned to the father. As time went on, the courts began to give custody to the mother, even though a child might be well beyond infancy. By the 1920s, mothers were given child custody in almost every divorce case.

In the last two decades, however, more and more people have questioned the assumption that mothers should always have sole custody. Many judges and courts are no longer presuming that mothers will have custody of all minor children. Today, in a small percentage of cases, custody is shared between mothers and fathers, and in some cases fathers are awarded sole custody (Ahrons and Rodgers, 1987; Luepnitz, 1982; Roman and Haddad, 1978).

All of these changes in the political and familial institutions occurred because of human actions. Some of these actions were dramatic and historic, and others were more gradual, but all were the result of human actions.

The general sociological point is that, every day, people affirm or challenge the society in which they live. Through their affirmations they keep the society as it is; through their challenges they often modify and change the society. Whenever modifications and changes are made, resistance usually arises from those who benefit from the existing social arrangements. Sociology is concerned with the way individuals affirm and maintain their societies or challenge and change them.

Social Influences on Human Behavior

A second fundamental view of sociology is that social settings (groups, organizations, cultures, and societies) influence and constrain human behavior. If we think of a newborn baby, for example, we have a human being who is apparently little more than a bundle of unrestrained reflexes. As the baby matures his or her character and general attitudes are molded by other human beings. In the early years of life, parents are usually most important in teaching the child the basic attitudes, values, and skills needed to survive in the social world. Later, teachers, friends, and others, along with the mass media, will shape the way a person behaves and thinks about all things, large and small.

Even as adults we are constantly being affected by social influences. Consider such everyday concerns as clothing and hair styles. At first a new style may not appeal to us. A new length of skirt or hair, or new clothing fashions, may seem odd and unattractive, and we vow not to change. But soon we see more and more people with the new styles and fashions, and perhaps someone comments that our own tastes are out of date. When this occurs, most of us change our preferences. Once we are wearing the shorter (or longer) skirt, longer (or shorter) hair, or new fashions, these styles come to feel natural and right because the social influences around us, from our closest friends to the mass media, have changed us.

Changes are not limited to the superficial level of styles and fashions. Our attitudes, beliefs, and behaviors about the most fundamental things of life—morality, politics, religion, work, entertainment—are also changed. Throughout our lives we are changed and modified as we enter different stages of life, different levels of education, new occupations, new communities, and new times.

Throughout this book we will see examples of how a wide range of social influences shapes people's lives. Yet even though we, as sociologists, are primarily concerned with the way human behavior is shaped by social influences, we should always remember, also, that individuals influence and modify the social groups and even the cultures and societies in which they live.

How Can Sociology Be Useful to You?

Since you are just beginning your first course in sociology, we want to tell you about the benefits you may derive from your study of sociology, even if this introductory course is the only one you ever take. Other benefits, such as jobs and careers in sociology, can be attained only if you go on to take other work and perhaps even advanced degrees (a masters or doctorate) in sociology. But let us begin with what you may gain from this course alone.

Facts and Information

Most sociologists are fond of accumulating and relating facts and information about social behavior and the society in which we live (as well as other societies). They have a special preference for facts that are not widely known. Even better are facts that run contrary to popular beliefs. Therefore, both in this book and in your class, you will learn a few things about human behavior that you did not know before. Suppose you were presented with the following statements and asked whether you believed them to be true. What would you say?

- At the beginning of this century Americans married at an early age, often in their teens.
- The rate of suicide is higher among teenagers than any other age group in the society.
- Most elderly people in the United States are poor; most live below the poverty level.
- Most Americans of Mexican descent are farm workers.
- Only 8 percent of Mexican Americans in the labor force are in farming, forestry, and fishing *combined*. Nearly 11 percent of Mexican Americans in the labor force are in managerial and professional occupations. (U.S. Bureau of the Census, 1990, p. 379.)

What is your reaction to these statements? Are they true or false? Every one of those statements is *false,* though they are widely believed to be true. The facts are:

- At the beginning of the twentieth century, men were about 26 years old at the time of their first marriages; women were about 22 years old. Perhaps it is surprising that these ages are similar to the ages at which men and women marry today (Kammeyer, 1987).
- In the United States the rate of suicide among 15- to 19-year-olds is *lower* than the suicide rate for people in every older age group (U.S. Bureau of the Census, 1990, p. 87). The suicide rate for people over 65 years is more than twice that for 15- to 19-year-olds.
- Most of the United States' elderly population (aged 65 and over) does *not* live in poverty. Among those people aged 65 and over, according to the current definitions of poverty, 12.1 percent are below the poverty level. This percentage is less than the national average, which is 13.1 percent. The percentage of children under sixteen living in poverty is 20.4 percent (U.S. Bureau of the Census, 1990, p. 460).

The facts about marriage age, suicide, occupations, poverty, and the labor force activities of Mexican Americans are statistical facts. Because statistical facts are fairly easy to obtain (often in government publications) the truth or falsity of such statements can be easily checked (although it is generally recognized that even statistical facts can sometimes be misleading). While sociologists try to document their statements of fact with statistics or research results, some statements of fact, including many in this book, are based on other kinds of data and observations. In chapter 2 we will describe the different research methods used by sociologists to establish social facts. Throughout this book you will be introduced to a wide range of social facts acquired by sociological research and analysis.

Knowledge and Awareness of Other Societies

Sociologists have always had a great interest in societies other than their own. Early sociologists were especially intrigued by the work of anthropologists (and others) who described remote societies and their cultures—often small, non-Western societies with unusual and exotic customs. It was both fascinating and instructive to learn how differently societies could be organized, and how much the beliefs and values of people could differ from one society to another.

Sociologists today continue to be interested in the small nonliterate societies, because there are still lessons to be learned and insights to be gained from such cases. The reports and descriptions of these and other distinct cultures have traditionally been called **cross-cultural studies,** and throughout this book we will be using them frequently to highlight or illustrate sociological points.

Today an even greater need exists for sociologists to understand other societies around the world. No longer are nations and societies on the other side of the earth simply regarded as unusual and exotic places with no relevance for our personal lives. Travel and commerce among all nations of the earth are now commonplace. For sociologists, this means that we are now able to obtain information, both quantitative and qualitative, from nations previously closed to sociological scrutiny. We must know about other societies, not just because they are sociologically instructive, but because we live in an interdependent global society.

In contemporary life it is just as important for Americans to learn, for example, about the Japanese education and economic systems as it is to know about their own. Americans whose military duty recently took them to the Persian Gulf, especially those who spent time in Saudi Arabia, needed immediate instruction on many aspects of Arabian culture. (This case will be discussed more fully in chapter 3, Culture.) Because of the importance of knowing about other societies we have purposely illustrated many sociological issues with examples from other nations around the world. These examples will, of course, supplement the many examples coming from U.S. society.

Many times the examples of sociological issues in other societies and cultures will be in boxes. These boxes will be of two types: *Cross-Cultural Perspectives* will reflect the more traditional anthropological studies of small, non-Western societies; *Cross-National Perspectives* will present research or analysis coming from one or more contemporary nations.

An Understanding of Human Behavior and Societal Life

As human beings we are always trying to understand ourselves, the people around us, and the events occurring in our society (or the world). To return to the example of Los Angeles police violence, no thinking person could watch the videotape of those actions without searching for some kind of explanation. One of the implicit promises of sociology is that it will offer some insights into human behavior and societal life that will improve your understanding of issues such as these. Furthermore, the insights offered by sociology are not limited to any specific case, but should be useful to you far beyond the questions of the day. You should be able to use sociological insights for problems and issues of the future, ones that we may not even be able to imagine now.

Throughout this book you will be introduced to many different sociological concepts (the technical terms of sociology). It is necessary in sociology, just as it is in economics or biology or physics, to learn the vocabulary of the field. We will alert you to the most important sociological concepts by providing a definition immediately after the concept is printed in boldface. These terms will also be defined fully at the end of the book. We believe that you will often find many of the terms and concepts applicable and useful, long after you have finished this course. For example, in chapter 13—The Economy and Work—you will learn about **role conflict.** One type of role conflict occurs when two or more people are expecting you to do different and conflicting things. Role conflict occurs mostly in the workplace, but it can occur in other areas of life as well (e.g., in your family life). This sociological concept and many others will prove to be useful throughout life.

In addition to concepts, we will also introduce you to a number of sociological theories. As we present and apply these theories we will show you how they can be useful tools for understanding current issues and problems. But equally important, these theories will provide the basis for understanding many issues and problems that will appear long after you have finished this college course in sociology. The usefulness of sociological theories is parallel to the way in which the theoretical principles of economics, biology, or physics can help you understand particular problems that you encounter in the economic, biological, or physical worlds. Thus, one of the important benefits of studying sociology is the general applicability of sociological theories to your personal and social worlds, in both the present and future.

To begin, then, we will use the final section of this chapter to introduce you to the historical beginnings of sociology and to some of the major scholars who have shaped the field. We will close by presenting the major sociological theories that currently prevail.

The Beginnings of Sociology

No precise date can be given for the founding of sociology, but its beginnings date back to the early 1800s. General agreement prevails that the work of the French scholar Auguste Comte (1798–1857) gave sociology its name and an identity that eventually led to its status as a scholarly discipline. Of course, long before the term *sociology* was coined there were intellectuals, philosophers, and religious leaders who made observations about the nature of human behavior and human society. A brief look at the ideas of the nineteenth-century scholars who formed this distinctive new field of study will add to our understanding of sociology. We will begin with the founder of sociology, Auguste Comte (Ritzer, 1992a).

Auguste Comte

Like many scholars of the nineteenth century Auguste Comte was influenced by the rapid changes occurring in European societies. During the years of Comte's young adulthood, French society had continued to experience repercussions from the French Revolution, which had started in 1789. The Revolution had brought about a considerable amount of chaos and disorder in France, and Comte viewed these developments negatively. Although Comte knew that a return to pre-Revolutionary conditions was impossible, he was looking for a way to bring greater order and tranquility to French society.

Comte thought that order could be restored if it were possible to understand more fully the way in which society worked. The fact that he lived in an age when the scientific approach had proved useful for understanding the physical world prompted Comte to put his faith in science. He rejected theological and philosophical approaches and concluded that the scientific approach was the way to achieve a better understanding of

Cross-National Perspectives

Sociology in China

Sociology in China dates back to the beginning of the twentieth century, when Chinese scholars who had studied in Europe and the United States returned to their homeland with the ideas of this new field. Through the early decades of this century the Chinese scholars translated into Chinese a number of the classic American and European sociological studies, including Durkheim's *Division of Labor*. Through the first fifty years of the twentieth century, Chinese sociology grew steadily. Chinese sociologists were interested in both sociological theory and sociological research. The Chinese had a special interest in the study of social problems such as poverty, overpopulation, problems of rural life, and social welfare. In this respect, Chinese sociology had many of the same interests as American sociology.

However, things changed dramatically after the Communists came to power in 1949. Within a few years sociology departments in Chinese universities were being closed, and soon sociology had disappeared completely.

There were several reasons why the study of sociology was banned in China. First, in the early years of the revolution the Soviet Union was taken as a model by the Chinese. Since sociology was insignificant in the Soviet Union, the Chinese concluded that it was unimportant for them also. Second, the Chinese believed that Marxian theory could take the place of conventional Western sociology (as late as the 1950s Marxian theory was not strongly represented in American sociology). Third, the Chinese decided that their revolution would solve existing social problems, therefore, sociological studies were not needed. Fourth, sociology was thought to be a *pseudoscience* that opponents of communism might use to attack the Communist party.

In 1957 a few Chinese sociologists tried to mount a defense of sociology, but they were severely criticized and seen as part of a right-wing conspiracy. The result was the complete disappearance of organized sociology in China. The only remnants of sociology during these years were the few sociologists who continued to work in academic settings, but as members of other academic departments such as history.

Chinese sociologists, like many other academics and intellectuals, suffered greatly during the Cultural Revolution of the 1960s. It was during this period that professors in many disciplines were forced out of universities and into the countryside, where they were made to do manual labor on farms.

However, with the death of Mao Zedong and the defeat of his allies, the country moved in a more liberal direction. In 1979, a symposium was held in which the president of the Chinese Academy of Social Sciences announced that sociology had been "rehabilitated." The next day the Chinese Sociological Association was founded. However, those who sought to rebuild sociology faced a difficult task since almost all work in the field had been discontinued in 1952. Almost three decades of sociological development throughout the world was unknown in China. Most of the sociologists who practiced in 1952 were either dead or too old to begin learning all the new developments in the field. Young people who were gravitating toward sociology faced a shortage of well-trained faculty, facilities, and written materials.

Through most of the 1980s, Chinese sociology made dramatic strides. A number of foreign universities developed formal and informal arrangements with Chinese universities. Foreign sociologists were routinely brought to China to teach and do research. Many foreign works in sociology, both classic and contemporary, were translated into Chinese. Most important, many Chinese students began studying sociology abroad, especially in the United States, and this promised to create in China a whole new crop of professors who were knowledgeable about the latest developments throughout the world. Finally, native Chinese sociologists were creating their own distinctive brand of theory and sociological research.

However, the brutal crushing of the democratic movement in May, 1989, has led to another round of setbacks for sociology in China. Steps have been taken to reduce enrollments in sociology programs. Efforts are being made to minimize the influence of Western sociological ideas on students. Research is being pointed in the direction of emphasizing the positive side of the Chinese social system. There is a movement to develop a socialist sociology, heavily infused with Marxian theory, that has distinctive Chinese characteristics. The fate of Chinese sociology throughout the remainder of the 1990s is clearly tied to the future of China's political system.

HANLIN, LI, FANG MING, WANG YING, SUN BINGYAO, and QI WANG. "Chinese Sociology, 1898–1986," *Social Forces* 65, 1987.

society. The appeal that the physical sciences had for Comte is revealed in the fact that he first called this new science of society *social physics*. Later, because that label had already been used by a Belgian scholar named Quetelet, Comte changed the name to sociology (Lazarsfeld, 1961).

Comte's work is important primarily because it advanced the idea that there could be (and should be) a science of society. He gave sociology a position among the other sciences of his time, and although it required the work of later scholars to solidify that position, Comte's pioneering effort deserves recognition. Also important in Comte's work is the idea that, as a science, sociology could solve social problems such as war, revolution, crime, and poverty. This idea continues to be a significant feature of sociology today.

As we move beyond the work of Comte and the beginnings of sociology, we encounter several major figures who either shaped the development of sociology as an academic discipline or had a major impact on the field. We will briefly examine their contributions to contemporary sociology, beginning with Emile Durkheim (Ritzer, 1992a).

Emile Durkheim

After Comte, no sociologist worked more diligently to give sociology a place among the established scholarly disciplines than the French scholar Emile Durkheim (1858–1917). In the scholarly and intellectual communities of Europe in the late nineteenth and early twentieth centuries, sociology was by no means completely accepted. Durkheim made it a personal crusade to advance sociology and sociological explanations of human behavior.

Durkheim often wrote in an argumentative style in which he first rejected nonsocial explanations of human behavior, especially those based on biological or psychological reasoning. He used this approach in one of his major works, *Suicide* (Durkheim, 1897/1951), in which he sought to demonstrate the importance of social factors in explaining what seemed to be distinctively individual behavior. Even today our normal first reaction to a report of suicide is to try to understand and explain this event in individual, usually psychological, terms. Durkheim, however, demonstrated that the social contexts in which people live can explain variations in the frequency of suicide. For example, he collected and analyzed statistical data on suicide rates in various European countries, and found that suicide rates went up during periods of social upheaval and change. He reasoned that, during times of revolution, war, or economic depression, the conventional rules of conduct would be in flux and, therefore, unclear. Durkheim called this societal condition *anomie*. **Anomie** literally means normlessness; it refers to situations in which individuals are uncertain about the norms of society. Suicide rates that go up during times of social upheaval (and thus presumed normlessness) illustrate what Durkheim called anomic suicide. Durkheim went on to identify other societal conditions that also led, in different ways, to variations in suicide rates.

Durkheim's analysis of suicide is considered by many sociologists an excellent demonstration of the science of sociology. One reason that his work is considered exemplary is his use of suicide statistics that allowed him to do his analyses and report his findings in a quantitative form. The statistical analysis of social data has become a prominent feature of sociology. The second reason for holding up Durkheim's work on suicide as a sociological ideal is that he used social factors (in this case, societal conditions) to explain individual behavior. Durkheim demonstrated a basic sociological premise, which is that human behavior can be explained in social terms.

Max Weber

The German sociologist Max Weber[2] (1864–1920), like Durkheim, saw problems in the way European societies were changing (Ritzer, 1992a). The key change, according to Weber, was the increase of rationality as the basis of human behavior. **Rationality** is a form of human action in which goals and objectives are set, and then achieved in the most efficient way possible. The choice of a behavior is based on how quickly and easily it will allow a person to reach a chosen goal or objective. Weber believed that, over the course of several centuries, the Western world had come to emphasize rationality so completely that it dominated every aspect of modern social life. Although rationality has obvious benefits, Weber also considered it a negative development in human societies. Furthermore, he believed that the trend toward an ever-greater emphasis on rationality would continue. For Weber, the problems of the modern world, with its emphasis on rationality, were like an "iron cage" from which there was no hope of escape (Mitzman, 1969).

We can illustrate Weber's concern with an example that will be familiar to anyone who has gone through the American educational system. Most large high schools and many colleges and universities are based to some degree on the principles of rationality. That is, they are set up to process the largest number of students (to give them an "education") in

---

[2] Sociologists use the German pronunciation for Weber, which is roughly *Vay-ber*.

the most efficient way possible. Often American college students receive their educations in large, mass-production-like classes. By assembling large numbers of students in a single lecture class, using multiple-choice or other objective examinations (often machine graded), only a relatively small amount of time will be required from one professor. Hundreds of students can earn credit for a course with a minimum of professorial effort. The emphasis on efficiency in systems of mass education is highlighted by comparing mass education with the undergraduate education in an elite British school, where a student may spend hours in discussion with a professor and where a personal relationship often develops between teacher and student. A mass education system makes it almost impossible for college professors to know more than a few of their many students personally. And the students usually know their professors in only a most superficial and impersonal way.

The most visible symbol of rationality and efficiency to Weber (and to many Americans) was the bureaucracy. A large university, of the type just described, is one type of bureaucracy, but many other organizations are equally familiar examples. In a bureaucracy, the standards of rationality and efficiency reign supreme; work is carefully divided into simple precise steps and made routine. The emphasis is only on speed and efficiency, with little regard for whether the work is meaningful for individual workers. We will examine bureaucracies more in chapter 4, where we will note, as did Weber, that although it is easy to criticize the bureaucracy, many tasks can be accomplished with precision, speed, and continuity within a bureaucratic organization (Weber in Gerth and Mills, 1958, p. 214).

Karl Marx

The German-born social philosopher and social analyst Karl Marx (1818–1883) has a somewhat different place in sociology's history than has either Durkheim or Weber (Ritzer, 1992a). Although he lived and did much of his writing before either of them, and therefore influenced the work of both, Marx was not a part of any effort to establish sociology as an academic or scholarly discipline. Marx was not a sociologist and did not consider himself to be one. He was an analyst and a critic of society, and as such, he and his ideas have had a profound effect on contemporary sociology.

Through his ideas, Marx has also had a significant impact on the events of world history—an influence that continues to the present. For Marx, as is well known, was not only an analyst of society; he was also a political activist. He believed that his ideas about society should play a part in solving the problems that he identified. It is important to recognize and keep in mind the distinction between Marx as the social theorist and Marx as the political activist. His social theories are the part of his work that make important contributions to current sociology.

When Marx examined the societies of his time, he was struck by the inequities that prevailed between the masses of people who were at the bottom of the society and those who were at the top. In societies that had a capitalist/industrial form of economic organization, the workers—the **proletariat**—sold their labor to the owners of the means of production. The owners of the means of production were the **capitalists,** the social class that owned the raw materials, the factories, the machines, and the equipment. Marx saw the relationship between the capitalists and the proletariat as one of struggle and conflict. The capitalists had the advantage in this struggle because they controlled not only the means of production but also the ideas, the values, and information that prevailed in society.

While Marxian theory is highly complex, especially in the interpretations of contemporary Marxian scholars, Marx's view of society is still one that emphasizes the struggle between those who have power and those who do not. In particular, Marxian theory points out that power often resides primarily in the hands of those who have economic dominance in a society. Throughout this book, but especially in our consideration of social stratification systems (chapter 8), we will see the pervasive importance of this Marxian insight—how those who control economic resources have a special ability to influence, and be the beneficiaries of, educational systems, health care and medical systems, and many other advantages of the society. For this reason, any societal analysis that employs a Marxian perspective is likely to look first at the economic system, and especially at the class structure.

In the next section we will see that a general sociological theory, called **conflict theory,** is built on the principle that social groups and societies are composed of units that are often engaged in some kind of struggle for power. Thus, conflict theory can be identified as a direct descendant of Marxian theory.

To a lesser degree some of the other pioneers of sociology have a connection with contemporary sociological theories. Durkheim, with his emphasis on the importance of social factors and the structure of society, was a forerunner of structural-functional theory, which will also be discussed below. Weber, in much of his work, emphasized the importance of ideas in shaping the direction and nature of societies. This emphasis is closely connected with some of the fundamental features of symbolic interaction theory, which will be discussed next.

Sociological Theories

A **theory** is a set of ideas that provides explanations for a broad range of phenomena. By extension, **sociological theories** are those that explain a wide range of human behavior and a variety of social and societal events. A sociological theory designates those parts of the social world that are especially important, and offers ideas about how the social world works. Every sociological theory has special words or terms that are unique to that theory.

Certain sociological theories are related to the microscopic level of sociological analysis. These theories are not inevitably bound to the microscopic level, but sociologists concerned with the behavior, actions, and interactions of individuals tend to use them. Two of these theories are symbolic interactionism and social exchange theory.

Symbolic Interactionism

As the name implies, **symbolic interactionism** deals primarily with the interaction between individuals at the symbolic level (Rosenberg and Turner, 1990; Stryker, 1990). **Symbols** are the words, gestures, and objects that communicate meaning between people. In any given society, people share a common understanding of these symbols. Words are the most important symbols from a symbolic interactionist viewpoint. If someone were to walk into the room where you are reading and shout "Fire!" no further description or detail would be necessary. That single word would convey the message that something significant is burning, and is possibly dangerous to you. Of course, the expression on the person's face might also convey a message, and we have learned to read messages in the faces, hands, and bodies of other people. If a friend were to describe the actions of another person and simultaneously roll his or her eyes skyward, you would understand that the friend is saying something like, "Can you believe that?" That facial gesture might not be understood by people from another society; however, it is a symbol that we have learned to interpret in a particular way.

Spoken and written words, as well as facial and bodily gestures, are important for symbolic interactionists. Human beings have an exceptional, and perhaps unique, ability to use words, and people make connections with other people through these words, or symbols. Infants and children acquire many of their early words from family members, especially parents. By the age of seven years, an average child has command of 8000 words (Pfeiffer, 1985) but the first words they learn are the symbols for observable, concrete things, such as *mama, daddy, mouth, nose, cat,* and *ball.* Gradually, children learn more abstract symbols—symbols that indicate not just things but evaluations as well (e.g., naughty puppy, pretty kitty, dirty garbage). Obviously, most of the evaluations that children learn are those held by family members, especially parents. Parents and other family members are referred to as **significant others** because their views have such a great influence on young children. Later in life, friends, schoolmates, marriage partners, fellow workers, religious and political leaders, and others will also be significant others.

In the process of learning language and symbols, children learn evaluations of themselves, just as they learn evaluations of other objects. In the same way that parents might convey the idea that "garbage is dirty," they might also convey the idea that "Doug is a good boy" when he plays nicely with his baby sister. It is through this process of learning symbols about themselves that children develop what symbolic interactionists call a **self concept,** that is, an individual's thoughts or feelings about himself/herself. (Rosenberg, 1979, 1990). Symbolic interactionism is, therefore, a theory that has something to say about how individuals think about themselves and thus how they act as individual human beings.

But symbolic interactionists also stress that the symbols people learn govern their responses to all other human beings and things. If someone were to show us a painting and say it was by Pablo Picasso, we would probably be in awe. We would probably respond as much to the name Picasso (a symbol) as to the painting itself. This example also illustrates how most members of any given society share a wide variety of symbols. The commonality of shared symbols at any given time gives symbolic interactionism a macroscopic dimension, as well as its predominant microscopic focus (Fine, 1990).

In summary, symbolic interactionists pay special attention to the symbols individuals use to interpret and define themselves, the actions of other people, and all other things and events. By understanding the meanings that people give to these things through the use of words and symbols, it is possible to understand much of human behavior.

Social Exchange Theory

A second important sociological theory is one favored by a substantial number of sociologists interested in individual behavior and especially in the interaction between individuals (or in some cases between groups). **Social exchange theory** (often simply called *exchange theory*) emphasizes that the motivations for human behavior are to be found in its costs and rewards. Every human action is seen as having some cost, and therefore, if carried out, it must have a reward. On the other hand, if an action is costly but unrewarded in some way, the individual will not likely repeat it (Blau, 1964; Cook et al., 1990; Ekeh, 1974; Homans, 1973).

As a simple example of the principles of social exchange theory, suppose you were to see an elderly man, with his arms full of packages, struggling to open a door. You might take the time to help him, even though you are in a hurry. The cost of your action is your time and energy. Your reward might be the thanks of the man, or perhaps the smiles of other people who were passing by and saw how helpful you had been. According to exchange theory principles, you would more likely aid the next person who needs help because you received a reward for your actions. On the other hand, if the elderly man were to tell you, "Stop interfering and mind your own business!" you would probably have felt punished for your action, and you would not be as likely to repeat it in a similar circumstance.

Social exchange theory principles—that people are likely to behave in ways that have been rewarding in the past and not to behave in ways that have been costly or painful—are thought by exchange theorists to explain most of human behavior and much interaction between people. Thus, for example, two young people dating will continue to see each other as long as each person is getting adequate rewards from the continuing interaction. It should be noted that the rewards can be anything that either of the two individuals finds of value, including gifts, opportunities for entertainment, the admiration of one's friends, an escape from boredom, the feeling that one is loved, sexual pleasure, and so on. When one person (or both) feels that there are more costs (e.g., time, effort, energy) than rewards coming from the relationship, then, according to social exchange theory, the relationship will probably end.

A key concept of social exchange theory is reciprocity. **Reciprocity** is the socially accepted idea that if you give something to someone, that person must give something of equal or near equal value in return (Gouldner, 1960). If a fellow student asks you for your class notes or solutions to some problems the night before an exam, and you give them, you will normally expect that person to give you something in return. Once again, what you receive in return need not be the same thing. Your fellow student may give you some concert tickets, invite you to a party, or simply tell other people what a generous and smart person you are. If you do not feel you have received an adequate reward (reciprocity), you are likely to feel slighted, and you will probably not be as generous if you are asked again.

The rules of reciprocity can be found at many levels of social life. We try to give people gifts that are similar in value to the ones they give to us; married couples try to entertain their friends in about the same way as they expect to be, or have been, entertained; friendly nations try to maintain a balance in their trading relations with imports roughly equal to exports. When there are violations of the principle of reciprocity, with one side returning less than it is receiving, relations between individuals, groups, or nations are apt to become strained. Too great a violation of reciprocity may result in anger and hostility and a breaking off of the relationship.

Although social exchange theory might have some applicability to the level of groups and societies, it is most often applied at the micro level of individuals. We will turn now to two theories that apply primarily to the macro level (groups, organizations, cultures, and societies): structural-functionalism and conflict theory.

Structural-Functional Theory

Structural-functional theory, often called *functional theory* or *functionalism,* emphasizes that every pattern of activity (that is, every structure) in a society makes some positive or negative contribution to that society (Abrahamson, 1978; Turner and Maryanski, 1979; Alexander and Colomy, 1990; Ritzer, 1992b). The two key words of structural-functional theory are *structure* and *function*. The term *structure* is used in this case as shorthand for social structure, which is a very basic sociological concept. A **social structure** is a regular pattern of social interaction or persistent social relationships. Examples of social structures include the socioeconomic status system of a society (the social class structure will be considered fully in chapter 8), the patterned social relationships between races and ethnic groups (chapter 9), or the patterns of family organization (chapter 11). These and other patterned social relationships are the structural features of a society.

Structural-functionalists are interested in why certain structures exist in a society and especially what purpose, or function, they serve. A **function,** according to structural-functionalists, is a positive purpose or consequence—one necessary for the continued existence of a society (or some other social system). With regard to the family system in a society, the functions might include producing children, caring for them when they are young, and training them in the ways of the society. If a society does not have a fairly persistent structure for producing new members, caring for them, and socializing them, the society is not likely to survive.

Early structural-functional theorists believed that every structure of a society had a function—that is, made a positive contribution to the continuation of the society (Malinowski, 1925/1955). Modern-day functionalists still look for the positive contributions that various structures provide, but they also emphasize that some structures are detrimental to the survival of the society. When a social structure has a detrimental effect or consequence for the existence or well-being of a society it is said to be **dysfunctional.**

To illustrate a possible dysfunction we consider again the example of marriage and family systems that produce children for the society. Throughout most of human history the death rates for infants and children were extremely high. In addition, many mothers died in pregnancy and childbirth. As a consequence, most societies developed marriage and family systems that encouraged people to have children, as many as they could. A marriage and family system that could produce many children under high-death-rate conditions was probably functional for most societies. However, in the twentieth century, the infant, childhood, and maternal death rates were greatly reduced in many countries. Nonetheless, the marriage and family structures continued to produce large numbers of children, who, consequently, had to be cared for and fed. The marriage and family system that had previously been functional was now viewed by many observers to be dysfunctional. The large numbers of children were seen as a threat to the survival of the society.

Structural-functionalists are also inclined to compare the obvious functions of social structures with the less obvious functions. The **manifest function** is the intended and well-recognized purpose of some social structure. The less obvious, unanticipated, or unexpected purpose of a social structure is called a **latent function.** To illustrate, we may ask the question, "Why do we have organized crime in the United States?" At the level of manifest function, the purpose of organized crime is for criminals to make money from illicit activities. But what is the latent function, the function that is less obvious? To answer this question we must look for the less obvious, unanticipated, or unexpected consequences of organized crime.

Functional theorists would ask if organized crime serves a purpose for someone other than the criminals, or for the society as a whole. For starters, organized crime is allegedly involved in providing illegal drugs, prostitution, and gambling. The users of these "services" are generally involved in an illegal activity, but many think of themselves as "law-abiding." (Most people who bet illegally on sports events consider this activity a part of everyday life.) Organized crime is also said to distribute most of the pornography in the society—again, a "service" that many citizens are willing to pay for without asking too many questions. But what of those of us who have no need for drugs, or prostitutes, or pornography, or gambling? We, too, may benefit from the services of organized crime. Newspaper reports claim that organized criminal groups have systematically engaged in buying gasoline without paying high federal taxes. The gasoline is then sold to independent retailers who, in turn, may pass the savings on to us, the gasoline consumers. Other reports state that organized crime is engaged in the toxic-waste-disposal business. When legitimate companies want to dispose of their toxic wastes they may contract with organized criminals who will agree to do the job cheaply because they will dispose of the toxic wastes in any way possible—legal or illegal. Thus, they "provide a service" by disposing of toxic wastes at a low cost. Of course, in the long run the effect of dumping toxic wastes in places where they will create health hazards will be dysfunctional to the society.

This functionalist analysis of organized crime helps to answer the otherwise perplexing question: "Why does organized crime persist in our society, even though most members of government, most law enforcement agencies and agents, as well as most citizens claim to want it stopped?" The answer is that organized crime, viewed as a structural feature of our society, provides a variety of services that are wanted and used by the rest of the society. It is in this sense that organized crime (as a structure) is functional.

The final major theory, conflict theory, also applies primarily to macroscopic analysis, that is, the analysis of larger social units such as social groups, social organizations, and societies.

Conflict Theory

In our discussion of Karl Marx we noted that his work sensitized sociologists to the fact that, in any kind of social group or system, from families to entire societies, inequities exist in the amount of power and resources held by the participants. Furthermore, these power and resource inequities are likely to persist over time. As we saw earlier, Marx believed that in a capitalist society the holders of the means of production are likely to have a persistent edge over the workers. Conflict theory is an extension of this idea, and thus as a general theory it emphasizes that in any social group, social organization, or society, certain positions (or statuses) are endowed with greater power than other positions or statuses. The incumbents of these positions, those with greater power and resources and those with less, are, according to conflict theory, engaged in a more or less continuous struggle. Those who have greater power and resources do not give them up voluntarily, and therefore those with less power and fewer resources try to wrest those resources from those who hold them (Collins, 1990; Coser, 1956; Dahrendorf, 1959; Ritzer, 1992b).

As an example of how conflict theory can be applied, we turn again to the family. Even though we usually think of the family as a highly cooperative social unit, one where feelings of love and affection exist between the members, the principles of conflict theory are clearly applicable (Collins, 1971; Scanzoni, 1972). In our society (and in most others) two family statuses almost always have more power and control more resources: adults (compared to children and adolescents) and males (compared to females). The adult male in the family is therefore usually able to exercise power over other members of the family, which means that he can make other family members do (or not do) what he wants.

A simple, and probably familiar, example of the way the family members who are in the subordinate status struggle to get more power is found in the relations between adolescent children and their parents. Until adolescence the power of parents over their children is usually unquestioned by both parties. However, adolescence in our society is often a period of considerable conflict between parents and their children because the adolescents are striving to have a greater voice in deciding what they can and cannot do. A 16-year-old or 17-year-old is likely to want greater freedom and independence than parents are willing to give. Outright conflict sometimes results, but disobedience and subversion are more commonly the tactics of adolescents as they push for greater personal autonomy.

If there are conflicts and struggles for power in the family (and we have said nothing about husbands and wives), then clearly the same is apt to be true of other social groups, social organizations, and societies. Conflict theory can also be useful for the analysis of sororities and fraternities, schools, religious organizations, majority/minority relations, the politics of nations, and, of course, the relations between nations. In later chapters many examples will be provided of the inequities between those who have power and resources and those who do not, as well as descriptions of the conflict that ensues when the group with less power and fewer resources struggles for greater equity.

Summary

Sociology is the study of human behavior, in all its many forms. There is no single sociology, however; there are many sociologies. Sociological specialties or subfields focus on some part of human behavior and/or some aspect of social life. Sociologists have different theoretical preferences, research preferences, and levels of analysis (microscopic or macroscopic).

Although sociologists differ on a number of issues, they generally share some fundamental ideas and views. One is that societies and other social settings are humanly created. Every day, people affirm and modify their social settings, but these same social settings, in turn, influence and constrain human behavior.

Sociology can be useful in a number of ways. It provides a wide range of statistical and substantive facts about social conditions and trends. Sociology also provides an awareness and knowledge of cross-cultural and cross-national information. Through sociological concepts and theories, sociology can aid in understanding many issues and problems beyond the subject immediately under study.

The beginnings of sociology can be dated to the early 1800s, when the work of Auguste Comte gave sociology its name and its place among other scholarly disciplines. Among the other pioneers of sociology, the most famous are Emile Durkheim and Max Weber. Karl Marx was an early analyst and critic of society whose ideas have had a profound effect on contemporary sociology.

There are four contemporary theories that dominate sociology. Symbolic interaction theory is oriented toward the interaction between individuals, especially at the symbolic level. The symbols that individuals learn through interaction govern their responses to other human beings, to things, and to themselves. Social exchange theory emphasizes the fact that the motivations for human behavior are found in the costs and rewards of human actions. Humans will continue actions and interactions that are rewarded, and will discontinue those that are not. Structural-functional theory focuses on macroscopic levels of analysis and emphasizes that every pattern of activity (structure) in a society makes some kind of positive or negative contribution to that society. Structural-functional theory also calls attention to less obvious functions of social structures; these are called *latent functions.* Conflict theory, which is an extension of some basic Marxian ideas, emphasizes that, in any social group, social organization, or society, positions of unequal power probably exist. The struggle for power is a source of conflict in these social groupings.

Appendix: Occupations and Careers That Use Sociology

In this first chapter you have been given a brief introduction to the field of sociology, but the emphasis has been mostly on the nature of sociology—its fundamental principles, its founders, and its major theories. You have seen that sociology can be useful to you, primarily through the facts and principles you will be learning. Little, however, has been said about the more practical applications of sociology, especially the occupational and career opportunities sociology offers, although there have been some hints about sociological jobs and careers in our discussions of some individual sociologists. In this brief appendix we will focus more directly on how the study of sociology can lead to occupations or careers.

What you might be able to do with training in sociology depends greatly on the degree or degrees you earn. With an undergraduate degree in sociology you can pursue a number of fields of advanced study. A bachelor's degree in sociology can be a basis for careers in social work, law, education, journalism, social policy, and other professional pursuits. The training that is part of a typical undergraduate degree program in sociology can also be useful for going directly into positions in government, research, marketing and sales, and human resources (personnel work). In addition, the skills learned in social research methods (see chapter 2) and statistical data analysis are skills often sought by businesses, research organizations, national and state associations and interest groups, and governmental agencies at all levels.

If you continue beyond the bachelor's degree and earn an advanced degree in sociology (master's or doctorate) the range of opportunities includes all those listed above as well as the role of professional sociologist. The most common career for professional sociologists is teaching, generally at the college level, from community and junior colleges to the largest and most prestigious universities. Some college teaching positions at the community and junior-college level may be held with a master's degree, but the Ph.D. degree is increasingly required for positions at any college beyond the two-year level.

More and more nonteaching jobs have become available for those with advanced degrees in sociology, especially for those with doctorates. Holders of these advanced degrees are often highly trained in research, data analysis, and in the analysis of organizational and governmental policies. Governmental agencies employ sociologists to carry out surveys and analyze data. Prominent federal agencies with sociologists on their staffs include the National Institutes of Health, the Census Bureau, the Civil Rights Commission, the National Science Foundation, and many others. Private organizations and businesses also hire sociologists who have been trained to design and carry out social research and policy analysis. Sociologists are employed by radio and television broadcasting companies, insurance companies, advertising agencies, and other businesses that must have valid information on public needs and interests.

Even though you may not go on to a career in sociology, it is our hope that you will take something useful from this introduction to the field. No matter what kind of work setting you enter, you can be assured that many of the principles and ideas presented in this book will be applicable and perhaps more relevant and useful than you can even imagine at this point.

CRITICAL THINKING

1. What types of subjects might interest sociologists? List three to five topics that might be the subject of a sociological study.
2. Compare and contrast the advantages and disadvantages of qualitative and quantitative research.
3. Suppose a sociologist wanted to study education in the United States. What would be the focus of a microscopic study of education? What would be the subject of a macroscopic study?
4. Which groups in society have a vested interest in keeping the existing social arrangements in place? Which groups in society are likely to promote change?
5. Give examples from your own life that show how social settings have influenced or constrained your behavior.
6. In what ways is a knowledge of sociology useful to you in your personal or professional lives? Generate a list of issues or questions for which sociological research might prove useful.
7. Describe and compare the major contributions made to the field of sociology by Comte, Durkheim, Weber, and Marx.
8. Give examples of important symbols on your college campus.
9. Assume the beliefs of a social exchange theory sociologist. How would the idea of reciprocity apply to your relationship with your parents?
10. Give a brief explanation of how conflict theory might apply to union and management relations in the United States.

2 Sociological Research

Jennifer Hunt describes an incident that occurred when she was riding in a police cruiser in a large city:

> One evening I was patrolling with a male officer when we observed people pouring out of a bar. A man then yelled, "You better get in here quick. There's a helluva fight going on!" The officer ran out of the car while I grabbed the radio and requested a backup. . . . When I entered the door, I looked to my left and noticed a man sitting at the bar. He looked relatively harmless . . . most of the action was occurring at the far end of the room. People were yelling and crying. Three wounded suspects were all armed with knives. The police officer seemed to be pointing his gun in three different directions. When I approached the rookie officer, I grabbed an hysterical waitress reaching for a knife that she had apparently dropped on a stool. Meanwhile the rookie disarmed one man while the other voluntarily discarded his weapon (Hunt, 1984, p. 290).

If Jennifer Hunt had been a regular police officer this incident would not have been extraordinary. But Jennifer was not, and is not, a police officer. She is a sociologist, and she was riding in the police cruiser to collect data for her doctoral dissertation. Her method of doing research is one that has a long history in sociology; it involves the researcher directly in the lives and activities of the people being studied. The researcher, then, is both a participant and an observer, and the research method is called *participant observation*. This research method will be discussed later in the chapter. (Some of the findings of Jennifer Hunt's research will also help to explain police violence of the type described at the beginning of chapter 1. See chapter 5, p. 155.)

Of course, very few sociologists are called upon to face dangerous citizens armed with knives when they do their research. In fact, many sociologists today carry out major sociological studies without coming into direct contact with people at all. There is some irony in such a situation because many people who become sociologists are initially attracted to the field through their interest in people and in human behavior. Yet it is only a slight exaggeration to say that significant sociological research is now possible without leaving the computer terminal. The information for such studies is obtained by others (often by skilled interviewers) and transferred to computer disks and tapes, where it is stored until needed.

These two different sociological research methods show again the diversity of sociology. In this chapter we explore the different ways of doing sociology by introducing and illustrating the most important research methods being used by sociologists today. But first we consider some of the underlying ideas that guide most sociological research. We begin with a brief look at what it means to use a scientific approach to study human behavior and social life.

A Scientific Approach to Knowledge

Most sociologists assume that human behavior can be studied by using a scientific approach. In today's world we are accustomed to having the results of scientific research for most major questions and issues we encounter. Certainly it is true of the physical world. We rely upon scientific studies to inform us about holes in the ozone layer that surrounds the earth and the dangers that such holes present. We look for scientific information about how the AIDS (acquired immune deficiency syndrome) virus is spread from one person to another because that information could help us make decisions about our own behavior. And, because most of us believe it is important to have scientific knowledge about the physical and biological worlds, we also expect to have scientific knowledge about our social and psychological worlds.

Although the scientific approach to understanding human behavior and the social world is widely accepted, studying humans is not quite the same as studying insects, the weather, or atomic particles. We therefore need to consider some of the basic elements of the scientific approach, but at the same time consider how the scientific approach must be modified to fit the subject matter of sociology.

Empirical Observation

One word that is critical for understanding the essence of a scientific approach is **empiricism,** which is the act of experiencing something with one's senses. Empiricism contrasts sharply with imagination and speculation, even though these two activities are also important parts of the scientific approach. We can imagine how some aspect of the social world will be, but we will not know what it is really like until we make some observations, or obtain information, either directly or indirectly.

Objectivity and Sociological Research

The central importance of empiricism in science leads directly to a consideration of a second feature of the scientific method—objectivity. **Objectivity** in science means, in general terms, that scientists conduct their research in such a way that their personal, subjective views do not influence the results of their research. This general statement may seem an easy rule to follow, but, for sociologists, objectivity poses some special problems.

Objectivity has two dimensions. Objectivity is first an attitude of the scientist who must try to keep his or her personal views, beliefs, and values from influencing either the conduct or the conclusions of the research. The second dimension of objectivity is the use of research procedures described in sufficient detail so that other scientists may, if they choose, repeat (or replicate) a study. The attitudinal dimension of objectivity is much more difficult to achieve and maintain than is the procedural dimension, and we will deal with that first.

Objectivity as an Attitude.   Scientists are expected to be objective about the subjects of their research. However, in everyday experience, scientists in all fields find it difficult to remain "value free." All scientists have personal views, attitudes, and values that could potentially affect the selection of particular problems for study, the conduct of the research, and the interpretation of the results.

In sociology, as well as in other social and behavioral sciences, special problems occur with this aspect of objectivity. Sociology often deals with issues, questions, and problems that are personally important in the lives of the sociologists conducting the research. Consider, for example, the issue of the death penalty for major crimes. One sociologist might be personally in favor of the death penalty, while another might be opposed. Will they likely ask the same research questions and carry out the same research? In an ideal world these two scientists with different views would not allow those views to influence the planning and execution of their research. However, in the real world these scientists might ask different research questions and reach different conclusions.

While some sociologists argue that all sociologists must be objective and value free at all times, others hold a more realistic view. This more realistic view acknowledges that sociologists have personal values, and, at least in some stages of their professional research, they may be allowed to use these values to influence their selection of issues and the types of questions they ask. For example, a sociologist might support the idea that women have a right to enter and succeed in occupations that have been previously male dominated. Such a sociologist could design a study to learn if women entering male-dominated occupations are treated and evaluated fairly. But, for validity, the study would have to be done fairly and the results reported honestly.

Attitudinal objectivity requires scientists to maintain an attitude of fairness and honesty when planning and conducting their research. Researchers cannot intentionally design their studies in such a way that the results will be predetermined to support their views. They cannot design the questions or measures in such a way as to influence the outcome of the research. They certainly cannot interpret their results in a biased or dishonest manner in order to obtain the results they desire. An objective attitude must be rigorously maintained in the conduct of research, or one of the fundamental elements of science is sacrificed.

Objectivity as a Procedure. **Procedural objectivity** refers to the performing and reporting of all research tasks in such a way that any interested person will know exactly how the research was conducted. The research procedure cannot include any methods of observation that other qualified scientists are unable to repeat. For example, if an astronomer claimed to have heard a message from intelligent beings coming from outer space but then asserted: "The messages can only be heard on my recording instruments, and no one else may use my instruments," such a report, no matter how interesting, could not be accepted by other scientists or, for that matter, by the public. To be scientific, the methods of observation must be reported in such a way that other scientists will be able to use those same methods. Only then can other scientists verify or reject the results of the original research.

Although this standard is widely accepted by scientists and the public alike for the natural and biological sciences, a tendency exists to hold the social sciences to a less rigorous standard. But the standards of scientific inquiry should be uniformly applied. If, for example, a sociologist were to report that a "sample of 200 adults completed a questionnaire" and then reported the results of the research without providing any additional information about the sample, we should be skeptical about the report. As a minimum requirement, any interested person should be able to ask for information as to where and how the sample was selected.

Sociological researchers must also report, or be prepared to provide more details about, the specific questions asked in interviews or on questionnaires. If questions have been combined in certain ways so as to create general measures, these steps would also have to be described. Finally, any statistical procedures used to analyze the data must be reported.

Some sociological research methods do not involve samples, questionnaires, or statistical analyses but rather involve the observation of individuals or groups in natural social settings. With these methods the precise research procedures are often more difficult to document, but the researchers are nonetheless obligated to provide full reports of their methods if they are to measure up to the standards of procedural objectivity.

Ethical Issues of Social Research

When sociologists carry out research projects they may cause problems for, or even do harm to, the people they study. This possibility makes it necessary for sociologists to consider the ethical implications of their research. The basic question that any social researcher must ask is: If I carry out this research, will it harm the participants or other people in some way? There are several types of potentially harmful or negative consequences that may come from social research.

Physical Harm

Although relatively rare, it is possible that a researcher's actions can cause physical harm to the people being studied. As an example, a social psychologist named Muzafer Sherif once conducted a field experiment with 12-year-old boys at a summer camp, and the final stages of the experiment had to be curtailed because the boys were in danger of being seriously hurt (Sherif, 1953). In this study the boys were divided into two groups, and then, through the manipulations of the researchers, the groups were brought into competition and conflict. For a number of days the conflict was limited to apple-throwing fights and to raids on each other's cabins, but in a final severe confrontation in the dining hall the two groups of boys faced off and the situation became dangerous. Some of the boys started to throw silverware and plates. The researchers quickly stepped in and stopped the hostilities (and that phase of the field experiment).

One of the objectives of Sherif's study was to observe how competition between groups could lead to conflict and then to learn about reducing conflict between those groups. Although that goal is surely desirable, it may have been outweighed in this case by the possible dangers to the subjects of the study.

Psychological Harm

The actions of a social researcher could possibly cause psychological harm as well, although anticipating when and how this might occur is often difficult. Researchers today frequently ask respondents about sensitive and personal issues, including questions about alcohol use, criminal acts, heterosexual or homosexual experiences, child or spouse abuse, deaths of relatives, mental illness, physical handicaps, and so on. For most people questions on these and similar subjects will not likely cause any psychological distress, but the possibility always exists that some respondents will suffer psychological harm. An example comes from a study of psychological depression in which interviewers asked subjects about an array of life's tragedies and about their symptoms of mental illness. The trained interviewers who conducted the pretest interviews reported that some of the interviewees were showing clear signs of depression after being questioned about these topics. The research directors became concerned that their interview was actually *causing depression*. Before the study could continue, the questions were broadened to include some more positive and "upbeat" topics (Converse and Presser, 1986).

Intrusions into Private Lives

Sometimes sociologists collect information on the private (even secret) lives of individuals and thereby raise ethical questions about the research. Sociologists occasionally study people whose behavior is immoral, improper, or illegal; when they do, the information they obtain could be damaging to the people being studied. The now-classic example of this type of research (and the ethical problems it raises) is a study of the homosexual activities of men in public restrooms (Humphreys, 1975). In order to study these men, Humphreys posed as a "watch-queen," a lookout who signals those engaged in homosexual acts that a stranger, or worse, a police officer, is approaching. Only a few of the men he studied knew that he was a sociological researcher. Although Humphreys took great care to disguise and protect the identity of the men he studied, a number of sociologists believed that, by deceiving the men under study, he was violating the ethical standards of social research. Humphreys subsequently reported that if he were to repeat the study he would spend more time "cultivating and expanding the [number] of willing respondents . . ." (Humphreys, 1975, pp. 229–231).

The Humphreys study is an extreme example of a concern that nearly every social researcher must have when collecting research data: How much must the researcher tell the respondents about the nature of a study in order to get their cooperation?

Sociologist Terry Williams experienced similar ethical problems when he studied cocaine users in "after-hours" clubs in New York City (Williams, 1989). Williams generally tried to pose as a normal customer in these establishments, but, because he would not use cocaine even when it was offered to him, the owners and other customers often became suspicious of him. (On at least one occasion he was openly confronted about being an undercover police officer.) But the ethical dimension of Williams's research was that he was routinely observing the sale, purchase, and use of cocaine, all of which were illegal acts. On one occasion, after his research was completed, Williams testified as an expert witness at a trial and was asked to name a man who had helped him in his research. The man was a major heroin and cocaine dealer, so when William refused to name him he was held in contempt of court by a federal judge. He was not remanded to jail, however, and eventually he was able to convince the court that his notes and contacts were anonymous and immune from prosecution (Williams, 1989, p. 30).

Both Humphreys's and Williams's studies raise serious questions about the rights and responsibilities of researchers when they study illegal or immoral acts. Can researchers collect information as a part of their research if this information may someday be harmful to the people studied? Do they always have an obligation to identify themselves as researchers and explain the purpose of their research? These questions reflect the ethical questions that arise to some degree in many kinds of sociological research.

Today most sociological research is conducted under rules of "informed consent," which means that, when people are asked to participate, they are told in a general way about the nature and purpose of the study and of any sensitive or dangerous aspects of the study. Of course, it must be clear that participation in the study is voluntary, and that the identities of participants will remain confidential. Most sociologists agree that, although it is sometimes inconvenient to go through the informed-consent procedures (and occasionally a study is changed or impeded because of them), it is better to err on the side of safety and to avoid problems of questionable ethics.

Research Questions and Hypotheses

All research starts with a question, but the questions may come from very different sources. Sociologists may study a question because it reflects a long tradition in sociology, or because it reflects a current societal development, or simply because it has a special importance in their personal lives.

As an example of a long sociological tradition there is the work of Emile Durkheim, some of whose ideas were introduced in chapter 1. As you will recall, Durkheim studied the ways in which suicide is related to social conditions. (Anomie, or normlessness, was one such condition.) Durkheim also speculated (or theorized) that social integration would be related to suicide. He defined **social integration** as belonging to, or being a part of, social groups or the society. Using data from various nineteenth-century European countries, Durkheim found that the more socially integrated segments of populations had lower suicide rates. Married people, for example, were presumed to be more socially integrated because of marriage and family ties, and married people had lower rates of suicide (Durkheim, 1897/1951).

Durkheim's theoretical insight—that the level of social integration can influence social behavior—has continued to stimulate research and analysis among present-day sociologists (Zimmerman, 1991). Studies still show that social integration, as represented by marriage, reduces suicide (Breault, 1986). Studies of the relationship between suicide and divorce are also built on Durkheim's ideas. Those who are divorced will probably have lower social integration than those who are married and thus will have higher suicide rates. Research in the United States (Stack, 1990a), Canada (Trovato, 1987), and Denmark (Stack, 1990b) supports the Durkheimian idea that being socially integrated through marriage puts one in less jeopardy of suicide than if one is divorced.

Durkheim's basic idea about the importance of social integration has also been employed in an explanation of divorce itself. For example, divorce rates in the United States are higher in areas where there are more recent migrants in the population. Recent migrants are likely to be less socially integrated and thus may contribute to the higher divorce rates in areas where they live (Glenn and Supancic, 1984; Glenn and Shelton, 1985).

These research results supporting Durkheim's theory of social integration can lead to other research hypotheses. An *hypothesis* is a statement about how various phenomena are expected to be related to each other. Since social integration (or the lack of it) has been found to be related to both suicide and divorce, other, new hypotheses may be suggested. A researcher might hypothesize that violence in the family (wife abuse, child abuse, elder abuse) would occur more often among families with low levels of social integration. The research literature on child abuse lends some support to this hypothesis, because it has been found that when parents are more isolated (few friends, little contact with other relatives) they are more likely to abuse their children (Garbarino and Sherman, 1980).

Theoretical Concepts and Research Variables

A theoretical idea such as social integration is called a concept. A **concept** is a word or phrase that summarizes some meaningful part of the social world. An important part of social research consists of translating key concepts into observable phenomena. For example, to translate the concept of social integration into an observable phenomenon, Durkheim used the percentage of the population that was married. Of course, being married is not the only indication of social integration. One could also get an indication of the social integration level of individuals by asking how many friends they have or how much time they spend with family members. These observable phenomena are called **indicators**—in this case, indicators of the degree to which people are socially integrated.

When concepts are observed through the use of indicators, researchers often refer to the indicators as variables. **Variables** are defined as objects or phenomena that can change from one size, state, or degree to another. Levels of social integration are variable because some people, or some groups, are more socially integrated than others.

Independent and Dependent Variables

Social researchers divide variables into two basic classes: independent variables and dependent variables. **Independent variables** are those that are thought to produce a change in some other variable. Durkheim expected, on the basis of his theory, that the independent variable, social integration, would produce changes in suicide rates, the dependent variable. **Dependent variables** are those that are changed or influenced by independent variables. In everyday terms, independent variables are the presumed *causes* of changes; they produce *effects* on dependent variables.

A researcher who wants to test the hypothesis that a low level of social integration will produce higher levels of child abuse would call social integration the independent variable and child abuse the dependent variable.

We have reviewed some of the basic elements of scientific research and turn now to the major research methods used in sociology. As we consider these research methods, further illustrations and elaborations will be given of the principles and processes already introduced.

Major Sociological Research Methods

Experiments

Experiments are typically set up in such a way that the independent variable is under the control of the researcher and its impact on a dependent variable can be observed directly. Such experiments are ideally suited for assessing causality (Brown and Melamed, 1990). A hypothetical experiment will reveal some of the important elements of social experiments.

Sociologists are often interested in how education and instruction can change the attitudes of individuals. For example, let us suppose that a community wants to change the attitudes of high school students about drinking alcohol and driving. A film is made showing how the use of alcohol contributes to automobile accidents and may cause serious injuries to young people. At the local high school, all seniors are given a questionnaire, called a pretest measurement, that will measure the students' attitudes toward drinking and driving. The **pretest measurement** is the measurement of the dependent variable (in this example, attitudes toward drinking and driving) before the introduction of the experimental variable (the film).

Shortly after the pretest measurement, the seniors are divided into two groups by some procedure that gives every student an equal chance of being selected for the experimental group (drawing names, for example, until half are selected and half remain). This technique, called *random selection,* is necessary to assure that all important characteristics of the students are distributed in the groups and that the two groups are as much alike as possible (Cook and Campbell, 1979).

After the two groups have been randomly selected, one group, the experimental group, is shown the film on alcohol-related accidents and injuries. An **experimental group** is made up of the subjects who are exposed to the experimental variable, the film. (The film can also be thought of as the independent variable, since it may produce a change in the attitudes of the students.) In an experiment, exposure to the experimental variable is often called the **experimental treatment.** The other group of students, called the control group, will not be given the experimental treatment (will not be shown the film). A **control group** in an experiment is made up of subjects who are not exposed to the experimental variable. Shortly after the film has been shown to the experimental group, the attitudes of the students in both the experimental and control groups are measured again. This is called a **posttest measurement.** If the film has had an impact on the students' attitudes about drinking and driving, the students in the experimental group will have changed their attitudes, while the attitudes of the students in the control group will have remained relatively unchanged.

The experiment in this illustration—conducted in a normal school environment and involving the relatively normal activities of seeing a film and filling out questionnaires—is a field experiment. **Field experiments** are conducted in settings that are natural and involve activities that are relatively normal.

Sometimes sociologists conduct experiments under much more controlled conditions. These are called **laboratory experiments** because they are conducted in specially designed rooms that are equipped with one-way mirrors, audio systems, and video recording equipment. In a typical laboratory experiment, subjects are brought into a room or laboratory and asked to engage in some activity or task (solve a problem, judge or evaluate something). The experimenter will usually administer an experimental treatment to some of the subjects but not to others (who serve as the control group). The effects of the experimental treatment are then measured in some way.

The laboratory experiment has the advantage of giving the researcher close control over experimental variables, but it is a research method that sees only limited use in sociology. Even in social psychology, the subfield of sociology where experiments have been used most, the experiment is not often used. In the words of two sociologists who are social psychologists, ". . . the experimental method remains the strongest model of scientific proof in science. Its chief limitation, from the [sociological] perspective is that it is poorly adapted to deal with many of the substantive questions of interest to sociologists." (Rosenberg and Turner, 1990, p. xi.)

Further, laboratory experiments are often highly artificial, unnatural, and contrived. Subjects are often asked to do tasks in the laboratory that they would not be likely to do in real life. Therefore, the results of laboratory experiments may be questioned for their applicability to real-life situations.

A distinction is often made between applied and basic research. **Applied research** is research designed and conducted to answer a specific practical question or to solve a particular social problem. **Basic research** tests hypotheses derived from theories, such as the test of Durkheim's social integration hypothesis discussed earlier. Applied research can be done with surveys and other research methods, but field experiments are often used to evaluate and assess the effectiveness of social programs or to test the desirability of proposed government policies that are designed to solve some social problem (Saxe and Fine, 1981).

Applied Research: A Field Experiment Example.   Sherman and Berk (1984) used a field experiment to evaluate different police methods for dealing with domestic disturbances. Domestic disturbances are disputes and violence between family members that are sufficiently serious for the police to be called to the residence. When police arrive at scenes of domestic violence, they may take one of several courses of action. They may try negotiating or otherwise "talking out" the dispute, they may ask one of the parties to leave, or they may make an arrest.

In Minneapolis, a field experiment was conducted to see which of three different police responses was most effective in reducing the recurrence of violence committed by the same suspects. When called to a residence where domestic violence of a misdemeanor[1] nature had occurred, the police were to take one of the following actions: (1) arrest the alleged offender; (2) separate the offender from the person who was attacked or threatened by making the offender leave the residence; (3) give some form of advice, counseling, or mediation. The action to be taken by the police in any given case was determined randomly through a color-coded pad of report forms. The color of the top sheet determined the officer's action. If, for example, the top sheet were blue, the officer would arrest the offender; if it were yellow, the officer would offer advice and counseling.

Conducting this field experiment required both the cooperation of the Minneapolis police department and careful supervision by the research team who took a number of precautions and made cross-checks to see that the police handled cases in the way called for by the experimental design. This experiment had no control group, since the objective was to determine which of the three alternative police responses would be most effective in deterring future violence. Each response was an experimental treatment, and its effects could be compared to the effects of the other two treatments.

Two methods were used to establish which treatments were most ef-

---

[1] A misdemeanor is a crime less serious than a felony; it is punishable by imprisonment for less than a year.

fective: (1) monitoring police records for six months to see if a suspect's name appeared again in a case of domestic violence and (2) interviewing the original victims by telephone over a six-month period to find out if there had been a repeat incident with the same suspect.

The clearest finding of this experimental study was that suspects arrested in domestic violence cases were less likely to be involved in violence at a later date. Specifically, suspects who were arrested and temporarily incarcerated were less likely to appear on police records in the next six months. Also, when interviewed, victims of the original violence were less likely to report a recurrence of the violence (Sherman and Berk, 1984).

The findings of this field experiment have some obvious implications for the way police officers respond to incidents of domestic violence: if the police make arrests and incarcerate individuals who engage in domestic violence, there is less likelihood that the violent behavior will continue. In fact, the implications of this study have not been ignored by the nation's police departments. After these results were publicly announced and published in a sociological journal, many police forces changed their policies with regard to domestic violence. In 1984, only 10 percent of police departments in cities over 100,000 had a policy of arresting suspects in domestic violence cases. In 1986, 43 percent of these same departments had such a policy. Spokespersons acknowledged that the results of the Minneapolis experiment influenced them to change the way they dealt with incidents of domestic violence (Sherman and Cohn, 1989).

Participant Observation

We noted at the beginning of this chapter that, when sociologist Jennifer Hunt collected data by riding in a police cruiser, she was engaged in a research method called participant observation. When sociologists do **participant observation** they make their observations by involving themselves directly in the lives and activities of the people whom they are studying. Participant observers observe what people say and do in the normal course of their regular activities; they talk to the subjects of their study about what they are doing and ask them what they are thinking. Participant observers may engage in informal interviewing by asking a number of subjects the same general questions. They also collect documents and other artifacts, and, most important, participant observers make extensive notes on what they see and hear (Simmons and McCall, 1985).

Participant observation is closely associated with the research method of anthropologists called *ethnography,* or sometimes simply *fieldwork*

(Anderson, 1990; Bernard, 1988). The essence of all of these activities is that the researcher is closely involved with the people being studied.

The degree to which participant observers become involved in the same activities as their subjects can vary greatly from one study to the next. For example, a sociological observer may actually be a member of some group of people (in an office or on an assembly line) and still observe what is happening from a sociological perspective. Sociological observers in these cases are called "insiders" (Burgess, 1984).[2]

One sociologist did participant observation where he was clearly an insider, by studying the hospital where he was confined with tuberculosis (Roth, 1963). Using his sociological training to observe the actions of doctors, staff, and other patients, he kept detailed field notes on conversations, routines, and activities. Even though he was like other patients, he was also acting in his role as a sociologist. After his recovery, he continued doing research by studying other hospitals, but as an "outsider" (Roth, 1963).

A second form of participant observation, more common than that involving true insiders, occurs when sociologists *act as if* they are bona fide members of the setting they are studying. A few people in the setting may be aware that sociological observations are being made, but most participants are not.

When sociologist Douglas Harper (1982) studied the lives of hoboes and tramps, he hitched rides on the railroad freight cars and participated as fully as possible in their way of life. He slept in hobo jungles and camps and shared food and company with those he met there. Although he did occasionally reveal his identity as "a writer and photographer," to most of the people he met in the tramp world he was one of them. By being accepted as a real hobo, he could observe their normal, everyday behavior.

In the third (and by far the most common) form of participant observation, sociologists approach the people to be observed and openly declare their intentions of doing a sociological study. Using this approach, they are clearly recognized as outsiders and, because they are outsiders, the researchers must gain the confidence of those being observed. They do so by involving themselves in the activities of the group so that they will become both familiar and nonthreatening to group members.

Sociologist Gary Fine (1987), who conducted participant observation research among Little League preadolescent boys, has reported how he first obtained permission from the league president to make his observa-

---

[2] Some sociologists prefer to make the distinction between participant observation and nonparticipant observation. Nonparticipant observers are equivalent to what we are calling "outsiders."

tional study. He described his research in general terms, explaining that he wanted to observe the behavior of preadolescent boys as they participated in Little League baseball and in their leisure time. When he was introduced to the coaches, and later to the boys, he made a similar statement. He informed the boys that he might eventually write a book, which gave him credibility and respect. In fact, the boys saw him as a kind of official chronicler and historian of the team, and occasionally asked him if some event were "going to be in the book."

Fine handled the issue of informed consent by telling the coaches that he would not study their teams unless they agreed. The boys were told that they did not have to answer his questions (including a questionnaire he handed out) or have anything to do with him if they did not want to. Each boy was given a letter to take to his parents that explained the central focus of the research; it invited the parents to ask questions, and informed them that if they had any objections he would respect their wishes. (Only two parents objected to the study.)

Sociological observers who are open about the aims and intentions of their research are often helped immeasurably by some members of the group who act as informants and interpreters (Johnson, 1990; Trice, 1970; Wax, 1971). When Fine studied the boys on Little League baseball teams, he soon earned the trust of several boys who became his confidants. They interpreted events for him and alerted him when something special was occurring. On one occasion, a young boy sidled up to him and said, "Moons are shining tonight," which was a signal that several of the boys were at the edge of the baseball park, "mooning" the passing traffic. It was at this point that sociologist Fine knew that he had gained the confidence of the boys.

Studying Police Behavior through Participant Observation. Two studies of police behavior are also examples of participant observation (Hunt, 1984, 1985; Martin, 1982). Both studies were done by female sociologists, a fact of some importance since males and male values tend to predominate in the police world. Despite the obstacles this predominance created, the reported findings of these studies are interesting and sociologically important.

Both Hunt and Martin became interested and involved in studying the police because women had recently been hired to work as patrol officers. Martin did her field work in the Washington, D.C., police department, and Hunt did hers in an unidentified large urban police department. (Hunt had previously spent a year studying New York City police officers.)

When Martin requested permission to do a study of women who had become patrol officers using police department data, the department re-

fused her request. However, she had also applied to join the Police Reserve Corps and was accepted. This status allowed her to wear a uniform
and join regular officers on patrol; it also gave her the access she needed
to carry out her observations. During a nine-month period, Martin went
out in patrol cars as often as three or four times a week. During the last
three months of her study she also conducted interviews with more than
50 patrol officers (28 female and 27 male), and about a dozen higher-
ranking officers. She did her research without specifically informing the
officials in her district that she was conducting a study, an action she later
regretted both for ethical reasons and because it may have limited the
scope of her research.

Several factors made it difficult for Martin to establish rapport with the
officers with whom she went on patrol. First of all, she was not a regular
police officer, only a reserve. The officers in her district soon learned that
she was a college professor, and she did make it a point to tell the officers
with whom she went on patrols that she was doing research. Martin believes that it was difficult to establish open relationships with some police
officers because she was of a different social and educational background
than they. The fact that she was a female in a department that was predominantly male was another problem and, finally, she feels that, because
she was white, her relationships with black officers (both male and female) were inhibited (Martin, 1982, pp. 221–233).

Hunt used a more direct and dramatic approach as she set out to overcome the resistance of the police officers (especially the males) in the department where she did her study. She believes that a participant
observer must change his/her perceived identity from being a person who
is "untrustworthy" to one who is "trustworthy" in the eyes of those
he/she is observing. Many police officers initially regard a researcher as a
"spy" for the police department administration. To avoid that suspicion
she deliberately displayed a defiant attitude and showed mild disrespect
toward some senior police officers.

More important, Hunt behaved in a variety of ways that made the
male officers either respect her or stand in awe of her. She displayed a
"combat personality," occupying herself with guns, judo, and hand-to-
hand combat. She repeatedly asked for patrols in high-crime areas of the
city. She used profanity freely and, by her own description, "acted
crazy." She behaved in unpredictable ways and deviated frequently from
the behavior that male officers expected of a woman. In Hunt's words,
". . . my fieldwork involved the construction of a new category of female
who combined elements of masculinity and femininity . . . . my new identity as 'street-woman-researcher' constituted a trustworthy category of
person in the policemen's eyes" (Hunt, 1984, p. 293).

The participant observation studies of Gary Fine (preadolescent boys) and Jennifer Hunt (police officers) show how individuals' attitudes and behaviors are influenced by their peers. We will examine their research findings on this point in chapter 5—Socialization.

Social Surveys

The research method most strongly associated with sociology is the social survey. A **social survey** is a method of collecting information from a sample of people by means of questionnaires or interviews. **Questionnaires** are written sets of self-administered questions that are delivered to respondents by hand or through the mail. **Interviews** are questions asked by an interviewer or researcher, either in person or on the telephone.

Survey research has two basic objectives: description and explanation. **Descriptive surveys** are designed to obtain some basic information about a population, the simplest being public opinion polls and market surveys. Public opinion polls, now routinely conducted and reported, are familiar parts of contemporary American life. Although such polls are sometimes conducted by sociologists and the results are of interest to sociologists, they are not a primary form of sociological research. The same holds true for marketing surveys, which are usually conducted by organizations specifically set up for the purpose of determining public tastes—for example, television viewing habits.

Sociologists conduct other types of descriptive surveys, often with the objective of identifying typical patterns of behavior or the distribution of attitudes in some population. For example, each year since 1975 the Institute for Social Research at the University of Michigan has conducted a survey among high school seniors in the United States. The reports of these surveys provide descriptive accounts of the life-styles, values, and attitudes of young people in their last year of high school. Among other things, this survey has asked high school seniors since 1975 about their use of marijuana. (The survey is funded in part by the National Institute of Drug Abuse.) Figure 2–1 shows the percentage of high school seniors who reported marijuana use during the preceding year. These data make it clear that marijuana use among high school seniors reached a peak in 1979 (50.8 percent) and has declined since that time. In 1990, the percentage who had used marijuana in the preceding year decreased to 27.1 percent, which is much lower than the 40.0 percent figure for 1975, the first year of the survey (Johnston, et al., 1989; University of Michigan, 1991).

Often descriptive surveys raise questions about the reasons for certain patterns of behavior or about the sources of particular attitudes. We want explanations and answers to our questions. This, then, leads to explana-

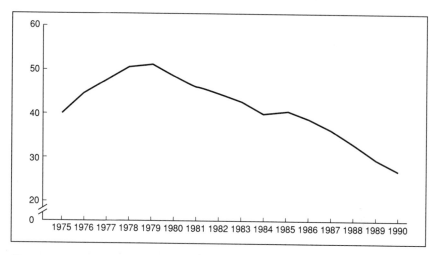

Figure 2–1.   Marijuana Use among High School Seniors, 1975–1990. (*Source:* Johnston et al. 1989; University of Michigan, 1991).

tory surveys. **Explanatory surveys** attempt to find independent variables that will be related to, and possibly account for, differences in behaviors and attitudes (as dependent variables). As an example of an explanatory survey, Bachman (1988) and his associates sought to explain why U.S. high school seniors reduced their use of marijuana after 1979. Using data from 11 classes of high school seniors (from 1976 to 1986), the researchers were able, through statistical analyses, to identify the most likely variables that could explain declines in marijuana use during the 1980s.

One hypothesis was that students used marijuana less because, like the larger society, they became more conservative. One measure of conservatism is religious commitment, which is negatively related to marijuana use: students who are more religious are less likely to use marijuana. However, religious commitment cannot explain declines in marijuana use during the 1980s because religious commitment among high school seniors *decreased* during that decade (Bachman, et al., 1988).

Further analysis revealed that declines in marijuana use during the 1980s were closely associated with changing student attitudes. Through the succeeding classes of high school seniors, students expressed increasing concerns about the *risks* of using marijuana, and they were more likely to *disapprove* of regular marijuana use. These changing attitudes about marijuana provide some explanation for the declines in marijuana use, but, of course, one can still ask why students' attitudes changed. The researchers speculate that changes in the social environment—possibly declines in the approval and use of marijuana among adults—contributed to the changing attitudes of students. As with many explanatory surveys in sociology, these explanations do not have the finality of an experiment, but they are informative.

Samples for Social Surveys. The respondents questioned in social surveys are sometimes loosely referred to as the sample. However, a careful use of this term requires that the people who are questioned be drawn in some random way from a specified population (or universe of people). For example, to draw a **random sample** of the adult population of the United States, researchers would have to use a sampling procedure that would give each adult in the population an equal chance of being selected in the sample. Methods for drawing random samples have been well developed and are used regularly by major survey–research organizations, public-opinion polling organizations, and the federal government.

While random samples are highly desirable, many researchers in sociology use respondents who have not been randomly selected. The resulting sample is called a **convenience sample,** that is, research subjects who are conveniently available to complete questionnaires or respond to interviews. (College classes often serve as convenience samples.) Convenience samples are usually justified on the grounds that the research is exploratory.

Secondary Analysis

When individuals or organizations carry out the costly process of selecting a large sample of respondents, the interviews or questionnaires are usually long, many different types of questions are asked, and they produce more data than any single researcher can analyze. For this reason the data collected in surveys are made available to other investigators. (If federal government funds have been used in the collection of data, they must be made available to other researchers after a specified period of time and at a nominal cost.) For example, the surveys of high school seniors discussed above collected data on 1,300 different variables (Bachman et al., 1987). These data are available in computer-readable form, which allows other researchers to have access to a large data archive at a minimal cost.

When new investigators analyze data sets from the surveys of other researchers it is called **secondary analysis.** These investigators often study issues that are very different from those studied by the original collectors of the data. Of course, in secondary analysis one is limited to the data originally collected, so some compromises are usually required. The advantage of secondary analysis is that it is relatively inexpensive and is therefore an excellent way for beginning researchers to get involved in so-ciological research.

Government Archives for Secondary Analysis. The federal government of the United States conducts surveys and censuses of various types on a regular basis, and data from these are available to researchers. When the population of the United States is counted every ten years through a na-tional census, the information obtained goes far beyond a simple count of men, women, and children. The census collects information on jobs, in-come, housing, marital status, childbearing, and many other aspects of American life. These data are available to the public and provide the raw material for many sociological studies.

The Census Bureau also conducts a monthly sample survey of the U.S. population called the Current Population Survey. Its primary purpose is to provide an ongoing evaluation of economic and social conditions in the U.S. population. Again, many opportunities exist for researchers to use these data banks for sociological research. For example, the Current Pop-ulation Survey data were used recently in a study of how having children influences the likelihood of parents' getting a divorce. It is fairly well es-tablished that when married couples have children their chances of mari-tal disruption are lessened (Morgan and Rindfuss, 1985; Waite et al., 1985). Now, using data from the June 1980 survey, researchers have found that whether a child is male or female also affects the likelihood of marital disruption. Specifically, the parents of a boy are less likely to di-vorce than are the parents of a girl. This fact is most clearly evidenced in the case of married couples with one child. If the child is a girl, the risk of marital disruption is 9 percent higher than if the child is a boy (Morgan et al., 1988). Researchers believe this difference indicates that fathers are more inclined to remain in the marriage when they have a son because they feel it is important to help with his training and upbringing.

The Historical-Comparative Method

Sociological researchers who use the **historical-comparative method** ex-amine the events and histories of whole societies, or the events and his-tories of major components of societies (e.g., religious systems, economic systems, governmental systems). The historical-comparative method is concerned with macroscopic types of social phenomena, to use the ter-minology introduced in chapter 1. This method also includes a compara-tive dimension, meaning, for example, that one society may be compared to itself at different historical periods or two or more societies may be compared to each other. Often the goal is to understand how historical

Sociology in the News

The 1990 Census of the United States

When the Census Bureau undertook its most recent count of the United States population in the spring of 1990 there were many news stories about the apparent shortcomings and inadequacies of the Census Bureau. The first reports emphasized how, three weeks after the census started, one-fourth of American households had not returned their census forms (Schrage, 1990). The other criticism is typified by the following headline: "New York City Disputes 1990 Census—Hundreds of Thousands of Residents Said to Have Been Missed" (Vobejda, 1990).

Throughout the year of the census there were frequent negative reactions and derogatory reports about the census. Newspaper columns, cartoons, and letters to the editor often portrayed the census takers as bumbling and incompetent. Politicians, especially mayors and governors who feared losing federal dollars because their populations might not be completely counted, questioned the competence of the Census Bureau and the adequacy of its procedures.

The charges that the Census Bureau is inept and its procedures inadequate need to be examined more carefully and with a bit more understanding than is typically the case among its critics. To begin with, only someone who has given little thought to the enormous task of locating and getting information from 250 million people—the approximate final total—would expect the count to be absolutely accurate. Perhaps if the United States had only five or six, or even twenty, million people to count, and if the population were homogeneous and concentrated in a small geographic area, it would be possible to complete a nearly errorless census.

Furthermore, the census procedure we use depends on citizens, themselves, to take a considerable amount of responsibility. Most people receive their questionnaire in the mail, where it is likely to be buried in (and perhaps mistaken for) the daily clutter of junk mail. In an earlier time (before the 1960 census) an army of census takers was hired to deliver a questionnaire to every household. Although that method also had its problems, there was less reliance on the citizenry to take the initiative.

There may well be some undercount in the 1990 census, which will cause some political leaders to call for adjustment, but, one might ask how they know that some people have not been counted. The answer is that the Census Bureau has been evaluating its own results for decades, and dutifully reporting how many and which types of people were probably missed. Most critics and average citizens would have no inkling of the extent and nature of undercounting if Census Bureau personnel had not persistently and conscientiously evaluated their own results.

We should also note that the Census Bureau has been limited in the last decade by budget restraints and cuts just as other agencies of government have. The people who conduct the census know what should be done to maximize responses, especially among hard-to-reach groups, but they are often limited in what they can do by a shortage of funds.

In the end, the Census Bureau must depend upon the attentiveness and cooperation of the people. If citizens ignore or reject the Bureau's attempts to gather information, the census results will suffer. It seems, therefore, both unfair and misguided to blame the Census Bureau if our census is not as good as it could be.

SCHRAGE, MICHAEL. "America's Lackluster Census Performance Is not without Justification." *The Washington Post*, May 18, 1990.
VOBEJDA, BARBARA. "New York City Disputes 1990 Census." *The Washington Post*, September 20, 1990.

events and conditions in different societies have led to different societal outcomes. Sometimes this method is used to explain why a society has changed in certain ways. To do this, researchers might study how conditions and events at one time in history led to different conditions at a later time. This study can be most effective when comparisons among two or more societies are made.

An example of historical-comparative research can be found in the work of Max Weber, one of the pioneering sociologists introduced in chapter 1. Weber, as we saw, was interested in rationality, that is, human action based primarily on the criterion of efficiency. He was especially interested in why the Western world, primarily Europe and the United States, had come to place so much emphasis on rationality. Using a historical-comparative research strategy to study this question, Weber compared the cultures of India and China with those of European countries. He was looking for historical factors that might have led to an acceptance of rationality in the West and that might have inhibited its acceptance in non-Western societies. Weber concluded that the rise of Protestantism and the acceptance of its belief system in Europe was a key factor that led to an emphasis on rationality and efficiency and a striving for material success. When Weber examined the religious ideas of Eastern societies he found none that encouraged rationality in the same way that Protestantism had in Europe. Indeed, some Eastern religions inhibited rational approaches (Weber, 1904–1905/1958).

Because the historical-comparative method of social research requires an extensive knowledge of historical conditions in different societies, it is not widely used in contemporary sociology. A similar approach that puts less emphasis on historical processes and more emphasis on collecting quantitative data from different societies is called *cross-national research* (Kohn, 1989a, 1989b).

Cross-National Research

Cross-national research is the collecting of similar kinds of data in two or more nations for comparison. A major example of cross-national research is found in the work of Melvin Kohn and his research associates (Kohn, 1977; Kohn and Schooler, 1983). Survey research studies of a similar nature were conducted over several years in the United States, Poland, Japan, Italy, and Taiwan. These studies showed that, in each country, the people who were higher in the social stratification system (more education, better jobs, higher incomes) were more likely to value self-direction. In raising their children, they tended to emphasize autonomy and to deemphasize simple obedience to rules. Since similar results were found in several different countries, these researchers concluded that a consistent relationship exists between social stratification and values that adults hold, especially with respect to rearing their children (Kohn, 1989b). (This study will be discussed more fully in chapter 5.)

Statistics and Sociological Research

Statistics are techniques used to process the numbers produced by research and measurement. Statistics should always help us in some way: if they do not explain or clarify, they are of no use. Basically, statistics will do one of two things: (1) make the communication of information easier or simpler; (2) help us to make certain kinds of decisions. Statistics that help us communicate information about numerical data are called **descriptive statistics.** Statistics that help us to make decisions are called inferential statistics.

Descriptive Statistics

Some of the most useful statistics are those that convey information about many numbers in a simple way—often with only a single number. When an instructor returns an examination to a class and says, "The average grade on the test was 92," he or she is using a single number to convey something about the scores of all the people who took the examination. The class is being told what the mean, the numerical average, is. The **mean** is calculated by adding all the scores together and dividing the sum by the number of people who took the examination. The mean is one type of statistic that is frequently used to say something about the central tendency of a group of numbers.

A second common measure of central tendency is the median. The **median** of the class's examination scores is the score in the center, or middle, of the distribution of scores. Roughly speaking, half of the students in the class would have scores that were higher than the median score, and half would have scores that were lower.

A third, less widely used, measure of central tendency is the mode. The **mode** on a set of examination scores would be the one single score received by the largest number of students.

Measures of Association and Correlation.   Sociologists, as we have seen, are often interested in how different parts of the social world are related to each other. A number of statistical techniques show relationships between variables, and simple percentages are frequently used for this purpose. Let us suppose that, in a study of the relationship between level of education and divorce, we found that 21 percent of the women with less than a high school education had been divorced, but only 10 percent of women with college degrees had been divorced. This comparison of percentages would suggest that level of education is related to divorce.

Statisticians (some of whom are sociologists) have developed other statistics to summarize, often in a single number, whether and how much two variables are related. A widely used, but fairly complex, measure of relationships is called correlation. **Correlation** is a measure of how much two variables are co-related. When two different variables are measured numerically, they can be correlated. In the example of educational level and divorce, the former can be measured numerically by using the number of years of completed education. Divorce cannot technically be measured numerically because it is an "all or nothing" characteristic. (Sociologists will, however, sometimes use the correlation technique for analyzing this relationship by arbitrarily assigning numbers 0 and 1 to the divorced and nondivorced states, respectively.) Educational level could also be correlated with another measure, such as number of months engaged before marriage. A sample of married people could provide information on their educational level and the length of their engagement before marriage. Every person would then have two measures: number of years of education and number of months engaged.

We will not go into the complex statistical calculation for correlation here except to say that the product of the appropriate mathematical procedures is a single number. This number can range from -1.00 to $+1.00$. Usually it will be a two-digit decimal fraction preceded by a sign (e.g., $-.43$ or $+.61$). This number, called a *correlation coefficient,* will conve-

Cross-National Perspectives

A Cross-National Study of Murder Victims

Murder rates vary from country to country, but one country stands out among all the rest. The United States' murder rate leads other economically developed countries of the world by a wide margin. (The murder rate is defined as the number of murders in a year for every 100,000 people in the population, so the larger population of the United States cannot account for the difference.)

Just how much the U.S. murder rate exceeds the rates of other countries is shown in a recent cross-national comparison of homicide rates conducted by Rosemary Gartner (1990). Gartner assembled data on homicide rates from 18 developed countries. The countries in her analysis included, in addition to the United States, Canada, New Zealand, Australia, Japan, and 13 western-European countries.[1] For the period from 1950 to 1980 the rate at which males were murdered in the United States was $3\frac{1}{2}$ times greater than the second highest country (Finland); the rate at which females in the United States were murdered was 2.6 times higher than the second-ranked country (Canada).

In comparison with most of the remaining countries, the United States murder rate was many more times higher. For example, the male murder rate of the United States was nearly 16 times higher than that of England and Wales. For females, the United States's the murder rate was more than five times greater than England and Wales's, and nine times greater than Ireland's.

Because the United States' murder rate has been so much higher than most other countries for many years, it has been the subject of much research. This research has produced several different types of explanations. These explanations can be divided into four categories (based on Gartner, 1990, pp. 94–96), and briefly summarized as follows:

1. *The distribution of economic resources.* Whenever there are more poor people in a population, or there are substantial economic inequalities between different population groups, the murder rate is higher.

[1] The 13 European countries included Austria, Belgium, Denmark, England and Wales, Finland, France, West Germany, Ireland, Italy, Netherlands, Norway, Sweden, and Switzerland.

2. *The degree of social integration.* Whenever the level of social integration is low (as indicated by high divorce rates, different ethnic and language groups), the murder rate is higher.
3. *The population characteristics.* The higher the percentage of the population aged 15–29, and the more people in the population who are engaged in activities away from the traditional-family household, the higher the murder rate will be.
4. *Exposure to official legitimated violence.* When the government of a country engages in legitimate violence, such as using the death penalty or engaging in war, the murder rate is higher.

All of these explanations for higher murder rates have found empirical support, especially from research conducted in the United States. However, the fact that most existing studies have focused on the country (U.S.) with an exceptionally high murder rate raises questions about whether it is possible to generalize from these research findings. This is the point of Kohn's (1989b) call for more cross-national studies as a way of testing theories. Only if theories find support in more than one society can we begin to have confidence in their general scientific validity.

Gartner's analysis of homicide in 18 developed societies sets out to test the cross-national validity of the four explanations of homicide summarized above. After completing the analysis of cross-national data on homicide rates, Gartner reached the general conclusion that the four explanations of murder presented above held true for other developed countries, just as they had in the United States. The countries that had more welfare spending, thus reducing poverty, had lower murder rates. Countries with less income inequality also had lower murder rates. Countries with lower divorce rates and less ethnic heterogeneity (indications of higher social integration) had lower murder rates. Countries that used the death penalty and had more wartime battle deaths (legitimized violence) had somewhat higher murder rates.

This cross-national study of homicide did not find support for the generally found pattern of more 15–29-year-olds in the population being associated with higher murder rates. In these 18 countries the percentage of 15–29-year-olds in the population was not associated with the murder rates.

This study did find a positive relationship between women in the labor force and higher murder rates of both adult females and children (but not males). Female employment, which engages women in activities outside the home, is somehow associated with higher murder rates for females and children. This finding raises a number of questions. The researcher asks, for example: "Where more women work outside the home, do all women and children, or only working women and their children, face higher risks?" Gartner (1990, p. 104). Also, who are the people committing these murders? Are they family members, or strangers? These questions await further research.

One additional finding of this study illustrates how the countries of the world (at least the developed countries) are linked or connected in a worldwide system. Almost all of the 18 countries studied had a similar pattern of homicide rates during the period between 1950 and 1980. Murder rates declined after 1950 and reached their lowest levels in the early 1960s. After the mid-1960s the murder rates rose in most countries, so that by 1980 they were experiencing their highest levels of the entire 30-year period. Only Japan and Italy experienced lower murder rates after 1967. For the other 16 countries, some similar set of forces or causes must have produced parallel patterns in their homicide rates.

GARTNER, ROSEMARY. "The Victims of Homicide: A Temporal and Cross-National Comparison." *American Sociological Review* 55, 1990.

niently summarize the degree and the direction of the relationship for anyone who understands correlations, even minimally. For example, if the correlation between educational level and length of engagement is .00 (or near zero), one would probably conclude that no relationship or association exists between these two variables. On the other hand, if the correlation is +.53 or +.61, one would say that the two variables are positively correlated. An interpretation would be that those people with higher numbers on one of the variables would also generally have higher numbers on the other variable. Persons with long engagements are likely to have high levels of education. Notice that nothing is said about cause and effect. We might reasonably say that people with higher levels of education have longer engagements before marriage because they are more likely to wait until they finish college before marrying, but the correlation value alone does not provide conclusive proof of this assumption. The correlation technique tells us only whether two things are related (co-related) and the direction and degree of that relationship.

Inferential Statistics

Inferential statistics are techniques that assist researchers in making decisions about whether, on the basis of a sample, statements can be made about the population from which the sample was drawn. For example, suppose we find a relationship between two variables in a sample of respondents in a social survey. Although the relationship holds for the sample, there is no certainty that it holds for the total population from which the sample was drawn. Even a randomly drawn sample may not *exactly* reflect the population. This is where statistical tests of inference become useful.

Some statistical tests will provide us with a probability statement that might, in a particular case, tell us something like the following: the chances are 99 out of 100 that the relationship found between two variables in our sample will also be found in the total population. If this probability is the result of the statistical test, we feel confident making an inference about the total population, even if we have studied only a sample from it. We could conclude that the relationship found in the sample is probably true of the total population, since the chances are only 1 in 100 that it would not be.

Summary

Although the research methods used by sociologists are varied and thus reveal the diversity of sociology, all are based on the idea that human behavior can be studied by using a scientific approach. A key element in the scientific approach is empiricism, a reliance on experiencing something with one's senses. Objectivity, a second key element, is both an attitude of value neutrality and a clear description of the research procedures used.

When carrying out social research, sociologists must be concerned about the possible harm they may do to their subjects. In extreme cases they may do physical harm, but the more likely danger is psychological harm. Ethical considerations demand caution when intruding into the lives of research subjects.

The social research process begins with a question. Research questions may come from the personal interests of researchers, current societal developments, or sociological theories. Research hypotheses are derived from reports of previous research or from theories. Concepts are measured by indicators that can be empirically observed. When concepts have been converted into measures they are called variables. Independent variables are those that are thought to produce change in dependent variables.

Experiments are research techniques that are ideally suited for assessing causality. Sociological experiments are classified as field experiments or laboratory experiments. Field experiments are often used to test the effectiveness of social programs or the desirability of proposed government policies. Field experiments are more closely connected with the real world, but laboratory experiments are under the closer control of the researchers.

Participant observation is a research method in which researchers interact with and observe the behavior of those whom they are studying. Participant observers may be involved to varying degrees in the groups and social settings they are studying, sometimes as full-fledged participants, or insiders, but more commonly as outsiders.

Social surveys often involve random samples of populations. The people selected in samples are questioned, either with questionnaires or through interviews. The two basic forms of surveys are descriptive and explanatory.

Secondary analysis is the use of data collected by other researchers for new and often very different kinds of research questions. Data collected by the government (e.g., the census) are often used for secondary analysis.

Historical-comparative research examines the histories of societies and compares either different periods in the history of a single society or the histories of several societies. Cross-national research is the use of survey data collected from two or more nations so that the results can be compared. Cross-national research is more quantitative than classic historical-comparative studies.

Statistical methods used by sociologists are descriptive or inferential. Descriptive statistics convey information about the central tendencies of numerical data and associations or correlations between measures. Inferential statistics are tools that help researchers make decisions about their data when they have drawn samples from larger populations.

Appendix: Sociological Research

Interpreting Statistical Tables

Most people, in every society, marry at some time during their lives. In the United States, for example, approximately 90 percent of all people marry at least once, and a substantial number marry more than once. In

Table 2–1. The Percentages of Females and Males Who Are Married at Ages
35–39 and 65 and Over, for Selected Countries

		Percentage Married	
Country	Age Category	Females	Males
United States	35–39	76	75
(1988)	65+	41	78
Sweden	35–39	73	66
(1981)	65+	38	67
France	35–39	85	84
(1980)	65+	35	73
Japan	35–39	90	89
(1980)	65+	35	81
Indonesia	35–39	88	96
(1980)	65+	25	81

Sources: U.S. Bureau of the Census, *Statistical Abstract of the United States, 1990.* Washington, D.C., U.S. Government Printing Office, 1990. United Nations, *Demographic Yearbook, 1982.* New York: United Nations, 1984.

many less economically developed and traditional societies such as India, the percentage marrying approaches 100 percent. However, even though most men and women marry, there is a much greater likelihood that, at the end of life, men will be married and women will not be. We will demonstrate this point with the accompanying table 2–1, which we present here as a way to illustrate the steps in reading and understanding a statistical table.

The first and most important rule for reading a table is to read the title carefully. Even experienced table readers can get confused if they fail to take the moment necessary to see what the title says. The title for table 2–1 is "The Percentages of Females and Males Who Are Married at Ages 35–39 and 65 and Over, for Selected Countries." Notice that the numbers in the body of the table are percentages.

We will return to the percentages in the table shortly, but first there is more to be learned from the title. The title says that the table will be providing information on the marital statuses of both females and males, at two different age periods (35–39 and 65 and older), for a few selected countries.

The second rule for reading a table is to begin at the left side of the table and examine the headings. The first heading is "Country," which obviously refers to the countries under consideration. The second heading is "Age Category," and it refers to age categories 35–39 and 65+. These age categories are shown for each country. It is customary to call the designations to the left of the data *stubs*.

The headings for the other columns of the table begin with an overall heading, "Percentage Married." Subheadings then divide the information according to gender: "Females" and "Males."

To see what kinds of information the body of the table provides we begin by inspecting the first percentage in the table—here the figure is 76 percent. This figure tells us that, in the United States among 35- to 39-year-old females, 76 percent are married. Moving along the same row to the next figure, we see that 75 percent of U.S. males in the same age category are married.

If we now move down to the next row we can examine the percentages of U.S. females and males who are married in the 65-and-over age category. We see that, while only 41 percent of the older females are married, 78 percent of the older males are married.

In a similar fashion we can examine the marital statuses of females and males in the other countries. We see the same pattern as that of the United States existing in all the other countries. In some cases it is even more extreme, as, for example, in Indonesia, where 81 percent of the males 65 and over are still married, while only 25 percent of the females in the older age group are married.

Table 2–1 shows that, in widely different countries, there is a consistent tendency for women in the later years of life to be unmarried. After age 65, only one-quarter to two-fifths of women are married, while two-thirds to four-fifths of older men are still married. The most obvious reason for this imbalance in marital status between males and females is the shorter life expectancy of males in many societies. However, an additional contributing factor is that, in many societies, males marry women who are younger than they, thus leaving many older women unmarried, even when there may be men of their age group still alive.

CRITICAL THINKING

1. What are the key features of a scientific approach? Why is it important in the study of sociology?
2. Sociologists must retain their objectivity about subjects that they study. If you were a sociologist, about which topics might you have difficulty maintaining a degree of objectivity?
3. Why should social sciences be held to the same rigorous standards of procedural objectivity as natural or biological sciences?
4. Discuss several ethical issues that need to be considered by sociologists when constructing research projects. Assume you are a sociologist interested in researching sexual behavior. Give examples of what you would consider to be ethical and unethical research practices for that topic.
5. Assume you wish to use twins to assess the degree to which heredity and environment influence our lives. What might be the dependent and independent variables in such a study?
6. Compare and contrast the advantages and disadvantages of the major research methods (i.e., participant observation, social survey, etc.) mentioned in this chapter.
7. Pretend you are a sociologist wishing to begin a research project on race relations in the United States. Develop several hypotheses that you might choose to test. What research methods would be most effective in testing these hypotheses?
8. Why must sociologists, and those who use sociological research, be wary of the statistics they use and see?
9. In what ways are statistics used in sociological research?

3 Culture

In the aftermath of the Persian Gulf war, Congresswoman Beverly Byron, along with a number of other members of the House of Representatives, visited Saudi Arabia. Representative Byron (age 58), who has served 12 years as a member of Congress, had a curious and probably awkward encounter with Saudi Arabian officials. It was an encounter that had its origins in the cultural differences between the Saudi and U.S. societies.

Representative Byron, along with other Americans, was visiting the ancient marketplace in Riyadh, the capital of Saudi Arabia (Conconi, 1991). As she walked through the market she was suddenly surprised by the Saudi police, who tapped a stick at her feet to get her attention. Through an interpreter she was told that her trousers were too tight *around the ankles.*

By American standards the Congresswoman's pants were entirely acceptable and proper, but they were improper and unacceptable by Saudi standards. The Saudi culture requires that, in public, women must wear loose-fitting garments—clothing that does not, in any way, reveal the shape of their bodies. Furthermore, as this incident shows, the Saudi police have the right and the responsibility to enforce these cultural standards of female dress, even if the offenders are visiting members of the United States Congress. (For a further examination of the differences between the Saudi Arabian and American cultures, see Sociology in the News, p. 92.)

Every society has its own special customs, its standards of acceptability, its way of life. These reflect what the people of that society believe is acceptable, desirable, and proper. The way of life of a society, or its culture, is a key element of social life, and is the subject of this chapter.

The Importance of Culture

The Meaning of Culture

Culture is the entire complex of ideas and material objects that the people of a society (or group) have created and adopted for carrying out the necessary tasks of collective life. As this definition suggests, cultures are human creations, but, of course, people inherit much of their culture from those who created it. In other words, every culture has a history. When children are born into a society they learn the elements of their culture, and they in turn pass them on, probably in some modified form, to those who follow them. Cultures, therefore, are also capable of change.

One convenient way to think about culture is to recognize that the people of every society have an array of tasks to perform and problems to solve. All people must have ways of providing food, clothing, and shelter, ways of producing and caring for children, and ways of solving disputes between members. Perhaps most important, all people must have a way of making life orderly and predictable.

We will present a fuller analysis of the components of culture later in this chapter, but two aspects of culture are important enough to introduce them here. They are *values* and *norms*.

Cultural values can be defined as the standards of desirability, of rightness, and of importance in a society. In Saudi society, to the Saudis, it seems desirable, right, and important that women should not be seen in public wearing tight-fitting clothing. **Cultural norms** are rules for what should and should not be done in given situations. Violators of the norms will be punished to some degree by other members of the society. In Saudi society, the police have the responsibility to enforce the rules of women's dress in public places.

A Cultural Explanation of Human Behavior

A cultural explanation of human behavior rests on the assumption that humans in any society will learn the basic cultural values and social norms of that society. To a considerable degree, the general behavior (and even individual behavior) of people in a society can be explained by that society's cultural values and norms.

Using culture to understand human behavior is not simply an abstract sociological exercise; it can frequently have practical applications as well. For instance, George Fields, an American advertising and marketing specialist, spent many years in Japan, where he worked at introducing American-manufactured products to the Japanese (Fields, 1983). Fields's parents were American, but he was born in Japan, and lived there during his youth. Fields's deep understanding of the Japanese people, their language, and their culture made him especially valuable when, as an adult, he worked for American businesses that wanted to market their products in Japan.

Although Fields was often successful in his efforts to introduce American products into the Japanese market, some of his failures revealed the significance of cultural factors even more clearly than his successes. One of Fields's more renowned marketing failures was his involvement in the attempt by General Mills to introduce cake mixes into the Japanese market in the 1960s. The problem was that, at that time, most Japanese kitchens did not have ovens. However, every kitchen had a rice cooker and, with some modifications in the mix, the cake could be baked in it. Fields helped introduce an intense advertising campaign; initially sales were good, but then they dropped off dramatically.

A group interview with Japanese housewives revealed that the reason for the decline was a concern about the vanilla and other flavorings in the mixes. One woman said, "I suppose you can wash it off, but . . . ." The Japanese women were worried about the possible contamination of their rice. Nearly every evening meal in Japan includes rice, which for the Japanese is not just a food, but a symbol of purity as well. The purity of the family's daily rice could not be jeopardized by baking a cake in the rice cooker.

When the Japanese women balanced the cultural significance of the purity of their rice against the attractiveness of serving cakes to their families, the purity of the rice was more important. The attempt to market cake mixes failed, and General Mills withdrew its product from the market. The power of a cultural symbol to influence human behavior was understood too late.

Two Competing Views of Human Behavior

Culture is not the only way to explain human behavior. Two other frequently encountered explanations are "human nature" and a scientific theory called *sociobiology*. In considering these alternatives, we will show that cultural explanations are more useful and significant.

"It's Just Human Nature"

Many people look for explanations of human behavior in what they call "human nature." The term *human nature* generally suggests that specific characteristics or traits that are found in all humans supposedly explain some particular behavior. Many times one hears people say, "It is just human nature to be selfish, . . . or jealous, . . . or friendly, . . . or aggressive." The speaker usually claims to explain some human or social behavior by invoking a particular characteristic.

On closer inspection, however, many aspects of human nature turn out to vary tremendously from one society to another. For instance, one society might value aggressiveness, while another might value nonviolence and peace. Quakers typically believe in and practice nonviolence. In contrast, some societies regard fighting as a pervasive way of life. The Yanomamo Indians, about 15,000 people who live in the Amazon rain forest, are constantly warring and fighting among themselves. According to data gathered over 23 years, 44 percent of the Yanomamo men over the age of 25 had killed someone (Chagnon, 1968; Rensberger, 1988).

When we compare the peaceful way of life of the Quakers and the violent way of life of the Yanomamo, we must question whether claims about a universally aggressive human nature have any validity or significance. A more satisfactory explanation of the difference between these two societies can be gained by examining the value that Quakers place on being peaceful and the value the Yanomamo place on violence and aggression.

The pervasive violence among the Yanomamo is evident in all parts of their lives, not just in their treatment of enemies. The males, for instance, are very violent with their own families. Yanomamo husbands often punish their wives brutally. As a minor punishment, husbands routinely jerk the small sticks that the women wear through pierced ear lobes. As a more severe punishment, they jab their wives with sticks or machetes, or burn them with glowing pieces of firewood. The Yanomamo women expect abuse by their husbands as a routine part of married life. An anthropologist who lived among the Yanomamo once heard two women talking about the scars their husbands had given them. One said that her husband must really care for her since he had beaten her on the head so many times (Harris, 1974).

As we would expect, the Yanomamo people rear their children in the tradition of violence. When small boys display aggressive behavior and engage in violence, they are encouraged and rewarded by their fathers. Understandably the Yanomamo have been called "The Fierce People" (Chagnon, 1968).

As the comparison between the Quakers and the Yanomamo shows, the human nature argument, which advocates the existence of universal, inborn, human characteristics, is extremely dubious. However, the idea that human behavior is shaped or determined by inborn, biologically based characteristics or traits continues to appeal to many people, and has formed the basis for a number of scholarly theories. For example, instinct theory, which dominated psychology during the early years of this century, attempted to explain any human behavior by attributing it to an instinct. Eventually it was recognized that positing an instinct for every human behavior was simply naming a behavior, not explaining it. (For example, having children might be attributed to a "parenting instinct.")

In recent years the most popular biologically based theory of human behavior has been sociobiology (Wilson, 1975). Because sociobiology has gained some prominence and popular acceptance in recent years, it is considered an alternative to the cultural explanation of human behavior.

Sociobiology. The fundamental idea of **sociobiology** is that human behavior reflects genetically inherited traits. Sociobiologists argue that humans are very much like other species of animals, that is, that human characteristics and behaviors are products of the Darwinian notions of natural selection and evolution. **Natural selection** is the idea that the fittest of any species will survive and spread its favored traits throughout the population (Gould, 1977).

According to this theory, we humans who are alive today have inherited the genetic characteristics that increased the chances of survival among our ancestors. The reasoning of sociobiology goes this way: if a specific trait appeared at some time in the genes of early humans, and that genetic trait made it more likely for the carrier and its offspring to survive, then that trait would more likely be passed on to the next generation. In the long run, through the process of natural selection, the traits that improved chances of survival would be found in the human population. Traits that detracted from survival, or were less advantageous for survival, would disappear or become rare. Sociobiologists conclude from this that any widely observed human behavior must have been beneficial for survival and, therefore, have been passed down genetically (Lumsden and Wilson, 1983).

As an example of the sociobiological approach, we have an attempt to explain the predisposition for human beings to feel love. The basic hypothesis was: "the great majority of women and men are born with a genetic capacity and need for forming durable attachments of an emotional character [love]" (Mellen, 1981, p. 139).

The sociobiological explanation for the human tendency to feel love is stated as follows: When early humans lived by hunting and gathering food, they had to cover a wide geographic area in pursuit of game and in search of other food. Hunting, especially, required speed and mobility. During the time when females were pregnant or were caring for their young, they were relatively immobile and needed assistance. The males, not similarly restricted, could range over large areas in search of food and game. If women and their children were to survive under these conditions, the males had to return with some food for them. Sociobiologists reason that males who were selfish might not return with the food, but if a male were born with a tendency to feel an attachment for the female who bore his child (a tendency to feel love), he would return to the female and child to share his food. If he did so, the child carrying his genes (perhaps including the gene that made him capable of feeling love) would be more likely to survive.

Or consider the opposite scenario—a male who did not have the genetic tendency to feel love for a female. Because this male would probably not return as often to the female and her child, this child might die from lack of food, and the male's genes would not survive to the next generation. In this way, in the course of hundreds of thousands of years, the genes that produced a capacity for love would have survived in the human species (Mellen, 1981).

Many features of this sociobiological description are not proved facts; many may be unprovable. In fact, no one has actually isolated a gene that gives people the capacity to love. We also know very little about the lives of prehistoric humans, so much of the scenario above is simply conjecture. Nevertheless, suppose it were all true. We are still left with the question, "Does it make any difference in our attempt to understand human behavior?" Perhaps all humans do have the capacity for love, but what difference does it make when love is viewed so differently in different cultures? Remember the Yanomamo wife who believed that her husband cared for her because he had beaten her on the head so much? A beating on the head is hardly considered an expression of love in American society.

Furthermore, although Americans believe in entering marriage on the basis of love, many societies consider love before marriage to be irrelevant. Often the bride and groom hardly know each other at the time of marriage, so they would not likely be in love. Why do the cultures of some societies emphasize love as a basis for marriage and other cultures deemphasize or ignore it? This interesting sociological question is one that the sociobiological point of view cannot address. Even if the socio-biological explanation were true (and that is by no means certain), socio-biology often misses interesting and important questions and issues such as why the people in different societies adopt such widely different be-haviors (Bock, 1980).

Another way of seeing the power of culture is to observe how the peo-ple of every society tend to believe that their way of life is best. We will examine this view next, as we discuss ethnocentrism.

Ethnocentrism

When the ancient Greeks heard people speaking in other languages, the sounds they heard seemed meaningless. To the Greeks, such talking sounded like "bar, bar, bar, bar." Thus they called people with other lan-guages *barbarians* (Ciardi, 1980, p. 18). The Greeks applied this word to all people who came from other societies whom they regarded as uncivilized.

People in all societies tend to think of themselves as the chosen people or, at the very least, as those at the center of humanity. From this view, it is understandable that people of any society would think their ways of doing things were the right ways, and the ways of other people were less right. This attitude is labeled *ethnocentrism*. **Ethnocentrism** is a view held by the people of a society that says that *they* are of central importance in the universe and therefore their way of doing things is the "right" way (Sumner, 1906).

Obviously not every group of people can be right, since often the cus-toms of one group are totally different from the customs of another. Also, if we had been born into another society, we obviously would have grown up thinking that the norms of that society were right and proper. It is the culture itself that makes things "right."

Cultural Relativism

The study of diverse cultural traditions often helps us to see how different customs can be equally acceptable. This view is the key to an important idea called *cultural relativism*. **Cultural relativism** is an approach that evaluates the behavior of the people of another society, not on the basis of the evaluator's culture but on that culture's own terms.

In an extreme version of cultural relativism there are no rights and wrongs, only different cultural values and norms. A more moderate version emphasizes the fact that cultures vary, and other people's patterns of behavior are best judged in the context of their own culture. The following example illustrates the point.

Staphorst is a town of about 11,000 people in the Netherlands (Newton, 1978). If you were to drive into Staphorst you would find a picturesque community where the people still dress in traditional Dutch clothing, reminiscent more of the time of Rembrandt than of the twentieth century. You might be tempted to photograph these people but, if it were a Sunday, it would be better to refrain, since the people of Staphorst are very religious and dislike having their photographs taken on their special day of worship. Indeed, the Staphorst people take Sunday so seriously that males and females do not spend time together on that day. They even separate their male and female farm animals on Sunday (Newton, 1978).

If you were to stay around Staphorst for a while, you would learn that their Sunday behavior is only a minor reflection of their conservative religious views. The people of Staphorst are 95 percent Protestant (75 percent Calvinist and 20 percent Dutch Reformed). They follow a conservative religious tradition, and believe strongly in a literal heaven and hell. They are conservative in other ways, also, rejecting most of the ways of modern Dutch life. (Polio vaccine was resisted until 1971, when the town experienced an epidemic.)

If you were to delve into the courtship and marriage patterns of the people of Staphorst, however, you might be surprised at some of the customs (Gibney, 1948). When a young man of Staphorst becomes interested in a young woman, he gives her a signal by trying to snatch the rain cape she keeps tied to her waist. If the young woman is interested, she probably helps him succeed. The actual courtship begins when the young man starts coming to the young woman's house (which he will do on Monday, Wednesday, and Friday evenings) after she has retired to her bedroom. Even though the young woman's parents are in a nearby room and can obviously hear what is going on, the young man will crawl through her bedroom window. He will spend the night with her but leave before morning. Quite understandably, this practice often leads to the young woman's becoming pregnant. When this happens, it is time for the two young people to marry, which they do shortly thereafter.

To summarize the courtship system of Staphorst, young people *must* have premarital sex and the young woman *must* be pregnant before marriage is possible. In our society and in many others, premarital pregnancy is typically viewed as an unfortunate occurrence. Indeed, often people who are most religious are especially apt to be upset by a premarital preg-

Cross-Cultural Perspectives

American Culture as a Foreign Culture

It is very difficult to see one's own culture as an outsider might see it. Many generations of American students in anthropology and sociology classes have had an outsider's glimpse of their own culture when they were asked to read a classic essay by Horace Miner on "body rituals" practiced in the *Nacirema* culture (Miner, 1956). Miner described the practices and rituals of the Nacirema with respect to the body. For example, he described a daily ritual associated with the mouth as follows:

> The daily body ritual performed by everyone includes a mouth-rite. . . . It was reported to me that the ritual consists of inserting a small bundle of hog hairs into the mouth, along with certain magical powders, and then moving the bundle in a highly formalized series of gestures (Miner, 1956, p. 504).

Miner described other rituals performed by the men and women of the Nacirema, beginning with a ritual practiced only by the males: "This part of the rite involves scraping and lacerating the surface of the face with a sharp instrument."; and one practiced by the females: "Special women's rites are performed only four times during each lunar month, but what they lack in frequency is made up in barbarity. As part of this ceremony, women bake their heads in small ovens for about an hour" (Miner, 1956, p. 505).

Miner's essay goes on to describe other strange customs of the Nacirema in a similar fashion, until almost every reader eventually guesses that the name *nacirema* when spelled backward is *American*. The customs described above are the American customs of brushing one's teeth, shaving, and having one's hair done.

This essay on the *Nacirema* allowed readers to look at their own culture as outsiders, even if only for a few moments. But there are many Americans today who have the actual experience of seeing their native culture as if they were outsiders. These are the Americans who have, for one reason or another, lived in a foreign country for a long and continuous period of time. When they reenter American society they often see this culture from a new perspective; for them, American culture is like a foreign culture (Austin, 1986).

Many Americans have occupations requiring them to live in other countries for extended periods of time. Included are foreign service and military personnel, United Nations specialists, employees of multinational corporations, members of the Peace Corps, relief organizations, religious groups, and educators. Even students who study abroad may be gone long enough to experience some "reentry" experience and reactions.

Many people who have lived in other countries for long periods of time report experiencing stress and a period of readjustment when they return to their home culture.

One problem for the reentrants stems from the fact that cultures change while one is gone, even for a relatively short period of time. Cultures are not static, especially that part called *popular culture.* Popular culture includes entertainment and entertainers, television shows, movies, music, clothing styles, and even language (slang is a special part of popular culture). Many details of popular culture are likely to be different from when one left, even a year or so earlier.

When they return to their home culture, people may feel "left out," not even fully understanding conversations among their friends and family. " 'We didn't feel as though we understood what was happening. . . . sometimes we felt as if we had returned from outer space!' " (Koehler, 1986, p. 91).

Many people who spend time in another culture find themselves more critical of their native culture when they return home. "When you come back from overseas you see America as a foreigner does. You view America through a sharper lens, and are able to pick up the strengths and weaknesses of the country more clearly" (Sobie, 1986, p. 97). In the words of one returnee from Germany, " 'When I came back to the states, I found Americans shallow and plastic . . .' " (Sobie, 1986, p. 97). Another woman describes her feelings about American wastefulness: " 'We had a water shortage on Okinawa and it disturbed us greatly to see how water was wasted here' " (Koehler, 1986, p. 91).

Some contemporary anthropologists offer us another perspective on U.S. culture as a foreign culture. Anthropologists, as we noted in chapter 1, have traditionally studied foreign, often exotic, societies, but they are increasingly turning their attention to American culture (Goleman, 1991). They are using their ethnographic methods to study parts of the contemporary United States, just as they previously used them to study foreign cultures. Recent anthropological studies in the United States have included the worlds of "New York art dealers and museum curators, advertising agencies, high-energy physicists, and pro- and anti-abortion groups in Fargo, North Dakota" (Goleman, 1991, p. B5).

Just as anthropologist Margaret Mead studied the lives of adolescents in Samoa and wrote the classic *Coming of Age in Samoa* (1928), a contemporary anthropologist has studied the lives of young Americans and written *Coming of Age in New Jersey* (Moffatt, 1989). Anthropologist Michael Moffatt lived for a period of time in a co-ed dormitory at Rutgers University and observed the lives of the residents there. His book describes the students' social relationships, drinking behaviors, race relations and racial attitudes, and their sexual attitudes and activities (Moffatt, 1989).

The trend of American anthropologists toward studying their own culture is, of course, simply an extension of the participant observation studies of sociologists described in chapter 2. It is possible to study one's own culture as an outsider, but in this case the ethnographer must be careful not to let his or her preconceived views and attitudes influence the observations and conclusions.

AUSTIN, CLYDE N. (ed.). *Cross-Cultural Reentry: A Book of Readings.* Abilene, Texas: Abilene Christian University Press, 1986.

GOLEMAN, DANIEL. "Anthropology Casts an eye on the Culture That Made It," *The New York Times,* April 2, 1991, p. B5.

KOEHLER, NANCY. "Re-entry Shock." In Clyde N. Austin (ed.), *Cross-Cultural Reentry: A Book of Readings.* Abilene, Texas: Abilene Christian University Press, 1986. pp. 89–94.

MEAD, MARGARET. *Coming of Age in Samoa.* New York: William Morrow, 1928.

MINER, HORACE. "Body Ritual Among the Nacirema." *American Anthropologist* 58, 1956.

MOFFATT, MICHAEL. *Coming of Age in New Jersey.* New Brunswick, New Jersey: Rutgers University Press, 1989.

SOBIE, JANE HIPKINS. "The Culture Shock of Coming Home Again." In Clyde N. Austin (ed.) *Cross-Cultural Reentry: A Book of Readings.* Abilene, Texas: Abilene Christian University Press, 1986. pp. 95–101.

nancy. Yet here we find the people of Staphorst, who are extremely religious, actually requiring pregnancy before marriage.

It would be difficult to argue that the acceptance of premarital sex and pregnancy by the people of Staphorst makes them "immoral." Judged by their standards, this practice is accepted as both moral and appropriate. Viewed from the perspective of cultural relativism, we as outsiders would accept the customs of the Staphorst people as part of their particular way of life.

The Staphorst example shows us that, if we take the time to look at the cultural traditions of other people, we can be more sensitive to the integrity of other cultures. In other words, we will be more inclined toward cultural relativity and less inclined toward ethnocentrism.

Cultural relativism, however, does not suggest that one must invariably accept the practices of other people regardless of what they might be. For example, when the Nazi government of Germany in the 1930s put into slavery or killed entire categories of people (Jews, gypsies, and the mentally retarded) one could not regard this phenomenon as just another example of cultural diversity. The idea of cultural relativity implies greater tolerance for cultural differences but not a blind acceptance of all forms of human behavior.

The Components of Culture

Earlier we defined culture as the entire complex of ideas and material objects shared by the people of a society. We are now ready to look more systematically at the major components of culture. We begin with a consideration of symbols.

People who live in the same culture generally understand each other, because they share the same symbols. **Symbols** are words, gestures, and objects that communicate meaning when people agree on and recognize what they represent. Every symbol has a social character because a group of people agree on the symbol's meaning (Charon, 1988; Meltzer, 1978). As we noted in our consideration of symbolic interaction theory in chapter 1, shared symbols are used by the people of any given society to communicate with each other and to create a certain order and predictability in daily life. Symbols can be divided into two types: nonverbal and verbal.

Nonverbal Symbols

In historical movies, when the Lord and Lady of the Manor ride through the village in their carriage, the tradesmen and shopkeepers often tip their caps and bow slightly. The symbolism of tipping one's hat to someone of high status is unmistakable: the lower-status person is showing respect for the high-status person. This act is an illustration of a **nonverbal symbol,** a physical display that has social meaning.

In a time when men wore hats, they used to tip their hats when meeting women acquaintances on the street; this gesture was a nonverbal symbol of their respect. Tipping the hat as an act of respect is rarely seen today, but a vestige of this custom can still be seen in some instances. When the President of the United States steps out of his helicopter, he usually exchanges salutes with the military personnel in attendance. The military salute is an evolved version of tipping one's hat and is initiated by the lower-status person and returned by the higher-status person. It is a nonverbal symbolic act, a sign of respect for someone in a higher social position.

Another example of using nonverbal symbols to show respect for people of higher status can be seen among students in many military settings (e.g., West Point), who come to attention when their instructors enter the room. They are seated only when told to do so. Coming to one's feet in the presence of someone of a higher status is a common display of respect found in many societies.

However, the meanings of nonverbal symbols are by no means the same from one society to another. Nonverbal symbols can sometimes have exactly opposite meanings in two different societies. In the United States, audiences and fans will often show their approval of performances by whistling. In Europe, however, audiences and fans whistle as a way of demonstrating disapproval and dissatisfaction.

The kiss, another nonverbal symbol, also varies widely in its meaning and use from one society to another. American male political leaders often have to brace themselves when they meet political leaders from the Middle East, some European countries, or the Soviet Union, because a common greeting among men in these countries is to exchange kisses on the cheeks. In American society, kisses on the cheek between men and women are used as a way of greeting friends and acquaintances, but men do not usually exchange kisses unless they are close relatives—fathers and sons and brothers may kiss after having been separated for some time.

The kiss on the lips between lovers is not as natural as it may seem. The lip kiss was invented by the people of ancient India, although the earliest Indian records (about 2000 B.C.) indicate that their earliest custom was a nose or "sniff" kiss (Pike, 1976). By the time the famous Indian manual of sex and love, the *Kama Sutra*, was written in the fourth century, the lip kiss was well established. The practice of kissing with the lips spread westward to Persia, Syria, Greece, Italy, and eventually to the countries that make up Northern Europe. For Americans, who inherited their culture from these European countries, the lip kiss between romantic partners has always been an expression of love and affection. In many societies, however, lip kissing between lovers was unknown until it was introduced by explorers, traders, and missionaries from the West. According to reports from these observers, the people of most African societies did not kiss on the lips, nor did the New Zealand Maoris, the Australian aborigines, the Papuans, Tahitians, or other South Sea Islanders. It is said that the Chinese considered kissing vulgar because it reminded them of cannibalism. Among Eskimo tribes of the Arctic, the custom was for lovers to rub their noses together (Pike, 1976).

Today the kiss on the lips between lovers is found in most societies around the world. This fact illustrates how a cultural trait can spread from one society to another as different peoples come into contact with one another. This process is called **cultural diffusion.** In the case of lip kissing, we may speculate that the worldwide distribution of American movies in the last 30 years greatly aided the process of diffusion. A few decades ago, American movies dealing with love had to be censored in Japan because the scenes showing men and women kissing were considered by the Japanese to be in very bad taste (Hughes, 1976).

Nonverbal symbols include many other things besides the physical acts performed by people. Many physical objects are also endowed with symbolic meaning. Flags, emblems, insignias, and coats-of-arms are some familiar examples of objects that have special meaning for people (Gusfield and Michalowicz, 1984). These objects are displayed on homes, automobiles, and clothing as a way of conveying messages to other people. In recent years the makers of clothing have adopted the practice of placing their names, logos, and trademarks on the outside of clothing. The successes of clothing lines carrying these symbols suggest that aesthetics is not the only reason for a brand name to be written on the outside of one's shirt, blouse, or pants. It takes only a little sociological imagination to see that recognizable names, logos, or trademarks send out a social message for the observers. Indeed, many different types of clothing convey messages to observers. Scientists, some of whom never go near a laboratory, nonetheless don their laboratory jackets as a symbol of their status as scientists (Joseph, 1986).

Verbal Symbols and Language

Although the nonverbal symbols of a culture are often interesting, it is the verbal symbols that have the most sociological significance. **Verbal symbols** are any verbal utterances that are part of the spoken or written language of a society. The language system shared by the people of a society serves as one of its most important social bonds. But more than that, language influences the way people of the same culture perceive reality.

The ability to learn and use verbal symbols is undoubtedly the most extraordinary ability that human beings possess, and using words and language is a critical element in people's social and cultural lives. At an early age, humans can learn hundreds—and then thousands—of different symbols, and can use them to communicate with other people. Not only do humans learn words, but they also learn the rules of grammar and sentence structure that are characteristic of their particular language. English-speaking children, even as toddlers, learn to add an *s* to the end of a noun when they want to speak of more than one object. We find it humorous when small children say "mouses" instead of mice, but they are simply following a generalized rule that, in all likelihood, no one has explicitly taught them. Small children hear the plural form used for many nouns and then, quite reasonably, adopt the rule as a way of using the language properly.

The capacity to learn symbols, as well as the rules for using them, allows humans to store and transmit information, thoughts, and ideas with great ease. This ability gives language its particular importance as a carrier of culture. Through language we share not just the names for things but also the rules and values that shape and influence how we relate to these things. An example of this principle can be found in some recent controversies surrounding the rights and responsibilities of biological fathers.

In American society the term *biological father* is important; a biological father has certain rights and responsibilities with regard to any children he produces. However, in recent years new reproductive technologies have allowed women to conceive babies by being impregnated with the sperm of male donors. This practice has raised questions and created problems in some cases about the rights of the "biological father." In some cases the sperm donors have claimed their rights as biological fathers. For Americans this raises a perplexing question because sperm donors would not ordinarily have rights to a child, but a biological father (which the donor seems to be) does.

In some societies the notion of a biological father does not have the same meaning and significance as it does for Americans. For example, a few societies exist where two or more men are married to the same woman.[1] In such a case, there is often no way to determine which husband is the biological father. In one such society in the foothills of the Himalayas, the lack of concern about the biological father extends to cases where wives become pregnant while visiting their home villages. The pregnancy is accepted (even welcomed) by the woman's husbands, and the infant is considered theirs. Apparently the biological father is of no importance and has no rights to the child (Zorsa, 1982).

Americans might have a difficult time understanding how these Himalayan people could be unconcerned about the actual biological father and about his rights and responsibilities. But again, the reason is that Americans cannot easily ignore the social meanings attached to the term *biological father*. The words and symbols shared by the people of a society are

---

[1] This form of marriage is called *polyandry*. For a more complete description of this form of marriage, see chapter 11.

important not simply because they convey information but also because they carry social rules and values.

The Sapir-Whorf Hypothesis. The words of any language seem to be symbols for elements that exist in the physical and social worlds. Clouds exist in the physical world, so a word has to be created so that we can refer to them. But another way to see the relationship between words and the physical and social worlds is to regard language as *shaping and influencing* what we see and perceive.

The idea that language shapes our perception of reality was developed by Edward Sapir and his student Benjamin Whorf in the 1930s; it is usually referred to as the **Sapir-Whorf hypothesis** (McCurdy and Spradley, 1979). This idea can be illustrated by observing how the people of some societies give to certain objects in their environment many different names with precise and detailed meanings. Among the Eskimos the constant presence of snow and its importance in their lives is reflected in their language. The Kobuk Eskimos of northeastern Alaska have many different words for types and conditions of snow, including: *snow falling on the ground, falling snow, swirling or drifting snow,* and *snow that collects horizontally on trees* (Boas, 1911; Williams and Major, 1984).

When a language system has many different words to represent variable aspects of the same object, it enables people to have much more complicated perceptions of that part of reality. Most of us have only one word for snow, and thus we do not usually make distinctions among different types of snow. However, avid skiers do make distinctions between *powder* and *machine-made* snow, and they also have special words for various snow surfaces. These words make skiers more sensitive to variations in snow, supporting the hypothesis that language shapes our perception of reality.

The idea that perceptions of the world are shaped by language systems can be illustrated by an example from our everyday world. Americans are increasingly conscious of health foods, and natural ingredients have come to be associated with healthfulness. Health food stores, specializing in grains, fruits, nuts, and other vegetable products, and *organic* foods (another term loaded with symbolic meaning), flourish around the country. However, the food and advertising industries have quickly become sensitized to the important symbolic significance of the words *natural* and *natural ingredients,* with the result that these terms now appear on the boxes and packages of many commercially produced food products. We tend to perceive these as health foods—even when most of the "natural" ingredients are sugar, corn syrup, starches, salts, and vegetable oils. (Both ice cream and potato chips can, if the producer wishes, qualify as *all natural.*)

Knowledge and Beliefs

Knowledge and beliefs taken together, constitutes a body of information created by the people of a society that influences behavior. Knowledge is presumed to be verifiable information, while beliefs are presumed to be difficult to verify. In practice, however, these forms of information are frequently interchangeable. Consider, for example, the following four statements about the sun:

- The sun is a god and should be worshipped.
- The sun is our primary source of heat and light.
- Sunbathing, which leads to a deep tan, is healthy for humans.
- Direct exposure to the sun over a period of time may produce skin cancer.

Which of these statements are knowledge and which are beliefs? Most of us would agree that the first statement is a belief, while the second is a factual statement and, therefore, knowledge. Statements three and four, however, are more troublesome. Some of us think that three is knowledge and four is only a belief, while others think the opposite is true. Furthermore, a true believer in a sun god would think it ridiculous to doubt the validity of the first statement. Knowledge and beliefs are not as easy to disentangle as one might suppose. An analysis of our reactions to this series of statements about the sun reveals the cultural nature of knowledge and beliefs. Those statements that we believe to be valid or true will influence how we behave. From a cultural viewpoint, knowledge and beliefs are accepted by substantial numbers of people in a society, and therefore shape general behavior. If we are to judge from the number of people who seek out beaches and swimming pools each summer, working assiduously at getting suntans, most Americans still seem to believe that a suntan is healthy (or at least attractive).

However, knowledge and beliefs in every society undergo continuous change. As knowledge and beliefs change, behavior also changes. Even today, some people have modified their views about suntanning and have changed their suntanning practices. It is ironic that, if Americans begin to shield themselves from the sun at the beach or the swimming pool, their behavior will parallel the behavior of Americans a century ago. In that era, women in particular kept their faces, arms, and legs shielded from the sun, not because of a fear of skin cancer but because a tanned skin was associated with laborers and peasants whose work exposed them to the full day's sun.

We return now to what many regard as the key or primary component of culture: cultural values, or simply values. In comparison with knowledge and belief that focus on *what is,* values are related to what *should be.*

Values

We noted earlier that values are a society's standards of desirability, of rightness, and of importance. Values are expressions of what is good or bad, beautiful or ugly, pleasant or unpleasant, appropriate or inappropriate. Cultural values are shared by a substantial number of people in a society and therefore influence the behavior of most people. The social rules governing behavior (called norms) are generally consistent with, or reflections of, cultural values.

Although it is possible to identify cultural values, not everyone in a society holds exactly the same values. Individual variation suggests the notion of personal values. **Personal values** are the values individuals use to make decisions about their personal lives and about the ways in which they respond to public issues. Personal values, like cultural values, deal, not with the trivia of life, but with fundamental and important aspects of our social lives. It is not a value to prefer The Grateful Dead or the movies of Eddie Murphy, although selecting any of them could perhaps reflect a more basic value. Personal values are likely to influence our occupational choices, our decisions about marriage mates (or about marriage itself), and our views about politics. Personal values influence our reactions to public issues: for example, our choice of a political party or our views on international relations, the environment, medical practices, and so on.

Values are not neutral; they are positively or negatively charged. Cultural and personal values can also vary in degree from very strong to very weak. Some values are more important, more pervasive, and more influential than others. Later, in our discussion of American cultural values, we will look for our most important ones.

Values vary from society to society. What one group of people considers desirable may be viewed as undesirable by another group. For example, in our society a high value is placed on youth, beauty, and vigor. Many people make strenuous efforts to remain youthful in appearance. Health clubs, weight-loss spas, cosmetic surgery facilities, the clothing industry, and many related businesses thrive on the desire of Americans to stay young looking. In other societies, youth is not so highly valued. In many societies around the world, older people are considered wise and valued advisors.

Engaging in competition in order to win is another value not shared by the people of all societies. Americans generally believe that winning is much better than losing, and that it is inappropriate to play a game without trying to win. However, among the Tangu people of New Guinea, winning is not the object of their game, *Taketak*. *Taketak* involves spinning around dried fruit rinds ("tops") into masses of stakes that have been driven into the ground. Players from each of two teams take turns spinning the tops in the palms of their hands and throwing them into the masses of stakes, trying to hit as many stakes as possible. Stakes that have been touched are removed. The object of the game is not to have one team "win" by hitting all the stakes, but to have both teams hit exactly the same number of stakes, at which time the game ends. Ending in a tie expresses one of the primary values of the Tangu culture—the notion of moral equality among all persons (Burridge, 1957).

While we have already touched on some American cultural values, we now examine more systematically the dominant values in American society.

Dominant Values of American Society

Observers and social analysts have tried since the earliest days of American history to identify the dominant values of the people who settled on the land that is now the United States (de Tocqueville, 1961; de Crevecoeur, 1782/1981). The effort continues into the present, as contemporary sociologists try to isolate dominant values held by most people in the United States today (Bellah et al., 1985; Gans, 1988). It is interesting to note that some of the dominant American values observed in the earliest days of this society still prevail today. The most prominent among these is the way Americans value individualism.

Individualism.   **Individualism** is the concept behind the special importance that Americans attach to the rights, freedoms and responsibilities of every person. Individual rights and freedoms and individual responsibility are key features of the American political philosophy that has its roots in the Judeo-Christian religious tradition. Americans believe that individuals have a fundamental responsibility for their own lives, and their successes or failures result from their own efforts and actions. This *belief* in individual responsibility leads directly to the *value* of individualism—the freedom of every person to do, think, say, and believe what he or she wants. Naturally, no individual has a right to harm other people or to infringe on their rights, but aside from those limitations, individuals have the freedom to lead their lives as they wish.

The spirit of American individualism is expressed in the words of a California man, a top-level manager in a large corporation:

> I guess I feel like everybody on this planet is entitled to have a little bit of space . . . one of the things that makes California such a pleasant place to live, is people by and large aren't bothered by other people's value systems as long as they don't infringe upon your own. . . . if you've got the money, honey, you

can do your thing as long as your thing doesn't destroy someone else's property, or interrupt their sleep, or bother their privacy, that's fine. (Bellah, 1985, pp. 6–7).

Personal Control.   Also a part of individualism, and closely related to personal freedom, is the notion of personal control. **Personal control** means that individuals cannot be made to do things they do not want to do by social, political, or economic forces. In concrete terms, a person has

> . . . the right to be neighborly or to ignore the people next door. It is the ability to be distant from incompatible relatives and to be with compatible friends instead; to skip unwanted memberships in church or union; to vote for candidates not supported by parents or spouses or not to vote at all; and to reject unwelcome advice or demands for behavior change from spouses, employer, or anyone else (Gans, 1988, p. 3).

Americans value the right to be in control of their own lives.

Not only do Americans believe they have a right to control their lives, but they are confident that they can do so and are optimistic about meeting and overcoming every challenge (Spindler and Spindler, 1983). Again this idea is expressed in the words of the California corporation manager who said, "Given open communication and the ability to think problems out, most problems can be solved" (Bellah et al., 1985, p. 7).

Action.   Americans also value being *active* over being passive when they face problems or encounter obstacles. This value is reflected in the way Americans respond to international problems, ranging from terrorism to the smuggling of drugs into the United States. Members of Congress have proposed using military aircraft to shoot down civilian planes suspected of smuggling drugs into the United States. The appeal of such a proposal is its direct and decisive action, although civilian pilots and passengers might be understandably apprehensive about this method of combatting drugs. In dealing with international problems, U.S. presidents who have taken direct military action (air strikes, invasions, and so forth) usually receive strong public support, as indicated by rising approval ratings in public opinion polls.

President George Bush's popularity rose to an unprecedented high (nearly 90 percent approval) among the American people during and immediately after the war against Iraq. As we noted in chapter 1, many Americans were impatient with the continuing efforts at negotiation once the Allied troops were in place in the Persian Gulf. They preferred action over inaction, even if it meant war and the loss of lives.

Hard Work, Success, and Personal Achievement.   Americans also place a high value on work, personal achievement, and success. These values are certainly found in the occupational world, where most people (especially males in our society) act them out. The emphasis on work and success often becomes so important that people sometimes forget why they are working and striving to succeed. These three powerful values are pervasive in American life. Indeed, they extend into many areas of life beyond the work world. Some observers note that Americans work even when they are engaging in leisure-time activities (Kando, 1980; Gunter and Gunter, 1980). Sports are no longer games but highly organized, serious competitions. Travel becomes a ceaseless driving marathon to see how many miles can be covered in a day, how many "points of interest" can be seen in a week. Childrearing is often measured more in terms of success and achievement than experienced as the joy of being with a child. Parents feel that they have "done a good job" when their children achieve good grades, win the most-popular-student award, make the football team or cheerleading squad, or graduate with honors.

Closely related to success is the value of materialism. **Materialism** is a preoccupation with acquiring more and more possessions and property. Sometimes the emphasis on acquiring cars, houses, video and sound systems, and recreational equipment is simply called greed. But material things are acquired for reasons other than the pleasure they give; possessions are also an indication of status. The term **conspicuous consumption** (Veblen, 1899), which is often used to describe this American tendency, means acquiring things simply to display them.

Many social critics claim that the late 1970s and 1980s saw an upsurge in materialism, reflected in the "me generation" philosophy (Wolfe, 1976). A major news magazine referred to the late 1980s as a period of "mindless materialism" (*Time*, 1987). Although not denying that materialism is an important value of Americans, one sociologist has argued that Americans in the 1980s, who were employed in factories, service jobs, and as clerical workers, were not excessively materialistic; instead they bought largely for "comfort and convenience" (Gans, 1987, p. 105). That could be true, for as Gans says, these Americans have seen their real wages and salaries decreasing since the mid-1970s, and could hardly have engaged in rampant materialism. Nonetheless, it is hard to deny that when economic circumstances allow, Americans at all levels of the economic structure are inclined to acquire more and more material things.

Rationality.   One important additional value of American society is rationality (Kalberg, 1980; Ritzer, 1983; Brubaker, 1984). *Rationality* as a value emphasizes the importance of setting goals and objectives and then achieving these goals in the most efficient way possible. Rationality reaches its peak when it is possible to calculate exactly which procedure will achieve an objective most quickly and with the least expenditure of effort.

Although the value of rationality has characterized much of the Western world in the last several centuries, it has a special prominence in the United States. Almost every part of life in the United States is in some way marked by an emphasis on efficiency and effectiveness. As a result, nearly everything is produced with an eye toward minimizing time and cost, and maximizing output and productivity.

McDonaldization: Rationality in Action. There is no better way to see the importance of rationality in our everyday lives than to look closely at a familiar part of our society: the McDonald's fast-food restaurant chain. McDonald's is built on the principles of rationality—*efficiency, predictability, control,* and *quantification* (Ritzer, forthcoming).

The McDonald's system offers us efficiency by getting us from being hungry to being satisfied (or at least no longer hungry) in the shortest period of time. Because both the customers and the management value the speed with which food can be delivered and eaten, the restaurants offer a limited, simple menu with food prepared and served in assembly-line fashion. While not noted by most customers, the speedy service offered is even more important for the restaurant than for the customer. It is in the restaurant's interests to move the customers in and out as rapidly as possible. To ensure this efficiency, the seating is made intentionally hard so that customers will not linger after finishing their meal (Luxenberg, 1985). Some McDonald's establishments go beyond that subtle encouragement, however, and post signs stating that customers may spend no longer than 20 minutes in a booth or at a table.

Predictability is also an aspect of the McDonald's system. We know that the "Big Mac" or "Egg McMuffin" we order in New York will be the same as the one we order on the outskirts of Santa Fe or in a shopping mall in Portland, Oregon (or, for the international traveler, in downtown Amsterdam or Moscow). The Big Mac or Egg McMuffin may not be gourmet eating, but it will be dependably acceptable as food. The predictability of McDonald's food is a result of the high level of control exercised over the preparation of the food and the routine measurement and quantification of all aspects of the process.

Control is another principle of rationality and, in the case of McDonald's, refers especially to the *substitution of nonhuman technology for human judgment.* One of the earliest technological developments at the McDonald's restaurants was a French-fry machine that determined precisely when the fries were done to perfection. The cooking of the French fries was not to be left to the judgment of a busy or disinterested worker.

In any McDonald's (as well as in most other fast-food restaurants) the soft-drink and milkshake dispensers automatically measure the precise, predetermined amounts that go into the paper cups.

Quantification, the exact measurement of every aspect of the process, is another feature of a completely rationalized system. When you eat a McDonald's hamburger you can be quite sure that exactly 19 percent of it will be fat, or, if you order the new "light" burger, it will be only 9 percent fat. Potatoes will be sliced so that each french fry is exactly nine thirty-seconds of an inch wide. Thirty-two slices of cheese, no more, no less, will be cut from a pound of cheese. Everything is measured and timed in the McDonald's system; the numbers are precise and unvarying.

The success of the McDonald's system, has, of course, been imitated by fast-food restaurants throughout the food-service industry (Hardees, Arby's, Kentucky Fried Chicken, Pizza Hut, Taco Bell, and many others). More important, the principles of rationality as employed by the McDonald's system have now become pervasive throughout businesses and the service industries of society. The vice chairman of Toys "Я" Us wants to be thought of "as a sort of McDonald's of toys." Jiffy-Lube, Midas Muffler, H & R Block, Pearle Vision Centers, Kampgrounds of America (KOA), Kinder Care, and Nutri-System all reflect the principles of rationality so successfully introduced by McDonald's. Even the services of lawyers and doctors (McDocs) can be obtained from an efficient, rationalized system.

The principles of rationality, as exemplified by McDonald's, have now been adopted throughout U.S. society. For this reason, one of the authors of this text has labeled this phenomenon the "McDonaldization of society" (Ritzer, forthcoming).

Norms

As we have previously noted in this chapter, norms are another major component of culture. While values are the general guidelines for evaluating behavior in society, norms deal with more specific situations and circumstances. We have defined norms as the rules for what one should or should not do in given situations (Williams, 1970, p. 442).

William Graham Sumner (1906) was one of the earliest sociologists to address the norms, or rules, of society. Sumner made the distinction between folkways and mores. **Folkways** are rules that generally govern everyday conduct. Violations of those rules usually bring no serious repercussions. The eating rules of a society often fall into the category of folkways. For example, eating an entire dinner with a spoon would be considered odd behavior for an adult, but it would not be a violation that calls for punishment.

Mores (pronounced *mor-ays*), by comparison, are rules relating to much more serious behaviors. Mores involve the moral standards of the society. Thus violations of the mores will result in severe punishments (often called **sanctions**) for violators. Stealing, robbing, killing, and espionage are considered to be immoral acts and are often punished severely.

Frequently the rules that a society considers important are written into **laws** by the government. When norms are made into laws, the government takes on responsibilities for enforcing the rules. Many laws reflect the mores of the society.

An illustration of the relationship between mores and laws can be found in the many towns and counties in the United States where business is prohibited on Sundays. These laws, called "blue laws," reflect a time when Sunday business was considered immoral. Today, some of these laws remain in effect, although most Americans do not consider shopping on Sunday immoral. This example shows that laws often reflect the norms of a society, but not invariably.

Variations in Following Norms. Although norms are the rules of behavior in a society, not everyone follows the norms at all times. One reason is simply a *lack of knowledge* about certain norms. Some people might not know what the rules are. Such is often the case with newcomers to a society, as illustrated by the immigrants in Israel who were unfamiliar with the norms that surround bus riding there. An Israeli bus driver described their plight:

> They don't know how to behave. They don't know what it means to stand in line; they haggle about the fare as if they were in the market; sometimes they even jump through the windows. (Toren, 1973, p. 103)

Faced with such violations of the norms, the driver may take the role of teacher, educating the immigrants about the norms of bus riding:

> The driver may have to convince these passengers that it is not customary to cook and eat on the bus. Less dramatic is the need to explain the basic rules of the game—that fares are fixed and have to be paid, that buses run according to a time schedule, and that the driver has to comply with traffic regulations. (Toren, 1973, p. 109)

Sometimes people are familiar with a norm, but they *do not accept it or choose not to follow it*. For example, although the norm of tipping for service in restaurants is generally understood in the United States, some people tip only when they consider the service to be of high quality. They do not accept the norm of routine tipping. (Some norms are easier to reject than others because penalties for rejection are not always severe.)

Often, societal norms are not followed because, although the norm still exists as an ideal, the behavior of substantial numbers of people has changed. In other words, many people may believe the norm is a good rule to follow, but in reality they deviate from it. A case in point is the norm prohibiting sex outside of, and especially before, marriage. In the United States, the prohibition against having sexual intercourse before marriage is a norm that most people are aware of and may even support, but evidence shows that more than 70 percent of American young people violate that norm (Hayes, 1987; Kahn et al., 1988; Zelnik and Kantner, 1980).

Ideal versus Real Culture

The norm prohibiting sexual intercourse before marriage is one example of a distinction often made between the ideal and real cultures. The **ideal culture** reflects the values and norms that most people of a society are aware of and accept (premarital chastity). The **real culture** reflects what people actually do in the conduct of their everyday lives (premarital sex) even though it may differ from the ideal culture.

A second illustration of the distinction between the ideal and real cultures concerns a dominant American value discussed earlier: individualism. This value is undoubtedly supported by the vast majority of Americans, and it does influence behavior in the society. However, there are limits to how much individualism is allowed in the real world, even by those who accept the ideal of individual freedom. If homeowners in a suburban neighborhood decide to let their front yard become a "natural yard" by letting the grass, wild flowers, and weeds grow without mowing, it is very likely that the value of individual freedom would be severely tested in the neighborhood. This is one case among many that could be cited in which the ideal culture is overridden by the real culture.

Material Culture, Technology, and Cultural Lag

The definition of culture presented earlier included both the "ideas and material objects that the people of a society have created. . . ." So far we have devoted most of our attention to cultural ideas, but now we will focus directly on the material objects of culture. **Material culture** includes all the artifacts, objects, and tools that are used in some way by the members of a particular society. In the United States, homes, cars, appliances, clothing, and works of art are all part of the material culture, as are the highways and roads, the machines that produce agricultural products and manufactured goods, television and radio networks and stations, and energy-producing facilities.

The concept of technology is closely related to the material culture, but the two terms are not synonymous. Technology includes machines and production systems, which are, of course, material things, but there is more to technology than machines. **Technology** is the interplay of machines, equipment, tools, skills, and procedures for carrying out tasks. This broader view, especially with the inclusion of procedures, allows us to see that a technology exists for running churches, providing medical care, or conducting political campaigns. For example, today's political campaigns combine the technology of television with the technology of public relations. Political candidates are instructed by their staffs what to say, as well as how to say it and where and when to say it, in order to maximize their coverage on the evening news (see chapter 16—Political Life). In this case the technology of media management is more important than the material aspects of television (cameras, videotape, transmission lines, etc.).

Technology in the contemporary world often changes very rapidly, usually much faster than social and cultural systems. Technological changes often make existing social practices or cultural forms obsolete, irrelevant, or even dangerous. Members of the society may not recognize the obsolescence of certain social or cultural practices and may continue to follow them. **Cultural lag** exists when social and cultural practices are no longer appropriate for prevailing technological conditions (Ogburn, 1922/1964).

For example, cultural lag exists between the level of productivity possible with modern machines and automatic production systems, and the expectations that most people have about working. In a modern industrial society, fewer people are required to produce objects (cars, wheat, bricks, household appliances, and so on). Yet we cling to the ideas that everyone should work and that their work should produce "things" (although increasingly we consider services, such as tax consulting, public relations advising, or beauty counseling useful and productive). We also tend to think that everyone should work productively at least 40 hours a week. As machines take over even more tasks of production (and services), we will have to give people economic rewards for what we now consider "nonwork." Perhaps someday people will be routinely paid for creating artistic works, traveling, thinking, meditating, or having therapy. If this idea strikes us as strange or impossible, we might recognize our own reaction as an example of cultural lag.

Cultural Diversity

As we noted earlier, within any society some diversity exists in how the culture is understood and accepted. Not every American places the same importance on hard work and achievement or, for that matter, even uses the same language. In this section we will discuss ways in which cultural diversity exists, even within a single society.

Subcultural Groups

For most societies we can identify a dominant culture. Our earlier description of American culture described the values, norms, and beliefs of the majority of Americans—the dominant culture. But often (and especially in the United States), identifiable groups of people have cultural characteristics that differ in some significant way from the dominant culture. These groups are called **subcultural groups,** or simply, **subcultures.** Some groups described as subcultures in the United States include Hispanic Americans, Native American Indians, Mormons, and residents of the "Old South" (Black and Reed, 1984; Mauss, 1984).

How does one identify a subculture? The illustrations above suggest that subcultures are identified by language, ethnicity, race, religion, region, or sometimes a combination of these factors. If one walks through certain parts of Miami, Florida, the prominence of Spanish, both in written and spoken form, signals that an Hispanic subculture (primarily Cuban) exists. Language obviously reflects an ethnic or national heritage, and therefore one would also find differences in foods, holidays, clothing, and other life-style characteristics. Although language and life-style differences are readily observable, the norms and values of a subculture are more subtle. They can, however, be identified by closer and more systematic observations, as we will see in our examination of Mormons and Hasidic Jews.

Because the people of any given subculture live in the context of a dominant culture, they often share the culture of the dominant society to some degree. Mormons, for example, have some identifiable norms and values that are distinctly Mormon, but they also hold many values and norms found in the dominant culture. Mormons of the nineteenth century had one norm that clearly set them apart from the dominant culture: the practice of polygyny (multiple wives). However, Mormons came to be influenced by the dominant culture, which vehemently opposed the practice of polygyny, and by about 1910 the practice had been officially dropped (Mauss, 1984). This example from the Mormon experience illustrates **cul-**

tural assimilation, a process by which members of subcultures come to accept the values, beliefs, language, and behaviors of the dominant culture.

A subcultural group must often take extraordinary measures to maintain its identity in the face of the dominant culture. In the Amish religious group of Pennsylvania, parents remove their children from the public schools as soon as legally possible in order to minimize contact with the secular world (Kephart, 1976). The Hasidic Jews have made similar efforts to maintain their cultural identity, even though they are tightly surrounded by the dominant culture.

Hasidic Jews. Hasidic Jews had their beginnings in Poland in the early eighteenth century (Harris, 1986). Hasidism was innovative "in the way it redefined traditional Jewish values by placing prayer, mysticism, dancing, singing, storytelling, and the sanctification of daily life on an equal footing" with the study of traditional law (Harris, 1985a, p. 42). There are about 250,000 Hasidim in the world today (about one-fifth of the number that existed at the turn of the century); 200,000 live in the United States—half of them in Brooklyn. The Hasidim are divided into a number of groups, or "courts," the largest of which is the Lubavitchers (named after the city in Belorussia that was its original home). Despite many similarities among all Hasidim (e.g., all adult males are bearded), some differences exist (e.g., Lubavitcher men do not wear *peyes,* or long sidelocks of hair).

The Lubavitchers live in the Crown Heights section of Brooklyn. They live in a well-defined area characterized by synagogues, kosher butcher shops, and ritual bath houses. They follow a number of notable customs:

- Husbands and wives are forbidden to kiss or embrace each other in public.
- No physical contact between the sexes is permitted outside of the family.
- Few men attend college and work is not seen as an end itself, but rather as a means to earn a living so that they can follow a religious existence.
- After they marry, women cut off most of their hair and wear wigs.
- Most families do not own television sets or go to the movies.
- Women are not allowed to sing in the presence of men.
- Boys and girls go to separate schools and men and women are separated in synagogue.
- A woman may not have any physical contact with her husband during menstruation, or for a week afterwards. At the end of this period the woman is required to have a ritual bath at the *mikveh* before resuming sexual relations with her husband.

Sociology in the News

A Crash Course on Saudi Arabian Culture

Beginning in the late summer and continuing through the fall of 1990, massive numbers of U.S. military personnel were abruptly sent to Saudi Arabia. Their arrival in that country put them in the midst of Arabian culture, about which they knew very little. Fearing that U.S. troops would inadvertently offend the Saudis, the U.S. military quickly put together a booklet instructing the troops on the "dos" and "don'ts" of Arabian culture (Goldstein, 1990).

United States military personnel were instructed on the ways in which Arabs interact and converse. On the issue of physical closeness, for example, Arabian men and women are not supposed to touch each other in public. Americans were informed that they should honor this custom, especially in cases where U.S. males might encounter Arabian women. Even two opposite-sex Americans were not to be seen holding hands in public, and, of course, they were not to engage in any other form of touching or romantic interaction.

By contrast, the U.S. soldiers were informed, it would not be uncommon for two Arab men to walk along holding hands. It would simply mean that they are friends.

In conversation, Arabs (if they are the same gender) are likely to have their faces much closer together than Americans generally prefer. Anthropologists have long noted the preference Arabs have for speaking to each other face to face and at very close range (Hall, 1973). Arabs prefer not to have a conversation with another person while walking. They feel it is important that people look at one another when they are speaking; interaction for them requires deep involvement and strong eye contact.

The military manual discussed the closeness issue:

> An Arab entering [an elevator] may stand right next to you and be touching, even though no one else is in the elevator. The same may happen on a bus, airplane, or park bench.

The Americans were also advised that they were always to shake hands with everyone (of the same sex) upon arrival and departure. But the nature of the handshake in Arabian culture is different from what it usually is in U.S. culture: "Handshakes between men are soft and gentle, not a test of strength."

In Arabian culture it is an insult to allow the sole of one's shoe to face another person. United States military personnel were advised that if they were in conversation with an Arab they must keep this in mind, "Sit properly and avoid crossing your legs."

The role of women is, of course, the area of greatest difference between Arab and American cultures. Women in the U.S. military were in Saudi Arabia carrying out a wide variety of activities, which was in distinct contrast to Saudi women, who are not allowed to be alone in shopping areas, drive cars, or participate in recreational activities with men. American women were generally expected to abide by these Saudi customs. When, for example, American women wished to use a recreational facility that had been made available to the men, it required the special permission of Saudi officials. But the women could only use it a few hours each week when the men were not there. The women were also required to wear loose-fitting blouses and knee-length shorts, even when they were swimming (Moore, 1990).

The Saudi Arabian experience was for many Americans a vivid and immediate introduction to the importance of cultural differences.

HALL, EDWARD T. *The Silent Language.* Garden City, New York: Doubleday and Co., Inc., 1973.
GOLDSTEIN, AMY. "Desert Culture Shock: For the U.S. Troops, An Arab Primer." *Washington Post*, August 23, 1990, pp. D1, D2.
MOORE, MOLLY. "For Female Soldiers, Different Rules." *Washington Post*, August 23, 1990, pp. D1, D2.

Since the Lubavitchers live in an enclave in Brooklyn completely surrounded by non-Hasidim, they frequently come into contact with people from the outside world. Even so they have been successful in maintaining their distinct cultural identity. Insofar as possible they treat outsiders as if they do not exist.

Countercultures

Often in a society, groups emerge that are not just different in their ways, but are consciously in opposition to the widely accepted norms and values of the dominant culture. This type of group is known as a **counterculture** group (Yinger, 1960).

Generally, counterculture groups are not exceptionally large, and they often seem to appear and fade rather quickly. A listing of some of the most prominent counterculture groups of the United States over the past 30 years reveals how shortlived most of them are. In the 1950s the "beatniks" appeared, led by a relatively small number of literary and artistic people. Their key countercultural note was a rejection of conventional morality regarding sex, drugs, and work. The beatniks were superceded by the "hippies" of the 1960s and 1970s, who generally subscribed to the same philosophy. Much larger numbers of Americans became involved in the hippie movement, carrying forward the themes of individual freedom, antiwar, and antimaterialism. In more recent times "punkers" appeared as a prominent counterculture group. Their most distinguishing features were their devotion to certain types of music, and their adornment of bizarre clothing, jewelry, and hairstyles. All these life-style choices seem designed to demonstrate a dramatic rejection of conventional ways.

One group that has maintained a relatively long-term identity as a counterculture group is the Hell's Angels. This loosely knit, nationwide organization centers its activities around motorcycles and the heavy use of alcohol and drugs. Once again the life-style manifested by this group seems designed to flaunt their rejection of conventional ways of life.

Counterculture groups are often highly critical of the established political systems, accusing them of being repressive, corrupt, or evil. These politically oriented groups often engage in illegal acts and terrorism. A recent example in the United States is a group calling itself "The New Aryan Nation." This organization models itself after the German Nazi party, is anti-black and anti-Jewish, and wants to return to a society in which whites are separate and in total control. Its members have engaged in killings and robberies in an effort to achieve their white supremacist objectives.

Also increasingly publicized are the activities of "Skinheads," a closely related counterculture group, easily identified by their shaved heads. They also hold explicitly racist and antisemitic views and have tendencies toward violence.

Summary

Culture is the entire complex of ideas and material objects that the people of a society (or group) have created and adopted for carrying out the necessary tasks of collective life. Cultural rules give the people of a society a guide for behavior and make their behavior relatively predictable.

As an explanation of human behavior, culture offers an alternative to a "human nature" explanation. The extensive differences in the behavior of people in different societies supports the importance of culture as an explanation.

Sociobiology offers another alternative explanation. It stresses that human behavior is influenced by genetically inherited tendencies. A major criticism of sociobiology is that it does not allow for cultural factors to override whatever genetically inherited tendencies humans might have.

Most people think of their own cultural practices as the best and right way—a perspective called *ethnocentrism*. The study of different cultures allows us to see that particular cultural practices are best judged in the context of the culture in which they occur—a view called *cultural relativism.*

The most important components of culture include the verbal and non-verbal symbols of a people. The verbal symbols, or language system, of a culture tend to shape people's perceptions of the real world (the Sapir–Whorf hypothesis). Knowledge and beliefs are also components of culture. Values, the standards of desirability within a culture, are centrally important for understanding culture. In the United States the most prominent value is individualism. Closely related is the importance placed on personal control of one's life. Other significant American values are action, hard work, personal success, personal achievement, materialism, and rationality. *McDonaldization* refers to a form of rationalization that has been adopted by businesses and service industries throughout the society.

Norms are the general guidelines for evaluating behavior in society. Folkways are norms that govern everyday conduct, while mores are norms that reflect the moral standards of the society. Norms are not observed uniformly by all people in a society.

An ideal culture does exist, which contrasts with the real culture—what people actually do in the conduct of their everyday lives.

Material culture and technology are also important elements. When the material culture and technology change, a cultural lag often results as other parts of the culture become obsolete, irrelevant, or, in some cases, dangerous.

Subcultural groups (or, simply, subcultures) are groups with identifiable cultural characteristics that set them apart from the dominant culture. Subcultures often get changed and influenced by the dominant culture through a process of cultural assimilation. To retain its distinctive ways, a subcultural group must make an effort to remain separate from the dominant culture. Groups with cultural characteristics that are consciously in opposition to the dominant culture are called *countercultures.*

CRITICAL THINKING

1. In what ways can a knowledge of the concept of culture be practical in business and travel?
2. Why (or why not) is a cultural explanation of human behavior more useful and significant than an explanation based on human nature or sociobiology?
3. Review the definition of ethnocentrism given in the chapter. Can you think of examples of American humor about peoples and cultures that are based on ethnocentrism?
4. The authors state that in order to be a cultural relativist one need not blindly accept all forms of human behavior. Give examples of human behavior (historical or other) that you feel are beyond the limits of tolerance. To what extent are your beliefs based on your culture's views of right and wrong?
5. Give examples of nonverbal symbols that you have used or seen in the past week.
6. Give an example of how new technology has shaped our verbal symbols and perceptions of reality.
7. Review the definition of cultural values presented in the chapter. List five values you feel are dominant in American society. Then list five values you personally feel are most important in your life. To what extent do your personal values match the societal ones you have mentioned? What might such a comparison indicate about your relationship to the dominant culture in America?
8. What norms govern your behavior as a college student? Would you classify these norms as folkways, mores, or laws?
9. Give three examples of discrepancies between our notion of the ideal culture and the real culture. How do you explain such discrepancies?
10. To what extent are technological changes responsible for cultural changes and cultural lag in the Third World today?
11. Make a fairly complete list of the subcultures and countercultures you believe exist in American society. Give an example of how each varies from the dominant culture. Is such diversity helpful or harmful for society?

4 Forms of Social Life: Interaction, Groups, Organizations, and Societies

Human behavior is not random; it is patterned. Regularity and order can be found in the actions of all humans, whether they are Tibetans living in Katmandu, aborigines living in the outback of Australia, or New Yorkers living on the Upper East Side of Manhattan. Average people living anywhere will know how to relate to the people with whom they come in contact in their daily lives. Imagine what would happen, however, if we were to take a person from any one of these places and put him or her in another society. The results would vividly reveal how the patterns of behavior in a society must be learned.

Because many of the social patterns of our own society are so familiar, we often give them little attention. In this chapter we will examine a wide range of different patterns of social relations. We will begin with a general concept that sociologists often use when describing a pattern of social relationships (social structure). Then, beginning at the microscopic level, we will see how interaction between individuals produces patterned behavior even in a two-person relationship. Next we will move to the level of groups and then to organizations. The chapter will conclude with a discussion of societies.

Social Structures

Social structures are regular patterns of social interaction and persistent social relationships. Social structures are constructed by the ongoing interaction of people, but at the same time, by observing these patterns of interaction, we can identify social structures. Social structures can be observed at any social level from the interaction between two people, through groups and organizations, to entire societies. To illustrate how a social structure is created through interaction, and, simultaneously, how social structures are observable in the regularities and patterns of everyday interaction, we will consider a familiar example.

Imagine a number of college students who come together at the beginning of a school year to live on the same corridor of a dormitory. When they first move in they are probably strangers, or perhaps they know each other only casually. Over a period of time, however, through their interaction, they will start sorting themselves into sets of people who spend time together. These sets of people will talk, go to meals together, help each other with homework, and so on. Some of the emerging groups are apt to have special interests and activities—sports, dorm politics, partying, practical jokes, or studying. Using the words of the social structure definition, we can say that regular patterns of social interaction and persistent social relationships will occur among these students.

When anthropologist Michael Moffatt (1989) lived among the residents of a dormitory at Rutgers University (see chapter 3, p. 74), he was able to observe the social structures that emerged during the first two months of the school year. He reports: "By late October, the residents of the floor had connected themselves together in the complex network of friendship [groups]" (Moffatt, 1989, p. 95). He describes some of the larger friendship groups and cliques, identifying their leaders, their special activities, and their differing styles. He also notes that there were some two- and three-person groups (see "Dyads and Triads," p. 105) that were either outside the larger groups, or in some cases connecting two different groups. Also, some first-year students "floated between this clique and others on the floor" (Moffatt, 1989, p. 96). These patterns of interaction (social structures) on a single dormitory floor were clearly identifiable after only two months of interaction. One can be quite certain that at the beginning of each academic year similar structures will emerge in dormitories and residence halls at every other college.

Because of the patterned nature of social structures, they can typically be sketched in diagrammatic form. For example, Figure 4–1 is Moffatt's diagrammatic presentation of the student social structure that emerged on the dormitory floor where he made his observations. In Figure 4–1, the

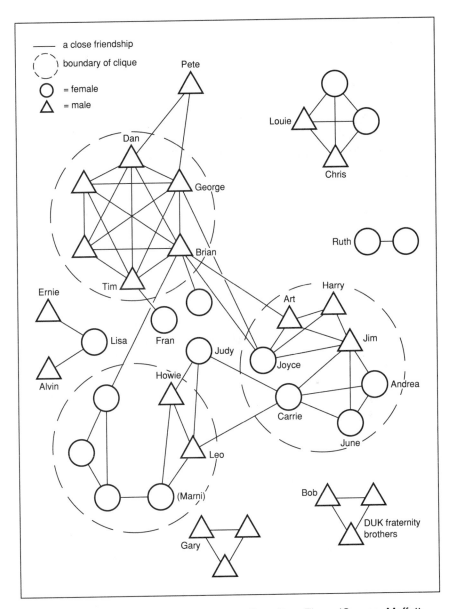

Figure 4–1. Student Social Structure on a Dormitory Floor. (*Source:* Moffatt, 1989)

lines drawn between individuals are based on mutual friendship choices as expressed on a questionnaire that Moffatt gave to the residents of the floor in late October. (Unnamed persons in Figure 4–1 are persons who do not live on the floor.)

Because social structures are created by people, they can change over time. But structures tend to have some persistence, and when sociologists speak of social structures they are talking about patterns of interaction and social relationships that persist over time. Included would be the major social structures found in societies, for they generally do not change rapidly. Examples in American society, to be examined later, are the socioeconomic-status system with its different social classes (chapter 8), and the major racial and ethnic groups (chapter 9). These stratification systems are, of course, social structures. The social class structure of the society is observable through the way people interact with each other, and these patterns of interaction do not change much over time. The same is true with respect to the relationships between racial and ethnic groups in the United States. Racial discrimination, for example, which places blacks and other racial minorities in disadvantaged positions, has existed for centuries and persists today.

Throughout this chapter we will be describing social structures at the various levels of social life. We will begin with the interaction between individuals, and then move on to groups and organizations. We will conclude, at the macroscopic end of the social continuum, with a consideration of societies.

Interaction

The ability of humans to meet and interact with other humans is a high-level skill, but most of the time we do it with ease. In an average day a person typically interacts with a wide variety of people, including friends, relatives, lovers, acquaintances, and strangers. As long as we share the same language with these people, we can negotiate almost any kind of situation, whether it is friendly or hostile, comfortable or awkward, casual or formal.

As we saw in our consideration of symbolic interaction theory in chapter 1, the human mind, with its ability to understand and use symbols (both verbal and nonverbal), makes interaction possible between people. People interact primarily through verbal symbols, or words, not only with others but with themselves. By using symbols to interact with themselves, people are able to evaluate other people and situations, and decide what actions to take. Again, this is an important principle of symbolic interaction theory.

When interaction occurs between two people, two things happen, almost simultaneously. Each person in an interaction situation is *sending* words and cues and *receiving and processing* words and cues as they come in from the other person. The important feature of any interaction is the way people use their minds to interpret the words and cues of another person, deduce their meaning, and respond accordingly.

This abstract description of interaction makes it seem complex and unfamiliar, but if we take an everyday situation we can see how the process of interaction works. Consider a hypothetical yet commonplace situation in which a male and a female college student are getting acquainted. If they are in college and happen to sit next to each other in a class, over a period of time they may have a series of interactions that could ultimately result in their dating and becoming romantically involved. Their early interaction is important in this process. Two people seated side by side may rarely talk with each other at first. Gradually, however, they may start to interact. Of course, the very act of engaging in conversation when it is not necessary is in itself a symbolic act. When two people find themselves engaged in conversation they may recognize that their interaction could imply a mutual attraction. Even as they talk about something as mundane as the sociology professor or the next test, the young man might reflect to himself that he is attracted to the young woman and that she might be attracted to him.

As this interaction continues, different things might be happening at different levels simultaneously. Noncommittal ideas may first be exchanged, as the students talk about the professor or about studying for the next examination. The young woman may say she doesn't have anyone with whom to study, but if she makes this remark, the young man must interpret what it means. He has only a second or two to decide if she is saying that it might be pleasant for the two of them to get together outside of class, ostensibly to do some studying. At the same time, as he is assessing what her words really mean, he is formulating his response. If he responds to her objective statement inappropriately, he may look foolish. If he treats it as a suggestion that they get together outside of class and she did not mean it that way, he may be embarrassed. The young man must quickly select from his many possible choices: "I don't have anyone to study with either," or "I always find it helps to study with someone just before the test," or "Why don't we get together before the test?"

If the young man made the last of these statements, the young woman would have to decide exactly what his words meant. He could be asking for a date, or he could simply be suggesting that they study together. The woman must weigh all the evidence, again in just a second or two, and make some appropriate response. As a rule, a person in this situation will reply in such a way that the response will be appropriate regardless of the real intent of the statement. Or the young woman could simply say, "Are you asking me for a date or do you want to get together to study?" However, before doing so she will have to weigh the consequences of this response. Will the young man be shocked by her directness? Will her statement have the effect of acknowledging the previously unstated attraction between them?

The interaction just described goes on within the context of the cultural values and the social norms we discussed in the last chapter. In some societies, the norms of courtship would make it totally inappropriate for two young people to make a date of any kind. Often parents would have to be consulted and a chaperon obtained before two young people of the opposite sex could spend any time together. We can see from these normative constraints why human behavior is not random but is, as we said, patterned. The interaction between two people who are getting acquainted is partially open to their own creativity and inventiveness, but it is also patterned by the norms that prevail in a society.

But there is another important social constraint on the interaction between the young man and woman we have been describing. Both people have social statuses, or positions, and attached to these statuses are social roles. Status and role are important sociological concepts because they reveal why there is a great amount of regular and patterned social behavior.

Status and Role

The words and actions of the young man and woman described above will certainly be influenced and shaped, especially in the early interaction, by the fact of their genders. Many American young people still believe it more appropriate for males to initiate invitations for dates than for females to do so. This view is changing, but many young women still say, "I think it is fine for a woman to ask a guy for a date, *but I wouldn't do it.*" This statement tells us that although some young women do not see anything wrong with a woman initiating a date, many still feel that it might be inappropriate behavior. But why is it viewed as inappropriate? In order to understand why someone would feel this way and why this feeling is shared by many other people—young and old, female and male—we have to examine the importance of the sociological concepts of status and role.

A **status** is a socially recognized position in a social system. A **role** is the behavior generally expected of one who occupies a particular status. Again we can use gender as an example of status and role. In all societies, males and females have socially recognized positions, with certain expectations about what one will and will not do. However, males and females are not expected to act in the same way in every society. In chapter 10 we will examine some societies in which men and women are expected to act in ways that are very different from those traditionally expected of them in American society. But—and here is the important point—gender is always a status that carries with it some expected behaviors. Roles are always connected with gender.

Statuses can be of two types: ascribed and achieved. An **ascribed status** is one into which individuals move or are placed, irrespective of their efforts or capacities. Examples of ascribed statuses include being male or female, young or old, black or white, son or daughter. We have little control over our ascribed statuses. (An example of an effort to control ascribed status would be a person who undergoes a sex change.) In contrast, an **achieved status** is one that people acquire through their own efforts. Examples include becoming a college graduate, getting married, having children, becoming an astronaut, or even becoming a bank robber.

A related concept is that of master status. A **master status** refers to a position so important that it dominates and overrides all other statuses, both for the person and all other people. For example, being an AIDS victim may well be a master status for individuals because the disease might be so overwhelming that it shapes the person's self-image as well as other people's view of him or her. More commonly in our society, a master status is related to one's occupation. A person who is a Supreme Court Justice, a nun, a major league baseball player, or an opera singer is likely to be seen primarily in terms of his or her major occupational role—a master role.

Another point about statuses and roles is that they have a reality of their own; they exist irrespective of the persons who fill them. Whoever occupies the status of the President of the United States, or is the center-fielder on a baseball team, or the anchorperson on a television news show must attend to certain expectations that accompany the status. In general, the people who fill a status understand the expectations and follow the behavior expected of them.

However, not everyone in a particular status behaves in exactly the same way. There are two reasons for this. First, the role expectations connected with a status are not fully detailed. Role expectations are not so precisely stated or understood that every detail of expected behavior is clear. Second, individuals who hold statuses may have their own orientations toward the role. Let us deal with each of these issues separately.

Roles do not specify every exact behavior that a person in a given status must follow. In fact, roles often have only broad requirements within which a person must operate. Airline pilots, for example, are expected to be competent to fly planes in all kinds of conditions, and handle difficult and emergency situations in a calm and collected way. When pilots speak to the passengers they generally present themselves as steady, serious, and relaxed, even though they may not always feel that way. However, some pilots will occasionally inject humor, irritation (with delays, for example), or other emotions into their public presentations. When they are not within hearing or sight of the passengers, their behavior may be even more at odds with the general role expectations for airline pilots. Behind the scenes they are able to introduce their unique, personal characteristics and still fulfill the role expectations connected with a status. In other words, people do not simply conform to role expectations; they also actively modify their roles. This ability of individuals to modify (at least to some degree) their own roles has been called **role-making** (Hewitt, 1984, p. 81).

Another way to see how individuals can vary their performance of a role is to note that the dominant view about what is expected of people in a given status need not be universal. Different orientations toward a role can exist. The college student role has broad outlines—enrolling, going to class, studying, taking exams—but different students might emphasize different features of the student role. These different emphases are called **role orientations.** Some students might emphasize the academic and intellectual aspect of the student role. With this orientation to the world of ideas and books, they take advantage of the opportunity they have to become involved in intellectual pursuits. Their role orientation toward their college-student status has been called the "academic-intellectual role orientation." In comparison, other college students are more oriented toward the vocational or professional training they receive in school. They see student life as an opportunity to learn a profession and gain entry into it. This orientation has been called the "vocational role orientation." Some students see their college experience as an opportunity to engage in an active social life or to learn social skills. For them, college is a learning ground for their future social lives. The fraternity/sorority scene may be a forerunner of the country club life that they expect to enter later. This role orientation of college students has been called the *social life role* (Bolton and Kammeyer, 1967).

As we have seen, the roles connected with statuses do not make individuals in the same status behave in the same way, but enough similarity is evident in role performance to produce some general patterns of behavior. These patterns, found among males and females, airline pilots, and students, and a vast array of other statuses, are sufficiently consistent to produce identifiable patterns in social life. However, statuses and roles can always be modified and changed over time, through the continuing actions and interactions of people.

Dyads and Triads

When two people engage in interaction it is called a **dyad.** When a third person is introduced into the interaction it is called a **triad.** While both dyads and triads involve interaction, and both can be seen as groups, there are some interesting differences between two-person and three-person interaction. From a sociological and practical point of view, the triad is a much more complicated social arrangement (Simmel, 1950).

A dyad has only one relationship, but a triad has three (A and B, A and C, B and C). That in itself makes the triad more complicated. Consider, for example, the common situation of a husband and wife dyad becoming parents of a new baby, thus becoming a triad. The relationship between the husband and wife becomes more complicated because each will now have a relationship with the baby. It is a fairly common occurrence for a new mother to devote so much attention to her relationship with the baby that her husband feels neglected. A substantial amount of research shows that satisfaction with marital relationships declines when married couples have children. Part of the reason can probably be attributed to the changes in interaction when a married-couple dyad becomes a triad.

Similar problems often emerge in three-person friendship groups. Although three-person groups can maintain a cohesive "three-musketeers" relationship, a balance is difficult to maintain. All pairs of relationships in a triad must be about equal in time spent together, displays of friendship, conversation, and so on. If this equality is not maintained, then one of the pairs will dominate, leaving the third person relatively isolated. Many people who have been in three-person friendship groups have had the experience of two members drawing closer together and shutting out the third.

Although dyads and triads are frequent forms of social interaction, the social group brings us to a more purely sociological level. We turn to this level next.

Social Groups

While the word *group* is used in various ways in everyday speech, and even in sociology, the technical sociological meaning focuses our attention on some important features of social life. A **group** may be defined as a relatively small number of people who interact with one another over time and thereby establish patterns of interaction, a group identity, and rules or norms governing behavior.

One of the key features defining a group is the interaction among all members. A larger entity such as a society (e.g., American society) differs from a group in that all the members of a society cannot possibly interact with each other because of their large number.

Although a large number of people cannot technically constitute a social group, a small number of people will not necessarily constitute a group either. Several people who meet briefly on an elevator are not a group, because they lack a group identity and because they do not interact on the basis of patterns they have established.

In-Groups and Out-Groups

According to our definition, a basic characteristic of a group is that the interacting individuals have a group identity. Therefore, to qualify as a group, the people who compose it must define themselves as members and, conversely, those outside the group must be defined as outsiders. The emphasis on group identity leads to the distinction between *in-groups* and *out-groups* (Sumner, 1904). An **in-group** is one that members are involved in and with which they identify, while an **out-group** is one to which outsiders belong. The importance of this distinction is the tendency for people to believe in the rightness and desirability of the in-group, and to reject the ways of the out-group. The in-group/out-group distinction usually takes on its greatest significance when two or more groups are in close proximity. Members of fraternities and sororities on a college campus may view members of other fraternities and sororities as out-groups. This can lead to an attitude of "us" against "them." In extreme cases, in-group/out-group attitudes may lead to conflict between groups. (See Sociology in the News, p. 108).

Primary and Secondary Groups

Sociologists also differentiate between primary groups and secondary groups. The concept of **primary groups** was developed by Cooley (1909) to describe groups "characterized by intimate face-to-face association and cooperation." Primary groups are typically small and close-knit. The relationships among the members are very personal. They strongly identify with each other as well as with the group as a whole. As a result of the closeness of the relationships, the primary group often has a profound effect on its members. As examples of primary groups Cooley cites the family, play groups of children, and neighborhood or community groups.

Secondary groups, in contrast to primary groups, are typically large and impersonal. Members do not know each other as intimately or completely as do the members of a primary group. Members' ties to a secondary group are typically weaker than the ties to primary groups. Secondary groups have a less profound impact on members. They are usually formed for a specific purpose, and the members rarely interact with each other outside of the activities that are oriented toward the group goal. The members of a local Parent–Teacher's Association or a labor union are examples of secondary groups.

Reference Groups

Another sociological perspective on groups is revealed by thinking of how groups (both primary and secondary) serve as reference groups. **Reference groups** are any groups that a person takes into account when evaluating his or her actions or characteristics. As humans we are always trying to evaluate ourselves and our behavior. Am I attractive? Am I doing a good job? Should I wear these clothes tonight? One way we answer these questions for ourselves is to refer to the performance or the qualities of the members of some group. Although individuals often use groups of which they are members as reference groups, a person does not necessarily have to be a member of a group in order to use it as a reference group. Take, for example, a woman who is making reasonably good career progress and, after some years, becomes a manager in a major corporation. If this woman's reference group is made up primarily of the circle of friends with whom she went to high school, she will undoubtedly have positive feelings about her career progress. Many of her high school friends have probably not gone on to jobs in the corporate world; compared to them she is doing well. On the other hand, if this same woman manager takes as her reference group the fastest-rising executives in her own corporation, she will evaluate her career success more negatively.

As this example shows, a reference group can be used to make comparative evaluations about oneself and one's performance. But reference groups can also provide a normative function by supplying an individual's norms and values. Thus, a young manager may not yet be a member of top management, but the latter can be his/her reference group, supplying the aspiring executive with the relevant standards of behavior. For example, if an aspiring young female manager notices that the successful female executives wear tailored suits and silk blouses, she too might stock her wardrobe with these items.

Religious group membership often provides an important reference group that has a profound influence on individual behavior. A study of American adults has shown that membership in different religious groups

Sociology in the News

Street Gangs in Los Angeles: An Extreme Case of In-groups versus Out-groups

Authorities in Los Angeles County estimate that there are some 800 street gangs in the county. These gangs have more than 90,000 members and were responsible for an estimated 650 killings in 1990 (Lacy, 1991). Gang members are primarily black or Hispanic, but there are also Asian, Samoan, and white gangs (Reinhold, 1988). The two most extensive groups are the Bloods and the Crips, who are arch rivals. The Bloods and Crips have many neighborhood groups subsumed under their general labels, e.g., the Grape Street Crips of Watts, the Hoover Street Crips, or the Inglewood and Avenue Piru Bloods.

Gang members attach an extraordinary importance to their names and other group symbols, revealing, of course, their intense in-group feelings. Out-group attitudes are also revealed by the hostility expressed toward the names and symbols of the other gang. It is said that a Blood will not ask a friend for a cigarette (since it starts with the letter C) but will instead ask for a "bigarette" (Reinhold, 1988).

In areas of Los Angeles where gangs thrive, a gang member who strays into the neighborhood of a rival gang or is found in the street wearing the wrong color clothing might get beaten up or killed. Many gangs have near-uniform clothing. Gangs connected with the Crips wear blue, while the Bloods prefer red. Members of one Hispanic gang are identifiable by their khaki pants, camp or prison jackets, plain Pendleton shirts, and head bandannas or brim hats (Stumphauzer et al., quoted in Mirande, 1987, p. 80).

Because of the dangers associated with wearing the colors of the Bloods and Crips, many Los Angeles-area schools have, for years, enforced dress codes that prohibit students from wearing either red or blue bandannas, shoelaces, or belts (Lacey, 1991). But the gangs have a new clothing fad—the wearing of professional sports team jackets and hats—that is now endangering the lives of nongang members living in Los Angeles (Lacey, 1991).

The Los Angeles Raiders football team is known widely for its black and silver colors and its menacing pirate symbol. Many Los Angeles gangs have adopted the black athletic jacket of the Raiders—it is said to be the favored attire at funerals when a gang member is killed. The problem arises when school children (and even school teachers and staff members) wear the Raiders jackets simply because they like the football team. In many Los Angeles neighborhoods they may be mistaken for members of a rival gang, and their lives may be endangered. School administrators are now banning the wearing of Raiders jackets in their schools because they fear one of their students will be mistaken for a gang member and beaten or killed (Lacey, 1991).

LACY, MARC. "Danger Links for Fans as Gangs Adopt Pro Attire." *The Los Angeles Times*, March 20, 1991.
MIRANDE, ALFREDO. *Gringo Justice*. South Bend, Indiana: Notre Dame University Press, 1987.
REINHOLD, ROBERT. "In the Middle of L.A.'s Gang Warfare." *New York Times Magazine*, May 22, 1988.

influences attitudes toward premarital sex, birth control, and abortion (Bock et al., 1983). Research evidence also reveals that religions as reference groups influence alcohol use (Cochran et al., 1988).

A person will likely have a number of reference groups, and those groups will probably change over time. Many college students have reference groups that include students who are socially popular figures, varsity athletes, and campus leaders. After graduation some of the characteristics and qualities of these types may seem superficial and irrelevant. Whatever one's reference groups are while in college, they are likely to change dramatically when one leaves the campus and enters the business or professional world.

Conformity—Three Classic Experiments

As the discussion of reference groups suggests, individual behavior is influenced by the groups to which one belongs and the groups to which one aspires. The tendency of individuals to respond to social groups and to allow them to influence behavior is one of the most intriguing aspects of human behavior. As we saw in the last chapter, Americans place great value on their individualism, and yet there is ample evidence that individuals have a tendency to *conform* to the behavior of other members of a group, even when no explicit demands are made to do so. That is, people seem to want to go along with the majority of group members even when those group members do not explicitly pressure them to conform.

The Sherif Experiment. An important study in this line of research is Muzafer Sherif's (1935) famous experiment, "A Study of Some Social Factors in Perception." Sherif was interested in studying what people would do when presented with an ambiguous phenomenon—one lacking in stable reference points. The phenomenon Sherif presented to his subjects was a single point of light in a completely dark room. Because no other objects in the room could be seen, there were no reference points, and the light appeared to move (even though it was not moving). This phenomenon is known as the *autokinetic effect*. In one part of this study individuals were first shown the light alone and then again in the presence of a group of people. When individuals alone were presented with the light, each one established a sense of the distance that the light had moved. When those individuals were then placed in the same situation with a group of people, each individual's judgment of the distance that the light moved tended to converge with the judgment of the group. It appears from this experiment that individuals prefer to be closer to the standards of the group; they preferred to be in conformity.

The Asch Experiment.   In another classic experiment, Solomon Asch (1952) studied groups of seven to nine college students to examine the effect of group pressure on individuals. In each group, all but one of the members (the subject) were confederates of the researcher. The group was shown pairs of cards—the first card with a single vertical line and the second with three vertical lines. One of the lines on the second card was equal in length to the line of the first card. The other two lines were sufficiently different that, when asked to match lines on the two cards, the vast majority of people making decisions alone chose the correct line.

In the crucial experiment, Asch had his confederates choose an incorrect line on the second card. These choices were made out loud, within hearing of the subjects, who were positioned toward the end of the group. Responding in turn, subjects showed that they were experiencing group pressure, even to the extent of making the same incorrect choice. In about one-third of the cases the subjects sided with the majority and made the incorrect choice. This tendency to conform to the majority opinion appeared even when the subjects apparently knew that they were making incorrect judgments. Although this experiment demonstrates the pressure to conform to group opinions, it is important to remember that in about two-thirds of the cases the subjects resisted the majority and made the correct decision.

The Milgram Experiment.   An experiment conducted by Stanley Milgram (1974) focused on a somewhat different aspect of conformity. He was able to demonstrate that many people will comply with the orders of someone who appears to be in a position of authority in an organization (the social form we will consider next). In the Milgram experiments subjects were asked to work with other individuals who, unknown to the subjects, were paid by Milgram to act out prearranged parts. The subjects always found themselves in the position of "teacher" in the study, while the confederates served as "learners." The learners were strapped into chairs and hooked up to electrodes. The teacher-subjects were placed in another room with a fake shock generator. Labels on the generator indicated the increasing intensity of its charge—from "Slight Shock" at the low end to "Danger: Severe Shock" and, finally, "XXX" at the other end. The shocks were not real, but the teacher-subjects did not know it. They were instructed to give the learner-confederates an electric shock for every wrong answer (intentional on the part of the confederate) and to increase the amount of shock each time. Learner-confederates reacted with screams, as if pained by the shocks. Almost two-thirds of the subject-teachers continued to administer shocks to the point marked "XXX"—a level they believed was potentially lethal. The researcher, dressed in white coat and projecting an aura of scientific respectability, was perceived by most subjects as an authoritative figure whose instructions were to be followed regardless of the resulting harm to other people.

Before the study, almost all of the subjects said they would never be able to bring themselves to inflict severe pain on someone in any foreseeable circumstances. The Milgram study indicates that, under certain conditions, many people, especially if they receive orders from authority figures, will violate their own moral norms and inflict pain, perhaps even at lethal levels, on other human beings.

These experimental studies reveal how people are influenced by the behavior of other members of groups and by authority figures in organizations. Furthermore, these reactions were produced in experimentally created groups and organizational settings. It is possible that the real groups and organizations to which individuals belong (families, friendship groups, schools, workplaces, and so on) may have even more influence on member behavior. Clearly groups and organizations can and do exert an influence on the behavior of individuals.

We are now ready to take a closer look at organizations and how they work. Of special importance is the bureaucratic form of organization that is so pervasive today.

Organizations and Bureaucracies

We live in a world that is increasingly characterized by large-scale organizations. Most of us were born in large hospitals or multipurpose medical centers; we have been educated in large school systems, have often worked for major corporations or businesses, and have dealt with complex governmental systems. Major portions of our lives are spent dealing with and working in large-scale organizations. We recognize increasingly that we cannot understand the society in which we live if we do not un-

derstand how organizations work and how the many different kinds of organizations—political, economic, and social—relate to each other
(Clark, 1988).

To see just how enmeshed we are with large-scale organizations, we
have only to open our wallets or purses. We carry social security cards,
identification cards, registration cards, driver's licenses, medical insurance
cards, credit cards, and a variety of other membership cards that verify
that we belong to organizations. In other words, we live in an "organizational society" (Presthus, 1978).

Sociologists use the term **organization** to describe a deliberately constructed collectivity aimed at achieving specified goals with clearly delineated statuses, roles, and rules. Thus, the U.S. Postal Service is an
organization of managers, supervisors, postal clerks, mail carriers, and
many others whose task it is to deliver the mail. Handgun Control is an
organization established to reduce the number of handguns in U.S. society. Any neighborhood improvement association, with officers, members,
and meetings, is an organization created to do something positive for a
neighborhood.

These three examples show that many different types of organizations
exist. Some are government agencies; some are private enterprises. Organizations may focus on causes or have special interests and may be national or local in scope.

Another way to make distinctions among types of organizations is on
the basis of how control is exerted over people who exist at or near the
bottom of the organization—called the "lower participants." Three types
of organizations have been identified on this basis (Etzioni, 1961).

Coercive Organizations.   A **coercive organization** uses force to control
those at the bottom of the structure. The major examples of coercive organizations are prisons and custodial mental hospitals. The lower participants in such organizations are prisoners and mental patients—people
who have no personal commitment to these organizations. Because they
are not deeply committed to the organization and, in fact, probably have
negative feelings toward it, coercion is needed to get them to do what the
organization wants.

A special name given to a certain extreme type of coercive organization is the total institution (Goffman, 1961). A **total institution** is an
organization that is cut off from the rest of society, forming an all-
encompassing social environment to meet all the needs of its members.
Not all coercive organizations are total institutions; for example, some
prisons and mental institutions allow inmates considerable flexibility
(e.g., weekend leaves, conjugal visits, open doors). (See Cross-National

Perspectives on extremes in prisons.) On the other hand, some total institutions may not have the key characteristics of coercive organizations. For example, many large naval ships remain at sea for weeks and even months, providing the personnel on board everything they need for a full and complete life (food, personal and medical services, entertainment and recreation, religious services, and so on). Although these ships are total institutions, the people on board are not absolutely coerced into being there. We will have more to say about total institutions in chapter 5—Socialization.

Utilitarian Organizations.   A second type of organization is the **utilitarian organization** that uses money to control the people at the bottom. Industries and businesses are the most common types of utilitarian organizations. All employees and workers, but especially those at the bottom (clerks and those who do menial labor), are in the organization primarily for the wages they receive. Such workers are not likely to be highly committed to their organizations, although they tend to have a higher level of commitment than the "lower participants" in coercive organizations. They do what the organization expects of them because they are paid for it.

Normative Organizations.   Finally, in **normative** or **voluntary organizations** participants are controlled by the norms and values of the organization. Mothers Against Drunk Drivers, which was founded in 1980 by Cindy Lighter of Fair Oaks, California after her 13-year-old daughter was killed by a hit-and-run driver, is an example of a normative organization (Weed, 1990, 1991). M.A.D.D. chapters appeared all around the United States because people in many communities shared a concern about the needless deaths caused by drunk driving and sought to do something about the problem.

Other examples of normative organizations include those organized around religious beliefs (Fellowship of Christian Athletes) and political ideologies (Young Democrats, Young Republicans). Those at the bottom of such organizations may be believers, members, or volunteers. They tend to be highly committed to the organization's purposes or beliefs, and they do what the organization expects of them.

All of these types of organizations, especially as they grow in population size, tend to become bureaucracies. The bureaucracy has become the most common form of organization in contemporary life. Although the term is often used in a negative or derogatory way, it is necessary to take a more neutral and objective look at this form of organization.

Cross-National Perspectives

National Extremes in Prisons

There are great variations in the way prisons are organized in different countries. Some prison systems are harsh, brutal, and repressive—consciously designed to break the spirit of inmates. Other prison systems give prisoners maximum freedom and show respect for individuality and privacy. Two examples will illustrate these extremes: the harsh and repressive political prisons of Uruguay in the 1970s and early 1980s, and the liberal system of the Netherlands prison, *Schutterswei*.

Actually, repressiveness began for prisoners in Uruguay even before they entered prison. They were first detained for long periods in military units and tortured in various ways. Among the methods used were electrodes strategically applied to their bodies, suspending the prisoners by their arms, and immersing prisoners' heads under water for long periods. The torturers were quite expert and were able to punish their prisoners without leaving any physical traces. In fact, physicians were ordinarily present to be sure that the torture did not go too far. One of the shocking aspects of the Uruguayan system was the active involvement and cooperation of members of the medical profession.

Once the Uruguayan political prisoners entered prison the physical torture stopped, but it was replaced by psychological torture. In effect, the physicians were replaced by psychiatrists and psychologists. Said one of the psychiatrists involved in the system: "The war continued inside the prison. . . . Day after day, rule after rule—all was part of a grand design to make them suffer psychologically" (Weschler, 1989). In fact, the prisons were designed by psychologists to inflict the maximum amount of psychological damage. For one thing, life in the prisons was totally unpredictable. Orders were to be strictly followed, but the orders changed arbitrarily, dramatically, and without notice from one day to another. Inmates who wanted to obey found it impossible to do so. For those prisoners who found it impossible to obey, and that was everyone, there was always the possibility of long stays in *La Isla*, the much-hated group of isolation cells to which errant prisoners were sent for long periods.

In addition, the inmates were systematically dehumanized. They were allowed no names and were referred to by number. The guards were taught to be revulsed by the inmates, and they referred to them as "cockroach" or "diseased one." Whatever few possessions inmates were able to accumulate were arbitrarily confiscated at various times. They had no privacy and were constantly under surveillance through a system of peepholes and bugging devices. The nerves of the prisoners were randomly shaken with faked escapes, complete with accompanying alarms, floodlights, and gunfire. After all this, and as a final humiliation, the prisoners or their families were expected to pay for the entire cost of imprisonment.

In contrast, the *Schutterswei* prison in the Netherlands is a model of a nonrepressive prison. One revealing feature of *Schutterswei* is that inmates have access to "sex cells," rooms with beds that prisoners can share with approved visitors. The only stipulation is that the visitor must be someone with whom the prisoner had a sincere relationship before coming to prison. The visitor may be a wife, a girlfriend, or a homosexual lover. The prison officials believe that such a system helps keep families together and personal relationships intact and keeps inmates from being broken mentally by incarceration.

The sex cells are not the only aspect of *Schutterswei* that stand in opposition to the more repressive types of total institutions. Prisoners are paid a wage of $27 a week that they can use as they wish, and many use it to furnish their brightly colored cells with television sets, stereo systems, and coffeemakers. Some buy and keep pets (parakeets and fish being the most popular choices). Individuality is encouraged in the furnishing of cells and in the clothes inmates wear. There is a snack room where they can buy food and a kitchen where they can do their own cooking. Private telephone calls are permitted. In the final year of their sentences, prisoners may be allowed as many as six leaves of up to 60 hours each. Some conservatives in the Netherlands label these prisons "Hilton hotels."

Do such liberal prisons work? No one really knows, but it is true that the streets of Dutch cities are comparatively safe and the crime rate comparatively low. And the Dutch prison system is comparatively cheap despite its high staff-to-inmate ratio.

"Doing Time the Dutch Way." *World Press Review.* 35 May, 1988:53.
WESCHLER, LAWRENCE. "The Great Exception." *New Yorker,* April 3, 1989.

What Is a Bureaucracy?

A **bureaucracy** is an organization with a special set of characteristics:

1. A division of labor among the members, with everyone having specialized duties and functions;
2. A well-defined rank order of authority among members;
3. A system of rules covering the rights and duties of all members in all positions;
4. Rules and procedures for carrying out all tasks;
5. Impersonality in the relations among members;
6. Selection for membership, employment, and promotion based on competence and expertise.

These typical features of a bureaucracy are what sociologists call an ideal type. An ideal type is not, as it might seem, a best possible form of something. Rather, an **ideal type** is a logical, exaggerated, and "pure" model of some phenomenon that one wishes to study or analyze. It is a methodological tool developed by the German theorist Max Weber, whom we discussed in chapter 1 (Weber, 1903–1917/1949). Weber developed the ideal type as a tool for analyzing and studying real bureaucracies. By specifying the characteristics of the ideal-type bureaucracy, it is possible to see if, and to what degree, actual organizations are bureaucratic.

As an ideal type, a bureaucracy consists of a hierarchy of positions, with each position under the control and supervision of the one above it. Each position is assigned the task of performing a set of official functions, and procedures in each position are defined by a set of official rules. The individual in each position is granted the authority to carry out the functions of that position, but that authority does not extend beyond it.

In order for bureaucrats to apply the rules attached to their positions, they must receive specialized training. In general, only those who are formally qualified through specialized training are entitled to hold positions within a bureaucracy. Bureaucrats do not own the means of production—the offices, desks, and machines; the organization owns them and provides them to the bureaucrats as needed. Bureaucrats are not self-employed; they are employees. The written word is the hallmark of a bureaucracy because administrative acts, decisions, and rules are all put into writing.

Only the highest authority within a bureaucracy can obtain his or her position without going through bureaucratic selection procedures such as testing or presenting certain educational credentials. Often in the federal government the heads of departments or agencies are political appointees, perhaps chosen more for their special relationship with the President than for their specialized skills. Although such appointees may obtain their positions through nonbureaucratic means, their authority, like that of those below them in the bureaucracy, is limited by the position they hold.

People become bureaucrats by their own choice, not because they have inherited a position in a bureaucracy. Bureaucrats are paid a salary, which is usually directly related to their positions in the bureaucratic hierarchy. The work associated with the official title is the sole, or at least the primary, occupation of the bureaucrat and is looked upon as a career. This opens up the possibility of moving to ever-higher positions within the organization. Upward mobility is based on merit and seniority. Promotion is determined by superiors within the organization.

Remember that this ideal-typical description may not pertain to any particular organization, but it should describe the characteristics that appear to some degree in any large organization (Blau and Meyer, 1987). One of these characteristics—the authority that is invested in the positions of a bureaucracy—requires some special attention.

Authority refers to "legitimate" power; it is the exercise of power accepted by those over whom it is exerted. It probably seemed quite natural when we stated above that people in the higher positions of an organization have authority over those in positions below them. But why is this true? How does a position in an organization give someone power over others in that organization? To understand the answer to this question we must examine how authority becomes legitimate (Weber, 1921/1968).

Legitimation of Authority.   In earlier times authority came primarily from the positions into which people were born. Kings and other royal family members in times past (and even in some places today) believed they were born with the *right* to exercise power over their subjects. But equally important is the fact that the people they ruled considered it their *duty* to obey the ruler's demands. This kind of authority is legitimized by **tradition**—the way things have been done for a long time in a society or social group. While traditional authority was more common in the past, tradition can also produce legitimacy for authority in modern organizations. In many businesses, leadership is passed directly from parent to child, and in some labor unions, parents have passed the presidency of the union to their children (Christie, 1956). Subordinates conform to the demands of such a ruler because it has been customary for them to do so. Therefore, one accepts the position of a traditional ruler because one has accepted it for a long period of time, or one's parents and grandparents accepted that rulership.

A second way authority can be legitimized is by the charisma a leader claims—and is believed by followers to possess. **Charisma** is the extraordinary, sometimes supernatural, qualities of a person. Leaders of revolutionary social, political, and religious movements frequently derive their authority from their charismatic qualities. Examples of charismatic political leaders are Hitler, Mao Zedong, Castro, and Gandhi. Charismatic religious leaders include Jesus, Mohammed, Reverend Sun Myung Moon of the Unification Church, and Ayatollah Khomeini. Even some entertainment stars are sometimes believed by their fans to have charisma or a "larger-than-life" quality that gives them extraordinary power. Charisma is derived more from the beliefs of the followers than from the actual qualities of leaders. As long as a person believes he or she has special qualities, or it is believed by followers, authority can be derived from charisma.

Charisma is a very short-lived form of authority, generally limited to the life span of the charismatic leader and perhaps a short while thereafter. Attempts are frequently made to extend a leader's charisma beyond his or her own lifetime. This process, called the **routinization of charisma,** is accomplished when the qualities originally associated with a charismatic individual are passed on and incorporated into the characteristics of a group or organization. As an example, even after the death of Martin Luther King, the civil-rights movement in the United States was able to keep his charismatic qualities alive in order to advance the movement's objectives. Once charismatic leadership is translated into an organizational form, however, it eventually evolves into either a traditional or a rational-legal form of domination (Weber, 1921/1968).

In a system of **rational-legal authority,** leaders are legitimized by the rule of law. They derive their authority from the rules and regulations of the system rather than from their personal qualities or from tradition. For example, the office of President of the United States is legitimized by the Constitution, which defines the President's rights and responsibilities. The President's authority generally does not stem from his personal charismatic qualities or from tradition, although it may in some cases. Presidential power is legitimized because people accept the rule of law and therefore accept the President's right to exercise the power of that office. When President Kennedy was assassinated, his Vice President, Lyndon Johnson, immediately assumed the powers of the Presidency. Whether people felt about Johnson the way they had felt about Kennedy was of no importance. The rule of law prevailed.

These ideas on the sources of authority relate closely to our concern with bureaucracy. Weber argued that each form of authority would manifest itself through some form of organizational structure. Rational-legal authority, with its emphasis on adherence to carefully defined rules and regulations, is conducive to the development of bureaucratic organization, while the other forms of authority spawned other types of organizational structures. Bureaucratization is the organizational form of rational-legal authority. Weber believed that as societies become increasingly rationalized, rational-legal authority will increasingly triumph over traditional and charismatic authority. In other words, the modern world would become increasingly bureaucratized.

In the early years of this century, before bureaucratic tendencies had reached nearly the proportions they have today, Max Weber predicted the triumph of bureaucracy in the modern world. His sociological prediction proved to be correct, but he was not happy about it. He deplored the tendency toward bureaucratization, saying that we were creating an "iron cage" from which there would be no escape (Mitzman, 1969). Weber thought that individuality and creativity would disappear in the face of the inexorable advance of bureaucratization. In Weber's view of the future: "Not summer's bloom lies ahead of us, but rather a polar night of icy darkness and hardness . . ." (in Gerth and Mills, 1958, p. 128).

The Realities of Bureaucracy

In the preceding section we have examined the ideal-typical features of bureaucracies: features that can be viewed as a rational system for accomplishing large numbers of tasks or great amounts of work. Indeed, bureaucracies do exactly that. Each year in the United States billions of pieces of mail are delivered, billions of checks are processed, and millions of student grade reports are placed on college transcripts. All of these tasks and many billions of others are accomplished by the people and computers of bureaucratic organizations. These monumental amounts of work are completed because the people and machines of bureaucracies apply precise rules and procedures in a uniform manner to every case processed. Also, because of the high degree of specialization, each person in a bureaucracy is doing a limited range of things in a highly repetitive manner. These features of the bureaucracy make it efficient in dealing with large numbers of tasks.

As everyone who has encountered a bureaucracy knows, however, bureaucracies are not very good at handling unusual or unique cases. The customer, or client, or student who has an out-of-the-ordinary situation or case nonetheless has the rigid rules of the bureaucracy applied, even though they are inappropriate or inapplicable. Under such circumstances many people become frustrated with bureaucracies and find them unfair as well as inefficient. But this reality of bureaucracies is just one of many that conflict with the organizational model of rationality and efficiency. We shall consider a few others next.

The Impersonal Treatment of Clients.   The ideal bureaucrat is supposed to perform in a formal and impersonal manner. When bureaucrats come into contact with clients, however, the clients often perceive this behavior style as disinterest or even hostility. The impersonal treatment of clients has been called "service without a smile" (Hummel, 1987, p. 27). The client feels like a nonperson in the face of this impersonal bureaucratic treatment. Of course, now that much bureaucratic work is done by computers there is literally no live person with whom the client can interact.

Paperwork and Red Tape.   As we noted earlier, the written word is the hallmark of bureaucracies. Not only is this true for the bureaucrats who must maintain written records of their actions, but it is also true for the clients of bureaucracies. Clients are frequently asked to complete various elaborate and detailed forms. Anyone who has ever applied for admission to a college, applied for a credit card, or visited a doctor knows that the first step is to fill out an application. Bureaucracies ask for many different kinds of personal information, and through their computers they are easily able to retain files on massive numbers of people. Every adult in contemporary society has left a paper trail of his or her activities through encounters with bureaucracies.

Rules and Regulations.   Bureaucracies have exact rules that are supposed to cover all situations and cases. The rules are to be followed precisely so that clients and cases will be uniformly treated. In this way the bureaucracy does not engage in favoritism and special treatment. However, sometimes the rules of the organization actually get in the way of what the organization is supposed to accomplish. The following account of an incident in a post office illustrates this point:

> I overheard a clerk telling a customer that he couldn't rent a post-office box unless he had a permanent address.

> "But the reason I need a box is because I don't have a permanent address," the man explained. "When you get a permanent address," the clerk politely explained, "you can get the box." "But, then I won't need it . . ." (Greenberg, 1979).

This example may be called a "Catch 22," a term first used as the title of a novel by Joseph Heller (1955). In this novel about military life during World War II, the protagonist, a bomber pilot named Yossarian, wanted to be excused from flying any more bombing missions by having the doctor declare him crazy. But the doctor explained that, even though there was a rule stating that a flier could be grounded if he were crazy, there was another rule—number 22—stating that anyone who wanted to get out of combat was not really crazy. This is the origin of the phrase, "Catch 22."

The term **Catch 22** has become a part of the English language, and is used for a wide range of encounters with bureaucracies. Generally, the term is applied to situations in which the rules of an organization make it impossible to do what these same rules require.

The Bureaucratic Personality.   Closely related to the issue of rules is the term **bureaucratic personality,** which is the tendency for bureaucrats to conform in a slavish manner to the rules of the organization. The person with a bureaucratic personality treats the rules as more important than the task or the objective of the organization. By adopting a bureaucratic personality, the bureaucrat can avoid guilt and personal conscience in dealing with clients (Hummel, 1987). The clerk who will not accept your check because the "company policy forbids accepting checks" can avoid personal blame or guilt when turning you down.

The Informal System.   According to the ideal-type characterization, bureaucratic organizations are built on the principle of impersonal relations among members. Members are supposed to be judged on the basis of objective measures of their performances, and relationships are based on rational principles. However, in reality, bureaucratic organizations always contain personal relationships and often close-knit social groups—primary groups of the type we discussed earlier. Some of the classic studies of sociology have shown how the informal groups in organizations, such as manufacturing plants, employment agencies, and the U.S. Army, influence behavior in ways that either subvert or override the objectives of the organization (Roethlisberger and Dickson, 1939/1964; Blau, 1963; Little, 1970).

The Tendency toward Oligarchy

Although positions in bureaucratic organizations, including leadership positions, are supposedly based on competence and expertise, such is not always the case. Apparently democratic organizations have an inevitable tendency to end up being undemocratic, or oligarchic. An **oligarchy** is characterized by a small group of people at the top of the organization having almost all the control and power. An early sociologist formulated the "iron law of oligarchy" to depict this tendency (Michels, 1915/1962).

To test out his thesis, Michels focused on the most unlikely places for oligarchies to arise—socialist political parties and labor unions. He felt that if he found oligarchical tendencies in such seemingly democratic organizations, he would find them anywhere and everywhere. In fact, Michels did find the existence of oligarchy in such organizations and concluded that the tendency toward oligarchy must be an "iron law" (Michels, 1915/1962, p. 50).

Michels attributed the oligarchic tendencies of organizations, in part, to the resources that came naturally to the people in positions of leadership. The leaders have higher-quality information and more information than is held by the membership. Leaders also control the flow of information throughout the organization, through the organization's news media and by an agenda they choose to present to the organization's membership. Leaders are also likely to have and develop a higher level of political skill—making speeches, writing editorials, and organizing group activities. Michels argued that leaders of organizations place their need to continue in a dominant position over the needs, interests, and values of the organization. In other words, power becomes more important to organizational leaders than does democracy. This means that the leaders of such organizations are perfectly willing to subvert the basic democratic principles of the organization in order to maintain their power.

Conflict in Organizations

The ideal-typical description of bureaucracy does not include conflict between individuals or groups within organizations. Yet conflict within organizations is pervasive. Of course, much conflict in organizations occurs between individuals, perhaps because they have incompatible personalities or because they are in competition for some scarce goal or resource. However, sociologists are often more interested in conflict that grows out of the characteristics of the organizations themselves (Clark, 1988; Perrow, 1986).

A major form of conflict within bureaucracies occurs when professionals such as physicians, lawyers, and scientists are employed in bureaucratic organizations. Professionals generally assume that their actions and performances should be judged and controlled only by other professionals. However, professionals employed in bureaucratic organizations are often subject to the supervision of nonprofessional superiors.

One study of Canadian doctors employed by large companies found the doctors in conflict with managers over various medical and health issues. For example, preemployment physical examinations were given to prospective employees, and the doctors were pressed by the company to disqualify any doubtful cases, even for minor medical reasons. The company wanted to minimize future risks, but this created conflicts with doctors who felt they were being pressured to violate their medical ethics. A number of other areas—plant safety, pressures for workers to return to work after injuries, and compensation for illnesses and injuries—revealed management interests that were in conflict with the medical autonomy of company doctors (Walters, 1982).

We have presented only one of many instances in which individuals or a sector of an organization has a nearly inevitable conflict with some other sector. For example, conflict almost always exists between sales and production people in industrial firms, between administrators and faculty in colleges, between doctors and nurses and administrators in hospitals, and between treatment and custodial staffs in prisons (Perrow, 1986).

Can Bureaucracy Be Eliminated?

While Max Weber was one of the first to fear and dislike the advance of bureaucracy, he was certainly not the last. Other scholars and intellectuals, as well as politicians and average citizens, have criticized the ever-larger bureaucracies and lamented the increasing number of bureaucrats (Blau and Meyer, 1987, pp. 194–195). Most contemporary observers, however, think that the clock cannot be turned back. "As much as we may wish otherwise, . . . large organizations operating on bureaucratic principles will remain part of the social landscape for some time to come" (Blau and Meyer, 1987, p. 195).

Another view of the future of bureaucratic organizations, however, sees profound changes occurring (Hage, 1988; Heydebrand, 1989). According to this view, the mindless rigidity of large bureaucracies is being replaced by smaller organizations characterized by informality and flexibility. Even though large organizations may continue to exist, their working subunits will be smaller, less formal, and more democratically organized. These working units will be mission- or task-oriented. Two decades ago Alvin Toffler (1970) coined the word *ad-hocracies* to suggest the idea of temporary work groups composed of a wide variety of highly skilled workers brought together to solve specific, nonroutine problems.

An example of an ad-hocracy can be seen in the way a movie might be produced by a set of creative and highly skilled people. Few rigid rules would guide their behavior, because most of the time they would be dealing spontaneously with emerging problems and questions. Some people believe that more and more circumstances will occur where these more informal and flexible work groups will emerge because they are best suited for the tasks at hand (Heydebrand, 1989; Toffler, 1970).

Although some social analysts foresee a future in which bureaucratic forms of organization will decline, the fact remains that the bureaucratization of life continues to expand. In the schools where we are educated, the organizations in which we work, and in virtually every other organization we encounter in our everyday lives, the form of organization is bureaucratic (Blau and Meyer, 1987; Meyer et al., 1985). On a worldwide basis the lives of more and more people are undoubtedly touched by governments and organizations that are increasingly bureaucratic. The bureaucratic form of organization may be modified, but it will not disappear in the foreseeable future.

Organizations of the type we have been considering are parts of larger social units called institutions. Institutions will be introduced briefly at this point, and illustrated in part 3 of this book.

Institutions

An **institution** is a set of groups and organizations with norms and values that center around the most basic needs of a society. The major institutions are the family, education, the economy, health and medicine, and the polity. All of these institutions are found in one form or another in all societies because they carry out necessary societal tasks. As an example, societies must have some orderly way of ensuring that males and females produce enough offspring and care for them well enough so that a sufficient number will survive and the society can continue. The institution that accomplishes these tasks is, of course, the family. Following the definition offered above, the family as an institution has identifiable groups (families and kinship units); there are norms associated with the family (e.g., rules specifying how many spouses one can have); and there are values associated with the family (loyalty to family members).

Descriptions of the major institutions help to define the nature of a society. Indeed, all of the institutions, taken together, give a fairly clear view of a society. We are now ready to consider this major social unit, the society.

Society

Although sociologists sometimes focus on large portions of the world (Chirot, 1985) or on the relationships between parts of the world (Wallerstein, 1974, 1980) the largest social entity studied by sociologists is the society. A society typically is the most complete, the most all-encompassing unit of sociological analysis. A **society** is a population living in a given territory, with a social structure, and sharing a culture.

This definition covers a wide range of actual societies and therefore encompasses considerable diversity. For example, the population size of a society can vary greatly. With a 1990 population of approximately 250 million people, the United States is a society, but other societies in the world have only a few thousand people (the Yanomamo described in chapter 3), and some have only a few hundred. Even China, with its population of over a billion people (1.2 billion in 1992), is described as a society, although great cultural differences exist from one part of China to another.

Societies are most commonly described in terms of their economic systems. The long history of human existence has had only a few basic types of economic arrangements. We will summarize them briefly:

Hunting and Gathering Societies

Through hundreds of thousands of years of human existence, until about 7000 B.C., all humans lived by hunting and gathering their food. They hunted wild game or fished, and gathered wild fruits and plants. Hunting and gathering societies were not permanently fixed in one place, because when the supply of food declined in a particular area it was necessary to move on to another. Only a few small hunting and gathering societies still survive in the world today. One, for example, is the !Kung[1] in the Kalahari Desert of Africa, a society that has been of great interest to anthropologists. The !Kung offer anthropologists an opportunity to study a hunting and gathering society and thereby gain insights into what the lives of prehistoric peoples might have been.

Horticultural Societies

Beginning about 9000 years ago (7000 B.C.), some humans started growing part of their own food rather than gathering foods growing wild. In horticultural societies, food is typically grown in gardenlike plots, which may be somewhat temporary in nature. When people started to grow their own food they also established more permanent communities and were not as likely to be nomadic.

Horticultural societies can still be found in the world today, as, for example, the Gahuku people of the New Guinea Highlands (Read, 1980). The Gahuku people have small personal garden plots that they cultivate

---

[1] The exclamation mark before the name Kung reflects the fact that the !Kung have a clicking sound in their language that does not exist in English.

with digging sticks. They raise mostly sweet potatoes, taro, and corn, though banana trees and other wild-growing fruits also provide food. These horticultural people also raise pigs, which provide food, especially for special ceremonial occasions.

Agrarian Societies

Agrarian societies appeared in about 3000 B.C. These societies differed from the horticultural societies by their larger scale of food production. Crops were regularly planted and harvested, often with the aid of plows pulled by draft animals. Generally the production of foods in agrarian societies was at a subsistence level, which means that the farm produce of one growing season was consumed during that year. As agricultural methods improved, however, some surpluses were produced, allowing some people in the society to engage in other kinds of productive activity. Since communities in agrarian societies could grow to larger sizes, the first cities emerged during this era.

The most prominent, early agrarian societies were in ancient Egypt, the Middle East, China, and later, in medieval Europe. Agrarian societies exist today wherever most of the people rely on agriculture for their livelihood and subsistence.

Industrial Societies

Industrial societies are those in which the predominant economic activity is the production of manufactured goods. The Industrial Revolution, which opened the way for industrialization, is usually placed in the last half of the eighteenth century. England led the way by introducing a variety of machines, powered by steam, that produced manufactured goods in factories. Agricultural production must, of course, continue in industrial societies, but in the most highly industrialized societies only a small proportion of the population is engaged in agriculture. In the United States today, the figure is less than 5 percent.

Postindustrial Societies

A recently introduced term for describing the economic base of a society is *postindustrial society* (Bell, 1973). The **postindustrial society** describes a society that was formerly industrial but is now primarily engaged in producing services and information rather than manufactured goods. In the

United States today most people in the labor force are providing services of some kind instead of producing things. The postindustrial economy will be discussed more fully in chapter 13—The Economy and Work.

A Sociological Classification of Societies

While the economic systems of societies have been widely used as a basis for classification, the classic sociological way describes societies in terms of the social relationships that predominate. A question that can be asked about societies is, How do people generally relate to one another? Or, looked at historically, do people relate to each other differently in contemporary society (especially the large urban-industrial—or postindustrial —societies) than they did in societies of the past? A nineteenth-century German sociologist named Ferdinand Toennies suggested that the relationships between people are different in modern societies than in societies of the past. He labeled historical societies *gemeinschaft* and modern societies *gesellschaft* (Toennies, 1887/1957).

Gemeinschaft **societies** are characterized by very personal face-to-face relationships such as those that exist in families, in rural villages, and perhaps in small towns. These highly personal relations between people are valued for their intrinsic qualities, not for the use they might be to us.

Gesellschaft **societies** are characterized by relationships that are impersonal and distant. People interact with each other only in limited ways. The relationships are entered into only for what they might provide. Social relationships in a *gesellschaft* society are seen as means to ends.

Obviously any modern, industrial society today has both *gemeinschaft* and *gesellschaft* relationships. No society exists in which close personal relationships are totally absent. Similarly in historical, traditional societies, people did enter some relationships for self-interested reasons. Toennies's distinction calls attention to the *prevailing* or *predominant* patterns of social relations in a society.

Summary

The way the people of any society relate to each other and organize their social lives is not random but patterned. Social structures are regular patterns of interaction and persistent social relationships. At a societal level, structures often reflect distributions of wealth, power, or authority, but structures can also be described along ethnic or racial lines.

Interaction between individuals is a complex process, but people do it with ease in their everyday lives. Although interaction has a creative and spontaneous dimension, it is patterned to some degree by cultural values and social norms.

Patterns of behavior are also produced by the statuses and roles that people occupy. Statuses are positions, and roles are the expected behaviors for a person occupying a position. However, people do not simply conform to a rigid set of role expectations, but may actively modify their roles.

Two people engaging in interaction is a dyad. When a third person is added, the dyad becomes a triad, making relationships much more complicated.

A key feature of social groups is that they are composed of a number of people who interact over time and thereby establish patterns of interaction, a group identity, and norms. Identifying with a group often produces in-group attitudes maintaining that the ways of one's own group are right, and those of out-groups are wrong. Primary groups are intimate, face-to-face groups, while secondary groups are larger and more impersonal. Reference groups are groups that people take into account in evaluating their behavior, even when they are not members of those groups. Experimental studies have shown that people tend to conform to the ways of groups they are in.

Organizations and bureaucracies are increasingly important in contemporary life. Organizations, divided according to how they control the members at the bottom, can be classified as coercive, utilitarian, normative/voluntary. Bureaucracies are organized along rational-legal lines, and in an ideal-typical sense are characterized by a division of labor, rank-ordered authority, a system of rules, impersonality, and membership based on competence or expertise.

The realities of bureaucracy include impersonal treatment of clients, paperwork and red tape, scrupulous observance of rules, a tendency toward oligarchy, and conflict. Although bureaucracies are often viewed negatively, they are not likely to disappear; however, the future may see modifications and changes in bureaucratic organization.

Institutions, such as the family, education, the economy, health and medicine, and the polity, are found in all societies. It is through the institutions that necessary societal tasks are accomplished.

Societies, the largest social entity typically studied by sociologists, are commonly distinguished by their economic systems: hunting and gathering, horticultural, agrarian, industrial, and postindustrial. Sociologically, societies can be described as *gemeinschaft* or *gesellschaft* types.

CRITICAL THINKING

1. Identify several social structures with which you might come in contact during an average week.
2. Give an example of a recent interaction that occurred in your life. How did your status affect your behavior in that interaction?
3. What statuses do you hold in life? Give an example of an expected behavior associated with each.
4. Are the following statuses achieved or ascribed: teacher, grandparent, female, judge, baby, nurse? How do you make the determination?
5. Give examples of groups that illustrate primary or secondary groups. Explain how the classification is made.
6. What reference groups are most important in your life? Explain how these groups may or may not influence your behavior.
7. Describe the Sherif, Asch, and Milgram experiments. What does each show us about human behavior in groups?
8. Use the first two pages of today's newspaper to identify two or three large organizations (using the term *organization* as sociologists would define it). Classify each organization as coercive, utilitarian, or normative.
9. The authors agree that the modern world is becoming increasingly bureaucratized. Give examples from this chapter and from your own life to support or refute this idea.
10. Give examples of both *gemeinschaft* and *gesellschaft* relationships in contemporary society.

5 Socialization

In earlier chapters we have seen how the people of a society share a culture with many common values and norms. We are now ready to examine more closely the process that results in the majority of the people in a society sharing similar values and norms.

An anecdote by the late, famous child psychologist Bruno Bettelheim (1985) will illustrate the process. Bettelheim described how children raised in Japanese and U.S. societies might come to have very different values. Their instruction in these values will likely begin at a very early age and in the most commonplace events. Bettelheim describes a familiar parenting situation: one in which a young child (say, a boy) does not want to eat his vegetables. A parent in the United States might say, "You must eat your food; it is good for you, and it will make you grow." In contrast a Japanese mother might ask her son a question. "How do you think it makes the man who grew these vegetables feel? He grew them for you to eat and now you reject them." Or, "How do you think it makes these carrots feel? They grew so you could eat them, but now you will not" (paraphrase of Bettelheim, 1985, p. 58). The Japanese mother is making the child consider how his behavior will make others (even the carrots) feel.

Thus, the Japanese teach even their young children to be sensitive to the feelings of others. In contrast, the admonition of the U.S. parent ("It will make you grow") emphasizes how the child himself will benefit from eating the vegetables. When the Japanese mother stresses how important it is for the child to be sensitive to the feelings of others, she is paralleling the notion of social responsibility and group loyalty found in the Japanese culture. Similarly, in the United States when the parent stresses the well-being of the individual child she is reflecting her culture's concern with individual self-interest.

In this chapter we examine this learning process in detail, noting that children learn not only from their parents but also from siblings and playmates, from teachers and classmates, and from television and other mass media sources. Furthermore, socialization does not end with childhood. It continues throughout life as we go into jobs and professions, new organizations, and different stages of life.

The Nature of Socialization

Socialization is the process by which a person learns and generally accepts the established ways of a particular social group or society. The principal purpose of socialization is to make sure that the new members will do things in about the same way as they are currently being done. In other words, societies, groups, and organizations maintain a certain amount of continuity over time because of the socialization of new members. Generally, new members accept what is taught to them as the right and proper way of doing things.

In a similar way, from a cultural perspective, socialization passes on the values and norms to the new members, which allows norms and values to persist from one generation to the next. Even when the new members of a society are not born into that society but come in as immigrants, various forms of socialization initiate these newcomers into the culture of the new society.

In addition to its significance at the level of the society and culture, socialization also contributes to the process of producing the characteristics and personality of the individual. The socialization that occurs early in life, in infancy and early childhood, is especially critical in this regard. Often called **primary socialization,** it is usually provided by the parents or other caregiver(s) and lays the foundation for personality development. In this process infants become social beings. The early stages of socialization nurture a tendency for the human infant to want and need interaction with other people—a tendency that generally endures for a lifetime.

Socialization continues throughout the lifetime of every individual. As people move into new jobs, organizations, communities, and even new life stages they will learn the values, norms, and behaviors expected of them in these settings. Later in this chapter we will turn to the socialization that occurs during adolescence, adulthood, and old age, but first we focus on the critically important socialization that occurs in infancy and early childhood.

The importance of socialization during infancy and early childhood can be understood by considering what human beings would be without contact with other humans. At this fundamental level we are not focusing on socialization per se, although some socialization is occurring, but simply on the contact and interaction between infants and other human beings.

Acquiring Human Qualities

The human baby—born with biological needs and limited capacities—can make sounds—primarily crying—and has senses that allow him or her to experience comfort and discomfort. In the early days of life, babies cry when they are uncomfortable and stay relatively quiet when they are comfortable. Their usual discomforts are hunger, wetness, coldness, and pain. They cry reflexively when these discomforts occur. Because human infants are helpless, they must have some other human present to give them food and keep them warm, or they will not survive.

Although babies in these early days of life seem to be very limited and almost entirely biological in their nature, increasing evidence shows that they are already orienting toward the humans in their environment. Video camera observations have shown that infants, even in the first hours after birth, have a "quiet-alert stage" when they are attentive to their environment, especially to people. In the first few days or weeks of life infants will make eye contact with a parent, and will respond to a parent's facial expressions and voice sounds. This research on very young infants seems to show that the physical dependence infants have on other humans is augmented by an early tendency to be attracted to their primary caregivers.

Since the human infant begins responding to other humans at such an early stage of life, we might too easily assume that many social and personal qualities normally found in humans are also inborn or inherent. But the evidence is to the contrary for, although human infants might have the tendency toward sociability, they must have sustained contact with other human beings or it will not develop. We can never know with complete certainty how an infant would develop if it were kept alive without contact with other humans, but a few documented cases of isolated children provide some insights. These substantiated cases of infants who have been raised in nearly complete isolation reveal all too clearly that, without human contact, the qualities we associate with humanness can be almost completely lost.

Children Isolated from Human Contact

Mythological stories have been told of children who were reared by animals instead of human beings, and some cases of children who were allegedly found living in the wild with animals have been minimally documented. (They are called **feral**—meaning wild—**children.**) In one such case in India two children were found living with wolves. They were brought to an orphanage where they were cared for, observed, and photographed over a period of years. Long after they were found, these children continued to display animal-like behavior, such as walking on all fours, eating food with their mouths, and preferring to play with dogs (Singh and Zingg, 1942).

The reported cases of feral children are generally not as trustworthy as the cases of children who lived in human settings but were kept virtually isolated from human contact (Curtiss, 1977; Davis, 1940, 1947). In each case a family member placed the child in some isolated part of the home, providing only enough food and water to keep the child alive but offering no human contact. When found, the children did not talk, nor did they show the range of emotions that humans usually display (crying, smiling and laughing, responding to human gestures of friendship, and the like).

In one such case, a father locked his daughter in a room from age two until she was discovered at age 13 (Curtiss, 1977). The girl (called Genie) was placed by her father in a restraining harness, seated on a potty chair during the day, and placed in a straitjacket at night. The mother of this girl, terrorized by her brutal husband and further limited by blindness, had almost no contact with Genie after infancy. When Genie was finally found she was unable to speak, because during her formative years her father had not allowed her to make any sounds. Even with intensive training after her discovery, Genie was unable to use language at more than a rudimentary level. Equally important, efforts to socialize her were only partially successful; long after she was found she persisted in behaviors that went beyond normal acceptability. One of Genie's teachers, who developed a close relationship with her, described how this 14-year-old girl "had many distasteful mannerisms and her behavior was often disconcerting and unpalatable" (Curtiss, 1977, p. 20). Genie would spit and blow her nose on everything and everyone around her. She also had a special fondness for plastic things and certain items of clothing or accessories:

> If anyone she encountered in the street or in a store or other public place had something she liked, she was uncontrollably drawn to him or her, and without obeying any rules of psychological distance or social mores, she would go right up to the person and put her hands on the desired item (Curtiss, 1977, p. 20).

Genie also masturbated whenever and however she could. Any object that she could use for masturbation attracted her. For more than four years after her discovery the professionals working with her were unable to limit this socially unacceptable form of behavior.

The information provided by Genie and the limited number of other cases of extreme isolation demonstrate that human beings do not become "human" if they do not have at least some human contact. Furthermore, there seems to be a critical formative period when infants and children need human contact and interaction or the effects upon their personalities are devastating and largely irreversible.

Early Socialization: "Getting Hooked on People"

How does a baby become human and develop personal traits? Most human infants eventually approximate the human qualities that are prominent in the particular group into which they happen to be born. To understand how this happens, we must go back to our earlier discussion of the human infant who cries when hungry and uncomfortable, and to the adult who attends to that crying by restoring comfort.

Because a baby absolutely needs adults for comfort and survival, adults control the situation. Although most parents first respond by freely gratifying their baby's every need, they do not do so for long. Eventually, adults start to assert their power. Parents continue to give what a child needs, but they start exacting a price. Mothers and fathers will feed and change the diapers of the baby, but eventually they want something in return, even if it is only a smile. If they get the smile, they may give something else—a hug, a cuddle, or a tickle. If the baby responds again, more comforting rewards are given.

This is the beginning of socialization for the norm of reciprocity (Gouldner, 1960). The **norm of reciprocity** calls for two interacting people to give one another things of equal or almost equal value. People want to continue to interact with one another if they are receiving something roughly equal in value to what they are giving.

Reciprocity in interaction is probably the earliest social lesson. Campbell (1975) describes reciprocity from the point of view of what is happening to the infant:

> The human infant is both highly dependent and pleasure seeking. Put these two things together, and it follows clearly that he must have the help of others in securing his own gratification. This simple fact is the root-source of a process that we shall call, quite unscientifically, "getting hooked on people" (Campbell, 1975, p. 17).

By "getting hooked on people," Campbell means that after a while the baby needs more than the food and the dry diapers that the adult provides. The baby also needs the smiles, the attention, the hugs, and the comforting words of the adult who delivers the other necessities.

At first adults will give warmth and comfort freely—but not forever. Adults soon start demanding more and more from their babies for what they provide. Thus babies must slowly give up their totally selfish ways. They have to start doing some things that they do not want to do and stop doing other things. Eating solid foods instead of warm milk, especially milk from the mother's warm body, comes just one step before sitting on the cold potty—and so the process of making a responsible member of society begins. Later, adults bestow smiles, praise, and affection for brushing teeth, keeping a room clean, sitting quietly during religious services, bringing home good grades on report cards, or writing thank-you letters promptly.

Parents and other adults also use negative sanctions, which they have at their disposal by virtue of their powerful position. They may augment their reward system by scolding, spanking, withholding desserts, or "grounding" to get the child or adolescent to do what is "right."

The use of reward and punishment to produce acceptable social behavior is not the only way to accomplish socialization; it is only a basic mechanism that is part of the larger process of socialization. Something else happens in this process that cannot be explained by the simple idea of rewarding good behavior and punishing bad behavior. Children do what their parents and others expect of them, even when their parents are not around to see what they are doing. Children will generally do the "right" things without constant reward or punishment. The following discussion explores how and why this happens.

Symbolic Interaction and the Social Self

In chapter 1 we introduced a theory called *symbolic interactionism,* and we noted that through symbols infants and children acquire an understanding of the world and themselves. Especially important is the way a child develops a sense of self through the process of interaction with significant others. **Significant others** are those people in an individual's life who shape the individual's self and provide definitions for other social objects (Mead, 1934/1962). Usually parents are the most important significant others in the early stages of life. The recognition by symbolic interactionists that the self is essentially a social creation is probably the single most important insight of this perspective (Fine, 1990).

One of the early symbolic interactionists, Charles Horton Cooley, emphasized the social nature of the self with his concept of the **looking-glass self** (Cooley, 1902). This concept conveys vividly the notion that every child develops a self-image that reflects how others respond to her or him. Both as children and adults, we can see ourselves mostly through the responses and reactions of others. It should be noted, however, that the actively creative human mind can also anticipate and imagine the responses and reactions of others. A boy who breaks a lamp while he is alone at home can probably anticipate or imagine his parents' response.

In a closely related sense, children and all humans can take an active, not simply a passive, part in the development of a social self. In taking some kind of successful action, a person does not necessarily need someone else to point out the success. A small child who bounces and catches a ball can evaluate that success independently. Humans have the capacity to assess the success of their own actions, and this ability contributes to their self-image (Gecas and Schwalbe, 1983).

Interacting with others gives people the ability to put themselves in the place of another person. As adults we do it almost constantly. If we are stopped by the police for a minor traffic violation, we try to decide quickly how to talk to the officer. Should we be flippant, aggressive, or humble? How will the officer respond to each of these approaches? Often we try to run through a scene as it might develop from these different approaches. We are not always successful in choosing the best strategy, but we try to anticipate how other persons will respond by putting ourselves in their places. The ability to respond to ourselves as objects, much as others respond to us, and the ability to anticipate how others will respond to our behavior or actions indicate a fairly high level of social being.

But one more step remains in the socialization process. We ultimately evaluate ourselves not only according to how specific individuals respond to us but also according to how others in general will respond. We consider what people will think if we do this or that. We want general social approval for what we do, not just approval from specific others.

Developmental Stages.   George Herbert Mead (1934/1962), an originator of symbolic interaction theory, first described how children arrive at the point where they are concerned about how others *in general* will respond to their behavior. Mead postulated a three-stage developmental process during childhood. In the first stage, the **preparatory stage,** young children simply engage in meaningless imitation of those around them. They have little use for symbols at this stage. In the second stage, the **play stage,** children learn how to evaluate themselves and other social objects from the point of view of significant others. In this stage children learn to put themselves in another person's place. Last is the **game stage,** during which children assume the roles of a number of other people simultaneously and respond to the expectations that these people have. During the game stage children acquire a sense of, and seek the approval of, what Mead called the *generalized other.*

The **generalized other** is the internalization of the norms of the larger social group or the society. As an example, most students will not cheat on an examination—even when there is no chance of being caught—because they have learned and internalized the idea that it is best to be honest. In a sense, they are rewarding themselves for living up to a standard they have learned and accepted. When people accept the ways of the society and generally behave in conformity to those ways, even when no specific punishment or reward will result from their conformity, then they are fully socialized.

To summarize, children learn to evaluate all objects (both abstract and concrete and including the self) largely from the people with whom they interact. Furthermore, their learning is not just superficial or calculated to get other people to bestow social rewards and approval. Nor is the learning of a society's ways done only to avoid punishment or penalty. The process starts there, but eventually humans internalize the ways of the society. They accept them as right for themselves and others, and they provide their own rewards when they conform to them.

This acceptance of societal ways does not mean that an effective social system will produce a society of conforming robots. People do cheat on tests; they also cheat in business deals and on marriage partners. Socialization to norms and values is never totally effective and certainly is not uniform throughout society. The rules and values of a society are themselves never universal or absolute. There is plenty of room for individual variation. Our description of early socialization explains why we have as much order and regularity in society as we do, and why it is possible to have a society at all. Although childhood socialization does not explain every individual's behavior, it does show how every individual is, to a great degree, a social product.

Agents of Socialization

Socialization is generally initiated by the people who are already members of a social system; they are called the agents of socialization, and they have the task of socializing new members. In the case of infants being born into families, the first socializing agents are the parents, but as children grow older, other agents of socialization also become important. Included among the other socializing agents are children's peers (often including siblings), teachers, and the mass media. We will begin with the most important early socializing agents, the parents.

Parents as Socializing Agents

Almost all parents recognize the responsibility of teaching their children the skills necessary to get along in life. From a sociological perspective, parents are responding to the social role of being a parent. Most adults learn the parental role through their own socialization.

Many parents also feel responsible for *shaping* the personalities of their children. Many contemporary parents have accepted the basic sociological and psychological view that personalities of children are shaped by environmental influences in general, and especially by parental influences on the child. However, parents cannot consciously set out to produce a certain kind of child and succeed in getting what they want.

Many young, modern, and well-educated parents seem to conceive of shaping the personalities of their children as a process of direct, straightforward teaching: "If I want my child to be independent, I will teach independence, and my child will be independent. If I want my child to be frugal or neat, I will teach those things." This naive view of the socialization process often causes parents to wonder "where they went wrong" when their children do not mature exactly according to their expectations.

Several factors explain why socialization is not a process of direct teaching. First, socialization is more complex than the direct-teaching idea suggests. To begin with, socialization usually involves two parents (or parent figures). Two socializing parents may send quite different messages to the child, and the result of mixed messages in the child's development cannot be anticipated. Even when parents are consistent, children often turn out differently from what their parents wish.

Second, the direct-teaching notion of socialization fails to take into account how pervasive and subtle socialization is. Socialization occurs as much by example as by direct verbal means. A father may tell his children to try to get along with other people and be friendly, but if he frequently engages in disputes with his neighbors and coworkers, the children get a different message. This father is socializing his children as much by his behaviors as by his words.

Furthermore, socializing agents other than family members influence a child. At a fairly early age children begin to be socialized by the communication media, especially television. Somewhat later, playmates and friends, the schools, and the print media (magazines, newspapers, and books) play a part in a child's socialization.

One final influence, biological inheritance, contributes an additional unpredictable factor. Although sociologists do not generally view personality characteristics as genetically inherited, the possibility does exist that certain natural endowments might moderate and interact with the socialization process (Rose, 1979).

Because socialization is complex, pervasive, and subtle, and because outside socializing agents compete with familial ones, parents cannot expect to shape their children exactly as they desire. The scientific analysis of socialization and the experiences of many parents do not support the notion of socialization as a process of direct teaching.

Parental Differences in Socialization

The parents in any particular society will usually be in accord on a wide range of things they teach their children to do and not do. (Almost no parent, for instance, will consciously teach a child to lie, cheat, or use profanity.) But despite this general agreement, substantial differences exist in what the parents value in one part of the society, compared to the parents in another. Parents coming from different subcultural, ethnic, or religious groups, different social classes, and different critical historical periods will have differing notions of what they should teach their children (Peterson and Rollins, 1987).

The most extreme variations from mainstream socialization values typically occur in cases where parents are zealous about some cause or belief system. Recent newspaper accounts of certain fundamentalist Christians reveal how some parents will take extreme measures to socialize their children into the ways of their religious beliefs. Two fathers gave nearly identical accounts of how they terrorized their five-year-old children with a fear of going to hell so they could be assured that the children would be obedient and God-fearing.

In the words of one of these fathers:

> My daughter is 5 years old and—people say how inhumane—I let my daughter lay and cry herself to sleep for a week straight about the flames of hell. See my daughter personally lay at night and said, 'I don't want to go to hell, I don't want to go to hell,' and she'd be laying there crying.

> I could have ran right in there and gave her the Gospel and she could have made a profession of salvation, but I let it get deep into her memory. Know what I mean? That there is a Hell. And that will affect her whole life. That's why she is an obedient child (Naughton, 1988).

Cross-Cultural Perspectives

Some Alternative Views of Children's Personalities

While Americans tend to believe that parents shape the personalities of their children, the people of certain other societies have distinctly different views. The Irish and the Hindus of India (to take examples from two very different cultures) place much more emphasis on the inherited characteristics of children. However, as we will see, there are other distinctive differences in the views of the Irish and the Hindus.

Irish parents do recognize that they play an important role in bringing up their children, and especially in teaching them right from wrong. They are likely to say, "Beware of the habit you give them" (Scheper-Hughes, 1979). But they also see a child's basic personality, talents, abilities, and nature as largely inherited. The Irish word that expresses this view is *dutcas. Dutcas* is translated as *blood, stock,* or *breeding,* but more specifically it refers to the personality characteristics one inherits from one's ancestors. Thus, when a mother throws up her hands in despair over her unruly sons, saying, "They're too full of their father's *dutcas*" (Scheper-Hughes, 1979), she is saying that the wildness of her sons is a trait they have inherited from their father.

An Irish child's *dutcas* does not have to come from an immediate parent, for the Irish believe that the characteristics of any ancestor can appear in the personality of a child. Thus, a daughter may be said to inherit her thriftiness from a particular grandmother, while a son may be seen as getting his laziness from a ne'er-do-well uncle.

A different view of inherited personality traits can be found among the Hindus of India (Kaker, 1979). Indian religious, medical, and folk beliefs hold that life begins at conception. It is here that the spirit from the body of someone who has lived previously is joined with the fertilized ovum. Thus, a major portion of the personality of a child comes not from immediate ancestors but from an already existing spirit that has lived in another body at a previous time. For the Hindu mother there is, however, an opportunity to modify the spirit while the fetus is still in the womb. The critical period for influencing the psychological development of the baby comes in the third month of pregnancy. According to Indian tradition, it is in that month that the feelings and wishes of the fetus, which come from its previous life, are transmitted to the mother. These are revealed to the mother in the form of cravings for particular foods. These cravings, which are really the wishes of the fetus, are not to be denied, for their fulfillment will ensure the proper psychological development of the child.

The personality of the Indian child is thought to be largely determined by the spirit from a previous life, though this might have been modified while in the womb. With this view in mind, it is not surprising that Indian parents are highly indulgent with their children. Mothers do not try to mold their children into a particular desired image. They are inclined to follow rather than lead the child in its development (Kaker, 1979).

These beliefs about the inherited personality traits of children, coming from the Irish and Hindu people, are not entirely unfamiliar to Americans. The personality traits of a child are sometimes seen as reflections of the personality of a particular family member — "She is just like her grandmother in her love of animals." There is also a long-standing folk belief in the United States that what a mother does during her pregnancy will affect the character of her baby. This parallels the Hindu belief described above. One American proponent of this view has collected cases that have led him to conclude that, from the sixth month of pregnancy, a fetus can begin to learn, and respond emotionally to its mother (Verny and Kelly, 1984). In one such case, a young musical conductor knew the entire score of a musical number, even though he had never seen it before. This is alleged to have occurred because his mother had played this piece of music while she was pregnant.

KAKER, SUDHIR. "Childhood in India: Traditional Ideals and Contemporary Reality." *International Social Science Journal* 31, 1979.
SCHEPER-HUGHES, NANCY. "Breeding Breaks Out in the Eye of the Cat: Sex Roles, Birth Order, and the Irish Double-Bind." *Journal of Comparative Family Studies* 10, 1979.
VERNY, THOMAS and KELLY, JOHN. *The Secret Life of the Unborn Child.* New York: Dell, 1984.

As a rule, parents try to teach their children lessons that they themselves have found to be useful or important in life. This rule has been most thoroughly documented with regard to the differences among socialization values of parents who are at different levels in the class structure (Kohn, 1977; Gecas, 1979, 1990).

Cross-National Findings. Studies conducted in the United States, Italy, Taiwan, Poland, and Japan have documented that parents at different

Sociology in the News

Programmed Socialization: Producing a Star Quarterback

Many contemporary parents see their newborn child as an opportunity to produce the perfect child. They firmly believe in the general sociological principle that the personality and character of a child are profoundly influenced by the actions and behaviors of parents. As the text points out, however, it may be exceedingly difficult, if not impossible, for parents to produce exactly the type of child they desire. Nonetheless, examples of parents who try to produce the perfect child are easily found. None, however, is more dramatic than the rearing of Todd Marinovich, former star quarterback for the University of Southern California football team.

Todd Marinovich's father Marv, a former college football player himself, apparently decided when his son was an infant that he would raise the boy to be a star football quarterback. The elder Marinovich started working on his son's physical conditioning when he was one month old. Todd could do push-ups and crawl on a balance beam before he could walk (Kornheiser, 1991). Through Todd's childhood and adolescence, nothing about his training and preparation was left to chance. His diet was so controlled that when he finished high school he had never eaten a Big Mac, or an Oreo cookie, or a Ding Dong (Looney, 1988). When Todd went to birthday parties as a child he brought along sugarless ice cream and a bag of carrot sticks.

Todd's mother Trudi worked on the mental aspects of his development. She played classical music and jazz in his room. She would not allow him to watch cartoons but instead showed him old movie thrillers (Alfred Hitchcock and Agatha Christie) to "spark his intellect" (Looney, 1991, p. 57).

As Todd grew older, his father employed an array of experts and specialists, who worked on every aspect of his son's physical and psychological development. Thirteen coaching specialists were at one time or another employed to develop his "speed, agility, strength, flexibility, quickness, body control, and endurance" (Looney, 1988, p. 57). A psychologist was retained for his mental development. Todd was described as "America's first test-tube athlete" (Looney, 1988, p. 57).

The lifelong training and conditioning regimen for Todd Marinovich paid off when he became a high school football star, breaking national records in his senior year (he also had a B+ grade average). Every major football college in the country tried to attract him, but he decided to attend the school his parents attended, the University of Southern California.

In his first playing year at U.S.C., Todd Marinovich quarterbacked the team through a successful season, which culminated in a Rose Bowl game. In his sophomore season, however, some ominous signs of change appeared in his behavior and his football play. Todd started missing team meetings, had some squabbles with his coach, and was finally suspended from the team when he failed to register for spring-semester classes.

In January of 1991 Todd Marinovich was arrested for possession of cocaine. This was one more sign that something was awry and he was breaking away from his father's ultracontrolled upbringing. Marv Marinovich acknowledged as much when he said, "I told him what to eat, when to eat, when to go to bed, when to get up, when to work out, how to work out. Now, I have a hard time getting him on the telephone . . ." (Kornheiser, 1991, p. E5). Todd probably expressed his feelings best when he told his mother, "I wish I could go somewhere else and be someone else. I don't want to be Todd Marinovich." (Kornheiser, 1991, p. E5).

LOONEY, DOUGLAS S. "Bred to Be a Superstar." *Sports Illustrated*, February 28, 1988.
KORNHEISER, TONY. "Marinovich: Inevitable." *Washington Post*, January 22, 1991.

levels of the class structure have different values that they communicate when they socialize their children (Kohn et al., 1983, Slomczynski et al., 1981, Naoi et al., 1985). The major findings of these studies can be briefly summarized: parents who are in the middle-class and upper-middle-class levels of the stratification structure (those with above average education and white-collar, managerial, or professional jobs) tend to value autonomy, creativity, and self-direction; by comparison, parents in the working class (especially those with blue-collar occupations) tend to value conformity to the rules and respect for external authority. In everyday terms, working-class parents are more likely to value obedience.

When parents engender in their children the value of autonomy and self-direction, they are portraying the world as a place that can be influenced by individuals who take initiatives. In contrast, parents who place a greater value on their children's obedience are reflecting their view of the world as a place of many rules and regulations, and where people in authority give orders. To make one's way in this world a person must learn obedience to the rules of those in authority.

When socializing their children, middle-class and upper-middle-class fathers wanted their children to be considerate of others, interested in how things happen, responsible, and self-controlled. These fathers were less likely to emphasize that their children should be well mannered, neat, clean, obedient, honest, and studious. These latter traits, however, were exactly the ones that the lower-class fathers strongly desired in their children.

Because of these different orientations, parents in the middle and lower social classes disciplined their children differently. Lower-class mothers punished their children directly or immediately after the child misbehaved, without asking questions. Middle-class mothers were more likely to punish or not punish their children according to how they interpreted the child's intention when committing the act. Middle-class parents judged the child's misbehavior by considering whether it seemed to violate the long-range goal that their child be able to demonstrate self-direction and individual responsibility. Working-class parents punished misbehavior if it violated some rule. They wanted obedience from their children—obedience to the rules that they had set down and obedience to the rules of the larger society.

In socializing their children, why do the middle classes value autonomy and the working classes value obedience to the rules? What is the relationship between position in the class structure and socialization values? According to the research of Kohn (1983) and his associates, the crucial factor is the occupational setting or work experience of the father. Middle-class fathers are typically employed in occupations that reward individual initiative and responsibility—autonomous behavior. The more they take initiatives, assume responsibility, and act independently, the more they are rewarded. In comparison, working-class fathers are typically employed in work settings where they must do exactly what they are told and where individual initiative is not especially valued or rewarded. People working on the assembly lines understand that they must do the work in the way they have been instructed if they want to keep their jobs.

Middle-class parents expect, at least implicitly, that their children will enter the occupational world at levels where they will be expected to show individual responsibility and self-direction. They socialize their children with this idea in mind, so that they will get along best and most successfully when they enter the white-collar, managerial, and professional occupations. Working-class parents have experienced a different kind of work world, one where they do what they are told, when they are told to do it. They assume that their children will enter the same kind of world, so they teach their children the importance of obedience in order that they will survive in that world. One might say that the arbitrary, absolute, and sometimes unfair demands for obedience that are often attributed to working-class fathers might be a way of forewarning their children about adult life. People in the lower strata of society are often treated arbitrarily by their superiors in the work world, as well as by other agents of authority (including police, the courts, and school personnel).

This line of research also shows how socialization is a contributor to the perpetuation of the existing class structure of a society. This socialization process may be *one* mechanism that pushes the children of working-class parents toward working-class occupations, whereas the children of middle-class parents move toward middle-class occupations. The different socializing influences that working-class and middle-class parents exert on their children actually help to keep the social class system more or less intact. As will be discussed in chapter 8, a relatively consistent and orderly continuation of the basic class structure persists from one generation to the next, perhaps due in part to class differences in parental socialization.

Reverse Socialization—Children Influencing Parents

Socialization is often viewed as a one-way process. In the case of parents and children the focus is primarily on the way the parents socialize their children. However, there is increasing recognition of the fact that children also influence their parents (Peterson and Rollins, 1987). Children's acting to change the behaviors, attitudes, or values of their parents is an example of reverse socialization. In general terms, **reverse socialization** occurs when people who are normally the ones being socialized are, instead, doing the socializing.

Reverse socialization in the family probably occurs most prominently after children have reached their teenage years. At this age the children are attuned to the mass media, where they learn about recent changes and innovations. The children can then serve as sources of information in the areas where the parents are not as attentive (clothing styles, slang, music, movies, and so on). Reverse socialization from children to parents is apt to be found in societies that are changing rapidly (Mead, 1970).

Parents of teenage and young adult children are likely to acknowledge that they are influenced by their children (Peters, 1985). Sports, for example, is one area where parents reported the greatest increases in knowledge and participation because of their children. To a lesser degree, parents acknowledged the influence of their children in the areas of leisure, personal care, politics, and religion. Parents also agreed that their children had influenced their attitudes on social issues such as drug use, sexuality, the handicapped, minorities, and, most important, "perceptions of youth" (Peters, 1985, p. 929).

Peers as Socializing Agents

We noted earlier that the peers and siblings of young children also act as socializing agents. Older brothers and sisters, with their superior knowledge and verbal ability, have an obvious opportunity for introducing their younger siblings to many different aspects of life. Oldest and only children do not, of course, have older siblings to socialize them, which could account for some of the differences between children who are in different birth-order positions in the family (Polit and Falbo, 1987).

Although older siblings have the earliest opportunities for socializing young children, neighborhood and school friends are also soon acting as socializers. By the time children reach school age they have extensive daily contact with other children. In this context, away from parents and other adults, the interaction among children is probably influential in shaping attitudes and values.

An example of the intensity of peer-group socialization is found in a study of preadolescent boys participating in Little League baseball (Fine, 1987, chapter 4). The potential for socialization among these boys, aged 9 through 12, is very great because they feel free to discuss openly any topic that interests them, including topics that they would not discuss with adults. Furthermore, boys of this age take the comments and ideas of their peers very seriously (Fine, 1987, p. 79).

Preadolescent boys participating in Little League baseball establish and enforce appropriate behavior among their peers. While the adults who are coaching them are emphasizing teamwork, sportsmanship, winning and losing properly, and "hustle," the boys are more concerned about proper self-presentations. They are learning from their peers when to be tough and, if the situation calls for it, when to be fearful. They are learning to control their aggression, fears, and, most important, their tears. They are also learning that they must display a desire to win and a loyalty to team unity.

Boys on these teams are treated harshly when they forget that the team is more important than their individual concerns. For example, a boy who cries when his team has won (because he made a poor play earlier) is described by his fellows as "strange." Similarly, a boy must not display happiness when something negative has happened to the team, such as a player who smiled when he had just made an out. This boy, usually a poor player, hit a hard line drive that was caught by the third baseman. Even though he had made an out for the team, he returned to the dugout smiling. Some of the better players immediately let him know that his response was inappropriate. One snarled, "God, Jason, that's stupid, don't smile" (Fine, 1987, p. 82).

In a Little League setting young boys are often learning traditional male behavior from their peers. Through the reactions and words of their peers they learn how to control and channel their behavior in ways that are consistent with the male gender role. The sociologist who observed hundreds of preadolescent boys over three years says explicitly that, through socialization by peers, "Boys learn to act like men" (Fine, 1987, p. 86). The socialization is effective and may, in some cases, run counter to the child-rearing goals of the boys' parents.

The Mass Media as Socializing Agents

The media of mass communication, especially television, movies, and radio, but also magazines and newspapers, convey thousands of visual, aural, and verbal messages each day. These messages are embedded in dramas, comedies, news reports, music lyrics, comics, cartoons, news stories, and commercial advertising. In myriad ways these messages are defining social life for people of all ages. From childhood to old age, the media of communication are continuing the process of socialization.

While all the media of communication are important, television has undeniably overtaken all others in reaching and influencing people. In American households television sets are on more than seven hours each day (Liebert and Sprafkin, 1988).

Television as a Socializing Agent for Children

An average six-month-old infant in the United States will be in front of a television set one and one-half hours a day. By three years of age most children will be selecting their favorite television shows (Liebert and Sprafkin, 1988, p. 5). Television viewing continues to increase until it reaches a peak at about 11 years of age, when an average child watches more than four hours a day.[1] Even among high-school seniors, however, television viewing is the recreational activity engaged in most often. (See Figure 5–1.) "It has been estimated that by the age of 18 a child . . . will have spent more time watching television than in any single activity besides sleep" (Liebert and Sprafkin, 1988, p. ix). This massive exposure suggests that television is an important socializing agent for the children of contemporary society.

Over the last three decades many studies have been done on the influence of television on children. The two topics that have received the most attention are violence and male/female roles. With respect to violence the question has been, Does the portrayal of violence on television produce higher levels of violent and aggressive behavior in children? Regarding male/female roles, the primary question is, Do children learn stereotyped views of males and females from television?

---

[1] The reported *average* amount of television watching by children does obscure the fact that substantial differences exist among children with different backgrounds. Children in the lower social classes and from minority backgrounds watch much more than middle-class white children (Liebert and Sprafkin, 1988).

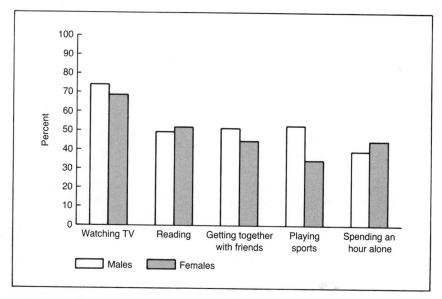

Figure 5–1.   Percentage of high school seniors participating in selected activities each day, by sex: 1985. Of the activities listed, the most common daily activity for both male and female students in the class of 1985 was watching television. (*Sources:* U.S. House of Representatives, Select Committee on Children, Youth, and Families, *U.S. Children and Their Families: Current Conditions and Recent Trends, 1987. Original Source:* University of Michigan, Institute for Social Research, *Monitoring the Future,* various years.)

Violence.   Even a casual viewing of television reveals that violence is the mainstay of many programs: killing, hitting, fighting, verbal abuse, and threats are pervasive. These kinds of violence are found on Saturday morning cartoons and other children's programs, as well as in police and crime dramas, military and war stories, and space adventures. Even music videos have their share of stylized violence and aggression, as we will see below. According to a widely used index of violence on television programs, there are 9.7 acts of violence in every hour of television programming. In cartoons, there are 21.3 acts of violence per hour (Liebert and Sprafkin, 1988, p. 118).

The hundreds of studies on the influence television violence has on children's behavior have produced an agreement that violence is learned from television (Liebert and Sprafkin, 1988). Aggressive behavior is found more often among the children who watch television most. A particularly interesting demonstration of the impact of television on the aggressive behavior of youngsters comes from a study conducted in Canada. This study focused on a Canadian community that did not have television reception until the mid-1970s because it was located in a geographic "blind spot" (Williams, 1986). The preschool and school-age children of this community—named "Notel" by the researchers—were studied both before and after television came to the community. Moreover, for purposes of comparison, the children in two other similar-sized communities were also studied. Both of these communities had received television broadcasts for many years, although one received only one channel (much like Notel was to receive). This natural field experiment provides important evidence on the impact of television on the aggressive and violent behavior of children.

The aggressive behavior of the children of Notel and the other two communities was measured before television came to Notel and again two years later. Aggressive behavior was measured by observations of children in their free-play time in school, and by teacher and peer ratings. Among the children of Notel, aggressive behaviors increased significantly after television was introduced into their community. During the same two-year period no similar increase was noted in the aggressive behaviors of the children in the two communities that had had television for many years. Further evidence was found when observations revealed that those children who watched the most television displayed the most aggressive behavior. Using several different measures and various kinds of analysis, this natural field experiment confirmed what other types of studies have also concluded: television viewing is related to more aggressive and violent behaviors among children (Joy et al., 1986).

Even though many studies have found television viewing to be related to violent and aggressive behaviors among children, the question still remains as to why a connection exists. Several types of answers have been offered (Joy et al., 1986; Liebert and Sprafkin, 1988):

1. *Observational Learning*—Children might, for example, see a "Kung Fu" kick on television and copy this method when fighting.
2. *Reduced Social Constraints*—Children who see violence used in many different situations might feel fewer social constraints against using violence.
3. *Arousal of Aggressive Tendencies*—Some children may have aggressive tendencies that may be aroused by seeing violence (or other exciting events) on television.

Male/Female Roles.   A second major concern of many people is that television may contribute to stereotypes about males and females. The content of television has been analyzed many times, and the conclusions concerning the treatment of women are that women receive little recognition and respect. Women occupy only a quarter to a third of the roles on entertainment programs, and, when they are shown, they are usually in lower-status jobs or are unemployed. The personalities of women on television are generally passive, deferential, emotional, and weak. In comparison, men are usually active, dominant, rational, and powerful. Television commercials also show women less than men, and males are seen much more in dominant, forceful, and active roles (Kimball, 1986; Liebert and Sprafkin, 1988).

The study of the children of Notel uncovered further evidence that television does influence how children view males and females. Both before and after television came to the community the children were asked about "how suitable it was for boys (and girls)" of their age to: cry when hurt, do dishes, play rough sports, go out alone after dark, swear, learn to cook and bake, and so on. They were also asked about the suitability of various kinds of jobs for men and women (e.g., medical doctor, librarian, principal of a school, Prime Minister of Canada). These questions and others served as measures of how traditional the views of the children were about male and female roles (Kimball, 1986).

Before television arrived, the children of Notel had more egalitarian attitudes about males and females than the children in communities where television had existed for some time. This was especially the case for the boys of Notel. Two years after television was introduced, both the boys and the girls of Notel had much more traditional views of males and females. The results of this Canadian study are consistent with numerous other studies, documenting in a forceful way that television does act as a socializing agent regarding male and female roles. The persistent portrayal of males and females in traditional roles does influence children's ideas (Kimball, 1986).

There is general agreement that television programs for young children, especially those shown on Saturday morning, are very traditional in their treatment of gender roles (Carter, 1991). Saturday morning programs on the commercial networks are dominated by cartoons and other shows in which males are in the dominant roles. The reason seems to be, in part, that girls will watch shows with male leads, but boys will not watch programs that have females as the leading characters (Carter, 1991). (For a fuller discussion of this issue see Sociology in the News in chapter 10.)

Television as a Socializing Agent for Adolescents and Adults

Adolescents and adults are also socialized by television. If we take only one small segment of television programming—daytime and evening drama—we can see just how enormous the influence of the mass media can be. The average American adult sees 12 hours of television *drama* each week. If we think of this estimate in relation to the pretelevision era of history, it is equivalent to *". . . five or six full-length stage plays a week!"* (Berger, 1987, p. 9).

One view among sociologists is that this vast amount of television viewing is very influential in shaping our definitions of the most basic features of social life. As a case in point, Taylor (1989) analyzed how the family has been depicted on American television between the 1950s and the 1980s. She argues that in each decade the television images of families have provided definitions of the nature of family life. For example, the harmonious families of Ozzie and Harriet and Beaver Cleaver provided the dominant definitions of the family in the 1950s and 1960s. In more recent times the families on television have been more varied. Some still show the intact family (the "Cosby Show," "Family Ties," and "Growing Pains"), but many others depict families broken by death and divorce, with the problems of single parenting ("One Day at a Time" and "Kate and Allie"), role reversals ("Who's the Boss"), and a half-dozen other variations on family life. Americans, according to this view of television, develop their personal responses to family problems on the basis of these television portrayals of contemporary families (Taylor, 1989).

We should not overlook the fact that television programs produced primarily for American television audiences are frequently sent to other countries around the world, where they also serve to socialize viewers. "Dallas," "Dynasty," and many other shows have enjoyed high levels of interest in Europe and elsewhere. One study revealed that German viewers of "Dallas" saw in this show a confirmation of their views of Americans. Although they knew that the Ewing family was exceptionally rich, and therefore not like most Americans, they also believed that many Americans had a life that was made easier by money. Even though German viewers recognized the exaggerated character of life on "Dallas"— ruthlessness, dishonesty, greed—they nonetheless incorporated some of what they saw in their attitudes about Americans (Massing, 1987). Very likely, the worldwide popularity of such television dramas as "Dallas" and "Dynasty" stem from their depiction of Americans as rich and aggressive.

Other television programs that have enormous potential for socializing adults and adolescents are the daytime talk shows—for instance, "Donahue," "The Oprah Winfrey Show," "Sally Jessy Raphael," and "Geraldo Rivera." These programs are immensely popular and are watched by millions of Americans each week. The standard format of these programs is to select a theme or issue for the day, invite special guests who have something to say on the topic, and then allow the studio and viewing audiences to ask questions or make comments. The topics under discussion purport to deal with important or interesting social issues or problems of the times. Viewers who perceive these programs as educational and informative, as well as entertaining, probably derive from them most of the information they possess on social issues. The opinions and attitudes of a great many people are very likely formed and reinforced by these television programs.

Although adolescents watch television dramas (including soap operas) and daytime talk shows, this age group, when compared to children and older adults, generally has the least interest in television (Williams and Boyes, 1986). One major exception is the great popularity of Music Television, or MTV. This part of television programming appeals primarily to the age group between 12 and 25. Since both the song lyrics and accompanying dramatic presentations are conveying messages, the audience is being socialized about a wide range of highly important matters in their lives—romantic relationships, love, and sex, as well as hair, makeup, and clothing styles. A number of critics have spoken out against MTV for the way sexual material is presented. They charge that sexuality is often portrayed in a sadomasochistic way, mostly with women as the victims (Strouse and Fabes, 1985). If adolescents are influenced by television fare in the same ways as younger children, the socialization they receive from MTV may produce more aggression in male/female courtship relationships.

Adolescent and Adult Socialization

We have already seen how television is an important socializing agent for both adolescents and adults, so obviously people continue to be socialized after childhood. Indeed, socialization continues throughout life, as we will see in the remainder of this chapter. Some adult socialization occurs in connection with changes expected from one life stage to the next, changes that come largely from the process of aging, such as adolescence, for instance, and old age. Other life transitions come unexpectedly and often with suddenness, such as the loss of one's job, or getting divorced, or being widowed. Other adult socialization occurs in connection with entering occupations or professions, organizations, work settings, or institutions.

Adolescent Socialization

Sociologists consider the adolescent stage of life a social creation more than a biological stage. In the United States, however, most people associate adolescence with the onset of puberty, and believe the associated biological changes are explanations of adolescent behavior (erratic, unpredictable, moody, uncommunicative, and so on). The sociological view is that some societies, but not all, create a period of life called *adolescence* and then socialize preadolescents in such a way that they know what is expected of them when they reach the appropriate age.

In earlier times, in many societies, there was no recognized adolescent period of life. When Shakespeare described the seven ages of man (in *As You Like It*) he moved directly from the "whining schoolboy" going "unwillingly to school" to the "lover" sighing ballads to his mistress. While the lover could be an adolescent, it is interesting that he makes no mention of an awkward, confused, or erratic teenager.

Contemporary anthropologists have also found societies that do not identify an adolescent period of life: after going through some form of puberty ritual, children go directly into adulthood. Both historical and cross-cultural evidence, therefore, support the sociological view that adolescence is a socially created stage of life.

The socially created adolescent period of life probably serves a useful societal purpose, especially in economically developed societies. Young people in many contemporary societies need formal education beyond childhood. By defining an adolescent period of life, young people are not obligated to enter into adult responsibilities until they have acquired the skills necessary for a highly technological and bureaucratic economic system.

People often learn what will be expected of them in a given status before they enter that status. Called **anticipatory socialization,** this process typically occurs in each stage of the life cycle. For example, young people learn, even before they reach the teenage years, that they will become adolescents. They learn that when they reach this stage their behavior and feelings will probably differ from the behavior and feelings of their childhood years. The words *adolescence* and *teenage years* become symbols with a self-fulfilling reality. In contemporary society, the economic system, augmented by mass advertising, sells the teenage years—a very lucrative market.

Teenagers are sensitized to the idea that they should like things that are clearly distinguished from childish and adult (or parental) things. Adolescents want to be clearly set apart from children and clearly set apart from parents and "old people." What adolescents define as their special domain is constantly being invaded by older and younger members of society. When preteen children start to idolize a music star first cultivated by teenagers, the teenagers quickly move on to someone else.

Adult Socialization

A number of important occasions arise in adult life when socialization occurs with special intensity. The term **adult socialization** refers to occasions in life when adults learn the new behaviors expected of them as they enter new occupations, professions, organizations, work settings, institutions, or life stages.

Socialization in Occupations and Work Settings

There is more to be learned in a new job or organization than the specific tasks that one is assigned. One must also learn the norms and the expected role behaviors of the work setting or organization. Anyone who enters a large office, an academic department, a service agency, an industrial shop, or any other work group enters an ongoing social system. Every social system, in addition to norms and roles, will have—as we saw in the last chapter—a social structure (prevailing patterns of interaction). The social structure will include friendship patterns as well as patterns of privilege, deference, and respect among members. Newcomers must be sensitive to these features of the group they are joining.

Some occupations and professions feature intense training at the time of entry; often this training is a conscious effort at socializing new members. Military organizations are especially likely to begin this socialization as soon as new recruits arrive. A less well-known but striking example of early training/socialization is found in the way the airline industry trains flight attendants (Hochschild, 1983).

The training of flight attendants extends far beyond the technical aspects of their work. Equally important is the socialization that flight attendants receive on how to present themselves to the flying public. Above all, they must perform their duties in a way that makes them seem friendly, helpful, cheerful, and composed at all times. Flight attendants, especially the females, must smile easily and often. They are taught to display a friendly and cheerful presence, even when they are hurrying to complete their work, are being harassed by demanding and unruly passengers, or are facing a crisis.

The socialization of flight attendants begins even before they are hired. In an airline publication for prospective flight attendants, candidates are told how to conduct themselves at the hiring interview. This book tells candidates to be sincere, modest, and to display a friendly smile. Interviewees are also told to be enthusiastic, but with calmness and poise, to be "vivacious but not effervescent" (Hochschild, 1983, p. 96).

After flight attendants have been hired they are sent to an airlines' school where, in addition to learning the fundamental skills and tasks of the job, they are drilled intensively on proper behavior and demeanor. Airlines often have strict rules about what flight attendants may and may not do. In the Delta Air Lines school, flight attendants are told they may not drink alcohol while in uniform or for 24 hours before flight time. While on flights they may not knit, read, or sleep (Hochschild, 1983, p. 99).

But the most important aspect of the socialization of flight attendants is that they must learn to control their real emotions and display the emotions that the airline demands. They must "manage" their feelings and emotions because they are being paid by the airlines to do so. Hochschild has called this behavior *emotion labor* (1983, p. 7). While we all learn to manage our emotions through the normal socialization processes, flight attendants are taught that managing theirs is part of their work. They are taught to deal with difficult passengers, and they are coached and drilled on how to control their anger.

Even though it is taboo to express anger toward passengers, flight attendants sometimes reach a breaking point. One flight attendant described an incident in which she finally did give vent to her anger toward a female passenger who had steadily complained about all the services, and then attacked one of the co-worker flight attendants with a racial slur. In the flight attendant's words:

> Then she began yelling at me and my co-worker who happened to be black. "You nigger bitch!" she said. Well that did it. I told my friend not to waste her pain. This lady asked for one more Bloody Mary. I fixed the drink, put it on a tray, and when I got to her seat, my toe somehow found a piece of carpet and I tripped—and that Bloody Mary hit that white pants suit! (Hochschild, 1983, p. 114)

Of course, this kind of incident is an exception, and most successful airline flight attendants are able to control and manage their emotions, even under very adverse circumstances. Most are thoroughly and effectively socialized to provide the "emotional labor" that the airline requires of them.

Even though this type of formal socialization occurs in various occupations, equally important informal socialization occurs when new employees begin working. Older members of the group take on the task of training newcomers, which they accomplish both by example and direct instruction. Often the socialization message of veterans differs from that in the formal training process. Such was the case in the police department studied by sociologist Jennifer Hunt (1985), a study that was described in chapter 2.

When rookie police officers went on active duty they were quickly taught by veteran officers that it was permissible to use force, and even violence, when dealing with citizens. The veterans were quite aware that a discrepancy existed between police academy training about force and violence and the advice they were offering to rookies. Veterans often said, "It's not done on the street the way that it's taught at the academy."

Veteran street police quickly informed rookie officers that the weapons and nightsticks they had been issued were not adequate for the job on the street. Rookies quickly replaced their wooden batons with the more powerful plastic nightsticks. In the police academy recruits had been taught to avoid hitting people on the head or neck because blows there could cause serious injury or death. In contrast, on the street the standard was to hit wherever it would do the most damage in order to avoid danger to oneself.

Veteran police officers carried out their socialization by showing their approval and support when rookie officers used force. One female officer was upset when she learned that she was the object of a brutality suit, and she was reluctant to face her male colleagues. When she did report for work, however, the men greeted her with a standing ovation. Their support also included a sexist compliment when they told this woman officer, "You can use our urinal now" (Hunt, 1985, p. 319). Thus, by praise and support as well as by example, rookie police officers learn that it is acceptable to use "normal" force on the street, even though the level of violence often exceeds what is legally permissible.

This research by Jennifer Hunt was done long before members of the Los Angeles police force brutally attacked a black motorist in 1991 (see chapter 1). Even though her research was done in a different city, we learn from her findings that young police officers are socialized by the veterans to use force that is far beyond the officially accepted level.

Both formal and informal socialization are likely to occur whenever one enters a new profession, organization, or work setting. Even when a person enters an organization or work setting in a position of authority, some socialization occurs. A new office manager or department head must usually take some time to learn the existing social system before making dramatic changes in working procedures (Gouldner, 1954).

Resocialization in a Total Institution

Some instances of socialization in adulthood are so intense and pervasive that they can be called resocialization. **Resocialization** is the process of unlearning old norms, roles, and values, and then learning new ones required by the new social environment. In the most extreme cases of resocialization the social self of the incoming person is stripped away or destroyed, so that the individual becomes dependent on the institution for a new self. This extreme often occurs when an adult enters a total institution such as a mental hospital or prison (Goffman, 1961).

As we saw in the last chapter, a total institution is usually cut off from the rest of society and forms an all-encompassing social environment that meets all the needs of the members. Prisons and mental institutions are prominent examples of total institutions. Total institutions are miniature societies, with all of the characteristics of societies: they have a cultural system with values and norms, as well as a social structure with statuses and roles. Another distinct feature of total institutions is the almost complete control they exert over the lives of people who exist within them. A total institution requires an extensive reorganization of the life of the entering individual. Because the old rules and roles of life can no longer apply completely in a prison or mental institution, resocialization must take place.

Jean Harris, a former headmistress of an elite girls' school who was convicted of murdering the best-selling diet-book author, Dr. Herman Tarnower, has vividly described her resocialization in a women's prison. One of the first things Harris learned is that prison discipline "has little to do with wrongdoing. It has a great deal to do with how people feel about you, or how fearful the staff is of the people who complain about you" (Harris, 1986, p. 201). In other words, discipline is often meted out arbitrarily. The same behavior by two different inmates will get different reactions from the guards. Harris describes how she received a misconduct charge for absent-mindedly leaving her government-issued coat in the exercise yard (the charge was "not taking care of government property"). In contrast, another inmate, sitting only seven feet from one of the guards, cut up her coat and made it into a vest. The guard said nothing.

Harris also describes the complex daily routine of obtaining an antidepressant medication. If an inmate needs medication she must go to the dispensary for each administration. However, it is no simple task to get there because the round trip requires getting through eight locked doors. The guards stationed at each of these doors often keep the inmates waiting for considerable lengths of time before allowing them to pass through. Inmates requiring medication three times a day spend a considerable part of their day making these trips to the dispensary. In prison, even the simple task of taking a pill requires learning an intricate procedure and coping with a variety of complications and frustrations.

Resocialization for life in prison means that inmates must learn both a formal and an informal social system. The formal rules are made and enforced by the administrators and guards. The informal social system of a prison is controlled by the inmates. A sociological study of a women's prison, conducted by Heffernan (1972), shows how a new inmate must learn the informal system quickly or risk getting into trouble with the more powerful inmates. In the bathrooms certain sinks and showers are reserved for women with the highest status. When movies are shown in the recreation room the best seats are available only to these high-status women. In the words of the women inmates, "Some can, some can't." Should a new and unaware inmate accidentally select one of these preferred places, the result is a verbal or sometimes physical attack. New inmates in a total institution have few options; they must learn the rules of the new system (both formal and informal) and abide by them. The socialization is generally quick and effective.

Since total institutions are also places of work for many people, it is not surprising that there is also an informal social system that influences staff members as well. A young woman who had recently been a youth counselor at an institution for delinquent girls describes what she learned about making changes in the institution:

> When I first began to work here I was fresh out of college. You have all these ideas about all the changes you're going to make—to apply all the things you learned in college to rehabilitate. You try to express your views to the rest of the staff—that other ways of doing things might be more effective. But after you're here a while, you become institutionalized [socialized]. You find out that's not what's wanted. People who have been here a long time are the ones that make the decisions. They're the ones who call the shots. They really don't want change. . . . After a while you change. You do things just like they've always been done here (Giallombardo, 1974, p. 107).

The lesson is the same for the new inmate and the new staff member: the ongoing social system of rules and arrangements must be learned when one enters a total institution. What distinguishes total institutions from other groups and organizations is that total institutions influence all aspects of a person's life, and the influence is continuous. In other settings, one must adapt to the norms and rules of a new place of work, for example, but one can escape for many hours each day. In a prison, mental institution, nursing home, or monastery, or aboard a ship, such escape is not possible, and therefore the socialization is both more intense and more pervasive.

Socialization during Unexpected Life-Stage Transitions

As we have seen with adolescence, the expected changes from one life stage to another are often preceded by anticipatory socialization. However, some transitions in life are often unexpected or sudden. The death of a husband or wife, or the loss of a job can occur suddenly and unexpectedly. In these cases, socialization for the new status occurs when the unexpected event is in the process of occurring or has occurred.

Loss of Job.   When people lose their jobs, especially if the loss means the termination of a long-time occupation or career, they are often ill-prepared to deal with their new status. One study of out-of-work scientists, engineers, and technical people reveals how unprepared many people are for being unemployed (Powell and Driscoll, 1979). Often, these professionals responded with relief when they were laid off because many had anticipated losing their jobs. After a period of relaxation, they made concerted efforts to locate new positions. When their best efforts failed, they often started to experience serious self-doubt. Continued failure to find a job usually led to feelings of cynicism and discontent. Eventually these unemployed professionals ceased looking for work and had to adopt a new view of themselves and their occupational lives. Many admitted that they felt apathetic and listless about most aspects of their lives:

> I've lost all my drive and don't care.
>
> What's the use of looking? I'll just be turned down.
>
> I'm sick of being humiliated by people who act like they're doing you a favor just talking to you (Powell and Driscoll, 1979, p. 317).

A study of unemployed Canadian workers, covering a much broader occupational range, identified the most important adjustments that unemployed workers had to make (Burman, 1988). Because their incomes were curtailed, they had to learn how to economize and modify their spending habits. They also had to reconcile themselves to the fact that they were "losing ground" in the race for economic mobility. One of the most serious problems for the unemployed was learning how to use the many hours of the day when they had no job to occupy their time (Burman, 1988).

Widowhood.   Losing a husband or wife through death is widely recognized as one of the most traumatic experiences of life. Learning to live without a spouse, especially after a marriage that has lasted a long time, requires a significant period of adjustment. Although the reactions of both males and females are likely to be similar, the chances are much greater for women to lose their husbands than for men to lose their wives. Women who have had traditional relationships with their husbands are often ill-prepared to take over many of the required tasks of contemporary life. The same is true of men if they have relied upon their wives for many of their daily needs. One woman, who lost her husband in middle age, describes the changes she had to make:

> It takes two years, say psychiatrists, before a widow absorbs what has happened and is capable of making decisions. Early [on] there is merciful numbness. . . . And the first thing you understand when your senses return is that

although you are the same person, nobody else believes it. And after a while you see that they are right and you have to grow up in middle age (Mooney, 1981, p. D1).

"Growing up in middle age" describes vividly the socialization experience that accompanies the loss of a husband or wife.

Socialization for Retirement and Old Age

The life stages of retirement and old age are like the stages of adolescence and adulthood in the sense that they, too, are socially recognized and expected stages in life. Therefore a certain amount of anticipatory socialization is expected for these later life stages.

The transition to old age, however, is becoming increasingly complicated because of changes in the physical and economic characteristics of those in the elderly category. Retirement from the labor force is no longer as closely associated with old age as it was in the past. At the beginning of this century, the majority of men aged 65 were still active in the labor force. Today fewer than 20 percent of men over 65 are employed; an even smaller percentage of women over 65 are still employed—about 10 percent.

Retirement occurs at or before age 65 today because a greater proportion of the older population is economically able to retire. The payments of retirement plans and Social Security benefits, combined with personal savings, are allowing more and more people to retire at age 65 or earlier. Combined with the better economic conditions of the elderly is their better health. For most people over 50 in the United States today, retirement is no longer associated with idleness, illness, and poverty. These people approach their retirement years with expectations for many years of healthy and active life. (Chapter 10 discusses the elderly in greater detail.)

Of course, as the aging process continues, and especially as individuals reach age 75 and older, health conditions do lead to other changes in social status. As individuals are afflicted with more physical infirmities and often suffer from chronic ill health, they become more and more dependent on the help of others. Frequently continuous care is required in this stage of life, many times in nursing homes and other institutions. In these settings they may be socialized to accept the inevitability of death.

Socialization for Dying.   The ultimate and universal stage in the life cycle is death. Social systems, then, must have mechanisms for preparing people for death. Anticipatory socialization is an especially appropriate concept in this case, since preparation for death must occur before the actual event.

Funeral services, for example, are increasingly common occurrences as people grow older. For the elderly, the deaths of family members and friends become regular reminders of their own impending deaths. The rituals connected with death legitimize death; people learn to accept the deaths of others and also their own (Berger and Luckmann, 1967, p. 10).

A sociological study of a community of very elderly people (average age was 80) revealed that much of the social organization of the community centered around death (Marshall, 1980). Residents of the community were repeatedly made aware of the fact that death was more or less imminent both for themselves and others around them. The administration of the community repeatedly urged residents to plan the arrangements for their deaths—the disposition of their bodies, bequests, and other details. The residents did not treat death as a major philosophical issue but as a normal and expected occurrence (Marshall, 1980).

This example of socialization reveals again that social systems do not leave unattended the important passages from one life-cycle stage to another. Instead, the people in the system are prepared (socialized) to accept their movement into the next stage, even if that stage is death itself.

Summary

Socialization is the process by which a person learns and accepts the ways of a particular social group or society. Every social system makes sure that new members joining the system learn the accepted ways of doing things. Socialization is also important in producing the characteristics and personality of the individual.

The process of socialization begins in the very early stages of life, and through this process human qualities are acquired. Infants who are isolated from human contact during the early years of life do not show the characteristics we normally associate with human nature. Human infants develop reciprocal relationships with adults in which they learn to satisfy their basic needs by behaving in the way adults want them to. Through socialization, a child develops a social self, that is, the learned perception that a person has about his or her qualities and attributes. People learn to evaluate themselves through interaction with others, just as they learn to evaluate all other social objects. Social objects include the values, norms, and roles that prevail in the society.

Parents are important primary socialization agents, and many parents take very seriously the responsibility of shaping the personalities of their children. However, socialization is too complex and subtle for parents to achieve exactly what they desire in the socialization of their children.

Research on childhood socialization has shown that working-class families socialize their children differently from middle-class, white-collar families. Working-class families socialize their children to be obedient and to observe social rules. Middle-class parents socialize their children to take initiatives and to participate in decision making (autonomy). These two forms of behavior are related to the kinds of roles that children from different social classes are likely to play in the adult work world. Reverse socialization occurs when children socialize their parents. Empirical evidence shows that children teach their parents about some aspects of contemporary life.

Peers are important socializing agents for young children, and often the socialization of peers runs counter to that of parents. The mass media, especially television, are pervasive socializing forces in contemporary society. Children spend much of their time watching television, and evidence reveals that they are influenced by violence and by male and female characterizations seen there.

Adolescents and adults are also socialized by television, which is just one aspect of adult socialization. Adolescents receive anticipatory socialization for the adolescent stage of life. Adult socialization occurs when people enter new occupations, professions, organizations, work settings, institutions, or life stages. The total institution provides a particularly vivid example of adult socialization; this socialization is so extensive that it is referred to as resocialization.

Several life-stage transitions require learning new roles, but for some of these there is little anticipatory socialization. Two examples are loss of job and a spouse's death. In contrast, a substantial amount of anticipatory socialization occurs for retirement and old age, and even death.

CRITICAL THINKING

1. Why is socialization important for the continuation of a culture? What would happen to a culture if all socialization ceased?
2. Explain how the socialization process in your culture taught you the following: how to say goodbye, proper table manners, and appropriate dress for religious occasions.
3. What evidence supports the claim that primary socialization is important to our "humanness"?
4. What is the norm of reciprocity? Give examples from your own life that illustrate this principle.
5. How do some of the values of middle-class and lower-class parents differ with regard to the socialization of their children? What accounts for this difference in values? How might this explain the perpetuation of the class structure in American society?
6. Explain how reverse socialization can take place between parents and children.
7. Evaluate some television shows in light of the information about violence and male/female roles presented in the chapter.
8. What evidence supports the notion that adolescence is a socially created stage in the life cycle rather than a biologically created one?
9. What is adult socialization? What changes in a person's life might cause such socialization to occur?
10. Under what conditions is resocialization likely to occur?

6 Deviance and Social Control

Ask a group of ordinary people to provide examples of deviance or deviant behavior, and you are apt to get an amazing array of responses. Indeed, when one sociologist asked people to do just that, he received 252 different descriptions. Among them, the following examples were offered:

> Movie stars, junior executives, perverts, perpetual bridge-players, psychiatrists, drug addicts, political extremists, conservatives, career women, prostitutes, liars, prudes, girls who wear make-up, priests, atheists, liberals, communists, alcoholics, the retired, criminals, divorcees, reckless drivers, and know-it-all professors (Simmons, 1965).

As we look at this list, we might wonder how the respondents could describe some of these examples as deviant. The fact that they did illustrates that deviant behavior is not as clear-cut and obvious as we might suppose, nor is deviant behavior as fixed and unchanging as we sometimes think. To arrive at a sociological understanding of deviant behavior, we must first see that deviance is *socially defined*, and that social definitions of deviance differ from one society or social group to another.

The Social Nature of Deviance

To say that deviance is socially defined means that whenever most of the people of a given society, or social group, consider a behavior deviant, *it will be deviant.* As a result, a vast array of behaviors have been and are considered deviant in different societies. Even within the same society, significant changes often occur in what people consider deviant behavior. Cross-cultural and historical evidence provides many examples of the shifting nature of deviant behavior, showing clearly that it is socially defined.

We have seen indications of the variability of deviance in earlier chapters when we encountered behaviors in other societies that would be considered deviant in the United States. We saw in chapter 3 how the parents of Staphorst in the Netherlands expect their daughters to have sexual intercourse and become pregnant before marriage. These very religious people do not consider this behavior deviant, because it follows their cultural norms. If, however, we were to hear of American parents who expected their teenage daughters to become pregnant before marriage, we would probably think of these parents as deviants.

Many other examples exist of different views about deviance from one society to another. Among the Plains Indians, young men were made to fast until they saw visions. A Plains Indian youth who could not see visions would probably have been considered deviant. Americans might consider a person who claims to see visions as a deviant. Among many Arabs the use of alcohol was prohibited, but smoking hashish was more likely to be accepted. An Arab who preferred alcohol to hashish would have been considered deviant by his own people, and yet most people in the United States would see the situation in exactly the opposite way (Simmons, 1965).

The Changing Nature of Deviance

The fact that deviance is socially defined becomes abundantly clear when we examine some recent changes in what Americans think of as deviant behavior. Some behaviors that, only a decade or so ago, were not considered deviant are now viewed as deviant. The reverse is also true.

Two centuries ago in the United States, for instance, being fat was considered good; it was certainly not considered deviant (Schwartz, 1986). But in the contemporary United States many people consider obesity a form of deviance. To be fat today is to have a blemish on one's appearance and to be a social disgrace. Fatness is considered to be a morally reprehensible condition (Millman, 1980).

From Acceptability to Deviance. Smoking, especially in public places, is a behavior that has undergone a rapid transformation in the United States in a short span of years. By the end of World War II smoking had reached a peak of popularity in the United States. Cigarette smoking was viewed as glamorous and sophisticated behavior. The tobacco industry even advertised that cigarette smoking was healthy ("as an aid to digestion," "to calm nerves," and "to control weight"). Smoking in public, even in closely confined places such as planes, cars, and restaurants, was perfectly acceptable behavior.

Personal attitudes about smoking began to change when the Surgeon General of the United States issued a report in 1963 showing that smoking was related to a number of illnesses, especially cancer and heart disease. Although many individuals decided to stop smoking, the social attitude toward public smoking did not change. Public smoking, even in confined spaces, continued to be acceptable behavior. Only gradually in the 1970s, and then rapidly in the 1980s, did the *social* definition of smoking in public change.

During the 1980s, more and more nonsmokers openly contested the rights of smokers to smoke wherever they pleased. Today, the social definition of smoking is almost completely the opposite of what it was 25 years ago. Smokers who "light up" in the presence of nonsmokers will likely be told in very strong terms that their behavior is unacceptable. Smokers now often complain that their rights are being violated because they are made to feel like "criminals" when they smoke.

The changing attitudes toward smoking is reflected in the growing ban on smoking on airplanes. For most of the history of aviation, passengers were free to light up on planes, but in April, 1988, smoking was prohibited on domestic flights of two hours or less. On February 25, 1990, that ban was extended to domestic flights of six hours or less (Reinhold, 1990). Thus, virtually all domestic flights, except for a few flights to Alaska and Hawaii, are now smoke-free. While nonsmokers are delighted, many smokers experience agony during such flights. To compensate, they often smoke right up to boarding time and as soon as they deplane (Yenckel, 1988).

Although driving a vehicle while under the influence of alcohol has always been illegal, and thus a somewhat deviant act, recent changes in social definitions have clearly made drunk driving more deviant. In the past, most people hardly gave a second thought to driving after they had had a few drinks or more. Now, with growing concern about death and injury caused by drinking drivers, especially when innocent bystanders are killed or hurt, the social definitions are changing. Active campaigns against drunk driving by organizations such as Mothers Against Drunk Driving (MADD) and Students Against Drunk Driving (SADD) have heightened public awareness that driving after drinking is now apt to be considered a deviant act. In fact, the courts, too, are treating the offense of "driving under the influence" as a more serious crime, and jail sentences are not uncommon—especially for multiple offenders and in cases where innocent people are killed or injured. In 1982, 27 states passed new, stiffer laws against driving under the influence of alcohol (and drugs). Among other things, penalties were made more severe, and the certainty of punishment was increased (Kingsnorth and Jungsten, 1988). On June 14, 1990 the Supreme Court ruled that roadblocks set up to check for drunken drivers were constitutional even though they constituted "slight" intrusions on privacy (Marcus, 1990).

While smoking and drinking are relatively common forms of behavior that are more likely to be considered deviant in recent years, it is worth noting that a similar fate has befallen a far less common form of behavior—dirt eating! (Forsyth and Benoit, 1989). Yes, eating dirt, usually fine clays, occurs in many parts of the world, including the rural United States. The dirt may be eaten "raw," or cooked with seasonings and vinegar. Those who eat dirt do so because they have done it since childhood, because it makes them feel healthier (it supposedly relieves stomach cramps), and because they enjoy it as a "snack." Said one dirt eater about dirt as a snack: "I don't know it is just crunchy, its satisfying, its like a craving or something you get used to like a candy bar . . . there is nothing else that will surpass that taste" (Forsyth and Benoit, 1989, p. 64). However, as rural residents have moved into urban areas, dirt eating has grown to be perceived as more deviant, even by those who engage in it. Those who still practice dirt eating generally conceal it from the public and even family members.

From Deviance to Acceptability. Just as some behavior becomes more deviant over time, other behavior becomes less deviant, or more acceptable. Cohabitation before marriage is a case in point. In the 1950s and early 1960s some couples lived together without being married, but most people regarded their behavior as unacceptable. Such couples were commonly described as "living in sin." If an unmarried couple remained together long enough, and especially if they had children, the label "common-law marriage" was applied, always carrying a negative stigma, however. Couples involved in common-law marriages were looked down upon by most people in the community and were clearly regarded as deviants. Now, just a few decades later, many Americans accept cohabitation as a natural stage between dating and marriage. Even people who would not accept cohabitation for themselves do not attach much of a negative stigma to those who do.

The open discussion of sexual behavior is no longer taboo. Part of this change is born of necessity, in response to the AIDS crisis. In large measure, however, candor in discussing sex reflects changing norms. For example, only a few years ago, condoms would never have been discussed openly, especially on television or in public settings. Since the spread of AIDS has become a national public concern, it has become acceptable, if not praiseworthy, to urge the use of condoms. Today, they are displayed, discussed, and demonstrated in a wide range of public forums. In the late 1980s the Surgeon General of the United States stood before a high school audience and demonstrated the proper use of a condom. Less than ten years ago that act would have been considered deviant.

Deviant Behavior as Defined by Specific Groups

Even within the same society, different social groups often define deviance differently. Groups of people who share the same norms and values will develop their own rules about what is and what is not deviant behavior. Their views may not be shared by members of the larger society, but the definitions of deviance will apply to group members. For example, the students in any high school will establish their own codes for dress, hairstyles, and behavior. Although not everyone has to have the same appearance, when an individual strays too far from the current fashion, that person is likely to be considered deviant.

The importance of group definitions of deviance among high school students can be illustrated by the case of gifted students who consider themselves deviant. One such student described all gifted students as "not really trying to get along with others, a little obnoxious about being smart" (Huryn, 1986, p. 178). Not only did gifted students consider themselves to be deviant, but 77 percent of them felt that their peers at school regarded them as deviants. While the larger society, especially the adults, might view gifted students as the ideal for young people, the gifted students themselves may be considered deviant in their own social environments.

These illustrations indicate clearly that deviance is profoundly influenced by the society or social group in which the behavior or act occurs. Although deviance is often associated with individual behavior (individuals are considered bad, weak, corrupt, dishonest, or evil when they commit deviant acts), the sociological view emphasizes that deviance is a social phenomenon. We can only understand deviant behavior if we first recognize that societies and social groups define what is deviant, and what is not. Therefore, the sociological definition of **deviance** is any behavior that members of a society or social group consider a violation of group norms.

The Social Functions of Deviance

As we saw in chapter 1, structural-functionalists look for the way societal structures (defined as regular patterns of interaction) may have some positive purpose for the ongoing functioning of the society. However, structural-functionalists also recognize that some social structures can have negative results (dysfunctions) for a society. At first glance, it would seem that most deviant behavior in a society (crime and other forms of unacceptable behavior) would be socially dysfunctional. However, since the work of Emile Durkheim (1895/1964), sociologists have recognized that deviant behavior can have positive functions for society. This paradoxical relationship can be explained by the fact that when a deviant behavior occurs, society's norms are reaffirmed. The deviant act serves to clarify the existing standards of social conduct. Without periodic violations of the standards of conduct, the standards would become less clear and thus less strongly held (Dentler and Erikson, 1959; Jensen, 1988).

Of course, we do not need cold-blooded murders to remind us that killing a person is a deviant act. Many areas of social life, however, lack clarity as to whether a behavior is deviant. These areas are ones in which the positive function of deviant acts is most clearly revealed. For example, during the Reagan administration, charges were brought against former White House officials (who had enjoyed close contact with the President and other staff members) for attempting to influence policy decisions in order to gain profitable contracts for their clients. Some charges resulted in convictions; in other cases, their actions were judged to be unethical.

These well-publicized activities—which highlighted what the media called "the sleaze factor"—have increased public sensitivity to the inappropriateness and illegality of "selling influence." When President Bush took office in 1989, one of his first acts was to appoint a commission that would prepare a code of ethics. He also spoke to all senior government officials, stressing the importance of avoiding even the "perception of unethical behavior." From a structural-functionalist perspective, this chain of events illustrates that deviant acts can have positive societal functions.

Sociological Theories of Deviance

Sociologists are concerned with why some people in a society engage in behaviors that violate, or run counter to, norms. Why do some people steal, rob, kill, and commit other illegal and antisocial acts? Theories of deviance attempt to answer these questions.

Strain Theory

The **strain theory** of deviant behavior approaches deviance from the level of cultures and social structures (in other words, at the macroscopic level). According to strain theory, a discrepancy, or a lack of congruence, exists between cultural values and the means of achieving them. The strain can be thought of as a pressure that occurs when the culture values one thing, but the structure of the society is such that not everyone can realize the values in a socially accepted way. As we saw in chapter 3, the culture of the United States places a value on material or economic success. The structure of our society, however, does not give everyone the same chance for economic success. Many people in the lowest social classes have almost no chance to succeed economically. The result is that they may accept the cultural goal of "getting rich" but reject the socially accepted means of doing so. (Chapter 8—Social Stratification—investigates the inequality inherent in the socioeconomic system.)

In the poor and minority areas of many American cities, many youngsters are pressured into deviant behavior because the conventional means for achieving economic success (education and careers) are both difficult and remote. For these youths, illegal activities represent other ways of achieving economic success, even extraordinary success. For example, selling drugs can be a means of making money. Many young men are willing to risk their lives selling "crack" and other drugs because in return they often make thousands of dollars a week.

As we will see later, however, deviance is also present in the upper levels of society. Wall Street traders and stock manipulators have made huge sums of money through a variety of illegal activities. In these cases, the cultural value of economic success has won out over prohibitions against breaking the law.

Merton's Typology. Strain theory does not excuse illegal behavior among the poor or the wealthy. Rather, it emphasizes that there are different ways of responding to cultural values (or goals), and some of the responses are deviant behaviors.

Sociologist Robert Merton (1938, 1957; Farnsworth and Leiber, 1989), who formulated strain theory, provides a typology of the different ways in which people respond to cultural values or goals. Merton labeled as **conformist** people who accept the cultural goals (achieving economic success) and who also accept the conventional or institutionalized means of achieving these goals (getting an education, working hard, and so on). In Merton's typology, conformists clearly are not deviants.

People who accept the cultural goals (economic success) but reject the conventional or institutional means of achieving them are called **innova-**

Table 6–1.   A Typology of Modes of Conformity and Deviance

	Culture Goals (getting rich, etc.)	Institutionalized Means (working hard, etc.)	
I. Conformity	Acceptance	Acceptance	Nondeviance
II. Innovation	Acceptance	Rejection	
III. Ritualism	Rejection	Acceptance	Types of deviance
IV. Retreatism	Rejection	Rejection	
V. Rebellion	Rejection and substitution	Rejection and substitution	

Source: Adapted from Robert K. Merton, *Social Theory and Social Structure*, rev. ed., p. 140. Copyright 1957 by The Free Press.

tors. When large-scale cocaine dealers make great sums of money, they are innovators because they come up with new ways of achieving the cultural goal of economic success.

Those resigned to being unable to achieve cultural goals such as wealth and recognition, but who nonetheless slavishly adhere to conventional rules of conduct, are called **ritualists.** Ritualists continue to work at bureaucratic or dead-end jobs even though they have given up on any significant advancement in life. Because they have abandoned cultural goals, they, too, are in some degree deviant.

The **retreatist** rejects both the cultural goals *and* the conventional, institutionalized means. The retreatist response can be found among people who have given up on the system completely. They have no interest in economic success and thus have no reason to involve themselves in hard work or any other conventional, institutionalized means. Such people are almost always seen as deviant.

A fifth type of response to cultural goals and institutional means is the rejection of both and the substitution of new cultural goals and means. These are the **rebels,** illustrated by revolutionaries who want to create a new type of society. The new society might have entirely new cultural goals (harmony and cooperation rather than individual economic success) and new institutional means (meditation, communing with the spirit world, etc.).

The different responses to cultural goals and institutional means are summarized in table 6–1.

Strain theory is most effective in showing how deviant behavior can be a product of the relationship between cultural goals and the structural characteristics of a society. As a theory of deviance, it is most closely associated with structural-functional theory (see chapter 1). Strain theory shows how some structural features of society (social classes, the poor, racial minorities) can be dysfunctional by keeping many people from realizing important cultural goals. Deviant behavior is often the result.

Strain theory is less effective as an explanation for deviance among those who are members of advantaged groups. As we noted earlier, when deviant behavior occurs among Wall Street brokers, it cannot be attributed to their position in the social structure. Their position in the social structure has not blocked their paths to success. Thus, the explanation for their choosing deviant behavior lies elsewhere (Akers and Cochran, 1985).

Deviance as Learned Behavior

As we saw in chapter 5, people learn both norms and values through socialization. We also saw that the norms and values that people learn vary greatly. Values and norms depend upon the society in which one lives and the social groups of which one is a member. Two theories of deviance are built on the idea that some people learn values and norms that lead to deviant behavior.

Differential Association Theory.   Edwin Sutherland (1947), who originated this theory, saw deviant behavior as the result of socialization. **Differential association theory** emphasizes that individuals may be socialized by a group of people who engage in and accept deviant behavior. The name of the theory reflects the idea that what people do is influenced by the differences in the people with whom they associate. This argument is akin to a folk belief about the dangers of "keeping bad company." People learn to be drug addicts, alcoholics, or car thieves by keeping company with others who engage in or admire such behavior.

In a classic sociological study, Howard S. Becker (1963) pointed out the importance of friendship groups in the process of learning to smoke marijuana. When people start using marijuana, they usually rely on their friends to supply the drug until they are relatively experienced users. Furthermore, people *learn* how to enjoy the effects of marijuana from their friends.

It is widely held in the drug culture that people who say they cannot get high on marijuana have been improperly instructed in how to smoke it, and that people who say they do not enjoy being high did not smoke with people they like or trust. Research has confirmed the importance of social support for marijuana use (Akers and Cochran, 1985; Goode, 1969).

Subcultural Theory. These studies are consistent with a second, and closely related, theory of deviant behavior, which is also based on learning deviant behavior from a social group. This second theory is called the *subcultural theory of deviance* (Cohen, 1955; Cloward and Ohlin, 1960; Campbell and Muncer, 1989). **Subcultural theory** puts the emphasis on the carrier of deviant ideas, and identifies subcultures that have norms and values quite different from those of the larger society. Therefore, deviant behavior is really conformity to a set of norms and values accepted and taught by a particular social group. But when these norms and values are not held by the majority of people, the resulting behavior will be frowned on and labeled deviant by the dominant groups in society.

One of the pioneering studies using this approach was Albert Cohen's (1955) analysis of a gang of delinquent boys. Considering this group as a deviant subculture, Cohen found that the group held values that constituted a sort of "anti-culture" or negative reflection of the "straight" middle-class world. The boys in the gang held other people's property in contempt and expressed their feelings by acts of wanton destruction and vandalism. They also seemed to derive malicious satisfaction out of making "straight" people feel uncomfortable. They were "negativistic" in that they often turned middle-class values upside down. Thus Cohen sought to establish that the deviant group he studied was a particular kind of anti-establishment subculture. He also generalized the idea that most deviant groups are simply negative reflections of the majority culture.

Deviant subcultures are very similar to the countercultures described in chapter 3. We noted there that in the United States many groups have held values and subscribed to norms that were in opposition to the most widely held values and norms. Various kinds of bohemian groups from beatniks to hippies to punks have been considered deviant because they held values and accepted norms that were at odds with the majority. Examples of deviant subcultures can be found in every large society.

The Violent Subculture of British Soccer Fans. In England today there are groups of fans, generally teenage and young adult males, who clearly reveal the way deviant behavior can be learned from a subcultural group (Dunning et al., 1986). These football hooligans (as they are called) generally come from the lowest rungs of the British working class. They consider drinking, fighting, and other aggressive behaviors a natural and normal part of being a fan at a soccer match.

Football hooligans identify passionately with their hometown teams, and when they go to matches they consider it part of the fun to attack and fight with the fans of other football clubs. These attacks include throwing objects (often dangerous items such as darts, metal discs, broken seats, bricks, slabs of concrete, and fireworks) at opposing-team fans. A common practice is for the fans of one team to "invade" the fans of an opposing team, either in the stadium or at the railway or bus stations as the visiting-team fans depart after the game. These invasions lead to fist fights, kicking, and other forms of violence. The most notorious of these invasions occurred at the European Cup matches in 1985, when a violent clash between British and Italian fans led to the deaths of 38 people. Many Britons consider it too dangerous to go to stadiums for the soccer matches because the threat of being accidentally harmed is too great. Most citizens clearly identify the football hooligans as deviants.

Various attempts have been made to explain the routine and nearly ritualized violence of British football fans. One explanation focuses on the norms and values learned by a segment of British youths, and thus it is consistent with both subcultural and differential association theories. Most of the violent youths come from working-class neighborhoods and housing projects where the norms and values are supportive of violence. In many of these neighborhoods it is a mark of prestige for a young man to prove his ability to fight and be aggressive. Indeed, many of these young men learn to enjoy fighting. A man 26 years of age describes the great satisfaction he gets from fighting:

> I go to a match for one reason only: the "aggro" [aggression and fighting]. It's an obsession, I can't give it up. I get so much pleasure . . . that I nearly wet my pants. I go all over the country looking for it. . . . every night during the week we go around looking for trouble (Dunning et al., 1986, p. 222).

In the neighborhoods and housing developments where these young English males grow up, they do not learn to value educational and occupational success. Instead, they learn to value "physical intimidation, fighting, heavy drinking, and exploitative sexual relations" (Dunning et al., 1986, p. 234). The deviant behavior of the football hooligans of England is easily identified as the product of the values and norms these young men have learned on the streets of their neighborhoods.

U.S. Outlaw Motorcycle Gangs.   In the United States there are subcultural groups who share norms and values that are very similar to the football hooligans of England. The most widely known are motorcycle gangs, such as the Hell's Angels, who also value fighting and getting into trouble. A related characteristic of male motorcycle-gang members is that they, too, are exploitative of their female companions. The female bikers are expected to engage in prostitution in order to earn money for the dominant males. But this is only part of the broader subordination of females to male bikers. Beyond prostitution, a biker's regular girl friend (his "ol' lady") can be bought and sold (for anywhere between 50¢ and $500), and the sexual favors of other females (those who do not have regular boyfriends) are freely shared by group members. Beyond sexual abuse, female gang members are generally treated quite brutally by the male members. Obviously, these and other forms of behavior are greatly at odds with the norms of the larger society (Quinn, 1987; Watson, 1980).

Puerto Rican Women Gang Members. Deviant female groups have also been the subject of sociological study. Young female members of several Puerto Rican gangs in New York City were studied and found to have a consistent set of values and beliefs (Campbell, 1987). The young women make a clear distinction between the recreational use of drugs and drug addiction. Gang members both use and sell marijuana, and at parties they occasionally use both amphetamines and LSD. However, they strongly condemn the use of heroin, and are very negative about "skin popping" (injecting drugs) because it is regarded as a sign of drug dependence.

In the subculture of these Puerto Rican women, many crimes are not considered criminal. Although they condemn people they do consider "criminals," they do not include as criminals those involved in ". . . drug selling, inter-gang warfare, organized crime, prostitution, domestic violence, stripping abandoned buildings and automobiles, shoplifting, and burglary of businesses" (Campbell, 1987).

Theories of deviant behavior that rely upon learning or socialization do not, of course, explain why different norms and values arise in the first place. When a general societal norm exists that is negative about criminal activity, why do some social groups (subcultures) place a positive value on criminal behavior? These theories also do not explain why some individuals do, and others do not, choose to associate with groups that hold different norms and values. Individuals do make choices; their behavior is not totally determined by their social environments. Examples abound of people who break away from the subcultural environments in which they find themselves.

Despite these criticisms, the importance of socialization as an explanation for deviant behavior cannot be denied. The evidence in support of socialization is found in virtually every form of deviance, from drug use and juvenile delinquency to adult and organized crime (Hazani, 1986; Orcutt, 1987).

Conflict Theory of Deviance

In chapter 1 we saw that conflict theory rests on the premise that, in any society, inequalities in resources and power will exist. When focusing on deviant behavior, conflict theorists emphasize the ways in which a society is organized to serve the interests of the rich and powerful members, often at the expense of other members of the society. To many conflict theorists, the ultimate source of deviance in U.S. society is the capitalist economic system (Gordon, 1981). This view is well summed up by the title of a book, *The Rich Get Richer and the Poor Get Prison* (Reiman, 1979). Since inequality is built into the very basis of the system, many conflict theorists hold that the only real solution lies in the system's total overhaul—a replacement by a much more equitable system in which the gap between the "haves" and the "have-nots" will be minimized.

Although deviance is found at every level of society, the nature, rate, and punishment of deviance are frequently related to the social-class position of the deviant individual (Berk, Lenihan, and Rossi, 1980; Braithwaite, 1981). Generally those from the upper strata of society—the wealthy, the powerful, the influential—play a major role in defining what is, or is not, deviant. These individuals are able to influence the moral and legal definition of deviance in numerous legal ways, including lobbying, making financial contributions to political campaigns, selecting candidates for office, and participating in various policy-making bodies. The result is that a society's moral and legal system reflects the interests of the powerful. The behavior of those whose interests are not represented is therefore much more likely to be defined as deviant. For instance, upper-class people are seldom, if ever, likely to be caught for, and charged with, vagrancy—an illegal behavior for which lower-class persons are frequently caught, charged, and convicted. As Anatole France (1922) once sarcastically commented, "The law, in all its majestic equality, forbids the rich as well as the poor to sleep under bridges on rainy nights, to beg on the streets, and to steal bread."

Elite Deviance. Although deviance is usually equated with acts such as vagrancy, burglary, robbery, kidnapping, and assault—for which members of the lower classes are more likely to be convicted—as we have seen, society's elites also break laws and deviate from the accepted morality. Conflict theorists have a special interest in **elite deviance,** or the deviant and criminal acts committed by the wealthy and powerful. Cases of elite deviance are often much more costly in economic terms than other types of crime, yet punishment is more lenient.

Elite deviance can take many different forms and may range from unethical or immoral acts to criminal acts punishable by fines and imprisonment. Stock manipulation and embezzlement of company funds, for example, are clearly illegal, although a public official who lies to his constituency or gives special favors to friends may be called immoral or unethical yet may be immune from prosecution. Some elite deviant acts result in personal economic gains (such as a senator's accepting a bribe). Other acts result in economic gain for a business or corporation (as in the case of price fixing or kickbacks or bribes to secure business contracts). While elite deviance is generally less visible, dramatic, and overtly violent than other forms of deviance, it may still be injurious to the public's health, safety, or financial well-being. For example, in 1967 the President's Crime Commission estimated that the nation's annual loss to white-collar crime was 27 to 42 times as great as the loss through traditional property crime (robbery, burglary, larceny, and forgery) (Thio, 1978, p. 355).

Even when criminal convictions are obtained, the penalties for elite deviance are often relatively light. When the E.F. Hutton company, a major financial institution, was caught in a fraudulent check "kiting" scheme, a crime for which ordinary citizens would generally be penalized, no company officials were criminally indicted. Even though the company officials were systematically writing checks when they had insufficient funds in bank accounts, and were therefore fraudulently taking the bank's money, the U.S. Justice Department did not choose to prosecute.

In the 1980s a scandal occurred on Wall Street involving the illegal buying and selling of stocks on the basis of "inside" or advance information about stocks that were going to rise in value. This is called *insider trading,* and it is illegal. The insider trading case that rocked Wall Street in 1986 centered around Ivan Boesky (nicknamed "Ivan the Terrible," or "Piggy" because he was so greedy). Boesky was a multimillionaire stock market speculator who ultimately admitted that his unbelievable economic successes (for which he was greatly admired) were the result of advance information he had acquired about corporate takeover deals. With this information Boesky was able to buy into the companies before their stock prices rose, and he could therefore make great profits. By the time these illegal dealings came to light, Boesky had amassed a huge fortune.

When his crimes were uncovered, Boesky agreed to help the government find others who were involved in insider trading. He eventually agreed to pay $100 million in penalties and was banished for life from professional stock trading. In exchange, the government allowed Boesky to sell $440 million in stock he controlled *before* the announcement of his penalties was made. In other words, Boesky was allowed to sell his stock before the price was to plummet *because* of the announcement of his penalties. Boesky was clearly treated quite gently by the authorities and emerged from the scandal with a significant portion of his fortune intact.

Boesky was also sentenced to a three-year prison term at the prison of his choice; he chose the minimum security facility in Lompoc, California. The California climate is gentle, and the prison is set on 44,000 acres of rolling hills and manicured lawns. It offers the inmates a gym, tennis courts, a weight-lifting room, and an outdoor track. It is hard to imagine a burglar or robber who has stolen hundreds of millions of dollars being given such preferential treatment and such a light sentence in a "country-club" prison.

Another prominent figure in the Wall Street scandals was Michael Milken, the pioneer of "junk bonds." Milken was involved with Boesky and, in fact, it was Boesky who, in order to aid his own case, wore a "wire" and helped gather the information that led to Milken's arrest (Kempton, 1990). Milken was eventually convicted of securities fraud and other business crimes and was sentenced to ten years in prison, a surprisingly harsh sentence for a white-collar crime. Prior to his conviction, Milken had agreed to pay a $200 million fine and a $400 million penalty. In spite of the forfeit of 600-million-dollars, it was estimated that Milken was left with a fortune of $700 million. Attorney General Richard Thornburgh said that Milken's conviction strongly suggests "that law enforcement has upped the ante considerably for 'crime in the suites' committed by the white-collar criminal" (McCartney, 1990, p. A22). However, Representative John Dingell said of the sentence that "its apparent harshness is more illusion than reality" (McCartney, 1990, p. A22). While Milken will spend several years in jail, unless he cooperates with government and is able to get his sentence reduced, the fact is that he will eventually emerge from prison a very wealthy man.

Conflict theorists argue, as we have noted, that elite deviants commit much larger crimes and receive lighter punishments than average citizens. This viewpoint can be illustrated by comparing the Boesky-Milken case (or the E.F. Hutton case) with that of William J. Rummel. Rummel was convicted of three offenses by the courts of Texas. His crimes were the following:

1. forging a check for $28.36;
2. obtaining $80 by fraudulent use of a credit card;
3. taking a check for $120.75 in return for a false promise to repair an air conditioner.

Although none of these crimes involved physical injuries to the offended parties, these convictions all happen to be felonies, and under Texas law conviction for a third felony carries a mandatory sentence of life imprisonment. The constitutionality of the law was sustained by the Supreme Court (*New York Times*, 1980a, p. A24). Thus, for crimes involving a total of $229.11, William Rummel faces a life behind bars.

Conflict theory emphasizes the inequalities of power and money in societies. Many conflict theorists, following Marxian theory, see the inequalities as growing out of a capitalist economic system. However, other conflict theorists have noted that inequalities in power and authority also exist in countries with socialist or communist economies (Dahrendorf, 1959).

We will turn next to a theory of deviance that shares with conflict theory the view that inequalities between groups of people in a society can influence who is and who is not considered deviant. Called *labeling theory,* it is associated with symbolic interaction theory (chapter 1) because it places great emphasis on the symbolic labeling of people as deviants.

Labeling Theory

Labeling theory focuses on the social nature of the process by which some individuals in the society are able to label other individuals as deviant. Also of interest is how the labeled person accepts or adopts the deviant label for himself or herself (Dotter and Roebuck, 1988; Gove, 1980).

Labeling theory is concerned with which people will be labeled "criminals," "alcoholics," "drug addicts," or "mentally ill" (Link et al., 1989). When such labels are applied, the labeling process begins. It involves a person or group doing the labeling (the labeler) and a person or group to whom the label is applied (the labelee). Those who do the labeling are social control agents. Often these agents, such as the police or psychiatrists, label as part of their official functions. Labeling also occurs in very informal contexts, such as when a family member or friend labels someone a drunk, a nymphomaniac, or a liar. Those who are labeled in this process are the deviants. Thus, from a labeling perspective, a deviant is someone to whom a deviant label has been successfully applied (Becker, 1963, p. 9).

The process of becoming deviant usually begins when people perform acts that are disapproved of by certain members of society. Some people rape, steal, or become mentally ill. These forms of deviance may be due to personality problems, a particular kind of home life, community conditions, peer-group influence, or other factors. Although some sociologists focus on the causes of deviance that lie within individuals or their environments, many have come to focus on the official and unofficial social control agents and the labels they create and apply. If no deviant labels were created by social control agents, then there would be no deviance. According to labeling theorists, in order for behavior to be considered deviant, it must be labeled as such:

> . . . social groups create deviance by making the rules whose infraction constitutes deviance and by applying these rules to particular people and labeling them as outsiders. From this point of view, deviance is not a consequence of the act the person commits, but rather a consequence of the application by others of rules and sanctions to an "offender" (Becker, 1963, p. 9).

In other words, no specific behavior is inherently deviant; behavior becomes deviant only when others define it as such.

As we have shown, the deviant label is not applied uniformly. The poor, minority groups, and the disadvantaged are more likely to be labeled deviant for a given act than are more advantaged individuals who behave in the same way. In cases of extreme offenses, such as murder, the community's selectivity in labeling people as deviant is not as clear, but it is quite clear in less extreme forms of deviance: "Some men who drink too much are called alcoholics and others are not; some men who act oddly are committed to hospitals and others are not; some men who have no visible means of support are hauled into court and others are not" (Erikson, 1964, pp. 11–12). These realities have led observers to argue that people are more likely to be labeled mentally ill when they are poor, work in low-status occupations, or are in similarly devalued circumstances (Goffman, 1959a). A person in a more advantageous social situation often escapes being labeled deviant, despite manifestations of the same forms of behavior.

Labeling theory has also been used to help us to understand deviance from the perspective of the victim of deviant acts. In cases where husbands have abused their wives, it is frequently the woman, the *victim*, who is labeled as the deviant (Carlson, 1987). The abusing husband will often successfully label his wife as deviant, charging her with being inadequate, perhaps not living up to the expectations of some ideal female role. Many abused wives report that their husbands convinced them, often for years, that *their* inadequacies were the cause of the beatings. Second, if an abused wife tries to do something about the violence, she is likely to be labeled as deviant by the larger society for revealing that her home and marriage are "defective." Thus, labeling contributes to violence against wives and to their reluctance to do anything about it. The abusive husband may ultimately be labeled as a deviant, but before that occurs, the female victim is likely to have acquired that label.

Primary versus Secondary Deviance. When deviance is viewed from a labeling perspective, the focal concern is not individual, isolated acts of deviance. Labeling theorists are not concerned with explaining why previously "straight" people steal their first orange from a fruit stand, embezzle their first dollar from their employer, or assault their first victim. Such early, nonpatterned acts of deviance are called **primary deviance.**

Virtually everyone commits some acts of primary deviance. In a study of 1689 adults in New York City, Wallerstein and Wyles (1947) found that 91 percent of the respondents in the study admitted that they had broken a law after their sixteenth birthday. Sixty-four percent of the men and 29 percent of the women could have been convicted of a felony. Between 80 percent and 90 percent of all the men and women studied had stolen something. One-fourth of the men admitted to having stolen an automobile, and one out of ten had committed a robbery. Thus, isolated acts that would be labeled deviant by social control agents are widespread.

Labeling theorists, however, are chiefly concerned with **secondary deviance,** which refers to forms of deviance that persist in individuals and that cause them to organize their lives and personal identities around their deviant status. Labeling theorists focus on the process whereby individuals become labeled as criminals, and the label comes to override all other definitions of self.

Although the labeling approach focuses on the degree to which others label an individual, it is also possible for individuals to label themselves (Thoits, 1985). For example, persons who are sick label themselves as ill in the hope that others will recognize this label and respond appropriately—by expressing sympathy, curing the illness, or excusing the sick person from normal activities and responsibilities. Deviants, then, sometimes label themselves before anyone else does and proceed to act in accordance with that label (Lorber, 1967).

Although a number of criticisms have been leveled against labeling theory, it persists as a powerful sociological perspective on deviance (Bazemore, 1985; Klein, 1986; Sommer et al., 1988). Much of the following discussion, in fact, is a reflection of the insights of labeling theory.

The Process of Social Control

Having defined deviance (and various theories of deviance), we now come to the problem of analyzing the reciprocal process of social control, which is an important part of labeling deviants. **Social control** refers to the process whereby a group or society enforces conformity to its demands and expectations. Social control involves those with power who seek (often successfully) to label as deviant those who do not conform. Those who develop labels and engage in the labeling process are the social control agents. Those successfully labeled are the deviants. From the perspective of labeling theory, deviants and social control agents cannot exist without each other. We also can differentiate between two broad types of social control agents: rule enforcers and rule creators (Becker, 1963).

Acting as Rule Enforcers

When we think of rule enforcers, we generally think of the formal agents involved in the social control process—the police, the courts, prisons, even parents (Birenbaum and Sagarin, 1976). Arrest by police, conviction and imprisonment by the courts, and punishment by parents are all examples of the exercise of social control through rule enforcement. Each of these social control agents is clearly implicated in the labeling process. Arrest and incarceration serve to label an individual as a murderer, thief, or rapist. Even parental admonishments can label a child lazy, dumb, or mean. **Rule enforcers** attempt to maintain social control and order through the threat or actual application of undesirable social labels.

Although most of us think of formal agencies when we think of rule enforcement, we are somewhat less likely to think of ourselves as rule enforcers. All of us, however, act as rule enforcers on a fairly regular basis in our day-to-day activities. If people around us violate a social norm, we act in a variety of ways to indicate that they have done so, in an effort to bring them back into line. We are likely to act as rule enforcers when we observe someone spitting on the floor, cutting in at the head of a line, or hassling an innocent passerby. Even a raised eyebrow, a grimace, or a frown can serve the function of social control. We can also engage in more extreme forms of rule enforcement such as a raised voice, a clenched fist, or even a blow to the head. Such interpersonal social control devices, both subtle and blatant, are far more widespread than the formal means employed by the police, the courts, and other social control agencies.

Rule Creators and Social Change

The **rule creator** devises the rules, norms, or laws. Without rule creators, we would have no deviance, since we would have nothing from which to deviate. This is what we mean when we say that deviance is created by social control agents who establish a society's normative system. While some laypersons may believe that norms, rules, and laws represent eternal and incontrovertible truths, sociologists see these rules as generally produced to protect the vested interests of the rule creators and those they represent.

A number of studies have shown that social rules are the product of the vested interests of social control agents. One illustration is found in Chambliss's analysis (1964) of the history of vagrancy laws—laws that came into being when feudalism was breaking up. Medieval landowners needed a large pool of cheap labor when they could no longer depend upon serfs to carry out their work. Vagrancy laws provided this cheap labor by forcing people to work in order to avoid being arrested for vagrancy. With the final breakdown of feudalism, the need for vagrancy laws disappeared. For a long time the laws lay dormant, little changed and rarely applied. However, as commerce and trade developed in Europe, the vagrancy laws were renewed and applied to different people. They were directed at the rogues and vagabonds who threatened to disturb the orderly flow of commerce by robbing and stealing. In short, vagrancy laws, first created to aid landowners, fell into disuse, only to be revived later and redefined to suit the new, powerful, commercial class. Vagrancy laws exemplify the fact that rules are the result of the vested interests of agents of social control.

Computer Abuse and Rule Creators.   A contemporary example of rule creation is found in the criminalization of computer abuse. **Computer abuse** is the unauthorized entry into someone else's computer data for the purpose of altering, stealing, or sabotaging it (Hollinger and Lanza-Kaduce, 1988). These acts are unusual types of deviance in that they can be committed without the use of force or even without the perpetrator's being physically present. The first law against such computer crime was passed in Florida in 1978. The interesting sociological question is why such laws came into existence.

The mass media played a key role in the development of computer crime laws. The fact is that few people would be aware of computer crime without the mass media's doing stories on them. The number of newspaper articles on computer crime, describing the threat it poses, has increased dramatically, as has public perception of computer crime as a serious problem. Unlike the case of vagrancy laws, no specific interest group played a central role in the passage of computer crime laws. (The news media have an interest in publishing stories on computer crime in order to help sell newspapers, but they have no vested interest in the passage of legislation against it.) A key role was played by state and federal legislators who were attracted to the issue by media attention and found in it a cause that would give them wide media exposure without alienating any powerful interest group. Thus, rules and laws may come into existence because of the action of groups with vested interests, but other forces (like the mass media) may also play a key role. Furthermore, laws may be created by interest groups, but they may also come into existence because social conditions (e.g., the rise of the computer, the increasing awareness of computer abuse) change and require new legislation (Hollinger and Lanza-Kaduce, 1988).

Sociology in the News

The Ultimate Computer Virus

The most visible computer crime in recent years was committed in November, 1988, by a Cornell University graduate student (since suspended by Cornell), Robert Tappan Morris. What made the case doubly interesting was the fact that Morris was the son of a senior computer scientist employed at the top-secret National Security Agency. The elder Morris has responsibility for the government's military computer security and electronic intelligence gathering. The crime committed by the younger Morris could have potentially endangered such highly secret operations. He created a "virus" (a program, or set of instructions, that replicates itself from computer to computer) that rapidly spread through a national network of interlinked computers. The virus succeeded in crippling approximately 6000 computers in government agencies and laboratories, companies, and universities. In some cases, it took days to restore normal operations on computers.

The government contended that Morris had knowingly launched a full-scale attack against the computer network. Morris claimed that he had not intended to disrupt the national computer network but rather was experimenting with a program that because of a design error multiplied rapidly throughout the computer system. In spite of this claim, in 1990 Morris became the first person to be convicted under the 1986 Federal Computer Fraud and Abuse Act. The judge rejected a prison term, but sentenced Morris to three years' probation, a fine of $10,000, and 400 hours of community service.

The case had been closely watched because of the fact that many felt that a message needed to be sent to computer "hackers" that this new form of criminal behavior was going to be taken seriously and dealt with harshly. Hackers are computer experts, some of whom take pleasure in penetrating the security precautions of the nation's computer systems. The dangers here are numerous. For example, company secrets can be uncovered and company funds can be diverted. A breach of the nation's defense computers could disrupt our ability to defend ourselves and, most dangerously, lead the military in the direction of offensive operations. Finally, national secrets can be discovered and passed on to unfriendly governments.

Some observers feel that the punishment meted out to Morris was not sufficiently severe and that Morris should have served some time in jail. They believe that the risk to national security requires stronger punishment. Said U.S. Representative Wally Herger (Republican from California), "I am very disappointed that the sentence did not include some prison time for this serious offense ... In this ground-breaking case, we must send a strong message that computer virus outbreaks will be punished severely" (Burgess, 1990, p. A1).

However, others argued that this was not a good test case of the law because many believed that Morris did not intend to breach the security of the nation's computer systems. Said one software specialist who testified for the defense, "He was playing with fire, but he didn't really mean to burn anybody" (Burgess, 1990, p. A1). Some feel that Morris had even done some good by pointing up vulnerabilities in computer systems and increasing the awareness of the computer community to the danger posed by viruses (Markoff, 1988).

BURGESS, JOHN. "No Jail Time Imposed in Hacker Case; Creator of 'Virus' Gets Probation, Fine." *Washington Post*, May 5, 1990, A1ff.

MARKOFF, JOHN. "How a Need for Challenge Seduced Computer Expert." *New York Times*, November 6, 1988, 1ff.

MARKOFF, JOHN. "Computer Intruder is Put on Probation and Fined $10,000." *New York Times*, May 5, 1990, 1ff.

The Personal Experience of Deviance

Becoming Deviant

Although some people come to be labeled deviant without having committed a deviant act, we begin our discussion with the assumption that some act has been committed that some rule-enforcement agents consider deviant. Some people who commit a deviant act once or twice may never commit another; others will proceed only partway through the process of becoming deviant; still others move from primary deviance to secondary deviance (Lemert, 1967).

If an act of primary deviance is observed, the person committing it may be punished by rule-enforcement agents. Despite punishment, some people commit additional acts of primary deviance. If these acts are observed by social-control agents, further and probably more severe punishments will occur. Although punishment may deter some people, others will engage in still further acts of deviance and possibly develop hostility and resentment toward those who punish them. This leads to a crisis level in the community's ability to tolerate more deviance. The most likely result is some formal action by social-control agents that labels the individual. For some, this strengthens their deviant identity and increases their deviant conduct. Ultimately, the individual who moves through the entire process comes to accept deviant social status and attempts to adapt to it. The end product is secondary deviance, or a person whose life and identity are organized around a deviant label.

Although some people consciously enter into a deviant career, most seem to simply respond to circumstances and situations in which they find themselves (Lemert, 1972, p. 80).

Coping with Deviance—Goffman's Theory of Stigma

More than anyone else, Erving Goffman has contributed to our understanding of how people, having been labeled deviant, cope with their own deviance. Goffman's work was done primarily in the tradition of symbolic interaction theory. He was especially interested in the way people interacted with each other, and in the messages they were sending by their words and gestures. In one of his most influential books, he studied people with certain characteristics that others would find unusual, unpleasant, or deviant (Goffman, 1963). Goffman called these characteristics *stigmas,* and he was particularly concerned with how people who have stigmas cope with them.

Goffman's analysis begins with physically stigmatized people and gradually introduces a wide array of other stigmas. In the end, readers realize that they have not been reading about a remote person who has a physical deformity, but about themselves. As Goffman (1963, p. 127) says: "The most fortunate of normals is likely to have his half-hidden failing, and for every little failing there is a social occasion when it will loom large, creating a shameful gap."

Goffman deals with two basic types of stigmatized individuals. The first type, the individual with a **discredited stigma,** "assumes his differentness is known about already or is evident on the spot." The second type, the individual with a **discreditable stigma,** assumes that his stigma "is neither known about by those present nor immediately perceivable by them" (Goffman, 1963, p. 4). Discredited or discreditable stigmas can take the form of physical deformities, as when a person has lost a limb; character blemishes, as when a person has a prison record or a history of mental illness; or membership in an ethnic or racial group that is often viewed negatively by others (gypsies, for example).

In Goffman's view, people with discredited stigmas (readily visible) face different problems from those with discreditable stigmas (not immediately obvious). With a discredited stigma, the person can be prepared for some expected (often hostile) responses in social interaction with other people. On the other hand, persons with discreditable stigmas often try to manage interaction so that others will not learn of their characteristic. Concealment often becomes cumbersome. For example, there is the case of Mrs. G., whose husband was in a mental hospital. In order to keep the neighbors from discovering what she believed to be a stigma, she told them that he was in the hospital because of a suspected cancer. Every day she would rush to get the mail before her neighbors picked it up for her as they used to do. She abandoned second breakfasts at the drug store with the women in the neighboring apartments to avoid their questions. Before inviting her neighbors in, she hid any material that identified the hospital, and so on (Yarrow, Clausen, and Robbins, 1955, cited in Goffman, 1963, p. 89).

AIDS and Stigma.   A major example of stigma in the United States today is AIDS. There is great fear of the disease and, at least in some segments of American society, substantial hostility toward those with AIDS. In the early stages of the disease, AIDS patients have a discreditable stigma, since there are usually not any overt signs of the disease. Victims will then often attempt to manage information so that others do not learn that they have AIDS. However, as the disease progresses, concealment of the stigmatized characteristics becomes increasingly difficult. AIDS victims are likely to lose substantial amounts of weight, look unwell, require frequent hospitalization, and perhaps develop the visible skin lesions of Kaposi's sarcoma. In Goffman's terms, AIDS victims in the later stages of the disease have discredited stigma; their disease is very visible. Rather than concealing information, AIDS victims come to focus on managing the tension produced by people who know that they have the dreaded disease. They may be shunned by friends, may lose their jobs, and may be badly treated by health personnel. The social aspects of having AIDS are easily understood as a contemporary example of Goffman's insightful analysis of stigma.

Leaving the Deviant Role

Once imposed, the deviant label is difficult and sometimes impossible to remove. However, many deviants do manage to shed the label and leave the deviant role. Our concern in this section is not with those who can escape the deviant label relatively easily (such as someone defined as slightly overweight, who can go on a diet), but rather with those whose label is difficult to remove. Although we will focus on alcoholics, the same points apply to many other deviant roles.

The problems of leaving a deviant role are illustrated by sociological studies of Alcoholics Anonymous (AA) (Trice and Roman, 1970; Denzin, 1986, 1987). In AA, one finds examples of successful **delabeling,** that is, cases in which alcoholics were able to shed their deviant label and replace it with a socially acceptable one, "recovering alcoholic."

Delabeling can occur in three basic ways:

1. Deviants can organize to change the rules, norms, or laws of society to make an offending behavior acceptable, as the gay liberation movement has done to delabel homosexuals.
2. Professionals, who frequently are the ones who initially apply a deviant label, also can establish delabeling ceremonies in which they publicly announce that an offending behavior has ceased to be deviant and an individual is eligible to return to the broader community. An event along these lines occurred when the American Psychiatric Association removed homosexuality from its list of mental illnesses (Spector, 1977).
3. Mutual-aid organizations can encourage the deviant individual to return to conformity to social norms. These organizations can also help create a socially acceptable stereotype about the reformed deviant. Alcoholics Anonymous is a mutual-aid organization that "provides opportunities for alcoholics to join together in an effort to cease disruptive and deviant drinking behavior in order to set the stage for the resumption of normal, occupational, marital, and community roles" (Trice and Roman, 1970, p. 539).

Alcoholics Anonymous uses various methods to help alcoholics shed their deviant label. AA believes that alcoholics have a biological predisposition to become alcoholics. This interpretation of the causes of alcoholism counters the alternate belief that alcoholics are responsible for their actions or that alcoholism is a form of mental illness. To help further in the delabeling process, AA argues that since alcoholics' deviance stems from their drinking, once they stop drinking, their deviant status ends. AA also has constructed a rather unusual repentant role. By admitting that they are alcoholics, alcoholics will supposedly embark on the road to delabeling and acquiring the new "more respectable role" of ex-alcoholic. AA also stresses the degradation of drinking. By showing how far down some alcoholics have descended, they set the stage for stories of glorious comebacks.

Although AA is more successful than most organizations in helping people leave a deviant role, few hard data are available on its success ratio. AA has been a middle-class organization with little attraction for individuals from the lower classes. Also, it could be argued that voluntary membership makes AA successful because those who decide to join AA are the ones most motivated to solve their drinking problem. AA, however, does help some people modify or change their deviant label.

Crime: A Major Form of Deviance

In this final section we turn our attention to a significant aspect of deviant behavior: crime. **Crime** is deviant behavior that violates the law and is subject to formally sanctioned punishment by the larger society (U.S. Bureau of Justice, 1983, p. 2). The study of crime, criminal behavior, and the treatment of criminals is a subfield of sociology called *criminology*.

Types of Crime

One way of differentiating crimes is to distinguish between crimes against people and crimes against property. **Crimes against people** (or **violent crimes**) involve the threat of injury, or threat (or use) of force, against victims. Violent crimes include four major types:

1. Murder and nonnegligent homicide (all willful homicides as distinguished from deaths caused by negligence);
2. Forcible rape (including assault to rape, threat of force, and attempted rape);
3. Robbery (stealing or taking anything of value by force or threat of force);
4. Aggravated assault (assault with intent to kill or to do great bodily harm) (U.S. Department of Justice, 1988a).

Property crimes do *not* involve the threat of injury, or the threat (or use) of force, against victims; the objective is to gain or destroy property unlawfully. The following are the major types of property crime:

1. Burglary (breaking or unlawful entry into a structure with the intent to commit a felony or theft—includes attempts);
2. Larceny-theft (unlawful taking of another's property without force, violence, or fraud—excludes embezzlement and forgery);
3. Motor vehicle theft (theft or attempted theft of a motor vehicle);
4. Arson (willful and malicious burning of, or attempt to burn, houses, buildings, vehicles, personal property, and the like, of another person).

The FBI calls all eight of these violent crimes and property crimes **index offenses.** They are also often called **street crimes**—a term used frequently in the mass media.

Another important way to differentiate crimes reflects the ways they are handled by the criminal justice system. **Felonies,** more serious crimes (e.g., homicide, rape, and robbery), are punishable by a year or more in prison. **Misdemeanors,** minor offenses (e.g., drunkenness, shoplifting, and disturbing the peace), are punishable by imprisonment for less than a year.

Although this section focuses on street crimes, at least five other major types of crime can be identified. A major social problem is **white-collar crime** (Braithwaite, 1985), or crime usually committed by upper-status people in the course of their occupations (e.g., computer data theft, embezzlement, consumer fraud, and bribery). Elite deviance, which we discussed earlier, is part of white-collar crime. Another type is **political crime,** which is misconduct and crime committed within or against a political system. As a result of government scandals such as Watergate, the Iran–Contra affair, and other questionable behavior of a variety of government officials (e.g., illegal campaign contributions and "influence peddling"), political crime is an issue of growing importance. Another facet of political crime is terrorism, which is an act carried out to influence or change existing governments. **Organized crime** refers to "those self-perpetuating, structured, and disciplined associations of individuals, or groups, combined together for the purpose of obtaining monetary or commercial gains or profits, wholly or in part by illegal means, while protecting their activities through a pattern of graft and corruption" (U.S. Bureau of Justice Statistics, 1983, p. 3). We usually think of the Mafia when we think of organized crime. In **victimless crime** (Schur, 1965) it is difficult to identify a victim: the participants choose to be involved in the activities (e.g., selling and buying pornography, prostitution). Finally, **juvenile delinquency** refers to illegal or antisocial behavior on the part of a minor.

Official Crime Statistics

The best-known crime statistics in the United States are gathered from official law enforcement agencies and collated and published by the FBI as the *Uniform Crime Reports* (U.S. Department of Justice, 1990). Local police agencies send the FBI monthly and annual summary reports on crimes in their jurisdictions, which provide the basis for the *Uniform Crime Reports* statistics. These reports include data on the number of offenses discovered by, or reported to, these law enforcement agencies.

For 1989, according to the FBI, 14.25 million criminal offenses were reported to the police in the United States. Of these, about 12.6 million (about 88 percent) were *property* crimes—burglary, larceny, motor vehicle theft, and arson. The 1.65 million *crimes against people* (violent crimes) included approximately 21,500 homicides, 94,500 forcible rapes, 578,000 robberies, and 952,000 aggravated assaults. The vast majority of crimes in the United States are crimes against property and *not* crimes against people (U.S. Bureau of Justice Statistics, 1990).

The great volume of crime in the United States is revealed by the frequency of various crimes. On the basis of the crimes reported in the *Uniform Crime Reports,* the FBI has prepared a Crime Clock, which is shown in figure 6–1. Among other facts, this clock shows that in the United

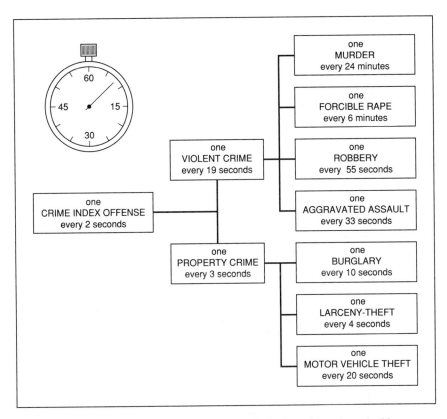

Figure 6–1.   Crime Clock, 1989. The crime clock should be viewed with care. Being the most aggregate representation of UCR data, it is designed to convey the annual reported crime experience by showing the relative frequency of occurrence of the Index Offenses. This mode of display should not be taken to imply a regularity in the commission of the Part I Offenses; rather, it represents the annual ratio of crime to fixed time intervals. (*Source:* United States Bureau of Justice Statistics, 1990).

States one violent crime is committed every 19 seconds, and one crime against property, every 3 seconds.

Murder in the United States.   The Crime Clock reveals that in the United States a murder is committed every 24 minutes. Compared to other countries, the United States has an exceptionally high homicide rate. For example, in 1980 23,000 murders were committed in the United States. This number of murders was committed by a U.S. population of 227 million people. As a comparison, the combined populations of Denmark, the Federal Republic of Germany, Greece, Japan, and Poland had populations totalling 230 million. Yet these countries had only slightly more than 2300 murders (U.S. Bureau of the Census, 1984, p. 181). In 1980 the United States had a murder rate that was ten times higher than these widely dispersed nations of the world. (However, it should be pointed out that since 1980 the number of murders in the United States has actually *declined*. It is likely, therefore, that, at the minimum, the differential between the United States and these other nations has not increased.)

Crime in Urban and Rural Areas

In 1989 the metropolitan areas of the United States (called MSAs, or Metropolitan Statistical Areas[1]) had a violent-offense rate of 779.7 per 100,000 (that is, there were 779.7 known violent offenses for every 100,000 people living in MSAs), whereas the comparable rate in rural areas was 188.7 per 100,000. In the same year, cities had a property-offense rate of 5,072.9 per 100,000, whereas the comparable rate in rural areas was 1,785.1 per 100,000 (U.S. Bureau of Justice Statistics, 1990). These figures underscore the extent to which crime is disproportionately an urban problem. Violent crimes are about four times more likely to occur in cities than in rural areas, and the likelihood of property crimes in cities is about two and one-half times that in rural areas.

One probable reason for the higher crime rates in urban areas is the greater likelihood of drug use in cities. An increasing body of evidence shows that drug sales and use are related to crime rates.

Women and Crime

Over the last two decades there has been an increase in the number of women arrested for crime (Simon and Landis, 1991). In 1963, 11.4 percent of those arrested for all crimes were women, while in 1987 that had increased to 17.7 percent. More striking was the increase in women arrested for serious crimes, almost doubling from 11.7 percent in 1963 to 21.6 percent in 1987. Almost all of the increase in female crime involves property offenses (especially larceny); there was very little increase in vi-

---

[1] A Metropolitan Statistical Area "includes a central city of at least 50,000 population or an urbanized area of at least 50,000. The county containing the central city and contiguous counties having strong economic and social relationships to the central city and county are also included" (U.S. Department of Justice, 1988a, p. 317).

olent crime (homicide, aggravated assault, and robbery) committed by females.

How do we account for this dramatic increase in female arrest rates? Four basic explanations have been offered. The first is the *masculinity thesis*, which argues that as women have become liberated, they have been freed to assert themselves in typically male ways—including crime. The second, or *opportunity thesis*, contends that, as women gain more education, enter the labor force in greater numbers, and assume positions of greater authority, they will have more opportunity to commit crimes, especially white-collar property offenses. The third position is the *economic marginalization thesis*, which maintains that because women still have poorer occupational and income opportunities than men, there is a greater need for them to commit crime. Finally, there is the *decline of chivalry thesis*, which asserts that while in the past chivalry served to hold down female arrest rates, such chivalry has disappeared, with the result that female criminals are now more likely to be treated like their male counterparts. While Simon and Landis (1991) find support for the opportunity thesis, it seems likely that all these factors are involved in the increase in female crime.

Drugs and Crime

Drug abusers, especially heroin addicts, frequently commit crimes in order to support their habits. In New York City, almost 80 percent of men arrested for serious crimes tested positive for the recent use of illegal drugs. It is estimated that 40 percent of New York's 1672 murders in 1987 were drug-related (Hamill, 1988); a similar percentage of the greater Washington, D.C. homicides in 1990 were drug-linked (Escobar, 1991). Furthermore, most people believe that official statistics greatly underestimate the actual amount of crime committed by drug addicts.

Many addicts become skilled criminal entrepreneurs in order to support their drug needs. Heroin addicts tend to specialize in a particular type of crime, which they refer to as their "main hustle." For males the most common main hustle is drug sales, while for females it is shoplifting and prostitution. As they specialize, they become increasingly adept at their particular crimes with the result that they will probably avoid arrest for committing the crime. This gives us one reason why the crime statistics on drug addicts, while still high, are probably greatly underestimated (Faupel, 1986).

The drug–crime linkage is rocking many American cities; in fact, it is disrupting many of the world's cities. Several Latin American countries are increasingly under the control of drug dealers. (See the box on Colombian drug traffickers: "Drugs and Political Power: The Case of Colombia.") Although the United States as a whole is not in the grip of drug gangs, certain areas of a number of our major cities are controlled by heavily armed drug gangs (with the Uzi machine gun as the weapon of choice) who deal viciously with those who seek to cut in on their territories. In Washington, D.C., during 1990, 483 people were killed, and many of these murders were drug related.

In order to deal with the increasing problems produced by drugs, a number of law enforcement and political leaders such as Kurt Schmoke, the mayor of Baltimore, have urged decriminalization of drugs. Decriminalization means that using drugs would not be a crime, and some agency of the government would dispense drugs to those who wanted them (perhaps even free of charge). Those who support decriminalization do not usually support the *legalization* of drugs, which would allow private business to sell drugs that are now illegal (e.g., cigarette companies could sell marijuana cigarettes).

The interest in decriminalizing drugs stems from a belief that little can be done at the moment about the seemingly insatiable demand for drugs in the United States. Slogans such as "Just say no" are not likely to have much of an impact on hardcore drug abusers. Furthermore, it is impossible to completely seal off the borders of the United States in order to cut off the supply of drugs. Therefore, with little to be done about demand or supply, decriminalization might be tried.

Decriminalization would squeeze the criminal element out of the business because, if the government dispensed drugs at no cost, or at a nominal cost, the profits would be taken from the illegal drug business. The presumption is that illegal drug dealers would lose interest in supplying drugs to addicts if they could not make enormous profits.

Decriminalizing Drugs: The Dutch Experience.   Those who advocate decriminalization cannot take much heart from the experience of the Netherlands. The Dutch have had a very liberal attitude toward drugs. Designated shops dispense marijuana. Amsterdam has a city-owned houseboat where cocaine and heroin are openly used. Specially designed buses travel around the city and dispense methadone at regular locations. In spite of this liberalness, or perhaps because of it, crime in Amsterdam has risen dramatically, with hard drug users blamed for the vast majority of the crimes. Drug abusers from many nations have gravitated toward Amsterdam because of its liberal policies. Some businesses have been hurt, and the city's image as a tourist attraction has been tarnished. However, there is some evidence that, contrary to what one might expect, marijuana use has declined, as has heroin addiction among young people (*Washington Post*, 1988, p. A18).

The American Justice and Penal Systems

Americans today expect that people who have been convicted of crimes will spend time in jail or prison; however, it has not always been that way. During the colonial period most convicted criminals were fined, whipped, or confined in stocks. If their crimes were serious enough, they were hanged. The colonists did not conceive of imprisoning criminals for a specified period of time (Rothman, 1971). Only after colonial times did the idea of imprisoning criminals become an accepted practice.

In the United States today the overcrowding of prisons has become a serious problem. The population of state and federal prisons in 1989 was 703,687 (U.S. Bureau of Justice Statistics, 1990). In the 1980s the number of people in prison a more than doubled, an increase of 113 percent. (See figure 6–2 for the growth of prison inmates since the 1920s.) One striking change is the increase in the number of female prisoners, which has grown faster than male inmates in every year since 1981.

The High Cost of Imprisonment.   Unfortunately, the mere custody of prisoners (let alone treatment) is very expensive. In 1983 (the last date for which data are available), municipal, county, state, and federal governments spent approximately $10.4 billion for corrections (U.S. Department of Justice, 1988b). This is more than a quadrupling of the $2.3 billion spent on such facilities a decade earlier, in 1973 (*Sourcebook of Criminal Justice Statistics — 1983*, 1984, pp. 2–3). Beyond correctional costs, the costs of police, courts, prosecutors, and public defenders swelled the total cost of the U.S. justice system in 1983 to almost $40 billion.

Arrest and Imprisonment as Deterrents to Crime.   The threat of imprisonment is supposed to serve as a deterrent to crime. We can differentiate between two types of deterrence. In **specific deterrence** the actual punishment of an individual is supposed to deter him/her from committing other crimes in the future. **General deterrence** involves the threat of punishment and the idea that people will not commit crimes because they fear they will be caught and sent to prison (Miranne and Gray, 1987).

The question posed by specific deterrence is whether an offender will be more or less likely to commit another crime after arrest or punishment. A recent study shows that arrested offenders will be less likely to commit a future crime than offenders who are released by the police. This was true for novice (first-time) offenders, but it was especially true of experienced offenders (Smith and Gartin, 1989). Persons who are arrested for criminal acts are less likely to commit a crime at a later date than those persons who are released by the police. This conclusion is nearly

Cross-National Perspectives

Drugs and Political Power: The Case of Colombia

One of the most ominous developments in the arena of drugs is the degree to which Latin American countries (Peru, Bolivia, and especially Colombia) are involved in the international drug trade and controlled by drug lords (Drozdiak, 1991). Government officials who stand up to, and attempt to arrest and prosecute, the drug kingpins have often found themselves in grave danger, and many have been killed for their efforts. In Colombia alone, between March, 1990, and March, 1991, the drug cartel killed three presidential candidates, as well as judges, police officials, and leading journalists and reporters (Rodriguez, 1991). In their efforts to control drug sellers, many hundreds of members of the police and the military have been killed.

Colombia supplies about 80 percent of the cocaine smuggled into the United States and earns between $2.5 and $3.0 billion from the business. In fact, the drug business is now larger than Colombia's other famous product—coffee. A leader of one Colombian drug cartel is Rodriguez Gacha. Gacha lives in a small town with his private military-style defense force of 110 gunmen. In addition, he controls the city government, which has responsibility for the transfer and promotion of police officers. Recently, Gacha's cartel participated in local elections and gained control over five more towns in the northern part of the country. This area could easily be turned into a "drug state" within the nation of Colombia. Beyond control over local governments, drug traffickers control one-twelfth of the productive farmland, one of Bogota's four main television stations, a nationwide chain of radio stations, car dealerships, office buildings, discount drug stores, and at least six of the nation's professional soccer teams. Said an executive of one of the country's largest newspapers: "These people are more powerful than the state" (Isikoff and Robinson, 1989).

Further buttressing the power of the drug lords is the fact that they employ many people who owe their livelihoods to them. In addition, the drug cartels have engaged in "narco-philanthropy," that is, giving money to the poorest members of society who, in turn, feel deeply indebted to and are ardent supporters of the drug traffickers. Another Colombian drug lord, Pablo Escobar, built 450 homes with running water, electricity, and telephone service—all rarities for the poor in Latin America. No one in the *barrio* has ever paid any rent. As a result, one of the people who lives in this *barrio* said: "We love Don Pablo [Escobar]. . . . He is a man of great tenderness" (*Washington Post*, 1989). A nine-year-old boy said: "He is the father of us all" (*Washington Post*, 1989). Not only is Escobar loved, but *Forbes* magazine rates him the fourteenth wealthiest person in the world.

In the last year Colombian officials have struck back with a plan not supported by the United States. The Colombian government has offered a deal to the drug lords—turn yourselves in and you will not be extradited to the United States. They have been promised that they will be tried in Colombia and that they will receive a reasonable sentence. Some of the leading drug leaders have already accepted the offer (including Escobar) and others are expected to follow.

Why have the powerful drug lords accepted this offer? First, as fugitives they are not able to freely enjoy their great wealth. Second, the government appears to be engaging in its own terrorism— assassinating and kidnapping drug lords and their families. Third, there is the fear of extradition to the United States and suffering the fate of Manuel Noriega, who was taken to the United States after the invasion of Panama in 1989 and is currently in prison awaiting trial on drug charges. While these new efforts may achieve some successes, it seems highly unlikely that the drug lords, or the Colombian drug business, will be seriously hurt.

It is possible to interpret what has taken place in Latin America from the point of view of Marxian theory. That is, one basic Marxian view is that those people in society who control the means of economic production are likely to control the government and the minds of the people. Marx, of course, focused on legitimate capitalists, but the drug lords can be seen as illegitimate capitalists who own the means (that is, the drug factories) of drug production. Given this power base, they are able to exercise control over the government and over the minds of the people through television and radio stations and newspapers they own.

DROZDIAK, WILLIAM. "Europe Finds Colombian Cartels Well Ensconced." *Washington Post*, April 11, 1991, p. A29.
ISIKOFF, MICHAEL and EUGENE ROBINSON. "Colombia's Drug Kings Becoming Entrenched." *Washington Post*, January 8, 1989.
RODRIGUEZ, CECILIA. "Colombia's Bid to End Narco-Terrorism." *Chicago Tribune*, March 22, 1991, pp. C23ff.
"Drug Lord's Largesse Wins Friends." *Washington Post*, January 8, 1989.

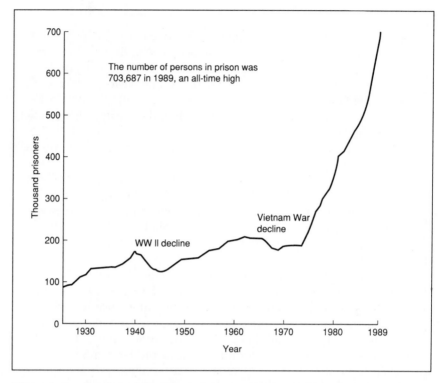

Figure 6–2.   Number of Persons in Prison: 1930–1989. (*Sources:* U.S. Bureau of Justice Statistics, *Report to the Nation on Crime and Justice* (Washington, D.C.: U.S. Department of Justice, 1983), p. 81; U.S. Bureau of Justice Statistics, *Prisoners in 1989* (Washington, D.C.: U.S. Department of Justice, May 1990).

the same as the field experiment described in chapter 2, in which men arrested for domestic violence offenses are less likely to repeat their offenses than men who are not arrested (Sherman and Berk, 1984).

Although arrests seem to deter people from future criminal acts, the same is not true for imprisonment. One study has shown that the severity of punishment (imprisonment) does not reduce the likelihood of a return to crime; being imprisoned actually *increases* the likelihood of another criminal offense (Shannon, 1980). Other studies have shown that about one-third of the people who serve time in prison, and are released, return to prison at a later date. This is called **recidivism** (Waldo and Griswold, 1979). If one-third of the people who spend time in prison are not deterred from further crime, it suggests that something about the prison experience may lead to further crime for some people. Moreover, even though it might be supposed that prison would be a special deterrent for white-collar crime, a recent study has suggested that even white-collar criminals are not deterred from future crime by prison sentences (Moore, 1987).

Capital Punishment. Between 1977, the year executions were resumed after a nearly ten-year lull due to unresolved legal issues, and the end of 1990, there were 143 executions in the United States. Furthermore, over 2400 people were on death row in January, 1991, more than have ever been on death row in the history of the United States (Paternoster, 1991). In executing people the United States stands in opposition to nations such as France, Canada, and the United Kingdom, which have outlawed capital punishment. On the other hand, the United States shares the death penalty with such repressive nations as Iraq, the People's Republic of China, and the Soviet Union.

Much of the support for the death penalty in the United States stems from the belief that it serves as a deterrence against major crimes. There is little question that it serves as a specific deterrence—the person executed will never commit a crime again. However, there is a real question as to whether capital punishment serves as a better general deterrent than imprisonment. For example, a substantial body of research shows that homicide rates in states with the death penalty are *not* lower than the rates in states that have abolished the death penalty.

Not only does capital punishment fail as a form of general deterrence, but it is also discriminatory, especially toward blacks. Blacks are more likely to be executed for murder than whites, and they are far more likely than whites to be executed for rape, especially if the victim is white.

Thus, while a number of people have been executed in recent years, and many more are in jeopardy of capital punishment, the fact is that there are real questions about the efficacy of the death penalty as a deterrent as well as about its fairness to minority groups.

Summary

Deviance is socially defined, which means that whenever most of the people in a given society or social group consider a behavior deviant, it will be deviant. It can be shown that many behaviors that were at some time acceptable are now deviant; similarly, many behaviors that were deviant at an earlier time are now acceptable. Deviant behavior can often serve to define for the society what is and is not acceptable behavior.

A number of theories of deviance exist: strain theory, deviance as learned behavior (differential association and subcultural), conflict theory, and labeling theory. Each one has a different perspective on deviant behavior.

From a social control perspective, there are attempts to keep most people in conformity with the prevailing norms of the society. Although the most powerful people in the society are most likely to define acceptable and deviant behavior, everyone at some time or another acts as rule enforcer and rule creator.

Three different stages of a career of deviance can be defined. The first stage is becoming deviant, the second is coping with deviance, and the third is leaving the deviant role. Important social aspects are involved in all three of these stages.

Crime is the most attention-getting aspect of deviant behavior. Several distinct types of crime can be defined, including crimes against people (violent crimes), property crime, white-collar crime, political crime, organized crime, victimless crime, and juvenile delinquency. Most crime in the United States is crime against property, but this country also has a high murder rate, especially compared to other nations. Crime is higher in urban areas than in rural areas, and this is probably attributable in part to the extensive use of drugs in today's society. The number of women arrested for crimes has increased substantially. Drug use has become such a serious problem in the United States that some law enforcement officials and political leaders have suggested decriminalizing drugs.

Persons convicted of crimes in the United States are expected to spend time in jail or prison. As a result, the American prison system has been charged with controlling ever-larger numbers of inmates. Serious questions have been raised about whether arrest and punishment will deter individuals from further crime. Recent studies have shown that arrest is a deterrent, but the severity of punishment is not. After a lull, capital punishment is once again employed in the United States. However, there are serious questions about how well it performs as a general deterrent, and it clearly is practiced in a discriminatory fashion.

CRITICAL THINKING

1. Use examples from the chapter to illustrate that deviant behaviors are socially defined behaviors that may vary from group to group.
2. What determines the nature of deviant behavior in a society or social group?
3. According to the structural-functionalists, how might deviant behavior have a positive societal function?
4. Depending on your cultural group, how might certain behaviors represent both conformity and deviance?
5. How can sociology be used to explain the extreme behavior of certain British soccer fans?
6. Use examples from the chapter to explain how conflict theorists explain deviant behavior. From the perspective of conflict theory, how does social class influence society's response to deviance?
7. How would a labeling theorist respond to a mother's statement that "her young son was just naturally naughty?" Would the sociologist consider her son's behavior an example of primary or secondary deviance?
8. In what ways have you acted as a rule enforcer in your day-to-day activities?
9. Give examples of rules that are produced to protect the vested interests of the rule creators in the following social organizations: United States Congress, high schools, prisons.
10. Use a daily newspaper to identify examples of the following types of crimes: property crimes, misdemeanors, white-collar crime, political crime, and organized crime. Compare society's punishments for each of these types of offenses.

7 Sexual Behavior from a Sociological Perspective

A NOTE FROM THE AUTHORS: *This chapter on sexual behavior has a special purpose at this point in the book. The first six chapters have introduced you to some fundamental concepts and ideas of sociology. Throughout the rest of the book, many of the concepts you have learned, such as values, norms, roles, reference groups, and so on, will help you to analyze and understand various aspects of social life. Similarly, the sociological ideas introduced in the preceding chapters will continue to provide insights about human social behavior in the remaining chapters. As an example, a fundamental sociological idea is that human behavior is influenced by cultural values, by social norms, by membership in groups and organizations, and by the verbal and nonverbal symbols that we share with other people. This chapter on sexual behavior will present applications of many of the basic concepts and fundamental ideas of sociology.*

Sexual behavior is a strategic area to choose for applying sociological concepts because it is explained so frequently by biological characteristics or psychological mechanisms. Although both biology and psychology are important in understanding sexual behavior, we will show that sociological concepts and ideas are also significant. With this approach we hope to strengthen your understanding of these concepts and ideas and, most important, give you the experience of seeing how helpful and relevant a sociological perspective can be.

- Sexuality is a basic human characteristic.
- Sexual behavior is universal, found in every society.
- Sexual behavior at its most fundamental level is a physical and biological act.

These facts are nearly indisputable, and as such they seem to suggest that a sociological perspective might have little relevance to sexuality and sexual behavior. Yet in chapter 3 we considered the people of Staphorst, who insisted that their children have premarital sex before marriage; this case reveals how important cultural customs can be in determining sexual behavior. To demonstrate more fully the importance of cultural norms and values, we begin this chapter with a brief examination of how much sexual behavior, and even sexuality, varies from one society to another. These cultural variations will make it clear that we learn much of our sexual behavior from the cultures of the societies in which we live (Reiss, 1986).

Sexual behavior undoubtedly has a biological basis in human beings, just as it has in every other animal species, but biology alone does not explain sexual behavior. This is obvious if we consider the cultural differences in sexual behavior among people in different societies.

There are societies, for example, in which a brother and sister eating at the same table is considered a mildly *sexual* act, and therefore they are prohibited from eating together (Davenport, 1977). In the United States, of course, there is nothing sexual about a brother and sister eating a meal together, even if they are alone. This illustration is but one example of the way in which sexual behavior is culturally defined and regulated.

Through the culture of a society, people learn what is acceptable sexual behavior and what is not acceptable. They learn when sex is appropriate or inappropriate and with whom it is acceptable or not acceptable. The very meaning of sex changes from one society to another. In some societies, sex is a pleasurable, nearly recreational, activity, while in others it is "dirty," and shameful, and rarely spoken of at all. There are some societies in which sex is a hostile battleground between the sexes, and other societies where sex is only for the purpose of reproduction.

In order to get a sense of how much sexual behavior is influenced by societal and cultural differences, we will first consider some cross-cultural and historical examples of sexual behavior. As we examine these variations in sexual behavior we should remind ourselves that we too learn appropriate sexual behavior from our own culture, in our time.

Cultural Differences in Sexual Behavior

One of the most unusual examples of sexual behavior comes from the classical period of Greek history (500 to 300 B.C.). During this period it was customary for many Greek men to have sexual relations with young boys. Often these men were teachers or military men, and the boys were their students or apprentices. Many of the men had wives and had fathered children, obviously having had heterosexual relations, but that fact did not preclude sexual relationships with boys as well (Flaceliere, 1962).

Although the practice of having sexual relations with young boys was widespread in classical Greece, it was not accepted universally. Aristotle, for example, one of the great philosophers of that era, thought that men who engaged in such relationships were depraved.

A similar cultural pattern has been observed among the Azande people of the Southern Sudan in Africa, where the men also routinely had sexual relations with young boys. Among the Azande the unmarried warriors had young boys who lived with them as personal aides. A boy would take care of the daily needs of his "husband," which included the soldier's sexual needs (Evans-Prichard, 1970).

Another cultural variation in sexual behavior is found in the way husbands and wives relate to each other during sexual intercourse. In chapter 3 we saw that among the Yanomamo people of the Amazon Valley, violence is common between husbands and wives, and this violence extends into their sexual relations. Similarly, the Gusii of southwestern Kenya define sexuality as a hostile and antagonistic relationship between men and women. Both sexes regard intercourse as a situation in which the man overcomes the natural resistance of the woman. Women are expected to frustrate men with sexual taunts and insults. Gusii men are said to experience greater sexual gratification when women protest and cry during intercourse (Davenport, 1977).

The Gusii view of sexuality is taught to the children when they are young and is especially emphasized at the time of puberty rituals. If girls display any signs of sexuality when they are young, they are punished; signs of sexuality among young boys, however, are both encouraged *and* punished. When these youngsters of the Gusii reach adolescence, they are taught sexual antagonism through the puberty rituals. The adolescent boys are circumcised at a secret initiation ceremony, after which the adolescent girls are brought to where the boys are. The girls are naked and perform erotic dances, while making negative remarks about the boys' mutilated genitals. The girls' dances are supposed to arouse the boys sexually, giving them erections, which will cause them pain since they have just been circumcised (Davenport, 1977). It is little wonder, then, after these childhood and adolescent experiences, that the Gusii think of sexual relations in the context of antagonism and hostility.

In contemporary Islamic societies, sexual relations between husbands and wives are greatly influenced by interpretations of female sexuality based on the *Koran*. Women's sexual needs are seen as very strong, and husbands must meet these needs if their wives are to remain virtuous. Female sexuality is often viewed as dangerous because women, if not under strict control, can be "fatal attractions" for men. A married man can too easily be distracted from his social and religious obligations by a woman other than his wife. Therefore, all women must be kept secluded in their homes, and when they enter public places their faces should be veiled and their bodies completely covered with clothing (Mernissi, 1987).

Cultural Definitions of What Is Sexual

Not only does sexual behavior vary from one culture to another, but definitions of what is considered "sexy" differ as well. For example, in the United States popular magazines often publish articles that claim to reveal which parts of the male and female anatomy are most sexy. Females are often said to favor the buttocks as the sexiest part of a male.

The newspaper *USA Today* has on occasion awarded honors for the best buttucks seen in movies (Beefiest Butt, Meanest Butt, and so on). Actors such as Mel Gibson and Arnold Schwarzenegger have been recently honored for their posteriors (Kurtz, 1991).

As for males, they too are said to be attracted by the buttocks as one of the sexiest parts of a woman, but breasts and legs also evoke some favor. Apparently, almost no American males select the armpits as one feature of a woman that arouses them sexually. Fewer still choose the neck as sexually exciting. Yet there are males in different parts of the world who would select these as the sexiest parts of a woman's body. Indeed, they would think it strange that men in other societies would not consider them sexy. For instance, among the Abkhasians, a group of people living in the southern part of the Soviet Union, the female's armpit is especially exciting sexually (Benet, 1974). It would be unthinkable among the Abkhasians for a woman to allow a man other than her husband to see her armpits. Japanese males, on the other hand, consider a woman's neck as a particularly sexual part of her body. They are especially attracted to a long, swanlike neck. For a number of years the Hollywood film actress Audrey Hepburn was very popular among Japanese men, precisely because one of her most striking features was a long, slim neck. Although this feature might have appealed to some U.S. males, it is doubtful that very many would have seen it as sexually arousing.

Women's breasts are considered objects of sexual attraction and erotic stimulation in almost every society, even those where the breasts are normally uncovered. However, among the Mangaia of Polynesia, women's breasts have no sexual significance. Because the males of this society do not find them erotic, women's breasts have no place in heterosexual foreplay or in sexual communication (Davenport, 1977).

History provides other examples of diversity regarding what was considered sexual. In Hawaii, before the influence of Western cultural ideals, extremely obese women were viewed as highly erotic, especially among the aristocrats and members of royalty (Davenport, 1977). In the United States, as recently as the beginning of this century, if one were to judge from the photographs of women who were considered sexually appealing, the ideal woman's body was much heavier and well rounded than the ideal body of today. The beginning of the twentieth century was also a time when women wore floor-length dresses, which made the sight of a woman's ankle or calf sexually arousing to males.

Although the sexual attractions of females are most often noted by contemporary Western people, sometimes the males of a society are the objects of sexual attention. Among the Wodaabe, a nomadic tribe in Central Africa, young males are the center of attraction, especially during ceremonies held several times a year. Dances are performed by the young males, who compete with each other to be chosen the most beautiful and charming (Beckwith, 1983). Their costuming and makeup, along with the parading and performing before tribe members, are comparable to a Miss America contest in the United States. The most handsome young men of the tribe stand in a kind of chorus line where their attractiveness is judged largely on the basis of their exaggerated facial expressions. An observer describes the scene as follows: "Eyes roll; teeth flash; lips purse, part and tremble; cheeks, inflated like toy balloons, collapse in short puffs of breath" (Beckwith, 1983, p. 508).

These facial features, especially the large rolling eyes, are particularly alluring to the women of the tribe, who may cry out in ecstasy when a man performs well. The charm and magnetism of these facial gestures may bring multiple wives to the most handsome young men of the tribe. American women would probably not find these facial gyrations sexually attractive, but the Wodaabe women clearly do.

These examples of cultural variations in sexual practices illustrate some of the many ways in which sexual behavior is culturally defined. Variations in definitions can also be seen in the context of a single society *over time,* when there are changing definitions of sexuality. As an example, definitions of sexuality and norms governing sexual behavior have changed dramatically in the United States throughout its history, as a brief review will reveal.

Historical Views of Sexuality in the United States

The historical evidence we have about the sexual lives of nineteenth-century married couples in the United States comes from diaries, journals, reports of doctors and midwives, folk songs, sayings, stories, and poems. As we will see later in this chapter, social research on sexual behavior, especially the systematic use of interviews and questionnaires (social surveys), were not undertaken until well into the twentieth century. Although the qualitative historical evidence we have must therefore be accepted cautiously, it does give us some insight into the views of many men and women of that time.

Social historians believe that marital sex was very different in the United States a century or two ago. In the nineteenth century the authority and supremacy of the husbands and fathers in many families (called **patriarchy**) dominated most of family life. In regard to sex, patriarchy meant that many husbands simply dictated when they would have sexual intercourse with their wives. In this powerful position, men often showed little regard for either the feelings of their wives or the physical repercussions of their actions (Shorter, 1982).

This example of the attitudes prevailing in the nineteenth century about marital sex shows one way in which sociological theories can be important in understanding sexual behavior. Conflict theory, which was introduced in chapter 1, emphasizes the importance of power and conflict in any social group, including the family. Power differences between husbands and wives, which were especially pronounced in this patriarchal era, made marital sexual relations an area of conflict within the family.

The indifference that many nineteenth century husbands displayed to the physical and emotional well-being of their wives is shown in the words of one social historian who said: ". . . intercourse in the traditional family was brief and brutal, and there is little evidence that women derived much pleasure from it" (Shorter, 1982, p. 9). Evidence reveals that many husbands did not abstain from having sex with their wives either during pregnancy or immediately after the birth of a child. Despite warnings of doctors and midwives that the health of women would be endangered during these periods, especially by infections, many wives reported with embarrassment that their husbands paid "no heed" (Shorter, 1982).

Of course, not every pretwentieth-century man behaved in this brutish and insensitive way. Certainly there were loving and considerate husbands who were sensitive to the emotional and physical feelings of their wives. We are describing only a general condition that prevailed in many marriages of that era.

And how did pretwentieth-century women regard sex? Many probably viewed it with fear because sexual intercourse often meant another pregnancy. Most women of the nineteenth century, especially those living in rural areas, had no knowledge of contraception or even of a safe period during their menstrual cycles. For women of a childbearing age, the only preventions against pregnancy were being pregnant already and—maybe—breastfeeding. An average married woman in the nineteenth century typically had seven or eight pregnancies, and perhaps as many as six live births. In addition to the difficulties of pregnancy itself, the very real danger of death during childbirth always existed. In the light of all these dangers, added to the insensitivity of many husbands, it is understandable that many married women would view sexual intercourse with apprehension and probably dread.

Another indication of the way definitions of sexuality have changed over time comes from the marriage manuals of the nineteenth and early twentieth centuries. One main theme found in marriage manuals of the 1800s was the belief that women have very little sexual desire. Women had sex with their husbands primarily because it was their wifely duty. An 1869 marriage manual asserted the following:

> As a general rule, a modest woman seldom desires any sexual gratification for herself. She submits to her husband, but only to please him and but by the desire of maternity . . . (Hayes, 1869, quoted in Gordon and Shankweiler, 1971, p. 460).

A second theme of nineteenth-century marriage manuals is also reflected in the statement above—the claim that women are interested in sex only because of a desire for maternity. This is often called the **procreative view of sex**—sex for reproduction only.

Writers of this period, including many who were doctors, also tended to see sex as a "draining," "exhausting," and "debilitating" activity. Men, especially, were thought to have a "loss of vital body fluids" when they had sexual intercourse, leading to negative effects on health and vitality. The view that men lose strength and vital fluids from having sex is a widely held notion in other cultures around the world. Many Hindus in contemporary India believe that men are born with a fixed amount of semen, which must be conserved if a man is to live to an old age (Harris, 1981).

Not until the twentieth century did marriage manuals start to acknowledge that women as well as men could have sexual desires, and that they, too, could enjoy the physical pleasure of sex. In the nineteenth century, this idea was only grudgingly admitted, and women who revealed their sexual desires too openly were often labeled mentally ill or deviant. Deviant behavior, as we saw in the last chapter, depends on what people, at a particular time, consider deviant. Thus, although a woman of the nineteenth century who was actively interested in sex was considered deviant, in contemporary American society a woman who claimed to have *no* sexual desire would probably be the one considered deviant (Barker-Benfield, 1976).

As we consider these changing historical definitions of sexuality and different norms for appropriate sexual behavior, we should note that views about sexuality and sexual behavior are in some way a reflection of the general characteristics of the society in which they are found. The place of women in the nineteenth-century United States was subordinate to that of the patriarchal male, so it is not surprising that sexual life would reflect this societal feature. But other general characteristics of society may also influence the nature of sexual behavior. We will consider this possibility next.

A Societal Perspective on Sexual Behavior

A basic sociological premise holds that the general nature of a society will shape and influence all types of behavior, including sexual behavior (Schur, 1988). In the case of the United States, it can be argued that sexual relations, as a reflection of the characteristics of the society generally, have become *depersonalized, commercialized,* and increasingly *coercive* and *aggressive.*

Depersonalization of Sex

Many social analysts have observed that social relations in modern society have become more and more impersonal. In chapter 4 we saw how the early sociologist Toennies used the term *gesellschaft* as a label for a type of contemporary society in which personal relations tend to be impersonal and based primarily on individual self-interest. A parallel feature of contemporary society is that many people are given much more personal freedom than are people who live in more close-knit traditional societies (Simmel, in Wolff, 1950). If these characteristics (impersonality, self-interest, and personal freedom) describe life in contemporary U.S. society, and there is considerable evidence that they do, we might expect that they would also be found in sexual relations. Thus, the **depersonalization of sex** is defined as sexual interaction that is impersonal and self-interested.

There is little disputing the fact that, since the late 1960s in the United States, personal freedom with regard to sex has greatly increased (Reiss and Lee, 1988; Talese, 1980). The most obvious example has been the acceptance of sex as a recreational activity. Many Americans, especially in the 1970s, came to see sex as an activity they could engage in simply for the pleasure it gave them. Sex was viewed as just one more pleasurable form of recreation, with little or no meaning beyond the immediate experience.[1] However, if sexual partners are seen only in terms of the pleasure they can provide, the relationship between the two people is very likely to be of no particular importance. Treating sexual acts and sexual partners as unimportant is the essence of depersonalized sex (Schur, 1988).

Commercialization of Sex

Commercialization prevails when everything can be bought and sold, when everything has a monetary value and can be purchased if one has the money to pay. The **commercialization of sex** refers to the fact that sex is bought and sold just like any other commodity in the marketplace. Americans are accustomed to purchasing their recreation, and since sex is seen by many as a form of recreation, it follows that sex is something to be purchased. Some obvious ways in which sex is purchased are prostitution, soft- and hardcore pornography, erotic telephone services, R-rated and X-rated movies and videos, and subscriptions to sexually oriented television networks. Also included is a substantial market in sexually oriented clothing and other sexual paraphernalia that are widely advertised and displayed. Almost all of these sex-related products and services can be legally purchased (the only exceptions being some extreme forms of pornography and prostitution).[2] It is estimated that the legal "sex industry" adds up to $5 billion yearly (Schur, 1988).

Another dimension to the commercialization of sex goes beyond the obvious commercial transactions for sex or sexually related materials. A widely held view exists that says that women are often "purchased" and displayed as the sexual property of men. Sociologist Randall Collins has said that, "With male dominance, the principal form of sexual property is the male ownership of females" (Collins, 1971, pp. 7–8). Even in dating situations, when males pay for meals and entertainment, there is often the implicit assumption that the females owe something in return. That something may be sex.

Our understanding of the commercialization of sex in the United States can be enhanced if we apply the insights of structural-functional

---

[1] Although many Americans came to view sex as recreational, that should not obscure the fact that most sexual behavior, in the context of a relationship, has some significance to the participants.

[2] Even prostitution is legal in a few Nevada counties.

theory. As we have just seen, the commercialization of sex is a structural feature of the society that maintains and perpetuates the exploitation of women. In functional theory terms, this commercialization is functional for males who often control more economic resources, but it is dysfunctional for females because it continues their exploitation.[3]

Functional theory also stresses how societies tend toward a consistency and integration among different structures. In the present case the general commercialization of many aspects of social life, but especially entertainment, is consistent with the commercialization of sex. The commercialization of sex "fits" with the commercialization of many other aspects of contemporary U.S. society—a point Schur also makes.

Sexual Coercion

The third aspect of sexual behavior in U.S. society is **sexual coercion,** which is forced sex, or rape. Rape is alarmingly widespread. Official statistics on rape reflect only reported cases, and the record shows 92,500 attempted or actual rape cases in the United States in 1988 (U.S. Bureau of the Census, 1990). Some people maintain that a level of "sexual terrorism" exists in contemporary American society that allows males to frighten, and therefore dominate, females. Sexual terrorism makes it necessary for women to ask themselves ". . . whether to go to the movies alone, where to walk or jog, whether to answer the door or telephone" (Sheffield, 1987, p. 171).

Official statistics on rape undoubtedly understate the case, however, since many instances of rape are not reported to authorities. Many women are forced to have sex against their will by men they know, such as acquaintances, friends, former boyfriends, and former husbands, as well as current dates and romantic partners (Brownmiller, 1975). The prevalence of date-rape or acquaintance-rape is literally uncounted, but surveys have shown that one-fourth to one-half of all women will experience rape or attempted rape in their lifetimes (Schur, 1988, p. 140). Rapes committed or attempted by acquaintances and dates are obviously related to the view that women are often regarded as sexual property.

An extreme view of coercive sex is expressed by feminist Andrea Dworkin, who argues that almost all acts of sexual intercourse are a demonstration of male domination (Dworkin, 1987). Dworkin's view is a minority position, but it does point to the potential for domination and coercion in sexual behavior.

---

[3] The usefulness of structural-functional analysis is not pointed out by Schur, but the argument presented here reflects his presentation (Schur, 1988, p. 13).

Cross-Cultural Perspectives

Societal Reactions to Erotica and Pornography

The people of prehistoric times produced artifacts, drawings, and paintings showing their keen interest in the sexual features and sexual acts of males and females. Most of the major historical cultures of the world—Greece, Rome, India, China, Japan, Africa—have produced art or writing that depict sexual behavior and sexuality. In the contemporary world there is a continuing outpouring of paintings, sculptures, photographs, films, and writing about sexuality and sexual behavior. Despite the universality of interest in sexuality and sexual behavior, the societal responses to sexual representations and descriptions are extremely varied, and often the source of great controversy.

The very words used to describe visual representations and written descriptions of the human body and sexual acts indicate how differently people react to sexual subjects. It is common to hear people speak of *dirty pictures* and *dirty books,* words that often reflect the speaker's negative feelings. The word *pornography* also carries a negative connotation about sexually explicit materials. On the other hand, the word *erotica* is apt to indicate a neutral, or even positive, reaction to sexual images, objects, or writing.

Sociologist Ira Reiss (1986) defines *erotica* as any material designed predominantly for sexual arousal. *Pornography* is the term applied to erotic material that is distasteful or obscene to the person who uses the label. From this perspective erotica is a more general, neutral, or less judgmental term, while pornography indicates that certain material is considered beyond a societal or personal standard of acceptability.

The differences and changes in the social acceptability of erotica is a sociologically interesting issue, because the standards and the justifications for acceptability are so varied. When Michelangelo, the Italian Renaissance artist, was asked by Pope Clement VII to paint a biblical scene on the wall behind the altar of the Sistine Chapel (25 years after he had completed the ceiling paintings) he painted all the figures, including Christ and the Virgin Mary in the nude. The Pope, however, considered these paintings objectionable, and, although he first wanted the paintings destroyed, he later agreed to have another painter (nicknamed by the Italians the *breechesmaker*) add clothing to the figures (Bullough, 1976; Lewinsohn, 1958). Indeed, over the next 200 years other painters continued to add clothing to the figures in Michelangelo's painting.

Late in his life Michelangelo painted *Leda and the Swan* for an Italian duke. This painting also depicted a nude woman, and if it had survived it would be invaluable today. It was ultimately burned, however, because the authorities of the time considered it objectionable (Bullough, 1976; Lewinsohn, 1958).

In India, many of the ancient temples of the Hindu religion are adorned with sculptures of a sexual nature. These sculptures do not simply show nude human figures, but depict males and females engaging in sexual intercourse. In fact, these Indian temple sculptures are noted for the variety of sexual positions of the participants.

In contemporary times, in many societies, sculptures and paintings of male and female bodies and people engaged in sexual acts continue to be produced and displayed. Especially important today are the erotic materials produced by photographers and the motion picture industry. Often, this form of erotic material makes no claim to being art, but is openly aimed at sexual stimulation. Reiss (1986) has called this form of sexual material *commercial erotica*. In the late 1960s Denmark and Sweden were among the first countries to change their laws about erotic materials, making them easily available. In these countries it has been possible for many years to purchase virtually any kind of visual or literary erotic material.

Many countries of the world, including the United States, have followed the lead of the Scandinavian countries and have made commercial erotica available to the public. The major exceptions are the Islamic and Communist countries (Russia, China, and Cuba, for example), where erotic materials are severely restricted.

In the United States the widespread availability of erotic materials is opposed and decried by several groups who consider such material pornographic. Among the most vocal opponents are religious leaders and political conservatives whose objections are on religious and moral grounds. But feminists, also, have raised an important challenge to pornographic materials, claiming that they perpetuate the subjugation, objectification, and debasement of women (Reiss, 1986).

BULLOUGH, VERN L. *Sexual Variance in Society and History*. New York: John Wiley & Sons, 1976.

LEWINSOHN, RICHARD. *A History of Sexual Customs: From Earliest Times to the Present*. New York: Harper & Row, 1958.

REISS, IRA L. *Journey into Sexuality: An Explanatory Voyage*. Englewood Cliffs, N.J.: Prentice Hall, 1986.

According to Schur's societal analysis of sex in American society, both the society at large and sexual behavior in particular are characterized by depersonalization, commercialization, and coercion/aggression. The fundamental assumption of this view is that the characteristics of a society will be reflected in the sexual realm. Although the resulting depiction of sex in American society may not be accepted by everyone (it is controversial), it does shed some light on contemporary American sexual patterns.

The Sexual Norms of Societies

All societies have rules and norms about sexual behavior. These norms sometimes require people to act in certain ways (have sexual intercourse if they marry, for instance); but more often, norms relating to sex prohibit certain behaviors. We will focus on two of the most widely recognized sexual norms: the incest taboo and the double standard.

The Incest Taboo

Every known *contemporary society* has a norm (almost always supported by laws) that prohibits sexual relations (and, of course, marriage) between close kin members—an *incest taboo*. In every case the norm prohibits sex between parents and children and between siblings. With regard to other relatives, the rules are much less consistent. In many societies, first cousins are prohibited from marrying and thus from having sexual relations. However, in every country of Europe and in 20 states in the United States, first cousins may marry (Ottenheimer, 1990). In many of the societies studied by anthropologists, marriage between cousins is actually preferred.

The prohibition of sex between close relatives has been nearly universal, but in a number of historical circumstances it has been allowed (Hopkins, 1980; Middleton, 1962). Generally, such exceptions to the rule permitted members of royal families to marry each other in order to retain royal power. In the Egyptian, Incan, and Hawaiian royal families, marriages between immediate family members kept the royal bloodline "pure," and retained privilege and power in the family. In one documented historical period, however, marriage between brothers and sisters, as well as fathers and daughters, occurred frequently among commoners. When the Romans ruled Egypt during the first to the third centuries A.D., such marriages were widely recorded. By allowing marriage between family members, Egyptians prevented family wealth and property from being confiscated by the Roman authorities through inheritance laws (Hopkins, 1980).

The exception to the incest taboo among the Egyptians shows once again how variable sexual behavior can be, but that should not obscure the fact that virtually every other society prohibits sex (and marriage) among close family members. One sociological explanation for the near-universal incest taboo is that it would be too disruptive to family relationships if sex were allowed between close family members. If such sexual relations were possible, they would probably lead to jealousies and alliances between some family members against others, which would produce family instability.

The Double Standard

After the incest taboo, one of the most pervasive sexual norms, found in many societies besides the United States, is the double standard of sexual behavior. The *double standard* is a set of norms that give males more sexual freedom than females. The *traditional* double standard includes the following specifics:

- Men may have sexual intercourse before marriage; women should not.
- Men may have sexual intercourse with women even when there is no emotional feeling or commitment; women may have sexual intercourse when they are in love, or when there is a mutual commitment.
- Men may have multiple sexual partners; women should not have multiple partners.
- Men may have sexual intercourse with women who are much lower in social status, or are "immoral" women; if a woman were to have sexual intercourse with a man of lower status, it would be viewed even more negatively than with a man of her own status.
- Men may have sexual intercourse for recreation or to gain sexual experience and expertise; women are not allowed to have these motives or objectives.

Because of the undeniable liberalization of sexual norms in the United States over the last several decades, some of these standards may have been somewhat relaxed. Perhaps among some individuals as well as in certain groups in the society, the double standard is not as rigidly enforced as it once was, but researchers continue to uncover evidence showing that significant aspects of the double standard are still with us.

One place the double standard can still be found is in the labels applied to males and females who are very active sexually. Males are given a great latitude in their sexual behavior before negative labels are applied. For example, among young people the word *gigolo* is sometimes applied to a male who has many different sexual partners, but it is only partially negative. If a female has many different sexual partners she is called a *slut,* which is unquestionably negative (Rubin, 1990). Sometimes young women today use the word *stud* in a sarcastic or hostile way when they refer to males who try to have sex with as many females as possible, but the term does not seem to have the same damaging force as the word *slut.*

Even preadolescent boys frequently use these negative terms to refer to girls. Sociologist Gary Fine, who spent a summer observing preteenage boys who were in Little League baseball, frequently heard these boys refer to girls as "sluts" and "prosties" [apparently a reference to prostitutes]. After listening to and observing these preadolescent boys, Fine concluded: ". . . boys generally wish to be seen as sexually potent, whereas girls lose status by having the same reputation—the double standard is very much in existence in preadolescence" (Fine, 1987, p. 107).

Another kind of evidence for the persistence of the double standard is an experimental study conducted among college students. The researchers asked the subjects to evaluate a specific person on the basis of his or her sexual behavior. (The person was fictitious, but the subjects were led to think it was a real person.) As one aspect of the experiment, subjects were asked to evaluate either a male or a female who had a first sexual intercourse experience in a casual relationship at age 16. Both male and female subjects gave more negative evaluations to a female than to a male who had done so. The researchers concluded that some aspects of the double standard still exist (Sprecher et al., 1987).

When Moffatt (1989) lived in the dormitory with Rutgers University students, he found students saying that no one should feel guilty about his or her sexual behavior. In actuality, however, these students, by their words and actions, still revealed their adherence to the traditional double standard. The men in particular still divided the women into the "good women" and the "sluts."

In her interviews with teenage women, Rubin (1990) found many who were reluctant to pass judgment on the sexual behaviors of other women. This appears to be a change from former times, when women were as severe as men in their condemnation of women who were sexually liberal. Today, young women with female friends who have casual or recreational sex are inclined to say that it is "none of their business" (Rubin, 1990, p. 70). While young women recognize that men can (and do) still apply negative labels to women's sexual behavior, they themselves try to be tolerant.

Sexual norms, such as the double standard, are learned through the process of socialization. In the next section we will examine how sexual socialization occurs and how it shapes sexual attitudes and behaviors, especially of young people.

Socialization for Sex

Most Americans say that children should learn about sex from their parents. The general assumption is that if parents take responsibility for the socialization of their children regarding sex, the values of the children will be healthier and their behavior will be more responsible. The alternatives to parental socialization about sex are formal sex education programs in the schools, learning about sex from peers, and learning about sex (either directly or indirectly) from the mass media—especially movies, magazines, music, and television.

Although most people believe that children *should* learn about sex from their parents, the fact is that parents do a very poor job of teaching their children about sex (Fox, 1980; Fox and Inazu, 1980; Roberts et al., 1978). To the extent that the sexual socialization of young people does occur in U.S. families, it is largely left to mothers, and the greatest amount of communication about sex is between mothers and daughters. Mothers are as likely as fathers (and some studies have shown them to be more likely) to discuss sex with their sons (Aldous, 1983; Fox and Inazu, 1980).

The minimal amount of sexual socialization received by sons, from either parent, is especially noteworthy. In one study of over 1400 parents in Cleveland, Ohio, less than 2 percent of the fathers and only 9 percent of the mothers had discussed premarital sex with their adolescent sons (Roberts et al., 1978). Furthermore, the sex education programs in schools have a tendency to focus on premarital pregnancy and thus give more attention to adolescent girls than they do to adolescent boys. This reflects the double standard of sexual conduct that assumes that boys can take care of themselves in sexual matters. The result is that adolescent males are short-changed in their sex education (Shapiro, 1980).

Since mothers and daughters are the most likely combination of parents and children to discuss sex, their communication has been studied most extensively. The topics mothers and daughters talk about most frequently are menstruation and dating/boyfriends. Over 90 percent of both mothers and daughters in one study said they had discussed these topics. The least likely topics are sexual intercourse and birth control, with about 70 percent of the daughters saying that they had discussed these matters with their mothers (Fox and Inazu, 1980). Since these percentages are higher than are reported in most other studies, they probably represent the best of circumstances.

On the basis of an observational study of parents and their ninth-grade-level children (both boys and girls), one sociological researcher concluded that *both* parents and children generally try to avoid talking about sex-related topics (Aldous, 1983). In this observational study the parents and their teenage child could choose to discuss or not discuss any of a series of topics presented to them. One of these topics was "The ABC's of Birth Control." While most parent–child groups did not avoid the discussion completely, they used a number of techniques to either keep the subject impersonal or otherwise limit the discussion. One method was the "cut-off," in which one member of the family would say something that effectively ended the discussion. When the parents of one boy started talking about birth control, the son cut off the discussion quickly by saying, "Um hum." Then, pushing on to the next topic, he said, "Next?" (Aldous, 1983, p. 33).

In another family, the father cut off the discussion of birth control by first saying to his son, "What do you think of that, Dale?" But then the father immediately blocked the reply by saying, "Of course, you're not thinking of anything like this yet, huh?" (Aldous, 1983, p. 33).

Even when parents did try to engage their children in a discussion of birth control, the children were very reluctant and noncommittal on the topic. The following one-sided conversation shows that the daughter, Debbie, wanted nothing to do with the topic:

MOTHER:	What do you think, Debbie?
DAUGHTER:	Nothin'.
MOTHER:	How would you plan your family?
DAUGHTER:	I don't know.
MOTHER:	Well, say you were 18 and married. Would you want a family right away?
DAUGHTER:	No.
MOTHER:	Well, how would you prevent it?
DAUGHTER:	I don't know. (Aldous, 1983, p. 35)

If, as it seems from this study, both parents and children prefer to avoid personal discussions about sexual topics, what is the explanation? One possible explanation grows out of the tendency of both parents and their children to act as if the other generation does not have a sexual life (Aldous, 1983; Jones and Placek, 1981). Thus, any conversation that moves into this area is likely to lead to embarrassing revelations. Children may not want to reveal how much they know or what their sexual experiences have been. Parents, for their part, may not *want* to know how experienced and knowledgeable their children are about sex, because to learn these things would require that they acknowledge the sexual nature of their children (Aldous, 1983).

Adolescents may not be eager to discuss sexual matters with their parents, but the topic is a very popular one when they talk with their peers. Among the 11-year-old and 12-year-old Little League boys observed by sociologist Gary Fine (1987), sexual topics ranked with aggression as the two major themes of their discussions. Boys of this age have relatively little sexual experience—apparently kissing and limited petting are the major activities of the most active boys—but their interest level is high. When they talk about it, they are trying to show that they are interested and knowledgeable about heterosexual relations. Through the talk, banter, joking, and teasing about sexual matters, the "boys learn what is expected of them by their peers" (Fine, 1987, p. 110).

While these preadolescent boys talk a great deal about heterosexual relations, they also make frequent references to homosexual topics. This often takes the form of derogatory expressions such as "God, he's gay," "He's the biggest fag in the world," and "What a queer." Although these phrases are not generally used to refer to actual homosexual behavior, and are often used among friends in a good-natured way, the rhetoric of homosexuality is a flexible and abusive part of the preadolescent's language (Fine, 1987, p. 115). Probably this negative use of homosexual terminology is a way in which many boys are trying to define their own sexual identity.

Socialization by the Mass Media

In the early 1960s the word *pregnant* was not allowed on television, and movies and television did not show married couples in the same bed (twin beds were the standard). However, in recent years the amount of sexual content in the mass media—especially television, movies, and magazines—has increased dramatically. Today television and movies are important sources of information and values about sexual matters for many children and adolescents. In 1977 a religiously oriented group that was concerned about the amount of sexuality on television monitored the networks and found 2.81 references to sex per hour of prime-time viewing. Their calculation was that over the course of a year television "viewers would be exposed to 9,230 scenes of suggested sexual intercourse or sexually suggestive comments" (quoted in Liebert and Sprafkin, 1988, p. 199). Although much of the sexuality on television in the 1970s was verbal, it is now much more likely that actual sexual behavior will also be shown (Liebert and Sprafkin, 1988). Perhaps most important, couples shown on television having sex are not usually married. Unmarried sexual intercourse "occurs five times as often as married intercourse on the prime-time series adolescents watch most often" (Liebert and Sprafkin, 1988, p. 201).

There is little doubt that television programs and movies are providing children and adolescents with information and normative standards about sexual behavior. Studies have shown that even young adolescents can understand the sexual talk and innuendos on prime-time television. When public opinion pollster Louis Harris asked youngsters themselves about the relative importance of prime-time television as a source of information about sex, they ranked friends, parents, and courses in school as more important; but, of course, the messages of television sex may be more subtle and indirect than adolescent viewers recognize.

Sex Before Marriage

In the United States, sex has traditionally been associated with marriage. The cultural ideal, which is still preferred by some people, is for young people to refrain from sexual activity until they are married. The popular way of expressing this ideal is to "save oneself for marriage." The evidence, as we will see shortly, indicates that among young people this ideal is not widely held, or at least not practiced, in the contemporary United States. Furthermore, there are historical data showing that from the earliest days of American history premarital chastity has been far from universal.

Premarital Sex Before the Twentieth Century

The Puritan period of American history is noted for its religious strictness and the close community scrutiny of all citizens' personal lives, and yet, even during that period, some couples had sex before marriage. A study by Calhoun (1945) found that approximately one-third of Puritan brides confessed to their ministers that they had had sex before marriage. Most of them confessed because they were already pregnant and wished to have their babies baptized. Other brides, who might have had sexual intercourse but were not pregnant, might not have felt as compelled to confess (Reiss and Lee, 1988).

There is other historical evidence showing that premarital sexual intercourse occurred at significant levels throughout the period between the seventeenth and nineteenth centuries (Smith, 1978). Social historians have used church records of marriages and baptisms to estimate how many first-born children were likely conceived before marriage (i.e., a first child born within nine months of a marriage was probably conceived premaritally). One such study, using this method on data coming from various New England communities, shows that, before 1700, about 11 percent of all births may have been premaritally conceived. This was, in fact, the lowest percentage found over the next 200 years. The highest percentages of premarital conceptions came in the period between 1761 and 1800, when slightly over one-third of the births were judged to be premaritally conceived. The data from this study suggest that in pretwentieth-century America about one in five first births were conceived before marriage (Smith, 1978; see also D'Emilio and Freedman, 1988, pp. 22–23).

These figures, however, reflect only premarital pregnancies, not all premarital sexual intercourse. There are two reasons why premarital pregnancies are underestimates of premarital sexual intercourse. First, it is unlikely that all women who became pregnant while unmarried went on to marry. Some might have intentionally aborted their pregnancies, had spontaneous miscarriages, or had children without marrying. These cases would not be reflected in the births occurring within nine months of marriage. Second, some couples might have had sexual intercourse while unmarried and yet not have conceived a child. This could have been the result of sterility on the part of either the man or the woman, the use of some elementary form of birth control (e.g., withdrawal), or having intercourse at a time when conception was not possible. If all these considerations are taken into account, it is possible to estimate from these data that at least one-fourth, and perhaps as many as 40 percent, of American young women had sexual intercourse before they were married. The percentages for young men were probably higher, because they were generally given more sexual liberty.

Premarital Sex in the Twentieth Century

The twentieth century saw the beginnings of social research that used interviews and questionnaires as primary data-gathering methods. The researcher whose name is linked most closely to the earliest studies of sexual behavior is Alfred C. Kinsey. Kinsey was a biologist who made his early reputation as a scientist by studying the gall wasp. In the 1930s, Kinsey shifted his focus of interest to the sexual behavior of humans, and his name is still remembered for the work that he did on human sexuality during the next two decades of his life. Kinsey and his associates conducted interviews with 5300 males and nearly 6000 females. The Kinsey interview, which was meticulously detailed and carefully recorded, was designed to provide the complete sexual life history of each respondent.

The Kinsey studies of male and female sexual behavior were published in the late 1940s and early 1950s (Kinsey, et al., 1948, 1953).

The Kinsey studies showed that a substantial number of women (and men) who reached adulthood in the twentieth century had sex before marriage. Among women born before 1900, about one-fourth revealed to the interviewer that they had had premarital sexual intercourse. Among women born after 1900, 53 percent said they had sex before marriage (adapted from Reiss, 1980, p. 170).

The percentages found in Kinsey's research may be slightly inflated, because his samples, while large, were notoriously biased toward the better-educated, higher-status segment of the population. At the time when he initiated these studies, many people were reluctant to discuss sex, even with scientific researchers. Kinsey was able to enlist the cooperation of organizations and groups, whose members were then asked for interviews, but organization members tend to have higher than average educations. Since the more highly educated women in the sample also had higher than average levels of premarital sex, the percentages were generally higher than might have been true of a representative sample of the population.

Even so, the findings of the Kinsey studies, along with the earlier historical research, leave little doubt that a great number of young women and men, throughout our history, had premarital sex. That having been said, however, we must add quickly that there have been some dramatic changes in premarital sexual behavior in the last 25 years. The percentage of unmarried young people who have sexual intercourse has increased greatly; sex starts earlier; the social relationships and social contexts in which sex occurs have changed; and attitudes about the connection between sex and marriage have become blurred. These changes will be considered in the next section.

Sexual Activity among Contemporary American Adolescents

The decade of the 1980s will probably be remembered as the "AIDS decade." AIDS (acquired immune deficiency syndrome) was first recognized in the United States in 1981, and while there was some early ambivalence about who could contract the disease, it was soon recognized as a major threat to public health. In 1987, then-President Reagan pronounced AIDS as "public health enemy No. 1" (Dickenson, 1987). The Surgeon General of the United States during that period made "safe sex" a personal crusade. AIDS-education programs were established in schools throughout the county to inform young people of the dangers associated with having sex. One might suppose that, in the face of this barrage of negative publicity about sex, the level of sexual intercourse among adolescents would have gone down. But, just the opposite occurred; sex among teenage women increased.[4]

Data coming from a study conducted in 1988 shows that sexual activity among teenage women increased between 1982 and 1988 (Forrest and Singh, 1990). In 1988, among nonmarried women between the ages of 15 and 19 who were not cohabiting, nearly half (49.5 percent) had experienced sexual intercourse. By comparison, when the same population was sampled in 1982, 42.1 percent had experienced intercourse. Among 15-to-17-year-olds, the percentage rose from 32 percent in 1982 to 38 percent in 1988. Thus, in spite of the educational and publicity efforts associated with AIDS, young people were more likely to be engaging in sex at the end of the decade than they had been at the beginning. Later in this chapter we will take a closer look at the ways in which the AIDS disease may have changed sexual behavior.

The increases in sexual intercourse between 1982 and 1988 among unmarried teenage women were due primarily to increases among white teenagers (see Figure 7–1). About the same percentages of black and Hispanic teenage women had sex in 1988 as had sex in 1982. It was the white teenage group that increased its level of sexual activity, narrowing the gap between them and black teenagers, especially at ages 18 to 19 (Forrest and Singh, 1990, p. 208).

Factors Associated with Early Sexual Experience

There are a number of factors associated with adolescents having sexual intercourse at a young age. Race/ethnicity is one of those factors. Despite the closing gap between black and white adolescent females, it is still young black women who have sexual intercourse earlier (Hispanic women start having sex later than either of the other two groups). Adolescent males have a similar pattern, except for the fact that Hispanic males have sexual intercourse earlier than white males (Mott and Haurin, 1988).

Studies of the school contexts of black adolescents have shown that black students in racially integrated schools will be older before they have sex than black students in predominantly black schools (Furstenberg et al., 1987). One study, however, found the racial composition of the

---

[4] The most recent data we have comes from the National Survey of Family Growth, which surveys only women. Many previous studies have shown, however, that males are more likely to be sexually active at an earlier age than females.

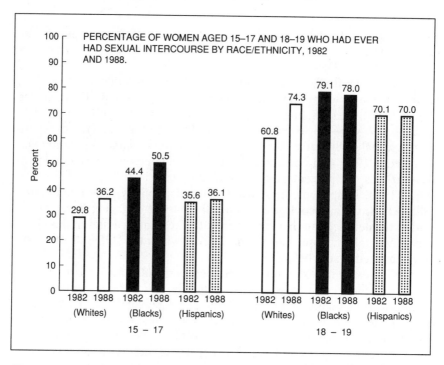

Figure 7–1.   Percentage of women, aged 15 to 17 and 18 to 19 who had ever had sexual intercourse by race/ethnicity, 1982 and 1988. [*Source:* Jacqueline Darroch Forrest and Susheela Singh, "The Sexual and Reproductive Behavior of American Women, 1982–1988." *Family Planning Perspectives*, 22 (1990): 206–214.]

school to be influential only for black males (Rosenbaum and Kandel, 1990).

Adolescents who have higher academic performances and educational aspirations are less likely to have sexual intercourse early. Teenagers who are more religious are also less likely to have sex. Those who attend religious services more often have more negative attitudes about premarital sex and are less likely to have premarital sex (Thornton and Camburn, 1989). United States teenagers who belong to fundamentalist Protestant churches are the most likely to be opposed to premarital intercourse. In general terms, young people have sex later if they have a "commitment to conventional values and institutions" (Rosenbaum and Kandel, 1990).

Earlier sexual activity is also related to characteristics of the families of teenagers. In particular, when young people come from single-parent homes they are more likely to start having sex earlier. Teenage girls in particular are more likely to have sex if they live in single-parent homes. Since sexual activity usually requires a degree of privacy, girls in single-parent homes may have more opportunity to have intercourse because they are less closely supervised (Miller and Bingham, 1989). Privacy in the home is not likely to be the only influential factor, however, since young people who come from large families (where privacy may be less available) are also more likely to have sex as teenagers (Rosenbaum and Kandel, 1990).

Adolescents who begin to use alcohol, cigarettes, and drugs at an early age are also more likely to start having sex early (Mott and Haurin, 1988; Rosenbaum and Kandel, 1990). For both males and females, the use of these substances before age 16 is strongly associated with having sexual intercourse at a younger age. Males who use alcohol and/or cigarettes before age 16 are 40 percent more likely to have sex before 16 than males who do not use alcohol and/or cigarettes. If males use marijuana early, they are almost three times more likely to have sex than boys who do not use marijuana. Adolescent boys who use other illegal drugs are more than three times as likely to have sex. For females, the importance of early cigarette, alcohol, and drug use is even greater. Early use of alcohol and/or cigarettes increases the chances of early sex by 80 percent. Early marijuana use makes early sex 3.45 times more likely, while use of other illicit drugs makes sex five times more likely (Rosenbaum and Kandel, 1990). The strong relationship between sex and early cigarette, alcohol, and drug use does not mean that drugs *cause* sexual activity. The research done so far has shown only that these behaviors are associated in the lives of teenagers.

It is often assumed that the behavior of teenagers is influenced by their friends, either because they learn from their friends or because they experience peer pressure. To evaluate this assumption with respect to sexual activity, the researchers in one study asked whether the sexual activities of one's friends might influence a young person's sexual activity (Billy and Udry, 1985). The assumption was that adolescents who had not had sex would be more likely to begin having sex if their friends were sexually active. Over a two-year period, in a study of both black and white teenagers, only white females were more likely to start having sex if their friends were sexually active. These research findings do not mean that, in general, friends are without influence in sexual matters; other studies have shown repeatedly that adolescents themselves rate their peers as a most important source of information about sex (Strouse and Fabes, 1985).

The First Sexual Intercourse Experience

While surveys of sexual behavior can tell us when and how many adolescents have sex, these surveys do not tell us much about how the young people themselves define and interpret the experience. What influences or motivates them to have sex? What meanings do adolescents give to sex? What is the first sexual experience like for most adolescents? For answers to these questions we must turn to studies that give young people an opportunity to describe their sexual experiences and their reactions to them.

First Sexual Intercourse: Gender Differences. Research evidence suggests that at the time of first sexual intercourse the *relationship* with one's partner is very different for males and females. Some evidence for this comes indirectly from the age differences of males and females (and their first partners) when they first have sex. Males, as we have noted, have sex for the first time at a younger age than females. One recent study found the average age for males when they first had sex was about 16, while the average age for females was about 17 (Rosenbaum and Kandel, 1990). This difference between males and females may not be surprising, but the ages of their first sexual partners may be. The first sexual partners of females are, on average, about three years older than they are. This age difference is about what one might find among romantically involved couples. The first sexual partners for males, however, are not younger females, but older females. The first sexual partners for males are, on the average, more than a half-year *older* than they are (Zelnik and Shah, 1983). These relative age differences suggest that the nature of the male/female relationship is different for young women than for young men. One possibility is that females have sexual intercourse for the first time with a committed partner. Males, on the other hand, may have their first sexual experience in a much more casual relationship (Zelnik and Shah, 1983).

Additional evidence from this study supports the view that most females have sex for the first time in the context of an established relationship. Sixty-five percent of the females described their first partner as someone they were engaged to or with whom they were going steady. Only about one-third of the males (37 percent) said that they were going steady with, or engaged to, their first partner. In fact, 43 percent of the males said their first partner was either someone they had "just met" or "just a friend" (Zelnik and Shah, 1983). Similar results were found among unmarried male and female college-age students who were asked about their first sexual experience. In this study, 65 percent of the males said their first partner was someone they were *not* in love with. Thirty-five percent of the females said they were *not* in love with their first partner (DeLameter and MacCorquodale, 1979).

These differences between males and females in their first sexual intercourse experiences are very likely a product of the different meaning that sex has for adolescent males and females. Traditional females often associate sex with feelings of love and affection for their partners. Sex is something that occurs in an emotional relationship with a male they love (or are infatuated with).

Young males, on the other hand, are much more likely to focus on sex as a physical activity. For boys, the objective is often simply to experience sex. Sex for them is an accomplishment, an achievement, and who their partner is may make little difference to them.

When adult men recall their first sexual experience they often use terms that show how important it was for their masculinity. In the words of one researcher: "They [men] characterized the experience as an 'important accomplishment,' a 'landmark achievement.' For them, it was a rite of passage, a crucial step on the road to manhood—a step in which they exulted . . ." (Rubin, 1990, p. 43).

To summarize, for young men, the first sexual experience is more often going to be a *measure of achievement*. For young women the first sexual intercourse experience is likely to mean *an expression of love*.

First Sexual Intercourse: Often a Negative Experience. Even though men were often pleased by the accomplishment of their first sexual experience, it does not necessarily mean they thoroughly enjoyed it. In fact, Rubin (1990) has concluded on the basis of her in-depth interviews with 75 teenagers and 300 adults, both males and females, that the overwhelming majority of both sexes look back on their first sexual intercourse as a neutral or negative experience. In her interviews only about one-tenth of the men and women used words of pleasure to describe the experience. The remaining 90 percent used words such as " 'overrated,' 'disappointing,' 'a waste,' 'awful,' 'boring,' 'stupid,' 'empty,' 'ridiculous,' 'awkward,' 'miserable,' 'unmemorable' " (Rubin, 1990, p. 43).

Once again, however, the disappointments that the males may have had with the actual experience were overshadowed by their "exhilaration of achievement" (Rubin, 1990, p. 44). The females had more complicated reactions, often tied to ambivalence about what was acceptable sexual behavior for females. It is noteworthy that those women who had the most positive reactions to their first sexual experience were the ones who had sex with men they had known for a long time and cared deeply about.

Changing Attitudes of Young Women. There is evidence that the attitudes of teenage women about sex are changing. One important change is that, unlike in the past, young women are discussing their sexual experiences with their friends, much as males have always done. It is apparently a staple in the conversations of teenage women to describe "my first time" (Sharon Thompson, 1990). But stories about "my first time" have two different themes: Theme 1 emphasizes how the first experience was one of physical pain, discomfort, or general unpleasantness; theme 2 describes the pleasure and excitement of the first sexual experience (Sharon Thompson, 1990). In interviews, approximately 75 percent of the young women reflect the first theme, which is consistent with the previous description of most people remembering their first sexual experience in negative terms.

Quite a number of females who describe their first sexual experience negatively also seem unsure about what actually happened. Often they tell of not anticipating or knowing what was going to happen until it was over. Often these girls are not sure whether they had sex because they wanted it or because their boyfriends coerced or forced them to have sex. These girls are also the ones who ". . . speak as if they had no sexual consciousness at all before the first penetration—no memories, no experiences" (Sharon Thompson, 1990, p. 344).

Many young women describe the fear they had and the pain they experienced when they first had intercourse. Some emphasize what a "nothing" experience it was, because everything happened so fast; it was over before they knew what was happening. Yet others use the experience to show their "superiority over other girls who don't have what it takes to be women" (Sharon Thompson, 1990). One such girl bragged "I really didn't feel nothing special. Most girls say, 'Oh, God, it really hurt,' and like that. It was nothing to me." (Sharon Thompson, 1990, p. 348.)

By contrast, about one-fourth of the teenage girls tell a very different story of their first sexual experience. They reveal excitement and enthusiasm, even in the retelling of the experience. Unlike the girls who tell the negative stories, these girls have a sexual memory that predates their first sexual intercourse experience. They describe how they had looked forward to sex, often for a long time. Many of them discovered masturbation at an early age and saw their sexuality as a very desirable personal quality. These girls also report experimenting sexually with boys, even in their prepubertal years (Sharon Thompson, 1990).

One of the most revealing and interesting features in the lives of these girls is that they describe how they related openly with their mothers about sex. The girls who had pleasurable first-sex experiences often had mothers who openly talked about sex and their own sexual lives. The mothers of these girls described their own sexual feelings and experiences in natural and positive ways. One daughter described her mother in this way:

> Mom had always talked very casually about sex. I mean, I have sat at the dinner table and discussed with mom what contraceptive she used when she was, uh, uh, you know, having an affair with my dad for the year before she married him. And, uhm, actually we have discussed what sex was like with my

father and what she did in—in the way of fooling around before she got married. (Sharon Thompson, 1990, p. 354.)

AIDS and Sexual Behavior

As we noted earlier, the emergence of AIDS in the 1980s increased greatly the number of open discussions about sex and sexual behavior. As AIDS came to be perceived as a health threat that might sweep through the population, sexual practices were discussed more widely and frankly than ever before. Public health officials, medical professionals, teachers, politicians, and many others began to speak openly about homosexuality, the use of condoms, anal sex, and oral sex—all topics that were nearly forbidden only a few years earlier. Perhaps most important, parents who were concerned about the welfare of their children started to be more honest about sex.

The facts about AIDS are that a person is most likely to contract the AIDS-producing virus (human immunodeficiency virus, abbreviated HIV) when the blood or semen from an infected person enters one's bloodstream. Sexual intercourse, therefore, is a principal way of passing the virus from one person to another. Of course, the virus can also be received by using a contaminated hypodermic needle (often the case among intravenous-drug users), by receiving a transfusion of infected blood, or, in the case of infected women, by the direct transmission to fetuses.

Sexual transmission of HIV is most probable when lesions or cuts are present through which infected semen or blood can enter the bloodstream. Thus, for example, a woman who has active herpes will be in greater danger of infection from a diseased partner, since the herpes lesions will admit the infected semen. Similarly, anal intercourse, which has a higher likelihood of tearing rectal tissue, will lead to a higher rate of HIV transmission.

The Centers for Disease Control now estimates that about one million people in the United States population are HIV positive, which is a decline from a previous estimate of 1.5 million (Larry Thompson, 1990, p. 6). These are only estimates, and debates are still going on about the number of HIV-positive people in the population. Once the disease of AIDS appears in an HIV-positive person it is more easily identified. Thus, we do have firmer information on the total number of AIDS cases and the incidence of new AIDS cases each year (United States Centers for Disease Control, 1991). Table 7–1 presents data on the total number of adolescent and adult AIDS cases since 1981 and for the year ending on April 30, 1991, according to exposure categories (probable source of infection).

Table 7–1.   AIDS Cases among Adults and Adolescents (13 and over) by Exposure Category, Cumulative Number of Cases from 1981 to April, 1991, and New Cases from May, 1990, through April, 1991.

	Cumulative Cases 1981 to April, 1991		New Cases between May, 1990–April, 1991	
	Number	*Percent*	*Number*	*Percent*
Male homosexual/bisexual contact	101,536	(59)	22,912	(55)
Intravenous (IV) drug use (female and (heterosexual male)	37,846	(22)	9,794	(24)
Male homosexual/bisexual contact and IV drug use	11,354	(7)	2,241	(5)
Hemophilia	1,482	(1)	313	(1)
Heterosexual contact	9,462	(6)	2,838	(7)
Blood transfusion	3,904	(2)	785	(2)
Other/undetermined	6,281	(4)	2,686	(6)
Adult/adolescent total	171,865	(100)	41,569	(100)

Source: Centers for Disease Control. *HIV/AIDS Surveillance Report,* May, 1991, p. 8.

The total number of adolescent and adult AIDS cases since 1981 had reached nearly 172,000 by the end of April 1991.[5] Over 40,000 cases are now being added each year, but there are some signs that the yearly number of new cases is no longer increasing.

The AIDS cases of the most recent twelve-month period reveal that, while homosexual and bisexual males still make up the majority of all new cases (55 percent), their percentage of the total is dropping. By contrast, heterosexual intravenous drug users are increasing their percentage of the total, from an earlier 22 percent to 24 percent.

The *number* of new AIDS cases coming from heterosexual contact continues to increase. The *percentage* of the total is also increasing. In 1988, new AIDS cases coming from heterosexual contact made up only 4 percent of the total, while in the year ending April 30, 1991, heterosexual contact accounted for 7 percent of the total. The majority of these het-

---

[5] AIDS cases among children under age 13 reached a total of 2841 by the end of April 1991. About 85 percent of these were infants infected by their mothers (most of whom were intravenous drug users or who had had sex with intravenous drug users).

erosexually contracted cases (56 percent) were the result of having sex with an intravenous drug user (not shown in table 7–1).

Knowledge about AIDS and HIV Transmission

The extraordinary effort to inform the American people about AIDS, and to urge them to change their sexual behavior, has been led by the government and the mass media. The federal government's National Center for Health Statistics conducts an ongoing national survey of 100,000 American adults to determine the extent of their knowledge about AIDS (Adams and Hardy, 1991). This survey (identified as Project HOPE) shows that while there are still some misconceptions about AIDS, there is nearly universal knowledge of the disease and a very high level of understanding of the three major modes of transmission (Russell, 1991). Ninety-six percent of adults know that the HIV virus is transmitted through sexual contact. When asked whether AIDS can be transmitted to *any* person through sexual intercourse, 86 percent say "definitely true" and 10 percent say "probably true." Ninety-five percent knew that the virus can be transmitted from a pregnant woman to her baby, and 95 percent knew that needle sharing by intravenous drug users is a means of transmission (Adams and Hardy, 1991, Table 1).

The most common misconceptions about AIDS are that it can be contracted from casual contact with someone who has the disease (shaking hands), or from some other source (toilet seats, doorknobs, insect bites). Many people (40 percent in one survey) still "mistakenly believe that AIDS is transmitted by *donating* blood" (Russell, 1991, p. 7). Within the adult population, those who have the lowest levels of knowledge are "the elderly, minorities, people with low levels of education, and those for whom English is a second language" (Russell, 1991, p. 7).

While this survey of U.S. adults reveals a significant level of knowledge about AIDS and its transmission, it also shows that most Americans do not consider themselves at risk of contracting the disease. Eighty percent of adult Americans say they believe there is no chance they have been infected with the HIV virus. "Fifteen percent said they thought there was a slight chance. Fewer than 1 percent said they thought they had a high chance of being infected now or in the future" (Russell, 1991, p. 7).

Since people in the United States know about AIDS and understand that it is transmitted sexually, one would expect some significant changes in sexual behavior. On the other hand, since the vast majority of Americans believe there is little or no likelihood that they will contract the disease, there would be little reason for them to change their sexual behavior. This leads to the obvious question: Have Americans changed their sexual behavior (and attitudes) since the beginning of the AIDS outbreak?

Has AIDS Changed Sexual Behavior?

For the population at large it has been difficult to ascertain just how much change has occurred in sexual behavior. The Project HOPE survey of adult Americans found that nearly 25 percent of those who said they were sexually active had reduced their number of sexual partners and/or used condoms.

There is also evidence that gay men, especially in the major urban centers where the earliest concentration of AIDS cases occurred (San Francisco and New York) have modified their behavior considerably. After an initial resistance, the gay community in San Francisco, for example, recognized that social and behavioral changes had to be made. The gay baths in San Francisco—where promiscuous and impersonal sex was the standard—were closed, and it was done with the support of the gay community (Fineberg, 1988).

A 1988 national survey of adolescent males has provided some interesting information about changes with regard to the use of condoms (Sonenstein, Pleck, and Ku, 1989). In this sample, 60 percent of unmarried males aged 15 to 19 had had sexual intercourse. By age 19, 86 percent had experienced sexual intercourse (blacks, 96 percent; whites, 85 percent; Hispanics, 82 percent). These adolescent males were asked a series of questions about AIDS to determine the extent of their knowledge of AIDS. They proved to be very knowledgeable about how AIDS was transmitted and indicated by their answers that they did not take the threat of AIDS lightly. Seventy-nine percent of these males *disagreed a lot* with the statement "Using condoms to prevent AIDS is more trouble than it's worth." An even higher percentage (82 percent) *disagreed a lot* with the statement "Even though AIDS is a fatal disease, it is so uncommon that it's not a big worry." Given these views, it is not too surprising to find that more than half (55 percent) said they used a condom the first time they had intercourse, and 57 percent reported that they had used a condom the last time they had intercourse (Sonenstein, Pleck, and Ku, 1989). In a similar survey conducted in 1979, only 21 percent of adolescent males had used a condom the last time they had had intercourse. Clearly, the campaign to instruct young people about the importance of using condoms to prevent the spread of AIDS has had an effect.

This 1988 study, however, found that the young men who were most likely to use condoms were those whose behaviors put them at the lowest

Table 7–2. Percentage of Never-Married, Sexually Active Males Aged 15 to 19 Who Had Used a Condom at the Time of Last Sexual Intercourse, by Risk Group

	Used a Condom at the Time of Last Intercourse
High-Risk Group (9 percent of the total) (One or more of the following behaviors: had engaged in homosexual activity, had had a sexually transmitted disease, had ever had sex with a prostitute, had used intravenous drugs, had a partner who used IV drugs.)	51%
Moderate-Risk Group (38 percent of the total) (Not in the high-risk group, but had engaged in one or more of the following: had sex with a stranger, had five or more partners in the last year, had sex with someone who had had many partners.)	45%
Low-Risk Group (54 percent of the total) (Reported none of the behaviors of the high- and moderate-risk groups.)	66%

risk for contracting AIDS. The researchers divided the sample into "high-risk," "moderate-risk," and "low-risk" groups on the basis of their sexual and drug-use behaviors. The criteria for determining the high-, moderate-, and low-risk groups are shown in table 7–2, along with the percentage in each risk group who used condoms at the time of their last sexual intercourse experience.

Table 7–2 shows that the low-risk group was most likely to use condoms; two-thirds reported using a condom the last time they had had sexual intercourse. The moderate-risk group had the lowest percentage using condoms: 45 percent. The high-risk group had a somewhat higher percentage using condoms: 51 percent. Condom use among the high-risk young men varied greatly by the type of high-risk behavior they reported. Those who engaged in homosexual behavior (3 percent of the sample) were very likely to have used a condom (66 percent). But the intravenous drug users and those who reported having sex with a prostitute had very low percentages using condoms (21 percent and 17 percent, respectively) (Sonenstein, Pleck, and Ku, 1989).

Although not shown in table 7–2, this study also found that young men who had had the *most* sexual partners during the last year were the *least* likely to use a condom; those who had had the *fewest* partners were the *most* likely to use a condom (Sonenstein, Pleck, and Ku, 1989).

The results of this study are encouraging on the one hand, since many more sexually active young men are using condoms than in the past, but discouraging because many of those who are at the greatest risk are the least likely to be using condoms. The small percentage of young men who are engaging in homosexual behavior are the exception. The high percentage of them who had used a condom at the time of last intercourse is further evidence that gay males are modifying their sexual behavior as a precaution against AIDS.

A Study of University Women. Random samples of the national populations are very important for our understanding of changing sexual behavior, but smaller studies of specialized populations, such as university women, can also be revealing. Such is the case with a recently reported survey of Brown University women who were given a questionnaire about their sexual behavior in 1989 that was nearly identical to ones completed by Brown University women in 1979 and 1986.

The 1989 survey did show, once again, that the educational campaign recommending the use of condoms has had some impact. In 1975, 6 percent of the Brown women said that condoms were used as their "usual method of birth control." In 1986, the percentage had risen to 14 percent, and, in 1989, the percentage was up again, to 25 percent.

With regard to sexual activity, however, the Brown women have made few changes since 1975. In both 1975 and 1989, about 88 percent of these women, who averaged about 21 years of age, were sexually active. In 1975, the pre-AIDS era, about 22 percent of the women reported that they had had more than six sexual partners in their lifetimes, and more than three partners in the year preceding the survey. In 1989, after having been told for nearly a decade that multiple sex partners may increase one's risk for getting AIDS, almost exactly the same percentage (21 percent) reported having had more than six sexual partners in their lifetimes and more than three in the past year. The percentages who said they engaged in oral or anal sex had also remained at about the same levels between 1975 and 1989 (DeBuono et al., 1990).

We started with the question: Has the AIDS epidemic changed sexual behavior in the United States? The evidence gives us a mixed answer. It appears that some homosexual males have modified their behavior. Condoms are now used more in both the gay and heterosexual populations, but condom use is certainly not universal. Many people in the heterosexual population have changed their sexual behavior very little. Claims that the AIDS scare dramatically reduced sexual activity among teenagers and young adults are not supported by the evidence.

Deviant Sexual Behavior

In our consideration of deviant behavior in chapter 6 we saw that almost every behavior has been defined as deviant by the people of some society at some time. We also saw that virtually every kind of behavior has been socially acceptable at one time or another. Thus, when we ask, "What is deviant sexual behavior?" we should be prepared to find that it depends upon who is defining the behavior and when.

In this chapter we have already seen that in Egyptian society for a period of more than 200 years (as long as the United States has been a country) many marriages occurred between brothers and sisters. Obviously sexual relations between brothers and sisters were not considered deviant by the Egyptians in that time. Yet, as we have also noted, societies existed in which a brother and sister were not allowed to eat a meal together because to do so had sexual connotations.

In light of these facts we can approach sexual deviance only from the social perspective of the people of one society during a particular time. We can try, for example, to assess what sexual deviance is in the United States during the last decade of the present century. Several ways have been suggested for evaluating whether a sexual behavior is deviant (Bryant, 1982).

One measure of deviance is whether a particular sexual act is *against the legal statutes* of a nation or state. Acts that are illegal are presumably deviant to some degree. The problem with using the law as a measure of deviance is that laws often remain on the books for many years, even when they are no longer enforced. For example, many states have laws against fornication, prohibiting sexual intercourse between people who are not married. A law against fornication would make almost every cohabiting couple lawbreakers. In the state of Virginia a cohabiting couple attempted to get the state's law against cohabitation declared unconstitutional, but Virginia's court of appeals rejected their lawsuit. From the legal perspective, the most important consideration is whether violations of a law are prosecuted. In the case of cohabitation, in Virginia as well as other states, it is unlikely that the laws prohibiting sexual intercourse between unmarried individuals will be enforced against cohabiting couples.

A second indication of sexual deviance is the *statistical frequency of some act.* If a particular sexual act is widespread, involving large numbers of people, it is not likely to be considered deviant. Again, the case of cohabitation is instructive, since the number of cohabiting-couple households in the United States now exceeds two and one-half million. A second example is adultery, which is contrary to existing social norms as

Sociology in the News

Should Alleged Rape Victims Be Named?

Since the 1970s, the news media in the United States have not published the names of the victims of sexual assault or rape (Goodman, 1991). But when William Kennedy Smith, a member of the newsworthy Kennedy family, was charged with sexual assault in Palm Beach, Florida, the principle of victim anonymity was breached by NBC television, the *New York Times*, and other news media (Kurtz, 1991).

This incident raised again the question of whether rape victims should be identified, as are their alleged assailants. In Smith's case, his name, certainly because of his being one of the famous Kennedys, was broadcast and published throughout the country. He was, of course, legally guilty of nothing at that time, since he had not been formally charged and had certainly not been convicted.

As soon as this story appeared in the media, many people automatically assumed that Smith was guilty of sexual assault. Regardless of the outcome of any legal proceedings, Smith's character and reputation were damaged, perhaps for life. In view of this, many people claim that there is a kind of equity or fairness in the victim's having her name published also. This view, however, neglects the point that, if a crime has been committed, it certainly should not be the victim who pays a price.

Some argue that, since the names of other crime victims are reported in the news media, the victims of sexual assault should be treated no differently. This position ignores the way victims of rape are typically perceived by the public at large and, often, by their friends and families. All too often, the public (and personal) reaction to a rape or sexual assault is "She asked for it." Or, in cases in which the victim knows her assailant, a common reaction is "Did she lead him on?" These reactions reveal a great deal about how many people perceive rape: as a sexual act in which women are responsible for controlling sex. These reactions do not define rape as a crime of violence against women. Furthermore, they ignore the right of every individual to engage in sexual acts of his or her own choosing. Regardless of any prior relationship or action, no individual should be forced to engage in a "sexual" act unwillingly.

Very often when women charge that they have been raped, their private lives are examined in detail and revealed publicly. Only the most saintly people could survive such public scrutiny. The result is that many women, knowing the treatment they will receive by the mass media, and all too often by the police, will not report a sexual assault.

In an ideal world, the crime of rape would be treated as every other violent crime. Rape victims would never be held responsible for the crimes committed against them and would not have their lives subjected to critical public scrutiny. But that ideal world has not yet arrived.

GOODMAN, ELLEN. "Woman, Rape, and Privacy." *The Washington Post*, April 20, 1991.
KURTZ, HOWARD. "Furor at N.Y. Times Over Rape Policy." *The Washington Post*, April 20, 1991.

well as against the law in most places. However, estimates show that at least 60 percent of all married men and 50 percent of all married women have adulterous sex before they reach age 40. Among high-income men—those earning $60,000 or more a year—an estimated 70 percent have extramarital affairs. Many of the women who are the mistresses of such men do not consider themselves deviant; they accept these affairs as a normal part of their lives (Richardson, 1985).

A third standard that can be used to evaluate the deviance of a sexual act is the degree to which *one person is a victim.* Being a victim indicates that one person in a sexual act is coerced or forced to do something against his or her will. Homosexual behavior, for example, almost always occurs between consenting adults, which leads some people to conclude that no deviance is involved. Similarly, prostitution is a sexual act that involves two people who agree, through a commercial transaction, to engage in sex. However, since many female prostitutes are addicted to drugs, have no other means of making a living, or are under the control of a male pimp, some question does arise about whether they are free in making their decisions.

Several sexual acts clearly involve victims. One obvious case is rape, in which one person, through force or threat, makes another person perform a sexual act. Closely related are all cases when children are sexually abused. The sexual abuse of children can occur either in the family or outside it. Inside the family, the most common circumstance is for a young girl to be sexually abused by either a father, brother, or other male relative living in the home. It is also possible for young boys to be sexually molested in similar circumstances, but the incidence is considerably lower. Even if the sexual abuse occurs outside the family, the aggressor is typically either a relative or friend of the family, or someone who has been charged with responsibility for the child. The results of a study conducted among college students at the University of New Hampshire showed that 19.2 percent of female students and 8.2 percent of male students had been "sexually victimized" sometime during childhood (Finkelhor, 1979).

A fourth measure of deviant sexual behavior is the degree to which a given act is viewed as *socially reprehensible.* One aspect of the sexual abuse of children is the revulsion that most people feel when they learn that a small child has been sexually violated or molested. The deviant nature of incest and rape is also reflected in the negative reaction that people have to the aggressors. Even some less deviant sexual acts such as voyeurism and exhibitionism are primarily deviant because the actors are considered socially reprehensible. The voyeur, or Peeping Tom, if unobserved, does no actual harm to his victim, but people abhor the way he invades another person's privacy.

Many kinds of sexual deviance, including some of those discussed above, depend to some degree on the situation or context in which they occur. For example, exhibitionism is the act of showing one's body in a public place, and yet people who go to nudist camps or nude beaches often emphasize that their action is neither sexual nor deviant (Bryant, 1982).

This sociological analysis of sexual deviance leads us back to where we started. Sexual behavior, both that which is acceptable and that which is deviant, is determined to a considerable degree by the norms, values, and roles of the particular society in which people live.

Summary

Sexuality is a basic human characteristic, sexual behavior is universal, and sex is a biological act; but many societal and cultural differences exist in sexual behavior and sexuality. All of these variations and differences, including historical changes from one period to another, indicate that sexual behavior is influenced as much by social factors as it is by biological factors.

A number of societal characteristics of the contemporary United States are reflected in sexual behavior. These characteristics include the depersonalization of sex, the commercialization of sex, and coercive and aggressive sex.

Sexuality is normatively controlled in every society. The most nearly universal norm is the prohibition of sex between closely related individuals—the norm prohibiting incest. However, the norms vary from one society to another, and there are historical exceptions to even the most widely held prohibitions—parent-child and sibling sexual relations.

The double standard is a complex of norms that gives males greater freedom in their sexual behavior than females. Although the rigidity of the double standard of sexual behavior might have lessened, it is still very much alive in American society today.

Children learn about sex through the socialization process. Although there is widespread agreement that children should learn about sex from their parents, evidence reveals that most parents communicate to their children very little information about sex. Children and adolescents learn about sex from their peers and the mass media, especially television and movies.

The traditional cultural ideal of not having sex before marriage has never been fully complied with in American society. Premarital pregnancies indicate a considerable amount of premarital sexual activity among young people prior to the twentiety century. Research by Kinsey and others in the first half of the twentieth century also revealed substantial numbers of young people having sex before marriage, but during the last 25 years the numbers have increased greatly.

Sex at an early age is associated with race/ethnicity, academic settings and performance, religiosity, and tobacco, alcohol, and drug use. The first sexual intercourse for males is associated with achievement; for females it is often an expression of love. In recalling their first sexual intercourse experience the majority of males and females describe it in negative terms. Young women today are discussing their sexual experiences more openly than in the past.

AIDS has introduced a new factor into the sexual behavior of people in the United States. More open discussions are held now about sexual matters, and awareness of sexual issues has increased. The chances of contracting AIDS can be reduced by certain modifications of sexual behavior, which most Americans understand, but, except for some gay males, and a general increase in condom use, there have been only moderate changes in sexual behavior.

Sexual deviance, like all other forms of deviance, is socially defined. Sexual deviance can be defined by the laws of a society, but the laws may fall into disuse. The frequency of a sexual behavior also indicates whether it is deviant; previously deviant acts often become more commonplace and thus less deviant. Deviance is also indicated by the degree to which a sexual behavior victimizes another person. Rape is one such deviant act. Sexual deviance is also indicated by the degree to which an act is viewed with revulsion. The sexual abuse of children is an act of sexual deviance that is considered especially reprehensible.

CRITICAL THINKING

1. Why is sexual behavior a good subject to demonstrate how fundamental human behavior is influenced by culture?
2. How do our beliefs about sexuality reflect the general characteristics of our society? Give contemporary and historical examples to support your answer.
3. Do the ideas of sexual coercion, commercialization, and depersonalization find support in any recent movies you have seen? Give examples.
4. In your view, are there still norms about sexual behavior that support a double standard for males and females? How do you explain the existence of such a standard?
5. What differences exist between the ideal roles and real roles of parents in socializing their children about sex? What other sources of socialization influence a person's sexual behavior and beliefs?
6. How do changes in the ability of sociologists and other researchers to gather data about sexual behavior reflect changing views about sex in society at large?
7. Two major modifications in sexual behavior have been suggested as a result of the AIDS epidemic. To your knowledge, to what extent has behavior changed to comply with these suggestions? What societal conditions might promote rapid compliance?
8. What standards might be employed in determining whether a particular sexual behavior is deviant?

CONNECTIONS

The Homeless

Introduction

The conditions under which people are made homeless have existed throughout the history of the United States (Rossi, 1989). However, homelessness became especially acute during the economic depression of the 1930s. When unemployment rates soared, some people were forced to "take to the road" in search of employment. Some became "hobos," unemployed wanderers who illegally used the railroads as their means of transportation. The struggles, sorrows, and desperation of these people were shared by folksong writer and singer Woody Guthrie (1912–1967), who traveled with the homeless and recorded their lives in such songs as "The Hobo's Lullaby."

"Hobo's Lullaby" takes on particular relevance in the 1990s because of significant increases in homelessness. The homeless today, however, are different from those in Guthrie's time because then homelessness was likely to be either a chosen life-style or a temporary condition based on extreme economic situations. Today, homelessness is a more serious problem because few people freely choose such a life and it is likely to be a far more permanent condition. Furthermore, the homeless are seen by most Americans as outcasts, deviants, and burdens to our society. Many wonder how it is possible that the United States, with its great wealth, can have 1 million people living on its streets without even the most basic human needs of food, clothing, and shelter (Burt and Cohen, 1989).

Who are the homeless and where do they come from? Fischer and Breakey (1986) have identified four categories of the homeless: (1) the chronically mentally ill who have been deinstitutionalized from hospitals or other mental health facilities, and who are more likely to exhibit the aberrant behaviors that people often associate with the homeless; (2) street people, such as "bag ladies" and "grate men," who live isolated lives, shun other people, and exist on what resources they can scavenge from the streets; (3) chronic or skid-row alcoholics whose lives revolve around ways to gain and drink alcohol; and (4) the situationally distressed who are unemployed (Belcher and DiBlasio, 1990), have been evicted from their homes, or are in transience seeking work. The last category includes families as well as single people. Elliott and Krivo (1991) found that the two best predictors of homelessness are the unavailability of low-income housing and insufficient mental health care facilities.

In Woody Guthrie's day, the homeless were very likely to be unattached men, but in recent years there has been an alarming rise in homeless families (Rossi, 1989; Wright, 1989). Bassuk and associates (1986) estimated that families comprised over 20 percent of the homeless population in 1985 and projected that their numbers would double in 1986. In New York City alone there are 4000 homeless families, totaling 14,530 individuals, of which 9590 are children. The typical homeless family in Boston was headed by a single black woman under 30 years old, who had not completed high school, and who had 2.4 children (Bassuk, 1986). These women had experienced trauma in their childhoods, had personality disorders, had inconsistent or nonexistent work histories, had extreme difficulty parenting, and sometimes physically abused their children. Not surprisingly, their children also had serious medical and emotional problems. The population composition of the homeless cuts across categories of gender, race, age, education, and occupation. The homeless are much younger than in the past, and are more likely to have psychiatric disabilities, to be drug abusers, and to have extensive medical problems. Women are also found more often among the homeless today than they were in the past (Garrett and Schutt, 1986).

From these descriptions of the homeless it is apparent that as a category the homeless are people who are often seen as deviating from the majority of the population on two counts. The very fact that they have no home makes them different from most people. But, in addition to being homeless, they may also have a mental illness, or be alcoholic, or be drug addicts, or be unemployed, or be in extreme poverty. The homeless often carry the burden of a double-deviant label.

For a fuller examination of the homeless, we will consider their conditions and problems from the perspective of the four major sociological theoretical perspectives.

Structural-Functional Theory

Structural-functionalists, as we saw in chapter 1, are primarily interested in the functions of different social structures. Functionalists look at the structures of a society and consider what purposes or functions they serve. For example, some functionalists see inequality in society as having a purpose or a function. Inequality is seen as the natural outcome of a system in which rewards are given to those who perform tasks that require special skills or talents. Some people live in affluence because they have these skills and talents, and use them to perform important societal tasks, while others live in poverty because they lack the skills and talents. According to this perspective, economic inequalities are functional because the important tasks of the society get accomplished. Inequality is also functional because the poor are motivated to work harder in order to rise above their deprived economic position.

The social position of the homeless can be seen as similarly functional in various ways. For example, the homeless are, as we have noted, deviant—often doubly so—but their deviance can be functional for the majority of the society. The aberrant behaviors of the homeless serve to reaffirm the values and norms of the rest of the society and thus strengthen their social unity. Further functions of the homeless can be found in their absence from the work force, for that opens up jobs for others. Also, the needs of the homeless lead to the expansion of various occupations such as social services, which can provide work for many members of the middle class.

Functionalists, however, are concerned not only with functions but also dysfunctions. Dysfunctions are the negative or detrimental outcomes of social structures. The homeless are dysfunctional to society by the strains they place on the economic and political systems. For example, when the homeless become ill, the costs of health care are borne by the public. The homeless certainly represent a severe drain on the time and resources of the police. Furthermore, many people feel that the presence of so many homeless people represents a threat to the quality of life within our cities.

Conflict Theory

For conflict theorists, the homeless provide an example of the inequality inherent in American society. The homeless often wander past, or set up "homes" on the grates near, the homes and office buildings of the most affluent members of our society. The inequality in our society is rarely clearer than when the affluent members of our society are forced to walk by, or step over, homeless people. There is clearly much mutual disdain and hostility between them.

Conflict theorists would also point to the powerlessness of the homeless, their lack of resources, and their resulting inability to change their situation. That our society largely ignores the homeless and the conditions under which they live on our city's streets provides conflict theorists with evidence of the extent of the powerlessness of this underclass.

The lack of power among the homeless is illustrated in their inability to gain affordable housing. In many cities housing once occupied by the poor has been either destroyed or purchased by corporations and renovated for rental or sale to the wealthy. Gentrification of inner city housing shoves the poor into smaller, more expensive living spaces, sometimes shared with many relatives. Continued increases in rents squeeze some people from these cramped spaces and into the streets.

In the past, the government has sought to satisfy the basic needs of the poor by building public housing. However, Kozol (1989) points out that the government is no longer building public housing, and "the waiting time to get to the top of the 200,000-family-long list is 18 years" (1989, p. 3G). The lack of affordable housing has led to an increase in public shelters that serve as temporary housing for the homeless. Bassuk (1986) has referred to shelters as "a stop-gap, band-aid response to a festering problem." Kozol describes these shelters as a "rational and antiseptic way to isolate and containerize the poor" (1989, p. 3G). Conflict theorists might view the growth of shelters as a way of placating the homeless and, more generally, the poor. Kozol contends that by the year 2000 the United States "may well be operating the most nicely decorated poorhouse in the world" (1989, p. 3G). To the conflict theorists, a poorhouse, no matter how nicely decorated, is a clear indication of profound inequality in society.

Symbolic Interactionism

Symbolic interactionists would be interested in how homelessness is experienced by people, how they make sense of their situation, and how they form relationships in the impersonal world of city streets. Instead of discussing homelessness in the abstract manner of the functionalists (e.g., the functions and dysfunctions of homelessness), symbolic interactionists are likely to observe it personally and to discuss it in far more individual terms. Those who have observed and talked to the homeless describe them in such a stark way that we may be shocked at the life-style of this segment of our population. For example, Jon D. Hull (1987) lived among the homeless on the streets of Philadelphia and described his interaction with a homeless man.

> Though he is now dying on the streets, . . . Gary Shaw, 48, . . . once worked as a precision machinist. But he lost his job and wife to alcohol. Now his home is an old red couch with the springs exposed in a garbage-strewn clearing amid abandoned tenements. Nearby, wood pulled from a building burns in a 55-gallon metal drum while the Thunderbird [a cheap wine] is passed around. . . . Gary has trouble standing, and he believes his liver and kidneys are on the verge of failing. His thighs carry deep burn marks from sleeping on grates, and a severe beating the previous night has left bruises on his lower back and a long scab across his nose. The pain is apparent in his eyes, still brilliant blue, and the handsome features of his face are hidden beneath a layer of grime (1987, pp. 94–95).

Symbolic interaction, as the name suggests, reflects a concern with symbols. From this point of view, it is interesting to reflect on "bag ladies" (Shulman, 1981). The "bag" is often a shopping bag. In our society a shopping bag is a symbol of success. Carrying a shopping bag out of a supermarket is a sign that the person is at least able to support her(him)self and perhaps a family. Carrying a shopping bag with a department store label is a symbol of an even higher level of success. Furthermore, there is even a symbolic hierarchy based on the prestige of the department store whose name is on the shopping bag. Thus, a bag from Nieman-Marcus is of higher status than one from Macy's which, in turn, is of higher status than a bag from K Mart.

The shopping bag has symbolic importance for bag ladies. It allows them to demonstrate that they are not very much different from most other women in society. As Shulman puts it, the shopping bag is a "universal female sign in our culture, [which] commonly adorns the arms of even comfortable women." In spite of this symbolic unity, there are clearly important differences between middle- and upper-class women and bag ladies. As Shulman says, "While most of us have drawers, closets, some even attics and cellars in which to store our possessions, the homeless . . . have only their shopping bags. Compare their contents with your dresser and kitchen drawers and the mystery of the bags disappears." Thus, in this case symbolic unity cannot conceal substantial material differences.

Social Exchange Theory

We can use exchange theory to look at one aspect of the lives of many homeless people—panhandling and begging. Homeless people do more than simply wander the streets, sleep in parks, sit on curbs, or scavenge garbage dumps for food. Some "earn" money by panhandling or begging. Some may simply sit with their hands out hoping for passersby to toss them coins; others are more aggressive and block the way of pedestrians; others are boys who jump on the hoods of cars to wash windshields, and still others are mothers with children who stand in busy intersections to solicit money from drivers. They may have signs that tell people such things as "Please help, have family, need job, money for rent, food, thanks!" or "God bless the happy giver" (Gibbs, 1988, p. 70).

Exchange theorists might look at panhandling as an example of reciprocity among drastically different economic segments of our population. When panhandlers are successful, they gain at least a meager subsistence. For their part, those who give panhandlers money relieve their guilt about the conditions under which panhandlers live in comparison to their own domestic comforts. For this reason, particularly successful beggars are the handicapped and women with small children, since most people feel especially guilty when passing them. Another gain for those who give to panhandlers is relief from fear. Many panhandlers create this sense of fear by yelling at people, acting menacingly, and approaching people in isolated and dangerous places, such as in subways. Thus, there is a kind of reciprocity in the relationship between panhandlers and those who give them money. The panhandler gains money to survive, while those who give reduce guilt feelings and feel less fearful.

People are ambivalent in their attitudes toward giving to panhandlers. Some feel that helping beggars simply encourages them to continue living on the streets, ripping off the hard-earned money of working people. For example, billboards of unknown sponsorship appeared in 1988 in El Paso, Texas, which said, "Please don't give to beggars, they cause traffic problems" (Gibbs, 1988). Others have a more charitable attitude and give to beggars because they feel they are victims of our society and should be cared for.

Looking at the Research

Research on the homeless is difficult for many reasons. For one thing, they are plagued with problems (e.g., drugs, alcohol, mental illness) that may make it difficult to get accurate information from them. For another, they may well resent talking to social scientists, who are apt to come from the far more successful sectors of society. Furthermore, the homeless may be difficult to study and restudy because they are such a rapidly growing and changing population. No one really knows exactly how many homeless there are, exactly what their demographic and social characteristics are, how they survive on the streets, or why and under what conditions they leave the streets. All these factors vary because homelessness is not necessarily a permanent condition; that is, many are only temporarily homeless. For example, they may have been evicted from their homes but after a few months move in with relatives. We do know, as seen in the research reported by Bassuk (1986), that the increase among homeless families is dramatic. Because these families are often headed by women, there has been a "feminization of homelessness" that is a reflection of the "feminization of poverty" in our country.

In general, the public is fearful of the homeless. Although they may toss the homeless some loose change, the public does not want to spend time with them and get to know them. As a result, misconceptions and myths about the homeless persist, that they are all mentally ill, alcoholics, or drug addicts. However, Wright (1989, p. 108) estimates that two-fifths of the homeless have alcohol problems, one-third experience psychiatric difficulties, and one-tenth abuse drugs. Since these problems often occur together, Wright estimates that a total of about 25 percent of the homeless have some combination of these problems. This, of course, means that the majority of the homeless do not suffer from these disabilities; they do not conform to the beliefs held by many Americans. Instead of being mentally ill (Snow et al., 1986), alcoholics, and drug addicts, most of the homeless are unskilled workers (and their families) who have gone in and out of the job market in dead-end, low-paying jobs that do not enable them to get off the streets. These people, like most of the homeless, are trapped in poor economic conditions that lead to further poverty and despair.

Although sociological theories and research help us to better understand the homeless, this work in and of itself does not help society to deal with the problem any better. Until there is a widespread consensus to do something about homelessness, and to use the work of sociologists and others in a constructive way, the future of the homeless, and their place in our society, is bleak.

References

BASSUK, ELLEN L. "Homeless Families: Single Mothers and Their Children in Boston Shelters." In Ellen L. Bassuk (ed.), *The Mental Health Needs of Homeless Persons*. San Francisco: Jossey-Bass, 1986.

BASSUK, ELLEN; RUBIN, LENORE; and LAURIAT, ALISON S. "Characteristics of Sheltered Homeless Families." *American Journal of Public Health* 76, 1986.

BELCHER, JOHN R., and DiBLASIO, FREDERICK A. *Helping the Homeless: Where Do We Go from Here?* Lexington, Mass.: Lexington Books, 1990.

BURT, MARTHA R., and COHEN, BARBARA. *America's Homeless: Numbers, Characteristics, and Programs that Serve Them.* Washington, D.C.: The Urban Institute Press, 1989.

ELLIOTT, MARTA, and KRIVO, LAUREN J. "Structural Determinants of Homelessness in the United States." *Social Problems* 38, 1991.

FISCHER, PAMELA J., and BREAKEY, WILLIAM R. "Homelessness and Mental Health: An Overview." *International Journal of Mental Health.* 14, 1986.

GARRETT, GERALD, and SCHUTT, RUSSELL K. "Homeless in the 1980s: Social Services for a Changing Population." Paper presented at the Eastern Sociological Society, New York City, 1986.

GIBBS, NANCY R. "Begging: To Give or Not to Give." *Time,* September 5, 1988.

HULL, JON D. "Slow Descent Into Hell." *Time,* February 2, 1987.

KOZOL, JONATHAN. "A Nicely Decorated Poorhouse." *The Kansas City Star,* April 9, 1989.

ROSSI, PETER. *Without Shelter: Homelessness in the 1980s.* New York: Priority Press, 1989.

SHULMAN, ALIX KATES. "Bag Ladies." *New York Times,* September 29, 1981.

SNOW, DAVID A., BAKER, SUSAN G., and ANDERSON, LEON. "The Myth of Pervasive Mental Illness Among the Homeless." *Social Problems* 33, 1986.

WRIGHT, JAMES D. *Address Unknown: The Homeless in America.* New York: Aldine de Gruyter, 1989.

8 Stratification: Living with Social Inequality

All societies face the basic problem of how to distribute scarce and desirable resources and social rewards—money, power, influence, and respect—among their members. Seldom, if ever, are they distributed equally; differences in social rank appear in virtually all human societies, even those that claim to be egalitarian. Throughout human history, some people have possessed greater wealth, prestige, and power than others, regardless of the society in which they lived, and this phenomenon shows no sign of disappearing. **Social stratification** refers to the structure of social inequality in each society—the manner in which scarce resources and social rewards are distributed among different social categories.

An individual's position in a system of stratification affects **life chances,** a term referring to the likelihood of realizing a certain standard of living or quality of life. For example, in American society the life chances of the poor for education, nutrition, life expectancy, quality of housing, and treatment by the criminal justice system differ dramatically from those of the rich. This chapter will be concerned with the nature and consequences of social inequality and social ranking: wealth and poverty, power and powerlessness, dominance and subordination, prestige and degradation, and the ways in which advantages and disadvantages are passed from one generation to another.

Although social stratification is virtually universal, societies differ in the ways in which they allocate scarce resources. Therefore, forms of stratification systems vary widely. Even though most societies have been stratified in some way, however, this does not necessarily mean that a society must be stratified. "A system of ranks does not form part of some natural and invariable order of things, but is a human contrivance or product, and is subject to historical changes" (Bottomore, 1966b, p. 10). In other words, social stratification is not "natural" or inevitable. A classless society is a possibility, if not a probability.

Social stratification is a *social* phenomenon. A system of stratification in any group or society is *not* determined by the biological characteristics of individuals or by supernatural laws. It results from human actions in both the present and the past. Earlier generations create a system of stratification that influences each succeeding generation. Throughout their lives people learn the structure of, and their places in, their society's stratification system.

Dimensions of Stratification

In a complex society such as exists in the United States, determining one's position in its stratification system is frequently difficult because several criteria may be used—wealth, prominence, prestige, influence, and ancestry. Although wealth is obviously an important determinant of one's place in the American stratification system, it is not the only one. People are evaluated differently depending on how their wealth is attained. For example, members of the U.S. House of Representatives have annual salaries of $125,100. However, they have a different location in the stratification system from a professional baseball player, a cocaine dealer, a plumber, a lottery winner, a small-town business owner, or a playboy whose annual incomes are the same or much higher. Each of these different sources of income carries differences in prestige and power which, in addition to wealth, must be considered in evaluating how people are distributed in a system of stratification.

Because social stratification in modern societies is influenced by different factors, Max Weber distinguished among three basic dimensions: class, status, and power. **Class** is a social ranking made on the basis of economic factors. **Status** in the context of stratification refers to a social ranking on the basis of *prestige,* that is, the esteem, honor, and social approval accorded an individual or group. **Power** is a social ranking based on the ability to make others do what you want them to do.

Class

Although Weber recognized wealth as an important dimension of stratification, it was Karl Marx who especially emphasized the role of economic factors in determining social ranking. He identified two basic social classes that are distinguished by their relationship to property. The dominant class—composed of landowners, slaveowners, and factory and business owners—owns and controls the means of production (such as land, machines, and tools). The subordinate class includes industrial laborers, peasants, serfs, and slaves who work for the dominant class.

In a capitalist society, industrial laborers (the **proletariat**) are forced to sell their labor to those who own the means of production (the **capitalists**). To achieve profits, capitalists exploit workers by paying wages that are less than the value of the goods the workers produce. As capitalists compete with each other and seek to achieve ever-greater profits, they try to cut costs by reducing wages paid to the workers. Marx described different ways—among them, employing children and lengthening the work days—in which capitalists in the nineteenth century sought to increase their profits.

Contemporary industrial capitalism differs greatly from capitalism in Marx's day, and critics have argued that his analysis no longer applies. Dahrendorf (1959), for example, contends that Marx focused too narrowly on the idea of ownership of property. The distinctive feature of capitalism today is the corporation, which is owned by hundreds of thousands of shareholders, not by one or even a handful. Such corporations, however, are controlled and run by a small number of people—corporate managers and executives. Therefore, *control,* not *ownership,* of the means of production is the factor that distinguishes classes in modern capitalist societies.

In analyzing changes in the economic structures of modern societies, several writers have suggested the emergence of an important new social stratum—a "**New Class,**" consisting of intellectuals, bureaucrats, managers, executives, scientists, and other professionals who wield power. This New Class appears not only in capitalist countries of the West but in the USSR, in its Eastern European satellite states, and in the Third World of developing nations as well. According to this analysis, economic changes have produced a changing occupational structure that creates new positions of power and authority in the economic, political, social, and cultural spheres.

Status

Although Max Weber did not ignore the special significance that Marx attributed to property and economic factors, he believed that stratification was based on prestige and power as well as on economic factors. Whereas one's class position is determined by wealth and income, Weber argued, one's status is based on the prestige that attaches to the positions that people occupy in society. Usually one's status position is intimately related to one's class position, but it is possible for individuals to be ranked differently on these two dimensions. Status, therefore, according to Weber, refers to groups of people who share similar life chances resulting from social estimation of honor or prestige.

For example, despite a popular egalitarian ideology, one source of status in American society is lineage or family background. Considerable prestige is connected with membership in such hereditary societies as the Daughters of the American Revolution, the Society of Mayflower Descendants, the United Daughters of the Confederacy, and the National Society of Colonial Dames. Although many such organizations tend to draw their membership primarily from those with considerable wealth, the primary criterion is ancestry. Similarly, inclusion in the *Social Register*, a published listing of about 65,000 families and single adults that has been used by sociologists as an index of the upper class in the United States, is based on social standing, not on wealth alone.

Power

Weber argued that a third dimension of stratification exists—power—that is different from class and status. Power refers to the ability to get others to do what you want, even against their own will. The nature and distribution of power and the struggle among groups vying for power have been among the central concerns of sociologists. Although class, status, and power are closely related, Weber felt that they were theoretically separate—that is, there are situations in which those wielding the greatest power in a society do not necessarily possess great economic resources or prestige. Thus power is a crucial part of any system of social inequality. The President of the United States, for example, has extraordinary power, both in this country and throughout the world, but he is not necessarily wealthy. We would not argue that basketball star Michael Jordan, pop star Michael Jackson, or even one of the wealthiest Americans—billionaire Sam Moore Walton (the founder and owner of Wal-Mart)—are as powerful or are accorded prestige equal to that of the President of the United States. We will examine the nature and distribution of power more fully in chapter 16, Political Life.

How Are Stratification Systems Justified?

Stratification systems are systems of inequality, and it is important that the majority of people accept that inequality. The people in privileged positions generally can accept the inequality easily, but even they can feel more comfortable if something justifies their position. People lower in the system must have some basis for accepting the inequalities they experience. For these reasons stratification systems usually have an ideology. An **ideology** is a set of ideas that explains reality, provides directives for behavior, and expresses the interests of particular groups. An ideology is used to legitimize and justify the existing social order and to maintain the inequalities in wealth, power, and prestige. The ideology, which contains a set of rules that explain how and why the society's resources are distributed as they are, frequently becomes accepted by those in subordinate as well as dominant positions. Different stratification systems have developed different kinds of ideologies, which may include religious, political, economic, or "scientific" elements.

Religion has frequently provided an ideology to support social inequalities. American slaveholders, for example, maintained that the Bible supported slavery—that blacks were condemned to eternal servitude by the curse of Ham. Similarly, the Indian caste system, characterized by a system of rigidly defined social ranks and an extremely high degree of social inequality that has endured for thousands of years, is justified by the Hindu religion. Hindu belief emphasizes the importance of reincarnation—the process whereby one's soul is reborn in another person after one's death. However, whether one's soul is reincarnated in a person higher or lower in the caste system depends on how faithfully one has accepted and observed one's duties in the previous life. Failure to observe the rules of the caste system could condemn someone to be reincarnated as an "outcaste," the lowest and most despised position in the system.

Science has also been widely used to justify social ranking. In American society for more than a century, so-called scientific findings have shaped views on race. In the nineteenth century scientists conducted numerous studies to prove the existence of a racial hierarchy in brain size, and therefore intelligence, with northern Europeans highest on the scale and blacks lowest. Today intelligence testing has replaced such anatomical studies as a way of "scientifically" validating the superiority of socially dominant groups. Differences in test scores between whites and blacks—affected by social class, cultural backgrounds, and the settings in which the tests are given—are frequently used to reinforce the system of racial inequality in the United States.

Finally, inequality in American society today is widely justified by **meritocracy** as an ideology. The basic belief in this ideology is equality of opportunity—all people in the United States have equal chances to achieve success, and inequalities in the distribution of wealth, power, and influence reflect the qualifications or merit of individuals in each stratum. Affluence is perceived to be a result of the personal qualities of intelligence, industriousness, motivation, and ambition, whereas poverty is perceived to exist because the poor lack those attributes. Thus Americans generally accept the idea that those at the top of the economic pyramid deserve to be there, and they attribute the responsibility for poverty to the qualities of the poor themselves (Huber and Form, 1973). Ryan (1971) labels this explanation of poverty "blaming the victim." He contends that this view fails to recognize the ways affluence and poverty are a result of the structure of opportunities available to people in different socioeconomic statuses.

Structural-Functional and Conflict Theories of Social Stratification

Sociologists have developed two broad theories to account for social stratification—structural-functional theory and conflict theory. These competing conceptions of social inequality have generated considerable controversy.

Structural-functionalists are inclined to see social stratification as an expression of common values in society. Therefore, since American society values economic success, it accords those with more money higher status in the stratification system. Since the stratification system supports basic American values, it contributes to societal integration and stability. In contrast, conflict theorists view stratification as an expression of conflicting group interests. The various strata are seen as emerging from the conflict over scarce, valued resources.

The **functional theory of stratification** views the stratification system as equitable because people get what society seems to say they deserve (Jeffries and Ransford, 1980). Those at the top are seen as deserving greater power, prestige, and life chances than those at the bottom, who deserve much less of each. Functionalists see inequality in the distribution of rewards as beneficial to both individuals and society because society's tasks are accomplished by the best-qualified people. Conflict theorists, on the other hand, view the existing distribution of rewards as unjust and detrimental to most people as well as to society as a whole.

To structural-functionalists, power and coercion do not play a central part in maintaining a system of rewards and privileges. In their view, the system is maintained because most of a society's members believe in and accept common values. Once again, conflict theorists disagree. They do not believe that most people in the United States accept the fact that some have a right to greater rewards. We accept it, they say, because those in power have forced us to, perhaps by propagandizing us into believing in their greater rights.

Structural-functionalists contend that the major function of stratification is to motivate the relatively few capable people to occupy higher-level, more prestigious positions in society. To encourage people to want to occupy these more "important" positions, Davis and Moore (1945) argue, they must be offered greater rewards, in the forms of more money, power, and prestige. Therefore, a society must not only be stratified, but it must be stratified in such a way that the higher a person rises in the system, the greater are the rewards attached to a position. So, the argument goes, if we want the most talented people to become physicians, politicians, or business managers, we must offer them greater rewards. If we do not, the structural-functionalist says, then not enough of the most talented people will enter these positions.

Conflict theorists ridicule this idea. They argue that these positions will prove intrinsically attractive to many people, with no need to offer greater rewards. Conflict theorists argue that since members of the upper classes occupy these positions in large numbers, they have a vested interest in attaching great rewards to them. They contend that the functional theory of stratification simply perpetuates the privileged position of people who already have power, prestige, and money. The functional theory also can be criticized for assuming that simply because a social structure has existed in the past, it must continue to exist in the future. Possibly future societies can be organized in other, nonstratified ways.

Critics of functionalism also challenge the idea that positions vary in their importance to society. Are garbage collectors really less important to the survival of society than advertising executives? Despite the lower pay and prestige of the garbage collectors, they may actually be more important for the survival of the society.

Even in cases where one position obviously serves a more important function for society, greater rewards do not necessarily accrue to that position. The registered nurse may be more important to society than the movie actor, but the registered nurse has far less power, prestige, and income than the actor.

Other critics question whether there really is a scarcity of people capable of filling high-level positions. In fact, evidence suggests that many people who may possess ability are prevented from obtaining the training needed to achieve prestigious positions. Moreover, formal educational credentials may themselves be unrelated to job performance and, therefore, serve to exclude capable people from jobs that they could effectively perform (Persell, 1977, pp. 158–163). In general, many able people may never get a chance to show that they can handle high-ranking positions.

Finally, functionalists see the American stratification system as open, with the ability to rise in it generally dependent on personal talent and motivation. This expresses the American belief that those with ability and ambition can make it to the top. Conflict theorists reject this notion as well. They argue that ability and motivation are insignificant; what really matters is being born into the upper strata where people have greater access to educational facilities, the best universities, and the "right" contacts. Conflict theorists hold that status in the American stratification system is often ascribed, rather than achieved. That is, more people remain in the position into which they are born than achieve higher positions through personal effort.

Social Inequalities in the United States

Having identified the various dimensions of social stratification and competing explanations for its existence, we now turn to an examination of social inequalities in the United States.

Inequalities of Class

What is the nature of economic inequality in American society? How equally is the economic "pie" divided? How concentrated are economic resources in the United States? In examining economic inequalities, we must first distinguish between wealth and income. **Wealth** refers to the total economic resources that people *have,* while **income** refers to how much money people obtain during a specified period of time, usually a year. Although there is frequently a close relationship between the two, an individual could possibly have substantial wealth and little income or vice versa. Therefore, wealthy landowners might be "land poor"—that is, they may own considerable amounts of real estate but derive little in-

Table 8–1.   The Distribution of Before-Tax Family Income among American Families

Year	Percentage of Total					
	Lowest Fifth	*Second Fifth*	*Third Fifth*	*Fourth Fifth*	*Highest Fifth*	*Index of Concentration*
1950	4.8	12.4	17.4	23.2	42.2	0.369
1960	5.2	12.7	17.8	23.7	40.7	0.353
1970	5.5	12.2	17.6	23.8	40.9	0.353
1980	5.2	11.5	17.5	24.3	41.5	0.365
1990	4.6	10.6	16.6	23.8	44.3	0.396

Source: U.S. Bureau of the Census, *Current Population Reports,* Series P-60, No. 159, 1988; *Current Population Reports,* Series P-60, No. 168, 1990.

come from it. On the other hand, some people might have a very high income but spend or lose most of it and thus have accumulated little wealth. In the discussion below we shall examine data on trends in the distribution of wealth and income in the United States.

Income.   Income is specifically the wages, salaries, dividends, interest, and rents received each year by individuals or family units. Median family income in the United States in 1990 was $35,353 (U.S. Bureau of the Census, 1991b). This means that half the families earned more than that amount and half earned less. However, this figure is somewhat misleading, because it tells nothing about the range of incomes above $35,353. Much more room exists at the top for high incomes than at the bottom for low incomes, as the annual earnings of many corporate executives, professional athletes, and entertainers demonstrate. In other words, the incomes of the bottom half of American families range from $0 to $35,353 annually, but the incomes of the upper half range from $34,210 to over $1 billion. However, the earnings of most American families are far closer to the figure of $35,353 than the huge sums earned by the super rich.

In 1990, the richest, 5 percent of American families earned more than $148,000 a year, and although most of them could be called rich, marked differences exist between the rich and the very rich. In a study based on 1982 income data, Avery and Elliehausen (1986) found that physicians and other health professionals, lawyers, and accountants are most highly represented in the $100,000–$279,000 range. However, the occupations producing the highest incomes (the top one-half of 1 percent—those with incomes in 1982 of $280,000 or more) were commercial and investment banking, insurance, and real estate.

The data in table 8–1 show the changes that have occurred since 1950 in the distribution of income in the United States. Table 8–1 provides two different measures of income distribution, each of which shows that during the 1950s and 1960s income inequality declined slightly, while during the 1970s and, especially, the 1980s, the gap between rich and poor has increased substantially; the rich grew richer and the poor poorer.

First, table 8–1 shows the share of income that was received by each quintile (one-fifth) of the population. In 1950 the bottom two quintiles (40 percent) of American families combined received 17.2 percent of the nation's income, and the top quintile received 42.2 percent. By 1970, share of the bottom 40 percent had increased to 18.0 percent while share of the top one-fifth had declined to 40.9 percent. However, by 1990 the two bottom quintiles combined had declined to 15.4 percent, while the top one-fifth had increased to 44.3 percent. Moreover, in 1989 the share of the poorest fifth of the American population (4.6 percent) fell to the lowest it has been since 1954, while the 44.6 percent of income received by the richest fifth represented an all-time high.

However, focusing on the top one-fifth of the population masks the increasing concentration of income at the very top. In 1990 the top 5 percent included families with incomes averaging $148,124. The top 5 percent received 17.4 percent of all income, which was more than the total income for the entire lowest 40 percent of the population. These recent increases in income inequality are reflected in the second measure of income inequality—an index of income concentration (technically called the *Gini index*). As overall income is distributed more equally, the index declines; as income inequality increases, so does the index. Although the index of income concentration has been characterized by periodic fluctuations, it declined between 1950 and 1970 and since then has risen steadily, in 1989 reaching its highest level (0.401) in the post-World War II period.

The income inequalities in the United States shown in Table 8–1 are especially striking when compared to other Western industrialized countries. As the data in figure 8–1 indicate, only in France and Austria do people at the lower end of the economic scale receive so small a share of income as in the United States. For example, the bottom fifth of the population receives more than twice as much income in Japan as in the United States (United Nations Department of International Economic and Social Affairs, 1985, pp. 6–9).

The Declining Middle Class. During the quarter-century after World War II, Americans experienced unprecedented prosperity and increases in family income. Average weekly earnings rose by 50 percent, and real median family income nearly doubled—increasing from $17,765 in 1947 to $35,474 in 1973 (in 1990 dollars) (U.S. Bureau of the Census, 1988c,

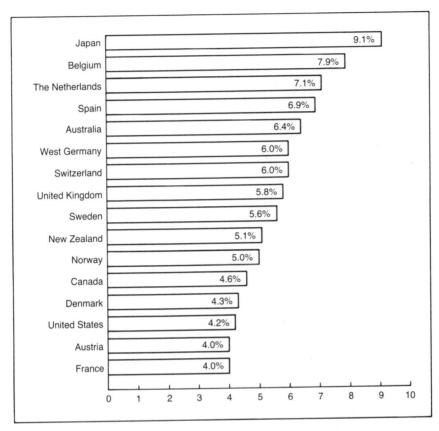

Figure 8–1. The Percentage of a Country's Total Income Going to the Poorest 20 Percent of the Population, for Selected Countries. The poorest 20 percent receive the greatest proportion in Japan and the least in Austria and France. (*Source:* United Nations Department of International Economic and Social Affairs, "National Account Statistics: Compendium of Income Distribution Statistics," *Statistical Papers*, Series M, No. 79. (New York, United Nations, 1985).)

p. 35; U.S. Bureau of the Census, 1991b, p. 201). Moreover, as we have seen in table 8–1, between 1950 and 1970 a trend toward more equitable income distribution appeared. Widespread prosperity and more equitable distribution of income contributed to the image of the United States as a "middle-class society" and reinforced the widespread belief among Americans that the quality of their lives would always improve over that of their parents and that the quality of their children's lives would exceed theirs.

However, since the early 1970s the economic position of the American middle class has stagnated. Real median family income, which achieved

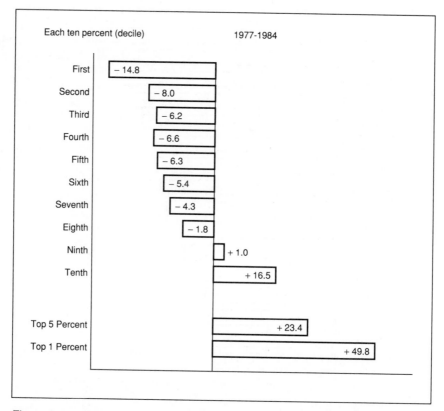

Figure 8–2. Percentage Changes in Average Family Income for Each Ten Percent of the Population, 1977–1988. (*Source:* Adapted from Congressional Budget Office, *The Changing Distribution of Federal Taxes: 1975–1990* (Washington, D.C., October 1987).)

an all-time high of $35,474 (in 1990 dollars) in 1973, failed until 1987 to reach that level again. Real median family income for 1990 ($35,353) was virtually the same as in 1973. The period of rapidly rising American prosperity had ended.

Moreover, as shown above, since the late 1960s a steady trend has been seen toward increasing income inequality, with the more affluent sectors of the population, not the broad middle class, receiving a greater percentage of the nation's income. A Congressional Budget Office study (1987) examined changes in income distribution between 1977 and 1984 and projected changes through 1988. Data from that study, shown in figure 8–2, showed that *all except the highest 20 percent of American families experienced a decline in income between 1977 and 1988.* The only substantial increase was in the highest decile (one-tenth) of income categories.

The incomes of the top 10 percent rose by 16.5 percent; the richest 5 percent, by 23.4 percent; and the richest 1 percent, by 49.8 percent.

However, studies of economic inequality that focus primarily on income distribution have been criticized because they generally focus on pretax income and therefore do not consider the effects of taxes on net income. The tax burden in any society may be distributed in three different ways—progressively, proportionately, or regressively. *Progressive* taxes are based on ability to pay—the percentage of income paid in taxes *increases* as income increases; the wealthier are taxed at higher rates than the poor. *Proportional* taxes place the same percentage burden on all income levels. In a system of *regressive* taxes the percentage of income paid in taxes *decreases* as income increases; the poor are taxed at higher rates than the wealthy.

The most familiar progressive tax is the federal income tax, which was established by the 13th Amendment in 1913. Precisely how high tax rates should be on different levels of income has been a perennial source of political controversy. One of the most dramatic changes in tax policy in the twentieth century occurred during the presidency of Ronald Reagan, when the rates for upper income categories were reduced substantially. Between 1981 and 1988 taxes on those in the highest tax brackets fell from 70 percent to 28 percent. When the decrease in taxes paid by the highest income categories is combined with the increase in other federal taxes (e.g. Social Security), the impact of the federal tax changes of the 1980s was that the overall tax burden for all but the richest ten percent of the population increased (Phillips, 1990, pp. 76–82).

While federal income taxes were becoming less progressive during the 1980s, state and local governments resorted with increasing frequency to regressive taxes as their primary sources of revenue. These regressive taxes include residential, business, and personal property taxes, sales taxes, and gasoline and cigarette excise taxes. A recent study of tax policies found that, because state and local governments rely heavily on regressive taxes, poor and middle-income families are taxed at rates significantly higher than the richest Americans, and the percentage of income paid in state and local taxes declines significantly as income increases. Thus in 1991 a four-member family with an income in the poorest quintile (one-fifth) annually paid 13.8 percent of their $12,700 annual earnings in state and local taxes; the second-lowest one-fifth (with an average income of $26,800) paid 10.7 percent; the middle fifth (averaging $39,100) paid 9.5 percent; the second highest fifth (averaging $54,000) paid 8.4 percent, while the richest 1 percent, whose incomes average over $875,000, paid only 6 percent. Moreover, there was considerable variation among the states. California, Delaware, Maine, and Vermont were the only states in which the rich paid a greater share of income than middle-

Table 8–2. Household Income and Homeownership

Thousands (1986 Dollars)	Number of Households (in thousands)		Percent Homeowners	
	1974	1987	1974	1987
Under 5	4,705	7,204	42.8	36.7
5 to 10	8,755	10,984	48.7	45.9
10 to 17.5	11,436	15,326	53.8	51.9
17.5 to 25	11,152	13,063	58.7	60.0
25 to 35	13,277	14,636	69.3	68.3
35 to 50	11,638	14,177	78.6	79.3
50 +	9,891	14,089	86.2	89.1
Total	70,854	89,478	64.7	64.0

Source: Apgar, William C., Jr. and Brown, H. James. *The State of the Nation's Housing.* Cambridge, Mass.: Joint Center for Housing Studies of Harvard University, 1988, p. 7.

income families, while Nevada, Texas, Florida, Washington, South Dakota, Tennessee, Wyoming, and New Hampshire taxed middle-income families at nearly twice the rates as the richest families. Poor families in Nevada, Texas, Florida, Washington, and South Dakota were taxed at five times the rate of the rich. (Citizens for Tax Justice, 1991).

The ability to own one's home has been a prominent component of the American dream and for many Americans it represents participation in the broad middle class. Therefore, another index of the declining middle class and the growing gap in living standards between the rich and the poor is in housing costs. Increasingly, the United States is becoming a nation of housing haves and have-nots. In 1987 the median price of a first home was nearly $67,000, four times the 1967 price ($16,530) and almost double the 1975 price of $34,800 (in 1986 constant dollars). In some regions of the country (especially the Northeast and the West), increases in housing prices have been even more dramatic. These rising costs have made it increasingly difficult for low-income and moderate-income—especially young—households to purchase a home. As table 8–2 indicates, between 1974 and 1987 the rate of homeownership declined for households with annual incomes under $35,000, and this decline was especially pronounced for households with incomes under $5000 (Apgar and Brown, 1988).

Wealth. Measures of income inequality alone do not adequately measure a society's stratification system. To gain an accurate picture of the distribution of a society's economic resources we must also examine wealth—which includes savings, investments, homes, and property. Wealth represents accumulated assets or "stored-up" purchasing power.

Historical trends in the distribution of wealth show that the Colonial and immediate post-Revolutionary periods were the most egalitarian in U.S. history (Smith, 1984; Williamson, 1980). In other words, wealth was more equally distributed during this period than at any other time. Between the early nineteenth century and the beginning of the Great Depression in 1929, economic inequalities increased. During the Great Depression and World War II the distribution of wealth became significantly more equal. From the end of World War II to 1963 an overall increase occurred in the concentration of wealth, but then it declined, so that by 1976, for the first time in the twentieth century, the wealthiest 1 percent of Americans owned less than 20 percent of the nation's total assets. However, the most recent data available indicate that that trend has reversed; wealth is again more heavily concentrated among the very rich. By 1983 the richest 1 percent of the population owned nearly one-third (32.9 percent) of the nation's wealth (Wolff, 1987; Joint Economic Committee, 1986). Today the distribution of wealth is much more highly concentrated in the upper extremes than income is.

Since the 1983 data probably do not reflect the impact of changes in national tax policies in the 1980s—changes that disproportionately benefitted the very rich—they may actually underestimate the current concentration of wealth. The Congressional Budget Office study cited above found that federal tax changes enacted between 1978 and 1986 had their most dramatic effects at the extremes of income distribution. Between 1977 and 1988 the tax burden of the poorest 10 percent of taxpayers increased by 20 percent, while the tax burden of families in the highest 10 percent of income declined 6.4 percent (Congressional Budget Office, 1987, pp. 43–48).

The concentration of wealth in American society is even more apparent if one distinguishes between net worth and net financial assets. Most studies of the distribution of wealth have relied on measures of **net worth,** which refers to the difference between a household's assets and liabilities. For example, the Census Bureau recently conducted a comprehensive survey of the net worth (which includes assets such as homes, bank accounts, stocks and bonds, and liabilities such as mortgages and loans) of American households in 1988. The study found that more than one-tenth (11 percent) of American households had zero or negative net worth—that is, their financial liabilities exceeded their assets. Moreover, the one-fifth of American families with the lowest incomes owned 7 percent of the total net worth, while the top one-fifth owned 44 percent. It also found that the net worth of a typical white household was more than 10 times that of a black household and eight times that of a Hispanic household. The median net worth for white households was $43,279; for black households, $4,169; and for Hispanic households, $5,524 (U.S. Bureau of the Census, 1990a).

However, the net worth of many Americans who have accumulated some wealth is held almost exclusively in the equity that they have in their homes and automobiles. Oliver and Shapiro (1989) have therefore argued that the most accurate measures of the concentration of wealth in the United States should exclude equity in homes and vehicles, since these can seldom be converted to other purposes (such as financing a college education, establishing or expanding a business, or paying for emergency medical expenses). The term **net financial assets (NFA)** refers to household wealth after the equity in homes and vehicles has been deducted. If this measure of wealth (rather than net worth) is used, figures on the overall wealth of American households and inequalities in the distribution of wealth in American society change dramatically. Although the overall household median net worth was $32,609, household median net financial assets were $2599. Moreover, whereas the top 20 percent of American households earned over 43 percent of all income (see table 8–1), the same 20 percent held nearly 90 percent of net financial assets (Oliver and Shapiro, 1988). Stocks, bonds, and trust holdings are especially concentrated among very wealthy families. The richest one-half of 1 percent of American families own 40 percent of the nation's corporate stock. As these recent trends indicate, then, the United States is a society in which both income and wealth are unequally distributed, and these inequalities appear to be increasing.

Poverty. For most of human history the vast majority of people have been poor. Because poverty was so widespread, it did not appear to be a significant problem. It was simply taken for granted and perceived to be inevitable, a perception that the Bible reinforced: "For ye have the poor always with you" (Matthew 26:11) and "The poor shall never cease out of the land" (Deuteronomy 15:11). In modern American society, however, the most affluent in human history, the existence of poverty appears as a glaring contradiction, one that has been the subject of considerable debate (Murray, 1984; Harrington, 1984; Sandefur and Tienda, 1988; Jencks and Peterson, 1991).

Obviously, poverty is a relative concept. The lives of poor families in rural Mississippi are considerably better than those of impoverished families in Calcutta, India, who are forced to live, eat, sleep, and die on the streets. Similarly, poor Mississippi families today live better lives than most families did in preindustrial times.

However, we do not live hundreds of years ago, or in Calcutta today.

Americans live in a society that takes for granted many gains in the quality and security of life. We find it intolerable that people should live on the streets or die at an early age of minor ailments (as they did in preindustrial times). Nevertheless, even in the United States today, the poor suffer from hunger, inadequate shelter, and premature death.

The most widely used definition of poverty in America is based on the idea of **income sufficiency**—the amount of money needed to purchase the basic necessities of life. Although several standards might be used to determine what level of income is sufficient, the measure used by the Social Security Administration has become the official government index of poverty.

The **poverty index** utilizes U.S. Department of Agriculture estimates of the costs of a minimal food budget, adjusted to the size of the family. The per person daily food budget is multiplied by three to determine the approximate level of funds needed for all other living costs—housing, clothes, medical care, heat, electricity, and other necessities. Therefore, in 1990 the index classified as poor all families of four with an income of less than $13,359 (U.S. Bureau of the Census, 1991a, p. 1). By this measure 33.6 million Americans, 13.5 percent of the population, lived below the poverty line in 1990.

Who are America's poor? Many Americans think of them as the "dregs" of society, its most disreputable members. The poor are often visualized as skid row winos, "bag ladies," able-bodied adults who prefer welfare to working, and so on. However, the reality is that the poor do not fit our stereotypes so clearly. For one thing, there are large numbers of **working poor**—people who earn so little from their work that their income is below the federal poverty line. For example, in 1989 the working poor totaled 2.6 million. Moreover, another 5.4 million people annually seek full-time jobs but have to settle for part-time work (U.S. Bureau of the Census, 1990b; Pear, 1986, p. 18).

Some recent data (U.S. Bureau of the Census, 1991a; Duncan, 1984; O'Hare, 1985; 1987) indicate the following characteristics of the poor:

- Most poor adults aged 22–64 are working or looking for work.
- Black poverty is three times as common as white poverty, and the poverty rate for Hispanics is nearly three times that for whites. However, two-thirds (66 percent) of the poor are white.
- Many poor people live in two-parent families. However, one of the striking trends in the United States has been the "feminization of poverty"—the increasing percentage of impoverished families who are headed by women. In 1990 more than half (53 percent) of families in poverty were headed by women.

- Of the 33.6 million poor Americans in 1990, 40 percent (13.4 million) were children under 18 years of age; of those poor 16 to 24 years of age, more than 40 percent were students.
- About 12 percent of the poor (3.7 million) were aged 65 and older.
- Of those poor over 15 years of age, nearly one-third were ill or disabled.
- Forty percent of the population below the poverty level do not receive welfare.

This profile of poverty in America shows that the stereotypical portrait of the poor is overly simplistic. First, many of those living in poverty are doing so because of economic conditions beyond their control. For example, thousands of blue-collar workers in "smokestack" industries have lost their jobs as manufacturing plants have shut down or moved; thousands of family farmers, caught between rising production costs and falling prices for their products, have been forced into bankruptcy. Second, many of those living in poverty are working or seeking more stable work. Third, many of those included in the categories discussed above—children under 18, some people over 65, the handicapped or disabled—are unable to work. Finally, the poverty category contains a disproportionate number of single mothers. Therefore, whereas some people are poor because employment is not available or because their employment does not pay a living wage, a great many poor people are unemployable under existing conditions rather than unemployed. The vast majority of the poor did not create their condition of poverty and are virtually powerless to change it on their own.

During the past quarter-century changes have occurred in the extent of poverty in the United States. In 1959, the first year for which comparable data were collected, 39.5 million people, or 22.4 percent of the population, were below the poverty line. Those figures declined steadily throughout the 1960s until by 1973 they reached low points of 23.0 million people, or 11.1 percent of the population. The major decline occurred during the middle 1960s, when poverty programs initiated by the Kennedy and Johnson Administrations were in full-scale operation. The **poverty rate** (the percentage of the population below the poverty line) remained fairly stable through the 1970s until the recession late in that decade, when it began to rise (see figure 8–3). This increase was further spurred by substantial cuts by the Reagan Administration in social welfare assistance programs. The number of people in poverty continued to climb until 1984, when the poverty rate fell to 14.4, its first decline since 1978. In 1990 the poverty rate stood at 13.5, about the same level as it had been in 1986.

The poverty rate provides us with an annual "snapshot" of the per-

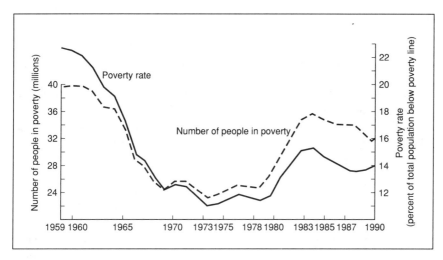

Figure 8–3.   Number of Poor and Poverty Rate: 1948–1988. (*Sources:* U.S. Bureau of the Census, "Money Income and Poverty Status in the United States: 1987." *Current Population Reports*. Series P-60, No. 161, 1988c. U.S. Bureau of the Census. "Poverty in the United States: 1986." *Current Population Reports*. Series P-60, No. 160, 1988e.)

centage of people experiencing poverty at one point in time—for example, in 1990 about one-seventh (13.5 percent) of the U.S. population lived below the poverty level. Such figures convey the impression of a permanent and well-defined group of "poor people." However, these figures obscure the turnover among the low-income population. An intensive study of U.S. families between 1968 and 1978 revealed that one-quarter of the U.S. population lived below the poverty level for at least one year during that period, but only slightly more than half of those living in poverty in one year were still poor the next year (Duncan, 1984). However, several studies have shown that poverty was somewhat more enduring in the early 1980s than it had been in the 1970s (Jencks, 1991, pp. 35–36).

The Underclass.   Although a substantial minority of the U.S. population lives in poverty at some point in life, for most of the poor this condition is not permanent. However, numerous scholars have recently begun to describe the lives of the most impoverished segment of American society— those who not only are economically marginal but are also concentrated in extreme poverty areas and are socially isolated from the rest of society. They contend that this social category at the very bottom of the social pyramid, referred to as the *underclass*, represents a steadily increasing and persistent form of poverty in the United States. Found primarily in the nation's inner cities, the underclass is characterized by high rates of joblessness, out-of-wedlock births, families headed by females, welfare dependency, school drop-outs, and serious crime. Although the underclass is disproportionately black and Hispanic, it also includes a substantial number of whites.

The concept of an underclass has been raised most prominently by William Julius Wilson (1987, 1989a, 1991), who has argued that the growth of the urban underclass—the "truly disadvantaged"—results from major economic changes in U.S. society that have caused extremely high levels of inner-city unemployment. Earlier in the twentieth century, relatively uneducated and unskilled native and immigrant workers were able to find stable employment and income in manufacturing. However, today, as a result of changes in the global economy, manufacturing jobs have moved from inner cities to the suburbs, the Sun Belt, or overseas; and the jobs created in the cities demand credentials that most inner-city residents do not possess. Thus inner-city residents find themselves without prospects for work. Moreover, as many stable working-class and middle-class residents with job qualifications have moved from the inner cities into better residential neighborhoods, the stability of neighborhood social institutions (e.g., churches, schools, and recreational facilities) has been undermined, and the social fabric of community life has deteriorated. The underclass has become increasingly isolated, socially and economically.

The notion of an underclass has been the subject of considerable debate (Wilson, 1989b; Jencks and Peterson, 1991). Some critics contend that the term *underclass* should be abandoned. For example, Gans (1990) has argued that the term has become a highly ideological and value-laden buzzword; people included in the underclass have become perceived as disreputable, the "undeserving poor," who could and should earn a living for themselves. Thus, the underclass has come for many people to refer not to a category of people made jobless by faults in the economy but rather by moral faults in the jobless themselves.

Moreover, critics have charged that the term is analytically imprecise and tends to lump together under a single rubric several different characteristics assumed to be found among all members of the underclass. For example, Jencks (1991) argued that there are several kinds of underclasses, including an impoverished underclass, a jobless underclass, an educational underclass, a violent underclass, and a reproductive underclass. He found that, while some conditions (e.g., job opportunities for those without higher education and the incidence of single-parent families) deteriorated during the 1970s and 1980s for those on the bottom of the social pyramid, on a number of other indicators—high school drop-out rates, teenage pregnancy rates, and violent crime—conditions improved. Given these contradictory trends, Jencks argues that the idea of a single uniform and growing underclass actually obscures, rather than helps to understand, what is actually happening to those at the very bottom of American society.

Inequalities of Status

The importance of status as a key dimension of stratification in U.S. society was demonstrated in one of the classic studies in sociology. Analyzing a New England community he called "Yankee City," W. Lloyd Warner began his research on the community's stratification system with the assumption that economic factors would be the most important in determining stratification (Warner and Lunt, 1941). But he found that the prestige of people's social backgrounds and life-styles (e.g., neighborhoods in which they lived, clubs to which they belonged), as well as their income levels, determined where they were ranked by others in the stratification system.

One of the most frequently used indices of status in modern societies is occupational prestige. Table 8–3 shows the prestige ratings given to various occupations in American society. The most prestigious occupations are usually compensated by substantial incomes, but they frequently require highly technical skills or are associated with political power. Thus, occupational categories with low prestige can possibly have incomes exceeding those with higher prestige. In many areas of the country the incomes of plumbers exceed that of college professors, despite the higher prestige associated with being a professor. In most cases, however, a close relationship exists between class and status positions.

One striking feature of the studies on occupational prestige is that occupational rankings in American society have shown little change since the first such studies were conducted in 1947. Moreover, considerable research has demonstrated that strong similarities exist in the occupational prestige rankings in most industrial countries and industrializing societies, such as China, as well (Inkeles and Rossi, 1956; Treiman, 1977; Lin and Xie, 1988).

As Warner suggested, however, status is not determined solely by occupation. Ancestry, religious affiliation, place of residence, life-style, amount of education, and many other factors have all been associated with an individual's status. There may be contradictions among these different factors: for example, sex and race might affect the prestige attached to occupants of a particular occupation. Acker (1980) found that predominantly female ("pink-collar") jobs have a lower average prestige than traditionally male occupations. This finding was reinforced by Bose and Rossi (1983), who found a substantial overall difference in the pres-

Table 8–3. Occupational Prestige Rankings

Occupation	Score	Occupation	Score
Physician	82	Real estate agent	44
College professor	78	Firefighter	44
Judge	76	Postal clerk	43
Lawyer	76	Advertising agent	42
Physicist	74	Mail carrier	42
Dentist	74	Railroad conductor	41
Banker	72	Typist	41
Aeronautical engineer	71	Photographer	41
Architect	71	Plumber	41
Psychologist	71	Farmer	41
Airplane pilot	70	Telephone operator	40
Chemist	69	Carpenter	40
Minister	69	Welder	40
Civil engineer	68	Dancer	38
Biologist	68	Barber	38
Geologist	67	Automobile mechanic	37
Sociologist	66	Jeweler	37
Political scientist	66	Watchmaker	37
Urban planner	66	Blacksmith	36
Mathematician	65	Bricklayer	36
Secondary school teacher	63	Airline stewardess	36
Registered nurse	62	Meter reader	36
Pharmacist	61	Mechanic	35
Veterinarian	60	Baker	34
Elementary school teacher	60	Shoe repairman	33
Accountant	57	Bulldozer operator	33
Economist	57	Bus driver	32
Artist	56	Truck driver	32
Actor	55	Cashier	31
Librarian	55	Sales clerk	29
Statistician	55	Butcher	28
Social worker	52	Housekeeper	25
Funeral director	52	Child care worker	25
Computer specialist	51	Longshoreman	24
Stock broker	51	Gas station attendant	22
Reporter	51	Taxi cab driver	22
Office manager	50	Elevator operator	21
Bank teller	50	Bartender	20
Electrician	49	Waiter/Waitress	20
Machinist	48	Farm laborer	18
Police officer	48	Peddler	18
Insurance agent	47	Maid/servant	18
Musician	46	Garbage collector	17
Secretary	46	Janitor	17
Computer operator	45	Bootblack	9

Source: Davis, James A. and Smith, Tom W. *National Data Program for the Social Sciences: General Social Survey Cumulative Codebook, 1972–1982.* Chicago: National Opinion Research Center, 1986, Appendix F.

tige ratings of traditionally women's jobs (e.g., housekeeper, dental assistant, private secretary, registered nurse) and predominantly men's jobs (e.g., garbage collector, electrical engineer, building construction contractor, plumber).

Some Consequences of the U.S. Stratification System

In this section we focus on the effects or consequences of one's place in the system of stratification. We will concentrate on the differences in lifestyle and life chances for people in various strata, especially the poor. We have already mentioned that life chances—the likelihood of realizing a certain standard of living or quality of life—are influenced by position in the social hierarchy. Numerous factors, including life expectancy, cause of death, and mental and physical health, are all related to the people's positions in the stratification system. Conversely, people's places in the system affect their life-styles—tastes, fashions, preferences, and other ways in which they lead their lives. Life-styles may include such items as one's type of home, vacation, leisure-time activities, reading habits, and sexual behaviors.

Health

As we will see more fully in chapter 14 on Health and Medicine, economic inequalities are significantly related to physical and mental health. In the United States and most other societies, people in the lower classes are more likely to suffer from poor physical and mental health than those in the higher socioeconomic groups (Syme and Berkman, 1981; Rainwater, 1968; Hollingshead and Redlich, 1958; Cockerham, 1986). For example, a disproportionate number of poor people suffer the disabling effects of chronic illnesses. In fact, the rates of disability among the poor for the major chronic illnesses—heart disease, arthritis and rheumatism, back and spine ailments, impairments of the legs or hips, and hypertension—are nearly double those of the nonpoor (Newacheck et al., 1980). Similarly, the relationship between health care and economic circumstances is reflected in a 1984 study of trends in infant mortality prepared by the National Center for Health Statistics. This study noted that in 1984 the infant mortality rate stopped going down partly because of cutbacks in federal medical funding for the poor (*Kansas City Star,* October 18, 1984, p. 7A).

On the basis of their systematic review of the relationship between income and illness, Newacheck and colleagues conclude that there is "a substantial health gap between 'poor' and 'nonpoor' families in the United States" (Newacheck et al., 1980, p. 143). Summarizing a considerable body of research dealing with the impact of social class factors on health, Cockerham (1986) comes to a similar conclusion: "On nearly every measure, membership in the lower classes carries health penalties. . . . To be poor is by definition to have less of the things (including health care) produced by society" (Cockerham, 1986, p. 49).

Life Expectancy

Life expectancy refers to the average number of years that people in a particular demographic or social category will live. The effect of social class on life expectancy is dramatically illustrated by the fate of passengers on the luxury liner Titanic, which sank in 1912. Of the 143 first-class female passengers on board, only four perished, and of those four, three chose to remain with the ship. Of the 93 second-class female passengers, 15 perished. However, 81 of the 179 third-class female passengers died as the ship went down (Lord, 1955). On the Titanic, as in society in general, life expectancy is related to one's position in the social hierarchy.

In a survey of a number of studies on the relationship between social rank and life expectancy, Antonovsky (1967) found that socioeconomic position has a significant effect upon life expectancy. In societies in which overall death rates are either very low or very high, only small differences exist between classes. Low death rates reflect great achievements in the battle against death, while high death rates reflect people's helplessness. In these extreme cases, position in the stratification system makes little difference. However, in societies where moderate progress has been made in reducing the death rate, differences are likely to be great because relatively scarce resources (such as new drugs and new medical techniques) are more available to members of the upper strata.

Studies conducted in American society for more than 50 years have persistently supported the conclusions of Antonovsky's research (Kammeyer and Ginn, 1986). Two national studies, one conducted in the 1960s and the other in the 1970s, found that when educational level is used as a measure of social class position, those with higher educational attainment have much lower mortality rates than those with lower educational attainment (Kitagawa and Hauser, 1968; Rosen and Taubman, 1979). Rosen and Taubman's study, which was limited to the white population, found that the least-educated people had death rates that ranged from 40 to 60 percent higher than the most educated people (Rosen and Taubman, 1979). A pronounced difference was also noted when family income was used as a measure of social class. The death rate for the lowest income groups was 2.75 times higher than for the highest income groups. A study of the causes of the deaths of over 48,000 white Oregon residents between 1976 and 1984 found that residents of the poorest census tracts had the highest mortality rates for all causes of death; the wealthiest had the lowest. The greatest difference between the poorest and wealthiest groups was found in deaths attributed to alcoholism, in which the lowest income group's index of potential life lost was 11.7 times higher than the index for the most wealthy group (United States Centers for Disease Control, 1988).

The higher death rates of people in lower social classes may be the result of a variety of factors. Since the economic resources of the middle and upper classes are greater, they may put their resources toward better environmental conditions or more extensive health care. The lower classes may have little money left for medical care after they provide for the necessities of food, clothing, and shelter (Rosen and Taubman, 1979).

People are also becoming increasingly aware that the occupations of members of the lower social strata are directly related to their higher mortality rates. One reason for the lower prestige of certain occupations is that they are more dangerous to health and life. Occupations such as underground mining, lumbering, oil drilling, and construction all have a greater chance of leading to accidental deaths. But although accidents may cause some deaths, evidence has also shown that conditions of the workplace may have delayed effects on health, thus reducing the length of life. Coal miners and cotton mill workers are known to have a high incidence of respiratory diseases (black and brown lung diseases) that lead to higher mortality rates. The long-term effects of working with asbestos materials, lead, and various petrochemicals are almost certainly injurious to health, and probably produce higher death rates (Fox and Adelstein, 1978).

Criminal Justice

The impact of social class on life chances is strikingly apparent in the area of criminal justice. The sociological literature on the relationship between social class and criminal behavior, however, has produced contradictory findings. On the basis of an extensive review of studies examining this relationship, Tittle, Villemez, and Smith conclude that "class and criminality are not now, and probably never were related, at least not in the recent past" (Tittle, Villemez, and Smith, 1978, p. 652). However, Braithwaite (1981), who conducted a review of studies of social class and juvenile crime, concluded that there is an inverse relationship between social class and crime; lower-class people commit more crimes against

Sociology in the News

The Class Factor in Health and Medical Care

During the 1988 presidential campaign Republican candidate George Bush asserted that class is "for European democracies or something else—it isn't for the United States of America. We are not going to be divided by class" (quoted in DeMott, 1990). Bush's sentiments reflect a widespread tendency among Americans to deny the reality of class. For example, Johns Hopkins University researcher Vicente Navarro argues that there has been a "deafening silence" in the United States on how class affects public health, and he points out that the United States is the only western developed nation that does not collect mortality statistics by class (Navarro, 1990, p. 1238).

Instead, U.S. data focus on differences in racial patterns of disease and mortality rates. However important racial factors are in determining how people live, die, and get sick, researchers such as Navarro argue that the focus on the substantial racial disparities in health has masked how closely linked class factors are to patterns of death and disease among Americans.

For example, the impact of class factors on health has been increasingly apparent in America's inner cities, where poverty and inadequate medical services have contributed to dramatic increases in the incidence of tuberculosis, hepatitis A, syphilis, gonorrhea, measles, mumps, whooping cough, ear infections, and AIDS. So severe is the crisis in health and medical care in poverty areas of the country that medical experts compare conditions in these areas with underdeveloped countries. One physician remarked, "We're seeing scenes here straight out of underdeveloped countries, diseases that haven't been seen in the United States since the turn of the century." For example, Dr. Harold P. Freeman, chief of surgery at Harlem Hospital in New York, has suggested that a black man in Harlem is less likely to reach age 65 than a man in Bangladesh (Rosenthal, 1990).

Numerous researchers, while acknowledging the impact of race, contend that class is a more important factor than race in predicting health. For example, one of the few studies in the United States that included information on class concluded that mortality rates were related to class: people with less education, less income, and blue-collar occupations were 2.3 times more likely to die of heart disease than managers and professionals. Similarly, researchers found that class differences in morbidity (illness) were more substantial than race differences. People making less than $10,000 were 4.6 times more likely to report having been sick than those earning over $35,000, while blacks reported getting sick 1.9 times as frequently as whites. Thus the racial difference was less than half the class difference (Gladwell, 1990; Navarro, 1990). Moreover, a 1991 study by the National Cancer Institute found that the most important factors influencing the incidence of cancer were low income and poor living conditions (Okie, 1991). Thus, as the income gap between rich and poor increases, it is probable that the gap in conditions of health will increase as well.

DeMott, Benjamin. *The Imperial Middle: Why Americans Can't Think Straight About Class.* New York: William Morrow, 1990.
Gladwell, Malcolm. "Public Health Experts Turn to Economic Ills." *Washington Post,* November 26, 1990.
Navarro, Vicente. "Race or Class Versus Race and Class: Mortality Differentials in the United States." *The Lancet,* November 17, 1990.
Okie, Susan. "Study Links Cancer, Poverty." *Washington Post,* April 17, 1991.
Rosenthal, Elisabeth. "Health Problems of Inner City Poor Reach Crisis Point." *New York Times,* December 24, 1990.

people—which are more likely to come to the attention of the police—than middle-class people do. Finally, depending on how social status is defined, Thornberry and Farnsworth (1982) found that social class background is not related to criminal behavior by juveniles. Among adults, however, an individual's educational attainment and job stability are both inversely related to criminal behavior; those with low educational attainment and unstable jobs have higher rates of criminal behavior.

However, most studies analyzing the relationship of social class and criminal behavior have not dealt with white-collar crime (including embezzlement, fraud, and bribery), which is almost exclusively an upper-class and upper-middle-class phenomenon. It is also more lucrative than other forms of crime. For example, the U.S. Chamber of Commerce estimates that white-collar crime costs over $40 billion annually, over 250 times the amount of all bank robberies, and more than ten times the annual amount in thefts (Reiman, 1979, p. 106). Yet the rates of arrests and convictions and lengths of sentences for white-collar crime are nowhere near as severe as those for index offenses, or street crimes.

The poor are disadvantaged in their relationship to the criminal justice system in several ways. First, they are much more likely to be victims of violent crimes. Moreover, they are more likely to be suspected of crimes by the police, and as a result, they are more likely to be arrested and charged with crimes. Higher-class individuals arrested for the same offenses are more apt to be released without being charged (Reiman, 1979). Once arrested, the poor are less able to afford bail. Often they must stay in jail until they are tried, which limits their ability to gather information for their defense. Because they probably cannot afford a private lawyer, they are forced to use overworked public defenders, who often lack the resources of private lawyers. In court they are likely to appear guilty because their dress, manner, and speech differ from that of judges and jury members, who are usually members of the middle or upper classes. If they are convicted, the poor cannot often afford to appeal their cases. When they do get out of jail, their poverty and their jail records prevent them from getting good jobs or perhaps any jobs at all. This situation, of course, leads some people into a vicious cycle of crime and incarceration that lasts a lifetime.

Education

In our society education is a crucial factor in determining one's chances of success in virtually every realm of life. College, postgraduate, and professional degrees are essential to occupational and economic success in our credential-oriented society, and socioeconomic factors have a strong influence on the level and quality of education that an individual is able to attain. Several studies have demonstrated that students with the same academic records but varying social-class backgrounds have different probabilities of obtaining education past high school. For example, Sewell (1971) found an extremely strong relationship between parents' socioeconomic status (SES) and college attendance: "the lower the SES group, the more limited the opportunities at each level" (Sewell, 1971, p. 795). He found that a student from a high SES background has almost 2.5 times as much chance as a low SES student *with the same academic ability* to attend some kind of post-high school educational institution. The advantage was 4 to 1 for access to college, 6 to 1 for graduation from college, and 9 to 1 for attaining a graduate or professional education. Similarly, Bowles and Gintis (1976) found that children from the lowest tenth in socioeconomic status are only one-twelfth as likely to complete college as those in the highest 10 percent.

A variety of factors prevent the poor from obtaining the amount and kind of education needed for vocational success. The quality of public elementary and high school education available to the poor is generally inferior to that available to the middle and upper classes. Also, many lower-class children either cannot afford to start college or are forced to drop out before they finish because they must go to work to support themselves and their families. Even when those from lower- and working-class backgrounds do attend college, they are much more likely to attend two-year community colleges or four-year colleges of lesser quality and prestige (Cohen and Brawer, 1982).

Open and Closed Systems of Stratification

Societies differ in the extent to which they permit and encourage **social mobility**—the movement of persons from one social class to another. An

open class system of stratification is one in which few obstacles exist for people who are changing their social positions; success is unaffected both by the constraints of disadvantaged social origins or by the privileges of advantaged social class backgrounds. All people, regardless of birth (sex, race, religion, ethnicity, social background), have genuinely equal opportunity to change positions and move up or down in the stratification system. The greater the degree of social mobility, the more open the class system is. In an open class system emphasis is placed on achievement.

By contrast, a completely closed stratification system allows virtually no social mobility. A **closed class system** is one in which children inherit their parents' social position. In a closed class system people's places in a social hierarchy are fixed or ascribed (that is, based on qualities such as race, ethnicity, social background, or sex, over which they have no control). In a closed class system little possibility exists for social mobility. People are born into a position and cannot, under normal circumstances, move out of it.

The most rigid and closed of all stratification systems is a **caste system.** A caste system is endogamous, which means that people must marry within their own caste. A person who does not marry within his or her caste will probably be punished severely. Intimate contact, such as eating with someone of a different caste, is prohibited. Typically elaborate systems of rituals and customs are developed to limit interaction between caste members. As an example of a completely closed system, we will consider the traditional caste system of India.

The traditional Indian caste system, the basis for organizing Indian society since the fifth century B.C., is the classic example of caste. The system can be divided into five broad strata, each of which contains thousands of internal distinctions based primarily on occupation. At the top of the hierarchy stand the Brahmans, the priests, scholars, and teachers of basic religious principles, who provide religious support for the social order (Mayer and Buckley, 1970). Occupying the lowest and most despised position are the *Harijans,* a term meaning "people of God," which was popularized by Gandhi. These people are the outcastes, whom Indians believe fall outside the caste system. They are frequently called "untouchables" because the outcastes are not permitted to touch members of the upper castes. Indians believe that they can be contaminated even if an outcaste's shadow touches their clothing, food, or person. Outcastes are so despised that in rural areas they are frequently barred from the villages during the early or late part of the day when they cast long shadows and are therefore more likely to contaminate other villagers.

Since 1949 discrimination on the basis of caste has been outlawed, and the coming of modernity to India has undermined and disrupted the traditional caste system, especially in large metropolitan areas. In the modern Indian world of bureaucracies, factories, and schools, contact among castes has increased. Despite these changes, however, the Indian caste system persists, especially in the rural areas, where 75 percent of the Indian population lives. In rural villages people still find it unthinkable to marry someone from another caste. How deeply the caste system is rooted and how harshly its rules are enforced is illustrated by a recent incident in a rural Indian village in which a 16-year-old girl, her 18-year-old lover, and a friend who had tried to help them elope were lynched by relatives and neighbors. The young woman was a *Jat*, the dominant caste in the region, while the young men were outcastes. The deaths of all three were decreed by the *Jat*-dominated village council after the young woman refused to give up her lover (Crossette, 1991, p. 60).

A caste system is not unique to India. For example, in Japan members of a caste called *Burakumin* are economically and socially discriminated against and are considered mentally inferior by the rest of Japanese society; marriages between the *Burakumin* and the upper caste are considered a tragedy (by upper caste members) and are strongly discouraged. (For a further discussion of the *Burakumin,* see "Japan's Outcastes: The Burakumin" in the Cross-National box.) As we will discuss more fully in chapter 9, the structure of relations between blacks and whites in the United States historically has resembled a caste system. Hereditary factors (skin color, hair texture, lip form) were used as the criteria for determining opportunities for full participation in society. African Americans were relegated to an inferior status, and their access to politics, education, jobs, and housing was restricted. Moreover, throughout the South, interpersonal relations between black and white were governed by what was known as the "etiquette of race relations," which required patterns of deference by blacks to whites. Although the legal basis for the caste system has been eliminated by judicial rulings and by federal legislation, the issue still remains controversial as to how closely black/white relations today resemble a caste system.

In the same way that a genuinely classless society probably has never existed, pure caste and class systems probably do not exist either. No stratification system is totally closed or totally open. Virtually all societies display ascription and achievement in some form, and thus fall somewhere between the two extremes.

A Sociological Analysis of Mobility

Lee Iacocca is one of the most prominent and celebrated businessmen in contemporary society. Born of parents who had immigrated to the United States from Italy, he experienced the hard times of the Great Depression as he grew up in Allentown, Pennsylvania. He worked his way through college, and, through the classic virtues of hard work, ingenuity, and industriousness, became president of two of the nation's largest corporations—the Ford Motor Company and, later, the Chrysler Corporation (which he rescued from near bankruptcy and transformed into a once-again prosperous company). His name has been prominently mentioned as a possible presidential candidate.

In 1984 Iacocca published his autobiography, *Iacocca.* Although books describing how to achieve success appear frequently on the best-seller list, *Iacocca* remained on the list for more than two years, a phenomenal feat for any book. One reason for the book's sensational success is that Iacocca's life story epitomizes the American dream. His is the classic success story—humble origins, an unquenchable desire to gain an education, a commitment to hard work, and a meteoric rise to the top of America's corporate world. Well publicized success stories such as Iacocca's reinforce the widespread belief among Americans that their society provides great opportunities for social mobility (Huber and Form, 1973).

Two types of social mobility can be described. One is **horizontal mobility,** which refers to movement from one social position to another of equal rank. Iacocca's shift from the presidency of the Ford Motor Company to the same position at Chrysler exemplifies this type.

However, popular interest in, and sociological research on, social mobility has centered on **vertical mobility,** which refers to movement upward or downward in the stratification system. Iacocca's rise to fame, fortune, and power is an example of upward vertical mobility; an example of downward vertical mobility would be if the son of a lawyer were to spend his career as a carpenter.

In analyzing the nature of social mobility, sociologists have focused on two main types: intragenerational mobility and intergenerational mobility. **Intragenerational or career mobility** refers to the movement of individuals in the stratification system during their lifetimes. Studies of this type of mobility focus on the life span of individuals, examining where people begin their careers and where they finish them. Someone who starts as a laborer and ends as a lawyer has clearly experienced upward mobility. On the other hand, someone who ends up on skid row after beginning as a physician has experienced downward mobility.

Intergenerational mobility refers to differences between the social-class position of children and the social-class position of their parents. Studies of this type of mobility compare the social class of parents with those of their children, most often with that of a son. If the children have more money, have more education, or occupy a higher-status occupation, they have experienced upward mobility. If they are lower than their parents on any of these dimensions, they have experienced downward intergenerational mobility.

Cross-National Perspectives

Japan's Outcastes: The *Burakumin*

The term *caste* refers to an extreme case of a closed system of strat-ification that is characterized by a hierarchy of social statuses into which people are born and must remain throughout their lives. The case of the Japanese *Burakumin*—Japan's "invisible race"—reflects the continuing impact of a caste system in one of the world's most modern, rational, and technologically advanced nations. Physically indistinguishable from other Japanese, the *Burakumin* are acknowl-edged to be completely Japanese, but of such lowly social origins that they are constantly subjected to prejudice and discrimination (DeVos and Wagatsuma, 1966).

The contemporary *Burakumin* are descendants of the untouch-able *eta* caste. The degree to which the *eta* were despised by the rest of Japanese society is revealed in the name itself: *eta* means "filth abundant." Under the feudal system of Tokugawa, Japan, from the seventeenth to the nineteenth centuries, the *eta* occupied an out-caste status below the four superior castes (the ruling caste of war-riors and administrators, the peasants, artisans, and merchants) that constituted Japanese society. The *eta* were discriminated against in every aspect of their lives, and a number of laws were enacted to reinforce their inferior status. For example, as outcastes they were restricted to the dirtiest, most defiling, and least desirable occupa-tions (e.g., butchers, leatherworkers, grave tenders, and execution-ers). They were legally segregated from the rest of the Japanese people and forced to live in isolated ghettos, the locations of which were deliberately omitted from maps. Moreover, they were required to walk barefoot and to wear special clothing that identified them as *eta*. Because they were considered innately inferior and "impure," their marriages were restricted to other *eta;* intermarriages with non-*eta* were virtually nonexistent.

The *eta* were legally "emancipated" during the mid-nineteenth century, at about the same time as American slaves were freed, and the laws that had formerly restricted their lives and discriminated against them were formally abolished. Although emancipation pro-vided legal freedom, discrimination against the outcastes (subse-quently known as *Burakumin,* or "village people") persisted. Among the popular prejudices about the *Burakumin* that persisted well into the twentieth century were the following:

One rib is lacking; they have a dog's bone in them; they have distorted sexual organs; they have defective excretory systems; if they walk in the moonlight their necks will not cast shadows, and, they being animals, dirt does not stick to their feet when they walk barefoot (quoted in Neary, 1986, p. 558).

Today there are an estimated one to three million *Burakumin* living in Japan, a nation of 123 million. Although the Japanese government has enacted legislation designed to end the cycle of poverty and discrimination and to improve their living conditions, *Burakumin* continue to be found in overcrowded slumlike ghettos and their lives are characterized by low incomes, high unemployment, and high dependence on welfare. They are often the "last hired and first fired." The *Burakumin* continue to be viewed by most Japanese as "mentally inferior, incapable of high moral behavior, aggressive, impulsive, and lacking any notion of sanitation or manners" (Wagatsuma, 1976, p. 245). The power of these stereotypes and the fear they elicit are reflected in the importance attached to family registration records, which certify "proper" social backgrounds. Such records are frequently required in connection with applications for jobs, loans, and admission to schools. Above all, it is not unusual for families to undertake exhaustive investigations of the lineages of their children's prospective spouses to ensure that their families will not be "contaminated" by *eta* origins.

During the twentieth century the *Burakumin* have organized social movements to protest the discrimination they encounter in employment, education, and housing. Recently, the militant *Burakumin* Liberation League has become a potent political force by using techniques of direct harrassment and intimidation against those who do not share its views of the *Burakumin* plight. As a consequence, Japanese book, magazine, and newspaper publishers, fearful of disruptions of their offices and homes by *Burakumin* "direct action" squads, have adopted an unwritten policy against any mention of the *Burakumin* in their publications (Fallows, 1990).

DEVOS, GEORGE and HIROSHI WAGATSUMA. *Japan's Invisible Race: Caste in Culture and Personality.* Berkeley: University of California Press, 1966.

FALLOWS, JAMES. "Japan's Hidden Race Problems." *New York Times*, October 14, 1990.

NEARY, IAN J. "Socialist and Communist Party Attitudes toward Discrimination Against Japan's *Burakumin*." *Political Studies* 34, 1986.

WAGATSUMA, HIROSHI. "Political Problems of a Minority Group in Japan: Recent Conflicts in Buraku Liberation Movements." In Willem A. Veenhoven and Winifred Crum Ewing (eds.), *Case Studies on Human Rights and Fundamental Freedoms.* Vol. III. The Hague: Martinus Nijhoff, 1976.

Any assessment of the extent of social mobility in American society must consider the effects of **structural mobility**—mobility occurring as a result of changes in a society's occupational structure. Structural mobility is caused by large-scale structural changes in the society as a whole. Among the structural changes that have had a profound effect on the class structure of many countries, including the United States, are technological innovations, wars, economic fluctuations (e.g., depressions or recessions), and urbanization. If the nature of the economy and the occupational structure change over time—for example, if the number of white-collar workers increases over blue-collar workers—then the possibility of upward social mobility from blue-collar to white-collar occupations will be increased because more higher-status jobs will be available. On the other hand, if an increasing percentage of the population has earned college degrees, the proportion of their children who can achieve mobility through college graduation will decrease. Thus Hout found that opportunities for changes between social origins and current occupations have recently diminished for both men and women. "[The] origins and destinations of workers in the early 1980s are more similar than were the origins and destinations of workers in the early 1970s" (Hout, 1988, p. 1382). This observation is especially true in high-status salaried professional and management occupations, where workers in the 1980s are more likely to have fathers with those occupations than was the case in the 1970s.

Patterns of Social Mobility in the United States

Some general conclusions can be drawn from the large body of recent sociological research on social mobility. First, most social mobility is modest; it occurs in steps between adjacent strata, that is, by moves from the lower-middle class to the middle class, or from a parent's occupation as a small-town merchant to the offspring's occupation as a lawyer or doctor. Large jumps from the lower class to the upper class (the classic rags-to-riches story) are rare; for example, Lee Iacocca's rise from humble origins to corporate success is the exception, not the rule.

Moreover, occupational inheritance is greatest at the top and at the bottom of the occupational structure. Men from upper-middle-class and unskilled blue-collar backgrounds are most likely to have occupations similar to their fathers, and children whose fathers had occupations between these two extremes are most likely to experience mobility. Studies of the highest levels of American society indicate that recruitment for the most powerful corporate positions is largely restricted to individuals from upper-class and upper-middle-class origins. A recent study of the social origins of the chief executive officers of 243 major corporations in 1986 showed that nearly two-thirds had been raised in upper-middle-class or upper-class families (Boone, Kurtz, and Fleenor, 1988; see also Kerbo, 1983; Tumin, 1985).

Second, patterns of social mobility in the United States have not changed substantially over time. Although most historical studies of social mobility are limited to cities and do not represent the nation as a whole, such studies tend to show that patterns of social mobility at the turn of the twentieth century and at mid-century were about the same. Furthermore, historical studies of business elites show patterns of recruitment from the upper class similar to the contemporary elite (Kerbo, 1983, pp. 346–348). However, Hout's recent analysis supports the notion of "expanding universalism." This phrase means that, increasingly, occupational status in the United States cannot be inherited but must be attained by actual achievement. Although high-status origins remain an advantage, advantaged offspring are less likely today than in the past to occupy high-status positions without competing with individuals from other social origins (Hout, 1988, p. 1381).

Finally, the overall rates of social mobility in the United States do not differ substantially from those in other Western industrialized countries. Although differences do exist in the historical experiences and occupational structures of the 16 countries they studied, Grusky and Hauser concluded that "industrialized societies share a common pattern of mobility" (Grusky and Hauser, 1984, p. 35). Similarly, Kerckhoff, Campbell, and Winfield-Laird (1985) found substantial similarities in the amount of intergenerational occupational movement of men in Great Britain and the United States. Consistent with the findings cited earlier, both studies found the greatest degree of inheritance of occupational position among the highest-status and lowest-status occupations, with the greatest mobility occurring among those in between. "The picture that emerges is one of severe immobility at the two extremes of the occupational hierarchy and considerable fluidity in the middle" (Grusky and Hauser, 1984, p. 35). Such studies contradict the notion that the United States is more open in terms of social mobility than other nations.

Social Stratification in the Soviet Union

Until this point our discussion of social stratification has focused primarily on patterns of social inequality and social mobility in the United States. The distinctive features of structured social inequality become even more apparent by a comparison with the Soviet Union, a modern, highly industrialized society that was, until the dramatic political upheavals of August 1991, the world's most powerful communist state. Although the social system of the Soviet communist state was legitimated by an egalitarian ideology, its system of social ranking and the distribution of scarce resources among those ranks differed considerably from the classless society anticipated by Marx.

Since its establishment of the USSR in 1917, stratification in that nation, as in the United States, has been shaped by economic and technological forces. Increasing division of labor and occupational specialization have produced an economic system in which technical expertise is highly valued, and the educational system has become a major factor in determining how people are distributed in the work force. As the number of skilled manual and nonmanual occupations has expanded, so also have opportunities for upward occupational mobility.

However, the occupational structures of the two countries differ substantially. The Soviet Union has continued to have a greater proportion of industrial workers than the United States because its economy has concentrated more on heavy industry and less on services, consumer goods, and marketing. The USSR also continues to have a higher proportion of farmers in its labor force than the United States does.

Despite differences in occupational structures, Inkeles (1968) found a remarkable agreement on the relative prestige of occupations among the United States, the Soviet Union, Japan, Great Britain, New Zealand, and Germany. Moreover, Soviet sociologists have identified a prestige hierarchy of occupations that is broadly similar to that found in the United States. Thus professional occupations, such as engineering and scientific jobs, are highly ranked, while agricultural, sales, and service occupations have low prestige (Dobson, 1977, p. 301). Yet in the Soviet Union the working-class or skilled manual labor categories have been consistently ranked above many low-level nonmanual or white-collar occupations. This fact may be explained by the communist ideology that extols the virtues of the worker and by the higher relative incomes obtained by the working class.

In Soviet society the state and the Communist Party were virtually identical. Until its monopoly of power was shattered in 1991, the Party, although it condemned the acquisition of private property, had become extremely wealthy, holding vast property throughout the nation. The Party's accumulation of wealth, coupled with the central role of the state in organizing and regulating economic forces, meant that power and privilege in the Soviet Union were more likely to flow from political position than from occupation. Consequently, the most highly ranked figures in Soviet society were political elites, who gained their privilege from their position within the structure of the Party, whose members consisted of less than 10 percent of the adult population.

The other path to elite status was to achieve celebrity status as a musician, writer, artist, dancer, actor, or athlete whose prominence was perceived as a contribution to the power and prestige of the Soviet system. However, although celebrities gained considerable prestige, they gained little power in the Soviet Union (Smith, 1976, p. 29).

Data on wage and salary distribution indicate that the pre-1991 Soviet Union was far from an egalitarian society. It had a wage ratio of 50 to 1, which means that the top salaries were 50 times greater than the minimum wage. In the United States, the ratio has been calculated at 300 to 1, or six times greater than the range in the Soviet Union (Lenski, 1978, p. 370). If one considers total income, including wages, stock dividends, and interest, the 50 to 1 ratio for the Soviet Union would hardly be affected, but the 300 to 1 ratio for the United States would be dramatically increased. In other words, income was far more equally distributed in the USSR than in the United States.

In contrast to official ideology, in Soviet society some people were "more equal than others." Soviet elites—the "privileged" class—had access to goods, services, and luxuries and enjoyed a life-style unavailable to ordinary citizens. The elites had access to special stores that insulated them from chronic shortages and provided them with scarce consumer items (Smith, 1976). Prominent Communist Party officials enjoyed the most conspicuous symbol of rank and privilege—chauffeur-driven limousines; they also had access to private cars, often foreign models, which were limited in number and extremely expensive. In a society with severe housing shortages, the elites received the most desirable housing—fashionably equipped urban apartments and lavishly furnished country estates. Moreover, admission to exclusive medical clinics, restaurants, and clubs was allocated according to rank. Overall, the Soviet elites were "far better clothed, fed, housed, and medically cared for than the rest of the population" (Smith, 1976, p. 43). In addition, they were among the few individuals who were permitted to travel to other countries, to vacation in expensive resorts, and to have access to Western movies, books, and magazines that were banned for ordinary citizens. Finally, in a society in which educational attainment is a critical determinant of upward mobility, elites were able to ensure that their children attended the most prestigious universities (Smith, 1976; Dobson, 1977; Matthews, 1978).

As much as anything, it was resentment of this vast system of privileges that Communist Party officials had allocated themselves that fueled the popular uprising that in 1991 ended the Party's reign. As one Moscow resident bitterly said of the dissolution of the Communist Party, "There couldn't be a better time to stop feeding the bellies of the party big-wigs. That was what the problem came down to" (quoted in Clines, 1991, p. 1).

Until recently, Soviet authorities maintained that poverty was a social ill found only in capitalist societies, and they officially banned public discussion of the existence of poverty in the USSR. However, the policy of *glasnost* (openness) initiated by Soviet leader Mikhail Gorbachev enabled economists and sociologists to examine poverty in Soviet society much more critically and publicly. Soviet sociologists estimate that at least 20 percent of the Soviet population—compared with 13.5 percent in the United States—live in poverty. However, Matthews contends that this figure is much too low, and that nearly 40 percent of the nonpeasant labor force earns less than the minimum subsistence level necessary to sustain an urban family. The existence of a substantial stratum of people living in poverty is therefore one of the primary social problems confronting the new political leadership of the country (Fein, 1989, p. 1; Matthews, 1986, p. 176).

Despite considerable social inequality and the existence of a substantial poverty class in the USSR, social mobility from the lower classes into the political elites appeared to be greater in the USSR than in the United States. Historically, a majority of the highest Party and administrative positions in the political bureaucracy were filled by males from peasant and working-class origins. Therefore political participation represented a very important channel of upward mobility for the children of peasants and workers in the Soviet Union. However, occupants of positions in the upper-middle stratum just below the elites—the "new class" of intellectuals, scientists, scholars, and managers—were likely to be drawn from upper-middle class backgrounds. Studies of trends in social mobility in the Soviet Union suggest that, especially among the urban intelligentsia, occupational continuity increased across generations; that is, children increasingly have not experienced mobility but have tended to have occupations similar to those of their parents (Dobson, 1977). Matthews (1978) suggests that in the late 1970s fewer and fewer people in the lower classes experienced social mobility because those selected for elite status were hand-picked by the incumbent elites for their talent as well as their support of elite policies. Nevertheless, Matthews contends that the Soviet elite was still more open in terms of class origins than other modern societies, including the United States. On the other hand, Dobson argues that the relatively high rates of intergenerational mobility found by Soviet sociologists result primarily from structural mobility—from changes in the economic structure of the Soviet Union, such as the expansion of bureaucratic and technical positions—rather than from "conscious socialist policies designed to promote mobility" (Dobson, 1979).

In addition to income inequality between classes, the Soviet Union has also been characterized by substantial inequalities based on gender (see chapter 10 for a discussion of gender inequality in the United States.) About 90 percent of Soviet women aged 30 to 49 work outside the home, which is roughly twice the percentage in the United States. About 68 percent of Soviet physicians are women, along with 75 percent of the teachers and 33 percent of the engineers. Yet most of the female labor force is found in unskilled manual positions or low white-collar jobs. Even those women in higher occupational positions usually have less authority than men (Swafford, 1978, p. 670; Browning, 1987).

The political power of Soviet women (or lack thereof) is similar to that of their American counterparts. Under the former Communist Party-dominated system, only one-quarter of the Party's members were women, and women held no real positions of power in the *Politburo,* the powerful elite body that made national policy. So striking was the absence of women from positions of power that it was a major news story in 1986 when Soviet leader Mikhail Gorbachev appointed the first woman in 25 years to the Secretariat, the 11-member body that carried out policies and supervised the nation's affairs (*New York Times,* March 7, 1986, p. 3).

The changes in the political structure of the Soviet Union following the failed coup attempt in August 1991 have been revolutionary. On the one hand, they ended the monolithic control that the Communist Party had exerted for nearly three-quarters of a century. On the other hand, they accelerated the movement for *perestroika* (restructuring) that Gorbachev had initiated soon after he assumed leadership of the nation in 1985. Nevertheless, precisely what kinds of social institutions will replace those that were overthrown is not at all clear. As the people of the Soviet Union seek to reshape and recast their society, it will be particularly interesting to see how these changes influence the structure of social inequality and patterns of social mobility in that country.

Summary

Social stratification, or structured social inequality, is a universal feature of human societies. Social inequalities and social ranking are usually justified by reference to an ideology, a set of ideas used to explain and justify the inequalities. The inequalities in American life are justified by a meritocratic ideology that emphasizes an ideal of equality of opportunity.

Sociologists have distinguished three basic dimensions of social stratification: class, status, and power. Class is an economic variable strongly emphasized by Marx as the determinant of social stratification. However, Weber argued that status, or prestige, and power were also important dimensions in a system of social stratification. An examination of the American stratification system reveals that, despite an egalitarian ideology, considerable inequality exists in contemporary American society. Inequalities in the concentration of wealth and income in the United States have been substantial throughout the nation's history, and they have become more pronounced during the 1970s and 1980s. Inequality is also manifested in differences among the social classes in both life chances and life-styles.

Stratification systems differ in the extent to which they are open or closed. An open class system is one in which there are few obstacles to social mobility, which is the movement between positions in a system of stratification. In a closed class system little possibility exists for mobility; people's positions in a social hierarchy are determined almost completely by birth. The most closed of all stratification systems is a caste system, which is exemplified by traditional Indian society.

There are different types of social mobility. Vertical mobility can be either upward or downward. Horizontal mobility involves the movement between comparable positions in the social structure. Sociologists have examined both intragenerational, or career, mobility and intergenerational mobility, in which parents' occupational positions are compared with those of their offspring. In general, studies of social mobility suggest that, despite a widespread belief that American society has provided unique opportunities for social mobility, upward social mobility is no greater in the United States than in other Western industrialized nations.

Despite an egalitarian ideology, patterns of social inequality and limitations on social mobility in the Soviet Union are clear. Elite status is drawn primarily from positions within the Communist Party and is reflected in unequal access by Party officials to scarce resources. Although the existence of poverty in the USSR was, until recently, officially denied, new studies indicate a substantial class whose incomes fall below official minimum subsistence levels. Social mobility from the lower classes is most pronounced in the political arena but is more limited among nonpolitical occupations.

CRITICAL THINKING

1. The authors state that a "classless society is a possibility, if not a probability." What conditions need to exist in order for such a society to be possible? Which existing society comes closest to this ideal?

2. Review the definitions of class, status, and power presented in the text. To what extent does each affect the following occupations in American society: judge, nurse, firefighter, mechanic, janitor?

3. Meritocracy has been a predominant ideology in American society. What are the basic tenets of this ideology? Review the data presented in the chapter to determine the validity of this ideology. Does it justify the existing social order? How did you learn about this ideology as you grew up? Give examples.

4. Explain the key differences between the structural-functional and the conflict interpretations of social inequality. What evidence presented in the chapter supports each theory?

5. How do the income data in the chapter support the contention that dominant and subordinate classes exist in American society?

6. The United States has been stereotyped as a "middle-class society" in which each generation is more successful than the previous one. Does the evidence in the chapter support this idea? How has the distribution of income been affected by America's move to a post-industrial society?

7. How can you explain the existence of an underclass in American society?

8. How are our lives (health, education, life expectancy, etc.) affected by social stratification?

9. What characteristics does a closed class system have? To what extent is American society closed?

10. Examine the experience of a grandparent, parent, and yourself to assess the intragenerational and intergenerational mobility in your family. In addition, assess each individual's horizontal and vertical mobility. Does your family's experience tend to prove or disprove the authors' main conclusions?

11. Compare and contrast social stratification in the United States and the Soviet Union. Be sure to include a comparison of ideology, occupational structure, power, and standard of living.

9 Racial and Ethnic Inequality

As we have seen in chapter 8, human societies are almost universally stratified or differentiated into categories of superiority and inferiority, dominance and subordination. Throughout history, racial and ethnic factors have frequently been used as criteria for ranking a society's members into categories of unequal wealth, power, and prestige.

Prejudice and discrimination and conflict and violence based on racial and ethnic distinctions are widely found throughout the world today—among black, white, colored, and Indian in South Africa, between English-speaking and French-speaking people in Canada, between East Indians and blacks in Guyana, between Kurds and Iraqis in Iraq, between Tamils and Sinhalese in Sri Lanka, between Chinese and Malays in Malaysia. Indeed, in the last few decades more people have died in ethnic conflicts around the world than in the Korean or Vietnam wars combined.

Indeed, the political ferment that unleashed dramatic political changes throughout eastern Europe during the late 1980s was fed by a resurgence of historic ethnic and national rivalries and antagonisms. The Soviet Union was rent by interethnic conflicts, such as those between the Armenians and Azerbajanis, as well as by demands from numerous other nationalities, such as Lithuanians, Latvians, Estonians, Georgians, ethnic Poles, and Ukrainians, for greater ethnic autonomy and even independence. Slavic nationalism in Yugoslavia, which earlier in the century had provided the spark that ignited World War I, has resurfaced, and conflicts among that country's several nationalities—Serbs, Croatians, Slovenes, Bosnians, Montenegrins, Macedonians, and Albanians—threaten the very existence of the nation. Prior to the fall of Rumanian strongman Nicolae Ceausescu in 1989 approximately two million Hungarians living in Rumania were subject to forced assimilation, the closing of Hungarian schools and social organizations, the suppression of the Hungarian language, and discrimination against those Hungarians who tried to retain their Hungarian ethnicity. Similar accusations of forced assimilation were raised by the Turkish minority in Bulgaria, where ethnic tensions led to the forced removal of thousands of Muslim Turks to Turkey. In this chapter we consider the dynamics of racial and ethnic relations. We will focus especially on how different patterns of racial and ethnic relations are achieved and maintained.

Ethnic and Racial Groups

The word *ethnic* is derived from the Greek word *ethnos*, meaning "people." **Ethnic group** refers to a group that is socially defined on the basis of its cultural characteristics. **Ethnicity**—the sense of belonging to a particular ethnic group—thus implies the existence of a distinct culture or subculture in which group members feel themselves bound together by a common history, values, attitudes, and behaviors. Other members of the society also regard them as distinctive. Ethnic groups may differ in cultural characteristics as diverse as food habits, family patterns, sexual behavior, modes of dress, standards of beauty, political orientations, economic activities, and recreational patterns. In its broadest sense, the term *ethnic* implies a sense of common peoplehood. In the U.S., Chicanos, Italians, Jews, Poles, Filipinos, and white Anglo-Saxon Protestants all can be considered ethnic groups.

The terms *race* and *ethnicity* are often used interchangeably, but they should be distinguished. An ethnic group is socially defined on the basis of its *cultural* characteristics; the term **race** refers to groups that are socially defined on the basis of *physical* characteristics. A group is defined as a race when certain physical characteristics are selected for special emphasis by members of a society.

The term *race* is meaningless in a biological sense, because there are no "pure" races. The crucial aspect of any definition of a group as ethnic or racial is that the characteristics that distinguish it are *socially defined.* Thus the criteria selected to make racial distinctions in one society may be overlooked or considered insignificant or irrelevant by another society. In much of Latin America, skin color and the shape of the lips—important differentiating criteria in the United States—are much less important than hair texture, eye color, and stature. A person defined as black in Georgia or Michigan might be considered white in Peru. Among the Tutsi (where men average a height of over six feet) and the Hutu (who stand slightly over four feet) peoples of central Africa, the physical characteristic of height is the basis for group distinctions. Therefore, the recent conflict between these two peoples, which resulted in the murders of thousands of the minority Hutus, is racial.

The principle that racial differences are socially defined is vividly shown by laws in the United States that prohibited interracial marriages. Until recently, many states stipulated that any person with one-fourth or more black* ancestry (that is, with one black grandparent) was legally defined as "black" and therefore prohibited from marrying someone "white." However, some states enacted more restrictive definitions of race. A recent example of this enactment occurred in Louisiana, when Susie Guillory Phipps, a light-skinned woman with Caucasian features and straight black hair, found that her birth certificate classified her as "colored." Mrs. Phipps, who contended that she had been "brought up white and married white twice," challenged a 1970 Louisiana law declaring that anyone with at least one-thirty-second "Negro blood" was legally classified as black. Under this law an individual who had *one* great-great-great grandparent who was black (and thus had only one-thirty-second "black" and thirty-one thirty-seconds "white" ancestry) was legally defined as black. Although the state's lawyer conceded that Mrs. Phipps "looks like a white person," the state strenuously maintained that her racial classification was appropriate (Trillin, 1986).

The South African system of *apartheid,* or racial separation, provided one of the most vivid examples of the way in which racial classifications are social, not biological, categories. Under apartheid, which was established in 1950 and formally abolished in 1991, all people were required to be classified into one of four legally defined racial groups—white, black, colored, and Indian. The racial categories into which people were (often

---

* Over the last two hundred years, a variety of terms—*Colored, Negro, Afro-American, Black*—have been used to refer to Americans of African descent. Recently, many black leaders have urged the adoption of the term *African American.* However, when this book was written, no consensus on terminology had emerged. Therefore, we will use both *African American* and *black American* in this chapter, and the more customary *black American* in the remainder of the book.

arbitrarily) placed determined whether or not they could vote or own land; the jobs they could hold; the schools they could attend; where they could live, eat, or play; and whom they could love and marry.

Although racial categories are arbitrary, because American consciousness of race is so pronounced, most of us are placed in a specific racial category—both by public perceptions and, more formally, by the categories (e.g., African American, Hispanic, Asian, American, Indian, European) used by the government and even by discussions such as this one.

What Is a Minority Group?

Sociologists usually use the terms *majority* and *minority* to refer to social relations in which racial and ethnic criteria are employed in the society's system of stratification. The distinctive feature of a **minority group,** or **subordinate group,** is that it occupies a *subordinate* or inferior position of prestige, wealth, and power in a society. A minority group is typically excluded from full participation in a society and is the object of discrimination by the majority group.

The term *minority* does not refer to the numerical size of a group. For example, in South Africa today, blacks are a numerical majority (69 percent) of the total population, yet they are systematically excluded from full social, economic, and political participation. Numerical superiority, therefore, does not necessarily ensure that a group will be dominant.

The crucial variable in majority/minority relations is **power**—the ability of one group to realize its goals and interests, even in the face of resistance. Power may be based on the superior population size, weaponry, technology, property, education, or economic resources of the dominant group. Superior power is crucial to the establishment of a system of ethnic or racial stratification. Moreover, having achieved power, a **dominant group,** or **majority group,** is reluctant to give it up voluntarily, but instead usually strives to maintain and perpetuate its privileged position.

Race and Ethnicity in the American Experience

The United States, which has been called a "nation of nations," is one of the most racially and ethnically diverse societies in the world. Despite an ideology formally committed to human equality, racial and ethnic criteria have frequently determined social status in American society. Figure 9–1 presents data on the distribution of major racial and ethnic groups in the United States. Presently members of the largest racial and ethnic minor-

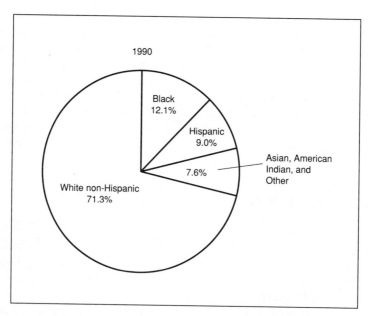

Figure 9–1. Racial and Hispanic Population of the United States, 1990. (*Source:* U.S. Bureau of the Census, *Census and You.* April 1991.)

ities (African Americans, Hispanics, Asians, and American Indians) comprise one-quarter (24.8 percent) of the population.

One of the most prominent features of the American experience is the competition among numerous racial and ethnic groups for economic, social, and political dominance. Moreover, in the future the impact of racial and ethnic factors will probably be even more pronounced. By the year 2000 one-third of all school-age children will be either Hispanic, African American, Asian, or American Indian (American Council on Education, 1988). Furthermore, in some states (e.g., California) the *majority* of working-age adults in 2000 will be members of these minorities (California Assembly Office of Research, 1986). Thus minority peoples will affect the nation's prosperity more substantially than ever before in U.S. history. In this section we sketch some key features of ethnic and racial relations in the American experience, beginning with the earliest inhabitants—Native Americans—and concluding with a discussion of some characteristics of contemporary immigration to the United States.

American Indians

The first Americans migrated from Asia 20,000 to 40,000 years ago, slowly dispersing throughout North, Central, and South America. Characterized by widely different levels of technology and cultural complexity, Native American peoples developed a great diversity of cultures, which persist to the present, despite the popular perception of North American Indians as a single distinct ethnic group. A good index of this cultural diversity is the number of languages—about 200—spoken today among American Indians. Although Indians represent less than 1 percent of the American people, the number of languages found among them is equal to the number of those spoken among the remaining 99 percent of the population combined (Hodgkinson, 1990, p. 1).

The Europeans invasion of North America had a permanent impact on American Indian peoples and cultures. From the 1600s onward, the insatiable European demand for land became the primary source of conflict with Native Americans. The process of European expansion westward involved the expulsion of Indians from their tribal lands. Although Indians resolutely resisted domination, the advance of white settlement eventually overwhelmed Indian resistance. Armed with superior military technology and bolstered by increasing numbers, whites moved inexorably westward. Indian tribes were forced to retreat as the control of lands they had formerly occupied was passed to whites. Their land base, which initially had been over 2 billion acres, dwindled to 155 million acres in 1871 and 90 million acres in 1980 (Dorris, 1981). Diseases such as smallpox, scarlet fever, measles, and cholera were fatal to large numbers of Indian peoples, who for centuries had been physically isolated from the Old World and had developed little or no resistance to these diseases. Moreover, substantial numbers of American Indians died as a result both of warfare with Europeans and of the deliberate extermination of Indians by European invaders. The Native American population, which had numbered between 5 and 6 million when Columbus arrived in the New World, dwindled to 237,000 by 1900 (Thornton, 1987, p. 32). Traditional Indian cultures and patterns of authority were undermined as their economic resources were eroded and as Indian affairs became controlled by whites.

By the turn of the twentieth century, whites believed that American Indians were a vanishing race, and that the few remaining Indians should be forced to assimilate—to give up their cultural heritages and to adopt the white values of rugged individualism, competition, and private enterprise. To ethnocentric whites, these values represented more "civilized" forms of behavior.

However, a striking feature of American Indian life in the twentieth century has been an ability to endure. Despite strong pressures to assimilate into the mainstream of American society, they have clung tenaciously to their cultures. Today nearly 2 million people identify themselves as American Indian, an increase of 40 percent over 1980. This places American Indians among the most rapidly growing ethnic categories in the United States.

A substantial portion of Indian lands were ceded to colonists and early settlers by treaties, first between Indians and colonial British governments and later with the United States government. These treaties form the basis of the unique legal and political status of Native Americans today. In contrast to other American racial and ethnic minorities, American Indian tribes "are due certain privileges, protections, and benefits of yielding some of their sovereignty to the United States" (Dorris, 1981, p. 54). Among these rights are the obligations of the federal government to protect their lands and to provide Indians with social, medical, and educational services.

During the nineteenth century, American Indians were removed to isolated areas not then coveted by whites. Solemn treaties signed with the United States government guaranteed that Indians would retain sovereignty over these lands in perpetuity—"as long as the grass shall grow and the rivers shall run." Although the lands held by Indians today represent only a small portion of those guaranteed in those treaties, they hold vast and extremely valuable agricultural, water, timber, fishing, and energy resources. However, these resources are being developed and exploited primarily for economic interests that are national and multinational, not Indian.

As a consequence, Indians are increasingly challenging their political and economic domination by outsiders, and are seeking to exert Indian control over reservation resources. Indian activists have mounted legal challenges to ensure that the federal government honors the terms of the treaties it has made with Indian tribes. Indian activism has also been reflected in their efforts to develop organizations to advance Indian economic interests by resisting external exploitation of their resource base. One of the most prominent of these has been the Council of Energy Resource Tribes (CERT), which was formed to promote Indian economic interests in the substantial coal, gas, oil, and uranium reserves that are found on Indian lands (Snipp, 1986). As the powerful economic and political pressures intensify over increasingly scarce and valuable Indian resources, it seems inevitable that conflicts will increase in the future (Erdrich and Dorris, 1988).

European Ethnic Groups

The first European immigrants to settle permanently in what is now the United States were almost exclusively English. The economic, legal, and political traditions that English settlers brought established the English character of American institutions, language, and culture. Ethnic groups who migrated later were forced to adapt to the cultural and social systems that the English had created.

Although the English composed the greatest proportion of the early colonial population, the middle colonies (New York, New Jersey, Pennsylvania, and Delaware) were settled by substantial numbers of Germans, Dutch, Scotch–Irish, Scots, Swedes, and French Huguenots. Here the idea of America as a "melting pot," in which diverse cultures come together to form a new people, was first formulated.

Immigration to the United States was greatest in the century between 1820 and 1920, when more than 30 million immigrants entered the country. Between 1820 and 1895 immigrants were drawn principally from countries of northern and western Europe—from Germany, Ireland, Great Britain (England, Scotland, and Wales), and Scandinavia (Norway, Sweden, and Denmark). With the exception of the Catholic Irish, the **"old" immigration** (as the immigration from these countries became known) was heavily Protestant.

Immigration to the United States reached its peak between 1890 and the outbreak of World War I in 1914, and those who entered were drawn from countries different than those of the old immigrants. The **"new" immigration**—including Greeks, Croatians, Italians, Russians (primarily Jewish), Poles, Hungarians, Czechs, and Lithuanians—hailed from southern and eastern Europe. Unlike the old immigration, which was heavily Protestant and followed agricultural pursuits in the United States, new immigrants were overwhelmingly Catholic or Jewish and were attracted primarily to the economic opportunities in the nation's rapidly expanding cities.

Native-born whites held deep-seated prejudices against the new immigrants, believing that they were innately inferior to previous immigrants. The U.S. Commissioner of Immigration described the new immigrants as "beaten men from beaten races; representing the worst failures in the struggle for existence. They have none of the ideas and aptitudes which fit men to take up readily and easily the problem of self-care and self-government" (quoted in Saveth, 1948, p. 40).

Such beliefs in the racial and cultural inferiority of new immigrants provided the foundation for American immigration policy from 1917 to 1965, which was designed precisely to discriminate against new immigrants by restricting their numbers while still permitting substantial numbers of old immigrants to enter.

Despite fears that they were undesirable and unassimilable and that they represented a threat to American society, the descendants of the new immigrants, today referred to as **"white ethnics,"** have achieved considerable socioeconomic success. Greeley (1976) has characterized their socioeconomic achievements as the "ethnic miracle." By the 1970s, Jews had attained the highest income levels of all European ethnic groups in American society, and they were followed by Irish, German, Italian, and Polish Catholics, not by white Anglo-Saxon Protestants. Moreover, when parental educational levels are held constant, Catholic ethnics show higher educational achievement than any other European group except Jews. Yet, despite their economic and educational achievements, many white ethnics still retain a sense of cultural identity with their ethnic and national roots.

African Americans

From the earliest settlement to the present, the principal racial division in American society has been between white and black; no other minority group has experienced discrimination so intense, pervasive, and enduring as African Americans. Numbering nearly 30 million—more than 12 percent of the total population—African Americans are today the largest racial minority in American society. Their numbers total more than the entire population of Canada or of the Scandinavian countries of Sweden, Denmark, Norway, Finland, and Iceland combined. Only Nigeria, Ethiopia, and Zaire have larger black populations than the United States.

Slavery and Caste.   During the first 200 years of their existence in American society, the lives of African American people were defined primarily by their role as slaves, a status in which individuals are involuntarily placed in perpetual servitude, are defined as property, and are denied rights generally given to other members of society.

Equally important in understanding the dynamics of race relations in the United States is that even those African Americans who were free during the slavery era (more than one-tenth of the black population) did not have the same rights and privileges as whites and were not accepted into society on an equal basis. In contrast to slaves in many other societies, slaves in the United States were subject to *racial* discrimination as well as legal servitude. Therefore, the most distinctive and enduring feature of black/white relations in the United States has been that African Americans—slave or free—have occupied a lower caste status, both during the more than 200 years of slavery and long after it was legally abolished in 1865.

The Aftermath of Slavery.   Bolstered by passage of the 13th Amendment, which abolished slavery; the 14th Amendment, which extended to them the equal protection of the law; and the 15th Amendment, which guaranteed the right to vote, African Americans actively sought to realize the opportunities and responsibilities of freedom. However, freed blacks were formally given freedom but not the means (that is, economic, political, and educational equality) to realize it. Through intimidation, violence, lynching, and terrorism, African Americans were kept in a subordinate status long after slavery had been legally abolished.

To ensure that white dominance would be perpetuated, the "Jim Crow" system of racial segregation was created. During the late nineteenth century, Southern legislatures passed a variety of statutes requiring racial separation. In 1896, in the famous *Plessy* v. *Ferguson* decision, the U.S. Supreme Court provided legal support for the doctrine of "separate but equal." Thereafter virtually every aspect of contact between whites and blacks was legally regulated.

From Plantation to Ghetto.   In response to these oppressive conditions, African Americans began to leave the South during the early twentieth century. They migrated primarily to Northern urban areas, where their settlement was both legally and informally restricted to areas in which other blacks lived. This migration out of the rural South has been one of the most significant aspects of the African American experience and one of the most important demographic changes in American history. In 1900, almost 90 percent of the black population lived in the South; by 1990 the percentage was only slightly more than one-half (53 percent). In 1900 African Americans were primarily rural residents, with only 22.7 percent living in urban areas. By 1980, more than four-fifths (81.3 percent) of the African American population lived in urban areas, indicating that blacks have become a more urbanized population than whites. Although a substantial portion of this increase in urban blacks occurred in the North, many Southern blacks also moved into cities. Table 9–1 shows the percentage of the African American population residing in major American cities for the years 1920, 1950, 1970, 1980, and 1990.

The massive migration of African Americans out of the South was one of the most important factors underlying the protest movement that swept the nation during the 1950s and 1960s. Although discrimination against African Americans in education, employment, housing, and the administration of justice also prevailed in the North, greater opportunities were available for them in Northern urban areas than in the South. Especially after World War II, an educated and articulate black middle class played an important part in legal challenges to the Southern Jim Crow system. These actions culminated in the Supreme Court's 1954 *Brown* v. *Board of Education* decision that segregated schools were unconstitutional. The *Brown* decision, which overturned the Court's 1896 "separate but equal" doctrine, symbolized the beginning of an era in which the legal basis for the caste system would crumble.

Table 9–1. African American Population as Percentage of the Total Population
of the 10 Largest U.S. Cities,* 1920, 1950, 1970, 1980, and 1990

	1920†	1950†	1970	1980	1990
New York	2.7	9.8	21.1	25.2	28.7
Los Angeles	2.7	10.7	17.9	17.0	14.0
Chicago	4.1	14.1	32.7	39.8	39.1
Houston	24.6	21.1	25.7	27.6	28.1
Philadelphia	7.4	18.3	33.6	37.8	39.9
San Diego	1.2	4.5	7.6	8.9	9.4
Detroit	4.1	16.4	43.7	63.1	75.7
Dallas	15.1	13.2	24.9	29.4	29.5
Phoenix	3.7	6.0	4.8	4.8	5.2
San Antonio	8.9	6.7	7.6	7.3	7.1

Sources: U.S. Census of 1920; U.S. Census of 1950; U.S. Bureau of the Census, *Negroes in the United States, 1920–1932,* Washington, D.C.: U.S. Government Printing Office, 1935; "Characteristics of the Population," *Statistical Abstract of the United States, 1972*, pp. 21–23; *Statistical Abstract of the United States, 1984*, pp. 28–30; U.S. Department of Commerce News Releases, Bureau of the Census, February 1991.

* These were the 10 largest cities in the United States in 1990.

† Figures pertain to "nonwhite" population, of which over 90 percent was black.

The Changing Status of African Americans.   During the late 1950s and early 1960s African Americans employed numerous forms of direct protest—such as nonviolent sit-ins, boycotts, and voter-registration drives — to effect changes in the existing system of race relations. During the 1960s federal, state, and local governments and private organizations made efforts to eliminate black inequality. The Civil Rights Act of 1964 substantially reduced public discrimination in restaurants, hotels, and business establishments. It also provided the impetus for substantial integration of public school systems in the South and for "affirmative action" efforts to ensure nondiscriminatory job hiring. The Voting Rights Act of 1965 enabled African Americans throughout the South to exercise their right to vote. Finally, the Civil Rights Act of 1968 banned discrimination in the sale or rental of housing.

The effects of these and other changes were most marked in politics and education. Between 1964 and 1990 the number of African Americans elected to public office increased from 103 to 7370 (still, however, less than 2 percent of all elected public officials). Moreover, the number of African-American mayors increased from *none* in 1964 to 313 in 1990. Many major American cities now have black mayors, including New York, Los Angeles, Chicago, Detroit, Philadelphia, Atlanta, Denver, and Washington, D.C. The increasing significance of African American political power was apparent in 1984 and 1988, when Jesse Jackson's presidential candidacy not only electrified the African American community (and was instrumental in registering thousands of new black voters) but gained the support of a substantial number of white voters as well.

Since the Civil Rights Movement of the 1950s and 1960s, African Americans have also achieved substantial gains in education. In 1957 the proportion of whites aged 25–29 who had completed high school (63.3 percent) was double the proportion of blacks (31.6 percent). By 1989 the proportions of each racial group who were high school graduates were nearly equal. Moreover, throughout the late 1960s and early 1970s a steadily increasing proportion of blacks began attending college, and the proportion of black college graduates increased as well.

However, these gains of the 1960s and early 1970s have eroded, threatening to reverse the movement toward educational equality. Between 1976 and 1989 the college attendance rate of black males dropped substantially (although the rates for black women increased). Moreover, the overall enrollment of black students in graduate and professional schools also declined. Finally, the percentage of college degrees awarded to African Americans declined between 1976 and 1989. In 1976 African Americans earned 6.4 percent of all bachelor's degrees but only 5.7 percent in 1989; the percentage of master's degrees awarded to African Americans also declined—from 6.6 percent in 1976 to 4.6 percent in 1989. Similarly, in 1989 811 doctoral degrees were awarded to blacks, compared to 1,056 in 1979. (Carter and Wilson, 1991).

Moreover, the overall economic status of African Americans has shown little improvement since the mid-1960s. Although many blacks have experienced socioeconomic mobility during the past decade, African-Americans remain underrepresented in high-status professional, technical, and managerial positions, and overrepresented in service occupations, traditionally recognized as low-status jobs in American society (Farley and Allen, 1987). Furthermore, an enormous gap still separates black and white family incomes. As figure 9–2 shows, since 1950 income levels for both African American and white families have risen substantially. White median family income nearly doubled, increasing from $18,683 (in 1990 dollars) in 1950 to $36,915 in 1990. The median family income for blacks increased more than 111 percent, reaching $21,423 by 1990. Although the gap between black and white incomes tended to narrow slightly during the 1960s, since 1970 this gap has increased (see figure 9–2). In 1970 black median family income was 61 percent of white family income. By 1990 it stood at 58 percent (U.S. Bureau of the Census, 1990b).

An even greater disparity between blacks and whites has been revealed

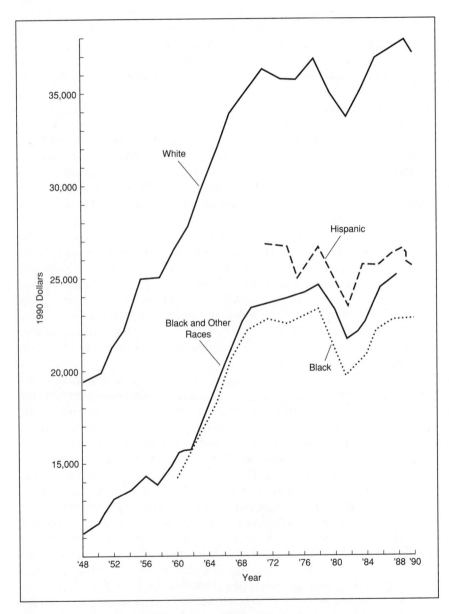

Figure 9–2. Median Income of Black, White, and Hispanic Families, 1948–1989 (in 1989 U.S. dollars). (*Source:* U.S. Bureau of the Census, *Current Population Reports*, Series P-60, 1948–1990).

by the Census Bureau survey of net worth of American households discussed in chapter 8. (In 1988, white households had a median net worth of $43,279, while the median net worth of black households was $4169.) As a result of all the economic inequities between blacks and whites, both past and present, white households average 10 times more net worth than black households (U.S. Bureau of the Census, 1990a).

The gap separating African Americans from the mainstream of American life is also reflected in residential patterns. Despite federal legislation outlawing discrimination in the sale of housing, blacks and whites remained nearly as residentially segregated in 1980 as they had been in 1970. This segregation is primarily a result of racial discrimination, not class differences; even affluent blacks continue to live in predominantly black neighborhoods. Other American racial and ethnic minorities—notably Asians and Hispanics—do not experience comparable levels of housing segregation (Massey and Denton, 1987, 1988).

The patterns of discrimination responsible for black residential segregation include efforts by some people in the housing industry who discourage blacks from buying homes in white neighborhoods and organized neighborhood resistance to proposals for low-income and moderate-income housing. Another crucial source of housing discrimination involves home loans. A study that analyzed over 10 million applications for home loans from every savings and loan association in the country between 1983 and 1988 showed that black applications were rejected more than twice as often as the applications by whites. Moreover, the applications of high-income blacks were rejected more often than those of low-income whites (Dedman, 1989). Thus the substantial differences separating black and white Americans economically, educationally, and residentially have not been eliminated, and in some respects they have widened in the past decade.

Hispanic Americans

Hispanic Americans constitute one of the largest and most rapidly growing ethnic categories in the United States today. During the 1980s the Hispanic, or Latino, population grew nearly five times faster than the rest of the population, reaching a total of more than 22 million, or 9 percent of the total population, by 1990. Although Hispanics are more likely than the rest of the population to be Spanish-speaking, Catholic, and poor, they do not constitute a single ethnic category; there are widely diverse cultural, historical, and geographic backgrounds among them. The Hispanic category includes representatives from more than 30 Latin American nations, as well as from Spain and Portugal. More than three-fourths of them are of Mexican, Puerto Rican, or Cuban descent, but there are also substantial communities from the Caribbean, Central America, and South America—for example, Dominicans, Colombians, Ecuadorians, Salvadorans, Guatemalans, Nicaraguans, and several other Latin nationalities—in the United States (see Levine, 1987). We focus here on the three largest Hispanic ethnic groups: Mexicans, Puerto Ricans, and Cubans.

Mexican Americans (or Chicanos) are the largest Hispanic group and (after blacks) the second largest minority group in American society. More than 13 million Chicanos live in the United States, about 90 percent of them in the southwestern states of Texas, New Mexico, Arizona, Colorado, and California. The earliest Mexican Americans became a minority through the annexation of Mexican lands by the United States in the nineteenth century. However, most Mexican Americans are descended from immigrants who came to the United States in the twentieth century. Mexican immigration is still a major factor in American society; today Mexicans are the largest national category of both legal and illegal immigrants to the United States.

Several indicators reveal that Mexican Americans lag considerably behind the mainstream of American society in socioeconomic status. Despite some evidence of improvement among younger generations, Mexican American educational attainment is less than that of both whites and African Americans. Long stereotyped as primarily rural farm workers, today Mexican Americans are overwhelmingly urban residents. However, they tend to be found primarily in low-paying blue-collar and semiskilled occupations (although some evidence reveals that during the 1970s the proportion of Mexican Americans in skilled, higher-paying occupations increased). As table 9–2 indicates, median family income for Mexican Americans is only 62 percent of median family income for whites (U.S. Bureau of the Census, 1990c).

Other Spanish-speaking peoples have immigrated primarily to urban areas on the East Coast, particularly since the end of World War II. Although the number of immigrants from countries throughout the Caribbean and Central and South America has increased markedly during this period, Puerto Rico and Cuba have been the two primary sources.

Puerto Ricans, who, unlike other immigrants, are American citizens, began migrating to the mainland primarily after World War II. Today nearly two-thirds of the more than 2 million mainland Puerto Ricans live in New York City, which has been the principal magnet for Puerto Rican immigrants. This migration to the mainland has been prompted primarily by economic pressures among the impoverished lower strata of Puerto Rican society. Consequently, Puerto Rican immigrants have been concentrated in blue-collar, semi-skilled, and unskilled occupations, and their

Table 9–2. Median Family Income, 1989

	Income	*% of White Income*
All races	$34,213	
White	35,975	
Black	20,209	56
Hispanic	23,446	65
Mexican	22,245	62
Puerto Rican	19,933	55
Cuban	31,262	89
Central and South American	25,460	73
Other Hispanic*	26,567	74

Sources: U.S. Bureau of the Census, "Money Income and Poverty Status in the United States: 1989," *Current Population Reports*, Series P-60, No. 168, 1990; "The Hispanic Population of the United States," *Current Population Reports*, Series P-20, No. 449, 1990.

* Includes those who identified themselves as from Spain or as Hispanic, Spanish, Spanish American, Hispano, or Latino.

income level (55 percent of white median family income) is the lowest among all American ethnic groups.

Cuban immigrants have been primarily political refugees. Approximately 750,000 Cubans have entered the United States since Castro's rise to power in 1959, and today they number more than 1 million. In contrast to most previous immigrations to the United States, early Cuban immigrants tended to be drawn mainly from the upper social and economic strata of Cuban society. With these backgrounds, they brought skills (educational, occupational, business, and managerial), entrepreneurial values, and substantial amounts of capital that enabled them to achieve rapid socioeconomic success. In the 30 years since their initial migration, Cubans have become the most affluent of all Hispanics and are an integral part of the economies of a number of American cities, especially Miami, Florida, which they have transformed into a major commercial center with ties throughout Latin America.

Asian Americans

Asian Americans are an extremely diverse category that includes Chinese, Japanese, Filipinos, Koreans, Asian Indians, Vietnamese, Cambodians, Laotians, and several other national or ethnic groups. By 1990 Asians numbered 7.3 million, which represented 2.9 percent of the American people (Barringer, 1991). Some have resided in the United States for generations; others have arrived very recently. Compared to the millions of Europeans who have immigrated to the United States, Asian immigration has been slight. However, today, as a result of changes in U.S. immigration laws, which before 1965 had virtually excluded them, Asians are proportionately the nation's fastest growing racial category. During the 1980s Asians constituted more than two-fifths (42 percent) of all legal immigrants, and the Asian population increased by 107 percent (compared to increases by Hispanics of 53 percent, by American Indians of 40 percent, and by African Americans of 13 percent) (U.S. Immigration and Naturalization Service, 1990). Although almost all states experienced substantial increases in their Asian populations during the 1980s, almost 40 percent of all Asian Americans lived in California, where they represent nearly 10 percent of the state's population (U.S. Bureau of the Census, 1991c).

Historically, the Chinese, Japanese, and, later, Filipinos have been the most prominent Asian groups; Asian Indians, Koreans, Vietnamese, Cambodians, and Laotians are more recent arrivals. The initial migration of Chinese, who were the first Asians to immigrate to the United States, reached its peak from 1873 to 1882. Initially welcomed as a source of labor, the Chinese soon became perceived as an economic threat to native labor, and they were subjected to various forms of discriminatory legislation. In 1882 Congress passed the Chinese Exclusion Act, the first law to restrict a specific nationality from immigrating to the United States.

Anti-Asian sentiment was revived when many Japanese immigrated to the United States in the early twentieth century. Although the Japanese represented an extremely small proportion of the total population, their presence generated intense hostility. Like the Chinese before them, the Japanese were the object of legislation to harass them and diplomatic efforts to prevent their further immigration. In 1924 all Asian immigration to the United States was restricted, and it remained limited until 1968, when a new immigration law went into effect.

Despite early anti-Asian prejudice and discrimination, in particular toward the Japanese during World War II (which resulted in their evacuation from the West Coast and their internment in concentration camps), Asians have recently made significant socioeconomic gains, especially in education. By 1980 more than half of 20- and 21-year-old Asian Americans were enrolled in school, compared with a third of whites of the same age (Hirschman and Wong, 1986, p. 1). By 1990 40 percent of the Asian population over 25 had completed at least four years of college, which was nearly double the figure (23 percent) for whites (O'Hare and Felt, 1991, p. 8). So extraordinary have Asian educational attainments been that charges have been raised that many of the nation's most prestigious universities have placed limitations on the percentage of Asian students they admit (Mathews, 1987).

Similarly, the income levels of Asian Americans are today slightly higher than whites; in 1989 better than one-third (39 percent) of Asian American households had incomes of $50,000 or more, compared to 32 percent of white households (O'Hare and Felt, 1991, p. 7). However, these figures obscure substantial differences in income levels among Asians. On the one hand, Chinese, Japanese, and Koreans had incomes above whites, while Filipinos, Asian Indians, Vietnamese, and Laotians earned less. On the other hand, in 1989 the poverty rate for Asians (14 percent) was nearly double that for whites (8 percent) (U.S. Commission on Civil Rights, 1988; O'Hare and Felt, 1991).

Contemporary Immigration

During the past quarter-century, traditional patterns of immigration into the United States have been radically transformed. This new immigrant wave promises to produce the most dramatic and far-reaching changes in the ethnic composition of the United States since the influx of "new" immigrants in the late nineteenth and early twentieth centuries. First, the number of immigrants to the United States has increased substantially. During the 1980s the number averaged over 633,000 annually, compared to 282,000 in the decade prior to 1965. In 1989 alone more than 1 million immigrants were admitted, a number greater than immigrants to all other nations of the world combined. Moreover, experts estimate that there is an additional net annual increase of 100,000 to 200,000 illegal immigrants (U.S. Immigration and Naturalization Service, 1990; Bouvier and Gardner, 1986.)

The changes in the national origins of contemporary immigrants are as dramatic as their increasing numbers. Until the late 1960s, immigration to the United States was overwhelmingly European, ranging from a high of 96 percent of all immigrants for the decade 1891–1900 to 53 percent between 1950 and 1960. Today, as a result of changes in U.S. immigration laws, only a small percentage (7.6 percent in 1989) of immigrants come from Europe. The predominant sources of immigration are Third World nations in Central and South America, the Caribbean, and Asia. In 1989 *none* of the ten leading countries from which the United States received immigrants—Mexico, El Salvador, the Philippines, Vietnam, Korea, mainland China, India, the Dominican Republic, and Iran—was a traditional European source (U.S. Immigration and Naturalization Service, 1990). Given the declining birth rate of the U.S. population, some demographers estimate that, if current trends in birth rates and immigration rates continue, a century from now 40 percent of the U.S. population will be made up of post-1980 immigrants and their descendants—at least 80 percent of whom will be Hispanic, Caribbean, or Asian (Bouvier, 1981).

The settlement patterns of today's immigrants differ from previous flows into the United States. Whereas previous immigrants settled primarily in the industrial states of the Northeast and Midwest (New York, Illinois, New Jersey, Pennsylvania), immigrants today are much more dispersed geographically. States with the largest foreign-born populations in 1980 were California, New York, Florida, Illinois, and Texas (U.S. Bureau of the Census, 1982, pp. 14–19).

When Americans think of immigrants to the United States, they often have an image of "huddled masses" who are poor, unskilled, and uneducated. That perception of immigrants may have been valid at one time, but today it is seriously out of date. The changes in U.S. immigration laws have affected the occupational composition of the present immigrant population. Today the range of immigrants' occupations much more closely resembles that of the native population than immigrant populations have in the past. Whereas immigrants during the first two decades of the twentieth century were overwhelmingly unskilled, blue-collar workers, preferences today for those with skills needed by the United States has meant that immigrants entering now are much more highly educated than in the past. Physicians, nurses, scientists, architects, artists, entertainers, engineers, and others with highly technical skills have contributed to a "brain drain," first from Europe and later from Third World nations that can least afford to lose such skills.

Today the overall educational level of immigrants to the United States is not especially low when compared to the United States' population as a whole. For example, 16.2 percent of U.S. adults aged 25 and over have completed college, while 15.8 percent of immigrants have done so. Immigrants from Asia and Africa are especially well educated; almost half of African (46 percent) and Asian (44 percent) immigrants in 1980 had completed college (Bouvier, 1986, p. 24). About half of all Asian immigrants between 1966 and 1975 were professionals; for Asian Indians the figure was 90 percent (U.S. Commission on Civil Rights, 1988, p. 5). The preference for immigrants with skills has meant that, unlike the situation between 1840 and 1920, it has become almost impossible for unskilled laborers to enter the United States unless they can claim a close family relationship or refugee status.

The emphasis on occupational skills has also meant that, increasingly, the less skilled have resorted to illegal means of entering the country. In 1989 nearly one million (954,000) illegal immigrants from 166 countries were apprehended, the vast majority from Latin America, especially

Mexico (U.S. Immigration and Naturalization Service, 1990). Although, as we noted earlier, the estimated annual net increase from illegal immigrants is lower than from legal immigrants, estimates of the total number of "undocumented aliens" living in the United States range from 1.5 to 3 million (Simon, 1989: pp. 283–284).

As was the case in the early part of the twentieth century, concern over the political, cultural, and, especially, economic impact of immigration has created a growing sense of alarm among many Americans. One debate about immigration that has a long history deals with questions regarding the impact that immigrants have on the domestic economy and on native employment and earnings, in particular. However, several scholars (e.g., Simon, 1990; Borjas, 1990; Reischauer, 1989), after reviewing the extensive research on the economic effects of immigration on native workers, have concluded that there is no conclusive evidence to support the idea that immigration has an adverse effect on the labor market prospects of native workers. No doubt many immigrants have in the past taken, and continue today to take, jobs and occupations that other American citizens do not want. The newest immigrants, especially those with low levels of education, often take the menial and service jobs that are the least desirable and lowest paid. Even immigrants with professional skills, such as medical doctors, often practice in less desirable settings and institutions.

Majority/Minority Relations

The diversity of racial and ethnic groups in American society provides an opportunity to examine several of the different ways in which racial and ethnic groups interact and to explore the conditions under which different kinds of intergroup relations occur. We examine first how members of the dominant group define the role of minorities and, next, the experiences of minorities in responding to the policies of majority groups.

Prejudice and Discrimination

Prejudice and discrimination are important elements in all majority/minority relations. The term *prejudice* (derived from two Latin words, *prae* [before] and *judicum* [a judgment]) denotes a judgment before all the facts are known. **Prejudice** refers to a set of rigidly held negative attitudes, beliefs, and feelings toward members of another group. **Discrimination,** on the other hand, involves unfavorable treatment of individuals because of their group membership. Unlike prejudice, which is an attitude and an internal state, discrimination involves overt action or behavior.

Clearly, however, a close relationship frequently exists between prejudice and discrimination. Because they are related, an extensive amount of research has been carried out concerning the nature and causes of prejudice. Attitude surveys conducted since the 1940s have shown a significant decline in antiblack prejudice; increasingly, white Americans have come to support broad principles of racial integration and equal treatment in public accommodations, employment, public transportation, schools, and housing. For example, in 1942, 32 percent agreed that whites and blacks should attend the same schools; by 1982 this figure was 90 percent. In 1944, 45 percent thought that blacks should have as good a chance as whites to get any kind of job, and by 1972, 97 percent agreed. The percentage approving integration in public transportation rose from 46 percent in 1942 to 88 percent in 1970. Moreover, whites have indicated increasing willingness to participate personally in desegregated settings (Schuman, Steeh, and Bobo, 1985). Illustrative is the decline in opposition to residential integration. In 1963 almost half of whites (45 percent) said they would move if black people moved next door, but by 1990 only 5 percent indicated they would (Gallup and Hugick, 1991, p. 27). These changes are a result of two factors. First, they reflect attitude changes among individuals over their lifetimes. Second, younger people generally exhibit less racial prejudice than their elders, and as younger, more tolerant, cohorts have replaced older, more prejudiced ones, overall racial prejudice has declined (Firebaugh and Davis, 1988).

However, the same striking agreement does not appear among Americans on how to combat discrimination or segregation (Jaynes and Williams, 1989). Although today white Americans endorse broad principles of nondiscrimination and desegregation in important areas of American life, they are much less likely to support policies for translating these principles into practice. For example, despite their strong support of the principle of integrated education, the percentage of whites who felt that the federal government should ensure that black and white children attend the same schools declined between the 1960s and the 1980s. Moreover, widespread white opposition was raised to busing as a means of desegregating schools (Schuman, Steeh, and Bobo, 1985).

The substantial gap between people's support for broad principles of equality and their support for specific programs to implement these principles indicates the complexity of racial attitudes. The relationship between prejudicial attitudes and discriminatory behavior is equally complex. Although prejudice is frequently seen as the cause of discrimination, it does not always produce discrimination. An individual can be prejudiced without *acting* in a discriminatory manner. Whether prejudice is expressed in discriminatory *acts* is strongly influenced by the social context in which the prejudice occurs. Discrimination is much more likely to occur in a social environment in which acts of ethnic and racial bias are accepted or not strongly condemned. This principle, which has been established from numerous social psychological studies, was recently underscored in a recent study at Smith College, where in 1989 racial tensions erupted after four black students received anonymous hate messages. Researchers asked students walking across campus how they felt about these incidents. Before the student could answer, a confederate, arriving at precisely the same time, would respond, by either strongly condemning or justifying the incidents. The researchers found that students' opinions were strongly influenced by those expressed by the confederates. Hearing others express strongly anti-racist opinions produced similar sentiments, whereas students who first heard expressions more accepting of racism offered "significantly less strongly anti-racist opinions" (Blanchard, Tilly, and Vaughn, 1991: p. 104). Clearly, the social climate strongly affects whether personal prejudices are translated into discriminatory acts.

Because sociologists are primarily concerned with understanding human behavior, the primary focus in our analysis of racial and ethnic relations is on discrimination, which is the means of preserving the inferior social, economic, and political position of minorities and the power and privileges of the majority. Discrimination can range from mild slights (ethnic jokes and slurs, for instance) to systematic oppression (slavery) to violence (lynching, pogroms, and massacres). We can distinguish two interrelated and mutually reinforcing types of discrimination: attitudinal and institutional.

Attitudinal Discrimination

Attitudinal discrimination refers to discriminatory practices that stem from prejudicial attitudes. The discriminator either is prejudiced or acts in response to the prejudices of others. Attitudinal discrimination is usually direct, overt, blatant, and visible. Despite increasing verbal acceptance by whites of principles of nondiscrimination and racial integration, African Americans especially have been confronted with attitudinal discrimination in virtually every public aspect of their lives. Many of the discriminatory acts encountered by blacks appear inconsequential to white observers—a white couple crossing the street to avoid walking past a black male; a "hate stare;" receiving poor service in restaurants, stores, hotels, or business services. Many whites also trivialize the discrimination resulting from racial slurs and epithets. Incidents of this kind are seldom reported in the press, yet they are demeaning realities to which African Americans of all social classes are consistently exposed (Feagin, 1991).

Much more dramatic incidents of discrimination have been reported in the news media (although many such incidents go unreported). For example, the 1991 brutal beating of Rodney King, a black motorist, by members of the Los Angeles Police Department was captured on videotape, was widely publicized, and drew widespread attention to the vulnerability of blacks to police harassment. Yet the King incident was only one of 15,000 complaints of police brutality filed with the federal government between 1985 and 1991 (Lewis, 1991, p. 1). Moreover, during the 1980s hundreds of incidents of intimidation, harassment, vandalism, and attacks occurred against racial and religious minorities, including more than 200 on college campuses between 1986 and 1988 alone (*Time*, 1987; Ehrlich, 1990; U.S. Commission on Civil Rights, 1990).

In a study involving interviews with blacks from throughout the United States, Feagin found that, despite antidiscrimination legislation and changing white attitudes, even middle-class blacks remain vulnerable targets for discrimination and that incidents of discrimination against them are far from isolated; they are cumulative—that is, a black person's encounters with discrimination are best described as a "lifelong series of such incidents" (Feagin, 1991, p. 109). One informant, a professor at a major university, described the constant tension that these experiences and the anticipation of them created.

> [One problem with] being black in America is that you have to spend so much time thinking about stuff that white people just don't even have to think about. I worry when I get pulled over by a cop. I worry because the person that I live with is a black male, and I have a teen-aged son. I worry what some white cop is going to think when he walks over to our car, because he's holding on to a gun. And I'm very aware of how many black folks accidentally get shot by cops. I worry when I walk into a store, that someone's going to think I'm in there shoplifting. And I have to worry about that because I'm not free to ignore it. And so, that thing that's supposed to be guaranteed to all Americans, the freedom to just be yourself is a fallacious idea. And I get resentful that I have to think about things that a whole lot of people, even my very close white friends whose politics are similar to mine, simply don't have to worry about (Feagin, 1991, p. 114).

Similarly, despite the enactment of antidiscrimination legislation and contrary to white perceptions that discrimination has been eradicated and that minorities receive preferential treatment in hiring, recent studies have demonstrated that African Americans and Hispanics continue to experience discrimination in employment. Pairs of white and black men with identical qualifications applied for 476 jobs advertised in Washington and Chicago newspapers. Whereas 15 percent of the white applicants received job offers, only five percent of the black applicants did. Moreover, white applicants advanced further in the hiring process and in the Washington area were much less likely to report receiving rude, unfavorable, or discouraging treatment than their black counterparts. These findings were similar to an earlier study of the hiring experiences of Hispanics and Anglos in Chicago and San Diego in which whites were three times as likely both to advance farther in the hiring process and to receive job offers as the Hispanic applicants (Turner, Fix, and Struyk, 1991).

Attitudinal discrimination does not always occur in so blatant or so obvious a manner. It can be manifested less dramatically merely by the adherence of members of the dominant group to social definitions of traditional subordinate group roles. Malcolm X, the charismatic black protest leader who was assassinated in 1965, recalled how his well-meaning white high school English teacher, Mr. Ostrowski, was bound by cultural norms concerning the "proper" caste roles for blacks.

> I know that he probably meant well in what he happened to advise me that day. I doubt that he meant any harm. . . . I was one of his top students, one of the school's top students—but all he could see for me was the kind of future "in your place" that almost all white people see for black people. . . . He told me, "Malcolm, you ought to be thinking about a career. Have you been giving it thought?" . . . The truth is, I hadn't. I never have figured out why I told him, "Well, yes, sir, I've been thinking I'd like to be a lawyer." Lansing certainly had no Negro lawyers—or doctors either—in those days, to hold up an image I might have aspired to. All I really knew for certain was that a lawyer didn't wash dishes, as I was doing.
>
> Mr. Ostrowski looked surprised, I remember, and leaned back in his chair and clasped his hands behind his head. He kind of half-smiled and said, "Malcolm, one of life's first needs is for us to be realistic. Don't misunderstand me, now. We all here like you, you know that. But you've got to be realistic about being a nigger. A lawyer—that's no realistic goal for a nigger. You need to think about something you can be. You're good with your hands—making things. Everybody admires your carpentry shop work. Why don't you plan on carpentry? People like you as a person—you'd get all kinds of work" (Malcolm X, 1966, p. 36).

Institutional Discrimination

Institutional discrimination, on the other hand, refers to rules, policies, practices, and laws that appear to be race- (or gender-) -neutral but have a discriminatory effect on minorities. Unlike attitudinal discrimination, institutional discrimination is not intentional or a consequence of prejudice, but it still has a disproportionately adverse impact on a minority group. Therefore, institutional discrimination is usually much more subtle, more complex, and less readily visible than attitudinal discrimination. Because it does not result from the motivations or intentions of specific individuals, but rather from policies that appear race-neutral, institutional discrimination is more impersonal than attitudinal discrimination, and its effects are more easily denied, ignored, or overlooked. (See the "Sociology in the News" box for an example of institutional discrimination in the severity of Minnesota's drug laws).

Institutional discrimination is central to one of the most controversial interpretations of recent American race relations. In *The Declining Significance of Race* (1978) and *The Truly Disadvantaged* (1987), William J. Wilson argued that in the past, attitudinal discrimination was the major factor responsible for the unequal economic, political, and social status of African Americans. He acknowledges that in many areas of American life, such as housing, education, and municipal politics, attitudinal discrimination is still pervasive and serves as a barrier to black participation in the mainstream of American society today.

However, Wilson contends that the overall economic position of urban blacks has recently deteriorated not only because of instances of attitudinal discrimination such as those cited above; it has also occurred because of impersonal economic changes that have little to do with race. These include "the shift from goods-producing to service-producing industries, the increasing polarization of the labor market into low-wage and high-wage sectors, technological innovations, and the relocation of manufacturing industries out of the central cities" (Wilson, 1987, p. 39). Relatively unskilled blacks concentrated in the nation's central cities are especially vulnerable to the relocation of manufacturing jobs that in the past provided economic opportunities for several generations of relatively unskilled workers—native and foreign, black and white. The economic opportunities of the African-American underclass, who lack the educational and occupational skills necessary for the highly technological jobs being created in the cities today, are therefore rapidly diminishing.

Although the African-American underclass's lack of educational and occupational skills reflect a legacy of historic attitudinal discrimination, institutional factors—the broad structural changes in the economy mentioned above—play a crucial role in sustaining black economic inequality. Even if all racial prejudice were eliminated, the African-American underclass would still lack the necessary qualifications to participate in the mainstream of the economy and would continue to be found primarily in the unskilled sector where unemployment is extremely high and wages very low. In other words, in the economic sphere institutional discrimination has become an important source of continuing African-American inequalities.

Institutional discrimination is thus more subtle, more complex, and less visible than attitudinal discrimination. Because it does not result from the motivations or intentions of specific individuals, it is more impersonal than attitudinal discrimination. Nevertheless, it has the same discriminatory consequences for minority group members. In examining institutional discrimination, therefore, we must consider the *effect* of a particular policy or practice upon a minority group rather than the motivations of the majority group.

Patterns of Racial and Ethnic Relations

The efforts of dominant groups to create and maintain their positions of power have been expressed in many different patterns of racial and ethnic relations, ranging from violent conflict to peaceful coexistence. The following discussion reviews the range of patterns of racial and ethnic relations. The patterns are not mutually exclusive; a majority group may adopt more than one of these policies at the same time or at different times. For example, as our discussion of Indian–white relations indicated, Native Americans at different times have been subjected to policies ranging from extermination to expulsion to forced assimilation.

Extermination

The most repressive and destructive dominant-group pattern of majority/minority relations is **extermination,** or **genocide,** which denies the subordinate group's very right to live. According to William O'Brien, genocide refers to actions intended "to destroy, in whole or in part, a national, ethnic, racial, or religious group." His definition includes:

> (a) killing members of the group; (b) causing serious bodily or mental harm to members of the group; (c) deliberately inflicting on the group conditions of life calculated to bring about its physical destruction . . . ; (d) imposing measures intended to prevent births within the group; (e) forcibly transferring children of the group to another group (cited in O'Brien, 1968, p. 516).

Although examples of genocide are not confined to the twentieth century, some of the most notorious examples have occurred relatively recently in human history. In 1915 1.5 million Armenians were massacred by the Turks. Between 1935 and 1945 the Nazis exterminated more than 6 million Jews and other "non-Aryan" groups (such as Gypsies). In the small African country of Burundi more than 100,000 minority Hutu (about 3.5 percent of the population) were murdered by the dominant

Sociology in the News

Institutional Discrimination in the War on Drugs

If all racial prejudice were suddenly and miraculously eliminated from the hearts and minds of Americans, would racial discrimination disappear as well? If discrimination is invariably rooted in prejudice, the answer would be yes. However, if we adopt the perspective that institutional discrimination plays a crucial role in maintaining racial inequalities in American society, then the answer is no.

Institutional discrimination refers to rules, policies, practices, and laws that appear to be race- (or gender-) neutral but have discriminatory effects on minorities. A recent controversial ruling by Judge Pamela Alexander of Minnesota's Hennepin County District Court provides an excellent example of institutional discrimination in the nation's war on drugs. Judge Alexander ruled unconstitutional a Minnesota law that punished the possession of crack more severely than comparable amounts of powdered cocaine. Similar laws calling for stiffer penalties for crack possession than cocaine possession have been passed or are pending in more than half of the 50 states.

The case involved five black defendants charged with possession of crack, a crime punishable by a four-year jail term for first-time offenders. On the other hand, the sentence for conviction of possession of the same amount of cocaine was simply probation. Testimony in the case indicated that crack is used mainly by blacks, while whites are much more likely to use cocaine. At issue was whether the difference in the severity of the sentences for possession of the two illicit drugs was justified. The Minnesota legislature had enacted the crack possession law in 1989 only after hearing considerable anecdotal testimony that crack was more addictive and harmful than cocaine. However, Judge Alexander maintained that there was insufficient scientific evidence on the effects of the two drugs to justify the disparity in the penalties for their possession. Although there was general agreement that the Minnesota legislature had enacted the penalties for the two crimes without any intent of targeting a specific minority group, Judge Alexander contended that the absence of racial prejudice or negative intent in the law's enactment was less relevant in considering the constitutionality of the crack law than whether it affected blacks disproportionately. "There had better be a good reason for any law that has the practical effect of disproportionately punishing members of one racial group. If crack was significantly more deadly or harmful than cocaine, that might be a good enough reason. But there just isn't enough evidence that they're different enough to justify the radical difference in penalties."

LONDON, ROBB. "Judge's Overruling of Crack Law Brings Turmoil," *The New York Times*, January 11, 1991, p. B9.

Tutsi people in 1972, and in 1988 another 5000 to 20,000 were killed. (Refer to the Cross-National box: "Ethnic Conflict in Africa" for further discussion of this topic.)

Since genocide violates the sanctity of human life, an ideology of racism is often developed to justify genocidal actions. **Racism** involves a belief in the inherent superiority of one racial group and the inherent inferiority of others. Its primary function is to provide a set of ideas and beliefs that can be used to explain, rationalize, and justify a system of racial domination. By denying that a racial minority has human qualities or by depicting it as subhuman or destructive of human values and life, the minority's extermination is made morally justifiable and acceptable. For example, in 1876 an Australian writer defended efforts to annihilate the native people of New Zealand (Maoris), Australia, and Tasmania: "When exterminating the inferior Australian and Maori races . . . the world is better for it. . . . [By] protecting the propogation of the imprudent, the diseased, the defective, the criminal . . . we tend to destroy the human race" (quoted in Hartwig, 1972, p. 16).

Expulsion and Exclusion

The objective of extermination is to reduce or eliminate contact between majority and minority, and to create an ethnically (or racially) homogeneous society. A similar rationale underlies the process of **expulsion,** that is, the ejection of a minority group from areas controlled by the dominant group. Expulsion can be of two types: direct and indirect (Simpson and Yinger, 1985, pp. 19–20). **Direct expulsion** occurs when minorities are forcibly ejected by the dominant majority, often through military or other governmental force. The policy of direct expulsion was at no time more pronounced in American history than during the nineteenth century, when thousands of American Indians were removed from the East to areas beyond the Mississippi River. During World War II, 110,000 Japanese Americans, most of them United States citizens, were forcibly removed from their homes and placed in detention camps in remote areas of the country.

Indirect expulsion occurs when harassment, discrimination, and persecution of a minority becomes so intense that members "voluntarily" choose to emigrate. Harassment and persecution of minorities, particularly religious minorities, led many groups to seek refuge in the United States. Persecuted Protestant sects were among the earliest European immigrants to the American colonies, and the tradition of the United States as an asylum for the oppressed has continued into the present. Since the early Christian era, Jews periodically have been forced—either directly

Cross-National Perspectives

Ethnic Conflict in Africa

Ethnic conflict and violence are not restricted to Western countries. During the past quarter century there have been several violent intertribal conflicts in Africa. In the process, thousands have died and many thousands more have been forced to flee their homes, creating in Africa one of the world's largest refugee populations. In Nigeria, conflict among Yoruba, Ibo, and Hausa tribes resulted in a bloody civil war that, between 1968 and 1970, cost a million lives. In Uganda, dictator Idi Amin slaughtered more than 100,000 Ugandans, mostly members of the Baganda, Langi, and Acholi tribes. Today ethnic divisions still create conflicts in many African countries, including Ethiopia, the Sudan, Benin, Ivory Coast, and Angola. While many Westerners have been aware of these conflicts, most know nothing about the severe violence and killing in the tiny east African country of Burundi, which in the past twenty years has experienced one of the largest massacres since the atrocities of Nazi Germany (Lemarchand, 1975).

Burundi is a landlocked country of central Africa, situated between the republics of Zaire and Tanzania. During its colonial period, which ended in 1962, Burundi was controlled by the Belgians. As in several other African countries, independence from European colonialism brought deep-rooted and long-repressed tribal rivalries to the surface. In 1972 a wave of violence swept the country. An estimated 100,000 people were killed, or 3.5 percent of the total population. A comparable annihilation of the American population would have resulted in the deaths of about 8 million people.

The violence in Burundi reflects the rivalry of the country's two major ethnic groups: the Tutsi and the Hutu. The Tutsi, a tall and slender people, make up only about 15 percent of Burundi's population. For centuries before the arrival of European colonial powers, the Tutsi had held the Hutu, a people of smaller stature, in a form of serfdom. During the colonial period the Belgians supported the social divisions of a Tutsi aristocracy and a Hutu servant class. When independence was achieved in 1962, many Hutu were hopeful that, since they represented 85 percent of the population, the promise of majority rule would bring an end to Tutsi domination. However, Hutu frustration grew in the years following independence as the more politically astute Tutsi effectively blocked Hutu efforts to change the status quo.

In 1972 small bands of Hutu revolted against Tutsi rule. They killed and mutilated any Tutsi they could find, including women and children, as well as any Hutu who refused to join them. The Tutsi-dominated government of Burundi responded with a wave of counterviolence. In many villages all Hutu of any wealth, community influence, or educational level above grade school were systematically shot or beaten to death. The killing was selective, aimed at all influential Hutu. The objective of the annihilation of the Hutu elites was to crush any Hutu threat to Tutsi power. The Tutsi sought to eliminate "not only the rebellion but Hutu society as well, and in the process lay the foundation of an entirely new social order" (Lemarchand, 1975).

This wave of genocide ensured Tutsi political and economic power in Burundi and led to the systematic exclusion of Hutu from the army, civil service, the university, and high schools. In 1988 the long-simmering tension between these two groups flared once again into violent conflict. At least 5000 more people were killed in another Hutu uprising and the Tutsi reprisal that followed, and more than 50,000 Hutu fled to the neighboring country of Rwanda, where Hutu are the tribal majority (Brooke, 1988; Perlez, 1988). The conflict between Tutsi and Hutu is but one example of how ethnic and racial hatreds continue to produce bloodshed and violence throughout the modern world.

BROOKE, JAMES. "In Africa, Tribal Hatreds Defy the Borders of State." *New York Times*, August 28, 1988.
LEMARCHAND, RENE. "Ethnic Genocide." *Society* 12, 1975.
PERLEZ, JANE. "Burundi's Army May Have Inflamed a Deadly Tribal Revenge Born in Fear." *New York Times*, August 29, 1988.

or indirectly—to leave the lands in which they have settled. The most dramatic emigration in modern Jewish history occurred in the late nineteenth and early twentieth century when millions (more than one-third of all Eastern European Jews) fled czarist Russia. Recently the persecution of Jews has revived in the Soviet Union and other former Soviet-bloc countries in Eastern Europe, forcing Jews by the thousands to seek refuge in other countries.

Several noted instances of expulsion have occurred throughout the world in the past decade. In 1989 more than 310,000 Bulgarians of Turkish descent (of a Bulgarian Turkish community estimated at between

900,000 and 1.5 million), whose ancestors had lived in Bulgaria for generations, fled to Turkey (Haberman, 1989). Similarly, at the end of the 1991 Middle East war, an estimated two million Kurds from northern Iraq fled to Iran and Turkey to escape Iraqi violence and terror. Turkish officials interpreted the massive exodus as a result of Iraqi leader Saddam Hussein's longstanding effort to empty Iraq of this troublesome minority (Haberman, 1991). In 1983 Nigeria expelled about two million immigrants from the neighboring countries of Ghana, Cameroon, Benin, Chad, and Niger. In 1985 another 700,000 people were forced to leave (*The Economist*, 1985). In Israel, Meir Kahane, a U.S.-born rabbi, gained considerable political support for his proposal to resolve Arab-Jewish tensions in that country by forcibly removing all Arabs from Israel and its occupied territories and making Israel into an exclusively Jewish state (Friedman, 1985).

Achieving or retaining ethnic homogeneity is also attained when a host society refuses to permit another group entrance because that group is perceived as a threat to the society's basic social institutions. When countries have policies that refuse to admit culturally different groups it is called **exclusion.** As we noted earlier, between 1917 and 1965 American immigration policy was based on the assumption that immigration from southern and eastern Europe and Asia should be substantially or completely restricted. This assumption was embodied in the 1924 immigration legislation, which established numerical quotas for each nation. More than four-fifths of the quotas were assigned to those nations of northern and western Europe whose ethnic characteristics most closely coincided with those of the "original" settlers of the country. Although Great Britain had an admissions quota exceeding 65,000, Italy was allocated less than 6000, and Hungary, less than 1000. Asians were almost completely excluded. This policy remained virtually intact until its repeal in 1965.

Oppression

Oppression involves the exploitation of a minority group by excluding it from equal participation in a society (Turner, Singleton, and Musick, 1984, pp. 1–2). Oppression "depends on exclusiveness rather than exclusion" (Bonacich, 1972, p. 555). Unlike extermination, expulsion, or exclusion, a system of oppression accepts the existence of minorities but subjugates them and confines them to inferior social positions. The majority group uses its power to maintain its access to scarce and valued resources in a system of social inequality.

Slavery, in which the slave's labor was a valuable resource exploited by the slave owner, was an example of oppression in American society. Even after slavery was legally abolished, the Jim Crow system of racial segregation that ensued was organized to exploit blacks for the benefit of the dominant whites. After taking a tour of the South at the turn of the century, a journalist remarked upon the exploitative nature of black/white relations:

> One of the things I saw in the South—and I saw it everywhere—was the way in which the people were torn between their feelings of race prejudice and their downright economic needs. Hating and fearing the Negro as a race (though often loving individual Negroes), they yet want him to work for them; they can't get along without him. In one impulse a community will rise to mob Negroes or to drive them out of the country because of Negro crime or Negro vagrancy, or because the Negro is becoming educated, acquiring property and "getting out of his place;" and in the next impulse laws are passed or other remarkable measures taken to keep him at work—because the South can't get along without him (Baker, 1964, p. 81).

A classic contemporary example of oppression is the South African system of **apartheid,** or "separate development," which has functioned to maintain the privileged position of whites, who have enjoyed one of the highest standards of living in the world but who represent only 15 percent of the country's population. On the other hand, South African blacks, who comprise more than two-thirds (69 percent) of the population, have been excluded from genuine participation in the nation's political system and have been legally confined to rural reserves, or "homelands," that represent only 13 percent of the land. However, black labor has provided a cheap labor supply for South African mines, farms, manufacturing, and domestic help that is essential to the South African economy and the system of white privilege. Therefore, the entire system of state controls restricting black political power, residence, and education has been designed to perpetuate the system of white privilege (Cohen, 1986).

Assimilation

In general, the majority group's response to ethnic minorities in America has been to seek their assimilation. **Assimilation** involves efforts to integrate or incorporate a group into the mainstream of a society. As with other majority group policies previously discussed, the objective of assimilation is a homogeneous society. In American society two distinct conceptions of assimilation have existed: Anglo-conformity and the melting pot.

Anglo-Conformity. The principal assimilationist model in the American experience has emphasized conformity by minority groups to dominant-group standards. In the United States this has been termed *Anglo-conformity*. **Anglo-conformity** assumes that ethnic minorities should give up their distinctive characteristics and adopt those of the dominant group (Cole and Cole, 1954). It can be expressed by the formula A + B + C = A, in which A is the dominant group and B and C represent ethnic minority groups that must conform to the values and life-styles of the dominant group if they want to achieve positions of importance and prestige in the society (Newman, 1973, p. 53).

A policy of Anglo-conformity not only seeks a homogeneous society organized around the idealized cultural standards, institutions, and language of the dominant group; it also assumes the inferiority of the cultures of other ethnic groups. Many Americans retain vivid and painful recollections of the ridicule of their cultural ways and the pressures for them to become "Americanized." Many tried to rid themselves of their traditional beliefs and practices. A daughter of Slovenian immigrant parents recalls her childhood:

> In the 9th grade, a boy said to me, "You talk funny." I wondered what he meant. I listened to my friends, and I did not think they "talked funny." Then, that great American experiment, the public high school, opened my ears. I heard the English language spoken as I had never heard it spoken. . . . I began to hear that I did indeed pronounce my words differently, and so did my friends. I practiced [English] in secret, in the bathroom, of course, until I could pronounce properly the difficult "th" sound, which seemed the most distinctive and, therefore, the most necessary to conquer. How superior I felt when I had mastered this sound . . . ! Alas, however, I refused to speak Slovenian (Prosen, 1976, pp. 2–3).

The Melting Pot.   Like Anglo-conformity, the ultimate objective of a melting pot policy is a society without ethnic differences. More tolerant than a policy of Anglo-conformity, the **melting pot** sees ethnic differences as being lost in the creation of a new society and a new people—a synthesis unique and distinct from any of the different groups that formed it. Unlike Anglo-conformity, none of the contributing groups is considered to be superior; each is considered to have contributed the best of its cultural heritage to the creation of something new. The melting pot ideal can be expressed by the formula A + B + C = D, in which A, B, and C represent the different contributing groups and D is the product of their synthesis (Newman, 1973, p. 63). As Ralph Waldo Emerson expressed it in the mid-nineteenth century:

> . . . in this continent—asylum of all nations—the energy of Irish, Germans, Swedes, Poles, and Cossacks, and all the European tribes—of the Africans, and of the Polynesians—will construct a new race, a new religion, a new state, a new literature . . . (quoted in Gordon, 1964, p. 11).

Cultural Assimilation and Structural Assimilation. To what extent has ethnic assimilation actually occurred in American society? Milton Gordon (1964) pointed out that assimilation is not a single phenomenon but involves several processes. The two most important of these are cultural assimilation and structural assimilation. Most of the previous discussion has concerned cultural assimilation, or **acculturation**—that is, the acquisition of the *cultural* characteristics of the dominant group, including its values, beliefs, language, and behaviors. But many ethnic groups have become fully acculturated to the dominant American culture and still have not been able to achieve full *social* participation in the society. Sharing the same language, norms, and culture does not ensure access to informal social organizations, clubs, cliques, and friendship groups.

Structural assimilation occurs when there is social interaction among individuals of different ethnic backgrounds. Two types can be distinguished: secondary and primary. Secondary structural assimilation refers to the ethnic integration of social situations characterized by impersonal secondary relationships: jobs, schools, political organizations, neighborhoods, and public recreation. However, even sharing membership in such secondary groups does not necessarily involve primary-group associations—informal social organizations, friendships, and, ultimately, intermarriage. Primary structural assimilation is achieved when these kinds of interethnic associations occur.

Considerable research has recently focused on measuring rates of assimilation among different U.S. racial and ethnic groups who have been compared in terms of educational attainment, income levels, occupational characteristics, residential distribution, and intermarriage (Hirschman and Wong, 1981). These data show that, overall, European ethnic groups and Asians have experienced considerable socioeconomic, educational, residential, and marital assimilation in American society. However, these patterns of assimilation are not duplicated among Hispanics, American Indians, and African Americans (Yetman, 1991).

Pluralism/Separatism

Pluralism refers to a system in which different cultures can coexist and be preserved. According to this notion, the strength and vitality of American society is derived from its ethnic diversity. Belonging to a "nation of nations," each group should be permitted to retain its unique qualities while affirming its allegiance to American society. This ideal can be expressed by the equation $A + B + C = A + B + C$, in which A, B, and C are each ethnic groups that maintain their distinctiveness over time (Newman, 1973, p. 67).

Pluralism is more tolerant of diversity than any of the policies we have previously considered, for it implies recognition of cultural equality among ethnic groups, not the superiority of one. It accepts and encourages—even celebrates—cultural differences but generally assumes that different ethnic groups will coexist within a common political and economic framework. As we point out in chapter 16, American religion has consistently been characterized by denominational pluralism, in which more than 1200 different religious organizations coexist. Members of most religious groups participate in the political and economic life of the country.

However, a number of groups, many of them religious—such as the Amish, the Hutterites, or Hasidic Jews—have sought to preserve their cultural identity by remaining both socially and geographically separate from the rest of the society. Groups who, in addition to retaining their cultural distinctiveness, refrain from extensive participation in the political, economic, and social life of the broader society in order to maintain their own subsocieties are examples of *separatism*, or self-segregation, which differs from pluralism primarily in the degree of geographic and social separation it emphasizes.

In the American experience pluralism and separatism have seldom been advocated by the majority; the primary advocates of each stance have been minority spokespersons. The basic difference between a policy of separatism and one of exclusion is that under separatism the minority is relatively autonomous and may voluntarily choose to place itself apart, whereas under a policy of exclusion the separation is dictated by the majority group. Under separatism the majority does not require separation of ethnic, religious, or racial groups; it simply permits it.

Minority-Group Responses to Dominant Group Pressures

How do minorities experience and respond to demands of the dominant group? The previous discussion has emphasized the role of the dominant group in setting the limits within which minority groups may function. Minorities, however, are not simply passive recipients of dominant-group policies; they actively respond in a variety of ways to majority pressures for subordination.

Sociologists have distinguished three broad and general categories of minority-group responses: acceptance, resistance, and avoidance. Acceptance involves the minority's moving toward the majority. Avoidance and resistance involve a rejection of, or moving away from, the majority. Depending on the situation, individual or group responses may change from one of these responses to another.

Acceptance/Acquiescence

A minority may accept the dominant group's definition of its subordinate status. Given the majority's superior power, acquiescence may be necessary for survival. The Southern caste system was for many years relatively stable because most blacks, at least on the surface, accepted the elaborate system of racial etiquette and segregation. The most severe violence against blacks—lynchings and terrorism—was committed when blacks made, or whites perceived them to have made, an effort to reject the traditional subordinate roles ascribed to them. Alvin Poussaint, a prominent African American psychiatrist, graphically recounted how he was forced to accept the traditional role of black submissiveness and deference toward whites.

> Once last year [1967] as I was leaving my office in Jackson, Miss. with my Negro secretary, a white policeman yelled, "Hey, boy! Come here!" Somewhat bothered, I retorted: "I'm no boy!" He then rushed at me, inflamed, and stood towering over me, snorting, "What d'ja say, boy?" Quickly he frisked me and demanded, "What's your name, boy?" Frightened, I replied, "Dr. Poussaint. I'm a physician." He angrily chuckled and hissed, "What's your first name, boy?" When I hesitated he assumed a threatening stance and clenched his fists. As my heart palpitated, I muttered in profound humiliation, "Alvin."

> He continued his psychological brutality, bellowing, "Alvin, the next time I call you, you come right away, you hear? You hear?" I hesitated. "You hear me, boy?" My voice trembling with helplessness, but following my instincts of self-preservation, I murmured, "Yes, sir." Now fully satisfied that I had performed and acquiesced to my "boy status," he dismissed me with, "Now, boy, go on and get out of here or next time we'll take you for a little ride down to the station house!" (Poussaint, 1971, p. 349).

The Southern caste system placed African Americans in a position of permanent subservience. Most European ethnic groups, however, were not so rigidly proscribed from seeking equal status with "native" whites. Nevertheless, the pressures of Anglo-conformity frequently led ethnic minorities to accept dominant-group standards. These standards included degrading perceptions of their own cultures, which caused them to feel ambivalent about their background and sometimes to reject it. The son of Italian immigrant parents describes his childhood in the following way:

> I enter the parochial school with an awful fear that I will be called Wop. . . . I begin to loathe my heritage. . . .

I am nervous when I bring friends to my house; the place looks so Italian. Here hangs a picture of Victor Emmanuel and over there is one of the cathedrals of Milan, and next to it, one of St. Peter's, and on the buffet stands a wine-pitcher of medieval design; it's forever brimming, forever red and brilliant with wine. These things are heirlooms belonging to my father, and no matter who may come to our house, he likes to stand under them and brag.

So I begin to shout at him. I tell him to cut out being a Wop and be an American once in a while. Immediately he gets his razor-strap and whales hell out of me, clouting me from room to room and finally out the back door. I go into the woodshed and pull down my pants and stretch my neck to examine the blue slices across my rump. A Wop! That's what my father is. Nowhere is there an American father who beats his son this way (Fante, 1966, pp. 391–394).

Some minority-group members have shown a willingness to lose their ethnic identity and adopt the characteristics of the majority group. The eagerness and intensity with which assimilation was sought are exemplified in Abraham Cahan's classic novel of immigrant adjustment, *The Rise of David Levinsky*. To enhance his ability to function in American society, Levinsky, a Russian Jewish immigrant, enrolls in an evening English class, where his teacher becomes one of his first American role models.

At first I did not like him. Yet I would hang on his lips, striving to memorize every English word I could catch and watching intently, not only his enunciation, but also his gestures, manners, and mannerisms, and accepting it all as part and parcel of the American way of speaking. . . . If I heard a bit of business rhetoric that I thought effective I would jot it down and commit it to memory. In like manner I would write down every new piece of slang, the use of the latest popular phrase being, as I thought, helpful in making oneself popular with Americans . . . (Cahan, 1917/1966, pp. 129, 292–293).

Resistance/Confrontation

Some minority-group members respond to majority-group pressures by refusing to accept majority-group definitions of their status. Resistance may include boycotts, strikes, legal action, political activity, nonviolent mass protest, and violence. Each of these techniques has been used by American minority groups to achieve greater equality in American life.

Despite murder, lynching, terrorism, and harassment—the tactics whites have used to enforce black subordination—black Americans have an enduring tradition of resistance to the caste system and discrimination. This spirit of resistance is typified by the following account by Fred Shuttlesworth, an African-American minister and leader of efforts to end racial segregation in Birmingham, Alabama, during the late 1950s and the

1960s. Shuttlesworth barely escaped death when his house was demolished by more than a dozen sticks of dynamite. Shuttlesworth recalls the experience:

> That house was about fifty years old, all that black dust and stuff, dynamite smoke and stuff, and I came out. On the way from around the back of the house, this Klans—this policeman who was a Klansman—said to me, . . . I think it shook him, he said, "I know some people. I know some people in the Klan. They're really after you." He said, "If I was you I'd get outa town as quick as I could."

> I said, "Well, you tell them that I'm not going out of town." I said, "You see all this I've come through?" I said, "If God could save me through this, then I'm gon' stay here and clear up this." I said, "I wasn't saved to run . . ." (quoted in Raines, 1978, p. 166).

Throughout the twentieth century the black protest movement has used the legal process to resist a minority status. Most noteworthy among these was the historic 1954 Supreme Court decision of *Brown* v. *Board of Education,* which declared segregated schools unconstitutional. Bolstered by the knowledge that segregation was unconstitutional, during the Civil Rights Movement of the 1950s and 1960s African Americans used a variety of tactics—public confrontations, boycotts, picketing, and civil disobedience—to bring about social change. Since the 1970s civil rights issues have more frequently been pursued through traditional political channels. Moreover, as Feagin's (1991) study of their responses to public discrimination indicated, today middle-class blacks especially no longer respond with the "deference rituals" expected in the Southern caste system. Instead, utilizing the resources (e.g., money, personal connections, knowledge of the law) that their middle-class status affords them, they vigorously contest, challenge, and confront such discrimination with increasing frequency and effectiveness.

The black protest movement has been instrumental in generating resistance among other racial and ethnic minorities. Although American Indians have for generations resisted pressures for assimilation, they have recently used many of the tactics of direct protest (such as sit-ins) employed by African Americans. Indians are also effectively using the legal system to challenge past and present treaty violations by whites. Resistance among Chicanos increased as well. One of the most dramatic manifestations of increased Chicano militancy was the armed confrontation of the charismatic Reies Tijerina, who advanced claims for millions of acres of Mexican land guaranteed to Mexican-American residents under the 1848 Treaty of Gaudalupe Hidalgo. On another front, Cesar Chavez has led agricultural workers, primarily Mexican Americans, in a struggle to improve their status. Such efforts have made apparent the political impact of the nation's 22 million Hispanics. Given their rapidly increasing numbers, Hispanics have become an important political factor, particularly because of their concentration in such key electoral states as California, New York, Texas, and Florida. Moreover, because Hispanics represent the nation's youngest population group, their political influence is likely to be even greater in the future (Gonzalez, 1991).

Avoidance/Withdrawal

Another response to minority status is avoidance, or withdrawal, in which the minority neither accepts nor resists the dominance of the majority. Rather, they seek to set themselves apart from the majority and to keep contact minimal. Such a stance shields minority group members from prejudice and discrimination by the majority group and enables them to preserve their own culture and social institutions with minimal outside interference.

Throughout the American experience many ethnic groups have tried to avoid the pressures of their minority status by embracing a form of ethnic pluralism or separatism as the most appropriate means of adjusting to American society. The adjustment of the immigrant Irish during the nineteenth century was typical of numerous other ethnic groups. Although the objects of discrimination by Protestant Americans, the Irish avoided much of the hostility directed toward them by creating a society within a society, a separate institutional system centered around the Roman Catholic Church. The institutional system that developed around the church—its schools, hospitals, orphanages, asylums, homes for the aged, charitable and athletic organizations, and informal groups—integrated the Irish community and served to maintain Irish-American solidarity and identity.

The most extreme form of avoidance is **separatism,** in which little, if any, interaction occurs with the majority. The impulse for separatism frequently has been created by conflict with the majority group and a desire to avoid a recurrence of the discrimination or oppression that a group has encountered. In other instances it is based on a resurgence or emergence of ethnic identity and a desire to form social institutions around it. Within the past decade the appeal of separatism has increased dramatically in numerous countries. This has been especially apparent in three eastern European countries—Czechoslovakia, Yugoslavia, and the Soviet Union—where decades of Communist-enforced unity have begun to disintegrate under the pressures for democracy and self-rule of each country's constituent ethnic groups.

The idea of separate ethnic areas or states has been advocated by spokespersons of a number of different ethnic groups in the United

States—by African Americans, American Indians, and German Americans, among others. Moreover, as we noted above, the idea of separatism has long appealed to religious groups seeking to protect their unique identity from the influences of the larger society. Today the value of racial and ethnic separatism is being hotly debated throughout the United States. This is especially apparent in the area of higher education. First, although the Supreme Court's 1954 *Brown* decision ruled that segregated public schools were illegal, enrollments in historically black public universities increased dramatically during the late 1980s and early 1990s. And, as traditionally white campuses have become more ethnically diverse, separate ethnic dormitories, ethnic studies departments, and even separate graduation ceremonies have emerged as ways of responding to the pressures experienced by minority students functioning in a white-dominated society.

Summary

Societies are frequently stratified by ethnic or racial categories. The terms *majority* or *dominant* refer to a group's relative power—its ability to realize its own objectives and interests. A minority group, in contrast, is subordinate to the majority group and is relatively powerless. An ethnic group is identified on the basis of its cultural characteristics. A racial group, on the other hand, is distinguished by its physical characteristics. Both racial and ethnic phenomena are socially defined—that is, the same racial or ethnic group may be perceived and responded to differently in different societies.

The ethnic diversity of the American people was reinforced by the migration of European, African, Asian, and Latin American peoples during the past three and one-half centuries. The greatest period of immigration to the United States occurred between 1820 and 1920. The old immigration, composed of peoples from northern and western Europe, occurred primarily prior to 1895. Immigrants from southern and eastern Europe—the new immigrants—came mainly between 1890 and 1920. Asian immigration, initially from China and Japan and more recently from Korea and Southeast Asia, occurred during the late nineteenth and twentieth centuries. During the second decade of this century, Spanish-speaking peoples began to enter the country in increasing numbers. The largest number of these were Mexican Americans, who entered in substantial numbers prior to the Great Depression of the 1930s and since World War II. Puerto Rican and Cuban migrations are essentially post-World War II phenomena.

African Americans are the largest racial minority in contemporary

American society. Both attitudinal discrimination and institutional discrimination have contributed to black inequality. Despite considerable changes brought about by federal, state, and local laws barring discrimination, African Americans still remain considerably outside the mainstream of American society.

The adaptation of ethnic groups is influenced by both the policies of the majority groups and the characteristics of the minority group. Among the range of majority-group policies toward racial and ethnic minorities, *extermination,* or *genocide,* is the most repressive. *Expulsion* and *exclusion* also aim for an ethnically homogeneous society but do not resort to genocide to achieve their goal. A system of *oppression* accepts the existence of ethnic differences but excludes minorities from full and equal participation in the society. *Assimilation* involves the integration or incorporation of a minority into the mainstream of a society. In the United States this assimilation took either the form of Anglo-conformity, in which there was an insistence upon conformity to the majority's cultural standards, or the form of the melting pot, in which diverse peoples each contributed to the creation of a new culture and society. Finally, *pluralism* and *separatism* involve a system in which different ethnic groups coexist equally and preserve their own cultural characteristics.

Minorities also respond actively and differently to majority policies, and their responses influence their adaptation. *Acceptance* involves acquiescence to the dominant group's definition of their status. *Resistance* may involve direct protest and action. *Avoidance* involves neither acceptance nor resistance; instead, minority people seek to separate themselves from contact with the majority. Its most extreme form is *separatism.*

CRITICAL THINKING

1. What is the difference between an ethnic and a racial group? Give examples to show that the characteristics of each of these types of groups are socially defined.
2. Give examples of majority and minority groups in American society. Does a majority group need to be numerically superior in order to be dominant? Give at least one example to support your ideas.
3. Why is the migration of African Americans from the rural South to the urban North an important demographic trend in American society?
4. Explain how legal decisions have changed the status of African Americans. Have laws produced true equality for African Americans in society? What would?
5. Compare and contrast the experience of Hispanic Americans and Asian Americans with that of African Americans. How do you explain the similarities and differences that you see?
6. Speculate about the impact of the population growth of minority groups on American society. Does an increase in numbers necessarily mean an increase in power? Explain.
7. Give examples of at least three ethnic groups in American society. How do the cultural characteristics of these groups differ? Which ethnic group do you feel is dominant in American society? Why?
8. In what ways are majority and minority groups in our society stereotyped? How do these stereotypes help perpetuate the existing social order?
9. Compare and contrast the power basis of the majority groups in the United States and South Africa.
10. How do dominant groups maintain control of subordinate groups? List the policies explained in this chapter and give an example of each.
11. How do minorities respond and adapt to majority policies?

10 Gender and Age: Stratification and Inequality

We are born either male or female, and, except for a tiny number of people who take the dramatic step of changing their sex, there is little we can do about it. The sex of a person is determined by certain physical characteristics, including the reproduction organs by which the sexes are biologically identified. Age is also a biological characteristic, but unlike sex, which is relatively stable, the process of aging goes on continuously. These two biological characteristics—sex and age—are part of our makeup at all times. What makes sex and age sociologically important is that every social group attaches significance to them.

The term commonly used to indicate that being male or female is socially significant is *gender*. **Gender** can be defined as the social distinctions made between males and females that are used to organize social arrangements and influence social behavior. Gender distinctions are made despite the many similarities between males and females, and the wide variations that can easily be observed within either gender category (Hess and Ferree, 1987).

Age is also used as a basis for organizing social activities and behaviors. Societies are strongly organized on the basis of arbitrary age categories despite the similarities of people in different ages, and the wide variations among people of the same chronological age (Riley et al., 1988).

The organization of societies around gender and age distinctions are of considerable importance because, as the title of this chapter suggests, the result is often one of inequities, or systems of inequality. We have already seen in chapter 8 on social stratification and chapter 9 on race and ethnic groups how inequalities exist in wealth, power, and access to many of society's opportunities. In this chapter we examine how being male or female, or being young or old, leads to different social arrangements and social behaviors. Although these differences do not inevitably lead to negative results, we will see that gender and age distinctions often produce inequalities.

We will begin by considering the positions of males and females, both in American society and in societies around the world. Later in the chapter we will focus on age groups, especially the elderly and the young.

Gender in Different Societies

Three key social dimensions describe the relationship between males and females, and define the position of each gender in a society. These dimensions are power, division of labor, and gender roles (Chafetz, 1991). Power is the ability to impose one's will upon others, even if they resist. Power can exist only when there is a relationship between individuals, between groups, or between classes of people. In this chapter we are interested in the power relationship between sexes—males and females.

Division of labor is also a general sociological term, commonly used to describe how the occupations of a society are specialized so that any individual has only one major occupation or task. When we use the term *division of labor* in connection with *gender,* we refer to the society wide assignment of different work tasks to males and females. We will refer to this as **division of labor by gender.**

Gender roles are the expectations that prevail in a society about the activities and behaviors that may and may not be engaged in by males and females. These expectations are widely understood and produce social pressures such that people feel the need to comply with them. These role expectations are socially learned through the process of socialization.

These three concepts—power, division of labor, and gender roles— are closely related to each other. They also reflect inequalities between different groups of people. With regard to power, obviously if one set of people has power over another, inequality results. With regard to division of labor and gender roles, the inequality is not as immediately obvious, but a closer examination will show how each concept leads to inequality between males and females. We will begin by looking at differences in male and female power in different societies.

Power and Gender

In most societies around the world, males have greater power than females, both in the personal and public spheres. For example, males have generally been the political leaders, historically (e.g., classical Greece, Imperial China, and the Roman Empire) and in contemporary modern societies. There have been a few notable women leaders in recent decades (Great Britain's Margaret Thatcher, the Philippines' Corazon Aquino, the late Golda Meier of Israel, and Indira Gandhi of India), but these women constituted only a tiny percentage of the world's national leaders. The male dominance of political leadership is also the standard among the vast majority of nonliterate societies on which we have ethnographic information.

At the private level the picture is almost identical. In the family, for example, males almost always have greater power than females. Much of the power of males within the family comes directly from a patriarchal tradition. Patriarchy means that a husband or father has unquestioned authority or dominance over other family members. Also, an organization—or, indeed, an entire society—may be based on the principle of patriarchy. In the case of Western societies, including the United States, support for patriarchy can be found prominently in the sacred writings of the Judaic and Christian religious traditions. Although these sources of male power might have diminished somewhat in recent years, their influence has certainly not disappeared.

In non-Western cultures the basis for male power in the family is also found in religious and ideological systems (Bernard, 1987; Giele, 1988, 1977). In the Islamic world males are given ultimate authority, both within their families and in the larger society where they predominate (Mernissi, 1987). Hinduism also gives primary power to males, again both inside the home and in the public world.

Before we examine some explanations as to why males in so many societies have been given more power than females, we should first note that considerable differences exist in the relative power of males from one society to another and in different historical periods. A careful examination of the anthropological record shows that in some societies, under certain economic and cultural conditions, women have power that is at least equal to, and sometimes greater than, that of men (Sanday, 1981; Tanner, 1974; Okonjo, 1976). Furthermore, in some societies where males have formal authority and dominance, females may have informal power.

Among the Mundurucu, who live in the tropical rain forests of South America, men monopolize the formal positions of authority, but the Mundurucu women do not think of themselves as inferior to men. In fact, the Mundurucu men do not think of the women as subordinate to themselves (Sanday, 1981).

In the societies where women have had power that is equal to, or greater than, men, one of two conditions has had to prevail: (1) the economic or historical circumstances make men dependent upon the activities of women; and (2) a long-standing magical or religious association exists between the fertility of women and the general well-being of the social group (Sanday, 1981).

When women in a particular society carry out an activity critically important for the physical survival of the group, they often increase their power. For example, among the African tribe called the !Kung, who live in the Kalahari Desert, food supplies depend upon hunting animals and gathering vegetation from the "bush." The !Kung women do the gathering, which requires that they go far out in the bush. From this activity alone they provide between 60 percent and 80 percent of the tribe's food. But the women do more than gather food; while out in the bush, they watch for signs of animals. Although the women do not hunt the animals themselves, they report their findings to the men who do the actual hunting. The contribution of the !Kung women is obviously great, and their power in tribal decision-making is equally great. The !Kung society is essentially egalitarian, as are other societies where the economic contribution of women is significant compared to that of men (Draper, 1975; Sanday, 1981).

A cross-national study of 111 contemporary societies confirms anthropological studies showing the importance of women's economic contributions (South, 1988). This study shows that the more that women participate in the labor force, the less males are able to exercise power over them. Specifically, men are less able to restrict women to traditional roles (early marriage, high fertility, and illiteracy) if women participate in the labor force (South, 1988).

Similar conclusions about the importance of women's economic contributions have been reached by studying families in the United States. For example, if we take husbands' helping with the housework as an indication of greater female power, some studies show that higher income from the wives is related to greater contributions by the husbands. A sample of couples in which the wives were college and university administrators showed that the higher the wives' incomes, the more likely it was that their husbands would share in family tasks (Bird et al., 1984). Two major studies using national random samples of adults have supported the same conclusion. As a woman's income increases relative to her husband's income, his share of the household work increases (Huber, 1986; Ross et al., 1983).

In the *public* sphere, however, there are only limited indications that women gain very much public or political power in societies where they make greater economic contributions. American women, for example, are contributing greatly in the economic realm, but, as we will see later in this chapter, their positions of power in the political or economic realms are still very limited.

In addition to the power that women may gain from their economic contributions, a second suggested basis of power for women is connected with religions or magic systems. Cross-cultural studies have shown that when religions or magic systems give prominence to women as the producers of life, they are also likely to have greater power. In many such societies the childbearing ability of women is closely associated with the fertility of the soil (Sanday, 1981). In West Africa, where such a view of women prevails, the women say, "Whether the male chief is big or small . . . what matters is that he was given birth by a woman" (Sanday, 1981, p. 115). The women may also express this power by action:

> Such women protest a chief's action by treating him like a child. They either rely on shame or ridicule to get their way or, if pushed to an extreme, will march scantily clad with bared breasts while men stand by in a state of embarrassed silence and passivity, as if they had been overcome by a superior military force (Sanday, 1981, p. 115).

A male in this case holds the political position of chief, but, despite this formal position of power, women exercise influence over him and other men. According to anthropologists, this occurs in a number of societies where women are portrayed positively in the magical or religious systems (Sanday, 1981).

The Iroquois tribe in North America provides an historical illustration of this point. The Iroquois believed the earth belonged to women, and they highly valued the fertility of the soil, for which the women were responsible (Sanday, 1981). As a result, the Iroquois women had considerable power in village and tribal decision-making (Wallace, 1969).

Despite the existence of societies in which women exercise power at least equal to that of men, in the overwhelming majority of societies males have had dominance over females.

Therefore, the question that needs to be addressed is, Why do males so often have greater power than females?

The oldest and most frequently used explanation for the greater power and prestige of males is biological (Goldberg, 1973). Contemporary sociobiologists argue that males evolved as the hunters and food providers, while females evolved as specialists in having and caring for babies and in taking care of the home (Tiger, 1969). The related assumption is that the male activities are more important, and thus they receive greater power and prestige. One major flaw in this argument is that it is not supported by the facts we have about food sources in hunting and gathering societies. In the hundreds of thousands of years before the development of agriculture, humans had to get their food by hunting animals and gathering edible vegetation. We know from contemporary hunting and gathering societies that women typically get most of the food (just as we saw in the case of the !Kung above). If preagricultural hunting and gathering societies were at all similar, it is hard to see how females could have been genetically programmed to leave the "breadwinning" activities exclusively to males (Collins, 1988).

One of the early economic theories of male domination goes back to the work of Friedrich Engels (1884/1972). The key to most economic explanations of male dominance lies not in who does the work, but in who controls the means of production (e.g., land, tools, machines). Contemporary scholars who advance the economic hypothesis point out that the power of women has usually been less in agrarian societies where women have not typically been the owners of the land (Blumberg, 1984). Women's power is especially low in societies where the inheritance system passes land from fathers to sons and where, at marriage, a woman must leave her home and live in her husband's family residence.

Division of Labor by Gender

In societies around the world, men and women are usually assigned different work tasks, which is another way of saying that labor is typically divided by gender. Exactly why a division of labor is so commonplace is a matter of considerable discussion. Some argue that certain tasks are assigned to men because of their greater physical strength. Whatever the validity of this explanation, it cannot account for all differences in gender-related work. An analysis of 50 types of work in 186 societies identified only two tasks invariably assigned to men: (1) the hunting and butchering of large animals, and (2) the processing of hard and tough materials, such as mining and quarrying rocks and minerals, smelting metal ores, and doing metalwork (Murdock and Provost, 1973). Women, on the other hand, were most likely to be responsible for grinding grain, carrying water, and cooking. At first glance, it would appear that this division of labor is based purely on physical strength, but carrying water—a woman's task—requires considerable physical strength. Furthermore, women in many societies carry heavy loads including—in addition to water—firewood, food, and various other products. According to reports, African women, who often carry heavy loads by balancing them on their heads, can carry as much as 70 percent of their body weight. This means that a woman weighing 140 pounds could carry nearly 100 pounds on her head (Rensberger, 1986).

In addition, there are more societies in which women are responsible for erecting and dismantling shelters than there are societies in which men have this responsibility. Women are responsible just as often as men for preparing the soil and planting seed, as well as for tending and harvesting crops (Murdock, 1937).

Evelyn Reed (1971) has argued that when agriculture was done primarily with a digging stick, this task was left most often to women. With the taming of animals and the development of the plow, agriculture was taken over by men. But farming done with a digging stick must have been just as backbreaking as farming done with draft animals and the plow. Physical strength alone, therefore, does not account for variations in the division of labor by gender.

Some scholars have suggested that differences in male and female work may reflect a desire, especially by men, to establish a clear male identity. Many people define themselves as male or female on the basis of what they do. For females, childbearing (and nursing) is unarguably their exclusive responsibility: "Perhaps because women have ways of signaling their womanhood, men must have ways to display their manhood" (Sanday, 1981, p. 78). From this point of view, men in all societies must have a way of demonstrating maleness in an activity prohibited to females. One activity frequently reserved for males is fighting battles and waging wars (Collins, 1988). There is an ironic symmetry in this idea: women are responsible for producing life, while men are responsible for taking life (Sanday, 1981). Even in contemporary U.S. society where women are widely used in the military, they have been prohibited by law from actually engaging in combat.

Gender Roles in Three New Guinea Societies

The well-known studies by anthropologist Margaret Mead (1935) provide vivid support for the argument that the gender-role differences familiar to us are not universal. Mead studied three separate tribes in New Guinea that happened to have dramatic differences in their gender roles. She lived first with the Arapesh, a society in which both the males and the females generally had characteristics and behaviors that we would associate with the feminine role. Both sexes among the Arapesh were passive, gentle, unaggressive, and emotionally responsive to the needs of others.

In contrast, Mead found that in another New Guinea group, the Mundugumor, both the males and the females were characteristically aggressive, suspicious, and, from a Westerner's view, excessively heartless and cruel, especially toward children. The striking feature of these two cultures is that males and females were expected to be very alike, and they were.

Mead then studied a third New Guinea tribe, the Tchambuli. In this group, the gender roles of the males and females were almost exactly reversed from the roles traditionally assigned to males and females in Western society. Mead reported in her autobiography that "among the Tchambuli the expected relations between men and women reversed those that are characteristic of our own culture. For it was Tchambuli women who were brisk and hearty, who managed the business affairs of life, and worked comfortably in large cooperative groups" (Mead, 1972, p. 214). The children also exhibited these characteristics. Girls were the brightest and most competent, and displayed "the most curiosity and the freest expression of intelligence." The Tchambuli boys "were already caught up in the rivalrous, catty and individually competitive life of the men" (Mead, 1972, p. 214). Mead reported also that while the women managed the affairs of the family, the men were engaged differently: "Down by the lake shore in ceremonial houses the men carved and painted, gossiped and had temper tantrums, and played out their rivalries" (Mead, 1972, p. 215).

This cross-cultural examination of gender roles shows vividly how the behavior and the seemingly "natural" personal attributes of the sexes can vary greatly. Most of what we think of as normal, typically male or typically female behavior is the outcome of the social life in which we are immersed and in which we become what is generally expected of us.

Traditional Gender Roles

We have now seen important variations in power, division of labor, and gender roles in different societies. These differences clearly imply that gender roles and associated behaviors are learned in the society where one is socialized. We now take a closer look at the nature of traditional male and female roles as they have prevailed in Western societies in general and the United States in particular. We begin by distinguishing two key dimensions associated with traditional views of males and females: personality traits and expected behaviors (Kammeyer, 1964).

Stereotyped Personality Traits of Males and Females

Many people believe that certain personality traits are inherently related to being either male or female, that males and females are born with distinguishing tendencies and characteristics. This way of thinking creates stereotypes. A **stereotype** is a belief that a certain category of people has a particular set of personal characteristics. Stereotypes exist for racial groups, religious groups, ethnic groups, and, in the case at hand, males and females.

For example, females are often stereotyped as emotional, whereas males are supposed to be unemotional. Males are believed to be less affected by things that would deeply touch females. Males are thought to be more aggressive, and women are seen as more passive. Many people believe that these and other personality traits come with the biological makeup of males and females. Refutations of these stereotypes are all around us, but the beliefs persist. Consider the following poignant statement by a young man describing an event with his girlfriend.

> There was an occasion when I went to Susan's one night, a happy man, and left feeling like a disheartened boy. She wanted to know why I didn't make a move on her and why I wasn't aggressive. . . . I know I'm not as aggressive as other men are or as I "should be" but I told her that it shouldn't matter. . . . I took her in my arms and asked her if she knew I loved her and she said she didn't know. I know she said it in disgust but it really hurt me. I began to cry. Man, I just about ran out of the door because I didn't want her to see me cry. I was not a man: I wasn't aggressive and I didn't hide my emotions and I really felt bad (Forisha, 1978, p. 160).

It is clear from this young man's reactions to his own behavior how deeply embedded the stereotyped views are of male personality traits. He shows shame and even disgust at his own characteristics and behavior. He feels that he failed by not being as aggressive as men are supposed to be, and he compounded the sin by displaying his emotions in front of his girlfriend.

A number of other personality traits are associated with being either male or female. Women are thought to be followers rather than leaders. Women are thought to be more sympathetic, sensitive, compassionate, and concerned about others. They are portrayed as more inclined toward artistic and aesthetic activities. They are assumed to be less inclined toward mathematics, science, and even intellectuality. Women are often thought to be more moral, more religious, or, in some cultures, "purer" than men.

Men are thought to be better leaders, more objective, aggressive, independent, active, dominant, competitive, logical, scientific, calculating, tough, strong, and unsentimental.

Believing in the stereotyped personality traits of males and females serves as a support or justification for many kinds of gender inequality. If males are believed to be better leaders and decision-makers, it would, of course, follow that men should be given positions of leadership. If women, on the other hand, are thought to be more sensitive, compassionate, and concerned for others, then they would "naturally" fit better into the tasks and jobs that call for these skills (caring for children, the ill, or the elderly, for example). But the occupations so often reserved for women have much less prestige than the leadership jobs allocated to men.

In general, a belief in stereotyped male and female personality traits is found among people who prefer a traditional allocation of tasks between the sexes. Most important, men are more likely to believe in stereotyped personality traits than women are. Studies have found also that age is related to beliefs about stereotyped personality traits, which means that older people believe in the stereotypes more than younger people do. Also, better educated people are less likely to believe in stereotyped personality traits, while religious people are more likely to do so (Mirowsky and Ross, 1987).

Although men are more apt to believe in the stereotyped personality traits of the sexes, a recent study has shown that husbands and wives are likely to influence each other's views. Interestingly, neither husbands nor wives seem to dominate in this process of mutual influence between spouses. Wives who do not accept the stereotyped view of the sexes pull their husbands closer to their views, but, on the other hand, husbands who do believe in the stereotype pull wives in their direction. Furthermore, husbands and wives who are in agreement, either for or against the stereotyped view, tend to reinforce each other's views and become more extreme (Mirowsky and Ross, 1987).

Expected Behaviors of Males and Females

The prescriptions for male and female behavior, according to the traditional gender roles, fit the stereotyped personality traits like a glove fits a hand. As we previously noted, whenever people hold stereotyped views of male and female personality characteristics, they are likely to hold traditional expectations about male and female behavior.

Although traditional gender-role expectations are found in almost every sphere of life, they are revealed most clearly in the family. According to the traditional feminine role, women are expected to perform supportive tasks within the family, and in general are expected to be subordinate to men. Women have the primary responsibility of taking care of home and children. The traditional expectation for men is that they will provide for and, if necessary, defend their families. Although these traditional female and male role expectations may seem exaggerated and even out of date, they still exist for substantial numbers of people in contemporary society. For example, in a modern-day family (with or without young children) it would still be acceptable for a wife to remain in the home while her husband was the sole wage earner. However, it would be considered very unusual if a husband stayed at home while his wife was the sole breadwinner.

Current Attitudes about Gender Roles

Traditional views about the feminine and masculine roles have been undergoing significant changes since the feminist movement began in the 1960s. The reduced support for the traditional gender roles that occurred during the late 1960s and early 1970s has been described as a "revolution in attitudes" (Mason and Lu, 1988, p. 39). Changes in attitudes have continued to move in the feminist direction since then. In 1985, a national sample of American adults expressed more profeminist views than a similar sample had in 1977. Both men and women, in every age group from 18 to over 65, showed less acceptance of the traditional feminine role in 1985 than they had less than a decade earlier (Mason and Lu, 1988).

Despite the declines in public expressions of support for the traditional female role, substantial numbers of adults still hold traditional views. For example, in the 1985 survey, 50 percent of the men and more than 45 percent of the women agreed with the statement: "It is much better for everyone if the man is the achiever and the woman takes care of the home and family" (Mason and Lu, 1988).

Surveys of adolescents show that many of them also accept traditional views about the feminine gender role. When a national sample of high school seniors was asked how they felt about the statement above, one-third agreed that it is better if the "woman takes care of the home and family." However, high school males agreed with the statement more than females (46 percent of the males, compared to only 21 percent of the females) (Bachman et al., 1987).

These survey results indicate that attitudes are changing about some of the strongest expressions of traditional gender roles, especially among women. Substantial evidence still exists, however, that many people in the United States consider it best if men are employed and women are taking care of home and children. For example, when high school seniors were asked about the most desirable arrangement for a married couple with preschool children, their first preference was for the husband to work full time and the wife not to be employed at all (Bachman et al.,

1987). These results among today's young people show the widespread acceptance of traditional gender roles in American society. To see how traditional gender-role expectations are learned, along with stereotyped views about male and female personality traits, we will examine the process of gender-role socialization.

Socialization for Gender Roles

To document the ways in which girls are socialized to exhibit female personality traits, and boys, male personality traits, is much like trying to document the ways in which people learn how to talk or use proper sentence structure. This socialization is such a continuous and ever-present experience that examples are both obvious and subtle.

Gender roles can be learned in a variety of ways, including direct training. Direct training occurs when significant others, especially parents, in the child's environment reward the child for behaviors that are consistent with traditional gender roles. If a three-year-old boy falls and skins his knee, his parent might say, "Oh, you are such a brave little man, you won't cry. Will you? If you don't cry we will let the puppy in the house." If significant others respond one way to boys and another way to girls, and if their responses reinforce the expected gender-role behaviors, then male and female behavior will likely be shaped and modified accordingly.

While everyday observations lead us to believe that such gender-role reinforcement does go on, it has not been easy to document this reinforcement in scientifically controlled observational studies (Losh-Hesselbart, 1987; Maccoby and Jacklin, 1974). What is demonstrable is that parents and others respond to children on the basis of their gender. Parents often provide toys and clothes that are consistent with their expectations of how children of each sex should behave. In one study, the homes of 120 infants were visited by researchers who compared the number and types of toys, the colors and types of clothing, and the colors and motifs of the children's rooms. Twenty baby girls and boys in each of three age groups—five months, 13 months, and 25 months—were included in the study (Pomerleau et al., 1990).

The researchers found that boys were provided with more sports equipment, tools, and large and small vehicles, while girls had more dolls, fictional characters, child's furniture, kitchen appliances and utensils, typewriters, and telephones. Girls' clothing was pink and multicolored more often, while boys' clothing was more often blue, red, and white. The color of girls' bedrooms was varied (not necessarily pink), but the bedrooms of boys were often decorated in blue (Pomerleau et al., 1990).

The tendency to identify infant males and small boys more often with

Cross-National Perspectives

A Comparison of Feminist Views in the United States and Three European Countries

The feminist movement that started in the United States in the 1960s was paralleled by similar movements in other parts of the Western world, especially Europe. While there are several different types of feminism and variations from country to country, there are some fundamental views that most feminists share. A basic concern of feminists everywhere is the inequality that exists between males and females, especially in the home, in education, and the workplace. A second near-universal concern of feminism is that efforts should be made or actions taken to reduce the inequities between the genders (Davis and Robinson, 1991). The action preferred by many feminists is for governments to ensure fairness and equity in education and employment.

Recently, sociologists Nancy Davis and Robert Robinson (1991) conducted a cross-national study to learn whether support for these feminist views are the same or different among the men and women of three European countries and the United States. Surveys were conducted in Austria, West Germany, Great Britain, and the United States, measuring the *perception of gender inequality* and *support for efforts to reduce gender inequality.*

For nearly two decades, survey researchers in the United States have asked how much agreement there is with the views and goals of feminism. These studies have shown increasing support for feminist views and objectives among Americans, both men and women (Mason et al., 1976; Thorton et al., 1983; Plutzer, 1988). On the question of *who* supports feminist views and objectives the picture has been more complex. Even gender is not consistently related to support for feminism. A number of U.S. studies, for example, have not found women to be any more supportive of women's rights than men (Cherlin and Walters, 1981).

The cross-national study of Davis and Robinson (1991) tested a number of different hypotheses, including the hypothesis that women would support feminism more than men. They called this the *underdog* hypothesis, since it is based on the assumption that any group disadvantaged by inequality will be more sensitive to it and wish to do something about it. On this hypothesis there was consistency among the men and women of the four countries studied. In every country women were significantly more likely than men to believe that there are gender inequalities and to support efforts to reduce inequalities (primarily in education and the workplace). This consistency among the four nations is noteworthy because, as noted above, not every U.S. study has found women more supportive of feminist views than men.

While there was consistency among the four countries on this hypothesis and several others, there were also several points on which the women of the United States were distinctly different from the European women. (American men and European men were generally much more similar.)

The ways in which women in the United States differed from the women of European countries are interesting enough to receive special attention. In all countries, women who were more educated were more likely to believe that there were gender inequalities in their societies. Well-educated women in the United States, however, were less likely than their European counterparts to support government actions to reduce inequality. The researchers suggest that, while educated women in the United States recognized gender inequality, they adopted a more individualistic solution to the problem. Influenced by the American value of individualism (chapter 3) and the ideology of meritocracy (chapter 8), American women were less likely than European women to favor government intervention to reduce gender inequality.

Women in the United States also differed from the women of some European nations in the way age was related to their support for feminist views. In West Germany and Great Britain younger women were more likely than middle-aged and older women to believe that there were gender inequalities and that the government should do something about them. In the United States it was middle-aged women who were more likely than either the younger or older women to agree with feminist views about gender inequality. Young women in the United States were less likely than middle-aged women to perceive gender inequality, but nonetheless, they were equally likely to favor government action to assure women's rights.

Perhaps young women in the United States grew up during years when feminist activism was more moderate than in the period when middle-aged women were reaching adulthood. Young women in the United States today may also face less discrimination than women of the 1960s and 1970s, and thus feel that there is less inequality. However, since these same young women do expect to spend many years of their lives in the labor force, they consider the government responsible for ensuring fair treatment (Davis and Robinson, 1991).

The differences and similarities between Americans and Europeans in this cross-national study shows once again it is important to conduct cross-national studies. While some relationships are found consistently from one country to another, other relationships may be unique to the particular culture or history of a country.

CHERLIN, ANDREW, and WALTERS, PAMELA BARNHOUSE. "Trends in U.S. Men's and Women's Sex-Role Attitudes." *American Sociological Review* 46, 1981.
DAVIS, NANCY J., and ROBINSON, ROBERT V. "Men's and Women's Consciousness of Gender in Equality: Austria, West Germany, Great Britain, and the United States." *American Sociological Review* 56, 1991.
MASON, KAREN O., CZAJKA, JOHN I., and ARBER, SARA. "Change in Women's Sex Role Attitudes, 1964–1974." *American Sociological Review* 41, 1976.
PLUTZER, ERIC. "Work Life, Family Life, and Women's Support of Feminism." *American Sociological Review* 53, 1988.
THORNTON, ARLAND, ALWIN, DUANE F., and CAMBURN, DONALD. "Causes and Consequences of Sex-Role Attitudes and Attitude Changes." *American Sociological Review* 48, 1983.

stereotypic colors has also been found in other studies. When mothers in public places were asked if strangers had made mistakes about their two-year-olds' gender, 70 percent of the mothers of girls said mistakes had been made, while only 30 percent of the mothers of boys said so. Parents of boys appeared to be more concerned that boys be seen as males and took more care to dress them and cut their hair so they would not be mistaken for females (McGuire, 1988).

This greater concern that boys be identified as boys indicates that adults consider it more serious when boys are misidentified, or in some way slip over into the female gender. It has often been noted that there is more adult tolerance for "tomboy" behavior in girls than feminine behavior in boys. Some observers have reasoned that this is true because "male-type" behavior is more highly valued in our society. Perhaps this is why it seems more tolerable when a girl behaves like a boy than when a boy behaves like a girl. At least, the reasoning goes, the tomboy female is aspiring to a "higher-status" position, while the boy who is more "feminine" is actually "lowering" himself. Perhaps this is why young girls can more successfully deviate from the traditional gender role. They cannot safely do so, however, much beyond the age of 10 or 11.

Modeling is a second way in which traditional gender roles may be learned. **Modeling** occurs when children observe significant others of the same sex (again, often parents) engage in a behavior and then imitate that behavior. For example, girls see their mothers (and other females) applying makeup and may imitate that behavior in play. Of course, modeling is based on the assumption that children can determine which sex they belong to and thus which behavior to model. This process may be aided by parents and significant others who will make it clear which sex is the appropriate or inappropriate model. If a boy begins to apply lipstick in imitation of his mother, he may be told that "little boys do not wear lipstick."

The mass media, and especially television, may also serve as important gender-role models for children. Evidence shows that children respond to television portrayals of the sexes, in that children who watch the most television are more likely to hold gender stereotypes (Losh-Hesselbart, 1987).

A Theory of Gender-Role Learning

In addition to acquiring appropriate gender-role behavior through social rewards, children also acquire gender roles as a result of the organization of the ideas and experiences they have encountered in early life (Kohlberg, 1966). The mental organization of ideas and experiences is a fundamental learning process and is actually an extension of the idea of the self-concept discussed in chapter 5. Children develop a sense of self from interacting with other persons. They learn that they are *boys* or *girls* because they are so identified by parents and significant others. Kohlberg describes this extension of the self for a boy:

> The . . . basic sexual self-concept (his categorization as a boy . . .) becomes the major organizer and determinant of many of his activities, values, and attitudes. The boy in effect says, "I am a boy, therefore I want to do boy things," therefore the opportunity to do boy things (and to gain approval for doing them) is rewarding (Kohlberg, 1966, p. 89).

Kohlberg's view of gender-role development starts with the idea that children organize their worlds as simply and efficiently as possible. Gender is already a part of most children's understanding by the age of three and is firmly fixed by the age of five or six. Once children have an idea of their gender, they tend to build their values and attitudes around this basic dimension. Parents start this process of gender-role differentiation, and normal developmental processes characteristic of all children then complete the process of acquiring a gender identity. **Gender identity** is a recognition of one's gender and an acceptance of characteristics typically associated with that gender.

Learning gender identity depends on symbolic communication with others, especially with significant others. At first children simply learn labels for themselves, much as they learn any other label for any other object. More than half of two-and-a-half-year-old children do not give the correct answer when they are asked their gender. By the time they are three years old, however, from two-thirds to three-fourths of children will answer the question correctly.

Although young children may recognize that *boy* or *girl* applies to them, they do not necessarily recognize that these words apply to entire categories of people. A young girl named Susan may know that she is both Susan and a girl, but she may not recognize that *girl* is a word that can be applied to a whole set of young females. At the age of two or three, children usually focus on superficial social characteristics, such as clothing styles and hairstyles, not on genital or other gender-related physical differences. This focus is reflected in the anecdote about the three-year-old who came home and announced to her mother that she had seen a new baby at her friend's house. When asked if the baby was a boy or a girl, she said she didn't know because "it wasn't wearing any clothes."

Kohlberg argues that the structuring of a child's world goes on at the same time as gender-role stereotypes are being learned. The male child recognizes not only that he is a boy but also that *boy* is a general category of people of which he is a part. Furthermore, he learns that boys are part of the general category called males and men. Girls learn the same kinds of things. When boys and girls begin to identify with their respective categories, they begin to value characteristics that are associated with their category.

Children tend to value things that are the same as, or similar to, things they already know and like. A boy, for example, learns to value certain games, toys, and active and sometimes aggressive behaviors because they are consistent with being a boy. Thereafter the boy will look for, and be interested in, activities that are associated with his already accepted male-like behavior. The same process occurs for girls.

There is a steady interweaving of the mental development of the child and the social learning that occurs with socialization. Through this process, males and females learn, and generally accept as appropriate, the major dimensions of the gender roles of their society. Through the remainder of this chapter we examine the ways gender roles continue to influence the behavior of males and females.

The Impact of Traditional Gender Roles

A few general statements describe the overall effects of traditional gender roles found in American society.

1. Gender roles, as traditionally defined, place women in subordinate and less-valued positions than men.

2. In the traditional feminine gender role, women are expected to make more sacrifices for other people than are men.

3. Traditional gender roles work to the disadvantage of women in most spheres of life, but especially in what is called the "public world" beyond the family.

Before examining evidence supporting these conclusions, we should note another point of view. Some argue that the traditional masculine role has significant disadvantages for men, just as the traditional feminine role has disadvantages for women (Lewis, 1981; Pleck and Sawyer, 1974).

An empirical study of college men uncovered many who experienced strains in their intellectual, sexual, and emotional relationships with women (Komarovsky, 1976). The source of these strains came, at least partially, from trying to live up to the standards of the traditional masculine role. For example, about one-third of these men—seniors in an Ivy League school—acknowledged that intellectual rivalries with women were troubling to them. One young man commented:

> I enjoy talking to more intelligent girls, but I have no desire for a deep relationship with them. I guess I still believe that the man should be more intelligent (Komarovsky, 1976, p. 49).

Another young man admitted that he had broken off a relationship with a young woman because "she bested me in arguments too often for comfort" (Komarovsky, 1976, p. 49). Although the majority of college men in this study did not display such attitudes and behaviors, those who did were disturbed when they could not live up to the masculine role ideal of being intellectually superior to women.

The catalogue of problems that men are said to experience because of the demands and limitations of the traditional masculine role include the following:

1. Males are not allowed to show their emotions because that would be seen as unmanly (recall the young man who cried in front of his girlfriend).

2. Males are expected to be brave and "macho" in the face of danger and threats.

3. Males are expected to perform sexually and, indeed, to be eager for sex at all times.

4. Males are expected to have jobs (unemployment is often very dis-

Sociology in the News

Children's TV Dominated by Boys' Programs

Saturday morning television programming for children (at least on the commercial networks) is dominated by programs featuring male characters (Carter, 1991). The reason, it seems, is not so much a matter of outright sexism, but is based on marketing considerations. The implications for gender role socialization may, however, be no different than if the decisions had been based on sexist attitudes.

Market research by the television networks has led them to conclude that girls will watch programs when they are male dominated, but boys will not watch shows that have a dominant female character. Even a show that featured males, a cartoon show based on the rock band "The New Kids on the Block," was cancelled by ABC because its audience was almost exclusively female. An ABC official in charge of children's programming said, " 'Only girls were watching the show . . . And you have to have boys watching the show for it to succeed' " (Carter, 1991, p. A1). Television industry executives readily acknowledge that children's television is, and has "always been male dominated."

Plans for the fall season of 1991 are, apparently, to have no shows that feature females in dominant roles. Among the new shows, for example, there will be a number based on real people, such as rap singer M.C. Hammer, child movie star Macaulay Culkin, and sports stars Wayne Gretzky and Bo Jackson. Some of these males, of course appeal to girls as much as boys. A show currently on TV called "Little Rosey," which was based on female comedian Roseanne Barr, is being cancelled (Carter, 1991).

Boys have an advantage over girls among the programmers of children's television simply because boys watch television more than girls. Girls are more likely, say on Saturday mornings, to find other things to do. (Of course, maybe girls are less interested in television *because* all the shows are male dominated.) Network decision makers see it the other way: they are firmly convinced that they must have shows that appeal to boys, which the girls will generally accept. In the words of one executive, after conducting focus group discussions with children, " 'The boys certainly didn't want to be seen liking the things the girls like' " (Carter, 1991, p. B6).

This last point is consistent with the theory of gender-role learning of Kohlberg, who claims that both boys and girls will actively seek out the things associated with the gender expectations of their society, and avoid those things associated with the other gender. Since television programs are oriented toward males, it is understandable that they would watch the programs, and reject female-dominated programs. If girls watch television, they are effectively forced to watch male-dominated programs, which may explain why they watch television less than boys.

But the most important socializing feature of children's television programming, dominated by male leading characters, is that females are shown at an early age that males play the most important roles in life. Since females are seen only in secondary roles, or are nonexistent, young girls are receiving a strong message about their importance (or lack of it) in society.

CARTER, BILL. "Children's TV, Where the Boys Are King." *New York Times,* May 1, 1991.

tressing for men) and to be competitive and successful in their work.

5. Males are often precluded from extensive contacts with their own children, often because of their intense work schedules and very often in the case of divorce (Seltzer, 1991).

Many scholars hold that such expectations and restrictions cause male stress and anxiety (Lewis, 1981). From this point of view, the traditional masculine role may explain why males exceed females in stroke and heart attack deaths, suicide, death as the victims of homicide and accidents, alcoholism, and mental illness (Lewis, 1981).

Although the pressures and constraints of the traditional masculine role may cause certain hardships and difficulties for males, moderating factors do exist. The first and most obvious point is that in many ways the traditional gender roles give males the dominant position in social relations. Furthermore, despite the importance assigned to the traditional masculine role, men may have much more latitude, or a wider range of options, than we sometimes assume (Goode, 1982).

Goode observes that relatively few men live up to the most frequently discussed prescriptions for traditional masculine behavior (tough, aggressive, striving, unsentimental). He notes further:

The *macho* boy is admired, but so is the one who edits the school newspaper, who draws cartoons, or who is simply a warm friend. There are at least a handful of ways of being an admired professor. Indeed a common complaint against the present system is that women are much more narrowly confined in the ways they are permitted to be professors, or members of any occupation (Goode, 1982, p. 135).

This observation about the relatively greater range of options for males, compared to those for females, illustrates a special case of the general sociological observation that "oppressed groups are *typically* given narrow ranges of social roles, while dominant groups afford their members a far wider set of behavior patterns" (Goode, 1982, p. 135).

We thus return to our original position: women are especially disadvantaged by traditional gender roles. We do not deny some negative impacts of the traditional masculine role, but women are adversely affected in more pervasive and critical ways.

We begin consideration of the impact of traditional roles by looking at several everyday behaviors. Gender roles, as we will see, are associated with the way people touch each other, how they sit and stand, and how they speak to each other. Although these behaviors may seem relatively unimportant and even trivial, their implications are often greater than we might first suppose.

Gender Roles and Male/Female Interaction

The pervasive influence of traditional gender roles can be found in many aspects of everyday life. For example, in daily behaviors, such as touching, standing, or sitting, males and females differ, and the differences are associated with traditional gender roles.

Touching, Sitting, and Standing. Observational studies of everyday interaction have shown that there is a general pattern of more powerful people touching less powerful people. Bosses, for example, are much more likely to touch workers than workers are to touch their bosses. With regard to male/female interaction, studies have shown that men are much more likely to touch women than women are to touch men. When males touch females, it may often be in a playful or friendly spirit, but it is also a way of demonstrating that the male has some control over the female.

Sitting and standing are both forms of body language. Again, observational studies of males and females indicate differences between the sexes. Males take up more physical space by the way they place their legs and arms. These differences in the way males and females sit and stand indicate that males are in a position of greater freedom and have greater control over space (Henley, 1977).

Speaking and Language. Studies have shown that when males and females engage in conversation, males are much more likely to interrupt females than vice versa. In one study, undergraduate male and female students who did not know each other were brought into a social laboratory for an experiment. They were introduced and told to get to know each other before the "actual" experiment. Their conversations during that get-acquainted period were recorded, and 54 deep interruptions were observed. Seventy-four percent of these interruptions were by males interrupting females, while only 26 percent were initiated by females. In same-sex couples the interruptions were nearly equal between the two conversers. In another study, where the same researchers observed conversations in "natural" settings—drug stores, coffee shops, libraries—males in cross-sex conversations made 96 percent of the interruptions (West, 1978).

In a recent study of groups made up of six college students, conversations were videotaped so that interruption patterns could be analyzed (Smith-Lovin and Brody, 1989). This study confirmed previous research: males were much more likely to interrupt females than they were other males. Females in these groups were also much more likely to yield to interruptions than were males. One interesting finding of this study is that females did not discriminate when they interrupted another speaker: they were just as likely to interrupt a male as a female. Males, however, were much more able to fend off an attempted interruption when it was coming from a female (Smith-Lovin and Brody, 1989).

This study, using college students as participants, supports the notion that males are following the traditional male gender role. The females in these groups, however, did not simply defer to males. "Women direct and accept interruptions in a way that does not differentiate systematically between males and females" (Smith-Lovin and Brody, 1989, p. 434). Nonetheless, this study shows once again that there is considerable gender inequality in conversational interruptions.

Some research shows that females are treated differently even by parents, who are more likely to interrupt their daughters than their sons (Weitzman, 1979). Other research has found that teachers in elementary and junior high schools also treat males and females differently in the classroom (Sadker and Sadker, 1985). Even though teachers claim that boys and girls are treated the same, observational studies of classroom behavior have shown that boys dominate communication in the schools. Even in language arts and English classes, where girls traditionally outperform boys, the boys still command more of the teacher's attention when they speak. In part, this male dominance in communication comes from boys' being more assertive, but, in addition, teachers respond differently to boys than they do to girls (Sadker and Sadker, 1985).

When boys call out answers without raising their hands, teachers are likely to accept their responses. However, when girls call out their answers, teachers have a greater tendency to reprimand them for not raising their hands. Teachers also give more attention to boys and praise them more often when they answer questions. The following dialogue illustrates a typical pattern in the classroom:

TEACHER: What's the capital of Maryland? Joel?
JOEL: Baltimore.
TEACHER: What's the largest city in Maryland, Joel?
JOEL: Baltimore.
TEACHER: That's good. But Baltimore isn't the capital. The capital is also the location of the U.S. Naval Academy. Joel, do you want to try again?
JOEL: Annapolis.
TEACHER: Excellent. Anne, what's the capital of Maine?
ANNE: Portland.
TEACHER: Judy, do you want to try?
JUDY: Augusta.
TEACHER: OK (Sadker and Sadker, 1985, p. 56).

This classroom interchange illustrates how males often receive support, which helps them move toward the right answers, and they receive praise when they answer correctly. Girls, on the other hand, are given less information about the quality of their answers and less praise (Sadker and Sadker, 1985).

The communications patterns in the family, in male/female conversations, and in the schools all reinforce the same general pattern. Female contributions are less highly valued than those of the male. If we think of how these patterns can make important differences in college, in organizations, in political groups, and in the work-world, we will realize that they are not trivial or inconsequential. When what men say is considered more important than what women say (perhaps by both men and women in many instances), then men will have an advantage in obtaining job positions, being promoted, and receiving career rewards. In the political world men will be more successful in running for office and getting elected. We turn now to the public world to see how women have fared in the worlds of politics, occupations, and careers.

Men and Women in the Public World

It is not difficult to document the dominance of men in all realms of public life. The political and occupational worlds are major areas in which males are greatly overrepresented in leadership positions. Using income as a measure of the positions people hold, or as a reward for their work, men have consistently had the advantage. The world of politics provides an excellent example of the underrepresentation of women in leadership positions of the U.S. system of government.

The Political Arena

When the Constitution and the Declaration of Independence were being written and were adopted, substantial debate centered on the inalienable rights of "men." When the founders of the new country used the word *men,* they may or may not have been using it to refer to *all* people, both men and women. Perhaps they were, but in fact they set up a form of government in which women (as well as slaves and Native Americans) were denied the right to vote. Not until the ratification of the Nineteenth Amendment to the Constitution in 1920—a century and a half later—did women finally receive the vote.

Although the United States was not the first nation in the world to grant women the vote, it was certainly not the last. On a worldwide basis, New Zealand was the first country to grant women suffrage, in 1893. Other countries that preceded the United States in giving women the vote include Australia (1902), Denmark (1915), the Soviet Union (1917), England (1918), and (in 1919) Luxembourg, the Netherlands, and Austria (Giele, 1988). Some European countries did not allow women the vote until after World War II (France, 1944; Hungary, 1945; Yugoslavia, 1946; Italy, 1947; Belgium, 1948; and Switzerland, 1971). Japan did not allow women to vote until 1945. A number of countries, especially in the Islamic Third World, still have not given women the vote (Giele, 1988).

Since women in the United States were not allowed to vote until well into the twentieth century, it is not surprising that women are poorly represented in the political realm today. Among the 100 members of the United States Senate in 1991, only two were women. In the House of Representatives in the same year, 29 of the 435 members were women. Among these national lawmakers, about 6 percent are women, although over 50 percent of the population is female.

The World of Work

Men and women hold very different positions in the world of work. Many occupations exist in which either men or women predominate. Figure 10–1 shows the gender distributions of some selected occupations in which there is a strong imbalance between males and females. As part of "Managers and Professionals," nurses, elementary school teachers, and librarians are overwhelmingly female. The professions at the opposite extreme, all having at least 80 percent male membership, are engineers, dentists, architects, physicians, and lawyers/judges. Not only are these male-dominated professions more highly paid but they also enjoy greater prestige than the female-dominated professions. The male-dominated fields are

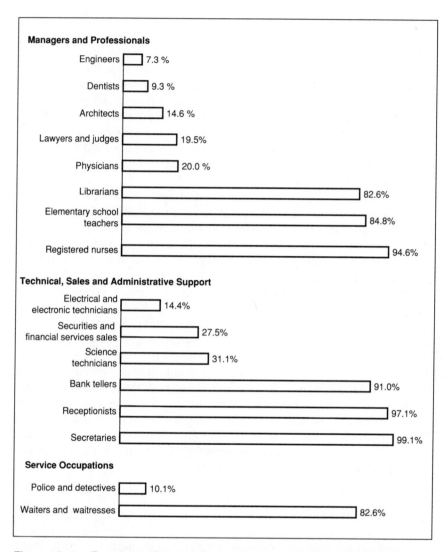

Figure 10–1. Females in Selected Occupations, as a Percent of the Total, 1988. (*Source:* U.S. Bureau of the Census, *Statistical Abstract of the United States, 1990* (Washington, D.C.: U.S. Government Printing Office, 1990), Table 645, pp. 389–391).

closely associated with traditional male roles (such as engineering), while the most female-dominated fields relate closely to traditional female roles (such as nursing and elementary school teaching).

However, finding men and women in gender-role related occupations, with different levels of compensation and prestige, is not entirely explained by the different gender-role orientations of the sexes. Factors contribute to the places of men and women in the occupational world that go far beyond gender-role socialization. One is sex segregation.

Sex Segregation in Occupations

Sex segregation in occupations means that certain occupations and jobs are filled primarily by women, while others are reserved for men. Sex segregation in the workplace is a product of both restriction and choice, but a study conducted for the National Academy of Sciences has concluded that restrictions, especially on women, have been more influential than choice (Baron and Bielby, 1985; Bielby and Baron, 1986; Reskin and Hartmann, 1986).

Studies of the occupational careers of women who work in organizations and bureaucracies have shown that sex segregation begins at the time women (and men) are hired. One influential study of over 400 work organizations in California, ranging in size from two to almost 8,000 employees, determined that sex segregation existed in the majority of organizations. Approximately 60 percent of the organizations studied were completely segregated by sex—"that is, workers of one sex were either excluded entirely or were concentrated in job titles filled exclusively by the same sex" (Baron and Bielby, 1985, p. 236). Even in the 40 percent of work organizations that were not completely segregated, less than 10 percent of the employees were in jobs that included both sexes. This overwhelming pattern of sex segregation in jobs makes it clear that the segregating was done by employers. It is highly unlikely that males and females, if they had been given free choices, would have been so consistent and thorough in selecting different jobs.

The widespread segregation of jobs by sex has significant influences on career mobility. It is not uncommon for men and women to have different entry-level jobs in an organization, even though the tasks are nearly identical. For example, in a California ordnance plant, the entry-level job for women was "assembler," while the entry-level job for men was "production worker." The tasks carried out were nearly the same, but the career opportunities for the male production workers were much greater, with a higher percentage of men being promoted to the next job level in the organization (Baron and Bielby, 1985).

A similar pattern was found in a study of federal government employees. This study is especially important because federal law makes it illegal to discriminate by sex, and one might suppose that the law would be more faithfully followed in the federal work force. However, that proved not to be the case, since female federal employees were generally hired at lower levels than male. Newly hired women were concentrated in female-dominated jobs in the lower tier of the job ladder, precisely the ones that offered the least opportunity for advancement. Even more important, women in the middle grades of federal workers were promoted at lower rates than men. This study also found that the most difficult kind of promotion for women was from the middle-level ranks to supervisory and managerial jobs (DiPrete and Soule, 1988).

Some alternative explanations have been offered for the widespread existence of sex segregation in occupations (England et al., 1988). One alternative has been offered by economists, who argue that women intentionally select occupations that are easy to get into and out of, while still providing moderately good incomes. An extension of this economic argument is that women also select occupations that allow them to take time out when they want to have children and remain at home. Obviously, this economic explanation is in line with the view that women *choose* to be in sex-segregated occupations. Although this economic theory sounds plausible, a national sample of male and female workers did not find support for its major assertions (England et al., 1988).

The results of this study and many others suggest a more sociological explanation for sex segregation of occupations and the accompanying lower wages for women. This explanation first emphasizes the mutual or two-way influence between gender-role socialization and discrimination by employers. Traditional gender-role socialization leads many women to the view that certain jobs are more appropriate and available for them. Employers conclude from this that women do not want certain male-dominated jobs. This may feed their already existing belief that women are "by nature" not suited to certain jobs. The general view that one sex is inherently superior to the other sex is called **sexism.** Sexism often serves as the basis for overt discrimination against women in the occupational world, keeping occupations sex segregated and, as we will see, women's pay less than men's pay.

Even in the absence of overt discrimination by employers, structural or institutional factors act to keep women in sex-segregated (and often lower-paying, lower-status) jobs. These structural or institutional impediments to promotion and higher pay have been called *institutional sexism.* **Institutional sexism** is defined as the day-to-day operations, rules, and policies of organizations and institutions that result in the discriminatory treatment of women. An important aspect of institutional sexism is that it can operate without individuals being prejudiced against women or intentionally discriminatory. However, when organizations and institutions have rules or policies that directly or indirectly impede or limit women, the effect can be just as important as when prejudice is blatant and discrimination, intentional.

An example of institutional sexism may be found in the practice of having female jobs in organizations that lead only to other female jobs — jobs that have relatively low pay and status. Other such institutional practices that work to the disadvantage of women include giving preferences to military veterans (which favor many more men than women), limiting public advertising for jobs (which might give the male friends of already employed men a better chance of being hired), and designing machines and tools for the average height and strength of men rather than women (England et al., 1988). As an example of the latter, some female police candidates in training programs are unable to use large caliber firearms effectively and are therefore unable to meet the training requirements. In actual police work, however, smaller-caliber weapons are often used by officers.

Another example of institutional sexism stems from employee policies about child care, which may have a significant effect on female employees. Few American employers provide child-care services in the work setting. (Employers in societies like Sweden are far more likely to provide adequate child-care facilities.) Since the traditional feminine role expectation is that women will care for children, women with children are apt to face more problems and strains than men working for the same employer. The employer cannot be blamed personally for creating the problems of their female employees with children, and the employer certainly cannot be charged with prejudice. The point remains that a company policy that does not provide adequate child-care services does affect some women adversely.

Then there are organizations and institutions that specifically limit the activities of women—particularly activities that are important for moving up in the organizational structure. For example, in the United States military women cannot serve on combat ships at sea or engage in ground combat. For the officer corps these are very important assignments during a career, since they are often considered prerequisites for gaining the highest military ranks. Obviously, if the rules of the military preclude women's serving in these positions, then women are severely disadvantaged when they try to compete for the highest military ranks.

A number of religious organizations have created similar institutional impediments for women. Barred from serving as ministers, priests, rabbis, or elders, women are automatically excluded from the higher offices and positions of authority within the religion. In most major religions today, males have retained the positions of leadership for themselves simply by blocking the first steps in the hierarchy. Opposition groups have occasionally emerged, however; an unofficial group of Roman Catholic priests has issued a "Pastoral Letter on Equality in the Church," which calls for ending the "sin" of gender discrimination (Hyer, 1985). This is a recognition of, and an effort to combat, the institutional sexism that exists in religion.

The Economic Impact of Sex Segregation on Women

Sex segregation of occupations, which is the combined product of gender role choices, discrimination in hiring and promotion, and institutional sexism, has some obvious impacts on the relative earnings of women compared to men. By 1990 the relative earnings of women in the labor force had reached about 70 percent of male earnings. Nearly 20 years earlier, in 1967, women in the labor force earned 62 percent of what men earned, revealing that, during these two decades, employed women made only small economic gains relative to men. Male and female incomes in the major occupational categories are compared in figure 10–2.

A recent study completed for the National Academy of Sciences estimates that 35 percent to 40 percent of the disparity in male and female income is accounted for by sex segregation (Perl, 1985). Although some reduction did occur in the amount of sex segregation during the 1970s, progress toward integrating workplaces slowed during the 1980s. The National Academy of Sciences report concluded with the following warning:

> Decreases in federal enforcement that have occurred since 1981 and recent changes in the philosophy of enforcement, including reversals of federal civil rights policy in some areas, are likely to negatively affect women's future employment opportunities (Perl, 1985, p. A15).

The future of women in the labor force is difficult to predict, although it appears from the above study that constant surveillance will be necessary if equality is to be achieved. In a study of 120 state agencies in California, researchers found substantial progress toward gender equity in job assignment over a six-year period (Baron et al., 1991). The types of state agencies that made the most progress were the younger and smaller organizations. More important, the agencies that did the best job of achieving gender equity in jobs were those whose hiring and job assignment practices were overseen by outside personnel authorities, rather than in-house affirmative action programs (Baron et al., 1991). It appears that some outside pressure on organizations prompts them to be more conscientious about gender equity.

Both overt discrimination and institutional sexism are still found

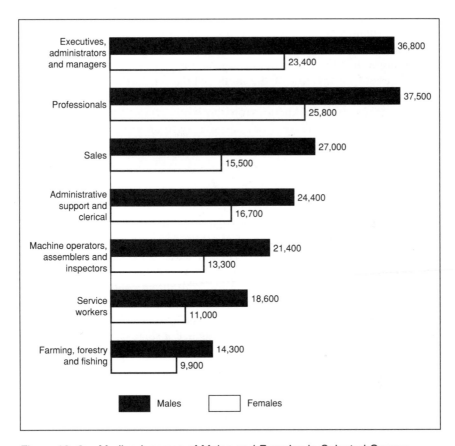

Figure 10–2.   Median Incomes of Males and Females in Selected Occupational Categories. (*Source:* U.S. Bureau of the Census, *Statistical Abstract of the United States, 1990* (Washington, D.C.: U.S. Government Printing Office, 1990), Table 673, p. 411.)

throughout U.S. society. On the other hand, increasing numbers of women are moving into a wide range of occupations and professions, and as they do some of the barriers created by sexist attitudes and institutional barriers are likely to be reduced and broken down. While gender equality in the workplace might be achieved in some future time, that time has not yet arrived (England and McCreary, 1987; Ferree, 1987).

Age Stratification and Inequality

A society may be stratified by age, just as it is stratified by economics, power, race, ethnicity, or gender. Age may be used to divide a population into significant categories that are treated in special ways. Different age groups in a society will be given different rights, opportunities, rules, and limitations. Often the old or the young age groups, since they tend to be dependent on the rest of the adult population, are at a disadvantage and therefore receive unequal treatment in the society. Although every society makes some distinctions on the basis of age, the nature of age stratification systems differs from one society to another and has changed from one historical period to another (Riley et al., 1988).

Children and Society

Since childhood appears to be a normal and natural stage of life, it is interesting to find that for much of Western history, childhood was not thought of as a distinct life stage. This, at least, is the view of social historian Philippe Ariés (1962), who assembled evidence to support the thesis that in the Middle Ages a child went from infancy directly into a kind of adulthood. The most common image of the medieval child, as Ariés found in the paintings of that period, was that of a kind of miniature adult. Obviously, if parents did not recognize a stage of life that we recognize as childhood, they were likely to treat their children differently than they are treated today.

Children at a very early age were expected to participate in productive work. Because of their size they could not do all things that adults could do, but they were not allowed to spend their time in frivolous play. In the nineteenth century in the United States, children of poor and working classes were expected to contribute to the family income and production by working. Even in the twentieth century, children of farm families often left elementary school to help with farm tasks.

Today, the situation is quite different, with children rarely entering the work force until at least high school age. Again the exceptions are likely to be on family farms, or other farm labor, and family businesses. Usually children are not expected to work, but they are also denied a wide range of rights and privileges. Children and adolescents in contemporary families are usually rather closely controlled and limited by parents. The assumption is that their immaturity makes it imprudent to give them too much freedom. Although some agitation has occurred for greater children's rights, no significant social movement has emerged (Farson, 1974).

Some rights that were earlier granted to adolescents and young adults have been withdrawn in recent years. Many high schools adopted liberalized policies of dress and behavior in the 1970s, which were withdrawn or retracted in the 1980s. Smoking, for example, was often allowed in specified areas of high schools, but in recent years many schools have discontinued this privilege. In a similar way, many states and localities in the 1970s lowered the age for drinking alcoholic beverages to 18. In the 1980s the laws were changed, raising the legal drinking age in most places to 21.

Again, these changes illustrate how the social definitions of age groups can change from one time to another, even in the same society. When age categories are socially defined, certain rights and limitations will be attached to the people in that category. This system is referred to as **age stratification.**

The attitude that limitations and restrictions can be based on age is called **ageism.** Although the term *ageism* is applied primarily to the treatment of the elderly, it can generally refer to any instance when an individual's age is the primary basis for evaluating and dealing with that person. An example of ageism would be a 63-year-old worker's being released from a job, while younger workers who are no more productive are retained. But ageism could also be illustrated by a brilliant teenager who has been denied entry into college simply because of age.

In the next section we will turn our attention to the elderly, a growing and increasingly important part of the population. Much of our discussion will reflect the work being done in a field of study called *social gerontology.* **Social gerontology** is the study of the impact of social and cultural conditions on the process of aging, and also the social consequences of age changes in the population of a society (Hooyman and Kiyak, 1988).

The Elderly Population

Old age cannot be precisely defined in terms of years of life, because just as the meaning of childhood has changed, so also has the meaning of old age. In the United States it is both the legal and social custom to use the 65th birthday as the beginning of old age. When the Social Security Act was passed in 1935, age 65 was set as the age when retirement benefits could be received. Thus, in the public mind, 65 became linked with old age. However, the laws have changed periodically, and for several decades Americans have had the option of receiving partial Social Security benefits at age 62. In the 1980s Congress passed legislation providing that, in the year 2000, full Social Security benefits cannot be received until age 67. Furthermore, as a way of combatting age discrimination in the occupational world, Congress also passed legislation that allows most classes of workers to work until age 70, if they wish.

Even though this legislation gives older people the right to remain in the labor force until they are well past 65, the actual trend in retirement has been in the opposite direction. For the last 100 years American workers have been retiring at younger and younger ages. In 1890, 70 percent of males over the age of 65 were still in the labor force. Today, less than 15 percent of Americans over 65 are employed (in 1986, 16 percent of males and 7 percent of females). By ages 62 to 64 less than half of all males (45.4 percent) are still in the labor force (Soldo and Agree, 1988). The percentage of women still working at that age is even lower, but the retirement trend for women is different from that for men. Among women aged 55 to 64 the percentage in the labor force has been edging upward since 1950, from 30 percent to over 40 percent. This increase among women, however, is probably just a reflection of the generally larger numbers of women in the labor force. The fact remains that between the ages of 55 and 65, less than half of U.S. men and women are still employed. Although some of these people may be unemployed or may have given up looking for work, the majority have probably retired voluntarily.

Who Are the Elderly Today?

The legal and social trends just discussed are indications of who the elderly are in our society, but some of these indicators are providing different pictures. If time of retirement means old age, then old age is coming earlier than ever before; yet the laws governing Social Security benefits, and prohibiting mandatory retirement, suggest that old age is coming later. Obviously, any definition of old age is very arbitrary, depending on the way in which age is socially defined. In the contemporary United States, many people still view age 65 as the beginning of old age, but new definitions are emerging, particularly from the older people themselves. Often people at age 65 and even older do not think of themselves as old because they have a level of health and a style of life that they do not associate with old age.

To reflect the changing conditions of older people, it has been suggested that we think in terms of the *third quarter of life*. The **third quarter of life** is defined as beginning at about age 50 and continuing until about 75 (Pifer and Bronte, 1986). Clearly, this concept minimizes the significance of reaching age 65 and emphasizes the fact that most people today continue to live active lives until age 75. The age of 50 is chosen in part because many people make important changes in their lives at that point—usually their children have established independent lives, their occupations and careers (and incomes) have often reached about the highest level that will be attained, and retirement emerges as a serious consideration. Age 75 is suggested as an upper limit for the third quarter of life because many people begin then to experience significant declines in physical and mental abilities (Pifer and Bronte, 1986).

Obviously a third quarter of life would have to be followed by a **fourth quarter of life,** the years between 75 and 100 years of age. The idea that an average person could live to 100 is not as extraordinary as it may sound. The life span (the maximum length of human life) has long been over 100 years, although only a few people in most populations reach this maximum. However, some responsible biologists and demographers are suggesting that by the middle of the next century (2050)—well within the lifetimes of many readers—life expectancy may be near or at 100 years (Siegel and Taeuber, 1986).

Another refinement on the definition of the elderly is found in the already widely accepted terms *young-old* and *old-old.* The **young-old** are people aged 65 through 74, while the **old-old** are aged 75 and older. Again, the young-old category is a recognition of the fact that many people over 65 are still vigorous, healthy, and active; the old-old category of 75 and older marks the beginning of, in many cases, physical and mental decline, although some people are still independent and active well beyond that age.

The Size of the Older Population in the United States

Regardless of how the older population is defined, it is certain that in the next half century both the *number* of elderly people and their *proportion* of the total population will increase.[1] In fact, the older population has been growing rapidly for the last 50 years. In 1990 over 31 million Americans will be aged 65 and older, while in 1940 there were only 9 million in that category. In a half-century from now, in 2040, there will be an estimated 67 million people aged 65 and over. If we look at the elderly as a percentage of the total population, we can see in figure 10–3 that people 65 and older have increased from about 8 percent of the total in 1950 to nearly 13 percent in 1990. However, the greatest increase in the percentage of older people in the population will come in the next century, when by 2030 the 65-and-over population will have grown to 21 percent.

Since about 1970 the increasing numbers of elderly in the population have been produced primarily by decreases in deaths due to chronic diseases (as opposed to infectious diseases). The major chronic diseases are heart disease, cancer, and stroke. Except for cancer, the death rates from these causes have declined since 1968. Furthermore, these three causes of

---

[1] Throughout the remainder of this chapter, unless we specify otherwise, the terms *elderly* and *old* will refer to the conventional age group of 65 and older. This designation is still necessary, because most available data use age 65 as the beginning of old age.

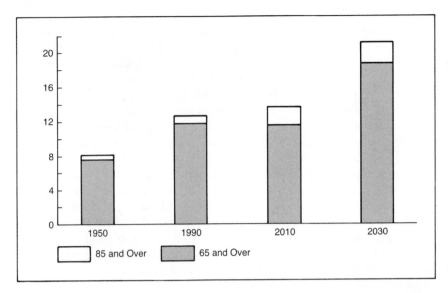

Figure 10–3.   Older Population as Percentage of Total U.S. Population: 1950–2030. (*Source:* Population Reference Bureau, Soldo and Agree, 1988.)

death, which account for three-fourths of the deaths among the elderly, are all occurring at later ages than they did 20 years ago (Manton and Meyers, 1987).

The Economic Condition of the Elderly

Just as the physical lives of many older people have been improving, so have their economic lives. There is definitely a bright side to the economic condition of the elderly population today, but there is also a dark side. We will deal with the bright side first, because it probably reflects the majority of the elderly. We have already seen an indication of the improved economic conditions of the elderly in the historical trends in retirement. We saw that in 1890, 70 percent of all males 65 and over were still employed, while in 1986 that figure was 16 percent and going down. The United States is not unique in the trend toward earlier retirement. A comparative study of Australia and Japan found earlier retirement in those societies, too (Schultz et al., 1991).

The high percentages of early retirement among men today probably reflects the fact that they are economically able to retire. Although the incomes of retired persons are lower than when they were working, they are not generally living in poverty. Nor are they wealthy, since the primary source of income for those 65 and over comes from Social Security benefits. In 1988 Social Security payments averaged about $500 per month for a retired worker. Of course, some retired workers receive additional pensions from previous private and public employment (Soldo and Agree, 1988).

Annual income is not the only economic resource of the older population, however. The majority of older people have some economic resources in real estate, savings, and investments. Over three-fourths of elderly householders own their own homes, which, in most cases, are mortgage free. Among elderly *couples,* 88 percent own their own homes, but only 65 percent of elderly females *living alone* own their own homes. Although the health care costs for the elderly are greater than for other age groups, Medicare now covers the major portion of their medical costs. In many cases taxes (both personal income and state and local property taxes) are reduced for people over 65. With these economic resources, many of today's elderly are able to live relatively comfortably, but certainly not in affluence (Soldo and Agree, 1988).

But now we turn to that part of the elderly population where the economic picture is much darker. Some people have reached old age who are perhaps in poor health and with physical disabilities, who do not own homes, and who have no savings or other assets. Often, their monthly rent takes a substantial part of their only money income—Social Security benefits. These elderly people live in very precarious economic conditions, often in poor, dilapidated housing. They are truly the impoverished elderly.

In 1988, according to the federal government's poverty standard, 12 percent of the elderly were living in poverty—with the old-old having a higher percentage in poverty than the young-old. However, the most serious poverty exists among elderly women and elderly minorities (Harel et al., 1990; Soldo and Agree, 1988). Elderly women have a significantly higher level of poverty (15 percent) than elderly men (8 percent). Elderly blacks have a much higher poverty level than elderly whites (31 percent compared to 11 percent), while elderly Hispanics are at an intermediate level (22.5 percent). The most seriously impoverished are elderly black women who live alone; a full 60 percent of these women are below the poverty level. These official poverty levels may actually be missing some of the poorest people in the society, for some elderly may be so poor that they live with relatives and thereby may reside in households that are not below the poverty level (Soldo and Agree, 1988).

Economic Comparisons between the Elderly and Children

Although many elderly in the United States are poor, even more poverty exists among the children of the society. In 1988, 20 percent of all children under 16 years old were living in households where incomes were below the poverty level. Among black children the percentage was 45.4 percent; among Hispanic children it was 38.9 percent. Since we have already seen that only about 12 percent of the elderly have incomes below the poverty level, clearly these children as a group are more disadvantaged than old people, especially because children (and their parents) are not likely to have the economic assets of many older people (homes, savings, investments). Furthermore, over the last 25 years the poverty rate among children has increased at the same time that the poverty rate among the elderly has decreased (Preston, 1984).

If one looks at expenditures by the federal government as a measure of the relative concern about the elderly and the children of the society, the balance is overwhelmingly in favor of the elderly. In 1984, federal expenditures per child for education, the Aid to Dependent Children program, food stamps, Head Start, nutrition, and health programs added up to only 9 percent of the per person expenditures for the elderly (Preston, 1984). If one considers government expenditures at all levels (federal, state, and local), and thus includes the educational system, expenditures are still estimated to be three times greater for the elderly than for children (Soldo and Agree, 1988).

The major source of income for the elderly (Social Security payments) is indexed to keep pace with inflation. By contrast, the major social program for poor children (Aid to Families with Dependent Children) has not kept up with inflation over the past two decades. Between 1970 and 1990 this form of aid to children has been diminished by 39 percent, simply because of inflation (Johnson et al., 1991).

Why are Americans choosing to devote more of their government expenditures to the dependent elderly than to dependent children? One explanation can be found in the competing voter interest groups, which have different levels of political power. In a democratic society the decisions that allocate different levels of resources to the dependent parts of the population are made by voters. Which groups of voters are more likely to support expenditures for the elderly? The elderly themselves would be justified in looking out for their own economic interests. As a group, the population over age 65 votes more than any other age category (U.S. Bureau of the Census, 1989). The elderly are now a significant voting block in the United States, and through organized interest groups, such as the American Association of Retired Persons, they are becoming stronger (Cockerham, 1991). But the middle-aged voting population is also likely to support expenditures for the elderly, for two self-interested reasons. The first is that, if the government does not support their elderly parents, it will fall to them to do so. The second is that the adults in the population, especially those who are middle-aged, may be looking ahead to when they reach old age, and they prefer to have governmental programs in place for their own support.

In contrast, none of these adult voting groups, except the parents of children, have a direct interest in supporting children. The matter has been put succinctly in the following statement:

> Children don't vote; and adults don't vote on behalf of their own children, which is water over the dam. I daresay that if we passed through life backwards, adults would insist that conditions in childhood be made far more appealing (Preston, 1984, p. 385).

A Cross-National View of the Elderly

Just as the older population is growing in the United States, it is also growing in much of the economically developed world (Schultz, et al., 1991). (See figure 10–4.) Most of the countries of northwestern Europe have a higher proportion of elderly in their populations than the United States does (12.0 percent in 1985). Among them the highest percentages in 1985 were Sweden (16.9 percent), Norway (15.5 percent), the United Kingdom (15.1 percent), and Denmark (14.9 percent). As figure 10–4 shows, the developing countries all have lower proportions of elderly because health and living conditions cause earlier deaths, and high birth rates add larger numbers of children to the population each year. The countries with the smallest proportions of elderly in their populations are found in Africa and the Arab Middle East (Soldo and Agree, 1988).

All of the countries of western Europe spend higher percentages of their gross national product (GNP) on their elderly than does the United States (7.4 percent). Austria has the highest expenditure on social programs for the elderly (21 percent of its GNP). In Scandinavian countries and Great Britain, when old people are taken care of by their relatives, the government provides some compensation for the services they render. Other European countries provide tax deductions and early retirement pensions for people who assist in the care of their older relatives (Soldo and Agree, 1988).

China, because of the sheer size of its total population, has a larger number of elderly people than any other nation on earth. In 1985 China had more than 50 million people aged 65 and over. In the culture of traditional China, elderly people were highly honored and respected. However, in the last 40 years, since its communist revolution, China has broken down many of the traditional cultural customs and values, and has at the same time engaged in an intense effort to modernize its economy.

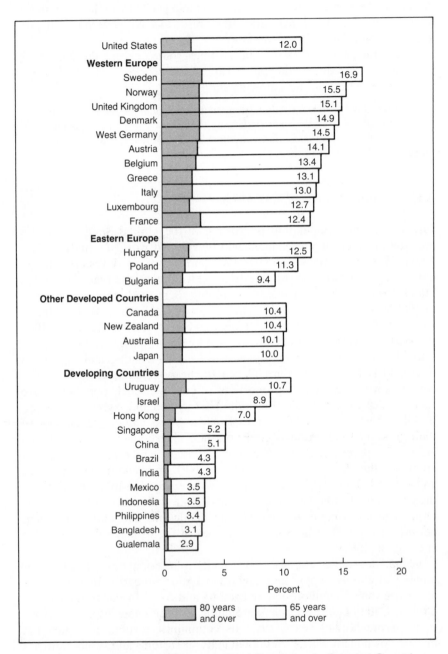

Figure 10–4. Percentage of Elderly in Total Population in Selected Countries, 1985. (*Source:* Population Reference Bureau, Soldo and Agree, 1988.)

This raises the question of how the elderly of China are being treated today (Olsen, 1988).

Evidence shows that China continues to give special attention to the elderly in its population through programs that have been created, especially since 1978. The most important of these programs are pensions and medical care for the retired elderly, homes for the aged, and special efforts to give the elderly Chinese satisfying activities after retirement. For economic and political reasons the Chinese are encouraging their elderly to retire at a relatively early age (60 for men and 55 for women). Early retirement allows the Chinese to bring younger and better trained workers into the urban labor force. The Chinese leaders are particularly concerned about the discontent among the retired elderly when they no longer have the meaningful activities of work. A prominent slogan of the Chinese today is "The old are entitled to continue doing, to study, to be cared for, to enjoy themselves, and to receive medical care" (Olsen, 1988, p. 255). It appears that the elderly do receive respect and consideration in contemporary China, but the reasons may have just as much to do with the political and economic aims of the government as with China's cultural tradition of venerating the elderly.

Summary

Every society is organized to some degree on the basis of gender and age categories, and often the results are inequities or systems of inequality. The inequalities between males and females can be analyzed in terms of three separate but closely related concepts: power, division of labor by gender, and gender roles.

In most societies males tend to have greater power and more privileges than females, but some exceptions are notable. Women have greater power in societies where they carry out activities on which men are dependent and where there are long-standing magical and religious associations between the fertility of women and the general well-being of the social group. In societies around the world, men and women are typically assigned to different work. The division of labor by gender often finds men doing heavy and dangerous work, but there are many instances when females, too, are assigned heavy and arduous tasks.

Cross-cultural evidence shows that the gender role differences familiar in American society are not universal and therefore are not inborn characteristics of the sexes. Anthropological studies give evidence that gender roles are learned through the socialization process.

The stereotyped personality traits associated with males and females attribute certain traits (emphasizing achievement and action) to males and other traits (emphasizing emotional support and comfort) to females. Therefore, traditional feminine and masculine roles in American society emphasize that females should participate in activities that are supportive and expressive, while males should participate in ones that are active and instrumental.

Attitude studies among Americans show that traditional gender-role attitudes have been reduced; but many Americans, both young and adult, still accept some traditional expectations, especially for women.

The socialization for gender roles occurs through social rewards provided by significant others and by models provided by males and females in the child's environment. Also, children themselves develop a gender identity and actively adopt the behaviors and attitudes associated with the different genders.

In general, the gender roles in American society (and many other societies) place women in subordinate and less-valued positions than men. However, the argument can be made that traditional gender roles also impose significant disadvantages on men. The traditional masculine role places expectations on men that may be stressful and perhaps places restrictions on their behavior. However, on balance, women are still more disadvantaged than men by traditional gender roles.

The impact of traditional gender roles can be seen in everyday behaviors, such as how males and females touch each other, how they sit and stand, and how they speak. In the schools the responses of boys and girls are treated differently by teachers.

In the public world, especially in political and economic life, women are underrepresented in the more prestigious positions. Sex segregation in occupations, produced in large part by sexism and institutional sexism, continues to leave women less rewarded in the work world.

In the stratification of society by age, the elderly and children are the most disadvantaged. Children and young adults are defined by the rest of the society as being less than mature, and thus limitations are placed on their rights.

The definition of old age is changing in the United States because of the improving health and economic positions of many people over age 65. The elderly population is growing rapidly, and will continue to increase in numbers and as a proportion of the population. Many elderly people today are reaching old age with considerably greater economic resources than in the past. However, elderly women who live alone, especially if they are members of minority groups, have much higher than average levels of poverty than other categories of the elderly.

When the poverty levels of the elderly and children are compared, higher rates of poverty are found among children.

Cross-national studies of the elderly find their numbers growing in most developed countries. All western European countries spend higher proportions of their economic resources on the elderly than the United States does. China, with the highest numbers of elderly in the world, has instituted special programs to care for this population.

CRITICAL THINKING

1. What relationship exists between economic contributions, power, and gender in our society?
2. How do Margaret Mead's studies of gender roles in New Guinea societies show that such roles are the result of society rather than biology?
3. List some common gender-related stereotypes. How are these stereotypes reinforced in the mass media?
4. Give examples of gender role expectations in your family.
5. Give examples from your own childhood of how you learned the gender roles expected of you in society.
6. In what ways are gender roles in evidence in everyday behaviors such as touching, standing, sitting, speaking, etc.? Can you think of examples of these differences from your own experiences?
7. Is sexism and gender stereotyping likely to decrease in the future? Explain, using information from the chapter as well as your own ideas.
8. Compare and contrast the rights and restrictions associated with old age and childhood.
9. Give examples of inequalities in our society related to gender and/or age.

CONNECTIONS

The United States–Mexico Border

Introduction

It is a warm spring Sunday as I drive into El Paso, Texas. The sun is shining, as it always does in this desert-mountainous region; my car windows are down to enjoy the warm rush of air, and a lively *conjunto* band is playing on a Mexican radio station. The Border Highway is aptly named as it follows the course of the Rio Grande River, which serves as the borderline between the United States and Mexico. On my left, on the Mexican side, families are picnicking on its banks and splashing and swimming in the shallow river, crossing the invisible borderline at times. Above the banks are the *colonias*, or poorest housing districts, in the huge city of Juarez, where adobe houses line dirt streets. Most homes don't have running water, so residents must wait for the water truck to come with their weekly supply. When it doesn't come there is no water, and some of their babies die of dehydration caused by dysentery from the polluted, contaminated waters in which they are now swimming. Farther down the river people walk through a large hole in the fence ("Tortilla Curtain") intended to restrict Mexicans from illegally entering the United States, to spend the day in El Paso. The green vans of *La Migra,* or Border Patrol, watch them but decide instead to chase another group and return them to the border. Since it is Sunday, not a work day, the daily cat-and-mouse chase game is played in a more relaxed way.

To my right, on the U.S. side of the highway, I also see *colonias* similar to those across the border; in them diseases that have disappeared in other parts of the United States are rampant. I wonder at these Third-World conditions as I drive farther north into El Paso, past sprawling homes with manicured yards, some with swimming pools, and others with maids' quarters that house the women who come from Mexico for low wages to take care of these homes and children.

On Monday morning a different picture emerges on the Border Highway. Traffic is congested on the bridges connecting the two cities; exhaust from cars sends pollution into the air to join with that from industrial smokestacks. Workers in Juarez take buses to the many *maquiladoras,* assembly plants built in Mexico by American corporations. There, American-made parts are assembled into consumer goods (e.g., televisions, refrigerators, clothing, toys) by Mexican workers and then returned, virtually duty free, to the United States for sale. These include many of the leading corporations in the United States—Ford, General Motors, General Electric, General Dynamics, American Telephone and Telegraph, Zenith, Union Carbide—as well as numerous smaller enterprises that have moved to the Mexican border cities to escape environmental, health, and safety regulations and the higher costs of real estate and labor in the United States. Plant managers across the bridge from the United States to join these workers, then cross back to their homes in El Paso, hoping to avoid the tangle of traffic compounded by trucks that carry goods from the factories.

Some people from Mexico come to work in the United States, both legally and illegally, for daily wages that far surpass the $3.00 minimum *daily* wage they find in Mexico. Most do manual labor, including the many women who work as maids. To avoid *La Migra* some cross on "mules"—a name for men who wade across the river with people on their backs so they will not get wet.

El Paso and Cuidad Juarez together comprise the second largest metropolitan area along the U.S.–Mexican border. The intersection of these two border cities reveals the economic, social, and cultural contrasts of the United States—an affluent, advanced industrial society—and Mexico, a less industrialized Third World country. In this discussion we will look at the complex set of social relations that characterizes the U.S.–Mexico border from the viewpoint of four theoretical perspectives, focusing especially on some of the consequences of the growth of *maquila-doras,* or American assembly plants, in Mexican border cities.

Structural-Functional Theory

In chapter 8 we saw that functionalists view stratification as a normal arrangement in societies, perpetuated by people's values and beliefs in a system that allocates jobs and wealth to people according to their training and expertise. This system is seen as functional because it ensures that all jobs in society get done and that people get what they deserve in terms of money, power, and prestige.

If we look at the development of U.S. corporations in Mexico from a functionalist perspective we would focus on how *maquiladoras* have been beneficial to both countries. During the 1980s the number of *maquiladoras* seeking to take advantage of cheap labor and low shipping costs and tariff duties increased from about 300 to nearly 1900 (Suro, 1991). A manifest function for corporations, then, is the greater profit earned on products made in Mexico than if the products had been manufactured in Asia, the Caribbean, or, especially, the United States. Functionalists would contend that *maquiladoras* have been beneficial to the Mexican economy and to Mexican workers because they have brought thousands of people into the work force who were previously unemployed or were working at even lower wages than the *maquila* workers.

Functionalists might also point to a latent function of *maquilas* in reducing the number of Mexicans coming into the United States illegally to seek work. This helps to provide a stability to the socioeconomic structures of both countries, as well as providing special benefits to the United States because Mexican workers spend approximately one-half of their paychecks there (Tiano, 1987).

Conflict Theory

Conflict theorists would disagree with the functionalists' view of the growth of American factories in Mexico. They point out that *maquiladoras* represent an excellent example of a "runaway shop" or "off-shore assembly plant" that has contributed to the process of deindustrialization in the United States. As we noted in chapters 8 and 9, manufacturing employment in many American cities has declined as employers have sought cheaper sources of labor, and one result has been the social problems associated with urban poverty.

Conflict theorists would also focus on the ways in which American corporate interests have exploited *maquila* workers in order to gain the greatest possible profits. For example, *maquila* workers are paid $0.55 to $1.40 an hour, less than one-third the U.S. legal minimum wage. For years, Mexican *maquila* workers received wages that ranged from one-fifth to one-seventh of those paid to American industrial workers, and recent devaluations of the Mexican peso have reduced these figures to as little as one-fifteenth of their American counterparts (Cockcroft, 1986, p. 110). Moreover, the absence of strict environmental, health, and safety regulations has led to environmental conditions so dangerous that one American medical official has characterized them as a "public health disaster waiting to happen" (Satchell, 1991).

Conflict theorists would also point to inequities in the division of labor by looking at age and gender stratification in *maquilas*. As many as 85 to 90 percent of *maquila* workers are women in the 16- to 25-year-old range; many of them become the economic mainstays of their families while still in their teens. María Patricia Fernández-Kelly, who has conducted extensive field research among women factory workers, summarized a typical reason given by plant managers for hiring females.

> We hire mostly women because they are more reliable than men; they have finer fingers, smaller muscles, and unsurpassed manual dexterity. Also, women don't get tired of repeating the same operations nine hundred times a day (Fernández-Kelly, 1983a, p. 181).

Fernández-Kelly challenges this assumption and says that *maquila* work has become a sex-segregated occupation as justification for subordinating women in the workplace and has resulted in a patriarchal power structure since most managers are men. Because there is an abundance of unemployed workers and these young, unskilled women are easily replaceable, they are relatively powerless to influence the conditions of their work. High turnover rates in *maquilas* further limit possibilities for career mobility among women, as does their lack of skills, which also keeps them in the lowest-paying positions. Finally, many women are made ill by unsafe and unhealthy working conditions, which would be illegal in the United States, and by age 30 are unable to continue working in the *maquilas*.

Symbolic Interactionism

As we have seen, symbolic interactionism is less interested in broad macroscopic issues, such as cross-cultural economic development, than on microscopic issues, such as the ways in which people communicate and interpret the meanings that situations have for them. People make plans and choose courses of action based on their interpretations of the meanings of situations. At times, there is a discrepancy between the expectations people have for situations and what they actually experience when in that situation. Again, let us look at *maquila* workers in Mexico to illustrate this idea.

Not all *maquila* workers are young, female, unskilled, and uneducated. Some are highly trained, educated females and males who have left the teaching profession. Why would *maquila* work appeal to teachers? In Mexico there is a discrepancy between the perception of teaching as respected work and the reality of teachers' lives. For example, although teachers are among the most highly educated in the country, the average teacher earns only slightly over $150 per month; most do not own a house or car; they pay 75 percent of their salaries for rent in the poorest areas of cities; and most teach in two schools, with few teaching materials for their large classes (Campa, 1989). This situation has led to widespread dissatisfaction among teachers and a strike of 100,000 teachers in Mexico City in 1989 (*Kansas City Times*, 1989). For Mexican teachers, symbolic representations, in the form of extrinsic rewards such as good pay and good working conditions, are lacking, as expressed in one man's comments: "What else can we lose, we've already lost our purchasing power and . . . maids earn more than teachers with 15 years of formal education?" (Campa, 1989, p. 9).

Symbolic interactionists might focus on the loss of self-esteem and role conflict that stems from the discrepancy between teachers' expectations for their work and the low rewards given to them. Zurcher (1983) says that this type of situation requires that some kind of action take place to reduce discomfort or strain. He says there are a number of kinds of action teachers might take, such as leave the role, stay in the role and "grin and bear it," "distance" themselves in such a way as to let others know they no longer care about the strain, or make a new role within the situation. From the symbolic interactionist perspective, we would assume that being a *maquila* worker would magnify role conflict between teachers' perceptions of the value of their education and training, and the semi-skilled work they must take to support their families.

Social Exchange Theory

Exchange theorists, like symbolic interactionists, are more interested in individuals' behaviors but in a different way. Whether people continue in situations or leave them is related to the rewards or costs they experience. If relationships are reciprocal, people will maintain them. As an example of this exchange relationship we will leave *maquilas* and look at another border situation: the relationship between Mexican domestic workers (maids) and their employers. Most Mexican domestics cross the border illegally because the benefits of domestic work far outweigh the work and wages available to them in Mexico—such as those in *maquilas*. The Border Patrol is not interested in stopping them, because they perform jobs that Americans do not want (Ruiz, 1987). Although on the border they earn less (about $15 to $20 a day) than domestics in other parts of the country, their wages far exceed those in Mexico ($3 a day). To support their own families, women domestics care for the homes and children of Americans while leaving their own children in the care of relatives. According to the rules of reciprocity, this arrangement is beneficial not only to domestics but also to their employers, who are relieved of housework and child care at a very low cost. Furthermore, for employers, the benefits are greater, because they typically do not pay social security taxes on the salaries of domestic workers (Ruiz, 1987).

Reciprocity is sometime strained, however, and violated to the point of termination of employee–employer relationships. As Ruiz (1987) has found, both Anglo and Mexican-American employers are unappreciative of their maids, and in fact some Hispanics treat them worse than Anglos do. Ruiz also found evidence of discrimination in newspaper ads for domestics through such statements as "must be clean" or, more blatantly, a refusal to accept Mexican domestics. Ruiz concludes that Mexican domestics experience a "quadruple whammy"—discrimination based on their low social class, their gender, their ethnicity, and their Mexican citizenship. In this example, the exchange relationship would not be equal, or reciprocal. Some women restore the balance by resigning, others by regarding other benefits as worth the costs they experience.

Looking at the Research

A growing body of research—called *border studies*—examines issues arising from the dynamic interaction along the 2000-mile U.S.–Mexico border. This research reflects some of the different perspectives discussed above. For example, sociologist and border scholar Ellwyn Stoddard (1987), who has conducted extensive research on the growth of *maquiladoras,* has found that most Mexicans who work in *maquilas* have no desire to move to the United States. *Maquila* workers receive higher wages and greater benefits, such as transportation to work, bonuses for good attendance, and cafeteria privileges, than do workers in Mexican-owned factories. He contends that the presence of *maquilas* has curbed unrest and actually prevented people from moving to the United States. Stoddard also reports that *maquila* workers are satisfied with their jobs and have little interest in union activities. Therefore, *maquila* growth has been beneficial to both countries—to Mexico by providing jobs, training, and capital, and to the United States by enabling corporations to produce goods at lower costs than would be possible in other parts of the world. Finally, he points out that *maquila* workers spend about one-half of their paychecks in the United States, thus stimulating U.S. businesses and the expansion of jobs.

However, critics of the *maquiladoras* point out that, no matter how contented workers may be in their *maquila* jobs, these factories serve as a magnet encouraging migration to the Mexican border cities for a population much larger than they can absorb (Bustamante, 1983; Fernández-Kelly, 1983b). By 1974 one-third of the people on the Mexican side of the border were migrants, but only 3 percent were employed in *maquiladoras* (Cockcroft, 1986, p. 109). Therefore, as the population of Mexican border cities increased after the introduction of the *maquiladoras,* so also did the unemployment and underemployment rates. One of the consequences of the extremely high proportion of women *maquila* workers is that employment opportunities for men in border cities, such as Juarez, are far less plentiful. Mexican men in these cities, therefore, seek work in the United States, while female members of their households work in the *maquilas* (Fernández-Kelly, 1983a, 1983b). Thus, critics contend that, rather than reducing the flow of illegal immigrants, the presence of *maquiladoras* has actually increased their numbers.

Finally, the *maquiladoras* are unstable; if threatened with labor unrest in the form of demands for higher wages or for improved working conditions, employers will simply move elsewhere in Mexico or to other countries where wages are lower and workers more compliant, leaving behind a mass of unemployed workers (Bustamante, 1983; Cockcroft, 1986). Critics also point out that, although U.S. corporations profit from the reduced labor costs of Mexican workers, U.S. workers who lose their jobs when U.S. plants are closed and moved to Mexico are the losers.

The *maquiladoras* are therefore influenced by a wide variety of social, cultural, economic, and political forces, and their presence in Mexican border cities such as Juarez has contributed to the unique quality of life on the United States–Mexico border. So closely intertwined are cities such as Juarez and El Paso that some have described the border region as a third country in which food, language, and music, as well as social, economic, and political structures, are shared. As described by Miller, border cities such as Juarez and El Paso "couple like reluctant lovers in the night, embracing for fear that letting go could only be worse" (Miller, 1985, p. xii).

The intricate linkage of the United States and Mexico that has been accelerated in the border region by the *maquiladora* program has served as a focal point for the debate over more extensive economic relations between the two countries. During the debate over the 1991 free-trade agreement with Mexico proposed by President Bush, the *maquiladoras* were frequently cited as a model of what the elimination of trade barriers between the two countries would bring. Indeed, both advocates and critics of the agreement felt that, because U.S. investment would not be concentrated along the border, it could transform Mexico into "one big maquiladora" (McConnell, 1991).

Critics argued that the free-trade agreement would prompt even more U.S. companies to take advantage of the lower wages and minimal health, safety, and environmental regulations by moving their factories to Mexico. Using the experience of the *maquiladora* as a model, they contended that in the process American jobs would be lost and the environmental degradation of Mexico and the border region would be accelerated (Armstrong, 1991). On the other hand, supporters of the agreement contended that, by opening up the huge Mexican market to U.S. exports and by increasing the purchasing power of Mexican citizens to buy U.S. goods, the number of American jobs would ultimately increase. Moreover, supporters argued that the economic expansion of Mexico that will result from the agreement will provide the resources and political stability necessary for it to enact more stringent environmental regulations and to improve their enforcement of them (Satchell, 1991).

References

ARMSTRONG, SCOTT. "Maquiladoras: Mint Plethora of Labor Disputes." *Christian Science Monitor,* May 21, 1991.

BUSTAMANTE, JORGE A. "Maquiladoras: A New Face of International Capitalism on Mexico's Northern Frontier." In June Nash and María Patricia Fernández-Kelly (eds.), *Women, Men, and the International Division of Labor.* Albany: State University of New York Press, 1983.

CAMPA, HOMERO. "Siete Veces Ha Cerrado La Puerta Bartlett A Los Lideres de la Disidencia Magisterial." *Proceso,* No. 643, February 27, 1989, pp. 6–9.

CROCKCROFT, JAMES D. *Outlaws in the Promised Land: Mexican Immigrant Workers and America's Future.* New York: Grove Press, 1986.

FERNÁNDEZ-KELLY, MARÍA PATRICIA. *For We Are Sold, I and My People: Women and Industry in Mexico's Frontier.* Albany: State University of New York Press, 1983a.

FERNÁNDEZ-KELLY, MARÍA PATRICIA. "Mexican Border Industrialization, Female Labor Force Participation and Migration." In June Nash and María Patricia Fernández-Kelly (eds.), *Women, Men, and the International Division of Labor.* Albany: State University of New York Press, 1983b.

Kansas City Times. "100,000 Striking Teachers in Mexico Demand Raises," April 25, 1989.

McConnell, Patrick. "Mexico Faces Free Trade with High Hopes and Skepticism." *Los Angeles Times,* May 25, 1991.

Miller, Tom. *On the Border: Portraits of America's Southwestern Frontier.* Tucson, Ariz.: The University of Arizona Press, 1985.

Ruiz, Vicki L. "By the Day or the Week: Mexicana Domestic Workers in El Paso." In Vicki L. Ruiz and Susan Tiano (eds.), *Women on the U.S.-Mexico Border: Responses to Change.* Boston: Allen & Unwin, 1987, pp. 61–76.

Satchell, Michael. "Poisoning the Border." *U.S. News and World Report,* May 6, 1991.

Stoddard, Ellwyn R. *Maquila: Assembly Plants in Northern Mexico.* El Paso, Tex.: Texas Western Press, 1987.

Suro, Roberto. "Border Boom's Dirty Residue Imperils U.S.-Mexico Trade." *New York Times,* March 31, 1991.

Tiano, Susan. "Women's Work and Unemployment in Northern Mexico." In Vicki L. Ruiz and Susan Tiano (eds.), *Women on the U.S.-Mexico Border: Responses to Change.* Boston: Allen & Unwin, 1987, pp. 17–39.

Zurcher, Louis A. *Social Roles: Conformity, Conflict, and Creativity.* Beverly Hills: Sage, 1983.

11 The Family

Because the family is a familiar social form, we can all describe what a family is and how it works. Our description would probably begin by stating that the family consists of a number of people with different statuses, such as wives and husbands, mothers and fathers, and children. But at this point we would have to pause because we may already have a problem. For example, there is a society in southern India called the Nayar who, according to the anthropological record, had a family system without husbands and fathers. In the eighteenth and early nineteenth centuries the men of the Nayar had no continuing relationships with their wives or children, nor did they assume responsibility for them. Thus, in the Nayar family system, the men did not occupy the status that we generally think is important for the family.

While the Nayar still live in southern India, their family system is no longer organized as it was in the eighteenth century, primarily because, when the British colonized India, they forced the Nayar to change. However, before the British arrived, young Nayar girls between the ages of 7 and 12 were married at a group ceremony. Each girl was given a specific boy as a husband, and for four days she would cohabit with him. At the end of that time, the boy would return to the home of his mother, and the girl would return to her mother's. Throughout her life this male would be her formal husband, even though she might never see him again.

The girl would reach maturity in the home of her mother, where she would receive overnight visits from her lovers. When she became pregnant, one of her lovers would be designated as the father of the unborn child. This nominal father would give a few symbolic gifts and pay the costs of the child's birth, but thereafter he would have no rights to, or responsibilities for, the child. The child would be reared in the home of its mother and grandmother.

The Nayar household was headed by the grandmother, who was the matriarch of the family. The sons of the matriarch also lived in the household, but only part of the time because the Nayar men were warriors. (In India's caste system the caste of the Nayar was responsible for military tasks and warfare.) These sons would help with economic support of the household, and when they were present they would also help with the childrearing (especially of the boys), but the Nayar household was primarily centered around the females (Gough, 1960).

It is easy to see why the Nayar might have developed a family system that deemphasized the importance and prominence of males. If the men of the caste were frequently gone on military expeditions or were taking part in military training, they could not be counted on to carry out key family tasks. Furthermore, since the men were engaged in fighting, they might be killed and thus lost to the family at any time. This example shows how family systems have a tendency to adapt to external conditions and why the family has been called an *adaptive institution*. This characteristic of the family will be discussed below.

Although the Nayar family system is unusual—nothing quite like their system has been observed in any other society—it does allow us to see some important sociological points. First, family systems can be organized in very different ways. In more sociological terms, the family structure and the statuses and roles of different family members can vary greatly from one society to another.

A second point to be made in the light of the Nayar example is that, in describing the family, we may find it best to begin with what the family does instead of what its organization or structure is. What activities, purposes, or tasks does the family perform? These functions of the family, as they are often called, are sometimes described as tasks necessary for a society's survival. Many efforts have been made to identify the *essential* or *universal* functions performed by the family, but these efforts usually reveal alternative (nonfamily) ways of accomplishing the same task (Reiss and Lee, 1988).

A better way to look at the functions of the family is to see them as variable from one society to another and from one historical time to another. This view still allows us to see that some important societal tasks, or functions, are nearly always carried out by the family. In the next section we will examine some major functions of the family, beginning with those that are found most widely, and moving toward those that are found less often or are of diminishing importance.

The Functions of the Family

An analysis of family functions has an obvious connection with structural-functional theory, described in chapter 1. Structural-functionalism focuses attention on the positive and negative contributions of a structure (in this case, the family) to a society. In chapter 1 we noted that the family contributes to society by producing children, caring for them when they are young, and training them in the ways of the society. Since these tasks are performed in some manner by the family in nearly every society, they are the near-universal functions of the society. There are, however, societies in which these functions are either not performed by the family, or they take such a different form that they deserve special attention.

Reproduction.   For a society to continue, replacements must be provided for the members who die, a task accomplished primarily through childbearing. (Sometimes the reproduction function is called *replacement.*) In almost every society, men and women who are married are the preferred producers of children. The Nayar family system, of course, is an exception, since the father was not part of the family unit. Also, societies exist in which children are produced by couples who are not formally married, but they may have **de facto unions** because they have cohabited for extensive periods of time. In addition, children are born to unmarried women, and in these cases, even with the fathers absent, mothers and their children are usually accepted as family units.

Care and Nurturance of Children.   As we have previously noted, the human infant is incapable of caring for itself. It must be given physical care or it will not survive. We also recognize more and more that the human infant must have emotional support and nurturance. Family sociologist Ira Reiss, who has searched for the universal family functions, has concluded that every family system, regardless of form, provides emotional support and nurturance for its children (Reiss and Lee, 1988).

Socialization.   If some degree of order and continuity is to exist in a society from one generation to the next, infants must also be taught the society's cultural and social ways. In chapter 5 we discussed the importance of parents' socializing their children, but we also noted that in many societies the mass media and schools are also significant socializers.

Meeting Economic Needs. The family is a societal unit in which members cooperate to satisfy their common economic needs. Sometimes people live in other larger social units in which there is economic cooperation (e.g., communes, *kibbutzim*). Also, many individuals in the United States today live alone; nearly one-fourth of all households (24.0 percent in 1988) had only one person. Obviously, for many people in contemporary American society, having family members in the same household is not a necessity for meeting economic needs. In many societies, however, the family has been, and continues to be, both an economic-producing unit and a consuming unit. Production within the family, through farming, a family business, or family handicrafts, has been most common through history. However, in contemporary, economically developed societies, the family is primarily integrated through its consumption, not its production. Nonetheless, the family continues to provide for the economic needs of its members, especially those who are dependent, such as children.

Intergenerational and Kin Support. Long after childhood, support—physical, economic, and emotional—continues between generations within families. Parents continue to help and support their adult children in a variety of ways, and adult children reciprocate by giving help, respect, and attention to their parents. In many societies, and among ethnic or nationality groups in the United States, more distant family members also give each other support and help. The nature and amount of family and extended kin support varies considerably, but the family continues to perform the support function in many societies.

Regulation of Sexual Behavior. Marriage is often a way of controlling sexual behavior. Many societies have norms prohibiting sex before marriage, as well as having strong prohibitions against extramarital sex. In restricting sex to marriage, these norms regulate sexual behavior. However, in such societies the restrictions are often imposed on women more often than on men—again, an example of the double standard of sexual behavior. Furthermore, in chapter 7 we saw that, in the United States and many other societies, the norms prohibiting premarital sex are not very effective. Although marriage systems can be, and often are, strong regulators of sexual behavior, many exceptions also exist.

Social Placement. In many societies, the family is a mechanism for placing new members into the existing structure of the society. In rigidly stratified societies, the family into which one is born will determine for life one's place in the society's structure. Obviously, in more open societies, this social placement function of families is much less determinant, but even when upward (or downward) mobility is possible, one still starts from the level of one's family of birth.

Reproduction, care and nurturance of children, provision of economic necessities, kin support, regulation of sexual behavior, and social placement, then, are the major functions of family systems; although other functions have been identified, such as education, religious training, and recreation, they are much less widespread and significant. The family system of every society will carry out at least some of these tasks, and in many societies the family performs most of them.

Even though the same functions are performed by the family systems of many different societies, the actual family structure may vary greatly from one society to another. We will consider next some of the major differences in family types.

Two Basic Family Types

The simplest distinction of forms of the family differentiates between nuclear families and extended families.

Nuclear Family. When a family unit is made up of a husband, wife, and children living in the same house, it is called a **nuclear family.** The primary bond of loyalty in the nuclear family is between the husband and wife.[1]

Most people are members of two different nuclear families during their lifetimes. The nuclear family into which one is born is one's **family of orientation.** (This is the family that gives a person his or her orientation, or socialization.) The nuclear family that one creates by marrying and having children is one's **family of procreation.**

Extended Family. When a family unit is made up of three or more generations living in the same household or very close together, it is an **extended family.** An extended family thus includes first-generation parents, their married sons or daughters, their spouses, and their children. Extended family units have a high degree of economic cooperation across all generations, and primary loyalty is usually given to the oldest generation.

---

[1] This description, and other family structures and norms, are *ideal types.* In chapter 4 an ideal type was described as a logical, exaggerated, and "pure" model of some phenomenon that one wishes to study or analyze. A nuclear family could still exist if a husband and father were living in another place (e.g., on military active duty).

Table 11-1 provides the names and descriptions for other major variations in family norms and structures.

The Family and Social Change

The preceding section and table 11-1 have shown that family systems can take many different forms, the norms that govern family relations can vary greatly, and the functions of the family differ from society to society, from one time to another. All of these facts indicate that the family is not a fixed and unchanging social arrangement, but that it can and does change. This statement raises the question about how and why the family changes from one time to another.

Because the family is widely accepted as a basic social institution of the society, it is often thought that the family shapes or influences the rest of the society. Although that can be true in some instances, it is usually the case that the alternative is true—the family as an institution is often shaped and changed by the rest of the institutions of the society. For this reason the family is appropriately called an *adaptive institution*. The family typically adapts, or makes adaptive changes, when some other part of the society changes.

The most familiar case of the family as an adaptive institution is found in the way the family adapts to changing economic conditions. History provides many examples: when economic times are bad—times of depression, for instance—families typically cut back on the number of children they have. In the United States, during the depression of the 1930s, people cut back on their childbearing, and this was before the time when contraception was easily and widely available. The birth rate was lower during that period, in part because people postponed marriage (an adaptation in itself), and if they were married, they had fewer children.

Ireland experienced a devastating famine in the middle of the nineteenth century (which killed more than a million of their 8 million people), and the people of Ireland thereafter completely reorganized their family system. Instead of allowing their children to marry early, as they had done before the famine, the Irish started using a system of inheritance and dowries that kept their children from marrying until they were quite old (men were often in their thirties or older). This new system also kept as many as a quarter of the Irish from marrying at all (Kammeyer, 1976).

These are but two examples of the way family systems adapt to changing external conditions. But the family also adapts to many political actions as well. Family systems are changed by immigration laws, tax laws, abortion laws, military conscription, social security systems, housing reg-

Table 11–1. Family Types

Rules of Descent		
Matrilineal	*Patrilineal*	*Bilineal*
Descent comes from mother and her kin Inherits property from, and owes primary allegiance to, that family	Descent comes from father and his kin Inherits property from, and owes primary allegiance to, that family	Descent comes equally from mother's and father's family Allegiance is shared.

Rules of Residence		
Matrilocal	*Patrilocal*	*Neolocal*
Newly married couples live with wife's family.	Newly married couples live with husband's family.	Newly married couples establish new, separate household.

Authority		
Matriarchy	*Patriarchy*	*Egalitarian*
Authority held by oldest female, usually mother	Authority held by oldest male, usually father	Husbands and wives share authority equally

Number of Marriage Mates	
Monogamy	*Polygamy*
One partner at a time	Two or more partners (either husbands or wives) at a time

Polygyny	*Polyandry*
A husband having more than one wife	A wife having more than one husband

ulations, and many other government actions and policies. Overall, the family is an institution that is more apt to adapt to changes in other parts of society than it is to produce basic social changes.

The Processes of Marriage and Family Life

To examine the marriage and family systems we can consider some typical processes that people experience as they enter marriage, have children, and, in many cases, divorce and remarry. We know that all people do not follow the same steps in the same order—some people have children before marriage, some married couples do not have children, spouses sometimes die at an early age, and not every married couple divorces. Nonetheless, a review of some of the typical processes, from courtship through remarriage, can reveal much about current-day marriage and family life.

Choosing Marriage Mates

In many countries of the world today, young people have almost complete responsibility for finding and selecting a mate for marriage. The United States is among the most prominent of these countries, and it has been so since the earliest days of the American experience. Even in colonial times Americans gave their children considerable freedom and autonomy in the selection of their marriage mates. Young people were allowed to spend time together in recreational settings where they could enjoy each other's company. Many European visitors in the eighteenth and nineteenth centuries believed that Americans, especially young women, were given far too much freedom.

The mate selection system in the United States has almost always been based on the idea of romantic love, or mutual attraction. The people of every society recognize that two people can develop an intense emotional attachment, but they often do not consider this emotion a sound basis for choosing a marriage mate. In fact, many societies regard it as foolish to select a mate on the basis of this heightened emotional state. Marriage is too important and serious an institution to be based on an emotion that will almost certainly diminish (Goode, 1959).

Nevertheless, the idea that romantic love should be a precondition of marriage did take root and thrive in the United States (Goode, 1959). It can be said that choosing one's marriage mate on the basis of attraction and love is consistent with the emphasis that early Americans placed on

Cross-Cultural Perspectives

Polyandry: A Rare Marriage Type

Polygyny and polyandry are forms of marriage that involve more than one mate. Polygyny—the practice of having more than one wife or female mate at one time—is very common in societies around the world. About 75 percent of all the societies that have been studied by anthropologists and sociologists allow polygyny. By contrast, polyandry—the practice of having more than one husband or male mate at one time—is very rare. Only about 1 percent of the world's societies have practiced polyandry (Stephens, 1963).

The most fully documented polyandrous societies are the Toda (a non-Hindu tribe of India), the Marquesan Islanders in the South Pacific, and various groups in Tibet and the Himalayan region generally. The Nayar, whom we have already described, are also usually classified as polyandrous, because Nayar women typically had several lovers. These lovers, however, did not live in the woman's household, and this sets the Nayar apart from other polyandrous societies. These few examples of polyandry provide the bulk of the information we have about this unusual marriage form.

Often the polyandrous men who share wives are brothers. This was true of the Toda, where women understood that when they married a man they were also marrying his brothers. Even a brother who might be born after the marriage would be considered a woman's husband. Tibetan polyandry, also, is typically a case of two or more brothers married to the same woman. The Marquesan Islanders are an exception, however, since the co-husbands were apparently not brothers.

The ethnographic reports of polyandrous males insist that there is very little jealousy among husbands. Anthropologists were generally told that jealousy is a ridiculous idea, and that displays of jealousy would be socially disapproved. Of course, if a wife with two or more husbands became pregnant, there would be no way of knowing who the biological father was. The people of polyandrous groups consider this a special advantage, since every baby will have several fathers to give it special care and attention.

Often in areas where polyandry occurs, resources and land are limited. Polyandry may emerge in these places as a way of eking out a living from an inhospitable environment that requires the energies of several men to provide for one family unit. For example, in

mountainous villages it can be advantageous if one husband culti-
vates the land, while another herds the sheep in a distant pasture. A
third brother can gather wood, or cut grass for cattle food. Also, a
wife in these places may be safer if at least one of her husbands is at
home while others are away (Zorsa, 1982).

One other economic advantage of polyandry is that the small par-
cels of land owned by a family do not have to be divided up among
their sons. When two or more sons marry one wife and live in the
same household, the land can remain intact from one generation to
the next (Goldstein, 1978).

In societies where polyandry exists, some families move toward
group marriage (multiple husbands *and* wives). If, for example, the
family's resources allow, the husbands of a woman may take a second wife. Since sexual relations may occur between any pair of
wives and husbands, the result is group marriage.

The dark side of polyandry is that it is frequently associated with
female infanticide. Since the ratio of males to females is normally
equal, or nearly so, there will be too many females for a polyandrous marriage system to work. In order to create an imbalanced ratio that has two or three times more males than females,
polyandrous societies are apt to let some female children die in
infancy.

The best theoretical perspective on polyandry is provided by
structural-functional theory. Polyandrous marriage patterns can be
functional in an environment with limited land and scarce resources.
Polyandry allows all men to have sexual access to a woman and to
experience parenthood. At the same time, this practice keeps the
society's birth rate in balance with its resources, the family's land remains intact, and cooperating husbands have an easier time of providing for the needs of a family. The females who reach adulthood
are likely to have an easier life with multiple husbands; in one polyandrous village the people said they pitied any woman who had only
one husband (Zorsa, 1982).

GOLDSTEIN, MELVYN. "Pahari and Tibetan Polyandry Revisited." *Ethnology* 17,
1978.

STEPHENS, WILLIAM N. *The Family in Cross-Cultural Perspective.* New York: Holt,
Rinehart and Winston, 1963.

ZORZA, VICTOR. "When Brothers Share Wives, Age Counts." *The Washington Post*,
May 2, 1982.

personal freedom and individual rights. The Declaration of Independence gave every individual the right to life, liberty, and the pursuit of happiness, a concept that was certainly consistent with choosing one's own marriage partner. Emphasizing romantic love as a basis for marriage gave participants great control over the selection of marriage mates in the past, just as it does today.

In contrast, most societies have had, and many continue to have, arranged marriages. In **arranged marriages** the parents select marriage partners for their children. Often the young people scarcely know each other, and it is not assumed that they will love each other at the time of marriage. In arranged marriage systems it is hoped that a couple will develop an affectionate and warm relationship after they are married, and that they will continue to have pleasant companionship for life.

Traditionalist support for arranged marriage is sometimes expressed in the slogan "Love matches start out hot and grow cold, while arranged marriages start out cold and grow hot" (Xiaohe and Whyte, 1990). The research on arranged marriages versus love marriages has not completely supported this slogan, however. In two separate studies, one conducted in Japan more than 25 years ago, and the other a more recent replication in China, the husbands and wives of both types of marriage were studied. The results of these two studies were very similar. The husbands of arranged marriages did, after some years of marriage, have higher levels of love and marital satisfaction than husbands of love marriages, but the wives of arranged marriages had lower levels of love and marital satisfaction than either the wives of love marriages or, the husbands of either type of marriage (Blood, 1967; Xiaohe and Whyte, 1990).

Many Islamic societies use systems of arranged marriages. In Iran, for example, the parents of a young man often interview the families of some potentially marriageable young women. They will inquire about the general characteristics of the family (their standing in the community, economic resources, educational attainments, occupational levels, etc.), and they will ask about the qualities of the marriageable daughter. The parents of the young man will then make a recommendation to their son, and in most cases he will follow their advice. In societies where arranged marriage is the custom, the young people often consider it a very difficult and imposing task to select a marriage partner. Young people in these societies will often say that they are too inexperienced to make this decision, and they would prefer to have their parents do so because they are wiser and more knowledgeable.

Social Influences on the Selection of Marriage Mates

Marriages in any society are likely to occur between two people with similar social characteristics. This pattern is called **homogamy**—marriage between people with similar characteristics—such as religion, race, education ethnicity, nationality, and social class.

Marriages are apt to be homogamous, even in a society like the United States, where the selection of a mate is based on love and personal choice. Homogamous marriages are the result of many social influences on the selection of marriage partners. Parents today may not choose marriage mates for their children, but they do influence their children's choices—sometimes directly, sometimes subtly. Parents make inquiries about the dating partners and the opposite-sex friends of their children. They ask about the families they come from, and in particular they ask about religion, socioeconomic status, and perhaps about nationality and race. Through such questions parents find out if their children are likely to be interested in someone coming from different social, cultural, racial, or economic origins. If these possible marriage mates are viewed as too different, and thus unacceptable, parents will often discourage the continuation of the relationship.

When children are still living at home, parents often try to influence the selection of mates by placing their children in social settings where they are less likely to meet members of the opposite sex who are "different." By selecting homes in neighborhoods with certain preferred characteristics, parents can reduce the chances of their children's meeting and ultimately wanting to marry someone of a different race, religion, ethnic group, or social class. Similarly, sending children to school, especially to college, may be done with an eye to the kind of young people their children are likely to meet. Whether or not parents fully recognize the significance of their actions, moving to a "nicer" neighborhood and sending the children to a "better" school makes it more probable that the children will meet, fall in love with, and want to marry someone who will be more acceptable to the parents.

Marriage to a person of the same (or similar) educational background—*educational homogamy*—has been studied over the last 50 years by Mare (1991). This study revealed that educational homogamy increased during most of that period (more men and women with similar educations married each other). In general, people who marry soon after leaving school (either high school or college) are most likely to marry someone with a similar educational background. People with higher levels of education also tend to marry someone with a similar educational background. During the 1980s, however, there was some decline in educational homogamy in the United States (Mare, 1991).

Religions and religious organizations frequently try to influence mate selection. Young members of most religions are encouraged by religious leaders to marry within their faith. Religious organizations often have rules that prohibit marriage to someone out of the faith, or procedures that must be observed if such a marriage is proposed. The religion's rules may require the nonmember to convert or to take religious instruction or training before the marriage is allowed.

Some impersonal forces in the society also lead to marriages within racial, religious, nationality, and socioeconomic groups. Because of discrimination, unequal opportunities, and economic sorting, people of the same race, religion, nationality, and social class are likely to live in the same neighborhoods, go to the same schools, have the same kinds of jobs, and belong to the same organizations. People who do not come into contact with each other obviously will not marry one another.

Cohabitation as a Premarital Stage

In contemporary American society, as well as many other societies, **cohabitation,** that is, unmarried couples living together, has emerged as an expected stage of premarried life. Yet, only two decades ago in the United States, cohabitation was relatively rare, and couples who did cohabit were engaging in behavior that was considered deviant. Often, cohabiting couples in the 1960s and earlier were people from the lower social strata of the society, or people who lived in some kind of Bohemian setting. In a fairly rapid transition, cohabitation became acceptable in the middle classes, and today cohabitation is found in every stratum of society.

In 1970, when the Census Bureau started collecting data on cohabiting couples in the United States, cohabiting households numbered slightly over a half-million. By 1988 the number of unmarried couples was up to 2.6 million (Surra, 1990). About one-third of women and men cohabit by age 23 to 24 (Thornton, 1988). By their early thirties, almost half of Americans have cohabited at some time during their lives (Bumpass and Sweet, 1989).

A similar pattern has emerged in many other societies. For example, in Australia in 1982 about 17 percent of all single persons aged 25–44 were in cohabiting relationships. This figure is not directly comparable to the United States figures above, but clearly, cohabitation is frequently found in Australia, just as it is in the United States (Khoo, 1987).

The most widespread pattern of cohabitation is found in the Scandinavian countries of Europe. In Sweden the cohabitation pattern has moved beyond being simply a premarital stage of life. Marriage rates have been going down rapidly in Sweden since the mid-1960s, and the reduced number of marriages is directly related to the increase in long-term cohabitation (Popenoe, 1987). For some, but not all, Swedes, cohabitation has become a substitute for marriage.

Almost all Swedes who do marry cohabit first—estimates are variously placed at 98 or 99 percent. In Sweden today, becoming pregnant or having a child is no longer a reason for marriage. One Swedish couple described their "marital history" to a researcher in the following manner:

> They met in 1967, moved in together in 1969, exchanged rings in 1973 (this was around the time their first child was born and was for the purpose of "showing others that they were attached"), and married in 1977. When asked what anniversary they celebrated, they responded, "The day we met" (Popenoe, 1987, p. 176).

In contemporary Sweden the customs, rituals, and ceremonies connected with marriage, if there is a marriage, have diminished in significance. Marriage ceremonies in most societies have social significance because they signal to the community, and to other social groups, that a couple is establishing a new relationship. Yet in Sweden the ceremonies and rituals connected with marriage are decreasing in importance. ". . . Swedish young people today are merely drifting away from their families of orientation, usually in stages, and eventually settling down with someone else, all seemingly without any form of public or social recognition" (Popenoe, 1987, p. 176).

When individuals enter into marriage or cohabiting relationships without the involvement of family members or other social groups, the sociological implications are considerable. The involvement of family and community members in any couple relationship, whether cohabitation or marriage, serves to keep the couple together. When relationships are formed on an individual basis, without the benefit of these social supports, they tend to break up more easily. Again, the case of Sweden is instructive, for even among cohabiting couples who have a child, the rate of breakup is three times as high as the rate for comparable married couples (Popenoe, 1987).

Entering Marriage

A paradox of married life is that newly married couples often consider their first year or so together as the happiest and yet the most difficult. There are numerous adjustments to make in early weeks and months, even if a couple has previously cohabited. One type of adjustment is dealing with mismatched marital scripts.

Marital scripts are the expectations one has about what is proper and appropriate behavior for husbands and wives. Each partner has these expectations, but they are likely to be unconscious and unspoken (Broderick, 1989, 1979). During the early stages of marriage, husbands and wives may have arguments and hurt feelings because they have different (or conflicting) marital scripts. Family sociologist Carlfred Broderick, who developed the concept of the marital script, illustrates with a personal example how a married couple with mismatched scripts can experience disappointment and even anger over the resultant misunderstandings. Even though Broderick had known his wife since they were both in kindergarten and they had dated from the time they were in the tenth grade, he learned early in marriage that he and his wife had mismatched scripts regarding what happens when someone gets sick:

> Every right-thinking person knows what you should do when you get sick—you go to bed. That is your part. Then your mother, or whoever loves you, pumps you full of fruit juice.

> Well, I married this woman I had known all my life, and in the natural course of events I caught the flu. I knew what to do, of course. I went to bed and waited. But nothing happened. Nothing, I couldn't believe it!

> I was so hurt, I would have left if I hadn't been so ill. Finally, I asked about juice and she brought me some—in a little four-ounce glass. Period. Because, as I learned later, the only time they drank juice at her house was on alternate Tuesdays, when they graced breakfast with a drop in a thimble-size glass. My family's "juice glasses" held 12 ounces and there was always someone standing by to refill them.

> It does not matter that an issue may seem foolish to an outsider, or that it may be solved simply. The point is that mismatched scripts can so easily derail a young couple (Broderick, 1979, p. 154).

Marital scripts, as can be seen from the illustration above, often come from unique family background experiences. Before we marry, the marriage relationship we have observed most closely is usually that of our parents. Whether that marriage was harmonious and idyllic or quarrelsome and stormy, we are likely to have picked up some deep-seated notions about the nature of the husband/wife relationship and of family life in general.

Marital Quality

Marital quality is a general term referring to marital satisfaction or marital happiness, and is an indication of how positive and satisfying a marriage relationship is. Sociologists who study marital quality are likely to ask people to agree or disagree with statements such as: "We have a good marriage," "My marriage with my partner is very stable," or "Our marriage is strong" (Norton, 1983). Other more elaborate measures of marital quality inquire into the degree of consensus about important matters such as philosophy of life, work and careers, or recreational activities.

Marital quality can also be ascertained by asking a couple about the amount of affection they display, or how frequently they express their love. Conversely, low marital quality can be identified by asking how frequently they have arguments and fights (Spanier, 1976).

Studies of marital quality have consistently shown that despite the adjustment problems of couples during the early years of marriage, they are likely to see their marriage relationship as good. Couples who are recently married and do not yet have children are especially satisfied with their married lives. Most studies of marital quality have shown that at no time after the first years of marital life do couples express a higher level of satisfaction with marriage (Anderson et al., 1983).

Parenthood and Marital Quality.   A marriage changes when couples become parents. Couples with a new baby experience a number of problems that tend to reduce their level of marital satisfaction. A most important factor is that they simply have less time together than they did before the arrival of the baby (White et al., 1986). Most new parents express some surprise about the sheer level of physical demands. One mother wrote in her diary when her daughter was a month old, "A month is only four weeks . . . but it has been an eternity for me. I'm a zombie. Four weeks of night feedings and little sleep. I haven't read a paper. I barely have time to shower and wash my hair" (Lowenstein and Lowenstein, 1983, p. 18). Among most new parents the overwhelming responsibility for caring for their baby falls to the mother. Most studies show that fathers carry less than 20 percent of the load in the routine tasks of infant care.

Naturally, if a new mother is too busy to take a shower and is not getting much sleep, a great many other aspects of married life are also being sacrificed, including a reduction in sexual activity because of decreased opportunities or fatigue (Sollie and Miller, 1980; LaRossa, 1983).

Married couples who have children when they are young and very shortly after they are married are particularly apt to experience feelings of dissatisfaction. A 28-year-old woman with three children describes her feelings:

> One day I woke up and there I was, married and with a baby. And I thought, "I can't stand it! I can't stand to have my life over when I'm so young" (Rubin, 1976, p. 81).

A husband describes how his wife's pregnancy and the baby made him feel resentful and jealous:

> When we were first married, I'd come home from work and she'd be kind of dressed up and fixed up, you know, looking pretty for me. Then she kept getting bigger and bigger, and she'd be tired and complaining all the time. I could

hardly wait for her to finish being pregnant. And when that was over, she was too busy and too tired to pay me any mind.

I used to get mad and holler a lot. Or else I'd stay out late at night and get her worried about what I was doing. We had nothing but fights in those days because all she wanted to do was to take care of the baby, and she never had any time for me. It sounds dumb when I talk about it now—a man being jealous of a little kid, but I guess I was (Rubin, 1976, p. 82).

Marital Quality through the Later Stages of Marriage.   Marital quality generally continues to decline after the first years of parenthood, especially after children reach school age (Anderson et al., 1983; Rollins and Galligan, 1978). The negative effects of children are especially severe for lower-socioeconomic-status women who are employed (Schumm and Bugaighis, 1986). When children reach adolescence, the relationships they have with their parents are related to the marital relationship between their parents. Mothers who report having difficulties with their oldest daughters, and fathers who report difficulties with their oldest sons, are both more likely to be less satisfied with their marriages than parents who have fewer problems with their children (Steinberg and Silverberg, 1987). Many different studies show consistent evidence that children put a strain on parents and make their marital relationships less satisfying.

The negative effects that children have on marital happiness is shown in a study of what happens when the last child leaves home. At one time it was widely assumed that parents (especially mothers) would be upset and at "loose ends" when the last child left them in an "empty nest." But a study of parents who had "launched" their last child showed that this event clearly improved marital happiness, and under some circumstances it improved general life satisfaction as well (White and Edwards, 1990).

Since marital quality is high during the early years of marriage, is low during the childbearing years, and improves when children leave home, there is a curvilinear (U-shaped) relationship between stages of marriage and marital quality. This curvilinear relationship has been found in so many studies over the years that one sociologist has described it as ". . . about as close to being certain as anything ever is in the social sciences" (Glenn, 1990, p. 823).

Power as a Dimension of Husband and Wife Relations

Power is the ability to impose one's will upon someone else, and the exercise of power is found in the family just as it is in other social groups. In family decision-making, power is partly a function of traditional male and female roles. In chapter 10 we discussed the way women, especially married women, have traditionally been expected to play a subordinate role to men. When married couples accept the traditional gender-role prescription of the wife as a subordinate to her husband, then she clearly has less power than her husband. Most couples today claim to hold an egalitarian view of marriage; they emphasize that family decisions are made jointly and that neither husband nor wife has greater power. Despite these egalitarian ideals, however, other factors influence the exercise of power in marriages, and these factors also tend to give greater power to husbands.

One important theoretical formulation about family power, called **resource theory,** explains the distribution of power in terms of the resources brought into the marriage by each of the spouses (Blood and Wolfe, 1960). Resources include income-earning ability, education, and occupational prestige, which are all closely tied to the economic world outside the home, where men have a distinct advantage over women. Of course, there may also be noneconomic resources, such as companionship, emotional support, and social skills—attributes that have been more closely associated with women (Safilios-Rothschild, 1970).

Although noneconomic resources may give some advantage to women, the fact is that in American society greater weight is given to money, status, and occupational prestige. These latter characteristics are exactly what gives husbands in most marriages a distinct advantage over their wives. The larger society, in which all marriages are embedded, gives men distinct advantages in money earnings and occupational status and prestige (Szinovacz, 1987).

Research over the last 25 years on the power relations between husbands and wives has continued to show that husbands have greater power in marriages than their wives (Allen, 1984; Olsen and Cromwell, 1975; Scanzoni, 1979; Szinovacz, 1987). Despite the fact that many husbands and wives seek an egalitarian ideal, they do not always achieve it. In the next section we will see one major manifestation of the continuing marital power of males: despite ever-greater participation of married women in the labor force, they continue to do the greatest proportion of family work, such as cooking, cleaning, and child care.

The Family and Employment

A very important feature of marriage and family life today is the relationship between family and employment. There was a time, not many years ago, when the family and employment were viewed as two separate worlds. That may always have been a myth, but today, in a very real sense, the worlds of family and employment are closely linked.

Sociology in the News

Japan's Bachelor Fathers

The newspaper photograph shows a neatly dressed Japanese man seated at the table in his "bachelor apartment." He looks up from a family photo album, while on the table, at arm's reach, stands a nearly empty bottle of scotch and a nearly full drinking glass. This man is one of a reported half a million Japanese mid-level executives who are living away from their families as "field office bachelors" (Reid, 1991).

The devotion of Japanese men to their jobs, often at the expense of their family lives, is well known. Even when Japanese men live at home they often spend most of their waking hours away from their families, generally working long days and then frequently unwinding in the evening with their working companions.

The field office bachelors in Japan are a new but growing example of devotion to the corporation (the numbers are estimated to be increasing by 10 percent a year). These men, and they almost invariably are men, are asked by their Tokyo-based companies to take positions in distant cities. Usually their transfer to a branch office is a step up on the corporate ladder.

Although their families could move along with them, couples often choose to live separately. There are several reasons for this decision, but the one cited most often (in 85 percent of the cases) is that children would have to leave schools they have worked very hard to get into (see chapter 12 on the Japanese educational system). Another reason is related to housing. Most of these men expect to be returned to the corporate headquarters in Tokyo after two or three years, and they are reluctant to give up their homes in the capital city. Another reason for leaving the family behind, although it is not often stated explicitly, is that men can devote even more of their time and energy to their jobs if they are living alone. One hotel executive said, " 'It's like a soldier; you don't want your wife and kids along on the battlefield' " (Reid, 1991, p. D9).

The field office bachelors will usually try to visit their families one weekend a month. These monthly visits, along with telephone conversations, constitute most of the family interaction. Of course, as already noted, many Japanese men spend very little time with their families anyway. One 16-year-old daughter said " 'Oh, Daddy always comes home so late anyway, what's the difference if he doesn't live here?' " (Reid, 1991, p. D9).

The Japanese have been concerned about the possible negative effects of the split-family arrangement on family relations, but the divorce rate in Japan continues to be low (about one-third of the U.S. rate). Studies of families who have lived apart have found that the separation is good for the family in the long run.

In the United States there is a comparable example of families being split up because of their work, but the cause is usually different. In increasing numbers, when both husbands and wives have careers, couples face the question of whether to move, or at least temporarily live apart. This has led to "commuter marriages" for some couples, because one spouse's career can benefit from a move but the other spouse's career requires staying in the same place (Gerstel and Gross, 1984). This difficult decision is most likely to be faced by college-educated husbands and wives when both have significant careers.

GERSTAL, NAOMI, and GROSS, HARRIET ENGEL. *Commuter Marriage.* New York: The Guildford Press, 1984.
REID, T.R. "Japan's Husbands in Exile." *The Washington Post,* April 18, 1991.

Prior to the industrial revolution, work and family were closely tied together. In the United States when the economy was largely agricultural and other industries were at the craft level (shoemaking and tailoring, for example), almost all work was done by family units. However, when industries became mechanized and powered by water, coal, and steam, the places of employment moved out of the home. Men went out into the work world—factories and offices—and the concept of the breadwinner emerged. At the same time, women, especially in the middle and upper classes, remained in the home. This situation led to the glorification of women as homemakers, and the breadwinner/homemaker division of labor came into being. In the United States the transition to the breadwinner/homemaker system reached its peak at the beginning of the twentieth century. At that time only about 5 percent of married women were employed outside the home (Davis, 1984).

The nineteenth-century movement that separated women from the workplace and kept them in the home as homemakers was supported by a new set of cultural values about women, motherhood, and the home. Historians have called this new cultural image the "cult of true womanhood" (Lerner, 1969; Welter, 1966). This image stressed that women had a moral duty and responsibility to remain in the home and care for their families. The "natural" place for women was the home where they could attend to the physical and moral development of their children and give comfort to their husbands, who were facing the cruel and difficult outside world of work (Piotrkowski et al., 1987).

During the twentieth century the ideal of the breadwinner/homemaker system has remained firmly embedded in U.S. culture, but at the same time an objective reality emerged that deviated from it. The percentage of married women in the labor force started going up at the beginning of

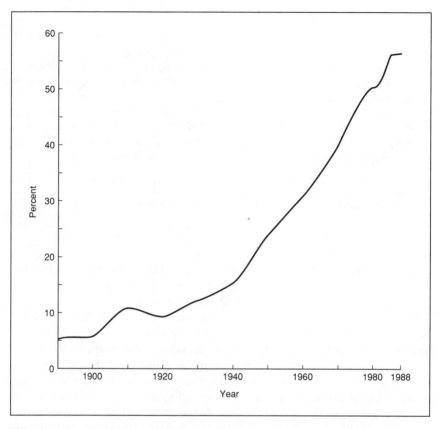

Figure 11–1. Percentage of All Married Women Who Are in the Labor Force, 1890–1988. (*Source:* U.S. Bureau of the Census, 1990).

the century and continued to increase through each decade up to the present time (see figure 11–1).

At the present time only a minority of married women conform to the homemaker ideal, because most are employed in the labor force. In 1988, 57.1 percent of married women with children under six years were employed outside the home; more than 72 percent of married women with children between 6 and 17 years were employed. Also in the labor force were 70 percent of divorced women with children below 6 years and nearly 84 percent of divorced women with children between 6 and 17 years (U.S. Bureau of the Census, 1990). Even though only a small percentage of American mothers are remaining at home as full-time homemakers, the role expectations embedded in the cultural ideal have not disappeared. Mothers rather than fathers are still expected to take primary responsibility for tasks related to children. Women also are expected to do much of the family work, such as cooking and cleaning (Blumberg, 1990; Piotrkowski et al., 1987; Spitze, 1988).

The expectation that women are still primarily responsible for family work is borne out by the research evidence. For example, both men and women today report conflicts between their employment and family obligations; however, men experience the conflict as resulting from the excessive number of hours they work, while women experience the conflict as coming from scheduling difficulties. For women, the scheduling problems reflect their dual responsibilities: their jobs, on the one hand; home and children, on the other (Voydanoff, 1988).

With regard to housework, many studies have been conducted in recent years to see if husbands are taking a larger share of family work. The most consistent conclusion is that women, regardless of whether they are employed, are still doing the great majority of family work. However, after years of finding few significant changes in husbands' contributions, there are indications that husbands are increasing their contributions to family work by a small amount. One study of time use among adults, aged 25–45, in both the United Kingdom and the United States, shows some increases by males. Between the mid-nineteen-seventies and mid-nineteen-eighties, slight increases were noted in both the amount and proportion of domestic work (cooking, cleaning, laundry) done by men. Women in the United States are still doing about three times as much domestic work as men, but this represents less of an imbalance than existed in previous decades. In both the United States and the United Kingdom, women have decreased the number of minutes per week they do domestic work, while men in both countries have increased their domestic work somewhat (Gershuny and Robinson, 1988).

Even when men do somewhat more housework, they often see themselves as "helping their wives" do *their* work. Husbands still see household work as "feminine home chores" (Barnett and Baruch, 1987).

Mismatched Work Schedules

When both husbands and wives are working, there is a fairly good chance that their work schedules will not be the same. Only 8½ percent of all working couples have perfectly matched schedules, which leaves over 90 percent with mismatched schedules. A substantial minority of working couples have extremely mismatched schedules because one is working during a "normal" work day, while the other is working **shift work.** Shift work, done at night or on an irregular schedule, is especially characteristic of many service occupations. Frequently, these are occupations filled primarily by women—nurses, waitresses, sales workers, and telephone operators (Presser, 1988).

Many couples with children may be making the choice to work at different times of the day so that one of the two parents will be available at all times to care for the children. This work arrangement eliminates taking the children to a babysitter or leaving them with a child-care service. Although there may be child-care advantages when the husband and wife work at different times, serious disadvantages may arise with respect to the marital relationship. One study has shown that 11 percent of employed couples have work schedules that may give them as little as an hour together between the time one spouse returns home and the other leaves for work. In some cases one spouse must leave for work before the other returns home (Nock and Kingston, 1984). When married couples are limited in the amount of time they have together, fewer opportunities are available for resolving problems, for intimacy, and for sexual relations (Piotrkowski and Gornick, 1986; Piotrkowski, 1987).

Research has shown that shift work does have the expected negative effects on marriage (White and Keith, 1990). Analysis of data coming from 1668 married women and men showed that shift work has a negative impact on every dimension of marital quality (e.g., happiness, disagreements, sexual life, and others). This research also showed that, over a three-year period, shift work increased the probability of divorce from 7 percent to 11 percent (White and Keith, 1990).

The concept of "work spillover" has been developed to emphasize how the pressures and demands of many kinds of work and professional occupations can intrude on family life (Small and Riley, 1990). In a study of 130 male executives and their spouses, the researchers were able to measure the amount of "work spillover" and show how marital relations, as well as other aspects of family life (parent–child relationships, leisure, and home management), were negatively affected (Small and Riley, 1990).

Conflict and Violence in the Family

The mass media have made most Americans aware of "abused children" and "battered wives." It is now well-known that violence occurs in families, although some confusion might still remain about its nature and frequency. Sociologists started examining the nature and extent of family violence in the 1970s, and as a result of their research, we now have a clearer and fuller understanding of this important social problem (Gelles, 1987; Steinmetz, 1987).

One misconception about family violence is that it is associated only with pathological or "sick" individuals. The most extreme and bizarre cases, often leading to serious injury and even death, are most widely reported; and on the basis of these cases, many people conclude that violence is the product of a mentally ill person. However, sociological studies have shown that violence is widely condoned as an acceptable way to deal with family problems, and is used frequently in "normal" or "average" families.

Many people in the United States accept the idea that it is legitimate to hit family members—under some circumstances. Marital partners, for example, often justify hitting a spouse, or being hit by a spouse, for one of two basic reasons: (1) the spouse is doing (or has done) something wrong in the eyes of the aggressor; or (2) the spouse "won't listen to reason" (Straus, 1980, p. 693). Both of these justifications can be found in interviews with a young married couple named Jennifer and Joe (LaRossa, 1980). Jennifer described herself as a strong-willed person who had been independent for much of her life and wanted to "run things" in her marriage. Her husband concurred in this evaluation, but he had opposing ideas about who should dominate the marriage. When the interviewer asked if Jennifer still wanted to run things, the following interchange occurred:

INTERVIEWER: Do you think you run things now?
JENNIFER: No, I tried, though!
JOE: She tries. One day we had a conflict and she more or less tried to run me and I told her no, and she got hysterical and said, "I could kill you!" And I got rather angry and slapped her in the face three or four times and I said, "Don't you ever say that to me again." And we haven't had any problems since (LaRossa, 1980, p. 160).

Joe analyzed his use of violence in the following way:

You don't use it until you are forced to. At that point I felt I had to do something physical to stop the bad progression of events. I took my chances with that and it worked (LaRossa, 1980, p. 160).

Later in the interview, Jennifer said:

Joe doesn't usually use force. That was the first and last time he'll ever do that. It was my fault. I was trying to dominate him, that's for sure (LaRossa, 1980, p. 161).

Joe, in this case, justified his use of violence by implying that Jennifer had gone too far in trying to dominate him. But, in addition, by saying that she was "hysterical," he was justifying what he had done on the grounds that she was beyond reason. For her part, Jennifer made it clear that it would be the last time he would hit her, but then she immediately added that it was her fault.

The case of Jennifer and Joe reveals that both the victim and the aggressor accepted violence under some circumstances. In this regard they are not unlike many other married couples. In a national sample of married couples, approximately one out of three husbands and one out of four wives agreed that it was at least "somewhat necessary," "somewhat normal," or "somewhat good" for couples to "slap each other around" (Straus et al., 1980, p. 47).

One of the most encouraging results coming from these studies is that family violence may have declined since 1975. Two national surveys, conducted ten years apart—the first in 1975, the second in 1985—allow comparisons to be made over that period of time. In these surveys, violence was measured by asking interviewees to think of situations in the last year when they had had a disagreement or were angry with a specified member of the family (e.g., wives might be asked about husbands). Interviewees were then asked if they had engaged in certain acts in that situation; these acts included throwing something at the other person, pushing, grabbing, shoving, slapping, spanking, kicking, biting, hitting with a fist, hitting with something else, beating, threatening with a knife or gun, and using a knife or gun (Gelles and Cornell, 1990; Straus and Gelles, 1986).

Between 1975 and 1985 *severe* violence (kicking, biting, hitting with fist, and more extreme) by husbands against wives declined from 38 cases per 1000 to 30 cases per 1000. As the researchers point out, this reduction may seem small, but when thought of in terms of the total number of United States' couples, this difference could result in 432,000 fewer beaten wives.

These changes at least give some hope that there has been a reduction of violence in the family, perhaps produced in part by women's having more options (shelters, support groups), greater police and law enforcement support, and a recognition on the part of males that they cannot use physical violence. It is possible that the reductions in violence, as reported in the national survey, may simply reflect people's greater reluctance to report violent acts to interviewers. While that may be, the researchers take some hope even from this possibility, arguing that the reluctance may reflect a change in public attitudes and may indicate new standards regarding the acceptability of violence in the family (Steinmetz, 1987; Straus and Gelles, 1986).

Survey research on violence in the family has often turned up the somewhat surprising finding that wives commit violent acts against their husbands at the same rate that husbands do against wives (Gelles and Cornell, 1990; Brush, 1990). This has been a very controversial finding, and has been debated vigorously in the social science literature. Feminist writers, especially, have pointed out how the statistics coming from surveys can be very misleading (Brush, 1990). Even though wives may say they have engaged in violent acts against their husbands, they very rarely *injure* their husbands. Males are bigger and stronger, and their blows do much more damage than those of females. Often wives are striking back after being hit or they are defending themselves (Saunders, 1986). Even when women are the aggressors (i.e., commit the first act of violence), husbands often respond with more violent acts and are apt to strike the most damaging blows.

Child Abuse and Maltreatment

Before 1960 public awareness of child abuse was low; that does not mean, however, that children were not abused in earlier times, for child abuse has a long and terrible history. One historian has said: ". . . the history of childhood is a nightmare from which we have only recently begun to awaken. The further back in history one goes, the lower the level of childcare, and the more likely children are to be killed, abandoned, beaten, terrorized, and sexually abused" (deMause, 1974, p. 1).

Today, child abuse is recognized as being much more widespread than just occasional sensational stories of severe abuse. Child abuse is now understood as covering a range of behaviors, including physical abuse, sexual abuse, and physical neglect. Emotional abuse, which is much more difficult to define and detect, is also recognized for the harm it can do to children. However, even with this increase in public awareness, parents commit a variety of physical and verbal actions against their children in the name of discipline and normal punishment.

In the 1940s Hollywood actress Joan Crawford reared her two children in a severe manner because she believed that, in this way, they would learn how to work and behave properly. When her daughter, as an adult, published an autobiographical account of the way she and her brother had been treated as children, many readers concluded that the children had been mistreated and abused (Crawford, 1978). And yet, it seems that Miss Crawford's colleagues, friends, and visitors saw her only as a strict and demanding mother whose children always behaved perfectly. Even today, some people might discount the daughter's account as exaggerated and, in any case, give the benefit of the doubt to the parent.

The abuse and mistreatment of children in the family have been called a hidden problem because the public generally accepts that parents may use physical methods to punish children. Corporal punishment is defined as an act intended to inflict physical pain on a person. Exactly when this physical pain is excessive is difficult to ascertain. In the range of physical punishments, U.S. legal and informal norms allow parents to spank and slap a child, or to hit a child with an instrument such as a stick, hair brush, or belt. In the 1985 survey of adult Americans, the rate of slapping or spanking children between 3 and 17 was over 549 per 1000 children. Thus, in any year the likelihood of a parent's hitting a child is more than 50 percent. The rate of hitting or trying to hit a child with some object was 97 per 1000—one in ten. The rate for very severe violent acts against children, including kicking, hitting with a fist, beating up, or using a knife or gun in some way, was 19 per 1000. It must be remembered that these figures come from the admissions of parents during telephone interviews, and may therefore understate the extent of violence toward children. However, again, some encouragement may be found in the declining rate between 1975 and 1985 of very severe violence against children. During these years, the rate of very severe violence against children declined 47 percent (Straus and Gelles, 1986).

Studies of family violence have shown consistently that families have a cycle of violence—violence in one generation is continued in the following generation. When children are treated with violence, they are more apt to become adults who see violence as a way of solving their problems. As adults they are more likely to hit their spouses and their own children. And in a final irony, children who have been struck by their parents are more likely to strike these same parents when they reach old age. Because of the cyclical nature of family violence, the family provides the training ground for violence (Steinmetz, 1987).

Separation and Divorce

Any discussion of contemporary marriage and family life must consider the issue of divorce. The divorce rate in the United States is higher than any other country for which there are acceptable data. The next highest rates of divorce are found in New Zealand and the Soviet Union (Reiss and Lee, 1988).

For the United States, statistical projections lead some researchers to conclude that nearly 50 percent of all marriages started in the 1970s could end in divorce (Weed, 1980). An even more extreme conclusion has been reached about marriages started in the 1980s, by two researchers who have concluded that nearly two-thirds of these recent marriages will be disrupted, by *either* separation or divorce[2] (Martin and Bumpass, 1989).

---

[2] This study is different from most studies attempting to determine the chances of divorce because it is based on a national sample of the U.S. population (Current Population Survey) rather than divorce statistics from the states. It is also unusual because separation is counted as a marital disruption, the same as an actual divorce.

This conclusion does not mean that two-thirds of these marriages *will* end in divorce. The researchers have simply projected this outcome because of the amount of separation and divorce that has already occurred in the first years of the early 1980s' marriages. So far, the disruption of these marriages seems to be outpacing that of 1970s' marriages, and thus could lead to the very high projected level of marital disruption. One must be very cautious, however, about projecting a number of years into the future because unanticipated events may make these projections invalid. It will be many years before we actually know how many of the marriages of the early 1980s will be disrupted by divorce.

The most realistic way to evaluate trends in divorce is to look at divorce rates, not the projected percentages of marriages that might end in divorce. A useful divorce rate can be obtained by determining the number of divorces in any year per 1000 marriages existing in the population. It is best to relate divorces to existing marriages, because any marriage in the population is "at risk" for a divorce. For the United States this divorce rate is shown in figure 11–2, which covers the years 1925 to the present.

Divorce Rate Trends in the United States

During the twentieth century the overall trend in divorce has obviously been upward, although there have been some notable ups and downs in the divorce rate.

One obvious pattern in figure 11–2 is the high peak of divorce in the middle 1940s. This peak corresponds with the end of World War II and probably reflects the way in which marriages were affected by couples being apart. The instability of marriages that were entered into hastily during the war is undoubtedly a factor here as well.

However, an even more dramatic increase in the divorce rate started in the 1960s and continued through most of the 1970s. During these two decades the divorce rate of the United States more than doubled. Several societal-level explanations for this rapid increase are possible. Since wars have sometimes been associated with increases in divorce, some sociologists have suggested that the Vietnam War might have been a contributing factor (Glick and Lin, 1986). However, that war could not account for the entire period of 20 years, since its societal impact was limited to the late nineteen-sixties and early nineteen-seventies. Also the proportion of the young population in the military was much smaller than in previous wars. Furthermore, a similar twentieth-century war—the Korean conflict—was associated with a *decline* in the divorce rate (South, 1985).

More frequently, explanations for the rising divorce rate of the 1960s

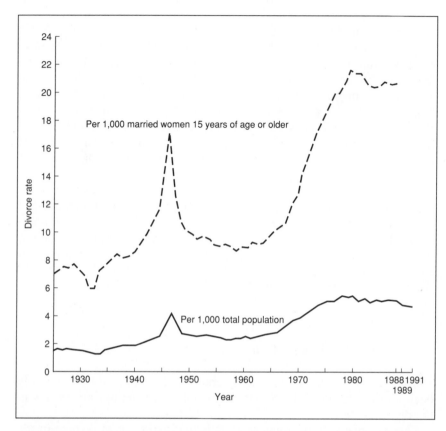

Figure 11–2. Divorce Rates for the United States, 1925–1990. (*Sources:* National Center for Health Statistics, 1981. "Advance Report on Final Divorce Statistics, 1981." National Center for Health Statistics, 1985. "Births, Marriages, Divorces and Deaths for 1981." National Center for Health Statistics, "Advance Report, Final Divorce Statistics, 1988. Vol. 39, Hyattsville, Md.: Public Health Service, 1991; National Center for Health Statistics, "Births, Marriages, Divorces, and Deaths for January 1991." Vol. 40, 1991.

and 1970s have centered around the major cultural and societal changes of that period. One notable change was the rise of the women's movement, or feminism, which emphasized, among other things, that women should have equal opportunities for self-realization and personal development. During this period women moved into education and the labor force in greater numbers than ever before, which may have had the effect of freeing them from marriages that were less than satisfactory. Of course, a general liberalization of social and sexual norms also took place during this time that may have freed many married people, both men and women, from traditional constraints and obligations (Raschke, 1987).

Although the United States' divorce rate is still at a high level, it has stabilized and even declined slightly during the 1980s. Some plausible explanations have been offered as to why the divorce rate is no longer climbing (Kammeyer, 1981). One factor may be that the average age of marriage in the United States has been increasing for some years. Viewed in another way, marriages among 18-year-old and 19-year-old women have sharply declined. The marriage rate for women in this age group in 1984 was only 35 percent of what it was in 1960. All available evidence points to the fact that when one marries early, especially in the teenage years, the chance of divorce is much higher (Booth and Edwards, 1985; Glenn and Supancic, 1984). Even during the 1980s, when the divorce rate for all other age groups was going down, the divorce rate among married women under 20 was *still increasing* (Glick and Lin, 1986).

A closely related factor that may account for the slight decline in the divorce rate during the 1980s is the reduction in marriages precipitated by premarital pregnancies. Some studies have shown that premarital pregnancy is related to higher divorce rates (Furstenberg, 1976, 1979a), while other studies have found that only premarital childbearing is related to higher divorce rates (Billy et al., 1986; Teachman, 1983).

Several reasons exist as to why premarital pregnancies and premarital childbearing are not leading to marriages as often as they did in the past. First, although higher percentages of unmarried young people are having sexual intercourse at earlier ages, they are more likely to use contraception than they did in the early 1970s (Zelnik and Kantner, 1980). Second, even when premarital pregnancies do occur, they do not lead to marriage as often as they would have in previous decades. Apparently less stigma is attached to an unmarried woman's having and raising a baby, so there is less pressure for some women to marry. But the more important reason that premarital pregnancy is not leading to marriage is the availability of legal abortion. Forty-two percent of teenagers who become pregnant have abortions (Henshaw, et al., 1991). Without abortion, some of these pregnancies would have led to teenage (pregnancy-prompted) marriages, which, as we have noted, have a higher chance of divorce.

Another factor that may be contributing to a decline in the divorce rate is that, for women, the economic consequences of divorce are often severe (Weitzman, 1985). Although men fare quite well economically after divorce, women have substantial declines in their levels of living. Weitzman concluded that divorced women had a 73 percent decline in their standard of living approximately one year after divorce. A reanalysis of her data indicates that the lowered level in income for divorced women may not have been quite as severe—perhaps only a decline of one-third—but the decline is still substantial (Hoffman and Duncan, 1988). Furthermore, when divorce occurs in families where the predivorce income is over $40,000, even the reanalysis of Weitzman's data shows declines of over 50 percent. If women can foresee that divorce will lead to substantial declines in level of living, they may choose to remain in less-than-satisfactory marriages. Effectively, then, the divorce rate would be somewhat reduced.

The combined influence of all these factors could produce stability or even a further decline in divorce in the future. And yet, as we noted earlier, early 1980s' marriages have a high level of marital disruption (Martin and Bumpass, 1989). The actual rate of divorce during the 1990s will be the only certain way of determining whether contemporary marriages are more or less stable than they were when the divorce rate was at its peak in 1979.

The Separation and Divorce Experience

Separation and divorce are almost always stressful and disruptive events in people's lives. Even though both parties may agree that divorce is the correct course of action for them, it is nonetheless a wrenching personal experience. Divorce, by all accounts, is a confusing tangle of emotional experiences, uncertain decisions, and difficult actions.

In an attempt to sort out some of the complexities of the experience, Bohannan (1970) has identified six different "stations" of divorce. These are:

1. Emotional divorce—the recognition that the emotional relationship with one's spouse is deteriorating and the marriage is ending.

2. Legal divorce—the process of learning and going through the legal and procedural steps required by the state.

3. Co-parental divorce—the determination of the custody of children, visitation rights, and child support.

4. Economic divorce—the division of money and property, and the establishment of levels of economic support (alimony).

5. Community divorce—the changes necessary, because of the divorce, in relating to friends, relatives, and associates.

6. Psychic divorce—the process of regaining an individual identity and autonomy.

The emotional divorce, which is when individuals conclude that their marriage may actually end and they begin to act on that conclusion, is the most stressful stage of the divorce process. A divorce means the end of a relationship that one has entered into with the expectation that it will last a lifetime. Divorce means a refutation of one's earlier decision, which makes it very hard for most married people, even when the marriage has been unhappy.

The legal divorce has changed greatly since 1970 because since that time almost every state has adopted some form of "no-fault" divorce. When no-fault divorce is possible—or required, as it is in some states— an adversary divorce procedure, in which one spouse charges the other with some wrongdoing (adultery, cruelty, mental cruelty, and others), is no longer necessary. Today couples can usually get a divorce by claiming irreconcilable differences, irretrievable breakdown, or incompatibility. Although divorce is easier to obtain than it was previously, no evidence supports the claim that liberalized divorce laws have been the cause of increasing divorce rates. Evidence does show that the change to no-fault divorce laws has had the positive effect of reducing the legal wrangling and rancor so often found in adversary divorce cases (Bahr, 1983; Raschke, 1987; Weitzman, 1985).

The economic divorce has also changed in recent years. As we noted above, women today fare much worse after divorce than men, for several reasons. If minor children are involved, wives receive custody in about 90 percent of the cases. There are clear economic costs to having children, including the additional costs for food, clothing, and shelter. Child support from fathers is almost always inadequate and frequently not received. Alimony or economic maintenance is rarely awarded to wives today after a divorce. Community property laws often require the sale of a couple's major asset, their home. When the proceeds from the home are divided, husbands, with their typically greater earning power, can usually repurchase a home of comparable value; wives frequently cannot (Arendell, 1987; Grella, 1990; Weitzman, 1985).

The community divorce is a reversal of the community aspects of marriage. When two people marry, they make a public (community) commitment through the wedding announcement and ceremony. Although norms and rituals exist for most other transitions in marriage and family life, there are no similar rituals for the end of marriage. The announcement of a separation or divorce is typically awkward for the person who makes it and the person who hears it. The confusion is reflected in the words of one man, who responded to the news of his associate's separation by asking: "Do I feel sorry for you or congratulate you?" (Bohannan, 1970).

The psychic divorce is almost always the last stage of a divorce. The process of adjustment that comes after the divorce itself involves the dual tasks of establishing a new life and a new personal identity. This process is often very difficult, especially for people who have been married for a long time. Not atypical is the statement of a woman who is about 35 years old:

> I feel this total lack of any direction. You know, I'm flailing around, "What am I going to do? What am I going to be when I grow up?" You know, one would like to know before one got one foot in the grave (Weiss, 1975, p. 69).

The Effects of Divorce on Children

Because a million children a year in the United States have parents who divorce, there is widespread concern about how the divorce affects these children psychologically, educationally, and socially. The research on this matter has demonstrated what is generally expected. When parents are in the process of separating, a great deal of stress falls on the children except, of course, if they are infants (Hetherington et al., 1978; Longfellow, 1979; Wallerstein and Kelly, 1975, 1976).

Children who are in the later preschool years, between the ages of three and one-half and six, often respond egocentrically to the separation and may blame themselves for what has happened. A child of this age might say, "Daddy left home because I was a bad boy—I didn't put away my toys that day" (Longfellow, 1979, p. 300). Children of school age, especially between 6 and 12, have a wide range of emotional responses to divorcing parents, but they commonly cover up their fears and negative feelings. Eventually, however, anger, fear, loss of identity, and loneliness are likely to emerge (Wallerstein and Kelly, 1976).

Children who are teenagers or older when their parents divorce also have feelings of anger, sadness, and a sense of loss or betrayal. However, at these ages they can also be more detached and analytical about their parents and their relationships with them (Longfellow, 1979).

Many studies have been conducted on the long-range effects of divorce on children, but the results are mixed. A recent study compared third- and fourth-grade children whose families had *recently been disrupted* with children in situations where disruption had occurred earlier, and with children in intact families. The children who had recently experienced family disruption showed somewhat lower academic achievement and performance than the other two categories of children (Kinard and Rein-herz, 1986). A study of 12-year-old to 16-year-old children found more behavioral problems among the youngsters whose families had been dis-rupted (Peterson and Zill, 1986). Evidence also shows that in adulthood the children of divorced parents (especially females) are somewhat more likely to divorce than the children of parents who did not divorce (Glenn and Kramer, 1987; Keith and Finlay, 1988). Although all of these results are negative for the children of divorce, their severity and depth should not be overstated. Most children of divorce do not show serious long-run impairments, either psychological or social (Kitson and Morgan, 1990; Kulka and Weingarten, 1979; Kurdek et al., 1981; Raschke, 1987).

Although the effect of divorce on children is complex, widespread agreement exists that conflict between parents during separation and divorce is likely to have negative impacts on children. But parents who remain married and have high levels of conflict are also apt to affect their children adversely. Finally, when divorced husbands and wives continue to have conflicts after divorce, their children will suffer (Demo and Acock, 1988; Kline et al., 1991).

Family Relations after Divorce

Divorced parents with minor children usually continue to have regular contact. Children often live primarily with the parent who has custody, but they may often be spending some time in the home of the noncustodial parent as well. The concept of the **binuclear family** describes a family system made up of the two households of divorced parents, in which minor children move from one parent's home to the other (Ahrons, 1981). This family system requires a considerable amount of coordination and cooperation between divorced spouses (Masheter, 1991). When the relationship between them is relatively friendly (or not hostile), the task of coordinating activities that involve the children can usually be handled with minimal problems. However, if divorced spouses have unresolved conflicts, a high likelihood exists that children will be used as a way of hurting or gaining advantage over the former spouse (Ahrons and Rodgers, 1987; Weiss, 1979).

Remarriage

About five out of six men and nearly three out of four women remarry after divorce (Glick and Lin, 1986; Thornton and Freedman, 1983). The chances of women's remarrying, however, vary greatly according to the age at which they divorce. A woman who divorces under the age of 25 has nearly a 90 percent chance of remarrying, but this percentage goes down to 60 percent for those who divorce in their thirties, and to just over 30 percent for those who divorce at age 40 or older (Bumpass et al., 1990).

The generally high rates of remarriage have led to large numbers of remarried couple households. A **remarried couple household** is a household maintained by a married couple, one or both of whom have been previously married (Cherlin and McCarthy, 1985, p. 23). When one or both partners in a remarriage bring children to that marriage, the resulting family is often called a **blended, or reconstituted, family** (Duberman, 1975; Spanier and Furstenberg, 1987).

The families created by remarriage, especially when there are children involved (his, hers, or theirs), are filled with complexity, uncertainty, and problems. One source of problems is the incomplete institutionalization of remarriage (Cherlin, 1978). Remarriage is an incomplete institution because the roles and norms and even the legal aspects of remarriage have not yet evolved enough to give order to this new family form. One illustration of incomplete institutionalization is found in the shortcomings of our language. We do not have terms or names for many people who may be, in a sense, part of one's kin group—what does one call the parents of one's father's new wife?

The most common problem connected with the families of remarriage results from the fact that the boundaries of families have expanded to include many new people for whom there are no clear role relationships. Many complications are introduced into family life by these greater numbers of people for whom there are ambiguous obligations and relationships (Spanier and Furstenberg, 1987).

Summary

The family can be organized in many different ways and still carry out a variety of functions that can be both necessary and useful for the society. Some important functions of the family, found in most societies, are reproduction, care and nurturance of children, socialization, fulfillment of economic needs, provision of intergenerational and kin support, regulation of sexual behavior, and social placement. Many different types of family structures exist, as well as many different norms governing the family life.

The family is an adaptive institution. Historical and contemporary examples support the idea that the family is likely to adapt to changes in other parts of the society, especially the economic system.

In many societies, including contemporary Iran, and to a lesser extent Japan, marriage is arranged by parents. However, in many Western societies the young people themselves choose their mates on the basis of mutual attraction and romantic love. The mate selection system of the United States has, throughout its history, been based primarily on romantic love. But, even when mate selection is left to young people, the family and other social groups can influence the process.

Cohabitation is now a stage of premarried life for many young people. The trend is more advanced in Scandinavia but is also prominent in the United States and Australia.

The early years of marriage are difficult in terms of adjustment, but these are also the years of high satisfaction with the marital relationship. Marital quality tends to decline with the arrival of children and continues to be negatively influenced by children throughout the later life stages. Most evidence shows that marital quality improves in the later years of marriage.

The relationship between family and work (both inside and outside the home) is the source of many complications and problems in contemporary family life. When both husband and wife are employed, they often have mismatched work schedules.

Conflict and violence in marriage is more widespread than is often suspected. The major serious forms of violence are spouse abuse and child abuse. Recent studies have shown slight declines in reported levels of both spouse and child abuse.

The divorce rate of the United States is among the highest in the world. Divorces increased gradually after 1920 and more rapidly in the 1960s and 1970s. Since the peak in 1979, the divorce rate has declined somewhat. The slight decline in the 1980s may be due to later marriage and possibly to the serious economic consequences that divorce has for many women.

Separation and divorce are stressful and complicated experiences. Six stations of divorce have been identified: emotional, legal, co-parental, economic, community, and psychic. As a result of divorce and remarriage, family relationships in contemporary society are becoming increasingly complex.

CRITICAL THINKING

1. Explain how the example of the Nayar shows that the family is an adaptive institution. Give examples of the adaptive nature of families in your society.
2. What functions does the institution of the family commonly serve in societies? Explain how each of these needs is met in your society.
3. Describe the various family types mentioned in the chapter.
4. Compare and contrast various methods for mate selection in different societies. To what extent do these methods reflect basic cultural values of the societies in which they are used?
5. How do you explain the emergence of cohabitation as a stage before marriage?
6. What is marital quality? How might marital scripts and parenthood affect marital quality?
7. What relationship exists between the family and work in contemporary society?
8. Describe the extent to which violence is a part of family life in American society. How do you explain this phenomenon?
9. How does statistical information about divorce and separation support the idea that the family is an adaptive institution?
10. How has divorce complicated the family structure in society? What other institutions in society have been affected by divorce?

12 Education

The United States has a long history of educating its citizens. The educational system of the nation was built on the principles of Thomas Jefferson, who proclaimed that an educated electorate is necessary for a democratic society. Americans value education and often look to the schools to solve social problems or to straighten out "wayward" youth. The statistics also tell us that educational opportunities are nearly universally available and that the actual percentage of youth enrolled in schools is as high as any other country in the world.

However, almost daily we hear or read criticisms of the schools. Critics say that schools are failing to educate our young people, and because the educational system is not doing its job the United States is falling behind in economic and technical competition with other countries. Still other critics say the schools are teaching the wrong things or are not intellectually rigorous enough. Complaints continue to arise about how the schools are run badly or how the teachers teach poorly. Concerns are voiced about too much violence in the schools, too many drugs, and not enough discipline. The list of concerns and complaints about the school system is never-ending.

The paradox is that in the United States, in a country where education is valued and universally provided, the educational system is often seen as a failure. In this chapter we take a sociological look at educational systems. We will direct most of our attention to the educational system of the United States, but comparisons will be made with other countries, especially Japan and Great Britain. We will see both the problems and the successes of educational systems, but, more important, we will see how educational systems are closely tied to the culture and the structure of the societies in which they exist.

A Brief Look at the History of Education in the United States

In the earliest settlements of colonial America, most youngsters were educated in the "real world" instead of the classroom. In 1647, however, more than a century before the American Revolution, the first mandatory school systems were established in the Massachusetts Bay Colony (Monroe, 1940). Education in the United States initially emphasized the four R's: reading, 'riting, 'rithmetic, *and religion*. Later, schools began to replace the emphasis on religion with a variety of occupational and economic concerns. This change reveals a feature of education that we consider more fully below, namely, the tendency for the educational system to reflect the needs and desires of those who control the society. Early in American history a major purpose of education, as defined by colonial leaders, was to serve religious needs. Later, however, economic leaders and economic interests took priority in defining the objectives of the educational system.

Between colonial times and the 1870s, elementary education became more democratized—that is, more widely available to all children. Following the principles of universal education advocated by Jefferson, a free public school system emerged by the mid-1800s. The widespread education of girls at the elementary level also became a reality during this era. By the middle of the nineteenth century, the first public high schools had been founded. This description of a universal and democratic American education has been labeled the *traditional view*. The **traditional view** of the *history* of American education is that the United States was founded on democratic political principles, which required an educated and informed electorate. The United States also had a social and economic philosophy that was highly democratic. According to the ideal, every person, regardless of origins or social background, should have an equal opportunity to achieve and succeed. A school system that is available to all the children of the society, i.e., a free and open system of mass education, is the major means by which equality is assured.

The traditional view of the history of American education still prevails today. Politicians, educators, and most citizens see the system of free and mass education as a way of ensuring that the society will have an informed citizenry, capable of making decisions in a democratic society. The educational system is seen as the key to success and achievement in the United States. However, among historians of education, this view has been challenged by the revisionist view.

The **revisionist view** of the history of American education emphasizes that the economic and social elites of the society will develop an educational system that meets their needs, not the needs of the masses of people. This view is a more critical, a less idealistic, perspective on education, based on the assumption that a fundamental conflict of interests always exists between the elites and masses of the society (Bowles and Gintis, 1976; Katz, 1968, 1987; Mennerick and Najafizadeh, 1987).

The revisionist historians of education contend that a major goal of mass education in the nineteenth century was to socialize the working-class and immigrant children so that they would be better workers in the nation's factories and businesses. The children were not learning the skills necessary for work as much as they were learning proper work habits. The educational system was teaching future workers the importance of punctuality, regular attendance, submission to authority, cleanliness, and order. Nowhere was the link between the needs of industrialization and those of the educational system more vividly revealed than in the "Lancaster system."

The **Lancaster system,** named after its founder Joseph Lancaster, was a school system based on the principles of efficiency and order. Although the Lancaster system was found primarily in urban places, near industries and factories, it became the model for centralized and efficient school systems emerging around the country. In the Lancaster system careful attention was devoted to every detail of student behavior and classroom procedures. Teaching in the classrooms of a Lancaster school was always conducted in precisely the same way: the emphasis was on rote memorization of facts and on strict discipline. The way in which students were seated and even the way in which they wore their hats were carefully regulated. The hats were to be attached by strings to shirt collars, slipped off at the proper signal, and left resting on the students' backs (Parelius and Parelius, 1978, p. 60).

As a way of increasing the efficiency of the system, the Lancaster schools made maximum use of a minimum number of teachers; only one teacher was assigned to every 400 to 500 students. To manage such large numbers of students, the system relied heavily on student "monitors" who had previously been taught the lesson by the teacher. The huge classes were divided into groups of ten, each of which was headed by a monitor.

Lancaster schools were like factories, except that their product happened to be students. It is easy to see how students who were often headed for work in factories were well prepared by a school system that was itself a factory. This interpretation is consistent with the revisionist view of education, since it would obviously be in the interests of factory owners to have well-socialized workers.

In some ways, the traditional and revisionist views of the history of education resemble two competing sociological interpretations of education: functional and conflict theory. Functional theory offers an explanation of education that has some of the same elements as the traditional view. Conflict theory picks up key features of the revisionist view.

Functional Theory and Education

One aspect of functional theory emphasizes that societies are made up of separate institutions that are integrated and interdependent. Thus, in an urban, industrial society, where families are less able to socialize their children for the work force, the educational system will take over some of the socializing functions. The educational system, according to functional theory, will ensure the social, political, and economic stability of the society. The schools can transform heterogeneous ethnic and religious groups into informed and productive citizens who have common values. Viewed in this way, the educational system contributes to an integrated, stable, and smooth-running society (Mennerick and Najafizadeh, 1987).

From a functionalist perspective, the schools perform more than an educational function; they provide a moral function as well. The **moral function** of the educational system is to teach children and young people the norms and values of the society. The norms and values are taught, in part, through the day-to-day activities of classrooms and schools, and, in part, through the content of what is taught to the young people. For example, even at the kindergarten level, children are being taught that they must conform to the expectations of those in authority and respect the rights of others. Kindergarten teachers organize the lives of the children in a way that prepares them for the order and conformity necessary at higher grades (Gracey, 1967).

The content of education, especially at the elementary level but to some degree at the secondary level, often depicts the culture of the society in ideal terms. The ideal culture, as we saw in chapter 3, reflects the cultural norms and values as they are supposed to be, not as they are. The materials presented by the schools, beginning with the earliest reading books and stories, are lessons in the "ideal" way of life. Families in these books and stories usually include a father, mother, probably two children (a boy and a girl, of course), pets, a pleasant house, a car, and so on. Even if a few of the contemporary books and stories show the mother working, or apartment life instead of a house in the suburbs, their depiction of life is far from the realities of life experienced by many children. Rarely will the stories describe divorced families, poverty, poor housing, large families (or, for that matter, married couples without children), illegitimacy, or sibling fights. Such books never show the more negative features of family life such as child or wife abuse or parental neglect. We are not arguing here that they should show this side, but we are emphasizing that education, particularly at the elementary level, tends to offer an idealistic version of the culture in which the students live.

The same kind of idealized treatment is given to all institutional spheres. Political affairs are typically described in their ideal form—a political system as it is supposed to work, not as it actually works. Courses in government teach about checks and balances, not about bribes, payoffs, corruption, excesses of power, falsification of records, or illegal use of government resources. As the educational process continues at the college and university levels, students are often given more realistic and critical assessments of their society and its culture. However, the early emphasis on the positive and idealized versions often causes these views to become deeply internalized.

Because schools transmit a society's norms and values, the student is likely to internalize and accept as proper most of the values and rules that guide the larger society. For example, competition and achievement are two widely accepted American values. The school is instrumental in conveying the idea that it is fair to give different rewards for different levels of achievement (Parsons, 1959). Children soon learn that those who get their lessons done quickly and accurately will be praised and rewarded with good grades. Furthermore, and this is a very important lesson, the highest achievers will be given additional rewards—being allowed to carry out special errands for the teacher, becoming room monitors, engaging in recreational activities, and receiving honors and recognition. The winners not only get the intrinsic reward of accomplishing their school work but they get the additional external rewards as well.

This familiar classroom experience teaches a variety of lessons that apply again and again throughout life. The lesson that most activities are competitive is reinforced later in dating, making athletic teams, winning college scholarships, being admitted to the best colleges, getting into a professional or graduate school, and getting the best jobs.

Functional theorists view this part of the school's teaching in a positive light because it provides a shared set of values for all the people of the society who have gone through the school system. The moral function of the schools helps to integrate and stabilize the society. Conflict theorists, as we will see below, view this matter somewhat differently.

Functional theory also emphasizes that an educational institution, especially one that rewards students for their ability and the quality of their work, provides an equal opportunity for every individual. The task of the schools is, therefore, to evaluate and sort the students according to their ability and performance (Mennerick and Najafizadeh, 1987).

Conflict Theory and Education

Conflict theory stresses that in any social system or society conflicts of interests will exist between different groups or categories of people. This theory also stresses that some groups will have more power than others and that the most powerful groups will take advantage of their position to maximize their interests. Thus, conflict theorists agree that the schools teach and gain acceptance for the prevailing norms and values of the society, but these are the norms and values that especially serve the needs of the advantaged and powerful people of the society.

When children in the schools learn that competition and achievement are the routes to economic rewards and high status, the positions of those who already have wealth and high status are legitimized. It is in the best interests of those who are already in advantaged and powerful positions to get the largest number of people agreeing that they have a right to be there. It is especially important that people who are in lower-status positions, and are likely to remain there, accept the legitimacy of a system of inequality.

Not only do children learn in school that competition and achievement are the routes to reward but, more important, they also learn to believe in the correctness of this method of obtaining rewards. For nearly everyone the method learned is so right that it seems natural or even instinctive. Even those who do not win the competition and thus do not get the rewards generally believe in and accept the system. Often losers blame themselves for not getting the rewards. Rarely do they question the legitimacy of the norms and values of the system (Sennett and Cobb, 1972).

Conflict theorists also see the educational system as organized to favor the interests of the most powerful members of the society in another way that is similar to the revisionist historical view of education: the educational system will produce the kinds of workers needed by the dominant economic interests of the society (Useem, 1986). The schools often do this, as we have seen, by providing well-socialized workers who have learned to be responsible and to carry out the assignments they have been given.

Another point of dispute between conflict and functional theorists concerns the fairness of the educational system. Conflict theorists see the schools as organized and operated in ways that give the children of the advantaged groups a better chance of succeeding, and thus the schools perpetuate inequalities in the social structure. The sharpest continuing dispute between conflict and functional theorists rests on this last point.

Instead of an educational system that gives everyone equal opportunities for success, conflict theorists argue that the system favors the children of higher-status families and works against the lower-status youngsters (Bowles and Gintis, 1976).

The differences between the views of functional theorists and conflict theorists regarding the educational system may be summarized around three issues:

1. Functionalists view the teaching of cultural norms and values as an integrating function of schools; conflict theorists view these norms and values as favoring the already dominant groups in the society.
2. Functionalists see the educational system as providing the skilled and trained workers needed by the economy; conflict theorists see the educational system as providing a docile work force that will be used by the dominant economic interests.
3. Functionalists view the educational system as fair and equitable— a system that gives everyone a chance at success, based on individual ability, hard work, and diligence; conflict theorists see unfairness and inequity in the educational system—a system that operates to keep lower-status youngsters in their place at the bottom of the social structure and that gives the children of the advantaged groups a greater likelihood of success.

Throughout this chapter, as we examine different aspects of educational systems and schools, we will see these issues reflected at several points: at the elementary, secondary, and college levels, and in educational systems of the United States and other countries of the world.

Education and Educational Systems Worldwide

The worldwide picture with regard to education has improved dramatically since the 1950s. The percentage of young people in primary and secondary schools has increased, and often greatly, in virtually every country of the world for which there are available data. In 1950, some European countries had only about half of their children in schools (Italy, 53 percent; Portugal, 40 percent; Romania, 50 percent; Spain, 53 percent; and Yugoslavia, 55 percent). Today, every European country has at least 75 percent of its children in schools, and in most countries the percentage is over 90. The United States stands out, even in comparison with the European countries, since nearly 100 percent of its children are in primary and secondary schools, and have been since 1950 (Najafizadeh and Mennerick, 1990).

In developing countries the percentage of youth enrolled in schools has also increased since 1950. However, even today only about one-quarter of the children in some African and Asian countries are in primary and secondary schools. The largest of these developing countries with low enrollments are Afghanistan (17 percent), Ethiopia (28 percent), and Pakistan (29 percent). Furthermore, the schools that the children attend in developing countries are often seriously inadequate. For example, the developed countries have an average of one teacher for every 28 students; the developing countries have only one teacher for every 87 students. Yearly per capita expenditures on education in developed countries average $477; in developing countries the average is only $79 (Najafizadeh and Mennerick, 1988).

Even the limited amount of money that the developing countries are able to put into education is not equitably distributed. The monies are often concentrated in urban areas, and among the social and economic elites. Subsidies for education are given more to upper-class youth. In a study of ten selected Asian and Latin American countries, youths from the richest 20 percent of the population received from 38 percent to 83 percent of the educational subsidies (World Bank, 1988). Developing countries also use more of their economic resources to support students in higher education than they do for primary and secondary students. This policy, too, benefits the elites of these countries more than people in the lowest socioeconomic classes.

In most countries around the world, females are not enrolled in primary and secondary schools as frequently as males. Again, major differences exist between the developed and the developing countries. In the developed countries of the world, the numbers of males and females enrolled in primary schools are nearly equal (the number of enrolled females is 97 percent of the number of enrolled males). At the secondary level in the developed countries, the number of enrolled females is 78 percent of the enrolled males. However, in the developing countries as a whole, at the primary level, 86 percent of the male children are enrolled compared to only 71 percent of the female children. At the secondary level in the developing countries, 35 percent of the males, but only 29 percent of the females, are enrolled. Although some exceptions do exist, the developing countries are more likely to educate their males than their females (Najafizadeh and Mennerick, 1988).

National Systems of Education

Many differences in the educational systems of different nations can be noted, but one of the most fundamental is the degree to which systems are differentiated and rigid. A **differentiated school system** is one in which different programs, tracks, or streams lead to different educational outcomes (Bidwell and Friedkin, 1988). In the United States a typical high school will have several different programs, usually including vocational, college preparatory, and perhaps a commercial or business curriculum. Obviously, students in the college preparatory program are aimed toward college to earn a degree. Vocational and commercial students are much more likely to go directly into the work force, although they may get additional training at technical or vocational institutes. Differentiation can also be found at the elementary school level, where different tracks are available for students with different ability levels.

The **rigidity** of an educational system refers to the ease or difficulty of moving from one educational track or program to another (Bidwell and Friedkin, 1988). For example, the United States is often thought of as a less rigid system than the systems of many other countries. As a cultural ideal, that is true, but in practical terms the United States' system is more rigid than we might suppose. It is certainly possible for a student who has graduated from a vocational or commercial high school program to enter college at some later date. Such a student might be limited initially in the type of college he or she could enter, but it is possible to make a change in educational and career paths. Also, anyone can choose to go on for more education at a later point in life. Moreover, one important value of American society is that everyone has the right to a higher education, at any time in life. For example, it is not uncommon at graduation exercises for elderly graduates to be given special recognition, and news stories delight in describing how an older person has returned to college and earned a degree.

Although the American cultural value supports an open educational system, actual practice is a different matter. Again, this point illustrates the considerable difference between a cultural ideal and reality. Few students probably begin in a vocational track in high school and then later go on to a college or university to earn a degree. Such a student would probably have to find a way to make up courses that are prerequisites for college admission or would have to find a college that would waive them. These and other kinds of barriers make the American system of education more rigid in fact than the cultural ideals would lead us to believe.

Nonetheless, the educational system in the United States is generally less rigid, both in the ideal and in practice, than are educational systems in some other societies. Many Asian and European countries have very rigid educational systems. Great Britain and Japan are examples of more rigid systems, although they are somewhat different in nature. Both, however, place great emphasis on special examinations administered to all students at critical stages in their educational careers. Since these examinations are often given at very young ages, educational careers, and often occupational fates as well, are determined early in life.

The British Educational System. Until about 1970, the British school system had three types of state-supported high schools: grammar schools, technical schools, and secondary modern schools. Since 1970 a new type of school, called the comprehensive high school, has been added (Kerckhoff, 1986).

The most prestigious British high schools have traditionally been the grammar schools. (Of course, Britain has also had very prestigious private secondary schools—called *public schools*—whose students are almost entirely the children of higher-status parents who can afford the tuition and boarding costs.)

The British technical schools are for talented students who are aiming for technical colleges and, later, technical occupations. The secondary modern schools, in contrast, are attended by students who have shown the lowest level of academic promise. The recently established comprehensive high schools of Britain are similar to American high schools in that all ability groupings attend the same school. However, within the comprehensive high school the children are still put in tracks, or "streams," on the basis of ability levels. The comprehensive school now enrolls about 60 percent of British students and 90 percent of Scottish students (Kerckhoff, 1986).

The introduction of the comprehensive high school in Great Britain may have made their system less rigid, but it remains more rigid than the educational system of the United States. British students who have been chosen for either an elite school or a higher ability track are consistently and effectively moved toward better colleges and universities, and later to more prestigious occupations and professions (Kerckhoff, 1986, p. 857).

The Japanese Educational System. In Japan the differentiation of students takes on a special meaning. Japanese children are differentiated by the particular schools they attend, even at the junior and senior high school levels but especially at the college level. The Japanese educational system is built around a series of examinations, each one determining admission for the next level in the system. The culminating examination occurs at the end of high school and is the one that determines admission to Japan's colleges and universities. The Japanese examination system, especially at the end of high school, is so intense it has been labeled "examination hell" or "examination war" (Duke, 1988; Rohlen, 1983).

The process of gaining admission to one of Japan's prestigious universities begins for some parents and children at the kindergarten level. Five-year-old kindergartners will sometimes take entrance examinations for the elementary schools that have the best records for getting their students into the most successful junior high schools. The ranking of junior high schools is determined, in turn, by their success in placing students in the best high schools. The examination hell near the end of high school allows a select few to be admitted to Tokyo University or to one of the major Japanese medical schools (White, 1987).

The Japanese educational system requires that students spend considerably more time in school each year than U.S. students. The school day typically begins at 8:30 A.M. and ends at 3:30 P.M., with a short lunch break. However, elementary school children often remain in school for another hour or more for additional class activities. Japanese children also attend school for a half day on Saturdays. Summer vacation is limited to the month of August, so the Japanese school year is 240 days, compared to the average of 180 days in American schools (Duke, 1986; White, 1987).

In addition to the regular schools, the Japanese have developed a private educational or tutoring system especially designed to prepare students for the next level of entrance examinations. These "examination cram" schools, called *juko,* drill the students on subjects that will be on the entrance examinations. Since about 80 percent of entering high school students aspire to a college or university education, almost all students attend *juko* schools after regular school hours. Furthermore, many Japanese students take one, two, or even three years off from their regular schools in order to attend the examination cram schools full time (White, 1987).

After all of this intense preparation, the Japanese students take the critically important university entrance examination. It is one of the ironies of Japanese education that the pace of work at the college and university level is rather leisurely, and very few students fail. Japanese students tend to see their college years as a time to enjoy life and indulge themselves.

Recent Trends in American Education

The schools of a society tend to mirror the characteristics and trends of that society. For example, during periods of war or national crises, the schools are likely to respond in the same way as the nation at large is responding. For example, during World War II in the United States, schools engaged the children in collecting scrap metals and other needed materials, buying war bonds and stamps, and participating in patriotic programs. In a similar way, general societal currents such as periods of political conservatism or radicalism are also reflected in the educational system. In the United States the 1960s and 1970s were periods of general change when many traditional ways were rejected in favor of more liberal ways. The schools, from the elementary level to universities, made parallel liberalizing changes.

It is not surprising, then, that schools also follow broader, more pervasive changes and trends in the society. For example, the increasing level of bureaucratization that has occurred in the United States—and most other societies—has also occurred in the educational system.

Increasing Bureaucratization

The bureaucratization of schools means, among other things, that many different, specialized statuses exist in contemporary schools. Although the early schools were made up mostly of teachers and students, with perhaps a few administrators, modern schools have large and specialized staffs. A large school system today will have, in addition to teachers and students, several layers of administrators, special education teachers of various types, counselors, psychologists, nurses, speech therapists, physical therapists, occupational therapists, nutritionists, and transportation specialists.

The bureaucratization of schools is also reflected in the increasing volume of formal, written communications, and quantitative analyses of the performances of students, teachers, administrators, and entire school systems. Student performances are evaluated with various tests that attempt to place a numerical value on presumed "inherent" abilities, such as intelligence, or on achievement in reading, mathematics, and other skills. Even entire school systems are evaluated on how effectively they are performing based on the average test scores of their students.

One justification for the objective and numerical testing of students is that evaluations are taken out of the subjective realm and made more impartial. The testing of students may have eliminated some biases, such as the cases of students admitted to high-prestige colleges just because their parents are alumni, but serious questions have been raised about the fairness of objective tests such as the Scholastic Aptitude Test (SAT) or American College Testing (ACT) examinations. Such tests might be oriented to the cultural backgrounds of higher-status students and give them an advantage over lower-status students (Crouse and Trusheim, 1988).

The bureaucratization of schooling also places increasing emphasis on formal credentials, especially college and professional degrees. The United States has been described as a society where great significance is attached to credentials with little or no attention paid to people's real qualifications (Collins, 1979). One interesting side effect of the great emphasis on credentials is that it has encouraged many people to fake their degrees, to buy "degrees" from commercial diploma mills, or to obtain "advanced" degrees without attending graduate schools.

The Liberalization of Schools in the 1960s

During the 1960s a variety of social and protest movements emerged in the United States—the civil rights, antiwar, women's, and the student rights movements. These social movements attacked the status quo of many institutions, including the educational system. The student rights movement began at the major universities in the mid-1960s, and within ten years its influence had been felt throughout U.S. education. It criticized the rigidity of the traditional grading system, the mindless bureaucratic requirements and procedures, the inflexible course requirements, the absolute power of teachers, professors, and administrators, and the irrelevance of academic courses to contemporary social problems.

As these criticisms worked their way through the educational system, many changes were made in U.S. schools and colleges. New courses were introduced; grading systems were modified; required courses were reduced; student participation in decision-making was increased; and many rules governing personal behavior, dress, and appearance were relaxed or abandoned. These changes loosened the educational system, making it less narrow and restrictive, but in the process, they might have lowered the intellectual quality of education.

Return to the Basics

With the beginning of the 1980s, many of the changes produced by the "loosening" of education still appeared in one form or another in the U.S. educational system. But the pendulum had clearly started to swing back (Apple, 1986; Ravitch, 1985). Many reasons can be cited for why the schools have reverted to a more traditional pattern, but one central explanation is the political trend in the United States during the decade of the 1980s, which was in a more conservative direction. This conservatism was epitomized for many of these years by former Secretary of Education William Bennett, who advocated a comprehensive revamping of U.S. education through a "return to the basics."

The return-to-the-basics slogan may have various meanings, but for many people it suggests a return to teaching the fundamentals of reading, writing, history, science, and mathematics. It also suggests a de-emphasis of many of the social sciences that are seen as intellectually "soft," subjects that tend to undercut absolute moral values and national patriotism. Thus, the advocates of a return to the basics reflect the conservative political agenda of the Reagan and Bush Administrations.

A return to the basics also calls for a more rigorous and intellectually demanding school system in the United States. Many Americans fear that our present educational system is not producing adults who can compete successfully with the graduates of other nations' schools. They are concerned that the American educational system is failing to produce well-qualified people, and thus the United States is not competitive in world economic markets.

One way to evaluate the U.S. educational system is to consider which young people are successfully completing high school and college. In the next sections we will examine who succeeds, especially in acquiring a college education in the United States.

Sociology in the News

"Political Correctness" on the Campus

The latest controversy associated with U.S. colleges and universities has been labeled the "political correctness" issue. This label, it should be noted, is a critical and negative label, generally used by those who wish to emphasize the excesses and dangers of this activity on U.S. campuses (Coleman, 1991; D'Sousa, 1991; Henry, 1991; Taylor, 1991).

Critics who are concerned about efforts to achieve "political correctness" attack the efforts of certain students and many faculty members who believe sexism, racism, ethnocentrism, and homophobia (among other things) are inherently bad and therefore should be eradicated in speech, in academic courses, in writing, and sometimes as subjects of scientific inquiry. These same students and faculty members are at the same time trying to awaken and sensitize people to points of view other than what they feel is the white-male-dominated, elitist, conservative point of view that now prevails.

It should be obvious that some of these objectives are partially linked to the subject matter of sociology. Throughout this book we have been considering concepts such as ethnocentrism, sexism, racism, the social class system, ageism, and others. We have seen, for example, that sexism and racism are deeply rooted in U.S. society and that they lead to unequal and unfair treatment for women and racial minorities.

As one dimension of the "political correctness" trend there are the efforts to eradicate language and speech that reflect sexist or racist views. Professors on many campuses, for example, would never get away with using derogatory slang terms for women or minority groups in their classrooms. But often, and perhaps inevitably, attempts to eliminate sexist or racist language, or any other language that offends any ethnic group, religion, or nationality will begin to encroach on freedom of speech and the free expression of individual opinion.

A number of colleges and universities have initiated policies that are trying to improve the sensitivity of students and faculty to these issues. Students are often required to take courses that will broaden their views of other cultures, nationalities, ethnic groups, women, racial minorities, gay males, and lesbians. Faculty members are challenged by students when they display sexist, racist, or homophobic tendencies. Student conduct rules are passed that make it an offense for students to make derogatory statements about groups or categories of people.

Political correctness gets its negative label from those cases where individuals or groups use extreme methods, or take extreme positions, in their efforts to eradicate intolerance or insensitivity. Students are not allowed to express their opinions in class, or they are penalized for "inappropriate" views; professors are accused, sometimes on flimsy grounds, of being racist or sexist in their classes; speakers are picketed, shouted down, or harassed; research projects are stopped because their scientific questions are considered by some to be unacceptable. Critics see these actions as dangerous encroachments on free speech, intellectual debate, academic freedom, and scientific autonomy.

The debate about political correctness is, as is so often the case, a conflict between two important sets of values. In this case one side is trying to eradicate intolerance and broaden perspectives (about the rights of women, racial minorities, gays and lesbians, etc.), while the other side sees these activities as infringements on individual freedom and academic or scientific autonomy.

COLEMAN, JAMES S. "A Quiet Threat to Academic Freedom." *National Review* 43, March 18, 1991.
D'SOUZA, DINESH. "Illiberal Education." *The Atlantic* 267, 1991.
HENRY, WILLIAM A. III. "Upside Down in the Groves of Academe." *Time,* April 1, 1991.
TAYLOR, JOHN. "Are You Politically Correct?" *New York* 24, January 21, 1991.

Who Succeeds in the American Educational System?

Functional and conflict theorists disagree about how well the educational system of the United States serves *the entire* population. One way to examine this issue is to look at the educational attainment of Americans. Table 12–1 shows what percentage of Americans—white, black, and Hispanic—aged 25 to 29, have completed various levels of education. Blacks and whites are apt to graduate from high school in almost equal numbers (82.2 percent and 86.0 percent, respectively), but the Hispanic population has a substantially lower percentage of finishing high school (61.0 percent). At the college level, whites begin to exceed blacks and Hispanics considerably. Whites enroll in college more, and graduate more, than

Table 12–1.   Schooling Completed among 25- to 29-Year-Olds: Whites, Blacks, and Hispanics, 1989

	Completed High School	Some College	Completed College
Whites	86.0%	44.8%	24.4%
Blacks	82.2%	34.6%	12.7%
Hispanics	61.0%	27.0%	10.1%
All Categories	85.5%	43.8%	23.4%

Source: U.S. Bureau of the Census, "Educational Attainment in the United States: March 1989 and 1988." *Current Population Report*, Series P-20. Washington, D.C.: U.S. Government Printing Office, forthcoming.

either blacks or Hispanics. Nearly a quarter of white Americans are now graduating from college (24.4 percent), while among blacks 12.7 percent, and among Hispanics 10.1 percent, are graduating (U.S. Bureau of the Census, forthcoming).

A recent study has examined the educational, occupational, and economic conditions of young U.S. adults, and has identified 20 million 16–24-year-olds as "the forgotten half" (William T. Grant Foundation, 1988). The forgotten half of American young adults are those who have not finished high school and high school graduates who are not college bound. Today, according to this report, even those who have high school degrees are often destined for low-paying jobs with limited chances for future economic advancement.

In the past a high school education was generally adequate for a reasonably well-paying job and an economically secure future. But recent technological and economic changes have altered the prospects for today's young adults who do not have college educations. Their economic futures are not bright, because even with a healthy economy, their opportunities are limited and their vulnerabilities great. In the years between 1973 and 1986 the median income of households headed by persons under 25 declined 26.3 percent. These households are largely made up of the young people who have not gone on to get a college education, but have married and entered the labor force. The drop in income for this group has been greater than that experienced by Americans between 1929 and 1933—critical years of the Great Depression in the United States (William T. Grant Foundation, 1988).

Economic Background and College Attendance

Conflict theorists argue that young people who come from advantaged economic backgrounds will benefit more from the educational system than the children of the poorer classes. Also, the children who belong to racial and ethnic minorities will benefit less often from the educational system than the children of the dominant white population. This contention can be checked by seeing if larger proportions of children from better-off families attend college than do children from poorer families, and if children from minority groups attend college least frequently.

Figure 12–1 shows how the economic, racial, and ethnic characteristics of families are related to having an 18–24-year-old child (or children) in college. The percentages show a general pattern of an increasing likelihood of at least one child, out of any 18–24-year-olds in the family, being in college. These figures on college attendance do support the conflict theory perspective. Young people coming from families making over $30,000 are about twice as likely to go to college as young people coming from families making under $20,000. Furthermore, when white families

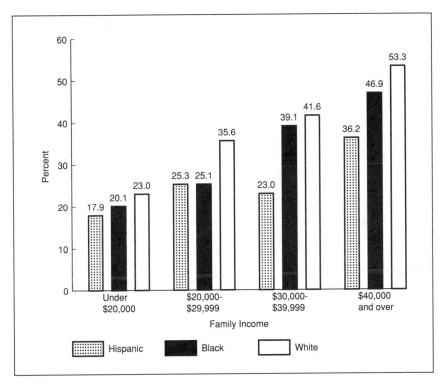

Figure 12–1. Percentage of Households with at Least One Primary Family Member, 18–24 Years Old, in College, by Family Income, Race, and Origin. (*Source:* United States Bureau of the Census, *Current Population Reports*, Series P-20, No. 443, 1990, Table 35.)

have incomes over $40,000, their children are much more likely than any other group to go to college (53.3 percent).

The Importance of an "Elite" College Education

Today it is nearly a necessity to have a college education if one aspires to a high-status position in any relatively large corporate business in the United States. The same is true of the other developed societies of the world. However, not all colleges are equal because the degrees they grant are not considered equal. Colleges and universities in the United States are hierarchically ordered, with a small set of elite schools at the top that have the best reputations for academic excellence, distinguished faculties, and carefully selected, intellectually talented students. Disagreements may arise about the rank order of particular schools, but a typical list of elite colleges in the United States includes Harvard (also the oldest), Yale, Princeton, Columbia, and Stanford, just to name a few.

A question often asked by the public as well as by sociologists is "Does the college that one attends make a difference in one's career opportunities and occupational advancement?" The question is more complicated than it first seems, for several reasons. The college one attends is associated with a number of other characteristics that can also influence career opportunities and occupational advancement. These other characteristics include family background, personal ability, academic performance, and motivation to succeed (Alwin, 1974).

One study found that, even when all these factors were controlled, some independent effect of the college attended still prevailed (Alwin, 1974). Furthermore, a study conducted among Japanese males also found that the graduates of the most elite colleges of Japan attained higher lifetime incomes and higher positions in organizations than men who had graduated from less prestigious colleges. Although this study was not able to rule out family background as a contributing factor, the author argues that in Japan the status of the college from which one graduates does make a difference in the occupational careers of males (Miyahara, 1988).

In a study of over 2729 senior managers and executives of 208 major corporations in the United States, researchers tried to determine if getting a degree from one of the elite schools of the country influenced the chances of attaining the very topmost levels of corporate America (Useem and Karabel, 1986). The researchers were especially interested in whether the social (family) backgrounds of these top corporate leaders could account for their positions, or whether degrees from elite schools were more influential. The researchers considered not just bachelor's degrees but also master's of business administration degrees and law degrees. Thus, they came up with somewhat different lists of elite schools for each type of degree.[1]

This study concluded that the main portion of these 2729 senior managers and executives who made it to the very top of the corporate and business structure were helped by their educational credentials. Holding a bachelor's degree from a prestigious school made it more likely that a person would be chosen as a chief executive officer (CEO) of one of the major U.S. corporations. A bachelor's degree from an elite school made the chances of becoming a CEO twice as great as a noncollege graduate in this group. (About 15 percent of the 2729 corporate managers had not

---

[1] The elite schools for bachelor's degrees were Columbia, Cornell, Dartmouth, Harvard, Johns Hopkins, Massachusetts Institute of Technology, Pennsylvania, Princeton, Stanford, Williams, and Yale. Elite schools for master's degrees in business administration were Columbia, Dartmouth, Harvard, M.I.T., Northwestern, Stanford, California—Berkeley, California—Los Angeles, Chicago, Michigan, and Pennsylvania. Elite schools for law degrees were: Columbia, Harvard, New York University, Stanford, California—Berkeley, Chicago, Michigan, Pennsylvania, and Yale.

gone to college or had not completed college.) Master's degrees in business administration from elite business schools, and especially law degrees from one of the elite law schools, also gave these corporate managers a better chance of being selected for the top corporate positions (Useem and Karabel, 1986).

However, elite social background—coming from a family listed in the *Social Register* or attending one of the nation's exclusive prep schools—also aided in moving up in the higher levels of corporate management. In particular, an upper-class family background led more often to the boards of directors of corporations and to leadership positions in the top-level business associations. Of course, combining a high-status social background with an elite education made it even more likely that these highest levels of corporate management and leadership in the business world would be reached.

Since these managers were almost all middle-aged and older, and thus had received their college and professional degrees many years earlier, it is not clear why the status of their schools should continue to aid them in their careers. It seems unlikely that what they learned in college would still be an influential factor. It may be that their personalities or styles, which had been developed or cultivated in elite schools, gave them an advantage in the corporate world. It may also be that at the highest level of corporate management a great deal of uncertainty prevails, and trust is a critical factor. Thus, the top level of promotions go to people who are most like those already in power, both educationally and socially (Useem and Karabel, 1986, p. 198).

The Effects of Beginning at a Community College

At the opposite extreme from the elite colleges and universities are the community colleges of the United States. Nearly half of all college students at any given time are attending community colleges (Monk-Turner, 1990). The most likely students at community colleges are women, minorities, and students from working-class backgrounds. Many of these community college students go on to graduate from four-year colleges, but their occupational achievement is not as great as students who begin at four-year colleges (Monk-Turner, 1990).

The Performance of the American School System

The task of the schools is to educate the children and young people of the society, and widespread concern exists about how the school system is performing its primary responsibility. The schools have many critics, who have pointed to failures and shortcomings in various areas. In the early 1980s a government report on the educational system was ominously ti-

Cross-National Perspectives

International Competition in Mathematics and Science

The Educational Testing Service has conducted tests for the National Science Foundation to determine the mathematics and science skill levels of 13-year-old students in six countries. The students came from the United States, South Korea, the United Kingdom, Ireland, Spain, and Canada. The students in these countries were given the same 63 mathematics questions and 60 science questions. For example, the students were asked to calculate the average age of five children aged 13, 8, 6, 4, and 4. More complicated questions required the students to know what the radius of a circle is, or how a plant would respond to artificial light (LaPointe et al., 1989).

In comparison with the students of the other countries, the United States students did not do well. In fact they were near the bottom in both the mathematics and science tests. It was the South Korean students who excelled on these tests. Seventy-eight percent of the Korean students could solve two-step mathematics problems, such as computing an average, compared to only 40 percent of the U.S. students. In science, 73 percent of the South Koreans could design scientific experiments and draw conclusions from them, compared to only 42 percent of the U.S. students.

It wasn't only the Korean students who outperformed the U.S. students in mathematics and science. In mathematics, students in four Canadian provinces performed above the mean, while those in two other Canadian provinces, Spain, the United Kingdom, and Ireland were about average. Only students from one Canadian province (French-speaking Ontario) and the United States scored below the mean. In science, students from British Columbia, Canada, performed about as well as the Korean students. Scoring at about the mean were those from the United Kingdom, Quebec (English-speaking), Ontario (English-speaking), Quebec (French-speaking), New Brunswick (English-speaking), and Spain. Joining students from the United States—well below the mean—were those from Ireland, Ontario (French-speaking), and New Brunswick (French-speaking).

This test is just one of several that has revealed how U.S. students perform poorly in comparison to students in other countries, especially those from Asian countries. While this relatively poor performance is a problem in itself, it is an even greater problem in terms of what it portends for the future. Said one official of the Educational Testing Service: "It's a pretty accurate prophecy of what the 23-year-olds of 1999 will be able to do" (Leff, 1989, p. A16). Said an official of the National Science Foundation: "The lack of preparation for further education and future employment that these teenagers demonstrated is nothing short of frightening" (Leff, 1989, p. A14).

At one level, the fear is that Americans will do less well than those in other countries in college and post-graduate education. This would seem to mean that the world's leading scientists, engineers, and physicians will be less and less likely to come from the United States. Furthermore, most experts believe that the work world is going to require more highly trained personnel in the future. But while the work world is demanding more, America's educational system is turning out students whose ability is declining in comparison to students around the world. Thus, a huge and growing gap is emerging between the demands of U.S. business and the students coming from the American educational system. The educational difficulties experienced by today's teenagers promise to translate into grave economic problems for the society as a whole in the future.

On the other hand, Asian nations like South Korea and Japan, which are already doing quite well both economically and educationally, should do even better in the future as their well-trained teenagers mature into productive adults. Thus, the United States could easily fall behind the Japanese economically and may even find itself threatened in several sectors by South Koreans and other Asians. Because of their ambition and diligence, now being combined with excellent educational training, the South Koreans will be daunting competitors for years to come.

LAPOINTE, ARCHIE E.; MEAD, NANCY A.; and PHILLIPS, GARY W. *A World of Differences: An International Assessment of Mathematics and Science.* Princeton, NJ: Educational Testing Service. 1989.
LEFF, LISA. "Survey of Math, Science Skills Puts U.S. Students at the Bottom." *Washington Post*, February 1, 1989, A14, A16.

tled *A Nation at Risk* (1983). The crux of this report emphasized that the American educational system was mediocre, and the threat that our schools posed for our national well-being and security was as great as any external threat. Many of the problems identified in *A Nation at Risk* are still in evidence. We will review some of the most important of these problems, including functional illiteracy in the United States and achievement levels of U.S. students. We will also consider the problems of teachers in the contemporary school systems.

Functional Illiteracy

To be illiterate is to be totally unable to read and write. Illiteracy in this sense is not a widespread problem in the United States today, at least compared to other countries of the world. But some adults who have gone through the elementary school system and even beyond have not yet learned to read, even though they are capable of doing so. The number of illiterate people is unknown because they often hide their inability to read and write. Also, residents of the United States who have emigrated from other countries may know how to read and write in their native languages, but they are not literate in English. Again, the numbers are not known.

Although the overall illiteracy rate in the United States is low, particular segments of the population have much higher rates. For example, estimates show that 60 percent or more of the prison population of the United States is illiterate. It is possible that illiteracy contributes to being in prison because those who commit crimes may have been unable to read about job openings or may have been afraid to apply for jobs because of the need to fill out application forms. Without legitimate jobs they may have turned to illicit acts and crime (Omang, 1982).

In recent years the concept of functional illiteracy has emerged. **Functional illiteracy** refers to the lack of basic skills needed to get along in society: for example, to read a newspaper, fill out job application forms, follow written directions, calculate prices, write checks, or understand bus schedules. Recent tests have been developed to measure the literacy skills (both reading and quantitative) of the young adult (21 to 25 years of age) population of the United States. One test measures "prose literacy," the knowledge and skills needed to gain understanding and use information from written materials such as editorials, news stories, and poems. To have a minimal score of 200, a person must be able to write a simple description of the type of job he or she would like to have. Among the total sample of young adults, including those who attended high school and those who did not, 3.9 percent scored below the 200 level. However, in the black population, 13.7 percent scored below the 200 level; among Hispanics, 6.5 percent scored below 200 (Snyder, 1989).

A second test measured the ability to locate and use information from documents such as indexes, tables, paycheck stubs, and order forms. Specifically, in order to score at a minimal level of 200 on this dimension, a young adult had to be able to match money-saving coupons to a shopping list of several items. On this test of "document literacy," 4.5 percent of the total sample of young adults scored below the 200 level.

A third test, dealing with "quantitative literacy," measured the knowledge and skills needed to apply the arithmetic operations of addition, subtraction, multiplication, and division, either alone or sequentially. A minimal score of 200 indicated an ability to total two entries on a bank deposit slip. Among the total sample of young adults, 3.6 percent could not achieve this level. Among blacks, 12.2 percent scored below 200; among Hispanics, 7.2 percent scored below 200 (Snyder, 1989).

Functional illiteracy was most pronounced among students who did not graduate from high school. Among them, the following percentages of young adults did not score at the minimal levels on the three tests: prose literacy—14.6 percent, document literacy—16.6 percent, quantitative literacy—13.9 percent (Snyder, 1989). Many critics of the schools regard these figures on functional illiteracy as a reflection of failure on the part of the school system to carry out its basic task of educating the population. This failure is especially serious with minority students.

Despite the fact that some U.S. students go through elementary school, and even through some years of high school, and still do not have the skills in reading and arithmetic that allow them to function in everyday life, the educational field may have some encouraging news. New evidence shows that performances on various standardized IQ and achievement tests are improving after a number of years of decline. We will review these new trends in the next section.

Performance on Achievement Tests

When *A Nation at Risk* was published in 1983, some disturbing trends were noted in the achievement levels of U.S. children, at both the elementary and high school levels. In international comparisons, especially with the Japanese, U.S. students were losing ground. Equally disturbing was the fact that U.S. students as a whole were averaging lower scores in the late 1970s and early 1980s than they had been a decade before. On standard IQ tests the scores of Japanese students had increased by more than ten points in a generation. The average Japanese student had a score of 111 compared to 100 for an average student in the United States. More striking was the fact that over 10 percent of Japanese had IQs above 130, while in the United States only 2 percent of students had IQs that high.

As a result of these concerns and others dating back to the 1960s, the Congress of the United States mandated that periodically the knowledge, skills, and attitudes of U.S. children and youth be assessed. Beginning in 1970–1971, schools initiated periodic assessments of U.S. students through a program called the National Assessment of Educational Progress (NAEP). The NAEP has measured reading achievement of 9-year-old, 13-year-old, and 17-year-old students five times since 1970–1971. The results of these tests indicate that students in these age groups were reading better in 1984 than they were in 1971. The 9-year-old and 13-year-old students started improving in the 1970s; the 17-year-olds, between 1980 and 1984. However, these reading assessments also reveal that 40 percent of 13-year-old students had not acquired "intermediate" reading skills and may therefore have difficulty reading the range of materials they encounter in school (Snyder, 1989).[2]

Changing SAT Scores

The decline in U.S. student performance during the 1970s was also revealed in lower average scores on the Scholastic Aptitude Tests (SAT). Between 1967 and 1980 the average SAT verbal scores dropped more than 40 points, and mathematics scores dropped by 26 points. One possible cause of the decline in average SAT scores may have been that a larger proportion of high school seniors were choosing to take the examinations. Perhaps due to the greater numbers of less-qualified students, the average scores were being depressed.

During the first half of the 1980s the combined mathematics and verbal scores did increase from 890 to 906, which seemed to be an encouraging sign (Stern and Chandler, 1987). That trend was short-lived, however, since the combined average started dropping again in the mid-1980s and was down to 896 in 1991. Verbal scores in particular have shown a decline, going down each year between 1986 and 1991 (Cooper, 1991). The 1991 verbal score average of 422 is the lowest in the history of the SAT examination. The mathematics scores, after remaining fairly steady through the 1980s, also declined in 1991 (Cooper, 1991). These declines have given support to the critics of American education who charge that the school system is not meeting the nation's needs.

The 15-year decline in average SAT scores reached its low point in 1980–1981 (combined average = 890). In 1990 the average total SAT score was exactly 900, though it has been as high as 906 in some of the intervening years (*Chronicle of Higher Education,* 1991; Ogle and Alsalam, 1990). Even though student SAT scores have moved up slightly from their lowest point (1980–1981), the scores are still far below what they were in the 1960s and early 1970s.

Social Dimensions of Schools and Classrooms

Schools and their classrooms are not just places for teaching and learning; they are also social settings. As with all other social settings there are roles, norms, values, and status hierarchies. From a sociological perspective it is important to see how social factors influence what happens in

---

[2] The intermediate level of reading is described as "the ability to search for specific information, interrelate ideas, and generalize from relatively lengthy passages dealing with literature, science, and social studies."

schools and classrooms—both to the students and to the teachers. We will begin our consideration of social dimensions of schools by examining the most basic of all relationships—the relationship between teachers and students.

Teacher/Student Relationships

Without a doubt, the relationship between a teacher and a student can have a great influence on the student's academic performance and, ultimately, on his or her academic achievements. Many successful people are asked if any teachers influenced them, and usually they can recall one or two who had a significant effect on their lives. This kind of anecdotal evidence showing that teachers "make a difference" is supported by a growing body of research that identifies how teachers' attitudes and behavior can and do influence the academic performances of children. Sometimes, however, the teachers themselves are unaware of just how much their attitudes and personal values can influence their evaluations of student performances.

For example, as children go through a school system teachers in that system often become aware of the qualities and characteristics of many students even before they are directly responsible for teaching them. Teachers are likely to communicate with each other about particular students and may form judgments on the basis of siblings or other relatives. Teachers may reach conclusions about ability levels and expect corresponding performances in class work or behavior. Thus, if teachers expect a poor academic performance or a good performance from a student, the student may be evaluated in a way consistent with that expectation. This is an example of the self-fulfilling prophecy. A **self-fulfilling prophecy** is an initial expectation that may be based on a *false* definition of the situation; it can actually produce a behavior that makes the original expectation become true (Merton, 1968). A teacher's self-fulfilling prophecy might be illustrated by the following instances. If a boy is told that he is good at arithmetic, he develops ideas about himself (expectations) consistent with the evaluation. These ideas lead him to behave in ways that make the evaluations come true. The boy who believes that he is good at arithmetic, for example, will try hard to do problems in arithmetic. This assumption, of course, is just as likely to operate in the opposite way: students who are expected to perform poorly tend to live up to those expectations.

In addition to forming expectations for specific children, teachers also develop positive or negative expectations for whole groups of children. One consequence is that members of the group tend to live up to these expectations, whatever a member's individual level of ability is. The following advice was given to a new teacher by a fellow teacher at an all-black California high school:

"Jim, you ever work with these kids before?"

"No," I admitted.

"I thought so. Well, now, the first thing is, you don't ever push 'em, and you don't expect too much . . . . you take them as they are, not as you and me [sic] would like them to be. That means, you find out what they can do, and you give it to them to do." (Cited in Silberman, 1970, p. 84.)

Rosenthal and Jacobson (1968) have done the best-known research study on the effect of teacher expectations on the performance of groups of students. At "Oak School," the site for the study, all the students were given IQ tests. At the beginning of the next school year, each of the 18 teachers in grades one through six were given the names of students (about 20 percent of the population) who, researchers told them, could be expected to show dramatic intellectual growth in the coming academic year. These predictions were supposedly based on the students' IQ scores of the previous year. In fact, the names of the 20 percent had actually been drawn at random from the school population as a whole; there were no differences between them and the other students. As Rosenthal and Jacobson (1968, p. 196) put it: "The difference between the special children and the ordinary children, then, was only in the mind of the teachers."

The crucial finding in this research was that teacher expectations made a difference: the IQs of the "special" children increased much more than the IQs of the control group (Rosenthal and Jacobson, 1968, p. 176). Rosenthal and Jacobson's research was admittedly limited; it was only one study of a single school. Subsequent efforts to replicate their study at other schools (e.g., Elashoff and Snow, 1971) have failed to produce such dramatic findings. Nevertheless, a variety of additional studies have supported the general notion that teacher expectations have an important effect on student performance (Boocock, 1980, pp. 154–160).

A somewhat different way of seeing the impact of teachers on the performances of their students comes from the study of a large and diverse sample of beginning first graders in the Baltimore, Maryland, public schools. Many of the schools in this study are inner-city schools serving minority (primarily black) populations. This study set out to see if it makes a difference when the teachers and parents of a student have different attitudes about what constitutes "good" and "bad" student behavior (Alexander et al., 1987a). The main hypothesis of the study was that if a student's teacher and parent had the same notion of a good student (or bad student), the student would perform better in the first grade. This hypothesis was *not* supported by the research, but something equally important was found. *The values of the teachers were related to the performances of the students in their classes.*

The researchers were especially interested in the way teachers' values were negatively related to the report card grades of black first graders. The researchers speculate that "Teachers who place a premium on 'proper values' and on 'following the rules' may be especially frustrated when their expectations for how pupils ought to behave are not fulfilled in the context of predominantly black inner-city schools, and they may find themselves, whether consciously or not, grading these students down as a result" (Alexander et al., 1987a, p. 74).

In another analysis with this same sample of Baltimore first graders, the researchers found that minority students performed less well when their teachers were from high socioeconomic backgrounds. The same findings occurred among nonminority students who came from low-socio-economic-status backgrounds. Both nonminority, low-status students and minority students had their greatest difficulties with teachers when the teachers had high-socioeconomic-status backgrounds. The high-status teachers were more apt to evaluate their students as less mature and to hold lower performance expectations for them. These high-status teachers were also the ones who had especially low scores when asked to evaluate the general climate of their schools. The picture that comes through is one of teachers who are not satisfied with their teaching settings and are, in the process, turning out low-achievement students. The sociological point of considerable significance is that the social origins of teachers can influence student academic achievement (Alexander et al., 1987a; Alexander et al., 1987b).

Long-Term Effects of Elementary School Teachers

The early evaluations that teachers make of particular students may have a long-term impact on academic performance. In a follow-up study of students who had been first, second, and third graders some four to nine years earlier, evidence showed that the early influences of teachers (and parents) were continuing to affect academic performance. When these students were first studied in the early grades, their grades and achievement levels were found to be closely related to the influences of their teachers (for some students) or their parents (for other students). The teachers and parents influenced the performances of the students even when their cognitive or intellectual abilities were the same. Four to nine years later, these effects of "significant others" were still related to the school performances of these youngsters (again, among students with the same levels of cognitive ability).

Different interpretations might be made of these long-term effects of early experiences in school, but one possibility is that children incorporate as a part of their self-image a view given to them by their early teachers or by their parents. Furthermore, in school systems the grades earned one year may influence the grades earned the next year. In the researchers' words, ". . . a 'paper person' is created that follows the child from grade to grade. Cumulative records that follow children through the school could support the children's high performance in later grades by affecting subsequent teachers' expectations" (Entwisle and Hayduk, 1988, p. 158).

Tracking and Later School Performance

One of the hotly debated topics of education is the impact that **tracking** (grouping children by ability level) has on the subsequent academic performances of students. The underlying assumption about tracking is that when students with similar ability levels are placed in classes together, the academic gains for all students will be maximized. High-ability students will not be slowed down by the less competent students, while students with less ability will be taught at a level and pace that will be more appropriate and thus beneficial for them (Kerckhoff, 1986).

Tracking is used widely in the United States and many other countries, sometimes at the elementary school level but especially at the junior and senior high school levels. The system appears to be widely accepted by teachers and administrators, but it has also developed a corps of critics (Oakes, 1985; Rosenbaum, 1976). One basic criticism cites tracking as a system that perpetuates inequality.

There is a concern among many critics about the fairness of the placement process. Some studies have found inconsistencies between the abilities of students and the tracks in which they are placed (Rehberg and Rosenthal, 1978). Kilgore (1991) has studied the factors that influence placement, and while her research does not find any arbitrariness, she does find that white students are able to match their educational aspirations with the appropriate track better than black and Hispanic students.

A second concern is that students who are placed in low-ability tracks will come to define themselves as poor students, unable to do academic work, and consequently they will do poorly. In other words, the tracking system also tends to become a self-fulfilling prophecy (Eder, 1981); being placed in a high track tends to elicit high-quality performance, while being placed in a low track tends to produce poor academic performance. The following statement by a student illustrates the negative effects a tracking system can have:

> I felt good when I was with my class, but they went and separated us—that changed us. That changed our ideas, our thinking, the way we thought about each other and turned us into enemies toward each other—because they said I was dumb and they were smart. (Schaefer, Olexa, and Polk, 1970, p. 12)

In a participant observation study of "Suburban High School," Finley (1984) examined the ways in which teachers shape and maintain a tracking system. Looking at English courses, Finley found four tracks—gifted, advanced, average, and remedial. Middle-class white children tended to be placed in the two highest tracks, while lower-class children, especially from minority groups, tended to be overrepresented in the lower tracks. The teachers defined high-track classes as desirable places in which to work, while low-track classes were regarded as undesirable. As a result, the teachers competed among themselves to teach the high-track classes and to avoid low-track classes.

Teachers evaluated themselves on the basis of the ratio of high-track to low-track classes they taught; the higher the ratio, the more positive the self-evaluation. This fact led teachers to create more higher-track classes, in which they could teach and thus increase their ratio. The key point is that the dynamics of the status system within the school led teachers to create and maintain a tracking system. In sum, "teachers created ability groupings for their own reasons," and the educational needs and fates of their students were affected by the ambitions of the teachers (Finley, 1984, p. 242).

Other studies of students in different tracks have found that students in lower tracks were likely to be more alienated, distant, and punitive toward each other. Lower-track students also had more negative attitudes about themselves, were less attentive in classes, and were more negative about their futures. Lower-track classes were more apt to be disrupted, which contributed to lower reading levels. Teachers of lower-track students had lower expectations for their students (Oakes, 1982; Eder, 1981; Femlee and Eder, 1983).

The critical question about tracking is whether it does, in fact, improve the academic achievements of *all* students, as its supporters claim. Does it improve the academic performances and achievement levels of the students in the low-ability tracks as well as those in the high-ability tracks? On this question, studies coming from the United States, Great Britain, and Israel all support the same conclusion: students who are in the high-ability track generally improve their academic and intellectual performances over what they would otherwise be, but students in low-ability tracks are more likely to lower their performances (Kerckhoff, 1986; Rowan and Miracle, 1983; Shavit and Featherman, 1988).

In the Israeli study, these effects of tracking were found on cognitive intelligence tests administered to young males when they were tested for military service (Shavit and Featherman, 1988). This study finds that the experience of having been in a high-ability track in high school actually improved a person's cognitive *intelligence* level between ages 13 and 17. Students in high-track classes apparently had certain kinds of intellectual stimulation that raised their intelligence, while students in low-track classes did not. The measured intelligence of students in the low track remained the same at age 17 as it had been at age 13.

The impact of tracking on students in British schools was measured by achievement-test performances in both reading and mathematics. The evidence from this study left little doubt that students in the low-ability tracks lost ground when compared to students who had the same earlier academic performance but who were not placed in ability tracks. The opposite occurred for students in high-ability tracks: they increased their average performance level relative to comparable students in ungrouped schools. Thus, tracking improves the education of only the students who get in the high track, while it lowers the achievement levels of the students in the low track (Kerckhoff, 1986).

At least three possible reasons can be given as to why the different ability tracks produce opposite results for students in the low and high tracks: (1) students in the high-ability track are provided with a different, and better, educational program; (2) teachers assigned to the high-ability track are more competent and more highly motivated; (3) students are influenced by their peers, so that students at each level adopt the standards of their classmates (Kerckhoff, 1986).

Order and Control in the Classroom

Classroom discipline and school violence are viewed by most teachers, as well as much of the public, as a critical problem in the schools. One-third of a sample of teachers said that discipline was the biggest problem in the schools (Dworkin, 1987).

Disruptions in the classroom can be of many different types, but their underlying characteristic is that they distract from the educational task. In the following vignette the student's behavior is not unruly or aggressive, but, nonetheless, it disrupts the class and is the kind of problem that teachers must confront.

> Pauline was in another part of the school picking up her year-book pictures when the bell rang, signalling the beginning of the period. She arrived in her English class late; and placing her books on her desk, immediately left the room. Ten minutes later she returned. . . . Once in class she devoted her attention to trying to close her purse, while her teacher presented a lesson from the textbook. Then she sashayed to the front of the room, casually sharpened a pencil, and returned at the same leisurely pace.
>
> Being a physically attractive young lady in an extremely short skirt, this jaunt captured the attention of everyone in the room, the teacher included. In her seat, she shortly began a whispered conversation with those around her, even though textwork had been given. Pauline started hers, which was to write a business letter, but suddenly decided she needed something from her purse. After a few minutes' search, she dumped its contents onto the desk with a clat-

ter, picked out an eraser, whisked everything else back into her purse, and resumed her work. Five minutes later she began another conversation with one of her neighbors. (Stebbins, 1977, pp. 45–46)

Such disruptions are not unusual, and indeed they often take a more serious and dramatic form. Maintaining order in a classroom is, from a teacher's perspective, frequently difficult. In his study of classroom discipline, Wegmann (1976, p. 77) concludes: "Regardless of what may be written in state law or school board regulations, the actual exercise of teacher authority is an uncertain, precarious enterprise."

The problem of maintaining discipline in the classroom, especially at the high school level, has been labeled by one researcher as "defensive teaching" (McNeil, 1986, p. 157). Defensive teaching occurs when teachers reduce the difficulty of academic work in order to keep the support and goodwill of the students, and thus the harmony and control of their classrooms can be maintained. Another way to describe what happens in many classrooms is to see it as an implicit "bargain" between teachers and students. The teachers, on their side of the bargain, keep the academic demands low, while the students, in return, are reasonably well behaved and passive (Sedlak et al., 1986). By "spoon-feeding" easy academic material, teachers are able to keep peace in their classrooms and avoid behavior problems.

Different explanations may be given as to why defensive teaching is necessary in today's schools. One reason already given is that life for the teacher can be easier by striking a bargain with the students. If the material is simple and can be evaluated as right or wrong through objective examinations and quizzes, classroom teaching is easier. But probably a more important reason, one that most teachers quickly learn, is that if discipline is not maintained in one's classroom, the repercussions are serious. School superintendents and principals judge classroom performance largely on the absence of problems. As one observer has noted:

A teacher will rarely, if ever, be called on the carpet or denied tenure because his [or her] students have not learned anything; he [she] will certainly be rebuked if his [her] students are talking or moving about the classroom, or— even worse—found outside the room . . . . (Silberman, 1970, p. 140)

The obvious result of defensive teaching and the classroom bargain is that educational quality is lowered. Knowledge is sacrificed for control, and the students are sold short in their educations (McNeil, 1986; Sedlak et al., 1986).

Summary

Government-supported education on the American continent had its beginnings in 1647. The first formal schools were influenced by religious interests, but later occupational and economic factors became predominant influences. In the 1800s a universal education system emerged, a system, which, from a traditional view, was important for a democratic society and provided equal opportunities for all children. An alternative historical view, labeled *revisionist*, emphasizes that the economic and social elites of the society develop an educational system that meets their needs. The Lancaster system of education is an example of a system that produced workers suited for the industrial workplace.

Functionalist theory, paralleling the traditional view of education, emphasizes how education is an integrating institution. Education helps to socialize children coming from diverse backgrounds, presenting them with an ideal version of the society and culture. Functional theory takes a positive view of education, emphasizing how students are rewarded for their ability and hard work.

Conflict theory, recognizing the conflicts of interest among different groups and categories of people, stresses that powerful interest groups in the society will control the educational system for their own ends. The educational system serves the powerful by providing the workers needed by the economic interests of the society. Conflict theorists also see the educational system as favoring the children of the advantaged groups over the disadvantaged.

The worldwide picture with respect to education has improved dramatically since the 1950s. Although great advances have been made, some areas of the world, notably in Africa and parts of Asia, still provide education for only about one-fourth of their children. Throughout many countries, especially the less developed ones, females receive less education than males.

School systems of nations vary in their differentiation and rigidity. Differentiation refers to different schools, tracks, or streams for different students, and rigidity refers to the ease of moving from one to another. The United States' educational system, especially from the perspective of cultural values, is less rigid than many European and Asian countries. Great Britain and Japan provide illustrations of more rigid systems in which universal examinations are key determinants of educational and occupational opportunities.

Changes in education tend to mirror trends in the larger society. These changes include the increasing bureaucratization of school systems, with a greater emphasis on quantification and formal credentials. In the 1960s in the United States, the schools underwent a liberalization process, which has more recently been reversed by a return to the basics.

The educational system does not serve different groups in the population equally. Blacks, Hispanics, and students from lower socioeconomic backgrounds tend to succeed less often in the educational system than those from the dominant white population. A college education today gives a great advantage in the occupational world, and therefore the economic world. An education from one of the elite colleges or universities is a key to top corporate management in both the United States and Japan.

In recent decades, many people have been critical of the performance of the U.S. educational system. A substantial number of Americans continue to be functionally illiterate. However, reading levels have increased in the last 20 years, but SAT scores, after declining in the 1970s, moved up for a few years, but then declined again.

A key social aspect of the educational system is the relationship between teachers and students. The evaluations that teachers make of students, even if based on false assumptions, can influence how they grade students. The values and social class origins of teachers also are related to how teachers grade students. The influence of teachers at elementary grade levels tends to be long-lasting.

Tracking students according to ability level is supposed to maximize the academic performances of all students, but the evidence shows that it has a positive effect on the high-track students and a negative effect on the low-track students.

Order and control in schools and in the classrooms is an important problem in American education. Many teachers lower their educational standards as a way of maintaining control of the students in their classrooms.

CRITICAL THINKING

1. Compare and contrast the traditional view of the history of U.S. education with that of the revisionists. Which view does the Lancaster example support?
2. Give examples from your own education of the idealization of culture at the elementary level. Why would or should colleges teach more realistic and critical assessments of society?
3. Assume, as the functionalists do, that the education system serves a moral function. Give examples of norms and values you have learned in school.
4. Compare and contrast the conflict and functional sociological interpretations of educational systems.
5. To what extent is U.S. education differentiated and rigid? Compare your conclusions with the educational systems found in Japan and England.
6. In what ways are U.S. schools becoming increasingly bureaucratized? Do you consider this to be a positive or negative trend?
7. Does our educational system provide equal opportunity for all individuals in society? Use information from the chapter to support your conclusion.
8. In what ways might schools serve the needs of the advantaged and powerful people in society?
9. Does tracking perpetuate inequality? Use evidence from the chapter to support your conclusion.
10. What effect does defensive teaching have on the quality of education? What suggestions can you make to reverse this situation?

13 The Economy and Work

In the past, the economy of the United States was able to cash in on its own technological innovations. For example, the automobile assembly line technology created by Henry Ford in the early 1900s was used nationwide to help build an exceptionally profitable automobile industry as well as hugely successful industries of various types (Womack et al., 1991). In more recent years, however, although the United States has continued to introduce a large number of important technological innovations, it has been left to the economies of other societies to implement them, realize their mass market potential, and reap the resulting huge economic rewards. For example, the video recorder was invented in the United States in the 1960s, but it was mass-produced by the Japanese who, until recently, had virtually the entire world market for this enormously successful and profitable technology. Similarly, the United States pioneered the television industry and at one time dominated the world market for television sets. Today, U.S. companies are a miniscule presence in that industry. Ironically, the production of television sets in the United States has grown from 10 million in 1980 to almost 15 million in 1989. However, 90 percent of those sets are being produced not by American, but by foreign-owned, manufacturers (Burgess, 1991).

The issue facing us today, and in the near future, is whether the

United States has learned economic lessons from the past and will be able to exploit its own technological breakthroughs. At the moment, the race is on for the development of commercial applications of advances in superconductivity that were largely made by Americans. Who, for example, will be the first to develop trains that travel, by magnetic levitation, *above* rails rather than on them? Obviously, the stakes are high, and the United States and its economy can ill afford many more failures. Although the outcome is far from clear, the signs are that, despite outspending the Japanese by a wide margin, the United States is behind in the race to commercialize superconductivity (Burgess, 1988).

The **economy** is the social institution involved in the production and exchange of a wide range of goods and services. These activities are accomplished by various economic elements, including businesses, industries, corporations, markets for goods, labor markets, the banking system, labor unions, relevant government agencies, and occupations.

In this chapter we look at economic systems, as well as many of their elements. We begin with an examination of broad changes in the economy, including the Industrial Revolution and the changing nature of capitalism and socialism. Then we turn more specifically to the changing nature of the U.S. economy, focusing on such issues as changes in the labor force, the decline of labor unions, deindustrialization, the growing strength of U.S. foreign competitors, projections on the future of the U.S. economy, and the post-industrial society.

Historical Changes in Economic Systems

Revolutionary changes in economic systems have occurred during the last century, and the next century promises many more to come. Because much of the future of the U.S. economy will be shaped by past changes, we need to understand the major developments of the past as well as the dynamics of the present (Hearn, 1988).

The Industrial Revolution

To understand modern economies and the nature of work in the United States today, we must go back to the nineteenth century and the **Industrial Revolution,** which introduced the factory system of production. In this system, machines replaced hand tools, and steam and other sources of energy replaced human or animal power. The many workers who operated the machines ranged from the highly skilled to the almost totally unskilled. Because much of the needed skill was already built into the machine, skilled workers could be replaced by adults and children with little or no training, who worked long hours for low pay. The transformation of workers into machine tenders led to a decline in the use of skilled workers and a rise in the use of unskilled workers.

Another defining characteristic of this age was the elaborate division of labor whereby a single product went through the hands of a number of workers, each of whom performed a small step in the entire production process. Adam Smith depicted this development in his famous description of the new method of producing pins. Under the old system a single person producing a whole pin could produce only a few each day, but in the new division of labor a group of ten workers could produce almost 5000 pins each per day. He describes the division of labor:

> One man draws out the wire; another straights it, a third cuts it; a fourth points it; a fifth grinds it at the top for receiving the head; to make the head requires two or three distinct operations; to put it on is a peculiar business; to whiten the pin is another; it is even a trade by itself to put them into the paper; and the important business of making a pin is in this manner divided into about eighteen distinct operations, which in some manufactories are all performed by distinct hands (Smith, 1937, pp. 4–5).

The first factories were primitive affairs, but they gave way over the years to larger and more efficient entities geared to mass production. **Mass production** had a variety of characteristics: products were standardized; parts were made interchangeable; precision tools were used so that parts could be made to fit universally; the production process was mechanized to yield high volume; the flow of materials to the machine and products from the machine were synchronized; and the entire process was made as continuous as possible. This, of course, is the assembly-line type of production that continues today in such industries as automobile manufacturing. These systems reached their fullest application in the United States in the mid-twentieth century and spread throughout the world.

Types of Economies

Economic systems can be organized in different ways to accomplish the fundamental tasks of producing and exchanging goods and services. The two major economic systems worldwide are capitalism and socialism, although most countries today are neither purely capitalist nor purely socialist. As we shall see in the pages ahead, the philosophies of both capitalism and socialism are moderated greatly in the actual workings of economies, including that of the United States. Furthermore, changes in the Soviet Union and Eastern Europe are leading to dramatic change in socialism—changes that are bringing it closer to capitalism.

The Changing Nature of Capitalist Economic Systems

Capitalism is an economic system that emphasizes the private ownership of property and the means of production. The owners of property and especially the means of production are expected to strive for economic gains called *profits*. Capitalism is the guiding economic philosophy in many societies, including most prominently the United States.

Karl Marx on Capitalism. As we saw in chapter 8, social theorist Karl Marx offered a critical analysis and description of capitalist systems. He saw capitalist societies as divided into two social classes, one of which exploited the other. One class, the capitalist, owned the means of production, which included land, raw materials such as mines and forests, and factories with all their tools and machinery. The other class, the proletariat, was forced to sell its labor time to the capitalist class in order to have access to the commodities produced by the economic system. The capitalists pay the workers for their labor time, but, as Marx emphasized, the workers are paid *less* than the value of what they produce for the capitalist. The gap between the costs of labor and production and the worth of what is produced is called the profit.

Marx saw the capitalist system as exploitative of the proletariat because the workers were paid only enough for survival for themselves and their families. The capitalists, by contrast, could reinvest their profits and expand their businesses. The general success of the capitalist class is therefore derived from exploiting the work of the proletariat.

Writing in the mid-1800s, Marx was describing capitalism in its heyday. Over the years capitalism has changed tremendously, and many neo-Marxian scholars have attempted to adapt Marx's ideas to the changing realities of capitalist society. For example, the capitalism of Marx's day can be described as **competitive capitalism.** No one capitalist, or small group of capitalists, could gain complete and uncontested control over a market. Although it was Marx who foresaw the growth of monopolies, Baran and Sweezy (1966) designated modern capitalist society as **monopoly capitalism.** In this updated type of capitalism, one or a few capitalists control a given sector of the economy. Monopoly capitalism weakens competition and introduces changes in the control structure of capitalist enterprises. In competitive capitalism an enterprise tended to be controlled by a single capitalist-entrepreneur. In monopoly capitalism, however, the modern corporation is owned by a large number of stockholders, although often a few large stockholders own most of the shares in a given company. Although stockholders "own" the company, managers exercise the actual day-to-day control. Managers are crucial in monopoly capitalism, whereas the entrepreneurs were central in competitive capitalism. One by-product of this distinction is that Marx's simple model of opposition between capitalist and proletariat no longer applies. Who are the capitalists? Are the millions of people who own a few shares of stock in General Motors capitalists? Are the managers of modern enterprises capitalists? Or are they members of the proletariat, since they are employees of the organization? These are just a few of the questions raised by changes in the capitalist system during the last century.

Another significant change in capitalism has been the growth of white-collar and service workers and the decline of the blue-collar workers whom Marx saw as the proletariat. Can Marx's theory of exploitation be extended to white-collar and service occupations? Making such an extension, Braverman (1974) argued that the concept of the proletariat describes not a specific group of people or occupations but a process of buying and selling labor power. Like blue-collar workers, white-collar and service workers are forced to sell their labor time to capitalists, although the impact of this exploitation and control is not yet as great as it has been on blue-collar occupations.

The Changing Nature of Worker Control.   Braverman recognized economic exploitation, which was Marx's focus, but he concentrated on the issue of managerial control over workers. Edwards (1979) sees control at the heart of the transformation of the workplace in the twentieth century. Following Marx, Edwards sees the workplace, both past and present, as an arena of class conflict—in his terms, a "contested terrain." Within this arena, dramatic changes have taken place in the way in which those at the top control those at the bottom. In nineteenth-century competitive capitalism, simple personal control was used. The "bosses exercised power personally, intervening in the labor process often to exhort workers, bully and threaten them, reward good performance, hire and fire on the spot, favor loyal workers, and generally act as despots, benevolent or otherwise" (Edwards, 1979, p. 19). Although this system continues to survive in small businesses, it has generally been undermined by the growth of large organizations. Simple *personal control* has been replaced by *impersonal technical* and *bureaucratic control.*

Technology is often used today as a way of controlling workers. The classic example is the assembly line found, for example, in the production of automobiles or farm machines, or in the processing of meat and other food. When workers are on an assembly line, their actions are controlled by the incessant demands of the moving line.

In today's industries and businesses many kinds of electronic automated equipment are used by management to increase control over workers. For example, telephone operators today do not have to be carefully watched and controlled by human supervisors because every operator's work is monitored by electronic equipment that records the exact amount of time an operator spends on each customer call. Operators know how long they should be spending to process each request, so there is no time for a friendly word before moving on quickly to the next caller. Technological control also diminishes the quality of the work experience (it is more boring, stressful, etc.) and demeans the lives of workers. Many kinds of jobs do not take advantage of the distinctive human ability to think, create, and be inventive (Shaiken, 1986; Zuboff, 1988).

Still another modern form of control is revealed in Nicole Biggart's (1989) study of direct-selling organizations such as Mary Kay Cosmetics, Tupperware, and Amway. Those involved in direct selling work largely on their own and therefore cannot be controlled through direct personal supervision, technology, or bureaucracy. Biggart shows instead that direct-selling organizations use *morality* to control those who do the selling for them. For example, the organizations seek to instill in the sellers the idea that such work is more than a job—it is a total way of life encompassing not just the material world, but the spiritual and civic realms as well. Direct-selling organizations also often wrap what they are doing in cloaks of religiosity and patriotism. Overall, direct-selling organizations create an elaborate moral system that controls those who do the selling for them.

The major direction in which capitalism has changed and modified is toward state capitalism. In **state capitalism,** capitalistic enterprises continue to exist, but there is also an array of state-owned branches of production, and the state regulates and manages the economy. The best contemporary example of this is Sweden, where state ownership and regulation coexist with capitalistic enterprises.

The Changing Nature of Socialist Economic Systems

Socialism is an economic system in which the means of producing goods and services are publicly or collectively owned. Sometimes socialist economies are found among small groups of people who share in the ownership of property and benefit equally from the production of their work. Many times small religious sects are organized along socialist lines. However, the typical socialist economy today is state socialism, in which the economy is controlled by the government. Under **state socialism,** the government—through its political leaders, officials, and bureaucrats—establishes what will be produced, manages how it will be produced, and controls the distribution of goods and services. The most familiar systems of state socialism today, although they are changing, are the Soviet Union and many Eastern European nations (Edwards et al., 1986).

The socialist ideology holds that socialism is a democratic system in which the people have a voice in the economic decisions that affect them. With no private ownership of property, wealth is supposed to be redistributed so that everyone has the resources needed for living. According to the ideology of socialism, workers are not supposed to be alienated from their work or from any other aspects of their society. Individuals should be able to express their distinctive abilities and capacities. These principles might be called the theory of socialism, but in practice, especially under state socialist systems, the reality often differs from the theory.

The state socialism of the Soviet Union, Poland, and other East European states has obviously not succeeded in all of these objectives. In chapter 8, we saw that the Soviet Union has a stratification system leading to the unequal distribution of material goods and other economic advantages. In the Soviet Union decisions about production have not been made by the people, but have been handed down from the top by government officials and bureaucrats.

The Changing Soviet Economy. Soviet leader Mikhail Gorbachev has used the term *perestroika* to describe the program for reforming Soviet socialism. Centralized economic planning and government control over every facet of the economy has defined the Soviet economy since the Communist revolution of 1917. Low productivity and goods of shoddy quality have been characteristic. Thus, for example, it has been claimed that "the most exciting thing about watching Soviet television was that the set was liable to catch fire" (*Fortune*, 1988b, p. 11).

Perestroika aims at increasing productivity and the quality of goods by moving toward more local control by factories, farms, and other economic enterprises. Instead of having centralized agencies make decisions, local units will make those decisions; and those judgments will be shaped, at least to some degree, by market forces. What is produced, how much is produced, and how much the goods will cost will be determined more by the market for the goods and less by fiat from Moscow (Parks, 1991).

The goal is to produce a system in which incentive exists for high levels of productivity and high-quality products. This means that some workers will need to be paid more than others and that consumer goods will be available to workers who are economically successful. Gorbachev has said that it is time that productive workers be rewarded "even if, Marx forbid, some of them get rich at it" (Ford, 1988, p. 74).

The current Soviet view is that workers need to be more motivated, more ambitious, more interested in earning money, and more concerned with accumulating material possessions. Workers will also be given more voice in running their organizations and in the selection of management. Organizations, too, will be motivated by allowing them to earn profits and to be free to decide what to do with those profits (expansion, higher pay, etc.). More entrepreneurship will be encouraged as people are allowed to go into various kinds of businesses for themselves or as members of a group. This program is obviously very revolutionary and ambitious, and it is unclear how far Gorbachev will succeed with *perestroika*. In the short run, much economic and social disruption (Wyle, 1991) and substantial price increases are forecast. But if Gorbachev is successful in weathering the storms (such as the attempted coup in 1991), a radically altered Soviet economy might emerge.

Table 13–1.   Changes in Labor Force by Occupational Group

Occupational Level	Percentage of the Labor Force					
	1900	*1930*	*1960*	*1970*	*1982*	*1995**
White-collar	17.6	29.4	40.8	45.6	53.7	52.5
Professionals	4.3	6.8	0.8	14.0	17.0	17.1
Managers	5.9	7.4	8.7	7.9	11.5	9.6
Clerical workers	3.0	8.9	14.1	16.9	18.5	18.9
Sales	4.5	6.3	7.2	6.8	6.6	6.9
Service	9.1	9.8	11.6	11.8	13.8	16.3
Manual	35.8	39.6	36.4	33.4	29.7	29.3
Farm	37.5	21.1	6.2	2.9	2.7	1.9
Not reported	—	—	5.0	6.3	—	—
Total	100.0	100.0	100.0	100.0	99.9	100.0

* The figures for 1995 are projections.
Source: Data for 1900 and 1930 adapted from Philip M. Hauser, "Labor Force," in Robert E. L. Faris, ed., *Handbook of Modern Sociology* (Chicago: Rand-McNally, 1964), p. 183. Data for 1960 and 1970 adapted from Constance Bogh DiCesare, "Change in the Occupational Structure of U.S. Jobs," *Monthly Labor Review* (1975), p. 24. Data for 1982 from *Employment and Earnings* (30) 1 (Washington, D.C.: U.S. Department of Labor, 1983), p. 157. Data for 1995 from George T. Silvestri, John M. Lukasiewicz, and Marcus E. Einstein, "Occupational Employment Projections Through 1995," *Monthly Labor Review* 106 (1983), pp. 37–49. Totals are rounded.

The Changing State of the U.S. Economy

Not only is the Soviet Union changing dramatically, but so is the U.S. economic system. In fact, the changes are so dramatic and so likely to be with us for the foreseeable future that one of the authors (Ritzer, 1989) has labeled this a "permanently new economy." Among the most important changes in the U.S. economy are changes in the labor force, the changing nature of labor unions, deindustrialization, the rise in America's foreign competitors, the development of some hopeful signs for the economy in the coming years, and the arrival of the postindustrial society.

Changes in the Labor Force

Overall, the labor force in the United States will grow by 18 million new jobs between 1988 and 2000, from 118 million to 136 million workers (Davis, 1990). Furthermore, there will continue to be enormous shifts within the labor force—changes that have been occurring throughout the twentieth century (see Table 13–1). The most dramatic of these has been the decline in the number of people who work on the farms or perform farm-related activities. In 1900 about 38 percent of the labor force was found on the farm, but by 1988 that figure had declined to slightly less than 3 percent. We have not yet reached the end of this decline: projections show that by the year 2000 farmers will represent about 2 percent of the labor force (U.S. Bureau of the Census, 1990, p. 395). A major factor here has been an array of technological changes that have allowed fewer and fewer people to produce ever-greater quantities of food. Today the independent farmer, being replaced by huge agribusinesses, is on the verge of extinction.

A second major change in the labor force has been the rise in the percentage of people in the professions (Abbott, 1988), which almost quadrupled between 1900 and 1982. Growth in this category has now stabilized and in 1995 the percentage of the labor force in the professions will be about the same as it was in 1982. Major factors responsible for the rise include increasingly sophisticated knowledge, technologies that require more highly trained people, and increasing wealth and sophistication that allow us to want and afford a wide array of professional services.

Third, something has occurred that could be labeled the *clerical revolution*. Clerical workers and those in related occupations constituted only 3 percent of the labor force in 1900, but by 1982 that percentage had multiplied sixfold to 18.5 percent. Projections indicate that by 1995 clerical workers will increase to 24 million, or nearly 19 percent of the entire labor force. The major cause of this increase is the rise of bureaucracies with their seemingly insatiable need for white-collar workers of all types. Another key factor is technological change: the rise of the computer has created an "information society" that needs workers to manage the computer's tremendous generation of information.

Finally, blue-collar or manual work has declined substantially. In 1930 the blue-collar workers were, by a wide margin, the largest occupational category, comprising almost 40 percent of the labor force. By 1956, however, the number of people in white-collar occupations exceeded the number in blue-collar occupations for the first time, and since then the gap between them has steadily widened. The forecast is for a further modest decline of people in blue-collar occupations through the mid-1990s. The decline in U.S. industry, technological changes that have eliminated the need for many blue-collar jobs, and the general shift to services all help to account for the decline in blue-collar occupations.

Fastest-Growing Occupations.   The fastest-growing occupation between now and the year 2000 will be that of medical assistant. This trend is part of a growth pattern for medical services (and service occupations in general) that will also include an increasing demand for home health aides, radiologic technologists and technicians, and medical secretaries. Still another cluster of occupations that is likely to grow substantially includes occupations linked to computers—data processing equipment repairers, systems analysts, programmers, and equipment operators. Therefore, the fastest-growing occupations are tied to basic changes in society in general and the workworld in particular—for example, greater attention to health matters and the boom in computer technology.

Increasing Importance of Women in the Labor Force.   One of the most dramatic changes in the last few decades has been the increasing number of women in the labor force (Shank, 1988). In 1890, only slightly more than 17 percent of the labor force was female, but by 1990 women constituted 58 percent of the labor force (Haughen and Meisenheimer, 1991, p. 15). Between 1970 and 1988, the number of women in the labor force grew by 74 percent, compared to a 31 percent growth rate for males (U.S. Bureau of the Census, 1990, p. 382). Between 1988 and 2000 the growth rate for women will continue to double that for men (25 percent to 12 percent), although growth rates for both will be down as a result of the overall decline in the birth rate. As far as the net change in the labor force is concerned, two-thirds of it has come, and will continue to come, from women. Not only are women more apt to be in the labor force but increasingly they are in high-status and high-paying occupations (Blum and Smith, 1988).

Although women appear to be doing quite well in the work world, many problems remain. For example, a stubborn pay gap (the percentage of male income earned by female workers) of between 60 and 70 percent (Ryscavage and Henle, 1990, p. 4) exists between female and male earnings, and women have a long way to go before achieving pay parity with men (Hodson and England, 1986). Another continuing problem for women is the lack of adequate corporate child-care facilities (Fernandez, 1986; Wash and Brand, 1990). This need has become particularly pressing in the 1990s, since 60 percent of women are working by the time their children are four years of age. Approximately 28 million children are living in households in which the mother works for at least part of the day on a regular basis (Wash and Brand, 1990, p. 20). These difficult problems are among many others that remain for women despite their significant gains in the labor force.

Changing Labor Unions

In 1900 only 3 percent of the labor force of the United States belonged to unions, but the percentage grew to 23 percent by the end of World War II. A decline began in the early 1960s and by 1990, the percentage had dropped to 16.1 percent (*Monthly Labor Review*, 1991, p. 2). An expected continuation of this decline leads to estimates that by the year

2000 union membership could drop to 13 percent of the labor force (Lipset, 1987).

Not only have unions lost members, but they have shown evidence of decline in other ways as well. Although in the past many unions could often negotiate large wage increases for their members, in recent years wage increases have generally been small. In addition, in order to get contracts with management, unions have been giving up rights and benefits they had won in previous contract negotiations (Katz, 1985). In a variety of ways, unions are weaker overall, including in their ability to negotiate with management. In numbers and in power, the U.S. labor movement is the weakest in the Western world.

Factors Involved in Union Decline.   Four key factors help to explain the decline in union membership: lack of competition among unions, worker resistance to unionization, management opposition to unions, and technological change. First, the union movement itself lost some of its dynamism because the internal competition between union organizations was reduced. The most notable case of reducing union competitiveness came when the two major unions, the AFL (American Federation of Labor) and the CIO (Congress of Industrial Organizations), combined to form the AFL–CIO, a single union organization.

Second, by the early 1950s, unions had already organized a large proportion of the group most receptive to unionization—blue-collar factory workers. When they had to look elsewhere for members, they found that other occupations proved resistant to union membership drives.

As one example, unions have not succeeded in organizing white-collar workers. Many white-collar workers are women, and females have historically been less likely to join unions, partly because of negative attitudes toward unions and partly because of their structural position in the work world. Among the structural factors is the fact that women are more apt to be in sectors of the economy (for example, bureaucracies rather than industries) where unionization is less common (Freeman and Medoff, 1984).

Unions have also failed to attract young people. As with the underrepresentation of women, the reason is not primarily a lack of desire to join unions but the result of a series of structural factors (Freeman and Medoff, 1984). For example, young people are often in temporary jobs, and temporary workers are clearly less interested in unions and more difficult to unionize than permanent employees.

The third factor in the decline of unions is management opposition (Goldfield, 1987). Management in the United States has never been favorably disposed to the union movement. (In other societies, especially in Western Europe, management has been much more accepting of unions.) In the earlier part of this century management hired thugs and killers to keep unions out. More recently, most companies came to accept unions, even though grudgingly. But in the 1980s management opposition to unions rose again. One successful move has been for companies to discontinue operations, or restructure the company, and thus break union contracts. Later the operations may be reestablished under a new name or different management, but the newly hired workers are nonunion. Also, many company managers have stepped up their efforts to avoid unionization (Lawler and West, 1985).

The fourth factor in the decline of unions has been technological change that reduces jobs. Often the jobs eliminated are blue-collar jobs, which were most likely to have been unionized. A good example of this trend is in the printing industry, once one of the bastions of union strength. In the old days when type was set by skilled hands, a large proportion of the workers was unionized. However, manual typesetting has been replaced by computer technology, and virtually all of the skilled manual jobs have disappeared. With the disappearance of those jobs came a decline in union membership, and consequently the decline and disappearance of unions in the typesetting industry (Scott, 1987). More generally, new technologies such as computers and robots often cost jobs, and these lost jobs often translate into declines in union membership and union power.

Union Responses to Declines in Numbers.   Unions have tried to adapt to their new, reduced situation by concentrating on new groups of workers like government employees, health workers, and professional athletes. They have also tried to develop a series of new goals such as job guarantees for members, the prevention of the loss of American jobs to other countries, and new benefits for members (Cornfield, 1989).

In addition to the four factors discussed in this section, union decline is also linked to the decline in U.S. heavy industry, where many unionized workers have been employed. As these industries have laid off workers, shut plants down, and "downsized," unions have lost large numbers of members. We turn now to a detailed discussion of this industrial decline, one that is often called **deindustrialization.**

Deindustrialization

While U.S. industry continues to dominate the capitalist world, it is not the powerful force it once was. Many U.S. industries, especially steel and automobiles, have declined—a process Bluestone and Harrison (1982) call "the deindustrialization of America."

A major manifestation of deindustrialization is the dramatic drop in employment in such key "smokestack" industries as steel, where the number of employees declined from 570,500 in 1979 to 274,300 in 1989, a decline of nearly 50 percent. Overall, between 1979 and 1989 employment in goods-producing industries declined from 29.5 percent of the total work force to 23.6 percent (Plunkert, 1990, p. 11). In addition, many workers have been "dislocated," which in most cases means they have lost their jobs forever. They not only lose their jobs but they also may forfeit their benefits (health insurance, retirement, etc.). They are apt to be laid off with few skills and with few opportunities for the training needed for many of the high-tech occupations now being created by our economy. For many, their only options are jobs such as selling hamburgers in fast-food restaurants. Many companies have been downsized or restructured. For example, USX (formerly the once-mighty U.S. Steel) went from about 100,000 employees in 1980 to less than 20,000 in 1987 (Ignatius, 1987). As a result of downsizing, many blue-collar workers have lost their jobs, but managers and professionals are not immune to major reductions in force (*Fortune*, 1988a).

As a result of deindustrialization, the standard of living in the United States has not risen nearly as rapidly as it has in other countries. The standard of living in the United States was surpassed by West Germany in 1977, and the gap has widened over the ensuing years. Japan, once near the bottom of industrialized nations in terms of standard of living, has been making rapid strides and is poised to pass the United States (Auerbach, 1988).

Disinvestment, Mergers, and Takeovers.   Another aspect of the deindustrialization of America is the fact that many U.S. companies have stopped reinvesting substantial sums of money in their own growth and development (Bluestone and Harrison, 1982, p. 6). To maintain productivity as well as to stimulate growth, industries must invest in basic plants and equipment. This kind of industrial investment made the United States the world's greatest economic power. However, in recent years, money has been diverted from such productive investment. For example, instead of investing in new plants and equipment in the United States, corporations are investing in similar facilities in other countries.

Another major source of disinvestment is the merger and takeover mania that has swept through the U.S. corporate world in recent years. Mergers between corporations cost money and, in themselves, produce no new factories, technologies, or jobs. Even more threatening are the huge multibillion dollar takeover efforts that have become commonplace in U.S. industry. In such efforts, one organization may borrow billions of dollars to take over another organization. Since the money is borrowed, it adds nothing to the productivity of the economy. In fact, in the case of takeovers, the economy may actually lose productive capacity as corporations that are taken over are dismantled and sold off in pieces in order to finance the takeover.

Multinationals.   One of the most dramatic economic changes in recent years has been the rise of multinational firms. Instead of being located in a given nation, the interests of many contemporary firms cut across a number of national borders. Many companies have become multinationals in recent years through mergers, acquisitions, and joint ventures with companies in other countries. The United States has 167 of the world's largest multinational companies, but it is closely followed by Japan with 111 such firms (*Fortune,* 1990).

While many companies have grown substantially by transforming themselves into multinational firms, there are at least three dangers to the U.S. economy. First, jobs may be transferred from the United States to foreign locales. Second, companies, even the U.S. multinationals, are more likely to be interested in their own profitability than the state of the U.S. economy. Thus, they may take actions (for example, closing a plant) that might increase their profits, but cause layoffs and other economic problems in the United States. Finally, there is the increasing tendency of foreign multinationals to acquire U.S. firms (as well as real estate and other sectors of the economy). Such acquisitions mean that profits earned in the United States will be sent to the home country of the foreign multinational (*Bondweek,* 1989).

Economic Competitors of the United States

Foreign manufacturers have become formidable competitors in the international marketplace. The products of Western Europe and Japan are marketed throughout the world in competition with United States' products. Furthermore, for many years Americans have purchased more goods from other countries than other countries have purchased from us, which leads to the often-reported negative "balance of payments" for the U.S. economy. There is no question that Asian economies, and especially the Japanese, have proved to be our most serious economic competitors. (See figure 13–1.)

The Growing Power of Asian Economies.   The success of the Japanese automobile and electronics industries is the most dramatic example of the growing power of America's foreign competitors. After World War II Japan had to rebuild its factories, and those new factories proved to be a big advantage over the aged factories already functioning in the United States. However, much of the success of the Japanese is traceable to the hard work and dedication of their managers and workers. Japanese workers are generally very loyal to their companies and are proud of the products they make. This pride and hard work makes Japanese products highly valued in the markets of the world (Halberstam, 1986).

However, the Japanese are now experiencing an economic threat from

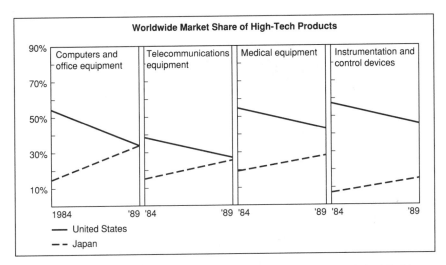

Worldwide Market Share of High-Tech Products

Figure 13–1.   The Decline of United States Companies' Share of the World-wide Market for High-Tech Products, in Percent, 1984–1989.
Source: Carla Rapoport, "The Big Split." *Fortune* 123, 1991.

their Asian neighbors—the "four tigers" of Taiwan, Hong Kong, Singapore, and South Korea (Amsden, 1989). South Korea has already made important inroads into the world market for small automobiles (Hyundai) and consumer electronics (Samsung), and it is likely to become a significant player in the world economy in other areas as well. The industriousness of the Koreans is revealed in their attitudes toward the Japanese, who are viewed as the "lazy Asians" (Halberstam, 1986). As if to support such a view, the Japanese passed a law that lowered the maximum workweek from 48 to 46 hours, and further reductions will lower the maximum workweek to 40 hours by the early 1990s (Shapiro, 1988). Therefore, the United States must compete not only with Japan but also with newer and more vigorous producers like South Korea and other countries on the "Asian Rim."

The U.S. Economy in the Coming Years

Although the recent history of U.S. industry has been somewhat negative, there are some hopeful signs. Many believe that manufacturing continues to be the key to the economic prosperity of the United States; signs of expansion are emerging in U.S. manufacturing, and greater success has been reported in the international marketplace (*Fortune*, 1988c). Even the smokestack industries have some bright spots, such as the revival of Ford and its record-high profits in the late 1980s, although that revival came, to some degree, from downsizing the company, which resulted in a

Cross-National Perspectives

"Lean Organizations" in Japanese and American Industries

Many attempts have been made to try to account for the great success of Japanese industry, in general, and its automobile industry in particular. Corresponding to these efforts have been attempts to understand the recent failures of the U.S. counterparts to the Japanese successes. One of the most influential recent works on this issue is *The Machine That Changed the World* (Womack, Jones, and Roos, 1990). While this book focuses on the automobile industry in the United States and Japan, it offers lessons for all types of manufacturing. According to Womack and his colleagues, "lean" organizations lie at the root of Japanese successes, and Toyota is given credit for creating this production system. In order to understand lean organizations it is necessary to first say some things about the U.S. system of mass production, a system that might be described as involving a "fat" organization.

The U.S. system of mass production, especially in the automobile industry, is characterized by numerous semi-skilled and unskilled workers tending very expensive machines. This system is oriented to the production of large numbers of standardized products. The machines involved cost a great deal of money, and the expenses associated with disruption are high. In order to ensure smooth production, U.S. companies believe that they must be certain that "extra supplies, extra workers, and extra space" are always available. All these extras make U.S. production organizations fat. For example, U.S. manufacturers feel the need to keep large inventories of parts and supplies in the factory in order to be sure that the expensive technology is utilized continually. The fear is that the shortage of a needed part or necessary raw materials will slow, or shut down, the production process. However, such a system is costly: (1) Large quantities of parts or supplies are usually bought on credit, requiring large interest payments. (2) If kept on site for a long period of time, material can deteriorate in quality or be stolen. (3) Keeping large quantities of supplies requires additional space, and the construction and maintenance of that space is also costly.

Not only do U.S. manufacturers keep huge inventories of supplies and materials, but they also maintain a large work force to back up and support their production workers. Thus, behind those production workers are battalions of fill-in workers, people who repair machines, workers who check the quality of what is being produced, people who perform housekeeping chores, rework specialists who repair defective products, first-line supervisors to oversee the production workers, and engineers.

Overall, the U.S. approach can be called the "just-in-case" system; that is, keep enough of everything on hand just in case it is needed. In contrast, the Japanese system of lean production has been labeled a "just-in-time" system. That is, parts and supplies arrive in the factory just as they are needed in the production system. There is no large inventory of parts and supplies, and thus all of the extra costs associated with such an inventory are eliminated by the Japanese manufacturing system. Almost all of the extra, "nonproductive" workers have been eliminated or greatly reduced. Instead of a supervisor, a work team has a group leader, who combines supervision with production. The production workers themselves do such things as housekeeping, minor tool repair, and the checking of quality, thereby eliminating the need for separate (and) nonproductive workers to perform these tasks. Instead of having staff specialists or consultants suggest ways of improving the production process, the workers themselves collectively suggest ways of improving production. The latter groups have come to be called the now-famous "quality circles."

Japanese manufacturers have made a number of other innovations that can be dealt with under the heading of *lean production*. In American assembly-line production, workers are discouraged from stopping the line under any circumstances. The idea is that the machinery is too expensive to be stopped, and too many people would be left idle by a stoppage of the line. Thus, a worker who sees a defective part, or a defect in the production process, is required to simply let it pass. The defect is supposed to be picked up at the end of the line by the quality inspector and dealt with by the repair people. The problem with this system, in addition to the fact that it requires extra workers, is that it is almost impossible to isolate and deal with the source of the defect.

In contrast, in the Japanese system a cord is placed above every production station and workers are urged to pull it, thereby stopping the line, whenever a problem arises that cannot be fixed immediately. Once stopped, the work team descends on the spot and seeks to discover the cause of the problem and to devise a way to fix it so that it does not recur. In this way, more and more problems are solved forever, whereas in the U.S. system the same problem occurs over and over. As a result, today Japanese assembly lines rarely stop, because virtually all problems have been solved. On the other hand, U.S. assembly lines stop constantly. Such stoppages are not the result of quality problems (only a line manager can stop a line), but because of inadequate supplies or poor coordination among the main production line and the many subassembly lines. Furthermore, Japanese assembly lines require almost no rework at the end of the line, because virtually all of the sources of poor quality have been eliminated. In contrast, U.S. manufacturing plants continue to do considerable rework—the fixing of mistakes takes about 20 percent of the area of a mass production plant and about 25 percent of the total hours worked. Clearly, such percentages reflect a "fat" manufacturing system, fat that has been all but eliminated in the lean organizations spearheaded by Japan. While there are efforts underway in the United States to create lean organizations, either among Japanese transplants or indigenous companies, the fact is that we have a very long way to go to create the kind of lean organizations found in Japan.

In sum, the Japanese system may be termed *lean* because it uses less of everything compared with mass production—half the human effort in the factory, half the manufacturing space, half the investment in tools, half the engineering to develop a new product in half the time. Also, it requires keeping far less than half the needed inventory on site, results in many fewer defects, and produces a greater and ever-growing variety of products (Womack et al., 1990, p. 13).

WOMACK, JAMES P., JONES, DANIEL T., and ROOS, DANIEL. *The Machine That Changed the World*. New York: Rawson Associates, 1990.

far smaller payroll. Outside of traditional areas of strength, other bright spots in U.S. industry include pharmaceuticals (for example, the drug t-PA that saves lives by dissolving clots that cause heart attacks [*Fortune*, 1988d]), biotechnology, "cosmeceuticals" (for example, Retin-A to remove wrinkles and Rogaine to stimulate hair growth in people with male-type baldness [*Business Week*, 1988a]), semiconductors, as well as the superconductors mentioned at the beginning of the chapter. All these examples demonstrate the strength of U.S. industries in terms of technological innovation.

The Postindustrial Economy

Many observers see the economy of the United States as moving beyond industrial capitalism into a stage called a *postindustrial society* (Bell,

1973). As we noted in chapter 4, a postindustrial society is one defined more by service industries than goods-producing industries. In 1940, 51.4 percent of the work force was in goods-producing areas like mining, construction, and manufacturing. In 1989 about 23.6 percent of the work force was in those areas. On the other hand, in 1940, 48.6 percent of the work force was in service areas, but by 1989 the percentage had increased to 76.4 percent (Kutscher, 1987; Plunkert, 1990).

The projections for the year 2000 are even more striking. Between now and 2000 the number of workers in goods-producing areas is likely to remain exactly the same, while the number of people in service-producing areas is likely to increase by 20 million people! (Kutscher, 1987)

In addition to the growth in well-known service areas in recent years, a number of new service arenas have emerged. Many organizations now provide services to other businesses. For example, accounting, computing, and security services have boomed (Tschetter, 1987). Also in this category are the organizations that provide temporary help to business. Processing knowledge and information and providing it to those who need it have become major sectors of the service area. Some have argued that instead of calling it a "service society," it should be called an "information society" (Lyon, 1986).

The Declining Economic Fortunes of the Younger Generation

With all of the changes occurring in the U.S. economy, many people in the younger generation will have a difficult economic future. Between 1945 and 1973, the wages of U.S. workers, adjusted for inflation, increased between 2.5 and 3.0 percent per year. But since 1973 wages have stagnated or even declined. People who were participating in the economy during the earlier time period were able to develop quite comfortable life-styles, which they continue today. They have job security through seniority, their housing costs remain stable because of fixed mortgages, and they have savings that grew dramatically during periods of high interest rates. In contrast, the generation coming into adulthood after 1973 has had a much more difficult time achieving the same life-style as their predecessors, and many are struggling economically. In order to achieve economic success, they will have to make many more sacrifices than the preceding generation. Many young U.S. couples today have both spouses working, and even so, they find it impossible to achieve what their parents did. Frequently they are unable to accumulate the capital necessary to purchase a home, and many incur great amounts of consumer debt. In addition, although many young couples want families, they must postpone or curtail having children because of economic considerations (Levy, 1987).

Experiences in the World of Work

Sociologists have studied the world of work in many different settings and occupations (Ritzer and Walczak, 1986). While many people enjoy their work and get fulfillment from their jobs or careers, many other people experience stresses and conflict through their work. Conflict is a major factor in occupational life and is often built into the work role.

Role Conflict

Role conflict refers to a situation in which a person who holds a position is confronted with conflicting or contradictory expectations so that compliance with one makes compliance with the other difficult. We will consider four of the major forms of role conflict: role overload, interrole conflict, person/role conflict, and intersender role conflict.

Role Overload.   **Role overload** occurs when an individual in a role is confronted with a large number of expectations and finds it difficult, if not impossible, to satisfy all of them in a given time period. Because of the nature of their position at the top of organizations, executives are prone to virtually every form of role conflict and are particularly likely to be confronted with role overload.

The president of a broadcasting company describes his day and his role overload, which, incidentally, he seemed to enjoy.[1]

> My day starts between four-thirty and five in the morning. . . . I dictate in my library until about seven-thirty. Then I have breakfast. The driver gets here about eight o'clock and often times I continue dictating in the car on the way to the office. . . . I will probably have as many as 150 letters dictated by seven-thirty in the morning. I have five full-time secretaries, who do nothing but work for (me) . . . (seven more) work for me part-time. This does not include my secretaries in New York, Los Angeles, Washington, and San Francisco. They get dictabelts from me every day. . . . I get home around six-thirty, seven at night. After dinner with the family I spend a minimum of two and a half hours each night going over the mail and dictating. I should have a secretary at home just to handle the mail that comes there. . . . Although I don't go to the office on Saturday or Sunday, I do have mail brought out to my home for the weekend. I dictate on Saturday and Sunday. When I do this on holidays, like Christmas, New Year's and Thanksgiving, I have to sneak a little bit, so the family doesn't know what I'm doing. (Terkel, 1974, pp. 390–391)

---

[1] Excerpts from *Working: People Talk About What They Do All Day and How They Feel About What They Do*, by Studs Terkel. © 1972, 1974 by Studs Terkel. Reprinted by permission of Pantheon Books, Inc., a Division of Random House, Inc.

Role overload is also illustrated by this school superintendent's comments: "There are times when I feel like I have about 15 balls in the air at one time, like a juggler. It's *so* many things. A committee working on this, a committee working on that, a dozen things going. Trying to keep abreast of all of them" (Blumberg and Blumberg, 1985, p. 151). Very often, as these two examples reveal, role overload is associated with the heavy time demands of high-status occupations and professions.

Interrole Conflict. **Interrole conflict** occurs when the expectations attached to one role are in conflict with the expectations of another role. Women in the labor force are especially apt to experience interrole conflict because the demands of their jobs are in conflict with the expectations their family members have about their family responsibilities. The interrole conflict comes between the job and family roles. Their bosses and fellow workers expect dedication to the job, while family members expect time and attention to their needs. Much has been written in the media about the "superwoman" who holds a high-prestige professional job and also fulfills relatively traditional family roles. However, as sociologist Myra Ferree (1987) points out, most women do not have jobs that conform to the media superwoman. The majority of employed women are employed as clerical workers, service workers, factory workers, or the relatively low-status professions of nursing and teaching. Despite the status level of these jobs, married women, especially those who have children, frequently experience interrole conflict between their employment and family roles.

Person/Role Conflict. Person/role conflict occurs when the expectations associated with a particular role violate a person's moral or personal values. This type of conflict is underscored in Robert Jackall's (1988) study of managers, *Moral Mazes*. One of Jackall's findings is that what is right in organizational life is usually simply what one's boss wants. Thus, person/role conflict occurs when what one's boss desires conflicts with the manager's moral sense of what needs to be done. Most managers, if they want to survive, resolve this conflict by ignoring their own morality and doing what their superiors wish. However, there are some who resolve person/role conflict by rejecting the wishes of superiors and doing what they think is right. This is clear in the case of "whistle blowers," or those who reject what the boss wants because it is immoral and go public with their grievances against the organization. Although whistle blowers may satisfy their own morality, they often suffer adverse consequences within the organization for failing to conform to organizational norms and for publicly announcing their dissatisfaction with the organization.

Intersender Role Conflict. **Intersender role conflict** occurs when two or more people have conflicting expectations of a person in a given role. As one illustration, college professors often experience intersender role conflict because two important groups, students on the one hand and fellow professors on the other, place conflicting demands on them. These two groups have radically different expectations of the professor, who is literally caught in a crossfire between them. Students expect their professors to do a good job of teaching: they should remain up to date on relevant material, prepare carefully for class, and work hard at communicating what they know in an interesting and informative manner. Furthermore, professors are expected to prepare and grade exams carefully, being sure to give students feedback on their performance and to comment on how they could improve in the future. Professors should also be available to students during office hours and at other times of mutual convenience. This all seems quite reasonable from the students' perspective. It clearly takes a lot of the professor's time, but, after all, isn't that what professors are supposed to do with their time?

From the point of view of professional colleagues, that is *not* what professors are supposed to do with their time. Fellow professors generally expect their colleagues to put in a minimum amount of time teaching. The majority of their time is expected to be devoted to research, writing, giving papers at professional meetings, and engaging in an array of other professional activities. Professors expect their colleagues to contribute to their discipline, primarily through research and writing. Increases in salary and promotions generally go to professors who do the most high-quality research.

The conflict between the expectations of students and colleagues often forces individual professors to make a choice. Does the professor conform to the expectations of students and carefully prepare a lecture? Or does he or she conform to the expectations of colleagues and work on a research project? This is the intersender role conflict experienced by professors on a day-to-day basis.

Conflict with Customers and Clients

People in service occupations often experience conflict with customers or clients (Peterson, Schmidman, and Elifson, 1982). Service occupations include, among many others, salespeople (Oakes, 1990), especially automobile salespersons, taxi drivers, airline flight attendants (Hochschild, 1983), male and female prostitutes, and physicians in private practice. Direct and spontaneous conflict is always possible in occupations that serve customers, as is illustrated by the following examples of waitresses, flight attendants, and salespeople.

Waitresses. Customers create all sorts of problems for waitresses, including complaints about service, belligerence, and drunkenness. Much conflict surrounds the waitresses' desire to be respected and the customers' propensity to act superior to them. Finally, the tip is significant to the waitress (as it is to the taxi driver), both as a symbol of success and as a source of income. The customer controls the size of the tip and, indeed, whether a tip is left. This is a continuing source of stress, as revealed by the following statement of a cocktail waitress:

> Tips? I feel like Carmen. It's like holding out a tambourine and they throw the coin. (Laughs) There might be occasions when the customers might make it demeaning—the man about town, the conventioneer. When the time comes to pay the check, he would do little things, "How much should I give you?" He might make an issue about it. I did say to one, "Don't play God with me. Do what you want." Then it really didn't matter whether I got a tip or not. I would spit it out, my resentment—that he dares make me feel I'm operating only for a tip. He'd ask for his check. Maybe he's going to sign it. He'd take a very long time and he'd make me stand there, "Let's see now, what do you think I ought to give you?" He would not let go of that moment. And you know it. You know he means to demean you. He's holding the change in his hand, or if he'd sign, he'd flourish the pen and wait. These are the times I really get angry. I'm not reticent. Something would come out. Then I really didn't care, "God-damn, keep your money!" (quoted in Terkel, 1974, p. 295)

Flight Attendants.   Flight attendants have many of the same conflicts as waitresses; in fact, a good portion of their job involves the service of food and drink. However, airline attendants have other kinds of conflicts with their customers, the passengers (Hochschild, 1983). For example, airline attendants are expected to act as if the cabin of the airplane is their living room and the passengers are their guests. Conflict arises here because no such expectation exists for the passengers, who are free to treat airline attendants as workers who are there to provide them with services. In other words, airline attendants are expected to be "nice" to passengers, but passengers need not be nice to attendants. Thus, attendants are expected never to express anger at even the most obnoxious passengers, but the latter are perfectly free to express their hostility to airline attendants.

Salespeople.   The livelihood of all salespeople depends on their ability to make sales, and, as in all relationships between worker and client/customer, the situation produces a struggle for control. Salespeople seek to persuade the customer to make a purchase, while customers try to resist these efforts and retain control of the situation by not agreeing to a deal. In almost all cases, the resolution of the conflict involves the use of **dramaturgy** (Goffman, 1959b): performances by individuals (in this case, salespeople) aimed at manipulating situations in ways favorable to themselves.

A good example of the use of dramaturgy to resolve conflict between customer and client appears in Miller's (1964) study of people who sold used cars. The heart of the drama is the "pitch," which begins when customers have made it clear that they really are interested in buying a car. The pitch involves a social drama in which the salesperson tries to understand the customer and modify sales tactics to fit the customer's character. In discussing a trade-in, taking a test drive, and seeing the customer's old car, the salesperson is able to discover things about the customer that help in selling the car. The salesperson tries to find out what the customer is thinking at all times. He or she accomplishes this by taking the role of the customer, as well as by keeping the customer talking. At all times, the salesperson "desires to keep control, in fact, achieve mastery of his relationship with the customer" (Miller, 1964, p. 19).

Alienation

The concept of alienation continues to be an important and powerful idea for understanding occupational experiences. **Alienation** is a Marxian concept that refers to a breakdown of the natural connections between people and their work, other people, and the natural world. A number of sociologists have expanded upon this basic meaning in various ways (Blauner, 1964; Schwalbe, 1986; Silver, 1986). For example, from a social-psychological perspective, alienation has four components. The first is **powerlessness,** or the domination of individuals by other persons or objects and the inability of individuals to reduce or eliminate that control. **Meaninglessness,** the second aspect of alienation, results from the inability of people to see their role in relation to other roles and to the purpose of their work. Third, alienated individuals suffer from **isolation:** they lack a feeling of belonging to the work situation and have little identification with the workplace. Alienation also involves a feeling of **self-estrangement,** which manifests itself in a lack of involvement in one's work. Self-estranged workers are unable to express their unique abilities, potentialities, or personality (Blauner, 1964).

Alienation on the Assembly Line. One occupation that epitomizes the characteristics of alienation is assembly-line work, where the major source of alienation is the relentless line itself. Assembly-line workers perform their assigned tasks at set intervals for eight hours every work day, with almost no variation allowed. In an automobile plant, a worker may tighten identical bolts hour after hour. In a poultry processing plant, a worker may stuff packages of giblets into turkey after turkey as they pass by on a conveyor belt. Respite comes only when the line breaks down, an event many workers hope for and sometimes contribute to by sabotaging the machinery.

Many assembly-line workers are almost totally powerless; they are unable to control the pace of the line, their superiors, or top management. This inability to control their own work pace is perhaps the most demoralizing aspect of the job. What distinguishes their work from virtually all other occupations is that both the rate of work and the kind of work are invariable and uncontrollable. Some degree of powerlessness exists in all occupations, but most workers can generally vary their own work pace and make their work more interesting by changing the tasks they perform.

Typically, assembly-line workers are unable to see what their specialized task has to do with the work of others on the line or at other levels in the organization. They are also unable to see what tightening a bolt has to do with the finished product (and, in many cases, they do not even know what the finished product is). The nature of the job contributes to a feeling of meaninglessness because it is so specialized, uninteresting, and unimportant that it is difficult for anyone to derive any satisfaction from the work.

The assembly-line workers' problems are compounded by their isolation. The noise and the demands of the line prevent interaction with co-workers on the job, making it difficult for an informal work group to develop. An assembly-line worker describes this phenomenon:

> You can work next to a guy for months without even knowing his name. One thing, you're too busy to talk. Can't hear. (Laughs) You have to holler in his ear. They got these little guys comin' around in white shirts and if they see you runnin' your mouth, they say, "This guy needs more work." Man, he's got no time to talk. (quoted in Terkel, 1974, p. 165)

Workers are also isolated from all levels of management because of the nature of their work and the desire of management to maintain what it considers to be proper distance. Assembly-line work is usually found in large plants, and their size also serves to inhibit the development of personal relationships.

Workers on the assembly line are particularly prone to self-estrangement. The work is so boring and anonymous that they derive little personal good feeling from it. Hence, workers spend a good part of their time daydreaming: "You dream, you think of things you've done. I drift back continuously to when I was a kid and what me and my brothers did. The things you love most are the things you drift back into" (quoted in Terkel, 1974, p. 160). Because no real skills or abilities are needed, assembly-line workers are unable to express themselves in their work.

Efforts to Cope with Alienation on the Job. One device often used by workers in alienating occupations is "working the system." In a participant observer study of a machine shop, Roy (1954) reports how the workers sought "to beat the system." "We machine operators did 'figure the angles,' we developed an impressive repertoire of angles to play and devoted ourselves to crossing the expectations of the formal organization with perseverance, artistry, and organizing ability of our own" (Roy, 1954, p. 257). For example, when a time study was being conducted to set piecework rates, the workers would take longer to do a job than they ordinarily would. They would run the machines at slower speeds or utilize extra movements such as "little reachings, liftings, adjustings, dustings, and other special attentions of conscientious machine operation and good housekeeping that could be dropped instantly with the departure of the time-study man" (Roy, 1954, p. 257). When the time-study person made a job difficult, the workers revised it to make it easier, even though the change might be harder on tools or reduce the quality of the product.

In another study, Roy (1959–1960) examined informal group practices that were not aimed against management but served to make work life more meaningful. Roy was interested in how machine operators prevented themselves from "going nuts." He was again a participant observer in a group of machine operators engaged in work that was repetitious and very simple and that required long hours and a six-day week. The following is Roy's description of the work:

> Standing all day in one spot beside three old codgers in a dingy room looking out through barred windows at the bare walls of a brick warehouse, leg movements largely restricted to the shifting of the body weight from one foot to the other, hand and arm movement confined, for the most part, to a simple repetitive sequence of place the die, punch the clicker, place the die, punch the clicker, and intellectual activity reduced to computing the hours to quitting time. (Roy, 1959–1960, p. 160)

Roy focused on the social devices that machine operators used to find some meaning in an essentially meaningless occupation. First, the machine operators made a little game out of their work: they varied their activities by changing the colors of the material or the die shapes used. Informal group activities made the work day more interesting and pleasant. During the morning "peach time" was announced, and one worker took out two peaches and divided them among the four workers. Then there was "banana time." The same man who brought the peaches also brought a banana, which was for his own consumption. Regularly each morning one of the workers would steal the banana and consume it gleefully while yelling "banana time!" The person who brought the banana would regularly protest, and just as regularly another worker would admonish him for protesting so vociferously. As the day progressed, there was "window time," "lunch time," "pickup time," "fish time," and "Coke time." Through these contrived activities, workers in an essentially meaningless job endeavored to make their work life more meaningful.

Runcie (1980) and Houbolt (1982) describe other coping devices among assembly-line workers. For example, workers can withdraw by being absent. In fact, Runcie (1980, p. 109) found that "on many mornings the line could not start due to the shortage of workers. Often we would stand around waiting for the company to find people to fill the holes in the line." Both Runcie and Houbolt found that workers use drugs as a means of coping with alienation. Said one worker: "If I smoke [marijuana], I can stare at a spot on the floor all day long and not get bored" (Runcie, 1980, p. 109).

Problems of Safety and Health in the Workworld

In addition to the conflicts and problems we have already considered, which tend to be connected with the psychological well-being of the worker, there are also physical problems. For larger numbers of workers than might be expected, work is hazardous. In 1989, about 6.3 million people suffered job-related injuries in the private sector. The government estimates that in that year there were 3600 work-related fatalities in the private sector in establishments employing 11 or more employees. However, it recognizes that this "significantly understates" the total number of work-related fatalities (*Monthly Labor Review*, 1990, p. 2). The National Safe Workplace Institute estimates that over 60,000 Americans a year die because of their work. About one-sixth of them die as a result of traumatic injuries associated with their work, while the other five-sixths die as a result of diseases, usually cancer, that come from prior exposure to some disease-causing agent on the job (Litke, 1988).

The hazards associated with the workworld take a number of forms. For one thing, various types of work can be unsafe and have the possibility of causing the worker physical harm. A machine operator can lose a limb because of a careless move, or a lumberjack can suffer serious injuries falling from a tree. Steel workers can be scalded, or crushed by equipment. A construction worker can fall from a scaffold or from a building, and a truck driver can die in a fiery crash. Firefighters have died as a result of using defective protective equipment while putting out fires. Hazards also exist for many people who have threatening forms of interaction on the job: the most obvious examples are military personnel and the police, but there are many others. The shopkeeper or the gas station attendant must deal with holdups, while the social worker faces the danger of forays into "tough" neighborhoods (Mayer and Rosenblatt, 1975).

Some workers confront a variety of unhealthy conditions that can bring on debilitating, and in some cases fatal, illnesses. Diseases are much more likely to kill or cripple people than on-the-job accidents. The best-known example is black lung disease among coal miners; out of the 100,000 cases of this disease in the country today, approximately 4000 people die from it each year. People who work with uranium run a risk of contracting cancer due to their exposure to radioactivity. Over 80,000 workers were exposed to radiation in 1980. This constitutes an increase in the number of people exposed and in the amount of radiation to which each worker was exposed; the exposure rate nearly quadrupled in a single decade (Omang, 1981). Another major occupational health hazard is asbestos (McCulloch, 1986). A large number of the one-half million people who have worked with asbestos can expect to contract cancer and other diseases (Stellman and Daum, 1973).

In addition to the danger to employees, we must also mention the danger to the population as a whole from economic undertakings. For example, the widespread production and use of chlorofluorocarbons is now known to reduce the ozone layer in the atmosphere, which can lead to dramatic increases in skin cancer.

Finally, a word about another health hazard—job stress. Many jobs are highly stressful, and prolonged stress can cause an array of physical and psychological problems. Certainly mine workers find their work, especially the threat of cave-ins, highly stressful. Similarly, being a firefighter, a police officer, or a paramedic can be highly stressful (Spitzer, 1988).

Many assume that high-status occupations produce the greatest amount of stress. According to a major study of the relationship between occupations and heart disease, that assumption is probably true, but it is not the entire story. The Framingham (Massachusetts) heart study found that males in professional and white-collar jobs—lawyers, doctors, dentists, and business managers—had the highest rate of coronary heart disease. Blue-collar men had the next highest rate, while male clerical workers had the lowest rate.

Among the women in the Framingham heart study, however, one group of employed women had a particularly high risk of coronary heart disease. Women who had clerical occupations, husbands in blue-collar occupations, and children living at home were far more likely to have coronary heart disease than any other working women or housewives. The researchers concluded that these women had heightened stress from the combined responsibilities and frustrations of their work and home lives (Haynes and Feinlieb, 1980).

Unemployment

Unemployment has been a persistent reality in the U.S. economy. During the last 30 years the unemployment rate has rarely been below 5 percent of the labor force (Flaim, 1990). During the early 1980s the unemployment rate was near 10 percent for several years. Five or 10 percent of the labor force translates into many millions of people out of work, many of whom are likely to be struggling economically and socially to survive. Traditionally, unemployment has plagued those in blue-collar, semi-skilled, and unskilled occupations. Although deindustrialization, downsizing, and restructuring have all served to increase the unemployment rate for white-collar and managerial workers, the rate for blue-collar workers still far outstrips that for white-collar workers. Other factors are highly related to unemployment. For example, those with less than a high school education have a far higher unemployment rate than college graduates. Race is also highly related to unemployment. Blacks since World War II have consistently had an unemployment rate that is double (or more) the rate for whites.

Unemployment is more than statistics; it involves highly personal effects on the people who are out of work (Burman, 1988). The most obvious problems for the unemployed person are the loss of income and the absence of a job in a society in which one is usually judged by one's occupation. But, as we saw in chapter 5, the unemployed person must learn how to structure the hours of the day that would normally be taken up by a job.

As symbolic interaction theory would suggest, an unemployed person is also likely to have some problems with his or her self-concept. Without work to think about, many of the unemployed have little to occupy their thoughts other than themselves: *"The only thing I have on my mind on those days is me. Nothing else"* (Burman, 1988, p. 188). More important, unemployment has a negative effect on self-esteem: *"On a bad day . . . I'll take it personally. Those are the days I feel incompetent, very unsure of myself"* (Burman, 1988, p. 200).

Obviously, structuring time and maintaining self-esteem are only two of the many difficulties facing those who are unemployed. The list is long, but the key point is that unemployment has a powerful impact on people. The unemployed are left to "kill time," and as a result end up in an endless process of "losing ground" occupationally, economically, and in a variety of other ways.

Satisfaction from Work

Many people go about their work each day without a feeling of personal gratification from what they do. The expansion of impersonal bureaucracies, factorylike offices, and assembly lines have all made it increasingly difficult for people to find satisfaction in their work. Yet many Americans do find satisfaction and even pride in their work.

The garbage collectors ("scavengers") of San Francisco (Perry, 1978) offer an interesting example. Collecting garbage is considered one of the dirty jobs of society; it is low in prestige and often low in pay. Garbage collectors have their problems with clients just as other service workers

Sociology in the News

Fetal Protection Regulations Are Illegal

In 1984 Gloyce Qualls, then 34, an employee of Johnson Controls (a battery manufacturer), was forced to transfer from a high-risk area where she welded posts onto batteries to a safer area, where she worked on vents for motorcycle batteries. However, the job change resulted in a 50 percent cut in salary. In order to get her old job and salary back, Ms. Qualls underwent an operation, a tubal ligation, that left her infertile. However, she later married and came to regret the decision and the fact that she could no longer have children.

Ms. Qualls became one of eight plaintiffs against Johnson Controls and, on March 20, 1991, the Supreme Court made an important decision in the case that relates to the issues of occupational safety and health as well as to the place of women in the work world. The Court ruled that employers cannot bar women of childbearing age from jobs that pose reproductive hazards. Johnson Controls had a general policy barring fertile women from holding jobs that exposed them to high levels of lead. (Lead is known to damage the fetus's brain and central nervous system.) While there are risks involved in such jobs, the Court ruled that the decision of whether to hold such jobs was up to the woman and not the employer. Employers should inform female employees of the danger and take adequate precautions against it, but they may not bar women from such jobs.

The company policy was clearly discriminatory. As Justice Harry Blackmun put it: "The bias in Johnson Controls' policy is obvious . . . Fertile men, but not fertile women, are given a choice as to whether they wish to risk their reproductive health for a particular job" (Smolowe, 1991, p. 60). The fact is that the lead is dangerous to *both* men and women of child-bearing age. For men, the danger lies in deformities in sperm that can either prevent conception or cause deformed fetuses. In spite of the risks to men *and* to the fetus, only women were involuntarily transferred to other jobs. One of the ironies of this case is that women are fighting for equal rights to expose themselves and their fetuses to the deleterious effects of lead.

The feeling was that such policies as this one involving "fetal protection" have often served as an excuse for not hiring women workers. The fear was that if this policy was allowed to stand, companies would find other reasons for not hiring women. The result would be a resegregation of the workworld just at a point when women have been making gains in at least some areas. An attorney for the American Civil Liberties Union hailed the decision for reaffirming "that women are full participants in public life in their country." However, a representative of the U.S. Chamber of Commerce argued that the decision had placed employers in the impossible position of complying with the new decision but, in the process, exposing themselves to huge damage suits. He argued that the American public would not "stand for injured children having no remedy against deep-pocket companies" (Marcus, 1991, p. A15).

MARCUS, RUTH. "Justices Find Bias in 'Fetal Protection'." *Washington Post* March 21, 1991, pp. A1ff.
SMOLOWE, JILL. "Weighing Some Heavy Metal." *Time* April 1, 1991, p. 60.

do. Customers complain about the noise the collectors make, and some customers demand special services. For these reasons we might expect garbage collectors to be dissatisfied with their work, but that is not necessarily the case.

In most cities, garbage is collected by a municipal sanitation department, but in San Francisco it is done by a private company. More important, the company is owned by the workers. The pay of these men is good, but pay is not usually the first reason given for the satisfaction of these workers. Some of the main sources of satisfaction include unusual sights (e.g., knife fights) very early in the morning, the feeling that they are their own bosses, and the surprising and sometimes valuable things found in the garbage. These workers are not in jobs in which they must mindlessly carry out someone else's commands. They have a degree of autonomy and decision making that allows them to feel that their work has personal meaning (Perry, 1978).

Occupations in which job satisfaction is apt to be greatest are those in which autonomy and a sense of personal accomplishment are greatest. A recent study of genetic counselors shows a high level of satisfaction in this group (Wertz, Sorenson, and Heeren, 1988). The main task of genetic counselors is to help clients make decisions about having a child. Clients often come to such counselors because they already have a child with a birth defect, because they are concerned that a family member may carry a gene that may cause birth defects, or because they have been exposed to some hazard that may have caused chromosomal damage. Counselors try to provide clients with needed information and allow them to voice personal concerns. In their study, Wertz and colleagues found that genetic counselors were satisfied or very satisfied with almost 95 percent of their counseling sessions. Counselors derived their satisfaction from a variety of things, including the perception that they had successfully communicated to their clients such specialized genetic knowledge as "etiology, diagnosis, risk, prognosis, and burden of the disease" (Wertz et al., 1988, pp. 44–45). High-status professionals, low-status garbage collectors, and the people in many occupations between these two extremes may be characterized as finding satisfaction in their work.

Summary

The economy is the social institution involved in the production, distribution, and exchange of the goods and services of a society. The major historical change in economic systems in the last 200 years was the Industrial Revolution. The factory system, an elaborate division of labor, and a system of mass production emerged during this era. Modern capitalism emerged concurrently as the dominant economic system in Western society. In the view of Karl Marx, capitalism is an economic system that exploits the proletariat. Since the nineteenth century, capitalism has evolved from being a competitive system to a monopoly system. Also, capitalism has shifted from being exploitative to being a system that manipulates and controls workers.

Socialist economic systems are the major alternative to capitalist systems. Socialism is an economic system in which the means of producing and distributing goods and services are publicly or collectively owned and controlled. Contemporary socialist societies, most notably the Soviet Union, are changing in the direction of less centralized state control, while greater democracy and free enterprise are being introduced.

The U.S. economy is changing rapidly. Dramatic changes have occurred in the labor force, especially in the distribution of occupational categories and the increasing numbers of women. Labor unions have undergone substantial declines since mid-century. Deindustrialization in the United States—the reduced importance of manufactured goods—has changed the nature of work and wages. Disinvestment, mergers, corporate takeovers, and multinational companies have become significant features of the U.S. economy.

The economic competitors of the United States, especially Japan and several other Asian nations, have been experiencing an economic boom.

The U.S. economy is creating difficulties for the younger generation in comparison to those who entered the economy after World War II. Although these and other problems are serious, hopeful economic signs are emerging as we move into the postindustrial and information society.

While many workers get satisfaction from their jobs and careers, there are also many conflicts, stresses, and hazards in the world of work. Workers cope with the stresses and strains of their jobs in various ways. Conflicts are a normal part of the workworld: managers and officials are prone to role conflict, while customer/client conflicts are frequently experienced in service occupations. Alienation confronts those in low-status occupations, and workers have found various devices to cope with alienation. Safety and health hazards exist in many different occupations. Unemployment is a persistent reality and poses grave difficulties for the millions who are out of work.

CRITICAL THINKING

1. Describe the major theories that attempt to adapt Marxism to contemporary capitalism.
2. Compare and contrast the major economic systems of capitalism and socialism.
3. Describe contemporary trends in the labor union movement in the United States. What general economic trends are partially responsible for the current state of U.S. labor unions? How have unions responded to change?
4. How has deindustrialization changed the U.S. economy? How has it benefitted overseas competitors?
5. What major changes in the labor force have occurred in American society since the turn of the century? How have these changes affected our life-styles?
6. In what ways has the Soviet Union sought to restructure its socialist economy?
7. According to the introduction to the chapter, what key issue faces the United States economy? What suggestions do you have for ways to deal with this issue?
8. Are the economic changes in the United States benefitting or harming the economic status of the younger generation? What evidence in the chapter supports your viewpoint?
9. What forms does worker alienation take in modern industrial economies? What solutions would you suggest for this problem? What is the economic cost of these solutions?

14 Health and Medicine

The twentieth century has brought dramatic changes in types of illnesses, causes of death, and the nature of health care. The illnesses and diseases that caused most deaths at the beginning of this century are no longer the scourges they once were. In 1900 half of the leading causes of death were infectious diseases, with tuberculosis ranking first and pneumonia second. Influenza was another major killer. These are diseases caused by bacterial and viral agents, and their victims at the turn of the century were often children and young adults. By 1987, tuberculosis was far down the list as a cause of death, accounting for only 1800 of the 2.1 million deaths yearly in the United States. In 1987, pneumonia was the *only* infectious disease in the top ten, having dropped from second to sixth (U.S. Bureau of the Census, 1990). Today infectious diseases cause death primarily among the elderly, not among children, as was the case at the beginning of this century.

Now, noninfectious diseases such as heart disease, cancer, and cerebrovascular disease (for example, stroke) have become the leading causes of death. These three diseases accounted for about two-thirds of all deaths in the United States in 1988 (National Center for Health Statistics, 1991, p. 80). In contrast to the infectious diseases, noninfectious diseases are related in large part to life-style and the aging process. Among young people, injuries from accidents, suicides, and homicides are now the leading causes of death. Because all of today's major causes of death are connected to life-styles and personal choices—in other words, social factors—sociologists have a keen interest in both health and medicine, as well as the medical profession itself.

Sociology of Health and Medicine

We may not be accustomed to thinking of sociology as a field concerned with health-related issues; these matters seem to fall within the exclusive province of physicians, biologists, and other health professionals. Yet the sociology of health and medicine, often called *medical sociology,* is one of the most popular specialties among sociologists.

The sociological study of health considers how human behavior contributes to disease and illness or detracts from good health. The sociological view is that both health and illness are not defined simply by physiological factors. Many social and cultural factors are involved, by serving as causes of illness, by influencing the course of an illness, or by affecting whether and how a person recovers from an illness. In addition, a powerful relationship exists between a person's health status and the social and cultural milieu in which the individual lives.

For example, consider how the food and dietary habits of the people in a society can influence their health. The Japanese prefer to eat fish, which has low levels of cholesterol, and they have very low rates of heart disease. In contrast, people in the United States have traditionally preferred red meat in their diet, which has a high level of cholesterol, and they have a relatively high rate of heart disease.

This comparison between the Japanese and U.S. dietary habits, and their apparently related heart-disease rates, illustrates an important aspect of medical sociology called *social epidemiology.* **Social epidemiology** is the study of the frequency and pattern of a disease within a particular population (Wolinsky, 1988). Epidemiologists focus on the prevalence of specific diseases or illnesses in different populations and then try to determine if a distinguishing social or behavioral factor can be isolated that could account for the differences. One of the early, classic examples of social epidemiology occurred in the late 1700s when Sir Percival Potts discovered that chimney sweeps had a higher rate of scrotum cancer than other groups in the population. It seemed probable that something in the nature of their work caused chimney sweeps to suffer more from this form of cancer, and ultimately the cause was found to be the excessive amounts of soot to which they were exposed.

Social Epidemiology and AIDS

Social epidemiology was a major tool in identifying how the AIDS virus was being transmitted. AIDS (Acquired Immune Deficiency Syndrome) was first reported in 1981, and it quickly became clear that the group in which AIDS was most prevalent was the homosexual male population. Early studies of gay men indicated that those who got the disease had engaged in sexual relations with a large number of partners. Therefore, it appeared that the sexual behaviors of these men were implicated in their contracting AIDS.

In 1982 further research revealed other high-risk groups in the population, indicating that the means of transmission could be other than sexual (Petrow, 1990). People who had received blood transfusions, especially hemophiliacs who need transfusions regularly, also had a high prevalence of AIDS. In addition, drug addicts who were taking their drugs intravenously appeared as a high-risk group. This evidence indicated that the virus was being transmitted by either infected blood or semen, and that victims were infected when the virus somehow entered the blood stream. These facts were further confirmed when infants were born with the AIDS virus, which they were obviously getting from the infected blood of their mothers.

After these early facts were uncovered, it was clear that AIDS was not exclusively a disease of the gay population but could be contracted by anyone who had direct contact with the blood or semen of a person carrying the virus. The direct contact that most frequently transmitted the virus, however, involved the sexual practices of gay/bisexual males and intravenous (IV) drug use (apparently because users were sharing dirty hypodermic needles). In 1989, gay and bisexual men and intravenous drug users still accounted for over 86 percent of new cases of diagnosed AIDS. For women in 1989, slightly more than 50 percent of the cases were the result of IV drug use, while one-third was traceable to heterosexual contact, mostly with IV drug users (National Center for Health Statistics, 1991, p. 25).

Other Interests of Medical Sociology

Medical sociology involves much more than studies of social epidemiology, however. Sociologists are interested in how different sociocultural backgrounds affect people's "attitudes, beliefs and behavior concerning health, illness, and death" (Wolinsky, 1988, p. 39). Medical sociologists are also concerned with the nature of the relationship between physicians and patients and the changes that have taken place over the years in that relationship. Some sociologists direct their attention to the study of hospitals as bureaucratic organizations. Others focus on medical and health occupations (ambulance personnel, laboratory technicians) and professions (physicians, nurses, and pharmacists). A growing concern of sociologists is the overall organization of health care in society and the changes taking place within the health-care system. This brief description provides only a glimpse of the field of medical sociology, but many of these issues will receive fuller treatment throughout this chapter.

The Changing Nature of Health and Medicine

The infectious diseases that were the major killers at the beginning of the century are called *communicable diseases.* **Communicable diseases** are diseases that can be transmitted to people in a variety of ways—by other people, by animals or other organisms, or from contaminated food or water that is ingested. Since, at the beginning of the twentieth century, there were few effective medicines or other techniques to combat these diseases, life expectancy was comparatively short (47 years in 1900 compared to almost 75 years in 1987); the infant mortality rate was high (the 1900 rate was about three times as high as the 1987 rate); and there was an ever-present likelihood of epidemics that could take massive numbers of lives in short periods of time. In many cases, contracting one of these infectious diseases had little to do with anything that people did or did not do. If a person happened to come into contact with the bacteria or virus, chances were that he or she would become ill. This point was proved most clearly in the case of the epidemics that swept through entire populations, often causing millions of deaths. (While these epidemics have all but disappeared in the United States, they continue to be problems in many other parts of the world. For example, in 1991 many countries in South America experienced a cholera epidemic [Okie, 1991].) People in the United States feared epidemic diseases in the earlier part of the century, but they had little fear of cancer. Cancer aroused less dread than tuberculosis, the greatest killer of that time (Patterson, 1987).

For an individual who lived at the turn of the century, contracting a disease and dying from it must have seemed largely a matter of chance or fate. Matters are quite different today. Most of the major diseases now prevalent can be traced to "problems of living" (for example, life-style, stress, environmental problems) rather than bacteria or viruses. In other words, diseases such as heart disease and cancer involve multiple causes, many of which are more closely related to the way people live than to strictly biological factors. To take just a few examples, eating foods high in cholesterol increases the likelihood of heart disease, smoking cigarettes is linked to lung cancer and emphysema, living in a community where pesticides are used heavily may contribute to a higher risk of cancer, and spending long hours sunbathing may lead to increased risk of contracting melanoma and other, less deadly, skin cancers. Diseases and illnesses today are apt to be tied to the actions we choose to take or not take. To a considerable degree, our individual chances of healthful living are much more in our own hands now than they were at the turn of the century.

In this context it is interesting to consider again the spread of AIDS. Like many of the infectious diseases that killed people at the turn of the century, AIDS is caused by a virus. Because the AIDS virus is not easily transmitted from one person to another, however, contracting the disease is closely linked to the choices people make in their actions and behavior. For example, people are more likely to get AIDS if they engage in male homosexual behavior, use drugs intravenously, and engage in heterosexual sex with high-risk partners. In addition, AIDS is tied to actions people fail to take, such as using condoms with a sex partner of whom they are uncertain, or using clean hypodermic needles when taking drugs intravenously. Thus, although AIDS is infectious, it is difficult to catch; the chances of being stricken with it are heightened by things that people do or don't do. People have much more control over this epidemic than they did over the epidemics that occurred in earlier times.

Individuals do not have complete control in all matters relating to their health, however, because illnesses are also influenced by the actions of other people and by societal conditions. For example, widespread use of chlorofluorocarbons in refrigerants, and in aerosol spray cans in many countries, is reducing the protective ozone layer in the atmosphere. This thinning of the ozone layer is linked to increases in skin cancer, including melanoma. Another example of an external threat to health is the use of pesticides and chemicals in the production and processing of foods. Most grains, fruits, vegetables, and meats today carry some residues of these chemicals, and are adversely affecting the health of entire societies.

Historical Causes of Declining Death Rates

Many people assume that advances in medical practices and medical discoveries are responsible for the victory over the infectious diseases that historically plagued humankind. However, historical studies of disease and death have shown that declines in the major infectious diseases cannot be attributed to medical discoveries, treatments, and practices (McKeown, 1976, 1979). Studies have shown that death rates for most infectious diseases were on the decline long before the most effective medical intervention was discovered or developed. For example, studies of England have shown that the death rate due to tuberculosis was declining at least 30 years before the tubercle bacterium was discovered in 1882. These declines were not produced by the medical treatments of that day, since they were generally ineffective. In some cases medical treatment may even have been harmful to the patient, as it probably was in the case of President Andrew Jackson's wife, who was advised by her doctor to start smoking as a treatment for her tuberculosis (Remini, 1984). Not until 1947, with the introduction of streptomycin, was an effective chemotherapy for tuberculosis available. By that time, the death rate due to tuberculosis was only one-sixth of what it had been a century earlier (McKeown, 1976).

The reduction in deaths from most other infectious diseases have followed a similar pattern. In the United States in the nineteenth and twentieth centuries, McKinlay and McKinlay (1977) discovered that, for nine infectious diseases, the death rate was declining for eight of them *before* vaccines were created or treatment developed. (Polio was the exception.) What did bring the death rates down in these cases? *Death rates for infectious diseases declined because of changes in social and environmental factors rather than medical factors.* Such changes included better sanitation, housing, and nutrition—in other words, an overall improvement in the standard of living (McKeown, 1971, 1979).

None of this discussion is intended to argue that medical care does no good or that medical discoveries are not important. The development of inoculation procedures and vaccines have certainly had a long-term impact on the health of people around the world. In fact, when the medical discoveries of the Western world have been applied to much of the developing world during the last half of the twentieth century, they have been highly effective. These more recent medical successes should not, however, obscure the historical fact that declines in infectious disease did not result primarily from improved medical practices and treatments. In both Europe and the United States, social and environmental factors were more important in reducing death rates (McKinlay and McKinlay, 1977).

The Medicalization of Society

In this century we have witnessed an increase in the power of the medical profession, and the increasing dominance of the medical approach to health and illness. One manifestation of this dominance is the **medicalization of society,** defined as the tendency to exaggerate the importance of medicine and to "medicalize," or treat as an illness, things that are not normally considered ilnesses (Conrad and Schneider, 1980; Conrad, 1986). The process of medicalization has been obvious in the area of deviance, where people who exhibit behavior that is considered deviant have come to be labeled as sick and therefore in need of medical help. The most notable example is the way in which alcoholism is now nearly universally defined as a disease. In the past the excessive use of alcohol was generally viewed as a result of a person's lack of willpower. Now most people regard this form of substance abuse as stemming from a chemical imbalance in the body, genetically transmitted, in many cases. Other compulsive behaviors and disorders have been similarly reana-

Cross-National Perspectives

An International View of AIDS

AIDS is an international problem. No major area of the world is free of the disease. Furthermore, the leaders and citizens of virtually every country in the world have expressed concern about AIDS, and often have taken stringent actions to keep the disease out of their countries. The Chinese, for example, insist that any student coming from another country be tested and found free of the disease.

Although AIDS is a global disease, there are important differences in the prevalence of the disease from one country or continent to another. The two areas that have the greatest prevalence, or rate, of the disease are North America and Africa, especially Zaire and Uganda. In many countries of the world, however, the number of cases is small. Sweden, for example, which has a very active program of testing for and identifying AIDS cases, has found only a very small number of cases in its population of 8 million.

At the present time most of the attention with regard to AIDS is directed toward the United States and parts of Africa where the disease is most common. Both social and economic factors are related to AIDS in these two areas and have produced important differences in the AIDS populations.

In general terms, AIDS is transmitted through sexual activity, blood, and prenatal contact. However, people in the United States and Africa get the disease in very different ways, which means that the distribution in the population also differs. In the United States the disease afflicts primarily homosexual men, and to a lesser, but increasingly important, degree, intravenous drug users. Since intravenous drug users are also more likely to be male, about 90 percent of the identified AIDS victims have been male (U.S. Bureau of the Census, 1990, p. 117). In Africa, by contrast, AIDS is widespread among heterosexuals, and thus there is a roughly 50–50 split between male and female cases (Makanjuola, 1991). These differences are traceable, in part, to differences in the sexual practices of the United States and Africa. For example, subordinate African women are unlikely to confront unfaithful husbands and they are not very apt to know about, or to be able to afford, condoms. In addition, many more Africans than Americans acquire AIDS through blood transfusions. In the United States, blood donors are now screened for the AIDS virus, but this is much less the case in Africa due to the lack of resources available for such procedures.

In the United States, in 1990, about 30 percent of AIDS victims were either intravenous drug users, or persons who had had sex with intravenous drug users. By contrast, Africans are much less likely to get the disease through intravenous drug use because such drug use is virtually absent there. The intravenous drug users in the United States typically get AIDS by sharing contaminated needles with someone who has the disease, but Africans are likely to contract AIDS from other kinds of contaminated needles. For example, because of improper sterilization, AIDS is transmitted in Africa through medical injections for diseases such as malaria and diarrhea. In one study of AIDS patients in Kinshasa, the capital of Zaire, 80 percent reported that they had received medical injections before the symptoms of the disease appeared (Mann et al., 1986).

Also, because of the prevalence of heterosexual transmission of AIDS in Africa, about 2.5 million African women are infected with the AIDS virus; "82 per cent of women with AIDS worldwide have come from Africa" (Makanjuola, 1991, p. 6). African mothers are more likely to carry the virus than U.S. mothers. This means that there is a greater likelihood of newborn children getting the disease before, during, or shortly after birth in Africa.

Of course, there are important differences between the United States and Africa in the ability to deal with the disease. While it is a burden, the United States has the resources to care for its AIDS patients and to see that they receive the latest treatments. In Africa, there is little money to treat AIDS patients, given the continent's limited resources and its many other problems. Furthermore, although the United States and other nations such as Great Britain have gone to great lengths to inform and educate their populations about AIDS, such programs are likely to lag in Africa because of a lack of funds. Low levels of literacy in Africa reduce the effectiveness of such programs.

An interesting aspect of cross-national comparisons of AIDS is that, in different societies, different groups have come to be stigmatized as carriers of the disease. In the United States, homosexuals and intravenous drug users are most likely to be stigmatized. In Africa, female prostitutes have come to be stigmatized because they have an unusually high rate of the disease. In other nations, it is sometimes Americans and other times Africans who are stigmatized because of the prevalence of the disease in their countries.

MAKANJUOLA, BOLA. "Living with AIDS." *West Africa,* January 14, 1991.
MANN, JONATHAN. "The Global AIDS Situation." *World Health,* June 1987.
MANN, J.; FRANCIS, J.M.; QUINN, T.; et al. "Surveillance for AIDS in a Central African City: Kinshasa, Zaire." *Journal of the American Medical Association* 255, June 20, 1986.

lyzed. A recent example is the medicalization of compulsive gambling. Described in the past as a personal weakness—a failure of will—compulsive gambling today is increasingly defined as a disease (Rosecrance, 1985).

A more controversial example of medicalization is the argument that hyperactivity in children is a medical problem (Conrad, 1975). In the past, children who were overly active, impulsive, and aggressive would simply have been seen as disruptive youngsters who needed to be controlled or perhaps punished. Today, children who have these characteristics are labeled as hyperactive and viewed as having a medical problem. The problem must then be treated by physicians, often with the use of mind-altering drugs (Conrad, 1975).

The medicalization process is not restricted to deviant behavior. For example, medicine has come to define childbirth as a medical problem that must be handled by physicians in a hospital context (Arney, 1982). What was once a natural process dominated by family and midwives came to be seen as at least a potential medical problem (Wertz and Wertz, 1986). Of course, one factor that contributed to the medicalization of childbearing was the extremely high rate of death associated with the birth process. Recent years have brought a resurgence of midwives as a reaction against the medicalization of childbirth (Weitz and Sullivan, 1985). A greater interest has also arisen in natural childbirth, and a few people are choosing to have babies at home rather than in hospitals. Despite these trends, medicine continues to control the childbirth process as reflected in the extraordinarily high rate of births by Caesarian section, a technique dominated by physicians.

Nor is the medicalization process restricted to the United States. For example, in Japan a number of extraordinary "diseases" have come to be defined as medical problems. For example, two diseases that now "strike" Japanese women are "kitchen syndrome" and "moving-day depression." A woman with kitchen syndrome might go on wild shopping sprees, while someone suffering from moving-day depression might complain that the water in their new home does not agree with them. Japanese doctors have come to define these afflictions as diseases and treat them by counseling the "victims" as well as by prescribing medicines (Lock, 1987).

Variations in Health Among Different Populations

In this section we will compare the health status of a number of populations or subpopulations in the United States, including differences between men and women and among races and social classes. As we proceed through the various comparisons between groups, we will rely heavily on the work of social epidemiologists, as described earlier.

Men and Women

Historically, there have been significant differences between men and women in patterns of health, illness, and death. Although some of these differences persist, indications are that greater similarities in the lives of men and women in the United States are producing more similarities in their mortality patterns.

Sex differences for some major causes of death have either stabilized, decreased, or are only slowly increasing (Verbrugge, 1985). Considerable speculation exists about the possible effects on female health of their increased participation in the labor force and changes in life-style, but it will be several years before these effects can be fully determined.

Gender, Smoking, and Lung Cancer. One important explanation for some equalization in death rates was the growing number of female smokers after World War II. As a former Secretary of Health, Education, and Welfare bluntly pointed out: "Women who smoke like men, die like men." In the 1980s we saw increased lung cancer among women because greater numbers of women began smoking cigarettes in the 1940s. Lung cancer has almost overtaken breast cancer as the leading cause of cancer deaths among women.

The relationship between the rise in smoking by females after World War II and increased likelihood of death from lung cancer is quite clear. Estimates show that smoking accounts for at least three-quarters of lung cancer deaths among females and slightly more (80 percent) among males (National Center for Health Statistics, 1988, p. 16). In figure 14–1 we see a comparison between males and females in terms of the percentage of people who have ever smoked cigarettes. Although males started with a much higher level of smoking, the increase for males was much less rapid than the increase for females. More striking is the fact that for males there was a decline in the percentage who had ever smoked from the cohort born between 1931 and 1940 as compared to the preceding cohort born between 1921 and 1930. On the other hand, females born between 1931 and 1940 were *more* likely to have smoked than the preceding cohort. In short, smoking among males had begun to decline, while smoking among females was increasing during this period (National Center for Health Statistics, 1988). During the 1980s, the number of female smokers declined, but not as rapidly as the number of male smokers.

What is striking is that changes in smoking are directly related to changes in death from lung cancer. As figure 14–2 makes clear, male cohorts demonstrated the same kind of increase in death rates from lung cancer as they did in smoking rates; and the same decline is shown in the death rate for lung cancer in the 1931–1940 cohort as is shown in the smoking rate for that cohort. Similarly, death rates for lung cancer for

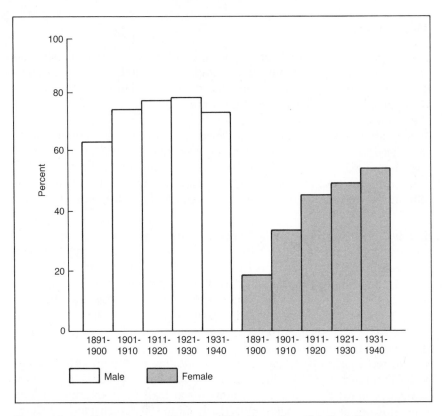

Figure 14–1. Percentages of Persons Who Have Ever Smoked Cigarettes, According to Sex: United States, Selected Birth Cohorts, 1891–1940. (*Source:* National Center for Health Statistics, Division of Vital Statistics, National Vital Statistics System.)

women have shown the same kind of steady increase as in the numbers of women who have ever smoked.

Other Health Differences Between Men and Women.   In spite of the increase in death rates due to lung cancer, women still have a higher life expectancy than men. Life expectancy for females born in 1987 was 78.4 years; for males, it was 71.5 years (U.S. Bureau of the Census, 1990). Male death rates generally exceed female deaths at all ages.

With respect to the two major causes of death, the male death rates due to heart disease and cancer are greater than the rates for women (at all ages). Women, on the other hand, tend to be sick more often, but their health problems are usually not as serious or as life threatening as those encountered by men. Women, for example, are 11 times more likely than men to have acute or short-term illnesses, such as infectious

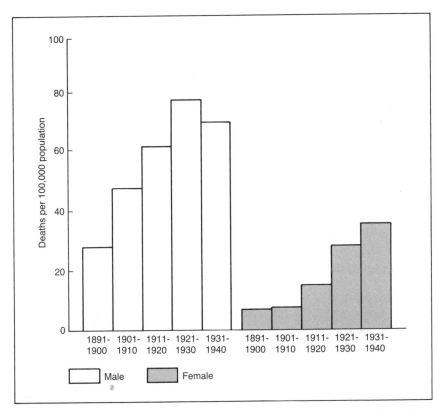

Figure 14-2. Death Rates for Lung Cancer among Persons 45–54 Years of Age, According to Sex: United States, Selected Birth Cohorts, 1891–1940. (*Source:* National Center for Health Statistics, Division of Vital Statistics, National Vital Statistics System.)

and parasitic diseases and digestive and respiratory conditions. But women, especially in later life, tend to die from the same causes as men. The difference is that men tend to develop these more serious illnesses much earlier in life and die from them at an earlier age (National Center for Health Statistics, 1988).

Some scholars suggest that women do not have more illnesses but are simply more sensitive to their bodily discomforts and more willing to report their symptoms. The best evidence indicates, however, that the differences in sickness are indeed real (Waldron, 1983). Verbrugge (1976, p. 401) observes: ". . . females experience a less comfortable and satisfying life with regard to a cherished attribute"—feeling healthy. To summarize, women are sick more often but live longer. Men are sick less often but die sooner.

The longevity of men is less than that of women because of both biological and social-psychological factors. The lesser biological durability of males is evident in mortality rates from the prenatal and newborn stages of life onward. The chances of male fetuses dying before birth are about 10 percent higher than for female fetuses (McMillen, 1979). In the newborn stage, males continue to have higher death rates because a variety of respiratory, circulatory, and other disorders are more common among male babies (Cockerham, 1986). Females are less likely to get childhood leukemia, and they have a better chance of survival when they do. When they are adults, their female sex hormones may protect them to some degree from heart disease up to the time of menopause.

For adults, social-psychological effects on life expectancy appear more important than biological differences (Verbrugge, 1985). These effects are seen in the health risks associated with various social roles, occupations, and life-styles. Males use more alcohol, illegal drugs, and cigarettes (despite the significant decline in male smokers), and they often have greater job-related stress. The life-style of the male business executive or professional, with its emphasis upon "career" and "success," is believed to contribute strongly to high rates of coronary heart disease. Among lower-class men, high levels of obesity and smoking, along with less leisure-time exercise and poor diet, join with the stress that accompanies a life of poverty to produce especially high rates of heart disease. The risk of dying from cancer is also higher than average for unemployed or underemployed men who live alone in poor, overcrowded, urban neighborhoods. They have less chance of early detection of cancer, and they are exposed to health conditions that make death more likely once cancer occurs (Jenkins, 1983).

The fact that accidents are also a major cause of death for males but not for females strongly suggests a difference in gender roles. Men are generally expected to be more aggressive than women in both work and leisure activities. High accident rates among males may be attributed to exposure to more dangerous activities, including jobs where the risk of death or injury is higher. Automobile accidents, too, kill or maim significantly more men than women, especially young adult males. Driving at high speeds is more common for males, as is participating in violent sports. Therefore, it would seem that the social psychology of the male gender role and male competitiveness are significant factors adversely affecting male longevity.

Women seem to take better care of themselves. They more readily admit that they are sick and more often consult with physicians. Whether women will assume the behavioral traits associated with the male role as they increasingly enter the same occupations as men is a question that sociologists will study with great interest in the years to come.

Health and Quality of Life in Old Age. Women live longer than men, but the quality of their lives in old age appears to be lower than men in old age. On a variety of dimensions women aged 74 and over are *worse off* than their male counterparts. Women at this age are more likely to live alone than men are. Beyond age 74 about 70 percent of men are married, but only about one-fourth of women are married after that age. Since traditional gender roles are likely to prevail in this age group, males are apt to benefit from having wives who take care of them. Another factor is that older women are less likely to have adequate incomes. On medical issues, older women have higher cognitive impairment, and their health tends to be poorer than males of the same age. Finally, older women have less ability to perform the basic activities of daily living (Haug and Folmar, 1986).

Race and Health

The health of racial minority groups, as measured by life expectancy and infant mortality, has improved significantly during the twentieth century. Between 1900 and 1987, the life expectancy of black females increased from 33.5 years to 73.6 years; for black males, the increase for this period was from 32.5 to 65.2 years. Although the life expectancy of black males has risen dramatically in the United States since 1900, black males still lag behind their white counterparts. (Strikingly, life expectancy for black males has actually declined slightly in the last few years as a result of AIDS and increasing numbers of crime-related deaths.) On the average, white females outlive black females by 5.3 years, and white males outlive black males by 7 years. In terms of infant mortality, for blacks the rate has declined from 43.9 (per 1,000) in 1950 to 17.9 in 1987, while for whites it declined from 26.8 to 8.6. Despite the substantial decline in the rates for both races, the black infant mortality rate in 1987 was still more than double the rate for whites.

Although some diseases that are especially prevalent among blacks (such as hypertension and sickle cell anemia) appear to have a genetic basis, differences in life expectancy between the races for many other health problems can be attributed to the fact that racial minorities are also most likely to be poor. Low-income groups living in poverty show high rates of influenza and pneumonia, lead poisoning, rat-bite fever, ear infections, murder, alcoholism, drug addiction, and lung cancer.

Social Class and Health

Membership in the lower class is closely associated with health disadvantages. The poor suffer more, not only from the infectious diseases that have been so devastating in the past, like influenza and tuberculosis, but also from the so-called "modern ills" like heart disease. In recent years the death rates from coronary heart disease have declined for all Americans, but more for the middle and upper classes than for the lower classes (Susser et al., 1983).

A study by the state of Maine further highlights the less favorable health situation of the poor. This study found that children from low-income families had higher death rates than children from more affluent families. Low-income children were ten times more likely to drown, 12 times more likely to die in fires, 16 times more likely to be murder victims, eight times more likely to die of disease, and four times more likely to be killed in automobile accidents (Cockerham, 1986).

Not only are the poor more apt to suffer ill health but they are also less able to afford to pay for needed health care. For example, the poor are much less likely to have health insurance (Davis and Rowland, 1986). Cutbacks in support of welfare programs by the federal government in the 1980s may increase further the inability of the poor to pay for health services, and some hospitals have limited the number of Medicaid patients they will accept. The poor receive fewer health services in relation to actual need, they cope with more bureaucratic agencies, and they receive lower-quality medical care. Although Medicaid has not met all the needs of the poor, it has provided health services where such services were not previously available.

Because the poor are less likely to go to doctors, they are more likely than affluent people to come to hospitals for treatment of preventable conditions such as diabetes and bronchitis (Abramowitz, 1988). Even when they do go to doctors, the poor are apt to receive service that is inferior to that of their middle-class peers. This lower-quality care is related, in part, to the fact that middle-class patients are more actively involved in consultations with doctors, while lower-class patients tend to be more passive (Boulton et al., 1986).

The most important relationship between social class and health is the manner in which social class has an impact on the opportunities that a person has for a generally healthy life. Crowded living conditions, poor diet, inferior housing, low levels of income and education, exposure to violence, and alcohol and drug abuse combine to decrease the chances of a healthy life for the poor.

Policy Changes in Health Care in the United States

The Problem of Escalating Costs

Health expenditures in the United States increased an average of 12 percent annually between 1965 and 1986. In 1965, U.S. citizens spent a total of $41.9 billion on health needs, as compared to 1989 expenditures of $604.1 billion (Friedman, 1991, p. 2493). Between 1980 and 1989, the rise in spending for health was particularly dramatic—considerably more than doubling from $248.1 billion to $604.1 billion.

Two major factors contributing to higher costs of health care are inflation and increased labor costs. *Inflation* means increases in the cost of medical equipment, supplies, and new construction, and it also serves to intensify the demands of hospital employees for higher salaries. *Labor* represents about 60 percent of a hospital's total expenses; therefore, increased labor costs are a highly significant component of rising hospital expenses. Inflation and the higher costs of operation have resulted in a more than 450 percent increase in semi-private hospital room rates since 1967. Doctors' fees have more than doubled during this period (Cockerham, 1986). Furthermore, the number of physicians in the United States has risen substantially, and this increase in numbers has contributed in some measure to national increases in health expenditures (Rushing, 1985).

Technology and Transplants. Another factor in the explosion of medical costs is the development and increasing use of new, highly expensive technologies such as CT (computerized tomography), MRI (magnetic resonance imaging), and PET (positron emission tomography). PET scanners currently cost about $4 million. A CT scan costs the patient about $400, an MRI about $800, and a PET scan approximately $1750 (Pollack, 1991).

Also very costly are the many new medical procedures. For example, heart bypass surgery accounts for about 20 percent of all health care costs in the United States (and for many people, such surgery did little good). Then there is the increasing frequency of organ transplants, of the heart and kidney, for instance. The cost of a heart transplant is well over $100,000, and a liver transplant costs even more. The drugs that patients need to prevent them from rejecting the new organs are also expensive. Furthermore, attempts by the body to reject a new organ are not uncommon, which requires further hospitalization and additional expense (Kutner, 1987). Even though transplants are still comparatively rare, they do contribute disproportionately to the explosion in health-care costs.

With the cost of health care continuing to rise, government measures have been aimed at controlling health-care expenditures. In the early 1980s came the establishment of Diagnostic Related Groups by the federal government that placed a ceiling on how much the government would pay for specific services rendered by hospitals and doctors to Medicare patients. This action was bitterly contested by hospitals and the American Medical Association. The cost of health care continues to be one of our most serious societal problems and is a source of considerable public dissatisfaction.

Sociology in the News

Crisis in American Health Care

An issue that is receiving a great deal of attention these days in the mass media, as well as in professional journals (*Journal of the American Medical Association,* 1991), is the crisis in health care. The high cost of health care is causing a wide range of problems, especially for the 33 million people in the United States without health insurance of any kind. Also at great risk are the estimated tens of millions of people who have limited insurance policies that leave them in danger of financial ruin in the event of a major illness (Lewin, 1991). Overall, one in four is uninsured or underinsured. The poor, especially from minority groups (Hispanic Americans are the worst off), are most likely to have little or no health insurance (Friedman, 1991). Thus, many people are in a situation like that of Betty Moore, who, although she has just purchased insurance, is not covered for a preexisting heart condition for one year: "It can happen any time that a hole in the valve gets too big and it has to be fixed . . . I'm just hoping that it doesn't get bad soon. I don't know what would happen if it does. You can't be sure there will be a surgeon who will take you if you can't pay" (Lewin, 1991, p. 29).

While a number of specific alternatives exist, there are three broad options open in terms of dealing with our health care problems (Eckholm, 1991). First, there are those who favor tax incentives that allow more people to purchase individual or household policies. The problem with this alternative is that many poor people would still not be able to afford these policies. Second, there are many ways in which the current system can be bolstered. The Medicaid program could be expanded so that the unemployed poor are covered. Employers could be required to offer insurance to employees. Employers could also be required to pay into a pool that would offer policies to uninsured workers. Finally, there is the possibility of setting up a national health insurance system financed by various kinds of taxes that would cover everyone. Those who favor the latter approach point to the success of the Canadian system.

The Canadian national health insurance plan is one of the most comprehensive in the world (Rosenthal, 1991). Tax money is used to offer free health care to all Canadian citizens. Thus, for example, Len Quesnelle had triple bypass surgery that would have cost $14,000 in U.S. dollars, but he had to pay only $200 to cover telephone calls and the rental of a television set. All Canadian citizens, rich and poor, are able to flash their insurance cards and virtually everything will be covered. And there is little of the enormous paperwork that hampers the U.S. system of insurance and adds enormously to the cost of health care.

However, there are tradeoffs in the Canadian system. There are sometimes long waits for medical procedures, even for people in need of such urgent procedures as heart bypasses. The government puts tight restrictions on the purchase of expensive technology (there are 15 MRI machines in Canada compared to the 2000 in the United States), on the number of specialists that can be trained, and on expensive procedures such as heart transplants. The result is that it is much more difficult to get medical services in Canada than in the United States. Middle- and upper-class U.S. citizens might balk at such a system, but the 33 million people in the United States without insurance would undoubtedly regard it as a god-send.

ECKHOLM, ERIK. "Rescuing Health Care." *New York Times,* May 2, 1991, pp. A1ff.
FRIEDMAN, EMILY. "The Uninsured: From Dilemma to Crisis." *Journal of the American Medical Association* 265, 1991, pp. 2491–2496.
Journal of the American Medical Association. "Caring for the Uninsured and Underinsured." 265, 1991, pp. 2491–2563.
LEWIN, TAMAR. "High Medical Costs Hurt Growing Numbers in U.S." *New York Times,* April 28, 1991, pp. 1ff.
ROSENTHAL, ELISABETH. "In Canada, a Government System That Provides Health Care to All." *New York Times,* April 30, 1991, pp. A1ff.

Organization of Health-Care Systems in the United States

Doctors in the eighteenth and early nineteenth centuries in the United States did not enjoy high social status (Starr, 1982). Few physicians were trained in either university settings or medical schools. Anyone who wanted to practice medicine usually could do so and could claim the title of "doctor." Many early doctors in the United States were trained as clergymen, pharmacists, or even barbers.

After 1800, the number of medical schools increased significantly, but their quality was not high. Several medical schools were organized for the primary purpose of making money from student fees. It was easy to be admitted and not difficult to graduate—provided that one's fees were paid. Doctors, in general, did not have a good reputation, and sometimes their procedures (such as "bleeding" patients) were more dangerous than the diseases they treated.

But this situation changed for the better with impressive developments in medical technology and increased control over medical education exercised by the medical profession. The Flexner Report, issued in 1910, which described the conditions in U.S. medical schools (some schools were called "plague spots" and "utterly wretched"), resulted in an overhaul of these schools. The better schools improved their training, while lesser schools eventually closed, as state licensing boards established quality standards for the training of doctors. The twentieth century has been characterized by significantly improved medical training.

The Autonomy of Physicians

As of 1987, 586,000 medical doctors and 27,000 doctors of osteopathy actively practiced medicine in the United States—25.2 doctors for every 10,000 people. There were also 1,627,000 registered nurses providing nursing services (U.S. Bureau of the Census, 1990, p. 101). Altogether, over 7 million people are employed in the health-care industry in the United States (U.S. Bureau of the Census, 1990, p. 404). Although medical doctors constitute much less than 10 percent of the industry's total workforce, at present the entire health-care delivery system is subordinate to their professional authority. Physicians usually control not only the conditions of their own work but also the working conditions of other members of the health profession as well. Consequently, the status and prestige awarded to the physician by the general public is recognition of the physician's monopoly of one of society's essential needs: health care.

Even though many changes in health care have occurred in recent decades, such as the increasing employment of physicians in for-profit hospitals, medical doctors continue to subscribe to a pattern of professional behavior that, in many ways, is based on an image of medical practice as it was around 1950. It is an image of the physician as an independent, fee-for-service, private practitioner. This image is of an entrepreneur completely free of lay control and totally in command of providing medical care. Medicine's autonomy rests on its supposed orientation of serving the public, its strong system of ethics, peer regulation, and professional expertise.

In practice, these bases of medical autonomy have not worked as well as they should. Peer regulation by physicians has generally been weak and ineffectual except in circumstances where errors and offenses have been blatant (Freidson, 1975; Millman, 1977; Bosk, 1979; Paget, 1988). Confronting a medical colleague is considered distasteful, even in private, and would be unthinkable in public. Freidson (1975) observes that rules of etiquette have restricted the evaluation of work and discouraged the expression of criticism. Millman (1977) contends that a "gentleman's agreement" exists among physicians, an unspoken agreement to overlook each other's mistakes, which grows out of a fear of reprisal and a recognition of common interests.

The American Medical Association has typically placed the self-interest of the medical profession over changes in public policy—especially when it comes to protecting the fee-for-service pattern of payment (Stevens, 1971). The medical profession in the United States has a consistent record of resisting social legislation that in any way reduces the authority, privilege, and income of physicians. As a group, the profession has opposed workmen's compensation, Social Security, voluntary health insurance, and health maintenance organizations (HMOs) in their initial stages. It has also opposed professional standards review organizations (intended to review the quality of medical work in federally funded programs), national health insurance, Medicare, Medicaid, and the Diagnostic Related Groups program. This has reduced societal confidence in medicine, since physicians in general are often viewed as placing the desire for financial profit ahead of the desire to help people.

A final example of the medical profession's self-serving position can be seen in the ways in which other health occupations have suffered because of the profession's manipulation. Chiropractors were at one time labeled *quacks* by the AMA, which continued its official efforts to discredit chiropractors until 1980. In 1987 a federal court decided that the AMA was guilty of unlawfully eroding the credibility of chiropractors (Shell, 1988). Physicians have also opposed acupuncturists; after they successfully drew acupuncture into the realm of medicine, they drastically limited its use (Wolpe, 1985).

The Changing Status of Nurses

Nursing is a major occupation in the health field. As physicians became the dominant profession in the United States, nurses have had great difficulty in achieving full professional recognition and, in fact, are usually considered by sociologists as semi-professionals. They have never achieved anything close to the power, prestige, and income level attained by physicians. Because physicians have most of the formal, official power over patients in hospital settings, nurses' power is limited, although they may find ways of exercising informal power within this system. Nurses certainly enjoy less prestige than physicians, and there is no comparison between the incomes of the two occupations: the average income for a physician in the United States is almost $120,000 per year, while the average nurse earns under $30,000.

How do we account for the failure of nurses to win full professional recognition? First, the overwhelming power of physicians within the health field makes it difficult for nurses to demonstrate their distinctive capabilities. Second, physicians have overtly opposed nurses' efforts to win professional recognition. Third, since nursing tends to be dominated by females (about 95 percent), males in general have opposed professional recognition for nursing. In fact, in male-dominated U.S. society, at least in the past, female-dominated occupations have found it impossible to win professional recognition. Finally, while physicians have generally assumed the high-status tasks (e.g., brain surgery, open-heart surgery) for themselves, they have relegated nurses to the "dirty work" in hospitals (changing linen, emptying bed pans, etc.). Occupations that do dirty work are obviously hard-pressed to win professional recognition.

Changes in Contemporary Nursing. Dramatic changes are occurring in nursing today. The most visible one is a widespread shortage of nurses. Every day, newspapers run advertisements by hospitals and other agencies trying to recruit nurses. A recent government report found almost 120,000 vacant nursing positions in hospitals and more than 20,000 open positions in nursing homes (Rich, 1988). In 1990, 12 percent of available nursing positions in hospitals were vacant, while in nursing homes, the vacancy rate was 19 percent (American Nursing Association). The problem is not the supply of nurses, which, since 1977, has increased by nearly 35 percent. Rather, the problem is whether the supply of graduating nurses can meet the needs of an ever-expanding health-care system and of the demands made on it. In addition, victims of severe diseases (such as AIDS) require intense nursing supervision, as do the rising numbers of elderly people with serious illnesses. More sophisticated technologies require great time and attention that, along with government and health insurance efforts at cost-containment, make the relatively poorly paid nurse a bargain to hospitals and other employers.

Complicating the problem of accelerating demand is the fact that a number of factors are forcing people out of nursing or are causing young people to rethink nursing as a possible career choice. (Nursing school enrollments are down dramatically.) One inhibiting factor is that, although starting pay (about $21,000) is competitive, the maximum that can be earned by a nurse is comparatively low—an average of about $29,000. (By way of comparison, an accountant is also likely to start at $21,000, but the average maximum is about $61,000.)

A third factor is nurses' lack of power, as noted above. Trained as professionals, they expect to command respect and to make autonomous decisions. However, nurses quickly confront the harsh reality that they must take orders, primarily from physicians. They are also realizing that their professional status involves doing society's dirty work—dealing with people (alcoholics, drug abusers, AIDS victims, schizophrenics) whom no one else wants to handle. More and more, nurses are showing signs of unwillingness to tolerate the difficult working conditions, the relatively low pay, and demeaned status of their profession. Therefore, in the near future the United States may be facing an increasing demand for nurses at the same time that their numbers are diminishing. As one nurse put it: "The old attitude toward nurses—'work long, work late, work hard'—is just not going to attract people. . . . Nurses aren't content to be the housewives of the hospital anymore" (*Time*, 1988, p. 78). Said another: "Unless you have this dying need to take care of sick people and clean up a lot of ——, why do it?" (*Washington Post*, 1988a, p. 13).

Doctor/Nurse Relationships

Traditionally, the work in medicine has been divided along gender lines. As mentioned earlier, doctors have been males and nurses have been females, and the authority of doctors has generally been unquestioned. Doctors make their medical decisions on the basis of medical histories, physical examinations, laboratory findings, and, sometimes, on the recommendations of other physicians who have been called in as consultants. Because nurses are often in close day-to-day contact with patients, they too, can give doctors useful information for making medical decisions. However, because doctors are supposed to be the medical authorities and decision makers, the advice given by nurses must be offered very carefully (Stein, 1974). When nurses advise doctors on appropriate medical treatments, they must do so without seeming to do so. For their part, doctors sometimes have to ask for the recommendations of nurses, but again without seeming to do so. This process has been called the "doctor–nurse game" (Stein, 1974, p. 202).

Hughes (1988) accepts Stein's views on the doctor/nurse game, but argues that it does not apply in all settings. Specifically, Hughes studied a casualty department in a British hospital. Although the formal authority for the sorting and initial diagnosis of acutely ill patients lies with doctors, in reality the need to make rapid decisions under great pressure falls mostly to nurses. The authority of the nurse is particularly clear in dealing with new doctors or with doctors recently returning to hospital work. Nurses in this setting often give doctors suggestions; they also reprimand doctors (especially young ones) and even question their competence.

Female Doctors

Although, as we have seen, medicine has often been divided along gender lines, changes are occurring. A particularly important development is the dramatic increase in female doctors. (It continues to be the case that relatively few males are entering nursing.) The increase in the number of women in medical schools is impressive: in 1971–1972, women made up only 10.9 percent of medical school students, but by 1987–1988 that percentage had more than tripled to 34.3 percent (National Center for Health Statistics, 1990, p. 213). In 1988–1989 women represented 37 percent of all first-year medical students (National Center for Health Statistics, 1991, p. 36). Less dramatic, but still indicative of a trend, is the fact that the percentage of female physicians increased from 10.8 percent in 1979 to 17.4 percent in 1986. (Figure 14–3 shows the increase in medical degrees granted to women.)

Several accounts of women medical students and physicians detail the problems women have in gaining recognition as equal colleagues by male

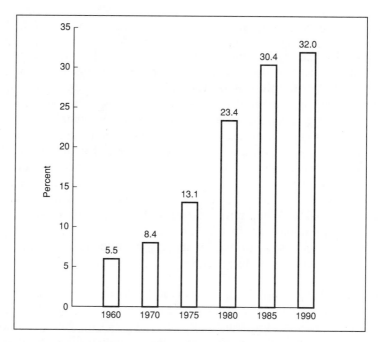

Figure 14–3. Percent of Medical Degrees Granted to Women, 1960–1990. (*Source:* U.S. Bureau of the Census, *Statistical Abstract of the United States.*)

physicians and as "real" doctors by patients (Hammond, 1980; Lorber, 1984; West, 1984). But the trend is clear: women physicians will be commonplace in the future, and the impact should be significant. As more women enter the medical profession, there is the potential for a change in the relationship between doctors and nurses and, more important, between doctors and patients. With more women as doctors, improved communication is possible, along with a greater willingness to relate to patients as people. Lorber (1984) found that when male doctors assessed their accomplishments during their careers, they tended to talk of their skills and choices of appropriate treatment. The personal side of the physician/patient relationship was rarely mentioned. Women doctors, on the other hand, stressed their value to patients and did so using words like "help" and "care." As one woman physician put it: "I think the best thing that I do is simply taking care of patients and being a warm and caring physician" (Lorber, 1984, p. 106).

As women doctors in increasing numbers choose to work in specialties like internal medicine, family practice, and even surgery, instead of the usual choices of psychiatry, pediatrics, and pathology, they will be treating a wider range of patients and extending their influence. With a somewhat higher percentage of women doctors, sexist attitudes on the part of male physicians will likely diminish, since these doctors will have had exposure to competent and professional female counterparts in medical school and later in clinical practice (Halpern, 1988).

In spite of the gains being made by female physicians, however, they continue to lag behind male physicians in several ways. Most notable is the fact that while male physicians earn, on the average, $120,000 per year, the average yearly income for a female physician is less than $75,000 (*Washington Post*, 1988b).

Emergence of the Business of Health Care

Important signs are now emerging that the professional dominance of the physician may be significantly reduced in the future. According to Cockerham (1986), three factors appear to account for this development. One is greater government involvement. Government intervention in health-care delivery remains limited at present, yet the evolving pattern is one of increased government regulation of medical practice. The second factor is the rise of consumerism in health care. More affluent and better educated people are attempting to take greater control over their health by making their own decisions about what medical services and health practices are best for them, and thereby interacting with physicians on a more equal basis.

The third challenge to the dominance of doctors is coming from a particularly powerful direction. A significant portion of the health market is being taken over by large business conglomerates (Starr, 1982; Ritzer and Walczak, 1988). Massive government funding of programs like Medicare and Medicaid have made health care a lucrative business. This fact has caused people to invest their money in private hospitals and nursing homes. Observing this trend, corporate chains began purchasing these facilities. This has been followed by a wave of mergers, acquisitions, and diversifications involving not only hospitals and nursing homes but a variety of enterprises such as hospital restaurants and supply companies, medical office buildings, emergency care centers, HMOs, health spas, and hospital management systems. The profit-making corporations expanded into markets that were underserved or into areas where they could compete successfully with nonprofit institutions by providing more attractive rooms, better food, a friendlier staff, and more efficient services.

In the context of corporate health care, the physician becomes an employee rather than an independent practitioner (Walsh, 1987). The doctor is bound to the rules, regulations, and procedures for practices established by the corporation, which, in all probability, is managed by people trained in business, not medicine. Hence, doctors who do corporate practice are not as likely to play the decisive role in decision making about policy, hospital budgets, capital investments, salaries, promotions, and personnel appointments. Work routines will undoubtedly be more regulated. Standards of performance will be developed, and the salaries of the doctors will be based on how well they perform. Physicians who do not meet these standards are apt to lose their jobs. Mistakes will also be closely scrutinized, not only to ensure quality care but also to avoid corporate liability for malpractice. In sum, the control of corporate medicine tends to be outside the immediate health-care facility and in the hands of a management system that is primarily business oriented. Within this system, the doctor's autonomy will be significantly reduced. And as the twenty-first century approaches, the definition of medicine as a "sovereign profession" shows signs of being increasingly less accurate.

As a result of the changes discussed in this section, medicine is losing some of its luster. For example, applicants to medical school peaked in the mid-1970s at about three applicants for every medical slot, and by 1987–1988 the number of applicants had dropped to less than two applicants for every position. Physicians themselves may be steering young people away from medical careers. As one physician said: "The realities of the new medicine are intruding on that relationship [between doctor and patient] and, for me and many others, are bringing this unique experience to an end" (Colburn, 1988, p. 9).

Patients and the Medical System

The Sick Role

The most influential theory explaining the behavior of sick persons in Western society is Talcott Parson's (1951) concept of the sick role. It is based upon the assumption that being sick is undesirable, and the sick person wants to get well. However, because the sick are seen as unable to take care of themselves, they must seek medical treatment and cooperate with care providers. Therefore, sick persons have, in Parson's view, a "duty to get well."

The **sick role** consists of four basic components: the sick person (1) is exempt from "normal" social roles, (2) is not responsible for his or her condition, (3) should try to get well, and (4) should seek technically competent help. Exemption from normal social roles because of illness is a temporary condition and is based upon the premise that the sick person will try to get well. Therefore, the person who is excused from normal duties assumes an obligation to get well. This includes a further obligation to seek help from a technically competent practitioner, typically a physician. The physician, on the other hand, has an obligation to return the sick person to as normal a state as possible.

The merit of this analysis is that it describes a patterned set of expectations that defines the norms and values appropriate to being sick, both for the sick individual and for others who interact with that person. This pattern allows us to predict the behavior of the ill in certain circumstances, such as situations where people are excused from school or work to try to improve their condition, including a visit to a doctor if necessary. Consequently, Parsons's concept of the sick role describes the behavioral norms appropriate to being sick in Western society.

Situations do exist, however, where the sick role concept has limited value for explaining illness behavior. Not everyone behaves in the manner the sick role suggests. Some people deny being sick when they have symptoms of illness; others refuse to go to the doctor even when they know they should. Some do not cooperate with doctors when they receive medical advice; and others may not feel any particular obligation to get well—especially if they can benefit from illness by avoiding responsibilities such as work. The sick role applies best to illnesses that are temporary and can be overcome by a physician's help. But some diseases cannot be cured and are not temporary, and in this case becoming "well" is impossible. In addition, the sick role described by Parsons incorporates the middle-class assumptions that rational problem solving (seeking medical assistance for illness) is the most effective behavior possible, and effort will result in positive gain (health). The concept fails to take into account attitudes typical of an environment of poverty, where success is the exception.

Yet the sick role does provide a reasonably good explanation of the patient/physician relationship in terms of mutual obligations and expectations. (Both are expected to cooperate in improving the patient's health.) The concept also helps us understand the role of medicine in controlling deviant behavior. Taking a structural-functionalist approach, Parsons suggests that illness is a form of deviance, since it is abnormal to be sick. Illness is not only deviant but it is also dysfunctional for society as a whole because it interferes with the smooth functioning of a social system. If too many people were sick and not functioning properly, social systems would become unstable. This could lead to social breakdown because essential functions like growing food and educating the young could not be carried out.

The medical profession thus functions to offset the dysfunctional aspects of illness by curing, controlling, or preventing disease. Hence, medical practice becomes a mechanism by which a social system seeks to control the illnesses of its deviant sick by returning them to as normal a state as possible. Consequently, implicit in the concept of the sick role is the idea that medicine is an institution for the social control of deviant behavior and represents society in maintaining social stability. Whether medical procedures should be used to control a wide range of human behavior is a debatable topic, but the trend in modern society is to have medicine assume more and more responsibility for behavioral problems.

(See our earlier discussion of the medicalization of society.) It has been argued, for instance, that there are few problems today that some group does not think of as a medical problem. Parsons helps us to see how medical practice operates as a form of social control.

Patients as Consumers

In contemporary times, health care has expanded beyond caring for the sick to the prevention of illness. Again, social class differences appear. The middle and upper classes feel more responsible for maintaining their health. The more affluent tend to visit doctors for preventive care, while the poor visit physicians primarily for the treatment of overt symptoms of illness (Dutton, 1978). Furthermore, there is widespread interest among college-educated persons in health-protective activities like dieting and exercise (e.g., jogging, aerobic dancing). All of this points toward a consumer orientation toward health among the middle and upper classes. The power of the health consumer lies in having the freedom to choose one's source and type of health care.

According to Reeder (1972), the concept of a person as a "health consumer" rather than a "patient" became established in the United States during the 1960s. In this context, physicians were defined as "health providers." In an age of consumerism, the traditional physician/patient relationship is significantly modified. The patient exerts more control and assumes a more equal footing with the doctor in terms of status, decision making, and responsibility for outcomes. The trend toward consumerism in medicine is similar to consumerism in other aspects of life in the United States, in which people make informed choices about the services available to them. This activity is usually more characteristic of the middle and upper classes, who have the resources to support it (Cockerham et al., 1986).

Lower-class persons, in turn, may have a more passive orientation toward life and less willingness to take responsibility for their problems (Arluke et al., 1979). When it comes to health, the lower class may place greater responsibility upon the health-care system to keep them healthy than the other classes do. Several studies have shown, for instance, that persons with low incomes are the most likely to agree that people should not be held responsible for their own illnesses (Wolinsky and Wolinsky, 1981). According to this view, if someone is sick (and poor), it is not his or her fault.

An important counter-influence on health consumerism, however, is medical technology. The development of a complex array of medical equipment and procedures has increasingly taken away the self-management of health from all patients, but especially from those at the bottom of society with their more limited levels of education and experience with technology. Although all patients are dependent upon physicians as experts, better educated persons are likely to be less in awe of medical "wonders."

Seeking Medical Care

Not everyone responds to the symptoms of illness in the same way, as mentioned earlier. Some people will consult with a doctor as soon as they feel sick, while others with similar symptoms will try self-treatment, ignore the symptoms, or perhaps simply wait to see what develops from them. Only about one-third of all symptoms that a person experiences will eventually be brought to the attention of a physician. The more uncertain someone is about the meaning of his or her symptoms, the more likely that person is to visit a doctor.

Typically, older people and females will see a physician about their health more readily than younger people and males. The aged visit doctors more often because, as a person becomes old, his or her bodily afflictions, even minor ones, tend to be more serious. Women visit physicians more often because they have more health problems. Even after subtracting doctor visits for conditions associated with pregnancy, women still show more visits to the doctor than men. Men visit doctors about four times a year, while women average over five visits annually (Cockerham, 1986).

Prior to the late 1960s, the poor in U.S. society were significantly less likely than the more affluent to utilize a doctor's services. However, because of Medicare and Medicaid public health insurance programs, the elderly and the poor have obtained more equitable access to professional health care. Although serious problems remain with respect to quality of care, research shows that people who are less able to pay for health care are still able to obtain it (Dutton, 1978; Rundall and Wheeler, 1979). The poor are visiting physicians more often than ever before, while the more affluent, in contrast, showed no change in the rate of physician utilization between 1983 and 1986 (National Center for Health Statistics, 1988).

The pattern of physician utilization in the United States is clear: middle-class and upper-socioeconomic groups continue to maintain the highest levels of health and participate more in preventive care. Preventive care is intended to keep healthy people healthy and consists of regular physical examinations and the like. The lower class has more illness and disability, and visits physicians more for treatment of symptoms. However, when the affluent really have need of doctors, they have the financial resources to seek the services of the best doctors whenever they want. (Rock Hudson, the movie star, who was afflicted with AIDS, chartered a jet liner to fly to Paris for the best available treatment for his condition.)

Doctor/Patient Communications

The concept of the sick role details the obligations of patients and physicians toward each other. Patients cooperate with doctors, and doctors attempt to return patients to a state of good health and as normal a level of functioning as possible. When people visit physicians for treatment and medical advice, doctors usually (but not always) take some type of action to satisfy the patient's expectations. Scheff (1966), for example, describes the medical decision role as the guiding principle behind everyday medical practice: the work of the physician is for the good of the patient, so it is better for physicians to impute illness to their patients than to deny it and risk overlooking or missing it. This perspective may promote "overprescribing" and is intended to satisfy the demands of patients. As Freidson (1970, p. 258) points out: "While the physician's job is to make decisions, including the decision not to do anything, the fact seems to be that the everyday practitioner feels impelled to do something, if only to satisfy patients who urge him to do something when they are in distress."

The interaction that takes place between doctor and patient is an exercise in communication. As is the case in any other face-to-face situation, the effectiveness of this exercise depends upon the ability of the participants to understand each other. A major barrier to effective communication, however, rests in the differences between patients and physicians with respect to status, education, professional training, and authority. Some doctors are very effective communicators, while others do poorly when it comes to communication with patients (Waitzkin, 1985).

Two groups in society, those with a poor education and women, have been identified as having the most communication problems with physicians. It has been found, for example, that poorly educated persons are the most likely to have their questions ignored and to be treated impersonally as a disease entity instead of an individual to be respected (Ross and Duff, 1982). Other studies show that physicians prefer upper-class and upper-middle-class patients and give them more personalized service (Link, 1983). A major reason is that doctors find these patients to be more like themselves; that is, higher strata patients reflect values, norms, and attitudes similar to those held by the doctor. Thus, doctors can be more comfortable in working with them. In contrast, Roth (1969) describes the way many physicians regard lower-class patients:

> They are considered the least desirable patients. The doctor has probably dealt with "their kind" during his years as a student and resident in outpatient and emergency clinics, and he has concluded that they are often dirty and smelly, follow poor health practices, fail to observe directions or meet appointments, and live in a situation which makes it impossible to establish appropriate health regimes (Roth, 1969, p. 227).

As for women, Fisher (1984; see also Todd, 1989) studied doctor/patient communication in a family practice clinic and found that many women patients were not satisfied with the explanations given them. Sometimes they did not believe they were being given the information needed to understand their health situation. "The women who called were often well educated and articulate, yet they did not feel they had enough information with which to make reasonable decisions or they felt they did not understand or could not trust the recommendation their physician made" (Fisher, 1984, p. 2). Their feelings were intensified when their medical problems were related to reproduction and their questions were always the same: How could they determine whether the treatment being recommended was in their best interest?

In one example cited by Fisher, her friend Andrea, a fellow graduate student, telephoned her to ask whether she should have a hysterectomy. The woman had developed a pelvic inflammatory disease, and treatment by antibiotics was unsuccessful. The doctor then recommended a hysterectomy, which meant she could never have children. Fisher suggested that she tell the doctor she was engaged to be married to another doctor who wanted a family and ask if there was any other way to treat her problem. Fisher states:

> Several weeks later my phone again rang. Andrea had followed my advice. Once the doctor learned of her impending marriage his attitude changed. He assured her that there were alternative treatments available and they would work hard to avoid a hysterectomy. She was treated with another course of antibiotics, her infection cleared up, avoiding unnecessary surgery (Fisher, 1984, p. 2).

Fisher found that Andrea's distressing experience was not an isolated case. Typically, the women patients in her study unquestioningly accepted the recommendations of the doctors in the clinic, and those recommendations were not always in the best interests of the women. Women tend to visit physicians not only more often than men but also for more intimate conditions. Yet medicine remains a male-dominated profession, and research like Fisher's calls for more insight on the part of doctors in dealing with female patients.

Summary

In contemporary urban-industrial societies the major illnesses are no longer the infectious communicable diseases; instead they are chronic disorders. The major chronic diseases, heart disease and cancer, are importantly influenced by life styles.

The sociological specialty called *medical sociology* focuses on many different aspects of health and illness. Among the important parts of medical sociology is social epidemiology, which is the study of the frequency and pattern of disease within a particular population.

It is often assumed that medical discoveries and practices were responsible for the victory over infectious diseases, but social and environmental changes were far more important than developments in medicine.

The medicalization of society is a pattern of defining a variety of behaviors, often deviant behaviors, as medical problems. Alcoholism, compulsive gambling, and the treatment of hyperactive children are examples.

Males and females differ in their health problems and their responses to them. Women are sick more often, but live longer; men are sick less often, but die sooner. There are both biological and social psychological reasons for the earlier deaths of men. Smoking is increasing among females, however, which is bringing the female death rate for lung cancer closer to that of males.

The aging of the United States population is an increasingly important factor in the health problems of the country, even though the health of people reaching old age is better than it was in the past.

Black people in the United States have generally poorer health and higher mortality than the white population. The lower social classes of the society have higher rates of infectious disease, as well as higher rates of the "modern ills" like heart disease. The life-styles, economic limitations, and social environmental conditions of the poor contribute to their higher illness rates.

Health costs have escalated greatly in the last 20 years, primarily because of increased labor costs, new and expensive technologies, and inflation. Attempts to control costs have had only limited success.

In the eighteenth and early nineteenth centuries, the training of doctors was limited and poor. The twentieth century has seen a great improvement in medical training. The health field has traditionally been dominated by the doctors, both individually and through their professional organizations.

Nurses are another important part of the health field, but they have failed to win the power, status, and wealth accorded to physicians. There is currently a major shortage of nurses as demand has increased and, with nursing school enrollments down, supply is beginning to fall.

In doctor/nurse relationships, doctors maintain a dominant position, even when they must rely on the greater knowledge of nurses. More and more women are becoming doctors, and their presence is likely to bring changes in the relationship between doctors and their patients.

Several changes are likely to reduce the dominance of physicians, including greater government involvement, increased consumerism among patients, and the rise of corporate health care.

The sick role is an undesirable role that carries with it both exemptions and expectations. The most important expectation is that patients will co-operate with medical practitioners in order to leave the sick role. People today are often thought of as "health consumers," who are expected to take an active responsibility for their health. Seeking medical care is one such responsibility that the more affluent, in the past, have been more likely to do. Those with greater economic resources could afford to get medical care because it caused them less financial hardship.

Communication between doctors and patients is largely controlled by the doctors. Some doctors communicate well and others, poorly. The quality of communication between doctor and patient is an important element in the treatment of disease.

CRITICAL THINKING

1. Explain how social epidemiology has been a useful tool in understanding the AIDS crisis in the United States.
2. How have the major causes of death in the United States changed since the beginning of this century? How do these changes move health even further into the realm of sociology?
3. How is the contraction of disease closely linked to people's actions and behaviors?
4. Give examples of the medicalization of U.S. society. Is this a positive or negative trend?
5. Compare and contrast the health status of various subpopulations in the United States. How important are gender, social class, age, and race in determining the quality of a person's health?
6. What accounts for the escalating costs of health care in the United States? Which groups in society will be most affected by rising costs? Do changes in medical technology necessarily benefit all of society or only a select few?
7. Describe the traditional pattern of physician behavior in the United States. Upon what has physician status and prestige been based? What forces in the medical community may change this pattern?
8. Contrast the status of nurses and doctors in the United States. What accounts for the differences you see? How might the impending nursing shortage force change in this profession?
9. How is doctor behavior affected by patient expectations? Which groups in society have trouble communicating with doctors? Why?

15 Religion

One of the most striking developments of the past decade has been the revival of the importance of religion throughout the world. Religion divisions have inspired bloody conflicts among Hindus and Sikhs and Muslims in India; between Catholics and Protestants in Northern Ireland; among Jews, Christians, and Muslims in the Middle East; between Shi'ite Muslims in Iran and Sunni Muslims in Iraq; between Buddhists and Hindus in Sri Lanka. Equally as striking has been the prominence of religion and religious leaders in the momentous political changes that have engulfed the Soviet Union and Eastern Europe. Moreover, religious fundamentalism has swept through the Islamic world, has formed the basis of a major Hindu political party in India, and has become established as a powerful force in American political and cultural life. Thus, despite earlier predictions of its gradual decline, religion remains of vital importance in the modern world (see table 15–1).

Religion, a universal feature of human existence, is one of the most dynamic, fascinating, varied, and complex of all human phenomena. Wallace (1966) estimated that, from the earliest human history to the present day, humans have practiced about 100,000 different religions. Religions are intimately involved with the working of societies. On the one hand, religions often provide social stability and inhibit social change. On the

Table 15–1. Estimated Memberships of the Principal Religions of the World

Religions	World	%
Christians	1,758,778,000	33.3
Roman Catholics	995,780,000	18.8
Protestants	363,290,000	6.9
Orthodox	166,942,000	3.2
Anglicans	72,980,300	1.4
Other Christians	159,785,700	3.0
Muslims	935,000,000	17.7
Nonreligious	866,000,000	16.4
Hindus	705,000,000	13.3
Buddhists	303,000,000	5.7
Atheists	233,000,000	4.4
Chinese Folk Religionists	180,000,000	3.4
New Religionists	138,000,000	2.6
Tribal Religionists	92,012,000	1.7
Sikhs	18,100,000	0.3
Jews	17,400,000	0.3
Shamanists	10,100,000	0.2
Confucians	5,800,000	0.1
Baha'is	5,300,000	0.1
Jains	3,650,000	0.1
Shintoists	3,100,000	0.1
Other Religions	17,938,000	0.3
World Population	5,292,178,000	100.0

Source: David B. Barrett. "Adherents of All Religions by Seven Continental Areas, mid-1990." Adapted with permission from *1991 Britannica Book of the Year*, p. 299. © 1991 by Encyclopaedia Britannica, Inc.

other hand, religious inspiration has been a dynamic source of social change. Therefore, to comprehend fully the nature of human life, it is essential to understand the intimate relationship between religion and the functioning of human societies.

Religion has been a social institution of great interest to sociologists. Almost all of the classical social theorists—Marx, Weber, Durkheim, Simmel—and many of the most prominent sociologists today have been interested in the role of religion in human societies and, especially, in the emergence of modern society.

For example, in *The Protestant Ethic and the Spirit of Capitalism*, a study that has become one of the classics of sociological theory, Max Weber suggested that the development of the emphases on acquisitiveness, systematic calculation, and the work ethic that characterize the economic system of modern capitalism was closely linked to the spread of Protestantism throughout Western society. This relationship was especially pronounced among sects that had adopted the doctrines of John Calvin, a sixteenth-century Swiss theologian. Chief among Calvin's tenets was the idea of predestination, the doctrine that held that the fate of all people—whether they would be going to heaven or condemned to eternal hell when they died—was predetermined by God.

Calvinist religious doctrine eliminated the Catholic sacraments that guaranteed being saved, and ruled out good works and feelings as ways of determining whether God had selected them to go to heaven. Therefore, Calvinists could never know their fate with certainty. They were perpetually insecure and had to look elsewhere for signs that would indicate whether they might be among the "elect," those who were in God's favor and would escape the fires of hell. Having accepted Luther's view that all earthly callings serve God, Calvinists came to believe that economic success in this life was a sign of salvation in the next. As a consequence, they struggled to accumulate wealth beyond their needs, and, in the process, they developed the character traits of hard work, self-discipline, and industriousness to achieve worldly success.

The Calvinist drive to achieve economic success was not simply a matter of personal greed but was rather an expression of a profoundly religious impulse. However, because Calvinists rejected worldly pleasures, they could not enjoy the fruits of their labors—the wealth that their hard work had enabled them to accumulate. Moreover, because they could never quite be sure whether they were saved, they could never relax. Instead, by reinvesting their profits and expanding their businesses, they were able to achieve additional worldly assurances of their otherworldly fate.

Eventually the religious basis of this constant quest for wealth was lost, and people came to seek the accumulation of profits, not as a sign of success in the next world, but as a measure of success in this world. However, the accumulation of profits was made legitimate by what Weber called the **Protestant ethic**—a system of beliefs and action involving a commitment to hard work, frugality, self-denial, and acquisitiveness. According to Weber, it was this legitimation (or justification) of the profit motive that contributed to the development of the values and personality traits that characterized the spirit of capitalism in the Western world and led ultimately to the development of the capitalist economic system (Weber, 1904–1905/1958).

The Sociological Perspective—Religion as a Social Phenomenon

A sociologist's perspective on religion differs from a theologian's or an adherent's. On the surface, a sociology of religion may seem to be a contradiction in terms. If sociologists are committed to an empirical and scientific analysis of social phenomena, how can they study something that is intimately related to the supernatural, which cannot be examined empirically?

Although we cannot scientifically study the supernatural, we can analyze the social phenomena that are related to the experience of the supernatural and expressed as religious feelings. These phenomena include religious behaviors, such as praying, missionary work, and preaching, and religious beliefs—for instance, in an all-powerful God, a vengeful God, an uninvolved God, or a benevolent God. In addition, the social roles (such as the clergy) connected with religion and the social organizations of religion (such as churches, sects, and denominations) are also frequent subjects of sociological investigation.

The **sociology of religion** examines the behaviors, beliefs, roles, and organizational structures of the world's major religions, such as Islam, Christianity, Hinduism, Judaism, Buddhism, and Confucianism, as well as newly emergent religious movements such as Rastafarianism, Cargo cults, and the Hare Krishnas.

However, the sociology of religion is also concerned with a variety of social activities and symbol systems that are not normally defined as religious. For example, for many years communism served many people as a kind of religion that provided a set of doctrines for explaining and giving meaning to human existence; it provided policies for achieving a "heaven on earth"; and it developed ceremonial rituals that united its followers into a community of believers. The dramatic changes that have accompanied *glastnost* and *perestroika* in the Soviet Union have led many to characterize communism as "the God that failed" (Marty, 1991).

Besides identifying political ideologies that assume a religious quality, some writers have suggested that for many people psychoanalysis and other therapeutic techniques have become religions that are based on a rational and scientific approach to "soul-building" (Glazer and Moynihan, 1963, p. 175; Dinges, 1988, p. 173). Finally, some commentators have argued that organized sport in contemporary society has taken on many of the characteristics of religion (Rudin, 1972; Novak, 1976; Prebish, 1984; Hoffman, 1985).

The essential element uniting these diverse phenomena in the category of religion is that, to some extent, each has developed a sacred quality. In his classic study of religion, *The Elementary Forms of Religious Life*, Emile Durkheim (1912/1965) argued that at the heart of religion is the idea of the sacred, as contrasted with the profane. The **profane** refers to the ordinary, the everyday, the commonplace, the utilitarian, the mundane aspects of life. The sacred, on the other hand, elicits an attitude of reverence, respect, mystery, awe, and sometimes fear. The respect accorded to certain objects transforms them from the profane to the sacred.

Although societies differ in what they define as sacred and profane, all societies make such distinctions. Often nonmaterial entities such as gods and spirits are defined as sacred, but "a rock, a tree, a spring, a piece of wood, a house—in a word, anything—can be sacred" (Durkheim, 1912/1965, p. 52). The **sacred** are those objects that people define and act toward with respect and reverence. Churches or temples are not merely buildings where religious meetings are held; they are also sacred places. They and their contents are treated with reverence and respect.

Above all, religion is a *social* phenomenon. First, religion involves aspects of human existence that are socially defined as sacred; what comprises the sacred varies among religious systems. Therefore, all religious systems are human phenomena, defined and constructed by people. Second, religion is fundamentally a shared, communal activity; it is expressed in communities of people who share common creeds, moral and ethical codes, and rituals. Thus religion is rooted in social processes, and its expression is shaped by the same factors—social class, ethnicity, technology, and language—that affect other social institutions. Sociologists are especially interested in examining how social conditions affect the expression of religious patterns.

Religion is a social phenomenon in still another sense; it is a socially defined way of interpreting and comprehending the realities of human existence, and of making them understandable. Religion provides a system of meaning, a definition and interpretation of life. **Religion,** then, involves those things that a society holds sacred; it comprises an institutionalized system of symbols, beliefs, values, and practices that deal with questions of ultimate meaning.

The Social Functions of Religion

Society and religion are closely interrelated. Neither can exist without the other. A useful way of viewing this interrelationship is to examine the functions and dysfunctions of religion for individuals and for the larger society. Such an examination underscores the social character of religion.

Meaning, Social Solidarity, and Social Control

Religion is a source of personal comfort and consolation. A religious system offers emotional support for people that enables them to endure very difficult circumstances. Human existence, after all, is precarious and uncertain. Religion enables people to accept the unacceptable and the inevitable—the disappointments, frustrations, sufferings, tragedies, and inevitable death—that are inherent in human existence. Religion provides a source of strength and meaning in the face of the ever-present possibility of the unanticipated, unexpected, and unanswerable.

One of the objectives of Durkheim's classic study of suicide was to demonstrate the role of religion in providing the individual with strength in the face of adversity (Durkheim, 1893/1951). In the 1980s Stack (1983) examined the relationship between religiosity and suicide rates in the United States. Using church attendance as his primary measure of religiosity, he found that the lower the rates of church attendance, the higher the rates of suicide. Indeed, the religious factor was more important than the unemployment rate in explaining suicide rates. He concluded that a decline in institutionalized religion will lead to a situation in which the individual is not integrated into a moral community and thus will be more vulnerable to suicide.

A recent study by Pescosolido and Georgianna (1989) of differences among religious denominations in the U.S. confirmed the general proposition that religion influences the suicide rate. However, they found that suicide rates are influenced by the denominations found in a specific geographic area, and that some denominations exert a stronger "protective" influence (that is, have lower suicide rates) than others. Counties with higher percentages of Catholics and evangelical Protestants (Nazarenes, Evangelical Baptists, Seventh-Day Adventists, Churches of God) had lower suicide rates than counties where mainstream Protestant denominations (Episcopalian, Presbyterian, United Methodist, United Church of Christ, Lutheran) predominated. The authors' explanation for these denominational differences lies in the nature of the social bonds and the sense of community that each of these denominations creates. Catholics and evangelical Protestants are much more likely to have their religious membership result in ties that bind people to a religious community and create a sense of belonging. Thus, by integrating individuals into a moral community, religion provides a source of strength, security, and emotional support that sustains people during difficult times.

Social Control. One of the basic problems for any society is to keep order and maintain social control. Society must deal with deviance and prevent those who have deviated from becoming fully alienated and thereby disrupting society. Religious ceremonies provide a source of social cohesion and unity for a society. Moreover, through various rites and ceremonies, such as the Catholic confessional or the Protestant communion, religion supplies ritualized ways in which those who have deviated from societal norms and values can rid themselves of their guilt. Religion provides an emotional release for the individual that also maintains the cohesion of the society. Religion thus serves as a means of social control, by which members of society accept and conform to dominant norms and values.

Religion not only provides psychological support for individuals; it also maintains the existing social order. Religions tend to support and to justify a society's norms and values, and to maintain the established and dominant groups within a society. Religion can also be used to legitimate the domination of one group by another. Although he had come to power as the leader of a secular Iraqi political movement, Saddam Hussein frequently employed tradtional Islamic rhetoric to justify his 1990 invasion of Kuwait. Moreover, he denounced as "infidels" the U.S. and Western defense of Kuwait and characterized his military compaign against them as a *jihad* (holy war). Religion thus often functions to legitimate, that is, to provide ideological support or justification for, the status quo or particular economic or political policies. Berger (1967) has argued that this legitimating function is the primary and defining characteristic of religion.

An excellent example of the use of religious authority to support the traditional social order involves the widespread religious opposition to certain aspects of the women's movement. Pope John Paul II, for example, has said that motherhood is at the center of Christian beliefs and should be promoted. "I want to remind young women that motherhood is the vocation of women. It was that way in the past. It is that way now and it will always be that way. It is a woman's eternal vocation" (*Washington Post*, 1979).

By interpreting the existing social order as ordained by God, religion can mask the fact that all societies are constructed by people; it can make a society's norms, values, and social arrangements appear to be fixed, permanent, and immutable—beyond human control. In the process, religion may obscure the humanly constructed nature of society and social problems, especially for those at the bottom of the social hierarchy. By acting as a conservative force in supporting the status quo, religion can undermine and retard reform and change. This was the essence of Karl Marx's critique of religion. Marx argued that because religion deflects attention from the humanly created inequalities in a society, it serves as the "opiate of the masses."

From this perspective, religion offers temporary relief for the poor and the dispossessed, but it prevents them from acting to change the structure of society and thus dealing with the basic sources of their problems. It leads the poor to reject earthly rewards—which they cannot achieve—as valueless when compared with the rewards promised by their religious belief system. Individuals may not be a "success" in this earthly existence, but because they have accepted the "other-worldly" values of a religious system, their ultimate salvation is ensured.

Critical, or Prophetic, Function

Even though religion often legitimates an existing social order, it can also challenge and change it. Therefore, religion can also perform a critical, or prophetic, function. Religion performs a **prophetic function** when it provides the standards for critically examining, challenging, and changing the existing social order. This prophetic function has occurred throughout the history of Judaism and Christianity, and it exists in constant tension with religion's tendency to support the status quo.

Many radical social movements have been grounded in religion. One of the most visible in the world today has been the development of "liberation theology" that has emerged as a force for radical change, especially in Latin America. Liberation theology is committed to social justice for the poor and the dispossessed and to the elimination of the injustices created by systems of extreme social inequality (Brown, 1986).

Group Identity and Adaptation

In addition to performing a prophetic function, religion can also provide a sense of identity. Participation in a religious group or institution provides a source of meaning, belonging, and group identity and helps to provide answers to the question, Who am I? Herberg (1955) has argued that the need to find a socially acceptable means of maintaining ethnic identity has contributed to the vitality of U.S. religion. Religion was especially important to European immigrants, whose primary identity was often tied to the religious community of which they were a part in Europe. For many immigrants, migration to the United States did not lessen, but rather heightened, their religiosity. However, in their desire to become fully Americanized, second-generation immigrants frequently abandoned many of their parents' cultural traits, including religion. Members of the third generation (the immigrants' grandchildren) were not as insecure about their status as Americans. Instead they desired a way of asserting and maintaining their ethnic identity in an impersonal urban society. According to Herberg (1955), membership in one of the "three religions of democracy"—Protestantism, Catholicism, or Judaism—provides a socially acceptable means of self-identification and thereby contributes to the integration and stability of the entire society. Thus religion is "an important part of the social cement that holds American social structure in place" (Hout and Greeley, 1987, p. 342).

Religion, therefore, is a complex and multifaceted phenomenon. It can have a variety of positive and negative consequences for individuals, social groups, and society as a whole. It can contribute to the integration of society and support the status quo. Or it can serve as a source of social conflict and challenge the existing social order.

The Changing Nature of Religion in the United States

Religion in the United States has been characterized both by relatively unchanging, stable features and by constant change. Religious organizations come and go; patterns of participation change; prevailing religious ideas vary from one generation to the next. At the same time, the basic patterns of commitment and participation are much as they were a century ago, and, despite evidence of a restructuring of American religion, the same broad religious communities (Protestant, Catholic, and Jewish) continue to be prominent features of American religious life. Here we examine three basic characteristics of American religion—its pervasiveness, its secularism, and its denominational pluralism—in light of its tradition of simultaneous continuity and change.

Pervasiveness of Religion

Religion has always been a conspicuous part of American life. From the earliest European settlements, religious factors have been uniquely prominent in this society; the dominant trends in American religion have been "profoundly different" from those in Europe (Caplow, 1985, p. 101). Almost all available data indicate that since colonial days, "the United States has been among the most religious countries in the Christian world" (Lipset, 1963a, p. 150).

The extraordinarily religious character of the American people persists even today. Numerous surveys have shown that, among industrial nations, Americans are among the most religious people in the world. Public opinion surveys conducted over the past 40 years indicate that the vast majority of Americans (between 94 and 99 percent) believe in God or a universal spirit, a percentage greater than in any other Western industrial society. In addition, when asked to rate, on a scale of 1 to 10, how important God is in their lives, the average rating of Americans is exceeded only by South Africans, with the highest rating reported by African Americans (see figure 15–1).

Religious behavior among the American people—as measured by membership or participation in a religious community—has remained relatively stable during the past four decades. As figure 15–2 indicates, church and synagogue membership among Americans has remained relatively unchanged since 1965, although, as we will note below, shifts have occurred in the religious groups with which people have been affiliated. The proportion of American adults who say that they are members of a church or synagogue rose to a peak of 76 percent in 1947 and gradually declined to 67 percent in 1972. Since then, church or synagogue membership has remained basically the same, standing at 69 percent in 1990.

Church and synagogue attendance also declined during the post-World War II period (see figure 15–3), especially during the 1960s among Roman Catholics who disagreed with Pope Paul VI's encyclical on "artificial birth control" (Hout and Greeley, 1987). Since 1975, however, religious

Cross-National Perspectives

Population Growth in Islamic Nations

Sociologists have long been fascinated by the influence of religion on social life. For example, in his classic study of suicide, Durkheim compared suicide rates among Jews, Catholics, and Protestants. Similarly, Weber's classic, *The Protestant Ethic and the Spirit of Capitalism*, examined how the doctrines of Calvinism influenced the development of modern capitalism.

Many sociological studies have noted that religious affiliation tends to be associated with a variety of demographic factors, including fertility levels. In the United States, for example, Catholics have generally had higher fertility rates than Protestants and Jews, although these historic differences have recently become less pronounced. Because Muslim nations are among the world's most rapidly growing, we will examine whether Islam, today the world's second largest religion with nearly a billion adherents, influences population growth.

Islam was founded in the seventh century by the Prophet Muhammad in what is today Saudi Arabia, and it is characterized by considerable continuity with Jewish and Christian traditions. Muslims share with Christians and Jews a belief in the same God and in the Old Testament prophets, and they acknowledge Jesus as a prophet. However, they believe that the Prophet Muhammad was the messenger through whom God's final revelation was communicated and transcribed in Islam's sacred book, the *Qur'an*.

From its Middle Eastern Arab origins, Islam quickly spread to Europe, Africa, and Asia. Today Muslims live in every nation of the world, although Islam's primary strength is found in the Middle East, Southern and Southeastern Asia, and Northern and sub-Saharan Africa. Muslims are a majority of the population in 40 nations, and in 7 others they represent a significant minority (25 to 49 percent).

Like most major religions, Islam is characterized by considerable diversity. The major sectarian division in Islam—between the Sunnis and the Shi'is (Shiites)—emerged in a dispute over who should lead Islam after the death of the Prophet Muhammad. Although a majority of Muslims in the world today are Sunnis, Shiites represent a powerful minority that has become most visible to the West in Iran, where postrevolution social change led by the Ayatollah Khomeini reestablished religious authority over many aspects of life that had become increasingly secularized under the monarchy headed by the Shah. In addition to sectarian divisions, there is substantial ethnic, regional, economic, and other religious diversity among nations that have large proportions of Muslim citizens. These various factors must be considered when the social impact of the "religious" factor is assessed.

The primary source of Islam's dramatic population growth, which is expected to reach nearly 2 billion by the year 2020, is the extremely high fertility rates in Islamic countries, which average 6 children per woman, in contrast to a figure of 1.7 for developed countries. However, this average obscures considerable regional variations, from an average of 3.6 in Islamic nations of Southeast Asia (Indonesia, Malaysia, Brunei) to 6.6 for nations in sub-Saharan Africa (Somalia, Senegal, Gambia, Niger, Mali, Guinea, Sierra Leone).

These very high rates of childbearing are not a result of religious objections to contraception; "Islam itself prescribes no special barriers to the use of contraception" (Weeks, 1988). The frequency of contraceptive use among married Muslim women ranges from 45 percent in Southeast Asia to 5 percent in sub-Saharan Africa, but in each case contraceptive use is lower in Islamic nations than in non-Islamic nations in the same region. Regional differences are also pronounced in the frequency with which women marry at a young age in Islamic countries, thereby increasing the probable number of pregnancies. As many as 47 percent of women under age 19 are married in South Asia (Pakistan, Bangladesh, Afghanistan) compared to only 18 percent in Southeast Asia. Early marriage, like resistance to contraceptive use, is a practice prescribed by tradition, not by Islam. Therefore, as the variations in fertility rates among Islamic nations indicate, current and future fertility trends among Muslim peoples are not influenced by Islam but rather by broader social, economic, and political factors.

KELLY, MARJORIE. *Islam: The Religious and Political Life of a World Community.* New York: Praeger, 1984.
MUNSON, HENRY, JR. *Islam and the Revolution in the Middle East.* New Haven: Yale University Press, 1988.
WEEKS, JOHN R. "The Demography of Islamic Nations." *Population Bulletin* 43, December 1988.

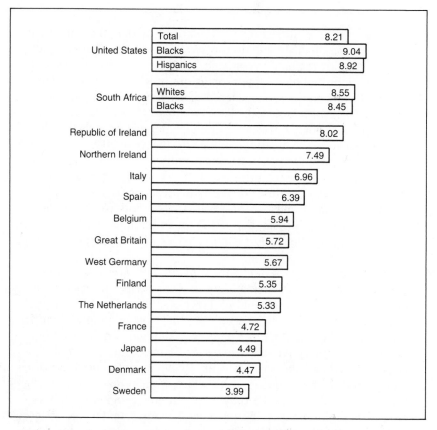

Figure 15-1. Importance of God in Life (1981) (average ratings on ten-point scale). (*Source:* Gallup Opinion Index, "Religion in America: 50 Years: 1935–1985," Report No. 236, 1985, p. 50.)

participation has been relatively constant, with about 40 percent of Americans indicating that they regularly attend religious services.

Secularization

Paradoxically, another feature of American religion has been its secular quality. **Secularization** refers to a decline in the authority of religious institutions, beliefs, values, and practices. Secularization is the process by which religious institutions and symbols cease to legitimate, support, and justify various aspects of society and culture.

Berger (1967) contends that secularization has occurred on three levels: societal, cultural, and individual. At the societal level, religious institutions no longer exercise substantial control or influence over the state

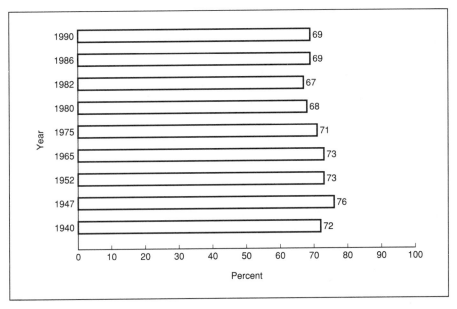

Figure 15–2.   Church and Synagogue Membership as a Percentage of the U.S. Population. (*Source: The Gallup Report.* "Religion in America," Report No. 259, April 1987, p. 35; George Gallup, Jr. and Frank Newport, "More Americans Now Believe in a Power Outside Themselves." *The Gallup Poll Monthly,* Report No. 297, June 1990, p. 37).

or other important aspects of society, such as the educational system. Or, to put it another way, secularization involves the separation of other institutions from organized religion and religious ideas. To illustrate, we can point to the degree to which functions such as education and social welfare, once the responsibility of religious institutions, have become the responsibility of the government. In this sense, religion has been relegated to a subordinate position in which its influence over the larger society has diminished.

Patterns of secularization have also influenced various aspects of cultural life. As secularization proceeds, the arts, literature, and philosophy less frequently draw on religious sources for inspiration.

Finally, secularization also has a subjective, psychological aspect, involving the secularization of consciousness. "Put simply, this means that the modern West has produced an increasing number of individuals who look upon the world and their own lives without the benefit of religious interpretations" (Berger, 1967, p. 107). In a presecular era, religious ideas were accepted as fundamental truths and were difficult, if not impossible, to change. Today many people are no longer sure of traditional religion because its authority has been undermined.

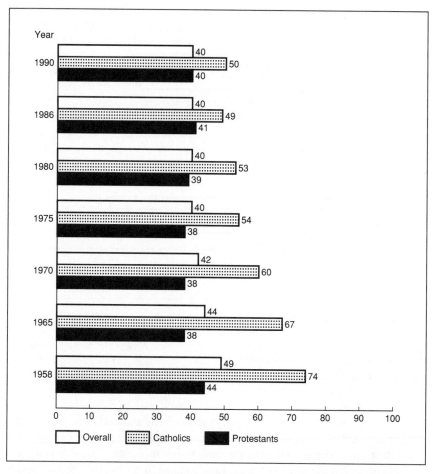

Figure 15–3. Percentage of Americans Attending Church during an Average Week. (*Source: The Gallup Report.* "Religion in America." Report No. 259, April 1987, p. 38; George Gallup, Jr. and Frank Newport, "More Americans Now Believe in a Power Outside Themselves." *The Gallup Poll Monthly,* Report No. 297, June 1990, p. 37).

Secularization is one aspect of the massive transformation of Western society that has included industrialization, urbanization, bureaucratization, and rationalization. Yet, despite the dramatic and pervasive impact of secular trends in the modern world, religion remains a vital force in most societies today.

However, today's society differs from earlier societies in which supernatural religion provided the dominant system of meaning, or meaning system. The first point of departure is that American society permits competition among a number of different religious systems. Second, in addition to competing among themselves, supernatural religions must also compete with a variety of other forms of religious consciousness, sacred symbols, and meaning systems. These new conceptions of the sacred are especially apparent in the religious consciousness and sacred symbols attached to nationalism (Crippen, 1988), and offered by other meaning systems, such as science, psychology, and Marxism, each of which provides alternative ways of defining and interpreting the world.

The Marketing of Religion

The necessity of competing for followers requires that traditional organized religion be "marketed." To compete in a secular society, religious groups are forced to tone down their religious message and to adopt the characteristics of secular organizations in making their appeals. Therefore, modern supernatural religions, like other modern organizations, compete in the open market. In their drives to sell their product—their distinctive religious message—and to finance the organizations and enterprises they have created to market their messages, religious organizations often resort to "hucksterism." When religious organizations adopt nonreligious characteristics in order to survive, their character becomes increasingly secularized, often to the point where religious and nonreligious phenomena become indistinguishable.

These trends have become most apparent in the development of television evangelism, which has dramatically changed the manner in which millions of people in the United States experience religion. In 1989 about half (49 percent) of American adults reported occasionally watching religious programs—a percentage greater than those reporting that they had attended religious services during the past week; about one-fifth (21 percent) said that they had watched religious programs on television during the preceding week (Colesanto and DeStefano, 1990, p. 18). Televangelists such as Jim and Tammy Bakker, Jimmy Swaggart, Oral Roberts, Pat Robertson, Jerry Falwell, and Robert Schuller have become national celebrities. The personal indiscretions of some of them have been sensationalized, and the scandals that have rocked the huge financial empires they have created through television contributions have been closely scrutinized by the media, the Internal Revenue Service, the United States Congress, and the courts.

Today the "electronic church" has adopted the formats of the most successful commercial television shows and the most sophisticated marketing techniques to become a highly rationalized multibillion-dollar enterprise. As a consequence, televangelism has become one of the most important political and cultural forces in modern American life (Frankl, 1987). Hadden and Shupe (1988) contend that the near-monopoly of television evangelism by evangelical and fundamentalist Christians has enabled them to mobilize very effectively religious and political conservatives into a powerful social movement. Not only has American religion been reshaped by television but televangelists have had a substantial impact on the conservative movement of the 1980s in American culture in general and American politics in particular.

Civil Religion

In the United States, people have historically regarded religion as a "good thing" and important for national well-being. Because of a strong tradition of separation of church and state, a national church has never been established in the United States. The common thread uniting people of diverse denominational affiliations is what Herberg (1955) has characterized as its underlying "culture-religion"—a secular, nonsectarian religion that unifies Americans around a cluster of sacred beliefs, symbols, and rituals that are a prominent part of America's civil religion, a public religious expression that reflects America's secular religiosity and serves as a source of cultural and social cohesion (Bellah, 1967).

Civil religion refers to the set of symbols, beliefs, values, and practices about the ultimate meaning of life in a nation, including patriotic and political phenomena not typically associated with religion. Civil religion is an important part of almost all political events. God is mentioned in the pledge of allegiance to the flag; the motto "In God We Trust" is engraved on the nation's currency. Political events of all kinds, from political party conventions to sessions of Congress, begin with invocations, frequently by members of the clergy. The existence and blessings of God have been explicitly invoked in the inaugural address of nearly every president. George Bush's first act as President was a prayer offered during his 1989 inaugural address that demonstrates the religious legitimation of political authority by the nonsectarian God of civil religion:

> Heavenly Father, we bow our heads and thank You for Your love. Accept our thanks for the peace that yields this day and the shared faith that makes its continuance likely. Make us strong to do Your will, and write on our hearts these words: "Use power to help people." For we are given power not to advance our own purposes nor to make a great show in the world, nor a name. There is but one just use of power, and it is to serve people. Help us to remember, Lord. Amen (*New York Times*, 1989, p. B1).

Civil religion in the United States is more than belief in a nonsectarian God who is deemed to have a particular interest in the destiny of the United States. Its pantheon of saints includes George Washington and Thomas Jefferson, the revered "founding fathers." Among its martyred saints are Abraham Lincoln and John F. Kennedy. Like other religious systems, American civil religion has developed elaborate rituals, sacred symbols, and a sacred literature. The Declaration of Independence and the Constitution are the religion's sacred scriptures. Its holy days include the Fourth of July, Memorial Day, Veterans Day, and, especially, Thanksgiving, each of which involves ritual celebrations that invoke the name and support of God for the nation. During its religious ceremonies sacred hymns such as the "Star-Spangled Banner," "America the Beautiful," and "God Bless America" are played and sung. Finally, among the religion's sacred symbols are the U.S. flag and monuments such as the Statue of Liberty, the Lincoln Memorial, the Vietnam Veterans Memorial, and Arlington National Cemetery, each of which has acquired a sacred quality that is perceived to embody the nation's basic values.

The notion of civil religion has generated considerable research since Bellah's formulation in 1967 (Richey and Jones, 1974; Gehrig, 1979; Bellah and Hammond, 1980; Demerath and Williams, 1985). Empirical studies have demonstrated widespread belief among the American people in an American civil religion. However, some writers (including Bellah, who has been most closely identified with developing the concept) have questioned whether its assumption of a cultural consensus, or unifying ideology embraced by most Americans, can be accurately applied today to a society that has become increasingly "fragmented, polarized, and fractured" (Demerath and Williams, 1985).

Denominational Pluralism

A civil religion is nonsectarian; it transcends denominational differences. Its symbols are uniquely American. It can be embraced by persons of all faiths and by people who have no formal religious affiliation. Civil religion is therefore consistent with one of the most distinctive features of religion in the United States—its **denominational pluralism.** Religious diversity has long been a feature of American life, but it is more apparent today than ever before. Melton (1987) has identified more than 1,200 different religious organizations in the contemporary United States.

The pluralistic character of American religion was established during the colonial era, when marked denominational differences existed among the colonies. Puritans were concentrated in New England; the Dutch Reformed, in New York; Quakers and German Moravians, Mennonites, and Lutherans, in Pennsylvania; Scotch-Irish Presbyterians, along the western frontier; Swedish Lutherans, along the Delaware River; Roman Catholics, in Maryland; Anglicans, in Virginia; and French Huguenots, in South Carolina—to name only some of the colonial religious groups. Despite this diversity, in only four of the 13 colonies—Rhode Island, New Jersey, Delaware, and Pennsylvania—were there genuine religious liberty and toleration of religious dissent. Not until the 1830s was full religious liberty available in all the states (Hudson, 1973; Marty, 1985).

Religious diversity in the United States, which at its founding was overwhelmingly Protestant, became more pronounced during the nineteenth century. Rapid population growth, westward expansion, the dramatic growth of towns and cities, and massive European immigration provided the dynamic conditions in which diverse religious groups developed and flourished. Niebuhr (1929) has shown the important role that class, ethnic, and regional factors have played in creating and maintaining religious diversity in the United States.

Social Class, Ethnicity, and Religious Affiliation.   Claiming more than 94 million adult members, Protestant churches comprise the largest religious category in the United States today (Kosmin and Lachman, 1991). The two largest Protestant groups—Baptists and Methodists—increased their numbers dramatically during the nineteenth century, primarily because they were what Niebuhr termed "the churches of the disinherited." Neither emphasized ritual nor a highly intellectualized theology. They also did not require an ordained, educated clergy. Consequently, they appealed to the common people both on the Western frontier and in the towns and rural areas of the East. Another major source of growth among Protestant churches was immigration. Most immigrant groups brought distinctive religious traditions with them. For example, different strains of Lutheranism were imported by Scandinavians and by Germans, who were the largest immigrant groups in the nineteenth century.

However, the most striking impact of nineteenth-century immigration upon the structure of American religion was the growth of the Roman Catholic church, which drew adherents from a great variety of ethnic backgrounds, including Irish, German, Italian, Polish, Czech, French, and Hungarian. German and especially Irish Catholics were prominent in the development of U.S. Catholicism during the nineteenth century. By 1900 membership in the Catholic church exceeded 12 million, and an elaborate Catholic institutional system of churches, schools, hospitals, and charities had been established. The "new" immigration from southern and eastern Europe and the later influx of Spanish-speaking immigrants from Mexico, Puerto Rico, Cuba, and Latin America further swelled the ranks of Catholics during the late nineteenth and twentieth centuries. By 1990 more than 46 million U.S. adults claimed membership in the Roman Catholic church, making it the largest single religious denomination in the country and the "wealthiest, most stable branch of world Catholicism" (Kosmin and Lachman, 1991; Duff, 1971, p. 73).

The growth of Judaism in the United States was also primarily a product of nineteenth- and early twentieth-century immigration. By 1880 there were about 250,000 Jews here, most of them German Jews who emigrated in the mid-nineteenth century. The predominant influence on contemporary Judaism, however, was the wave of more than 2 million

Eastern European Jews who entered the country between 1880 and 1924. Today more than 3 million adults in the United States identify themselves religiously as Jews (Kosmin and Lachman, 1991).

Another major source of America's religious pluralism has been the creation of new religious groups. Religious movements have frequently emerged during periods of intense religious enthusiasm. This was especially true during the Second Great Awakening, which took place in the first three decades of the nineteenth century. During this period of religious ferment several new religious movements appeared, emphasizing utopian ideals of community and religious brotherhood. Many utopian communes, such as the Oneida Community, were relatively short-lived. Other religious innovations, such as Christian Science, the Millerites (later known as Seventh-Day Adventists), the Campbellites (which later included both the Disciples of Christ and the Church of Christ), survived. Most dramatic and vigorous of the movements that endured from that period is the Church of Jesus Christ of Latter-Day Saints (the Mormons), which grew from an impoverished and persecuted cult in the 1840s into one of the most distinctive and firmly established religious groups in the United States today. More than 2.5 million American adults claim membership as Mormons, who have the distinction of having their religious doctrines and ideals provide the basis for a unique cultural region in Utah and in many communities in surrounding states (Kosmin and Lachman, 1991; Shepherd and Shepherd, 1984).

Recent Trends in Religion in the United States

During the 1950s several sociologists argued that the United States was undergoing a religious revival, a "surge of piety." Church attendance and membership reached all-time highs, and public professions of religious faith became fashionable. The religiosity of the 1950s ended dramatically during the 1960s, when church attendance, particularly among Roman Catholics and the young, dropped sharply. Public opinion polls indicated a substantial decrease in the importance that Americans attributed to religion. During the 1960s, the authority of many traditional institutions, including the government, the family, schools, and religion, was challenged. Churches became deeply divided over political and social controversies, particularly over the civil rights of minorities and the Vietnam War. The counterculture that challenged the prevailing cultural values of the Protestant work ethic, materialism, and conventional sexual mores also threatened traditional religion. These issues produced a crisis in American religion that led not only to tension and division within and a defection from established religious organizations but also to spiritual experimentation and to the creation of new religious movements (Pritchard, 1976; Roof and McKinney, 1987; Wuthnow, 1988b).

Sociology in the News

Religious Ethics and Sexuality in Tension

Religion has never existed in a social vacuum, but its form and content are shaped by the broader society. Organized religion has not escaped the impact of the sexual revolution that liberalized sexual behavior throughout U.S. society. Although numerous social issues (e.g., race relations, women's rights, abortion) have recently been the subject of heated debates within religious bodies, none has been so divisive or has elicited greater turmoil than the issue of sexual morality. Christian and Jewish teachings have traditionally limited sexual relations to heterosexual relations within marriage and have excluded homosexuals from the clergy. However, several prominent religious groups—the Presbyterian Church (U.S.A.), the United Methodist Church, the Episcopal Church, the Evangelical Lutheran Church in America, and Reform Judaism have recently begun to explore the implications of their restriction of sexuality to relations between married heterosexual partners.

Among Protestant denominations, the Presbyterian Church (U.S.A.) has produced the most ambitious and comprehensive of several denominational efforts to consider changes in their traditional stance on sexuality. The furor that greeted the 1991 publication of a church task force report on human sexuality mirrors the controversy that the issue of human sexuality has aroused, even among more liberal religious bodies. Public opinion polls showed overwhelming opposition among Presbyterians to changes in church policy barring homosexuals from the ministry and declaring homosexual relationships sinful. However, the task force responsible for preparing the report heard extensive and often agonizing testimony from people—gays and lesbians, the aged, young unmarried people living together, the physically handicapped, women trapped in destructive marriages—who had been alienated from the church by its restriction of sexuality to heterosexual marital relationships. For example, 40 percent of adult Presbyterians are single, yet adherence to the church's teaching would prevent them from experiencing sexual intimacy.

The explosive report sharply criticized the church's traditional notions of sexuality as grounded on a patriarchal model that legitimates traditional gender roles and, especially, male gender privileges. As an alternative to the single sexual outlet currently sanctioned for Presbyterians, the report called for "offering a diversity of responsible sexualities in the church, including the lives of gay men and lesbians, as well as new patterns among non-traditional families." Rather than fearing sex, the report views it as a divine gift that can enhance the quality of life by bringing people into "loving, caring, mutual relations with others; sexual intimacy should be celebrated, not denied." The church's primary concern, therefore, "should not be focused in a limited way on rules about who sleeps with whom" or whether sexual activity is premarital, marital, or postmarital, but rather "whether the relation is responsible, the dynamics genuinely mutual, and the loving full of joyful caring. . . . What matters morally and ethically is how we live our lives as faithful people, regardless of our sexual orientation."

Criticism of these proposed changes in the Presbyterian Church's traditional stance toward sexuality was vehement and led ultimately to rejection of the report. However, the efforts to consider these issues among numerous religious groups indicates that religion is intimately linked with the political and social controversies of the larger society in which they are embedded.

CAREY, JOHN J. "Body and Soul: Presbyterians on Sexuality." *The Christian Century* May 8, 1991, pp. 516–520.

"Churches in Change." *USA Today*. June 4, 1991, p. 11A.

The General Assembly Special Committee on Human Sexuality, Presbyterian Church (U.S.A.). "Keeping Body and Soul Together: Sexuality, Spirituality, and Social Justice." Reports to the 203rd General Assembly (1991). Baltimore, MD, 1991.

GITTINGS, JIM. "A Bonfire in Baltimore." *Christianity and Crisis*, May 27, 1991, pp. 172–177.

STEINFELS, PETER. "What God Really Thinks about Who Sleeps with Whom." *New York Times*, June 2, 1991, p. E4.

WATTS, GARY L. "An Empty Sexual Ethic." *The Christian Century*, May 8, 1991, pp. 520–521.

Neither the political movements nor the counterculture itself extended much beyond the 1970s, but the impact of that period on American religion today has been substantial. Religion in the United States has undergone several critical changes during the 1970s and 1980s.

Decline of Mainstream Protestantism

The Protestant majority—the "religious establishment"—has declined substantially. Protestants comprised 69 percent of the American population in 1947 but only 59 percent in 1986 (see table 15–2). This decline has occurred primarily among mainstream Protestant denominations (Episcopal, United Methodist, Evangelical Lutheran, United Presbyterian, United Church of Christ). Since 1965 mainstream Protestant churches have stopped growing or have experienced substantial membership losses, and have experienced declines in participation and institutional support, resulting mostly from a scarcity of new members (Roof and McKinney, 1987).

Not all Protestant churches were declining, however. During the 1970s and 1980s a new wave of religiosity has been especially pronounced among evangelical and conservative Protestant groups, such as the Assemblies of God, the Church of Christ, Pentecostal and Holiness groups, the Mormons, Seventh-Day Adventists, Jehovah's Witnesses, and South-

Table 15–2.   Religious Preference in the United States, 1947–1986 (by percent)

Religion	1947	1957	1967	1977–1978	1986
Protestant	69	66	67	60	59
Baptist	*	*	21	19	20
Methodist	*	*	14	11	9
Lutheran	*	*	7	6	5
Presbyterian	*	*	6	4	2
Episcopalian	*	*	3	2	2
Roman Catholic	20	26	25	29	27
Jewish	5	3	3	2	2
All others	1	1	3	1	4
No religious preference	6	3	2	8	8

Source: The Gallup Report, 1987.
* Data not available

ern Baptists (Kelly, 1972; Hoge and Roozen, 1979; Roof and McKinney, 1987). Similarly, Roman Catholicism has experienced a conservative movement (Dinges, 1988), and Orthodox Judaism has grown more rapidly than either of Judaism's two more liberal branches—Reform and Conservative. Not only has membership in such conservative religious bodies been rapidly increasing but these groups have become particularly adept at using the electronic media—television, in particular—to spread their doctrines. The most substantial impact of religious conservatism has been seen on American political life, where the "New Christian Right" has had a powerful influence on the debates over such issues as school prayer, abortion, gay rights, women's rights, and pornography (Liebman and Wuthnow, 1983; Hadden and Shupe, 1988).

Growth of the Roman Catholic Church

The Roman Catholic church has grown in numbers and influence, increasing from 20 percent of the U.S. population in 1947 to 27 percent in 1986, making it the largest single religious denomination in the United States. Moreover, Catholics have increasingly become part of the social, cultural, political, and religious mainstream of American life. Today, more affluent and better educated than ever before in American history, they have become virtually indistinguishable from other Americans in their social and cultural characteristics (Berger, 1987).

Proliferation of New Faiths

A wide array of new religious bodies, both Christian and non-Christian, has emerged. For the first time in American history, groups drawn from

Eastern religions (especially Islam, Buddhism, and Hinduism) have attracted substantial numbers of devotees. As a consequence of increased spiritual experimentation with "foreign" religious faiths and changing patterns of immigration to the United States since 1968, the number of adherents of Eastern religions has increased. Some of these, such as the International Society of Krishna Consciousness (Hare Krishnas), the Divine Light Mission (followers of the Guru Maharaji), or the Rajneesh movement (followers of the Bhagwan Shree Rajneesh), were highly visible and gained national notoriety. By 1986, 4 percent of the population (more than 9 million) indicated identification with a faith outside of the three major religious categories of Protestantism, Catholicism, and Judaism. Observers have noted especially the rapid growth of Islam and have estimated that the number of Muslims in the United States was as high as 6 million by 1989 (Melton, 1987, p. 147; Goldman, 1989, p. 1). However, in 1990 the largest and most comprehensive survey of religious affiliation yet undertaken placed the number at 1.4 million (Kosmin and Lachman, 1991), which still demonstrated that the Islamic population in the United States was rapidly increasing.

Included among the new Christian groups are those with a fundamentalist Christian basis: the Children of God, Marantha Christian Ministries, the Way International, the Calvary Chapel Movement, and a host of local groups with no national relationship. Moreover, a number of religious innovations have had a substantial appeal. Like some religious groups drawn from Eastern religious traditions, some of these have proved to be widely publicized and highly controversial: the Church of Scientology, which combines elements of popular psychology, folk wisdom, and spiritualism; and the Unification Church, founded by Reverend Sun Myung Moon, who claims to be the prophet of a religion that fulfills traditional Christianity.

Rise of Privatized Religion

Religion has increasingly become a private, individualistic, and personal affair. Many people today fashion their own individual religious belief systems without communal support and without participation in traditional institutionalized religious bodies. Many of those embracing a private faith are apt to be nonaffiliates, people indicating no religious preference, whose number rose from 2 percent of the U.S. population in 1967 to 8 percent in 1986 (see table 15–2). The primary goal of privatized religion is self-fulfillment, and the focus of such religious forms is therefore on the techniques—mystical, magical, psychotherapeutic, and technological—whereby fulfillment can be achieved. This focus has been the common denominator of what has been termed the "New Age" movement, which includes a great number of consciousness-raising groups (such as est, Transcendental Meditation, Silva Mind Control, biofeed-back, Gestalt Awareness Training, and Lifespring), designed to heighten an individual's physical, social-psychological, and spiritual awareness, and to enhance individual self-discipline and personal effectiveness. Although the publicity they have received has tended to exaggerate their numbers (Kosmin and Lachman, 1991), what these diverse New Age groups have in common is their "belief in a cosmic destiny for [humankind], which in-dividuals pursue mainly through mystical examination of the self; and in a 'new age' of existence that will be peopled by superior beings who have undergone a process of inner 'transformation' " (Bordewich, 1988, p. 38).

Return of the Baby Boomers

Members of the "baby boom" generation, who were born between 1946 and 1964, were those most likely to have rejected established religion in the 1960s and 1970s. However, as baby boomers have approached mid-life, many have returned to organized religion and are especially likely to view religious institutions as important for "rites of passage"—baptisms, marriages, and funerals. The religious participation of baby boomers who had previously dropped out has been especially affected by their location in the life cycle; in the 1980s baby boomers were likely to be involved in family formation and parenting. Those who had dropped out of organized religion earlier in their lives were far more likely to have renewed their religious participation if they had children (Roof, 1990; Roozen, Mc-Kinney, and Thompson, 1990).

Changing Role of Women in Religion

One of the major issues that grew out of the "equality revolution" of the 1960s and has since become more pronounced in American religion con-cerns the role of women. Although women have traditionally been more active participants than men and have played very crucial support roles in most religious organizations in the United States, they have until recently been virtually excluded from formal positions of authority and leadership. Today women cannot be ordained in the Roman Catholic church, the Eastern Orthodox church, many conservative Protestant denominations, and Orthodox Jewish congregations. However, reflecting the impact of the feminist movement, since the 1970s significant challenges have been brought to the traditional definitions of male and female roles within sev-eral religious organizations. Although overall seminary enrollments in re-cent years have been declining, between 1972 and 1989 female enrollments in Protestant seminaries increased by nearly 400 percent; in 1972 only one-tenth (10 percent) of the country's Protestant seminary stu-dents were women, but by 1989 that figure stood at more than one-fourth

Table 15–3.   Ten Protestant Denominations with Largest Number of Women
Clergy, 1986

Denomination	Number of Women Clergy	Women Clergy as Percentage of Total
Assemblies of God	3718	13.9
Salvation Army	3220	62.0
United Methodist	1891	5.0
Presbyterian Church, USA	1519	7.8
United Church of Christ	1460	14.5
Episcopal	796	4.5
Christian Church (Disciples of Christ)	743	10.9
International Church of the Foursquare Gospel	666	19.1
Lutheran Church in America	484	5.6
American Baptist Church	429	5.6

Source: Constant H. Jacquet, Jr. *Women Ministers in 1986 and 1977: A Ten Year View.*
New York: National Council of Churches, 1988b.

(29 percent) (Jacquet, 1990, p. 282). Moreover, as table 15–3 indicates,
the number of female Protestant clergy nearly doubled between 1977 and
1986. Women clergy were most numerous in certain theologically conservative denominations (e.g., Assemblies of God, Salvation Army,
Foursquare Gospel Church) and in some theologically liberal denominations (e.g., United Methodist, Presbyterian Church, USA, United
Church of Christ, Disciples of Christ) (Jacquet, 1988b). The feminist impact was also reflected in movements within the Roman Catholic church
seeking to obtain the ordination of women and within Conservative Judaism to permit women to participate more fully in religious observances
and in policy-making bodies (Wuthnow, 1988b, p. 229).

The increasing presence of women in the clergy and in policy-making
positions—primarily in mainstream Protestant denominations—also
sparked controversies over other issues related to the status of women. Illustrative of these controversies has been the movement for "inclusive
language"—the effort to alter the terminology in which conceptions of
the sacred are communicated. Critics of traditional religious discourse argue that the very symbols and language that have been used to describe
God in Judaism and Christianity—King, Lord, Master, and Father—not
only reflect a tradition of male domination, power, and authority but also
limit and circumscribe conceptions of what is virtually impossible to describe in human terms. The movement for inclusive language seeks to
"minimize the male bias reflected in . . . language about human beings
and language about Christ and God," and reflects one of the major issues

in contemporary American religious life (National Council of Churches, 1983, p. 6).

Personal Religious Experience

Religious experiences vary widely in form and intensity. For many whose lives have been secularized, religious interpretations have little meaning. For many others, religion is a purely formal and social obligation that may involve activities such as attending religious services, but it has little other effect on their lives. However, nearly nine of ten (87 percent) people in the United States claim that religion is very important or fairly important in their lives; only 13 percent said that religion was not very important to them. Moreover, a substantial number claim to have had one or more dramatic and intensely personal religious experiences. In 1990 more than half (54 percent) claimed to have been aware of or influenced by a power greater than themselves, while 38 percent of adults who were questioned indicated that they had had a "born-again" Christian experience (Gallup and Newport, 1990).

On the basis of extensive research on the diversity of religious experience in American society, Glock and Stark (1965) have developed a typology of religious experience, which we examine in the order of the frequency with which each type of experience occurs. The four types of religious experience are *confirming, responsive, ecstatic,* and *revelational.*

Confirming Religious Experience

The most frequently reported form of religious experience in contemporary American society is a confirming experience, "a sudden feeling, knowing, or intuition that the beliefs one holds are true" (Glock and Stark, 1965, p. 43). The individual becomes aware of the existence or presence of the sacred. A confirming experience is not a spectacular, overwhelming, or particularly dramatic event. However, it has deep personal meaning and significance to the individual. The sudden intensification of feeling that occurs may take a general form in which the individual experiences a sense of reverence, awe, solemnity, or calmness. Or the individual may have a distinct awareness of the closeness of a divine being, such as may be elicited by the wonders of nature (Hay, 1979). During the mid-nineteenth century Henry David Thoreau described such an experience during his solitude at Walden Pond.

> Once, . . . in the midst of a gentle rain, . . . I was suddenly sensible of such sweet and beneficent society in nature, in the very patterning of the drops, and in every sight and sound around my house, and infinite and unaccountable friendliness all at once, like an atmosphere, sustaining me, as made the fancied advantages of human neighborhood insignificant. . . . Every little pine-needle

expanded and swelled with sympathy and befriended me. I was so distinctly made aware of the presence of something kindred to me, that I thought no place could ever be strange to me again. (Thoreau, 1854, p. 116)

Responsive Religious Experience

The confirming experience is passive; the individual merely feels aware of the presence of the divine. The responsive experience, on the other hand, is marked by reciprocity; the individual feels that the divine is responding to him or her as well. Rather than merely being made aware of the presence of the divine, individuals sense that the divine has taken special notice of them.

The responsive experience can take a variety of forms. It frequently involves an awareness of an external power controlling and guiding the individual. It can also produce a sense of peace, serenity, and joy, a feeling that the divine has chosen the individual (Hay, 1979). A responsive experience is frequently reported among those who pronounce themselves "born-again Christians." Responsive religious experiences frequently occur during periods of stress (Hay, 1979, p. 176), as when individuals perceive the divine to have helped them in a time of crisis, such as an illness, a miraculous escape or rescue from danger, or a positive turn in one's economic fortune.

Ecstatic Religious Experience

The ecstatic religious experience involves not only awareness of the presence and responsiveness of the divine but also a feeling of an intense and intimate emotional relationship with the sacred. So powerful is the intensity of the ecstatic experience that one of the most prominent features reported about them is the imagery of light or the physical sensation of being electrified. Probably the most famous conversion in Christian tradition was that of the Apostle Paul, whose experience is described in the New Testament: "Now as he journeyed he approached Damascus, and suddenly a light from heaven flashed about him. And he fell to the ground and heard a voice saying to him, 'Saul, Saul, why do you persecute me?' " (Acts 9:3–4).

In his analysis of religious experiences among British graduate students, Hay (1979), within the category of ecstatic religious experiences, has found extrasensory perceptions, out-of-body experiences (in which an individual's soul or mind is reported to have left the body and observed the body from outside), and visions. He reports the following visionary experience.

A week after I met _____ , we were sitting looking at each other's eyes in a bedroom and there began to be a beam passing between our eyes and also a third eye in the middle of our foreheads. This lasted for about two hours and we didn't say a word to each other. Towards the end of the two hours . . . [it] came and went in waves, and we began to know that we had known each other in a previous life. Because we had known each other, we *knew* each other (Hay, 1979, p. 171).

Revelational Religious Experience

The least common type of religious experience, but perhaps the one that receives the most publicity, is the revelational. While other types of religious experiences may involve a sense of the divine speaking, the distinctive characteristic of the revelational experience is that the individual receives "confidential information about the future, divine nature, or plan" (Glock and Stark, 1965, p. 55). Such relevations may be **orthodox**—that is, supportive of the existing religious and social order—or **heterodox**—that is, critical and potentially disruptive of the status quo.

An example of an orthodox revelation is the reported appearance or apparition of the Virgin Mary, a religious experience with a tradition in Christianity dating back to the Middle Ages (Zimdars-Swartz, 1991a). Between 1928 and 1973 more than 200 such encounters were reported to Roman Catholic authorities, and since then apparitions have been reported by devout Roman Catholics in Ireland, France, Yugoslavia, Italy, the Soviet Union, Rwanda, Egypt, Spain, and the United States (Zimdars-Swartz, 1988, 1989a, 1991a, 1991b). Reports of such experiences have frequently had a dramatic public impact. Some have been memorialized by the establishment of sacred shrines, such as that in Lourdes, France. Reports of appearances by the Virgin Mary have often drawn great crowds. In 1950 an estimated 100,000 people traveled to the Wisconsin farm of Mary Ann Van Hoof to witness messages that were transmitted through her from the Virgin Mary (Zimdars-Swartz, 1989b). In 1988 over 13,000 people from all over the United States gathered in Lubbock, Texas, after three people reported that they were receiving messages of peace and hope from Mary (Pratt, 1988, p. 1; Zimdars-Swartz, 1991a, pp. 17–18).

These experiences of encounters with the Virgin Mary are orthodox in the sense that they usually encourage people to become more devout in their adherence to established religious practices and authority. Heterodox revelations, on the other hand, are important sources of social change, for they provide visions of a new social order and a basis for rejecting and challenging established authority.

Many examples of revelational experiences have been recorded among the world's religions. The Islamic and Christian faiths, as well as many sects in both religions, originated with their founder's claims of having received divine revelation.

One of the most dramatic revelational experiences in American religious history was that of Joseph Smith, from whose experiences the Latter-Day Saints (Mormon) churches have developed. As an adolescent, Smith, who had been deeply troubled by the competing claims of truth offered by various denominations, had a striking revelational experience.

> After I had retired . . . I kneeled down and began to offer up the desires of my heart to God. I had scarcely done so, when immediately I was seized upon by some power which entirely overcame me, and had such an astonishing influence over me as to bind my tongue so that I could not speak. Thick darkness gathered around me, and it seemed to me for a time as if I were doomed to sudden destruction. . . . just at this moment of great alarm, I saw a pillar of light exactly over my head, above the brightness of the sun, which descended gradually until it fell upon me. . . . When the light rested upon me I saw two personages, whose brightness and glory defy all description, standing above me in the air. One of them spake unto me, calling me by name, and said—pointing to the other—THIS IS MY BELOVED SON, HEAR HIM. (*History of the Church of Latter-Day Saints*, 1902, pp. 5–6)

Revelational experiences have frequently provided the inspiration and source of authority for new social movements. Weber called the authority derived from such experience *charismatic*. As noted in chapter 4, *charisma* refers to qualities of an individual personality that are believed to be exceptional and sometimes of supernatural origin that give the individual authority over others.

Persons with charismatic qualities frequently become the leaders of **revitalization movements:** "deliberate, organized efforts by members of a society to create a more satisfying culture" (Wallace, 1966, p. 626). A revitalization movement provides a new belief system for interpreting and explaining the universe. Faith in a charismatic leader elicits a total commitment among movement followers, which accounts for the extremely well-disciplined nature of many such groups. Throughout the American experience many revitalization movements have developed into organized religions. Among the more successful and enduring are the Mormons, Christian Scientists, and the Black Muslims. More recently, sensational publicity has been directed toward such revitalization movements as the Unification Church, the Children of God, and the International Society for Krishna Consciousness (Hare Krishnas), among others.

Leaving Religion

Most of our discussion of religious experience has focused on processes whereby people affiliate or identify with a religious tradition. However, people may also become disillusioned with and reject or disaffiliate from religion. Therefore, it is necessary to consider the experience of leaving religion.

We noted above that a substantial minority (40 percent) of American adults reported attending religious services regularly. However, an almost equal proportion report being relatively uninvolved in religious activities. In 1978, 41 percent of adults sampled in a national survey were "unchurched," that is, they had not participated in a formal religious service during the previous six months (Princeton Religious Research Center, 1978). The vast majority of the unchurched are people who report a religious preference but who seldom attend religious services. Only a small proportion of people in the United States—about 7 percent—report no religious preference. Among these are people who never had a religious identity and those who once had a religious identity but rejected it later in life.

Religion is always a dynamic, changing phenomenon, and many people change their religious identities during their lifetimes. Many people at some point leave the religion in which they were reared (Bromley, 1988). Many of these will switch to another religious affiliation (Roof and Hadaway, 1979; Nelson and Bromley, 1988).

Hadaway and Roof (1988) focused on **apostates**—those who earlier in their lives had had a religious identity but who later came to reject any religious identity. They found that apostates are most likely to be young, single, male, highly educated, politically independent, geographically mobile, more involved socially with friends than with family, urban and suburban residents, and much more accepting of the "new morality" on issues such as drug use and sexual behavior. The peak period of rejection of religion in the post-World War II period occurred during the 1960s and early 1970s, when many young Americans questioned traditional institutions. However, since the early 1970s religious apostasy appears to have declined (Hadaway and Roof, 1988).

The Institutionalization of Religious Experience

The origins of many religious organizations, beliefs, and forms of worship can be located in the religious experiences of a religion's founder, frequently a charismatic leader claiming to speak for the divine. Whenever a new religious movement is founded and dominated by a charismatic leader, the death of that leader threatens the religion's continued existence. Members must adapt to new circumstances if they want to continue the practice of their religion. If charismatic leaders want to ensure the success of the group beyond their lifetimes, some means for governing the religious organization must be created. The authority of the charismatic leader may be transferred to relatives, to trusted colleagues, or to impersonal positions in the organization itself.

The crisis of continuity for a religious organization on the death of a charismatic leader is resolved by the institutionalization of religious experience. Many religious rituals are methods developed to continue the religious experiences of a movement's earliest participants. Thus, a relatively spontaneous and subjective experience becomes institutionalized, patterned, and routine. Institutionalized behaviors and structures then become the ways of eliciting, creating, or maintaining religious experience. O'Dea and Aviad (1983) have identified three aspects of the process of institutionalization in a religious movement: cultic activity or religious behavior that involves patterns of worship or ritual; beliefs, which are a religious movement's pattern of ideas; and organization, that is, the social organization, or social structure, of a religious group.

Religious Behaviors

Rituals are complex, communally shared, ceremonial forms of religious behavior. They symbolically express spontaneous religious values and experiences that have become standardized and institutionalized over time. Rituals occur during worship services and around events, such as christenings, weddings, and funerals, that mark important stages in the life cycle. In Christianity, for instance, the Mass or Liturgy "became both the representation of the original experience and the way in which the worshippers expressed their relationship to the sacred" (O'Dea and Aviad, 1983, p. 42). Similarly, a Jewish seder at Passover is characterized by a prescribed series of prayers, the recitation of sacred literature, a huge feast, and a congregational gathering that both commemorates the historic experiences of the Jewish people and unites them in a community. As time passes, proper performance of a ritual becomes increasingly important, and any effort to change it is upsetting.

Religiosity can be expressed in a variety of rituals. It would be difficult to describe all religious behaviors because many that are not usually defined as religious actually are manifestations of religious sentiments. For example, for the strongly patriotic who perceive their particular brand of nationalism as deriving from God, standing at attention for the raising of the flag or the playing of the national anthem is a religious behavior. On the other hand, some behaviors commonly defined as religious (for example, attending church) may involve nonreligious motivations, such as making social contacts, impressing business associates, or finding a suitable marriage mate for one's child.

Prayer, a form of addressing the sacred, is one of the most widespread forms of religious behavior and is found in virtually all religions. A prayer can take the form of asking the sacred for a favor or giving thanks to the sacred force for a past blessing. It can also serve as an affirmation of faith in the religious system itself.

Another basic religious behavior involves some form of physical exercise. Guttman (1978, p. 16) has pointed out that many societies have "incorporated running, jumping, throwing, wrestling, and even ball playing in their religious rituals and ceremonies." The ancient Olympic games, conducted in honor of the god Zeus, were sacred festivals, an integral part of ancient Greek life. In Iran's national religion, Shiism, a branch of Islam, religious activities among the most devout adherents involve an exhausting and arduous athletic ritual designed to purify the minds of participants ("The Sport of Religion," 1972). Sufism, a mystical Islamic tradition that has recently gained increasing numbers of American adherents, uses physical exercises, including breath control, body movement, and dance, to gain control over the senses and achieve a mystical experience (Awn, 1987, p. 119). Similarly, sumo wrestling, Japan's most popular spectator sport, has its roots in Shinto, the national religion. Early sumo contests were part of Shinto religious festivals (Halloran, 1974, p. 10:1). For the Shakers, a communal religious group that flourished in the eighteenth-century and nineteenth-century United States, physical exercise in the form of an elaborate communal dance was an integral part of their religious ritual (Nordoff, 1875/1971).

Drugs may be used as a means of producing physiological changes in the individual that could induce a spiritual state. Although many religious leaders deny the religious authenticity of a drug-induced experience, drugs have been used for sacramental purposes in many societies. The ancient Greeks, for example, chewed the intoxicating leaves of ivy to induce an ecstatic state. In the Native American Church, a religion that has become popular among North American Indians since the turn of the twentieth century, an elaborate ritual surrounding the use of peyote has developed. A participant in the peyote rites recalled:

> For three days and for three nights I had been eating the peyote and not slept at all. Now I [suddenly] realized that throughout all the years that I had lived, I had never once known a truly holy thing. Now, for the first time, I knew it. (Radin, 1926, p. 182)

Drugs or physical exercise are not the only methods by which religious experiences can be elicited. Other methods of physiological inducement of religious feeling include the mortification of the flesh by pain, sleeplessness, or going without food or water. All these methods were employed among the Plains Indians, for whom fasting and self-torture were a necessary prelude to a young male's acquiring a vision or communication with a "guardian spirit," which served as a ritual transition from adolescence to maturity (Benedict, 1922; Powers, 1987).

Religious behavior often involves notions of mana and taboo. **Mana** refers to the power inherent in sacred objects. To a believer, touching sacred objects will cause the powerful qualities of those objects to be transmitted to them or will bring them good fortune. Touching the Western Wall in Jerusalem is a sacred rite for Jews. Many Christians claim miraculous cures by visiting sacred shrines, such as the one in Lourdes, France. On a more mundane level, mana is exemplified in the belief that luck follows from carrying a rabbit's foot or kissing the Blarney Stone.

The converse of the notion of mana is a **taboo,** a religious proscription against having physical contact with certain objects in order to prevent the power embodied by these objects from affecting a person. The Polynesians, for example,

> . . . maintained an elaborate set of taboos on contacts of one kind or another between status groups, particularly between royalty and commoners. The chief's body could not be touched by the body of a commoner; even if the contact were accidental, death would be the result for the commoner. The commoner could not look down upon his chief from a higher elevation (looking is, in a sense, like touching), and so the chief had to sit upon a raised platform and be carried on a raised litter above the shoulders of his subjects. (Wallace, 1966, pp. 61–62)

Taboos are often related to food, drink, or other substances that may be taken into the body. Among Orthodox Jews and among Muslims a wide variety of foods are taboo. Similarly, several contemporary religious sects, such as the Hare Krishnas, forbid the use of drugs. Mormons proscribe the use of tobacco, alcoholic beverages, and drinks containing caffeine, such as coffee and tea.

Another type of religious behavior involves the creation and use of various forms of religious symbols or icons. These symbols represent either sacred entities, or the values, relationships, processes, or events associated with the sacred. Examples of religious symbols include the Christian cross or fish, the Jewish Star of David or menorah, and (in civil religion) the flag of the United States.

Religious Belief Systems

Religious belief systems include both myth and theology. A **myth** is a sacred story, a parable, or a graphic way of communicating a basic idea concerning the activities and moral prescriptions of divine beings. It provides a concrete and emotionally charged explanation of the historically significant events in a religious system. To a sociologist, the importance of a myth is not its truth or accuracy, but its ability to bind believers into a common community and to reinforce belief in a society's basic values and social institutions. The Christmas stories of the shepherds, the angels, and the three kings are part of Christian mythology. Their historical accuracy or inaccuracy is irrelevant; their importance lies in uniting Christians into a sacred community for the celebration of Christmas.

Of particular importance are "origin" or "creation" myths, found in many different societies. Creation myths describe the origins of the universe and humans' place in it. They usually include descriptions of the origins of societal norms and values, family organization, law, and government. They are kept alive by periodic recitation. Although such myths persist in contemporary society, recitation today most often takes the form of reading or repeating aloud the basic truths as they are recorded in sacred documents, such as the Old and New Testaments in the Christian tradition.

The belief system of a new religion is born in the experience or inspiration of the religion's founders. The rational and logical development and extension of these ideas is the task of theology. **Theology** applies the process of rationalization to a religious belief system. A theology usually develops when a priestly class is differentiated from lay members of a religion. The more clear the distinctions between clergy and laity become, the more specialized the clergy's functions become, and the more likely it will be that a system of religious ideas, a theology, will become elaborated and rationalized.

Religious Organizations

The process of institutionalization is clearly apparent in the organization or structure of religious groups. An important distinction in religious organization appears in the two ideal types that the German sociologist Ernest Troeltsch (1931) called *sect* and *church*. A further distinction is made between these two forms of religious organization and cults.

Sect.   A **sect** is a small, voluntary group of members who join the group of their own conscious choice. A sect is the type of organization that characterizes a religion in the first stage of a revitalization movement. Primary emphasis in a sect is placed on a personal religious experience, and its leadership is usually composed of laypeople with no specialized training. The primary source of guidance for the sect's members is the sacred scriptures or personal inspiration. Rather than accepting the existing society, sect members tend to reject or feel alienated from it. Consequently, membership is often drawn from the lower classes—the "disinherited," who have no vested interests in maintaining the status quo.

Sect members withdraw into their own community, which develops its own rigorous standards of perfection (such as a conversion experience, renunciation of all worldly possessions, or renunciation of "vices," such as smoking, drinking, or gambling). Sects are exclusive religious organizations; they do not admit people who do not conform to their rigorous norms. Membership in a sect is total; the group's code of ethics is uncompromising and absolute, demanding full conformity. This characteristic is reflected in the group's limited interaction with outsiders and its refusal to participate in many societal activities (such as military service, saluting the flag, or medical treatment). Frequently, sects set themselves apart by such things as peculiar dress or dietary restrictions. Sect members may live in territorial isolation from the world, as the Amish do, or within the general society but with limited social interaction with nonmembers, as Hasidic Jews do. (See chapter 3.)

Church.   Distinct from a sect, a **church** is a large, socially acceptable, institutionalized religious group into which one usually is born, rather than converted. No special requirements are prescribed for membership; some members join only for secular or social reasons. While the sect is exclusive, a church is inclusive and often national in scope. It tries to extend its spiritual influence to as many people as possible. A church is characterized by a bureaucratic structure made up of a professional clergy within an established hierarchy. Ritual and belief systems tend to be elaborate and highly prescribed. Because most members are born into a church and do not actively choose membership, a strong emphasis is placed upon education as a means of perpetuating the faith.

One further distinction between a sect and a church is that a church accommodates itself to the secular world, while a sect resists such accommodation. Churches tend to be relatively larger and more socially inclusive than sects, but sects make stronger demands on and elicit greater commitment from their members. "Churches attempt to regulate or fulfill a few of the activities or needs of large numbers of people; sects attempt to regulate or fill many of the activities or needs of small numbers of people" (Wuthnow, 1988a, p. 495). That sects elicit greater commitments from their members is reflected by the differences in levels of financial contributions among American Protestant denominations. The nine Protestant denominations with over a million members average $348 per capita in annual contributions. However, as table 15–4, indicates, the Protestant groups with the highest per capita giving tend to be relatively small in membership. Of the nine groups with the highest per capita contributions, six had memberships of less than 100,000 and only one—the Seventh-Day Adventists—had a membership exceeding a quarter million (Jacquet, 1990, p. 266). Similarly, a national survey found that the level of religious commitment, as measured by frequency of attendance at religious services, was directly related to contributions to and volunteer activities for *both* religion and other charities; those who were highly involved in religious activities contributed and volunteered much more substantially than those who were only minimally involved or uninvolved. The authors conclude that "generosity with money and time is not so much determined by income as by level of religious commitment" (Hodgkinson, Weitzman, and Kirsch, 1990, p. 109).

Because their appeal is oriented primarily to the middle and upper classes, churches are frequently alien to the lower classes in decorum and

Table 15–4. Differences in Annual Per Capita Contributions among American Protestant Churches: Denominations with a Million or More Members and the Denominations with the Highest Per Capita Contributions

	Membership	Per Capita Contributions
Largest Denominations		
Presbyterian Church (USA)	2,930,000	$559.00
Episcopal Church	2,455,000	493.00
Evangelical Lutheran Church	5,252,000	336.00
United Church of Christ	1,645,000	326.00
Christian (Disciples of Christ)	1,073,000	316.00
Southern Baptist Convention	14,813,000	297.00
Lutheran Church—Missouri Synod	2,605,000	296.00
United Methodist Church	9,055,000	284.00
American Baptist Church	1,550,000	224.00
Average	4,598,000	$348.00
Highest in Contributions		
Reformed Episcopal Church	6,247	1,289.00
The Missionary Church	26,332	1,184.00
Evangelical Mennonite	3,888	1,101.00
International Pentecostal Church of Christ	2,628	1,008.00
Evangelical Covenant Church	87,750	905.00
Presbyterian Church in America	208,394	890.00
Seventh-Day Adventists	687,200	836.00
Free Methodist Church of North America	73,647	798.00
Baptist General Conference	135,125	789.00
Average	136,804	$986.00

Source: Constant H. Jacquet, Jr., ed. *Yearbook of American and Canadian Churches,* 1990. Nashville, TN: Abingdon Press, 1990, p. 266.

social composition. Sects emerge from the dissatisfaction felt toward these established expressions of religiosity. However, the sectarian character of a religious group is almost always short-lived. It is either modified over time, or it ceases to exist.

The transition of an organization from sect to church illustrates the process of routinization or institutionalization, which is a common characteristic of religious movements. As Niebuhr has pointed out, "by its very nature the sectarian type of organization is valid only for one generation" (Niebuhr, 1929, p. 19). Numerous Christian denominations that began as sects appealing to the disinherited, such as Baptists, Methodists, and Quakers, gained social respectability and became churches. Although an individual may join a sect by choice, his or her children are born into the group and do not necessarily share the enthusiasm and fervor that prompted the parent's participation. To convince a new generation, the sect must modify entrance requirements, usually by making them less stringent, and it must emphasize the role of education. If a sect is successful and attracts increasing numbers, an organizational apparatus becomes necessary.

As the organization expands, it begins to develop a life of its own. Those who work within the religious organization develop the need to expand their own power bases, to advertise the good deeds of the organization, and to develop educational techniques to ensure the support of the succeeding generations. All of these needs lead to an ever-expanding bureaucratic structure. In addition, the organization develops an interest in its own survival that leads to the support of the status quo. If the group is prospering in its environment, it will resist efforts to change it. Religious routines tend to become less dynamic and spontaneous and more routine. All of these developments signal the loss of characteristics that initially marked the sect. Once the organization becomes institutionalized, it tends to become rigid and formal. Inevitably some people find that its prescribed formulas do not meet their religious needs. Sectarian groups that respond to this dissatisfaction are apt to develop. Thus a religious organization may be subject to the same kinds of disaffection, change, and revitalization that originally led to its own formation.

Cults.   The basic distinction between a church and a sect is that a church accepts the status quo while a sect rejects it. However, Stark and Bainbridge (1979) have argued that sects should be distinguished from cults, even though both stand in tension with their surrounding sociocultural environment. **Cults** are small, voluntary, and exclusive religious groups that have created new religious systems. These two types of religious organizations are distinguished primarily by their origins—the manner in which they begin.

Sects are the result of schisms; they break off from existing religious organizations. Founders of a sect do not seek to create a new religious body but to realize what they perceive as the "original" beliefs and practices of the organization from which they have split. They begin as internal factions of a religious body. They are religious conservatives, seeking to reestablish the "true faith," which they claim the established religious body has abandoned. For example, many Protestant denominations in the United States were organized not as efforts to establish new religious faiths but as attempts to realize more fully the essence of the Christian church.

Cults, on the other hand, are not schismatic; they are not splinter groups breaking away from an established religious tradition. With no previous organizational attachment to an existing religious body, they represent a new religious tradition altogether. Because they introduce new religious beliefs or practices that may be completely alien to an established religious tradition; founders of cults are religious radicals. Cults may take the form of either religious innovations, which are based on new revelations or insights, or importations, which involve acceptance of a tradition or faith well established in another society but new and different in the receiving society. Examples of innovative cults include the early Mormons and the Unification Church of the Reverend Sun Myung Moon, the founders of which both claimed to be introducing new doctrines that fulfilled traditional Christianity. Among recent imported cults are several groups drawn from Eastern religions, such as various Muslim and Buddhist sects.

Summary

Religion is one of the most pervasive and complex of all human activities. The sociology of religion is concerned with understanding the role that religion plays in society and the influence of social factors upon religious activity. Religion is what is socially defined as sacred, encompassing entities that evoke a sense of awe, mystery, respect, and honor. For many people the sacred involves supernatural entities. It can also include a variety of other phenomena, such as political ideologies or even scientific systems, that provide a system of ultimate meaning.

Religion has several social consequences, both positive and negative, depending upon one's individual perspective. By providing an explanation and interpretation of the universe, religion deals with the problems of meaning that are inherent in the precariousness of human existence. It serves as a source of strength, comfort, and consolation for the individual, a means of warding off uncertainty. It provides a sense of individual and group identity. Religion also often functions to legitimate the existing social order. By interpreting society as something other than a human creation that is difficult, if not impossible, to change, religion reinforces the status quo. However, religion also frequently performs a critical function by providing a basis from which to criticize and challenge society. Many revitalization movements, which are efforts to create a more satisfying society, have their origins in a religious impulse.

Religion in American society has been characterized by three basic features: pervasiveness, secularism, and denominational pluralism. From colonial times to the present, religion has been a prominent feature of American life. Yet, despite this pervasive attachment to religion, the authority of religious beliefs, values, and practices has declined. Religious diversity, or denominational pluralism, has characterized religion in

America. It is a result of social class, racial, and ethnic factors, and the spontaneous creation of new religious groups within American society.

Religion involves several different but related features: personal experiences, behaviors, beliefs, and organizations. Personal religious experience takes many forms. New religions or religious revitalization movements often are based on a charismatic leader's claim of having had a revelational experience. New religious movements can take the form of sects or cults. Sects are offshoots of existing religious organizations, while cults represent religious innovations or importations. Once new religious movements are founded, they attempt to institutionalize the religious experience of their founders. This involves the development of rituals, beliefs, and organizational structures. As a group's organizational structure becomes established, new movements, with different social bases, may emerge to start the process again. Thus, change in religious organizations is a dynamic and recurring process.

CRITICAL THINKING

1. Is religion a source of social stability or social change? Give examples to support each viewpoint.
2. Why are sociologists so interested in the role of religion in society? Use Max Weber's study on the Protestant ethic to show how religion and economics might be intertwined.
3. How can sociologists who believe in the scientific method study a subject that is associated with "faith" rather than "facts"?
4. What is religion? Why is it considered by sociologists to be a social phenomenon?
5. What aspects of religious behavior in the United States are relatively unchanging?
6. What is "liberation theology"? With which part of the world is it most commonly associated? How does the existence of liberation theology show that religion is a social phenomenon that affects other parts of society?
7. Describe the major social functions of religion and give examples to illustrate each function. Does religion provide social stability or promote social change?
8. What is secularization? How is secularization related to other major trends in American society such as industrialization, urbanization, bureaucratization, and rationalization?
9. In what ways is religion "marketed" in American society? How does this trend show religion to be social behavior related to other aspects of society? Is this a positive or negative trend?
10. Describe civil religion in the United States. Speculate as to the nature of civil religion in the "atheist" society of the Soviet Union.
11. What is privatized religion and why is it on the rise in the United States? In what ways does such religion circumvent the traditional functions ascribed to religious behavior?
12. Compare and contrast the various types of religious organizations mentioned in the chapter. What function might each serve in society?

16 Political Life

The political system of the United States was designed to give people a strong voice in determining what their government should do. Voting for political leaders is an important way for people to express their will. In contrast to many democracies, however, especially those in Western Europe, a comparatively small percentage of the population participates in the voting process. For example, in the 1988 presidential election only about half of those eligible to vote bothered to cast a ballot. The youngest eligible voters in the population are least likely to vote—those between 18 and 29 years of age. The paradox is that young people have the greatest stake in political elections. If elected leaders get the country into a war or undertake other military adventures, young people will most likely do the fighting and dying. Young people have the longest time to live, and political decisions made now (for example, increasing the national debt) are apt to have a great effect on them for many years.

Even among older age groups, from one-third to one-half of eligible voters in the United States do not vote in presidential and congressional elections. Although Americans give great lip-service to democracy, their voting behavior is very low compared to other democratic nations (Piven and Cloward, 1988). Americans think of their government as the most democratic in the world, but large numbers of them do not participate, even in the simple act of voting.

Power, the State, and Government

The central concern of the political institution, or polity, is power—the ability to control other people's behavior and carry out one's will despite resistance. Obviously there are some situations in which people comply more willingly to the imposition of power than others. As we saw in chapter 4 in our discussion of bureaucracy, the German sociologist Max Weber (1918/1946) distinguished between legitimate and illegitimate power. Legitimate power, or *authority,* is power exercised by leaders that is generally approved or accepted as appropriate by members of a group or society. Although they may strongly disagree with laws that their elected officials enact, most people in the United States accept the right of those officials to pass such laws and hence accept them as legitimate.

On the other hand, there are circumstances in which people do not recognize the power exerted over them as legitimate and do not comply willingly to its exercise; they comply only because they are forced to do so. **Coercion** is power based on the threat or use of force, and is therefore considered illegitimate by the people who are forced to act against their will.

The State and Government

The state is the dominant political institution in modern societies (Lehman, 1988). The **state** is the sole source of legitimate physical force (Weber, 1918/1946); it is the only institution that can impose taxes, declare war, and imprison law violators.

The enormous power of the state appears in the variety of functions it performs (Weber, 1921/1978, p. 905):

1. The enactment of law (legislative function).
2. The protection of personal safety and public order (police).
3. The protection of vested rights (administration of justice).
4. The cultivation of hygienic, educational, social-welfare, and other cultural interests (the various branches of administration).
5. The armed protection against outside attack (military administration).

Sociologists sometimes use the term **nation-state** when referring to a state that has power over people living in a distinct geographical area known as a nation. The nation-state developed in Europe only about 500 years ago, and it has emerged in most Asian and African societies during this century. However, the nation is not found in all societies. Some preindustrial societies in Africa and Asia exist without clearly defined state structures.

The principal organization of the state is the government. Governments can be organized in a number of different ways and can take different forms. Governments typically take one of three major forms: autocracy, totalitarianism, or democracy.

Autocracy. In an **autocracy,** ultimate power is held by a single person. An autocrat may gain the position through heredity (an absolute monarch) or by rule of force (a dictator). Among the most recognizable autocratic rulers in the world today are Muammar Qaddafi of Libya and Kim Il Sung of North Korea. Autocrats rely on their ability to control the military and police systems of their countries, and to maintain the unquestioning loyalty of large numbers of their subjects. Criticism of the government and the autocrat is usually prohibited. The government often censors the media and sometimes uses terror to stifle public dissent. However, an autocracy tends to separate the private and public lives of its subjects, allowing individuals some degree of freedom in private matters of family and religion.

Totalitarianism. **Totalitarianism** is a form of government involving state control and regulation of all major institutions in a society. The state is represented by a small ruling clique that relies on physical force and terror to maintain social order. A totalitarian government exerts total control over a nation and makes little distinction between public and private concerns. A totalitarian regime seeks to control family life as well as economic and political institutions. Friedrich and Brzezinski (1965) have suggested six elements of totalitarian rule:

1. *A single political party.* Totalitarian states are one-party governments led by dictators or by a ruling clique. The one political party is the only legal party in the state.

2. *Control of the economy.* Totalitarian states exercise control over virtually all portions of the economy. The state may set goals for economic production, establish prices and supplies for goods, and dissolve private ownership of either industry or farms.

3. *Control of media.* Totalitarian states control television, radio, newspapers, and magazines. They deny a public forum to dissenting opinions so that only the official party position is communicated to the people.

4. *Control of weapons.* Totalitarian states monopolize the use of weapons, denying the individual the right to own arms.

5. *Ideology*. Totalitarian states use an elaborate ideology to explain virtually every aspect of social life. Social goals and values are described in simple terms, and distortions are often made about the state's enemies.

6. *Terror*. Totalitarian states rely on terror to maintain social control. Secret police, torture, and punishment without trial are common in totalitarian states.

Nazi Germany is a major example of totalitarian rule in this century. Anti-Semitic ideology, concentration camps for Jews and others, and the terror of the Gestapo (Hitler's secret police) were key elements of Nazi Germany's totalitarian power. Many of these features have also characterized the Soviet Union and its client states in Eastern Europe.

Democracy. The word *democracy* is derived from the Greek roots *demos,* which means people, and *kratia,* which means rule. Literally, then, democracy means rule by the people.

In everyday conversation the political system of the United States is usually referred to as a *democracy*. A **democracy** is a form of government in which there are periodic opportunities for the people being governed to retain or replace governing officials. A country is democratic when a large part of the population is able to "influence major decisions by choosing among contenders for political office" (Lipset, 1963a, p. 28). By this criterion it appears that the United States is a democratic society. We do have periodic elections to select the president, senators, representatives, governors, mayors, and other elected officials. In choosing among aspirants to political office, voters are presumably able thereby to influence the programs and policies of the government.

Three Views of the Political System of the United States

Considerable controversy exists among sociologists concerning the extent to which the U.S. political system is actually democratic. There are three different views of the U.S. political system: pluralist, neo-Marxian, and elitist. Of these three views, only the pluralist is consistent with characteristics of a democratic system. The neo-Marxian perspective emphasizes how power is held by those who control the economic system. The elitist view also contends that power is held by a relatively small group, but that group is not limited to capitalists controlling the economic system.

The Pluralist View

Pluralism describes a society that is made up of a number of competing interest groups (Rose, 1967). These competing groups serve to disperse power in a pluralistic society (Wasburn, 1982, p. 299). Such groups may represent the interests of business, labor, education, medicine, sports, or others. Each group has power within its own realm, and exerts power and influence over the federal government. Although the government is not a pawn in the hands of various interest groups, it is seen as directed and influenced by each of these powerful interests. Which interest group, or coalition of interest groups, wins out on a particular issue depends upon which one is most powerful at a given time in a particular sphere. Since each group can exert greater power on some issues than on others, no single interest group ever fully realizes its goals and dominates other groups. In a pluralistic society the political process is not run by a single powerful elite but is characterized by shifting patterns of interest-group influence. In fact, in the pluralist view, the balance of power among interest groups makes the United States a democratic society (Dahl, 1967).

An ideal pluralistic system operates under four basic conditions (Gamson, 1975). First, everyone must accept the norms and values of constitutional democracy. Second, there must be a set of groups whose interests overlap so that individuals are linked to a variety of groups in which they encounter people with different orientations. This prevents people from developing a single image of what should be done in society. Thus, a given individual is likely to be a member of a wide array of very different groups, including family, community, work, religion, ethnic, and social class. Third, in a pluralistic political system, access to the political arena should be open so that any group has the opportunity to receive a fair hearing for its point of view. Fourth, a balance of power must exist among competing groups so that no one group can dominate on all issues and so that coalitions among groups can shift, depending on the issue.

A Theory of Power Based on a Pluralist View. The sociologist David Riesman (1961) has advanced a pluralist view of power based on the notion of veto groups. A **veto group** is a special interest group that attempts to protect itself by blocking the actions of other groups. Riesman suggests that the U.S. has two levels of power—an upper level of competing veto groups, and a lower level of the unorganized public. Veto groups compete for dominance on particular issues and they seek public support in their efforts. An example of veto group competition is the fight over handgun regulation between the National Rifle Association (opposed) and Handgun Control, Inc. (in favor). In Riesman's view, power is diversified among the plurality of veto groups, and no single group dominates political decision making. The emergence of veto groups has been an important political development. Indeed, Riesman suggests that the "only leaders of national scope left in the United States today are those who can placate the veto groups" (Riesman, 1961, p. 213).

Political Action Committees.   In recent years political action commit-tees, usually simply called PACs, have emerged as influential veto groups (Stern, 1988; Sabato, 1985). PACs are political organizations that operate independently of political parties, channeling money from special interest groups into the election campaigns of political candidates. The special in-terest groups are sometimes representatives of some part of the political spectrum, such as conservatives or liberals, but more often they represent some special economic or demographic group. Thus, for example, PACs sponsored by insurance companies spent almost a million dollars on the 1990 congressional elections (Rowe, Jr., 1991). The number of PACs grew from 113 in 1972 to 4211 in 1987. Between 1972 and 1986 total PAC gifts to congressional candidates grew from $12.5 million to $132.2 million (Stern, 1988, p. 24). PAC contributions have become an important means of funding political campaigns. Although individual contributions to fed-eral candidates are limited to $25,000 in a given election, the total amount that a PAC can contribute has no legal limit. For example, in 1985–1986 NCPAC (National Conservative PAC) spent over $9 million on political activities (E. Zuckerman, 1988).

PACs vary greatly in size, strength, and political ideology. The Peanut Butter and Nut Processors Association has its NUTPAC, the beer distrib-utors have their PAC (once called SIXPAC), and the snack food industry has its SNACKPAC (Carlson, 1988). The objective of a PAC is to gain influence over, and access to, members of the House and Senate in order to advance its interests and/or adversely affect the interests of other groups. Given the large amounts of money at their disposal and the fact that there are no legal limits on their total contributions, PACs are grow-ing in influence; many (e.g., Stern, 1988) would say that their influence is excessive and dangerous.

PACs were originally founded by labor unions and were heavy contrib-utors to the Democratic Party. Within a few years businesses moved in to form PACs that were largely oriented to supporting the Republican Party. Since 1980, the new PACs that have been formed show a marked preference for Democratic candidates (Wilcox, 1988). In the 1988 elec-tion PAC support for Democratic candidates for the House of Represen-tatives and the Senate far outstripped support for Republican candidates. (This is, in part, due to the fact that PACs give almost 90 percent of their contributions to incumbents.) In fact, one official attributed much of the Democrats' success in the 1988 House elections, despite the overwhelm-ing vote in favor of the Republican candidate for president, to the Dem-ocrats' big advantage in PAC support. One interesting point here is that in the late 1970s Democrats opposed PACs, but, with the success of pro-Democratic PACs in the 1980s, some Republicans are now calling for leg-islation outlawing PACs. However, one expert concluded that it is unlikely that PACs would be made illegal: "Believe me, the genie's out of the bottle" (Berke, 1988a, p. B17).

The Neo-Marxian View

Neo-Marxian theory is derived from Karl Marx's idea that the legal and political systems are built upon, and are a reflection of, the economic base of the society. Neo-Marxians generally accept this idea but have often modified it to correspond with contemporary realities in capitalist countries. Some neo-Marxists have taken an even more extreme view of these matters than Marx did. They have seen the state as *wholly* determined by economic forces. Lenin, for example, saw the state as simply a tool used by one social class to oppress another. Thus, he felt that if economic inequality were ended, it would lead to a withering away of the state, at least as an instrument of oppression. Of course, the history of the Soviet Union since the revolution of 1917 indicates anything but a withering away of the state. The Soviet state has become huge, powerful, and often oppressive, capable, at least in the past, of murdering millions in what Solzhenitsyn (1973) called the "Gulag Archipelago."

Most modern neo-Marxists no longer accept this simplistic view of the relationship between the state and the economy. At one time, neo-Marxists argued that in American society the state was simply a tool of the capitalist class, but such a view is no longer considered tenable. A moderated neo-Marxist view is that the state is not dominated by economic interests, but it still usually protects the interests of the capitalists (Poulantzas, 1973).

The Military-Industrial Complex. A good example of the continued applicability of the neo-Marxian perspective is found in the idea of a military-industrial complex. The **military-industrial complex** refers to the close alliance between the military establishment and the industries that make a major share of their profits from producing military equipment (Dye, 1983).

The two sectors—the military and industrial—tend to foster the interests of each other. It is in the economic self-interest of the military-weapons industry to support the military; conversely, it is in the interest of the military to support industries that enhance its power and ensure its existence. Critics of the military-industrial complex charge that it adversely affects the military, industry, and the society as a whole.

Although the idea of a military-industrial connection had been recognized some years before by sociologist C. Wright Mills (1956), public awareness was increased greatly when President Dwight D. Eisenhower, in his farewell address, warned of the dangers of this connection. Eisenhower told the nation that the combined influence of the military establishment and the industries that benefitted from producing weapons could become too powerful. With too much power the military-industrial complex could "endanger our liberties and democratic processes" (Eisenhower, 1972, pp. 31–32).

In the years since Eisenhower's warning, both the military and the industries supplying the military have grown immensely. Weapons systems and defense systems have been created, only to be abandoned when they became obsolete, leading to the expenditure of billions of dollars. The 1991 military budget is nearly $300 billion (Kaplan, 1990). Serious questions have been raised about many costs within the military system, especially because of repeated scandals that revealed waste, corruption, and crime.

The most obvious examples of a large and uncontrolled military-industrial complex have involved industries' overcharging the government for military materials. For example, in late 1985 several executives of General Dynamics, the third largest military contractor, were indicted for improperly billing the government for $7.5 million. This incorrect billing was, however, only a small part of a larger scandal. The billing was related to DIVAD, the name of a prototype for a General Dynamics gun (later known as the Sergeant York) that was supposed to protect troops from air attack. A contract for its production had been awarded in 1981. By 1985, following the expenditure of almost $2 billion, the DIVAD project was scrapped because this anti-aircraft gun had repeatedly failed to perform satisfactorily. It was the close connection between the military establishment and defense contractors that explains how such a vast amount of money could have been spent on a failed weapons system (Rasor, 1985). Investigations have now revealed that for many years the Pentagon withheld information from Congress that would have revealed the ineffectiveness of the gun under combat conditions. It seems that within the military the program managers for any weapons system have a vested interest in keeping the procurement process going once it has been started. Of course, the latter is clearly in the interests of the weapons makers. A Pentagon watchdog describes the situation this way:

> Because of the high stakes created each year by a $100 billion procurement budget, the system puts tremendous pressure on each individual [military program manager] to not rock the boat and then places him in a position to become very cozy with the contractor. (Rasor, 1985, p. 137)

Military officers who are in charge of procuring weapons for the Defense Department are often well rewarded if they remain "cozy" with defense contractors. Upon retirement from military duty, many high-ranking officers join the same corporations whose products they have been purchasing and approving (Rasor, 1985). This practice is so widespread that it has been called the "revolving door." It is good business for the defense contractors to hire former military officers because the knowledge they bring to the company can greatly aid in retaining present contracts and gaining new ones.

This close connection between military people and industrialists enhances the possibilities for corruption and crime. With billions of dollars to be made from Defense Department contracts, defense industry executives and military officials can be tempted. For example, in 1989 a former top executive with the Unisys Corporation (a major electronics firm) pleaded guilty to bribing an assistant secretary of the Navy. During the same period that the bribes were made, the Unisys Corporation received two Navy contracts totaling over $300 million. This incident is only one in a series of corrupt and illegal actions described as the military procurement scandal (Murphy, 1989).

When military purchases are influenced by bribes, corruption, and various levels of collusion, it is not surprising that many purchases made by the military are outrageously priced. Some widely publicized examples of overcharging include:

- A rechargeable flashlight that costs the commercial airlines $35. Cost to the Air Force was $181.
- A flight engineer seat priced at $5065 for the private airlines. Cost to the Air Force was $13,905.
- A coffee brewer for a private airline that costs $2125. Air Force cost was $7622 (Rasor, 1985).

Among other examples of exorbitant prices paid by the military, it is difficult to find a case that exceeds the boxes of tools the Gould Corporation sold to the Navy for $10,168.56 each. When Congressman Berkley Bedell's staff went to a hardware store and bought the same tools, the cost was $119.23 (Rasor, 1985, p. 164). The Navy audit system found the tools overpriced but concluded that the costs were "legal." The Navy then negotiated with the Gould Corporation, which returned 10 percent of the overcharge. The Navy held a press conference when the refund check was received from Gould, apparently feeling that this represented "a big victory" (Rasor, 1985, p. 166).

The military-industrial complex constitutes a huge economic bloc that wields substantial power and strongly influences U.S. policies and actions. This exceptional power lends support to the neo-Marxian view that the political and social aspects of a society will be shaped by its most powerful economic interests.

The Elitist View

The third approach to the state emphasizes the existence of a political **elite,** or a small group of people who come to power and dominate the

Sociology in the News

Successes of the Military-Industrial Complex, Or Are They?

While we have assailed the military-industrial complex on a variety of grounds, including huge expenditures for exotic weapons systems that do not work, there is the matter of the 1991 war with Iraq. Arrayed against an army of at least equal numbers, the Allied forces won a decisive victory largely on the basis of superior military technology. Among the technological marvels of Operation Desert Storm were

- Patriot missiles (the "SCUD busters"), which knocked many Iraqi missiles from the sky.
- The M1A1 Abrams tank, which bested one of the Soviet Union's best tanks, the T-72, because of its ability to fire on the run, using thermal sights.
- Stealth fighters, which flew with virtual impunity through Iraqi radar defenses.
- Laser or optically guided "smart bombs" and cruise missiles, which hit target after target with great precision.
- Destruction of Iraq's antiaircraft defenses with precision bombing and electronic jamming.

It is clear that the military-industrial complex has had its successes, and it has caused other nations to rethink their military philosophies. No longer can nations such as Iraq and China rely on human waves of troops to win a war against a modern army. The Soviet Union had relied on large numbers of troops equipped with merely adequate weapons, but it too will need to reassess its position in light of Desert Storm. Many countries are now interested in buying technologies like the Patriot missile.

Although Desert Storm was a nearly unprecedented success, we must be wary of exaggerating the strength of U.S. military technology. For one thing, many of the successful technologies like the B-52 bomber and battleships like the Missouri and Wisconsin were built in the 1940s and 1950s (*The Economist,* 1991). For another, many of the successful weapons turn out to be dated technologies when we examine them closely. Many people have more sophisticated technologies in their home computers than is found is most modern weaponry. The Patriot missile was conceived over 20 years ago, and it was originally designed to intercept and destroy incoming aircraft. It had to be adapted and modified to deal with the SCUD missiles. Furthermore, it was able to intercept those missiles only within a few miles of the launch site, causing destruction on the ground from the debris from both SCUDS and Patriots. The TOW antitank missile first became operational in 1970 and was successfully used by the Israelis in 1982. Thus, although there is cause for the military-industrial complex to rejoice, in many cases Operation Desert Storm was not fought with state-of-the-art technology. The success of modern weapons will lead to a call for a new, even more advanced generation of weapons. In our euphoria over the successes in the war with Iraq, we must remain vigilant that the military-industrial complex produces advanced weaponry at reasonable cost.

CLIFFORD, TIMOTHY, and LANE, EARL. "Allies' Technology Tipped the Scales." *Newsday,* March 4, 1991, p. 15.
Economist. "Weapons; Old but Good." March 9, 1991, p. 40.

population. Proponents of this approach also dispute the pluralist idea that the U.S. is democratic. Elite theorists developed their orientation in direct opposition to the Marxian belief that it is possible under communism to develop a society characterized by political, social, and economic equality. In their view, an elite evolves to govern any and every form of society.

Elite theorists believe that political systems are run by a small elite. One elite theorist describes the United States this way: "Great power in America is concentrated in a tiny handful of people" (Dye, 1983, p. 3). However, elite theorists sometimes differ in their evaluation of this condition. Some favor the concentration of power in the hands of the elite rather than in the hands of the masses (Ortega y Gasset, 1932). This group of elite theorists is fearful of democratic rule and favorably disposed toward control by a small elite. Others who subscribe to elitist political theory tend to be critical of elites and to see them as having a negative effect on society.

The Power Elite.   C. Wright Mills (1956) suggested such a negative elitist model of power, which he called the "power elite." The **power elite** is a small group of influential persons who occupy key positions in large corporations, the executive branch of government, and the military. Members of the power elite share common interests and goals; many have attended the same colleges, and many know one another personally. The members of the power elite are powerful not because of extraordinary personal skills and abilities but because they occupy important bureaucratic positions:

No one, accordingly, can be truly powerful unless he has access to the command of major institutions, for it is over these institutional means of power that the truly powerful are, in the first instance, powerful. Higher politicians and key officials of government command such institutional power; so do admirals and generals, and so do the major owners and executives of the larger corporations. (Mills, 1956, p. 9)

Mills suggests three basic levels of power in the United States. At the top, of course, is the power elite. Interest group leaders, legislators, and local opinion leaders compose the middle level. The bottom level consists of the mass of unorganized citizens who are controlled by the "higher-ups" and are often unaware of how important political decisions have been made.

G. William Domhoff (1967, 1978, 1983) presents an elitist model of power based on the idea of a "ruling class":

> . . . the ruling class is socially cohesive, has its basis in the large corporations and banks, plays a major role in shaping the social and political climate, and dominates the federal government through a variety of organizations and methods. (Domhoff, 1983, p. 1)

Membership in the governing class is based on an individual's being listed in the *Social Register*, attending a prestigious preparatory school, belonging to an exclusive men's club, or being a millionaire. Domhoff estimates that the governing class consists of not more than 0.5 percent of the population, or about 1 out of every 200 people. This uppermost social class is extremely wealthy and exerts control over the executive branch of government, major corporations, the military, the mass media, major regulatory agencies, and boards of trustees of major universities. Through its control of these organizations and institutions, the ruling elite is able to formulate political and economic policies that will be of greatest benefit to their interests. This policy-planning process begins in the boardrooms of the largest corporations in the United States, and it extends into policy-discussion organizations where the issues of the day, such as "foreign aid, tariffs, taxes and welfare policies," are discussed (Domhoff, 1983, p. 84).

Another useful mechanism of the ruling class for establishing policy is the nonprofit foundation. Foundations are tax-free institutions that are "an upper-class adaptation to inheritance and property taxes. They provide a means by which wealthy people and corporations can in effect decide how their tax payments will be spent, for they are based on money that otherwise would go to the government in taxes" (Domhoff, 1983, p. 84). The most famous and influential of the "old money" foundations are those created by the Ford, Rockefeller, and Carnegie fortunes.

After the ruling elite has established which political and economic policies are most advantageous, the next step is to get them implemented. This goal is accomplished, in part, by shaping public opinion through the public schools, churches, and voluntary associations. Opinions, beliefs, and attitudes of the people are also shaped through ". . . movies, television programs, books, pamphlets, speakers, advice and financial support" (Domhoff, 1983, p. 99).

However, the ruling elite, according to Domhoff, need not rely heavily on shaping public opinion, because policy objectives can be attained much more effectively by affecting the operations of the government directly. One method for doing this is to influence the candidate selection process of the major political parties. The method of the ruling elite is simple and direct: ". . . large campaign donations that far outweigh what other classes and groups can muster" (Domhoff, 1983, p. 117). But even this method can be unstable and unreliable as a way of influencing policy. A more direct approach is to influence the elected officials after they are in office, regardless of who they may be. This effort is accomplished through a variety of lobbying and influence groups.

Influence groups include specially created presidential commissions that deal with specific problems, and quasi-governmental groups such as the Business Council (Domhoff, 1983). The Business Council is composed primarily of the chairs or presidents of the largest corporations in the country. Members of the Business Council invite government officials to attend friendly, relaxed, and semi-social meetings, often at exclusive resorts near Washington, D.C., with all expenses paid by the Business Council. Through speeches, panel discussions, and reports, as well as informal conversations, the policies favored by the Business Council are conveyed to governmental leaders.

The Business Council prefers to work in the background or behind the scenes, but it also has a more public counterpart called the Business Roundtable. The Business Roundtable is an active and direct advocacy organization that sends representatives to lobby members of Congress, as well as the president and cabinet members (Domhoff, 1983).

Domhoff's notion of a ruling class closely parallels Mills's "power elite" model. Both views see the masses as unorganized and powerless. Both models suggest that Congress has relatively little power compared to the executive branch, and, most important, both argue that power resides with a small and cohesive group of individuals who share similar social backgrounds. The major difference in the models is that Mills considers the military leadership and the executive branch more or less coequals with the corporate rich, while Domhoff views the upper social class as completely dominant; it controls the power elite.

There is no certain way of judging whether the pluralist, the neo-Marxian, or the elitist view of politics is the best description of the U.S. political system or any other political system. All three views provide insights into the workings of political systems, and thus they help us to understand the political process, both in our own country and elsewhere. As each new political issue arises, we can observe whether the pluralist, the neo-

Marxian, or the elitist view provides the best explanation of the outcomes.

The American Presidency

The framers of the Constitution tried to prevent any occupant of the presidency, or any other branch of government, from acquiring inordinate and arbitrary powers. In so doing they tried to create a balance of power among the three branches of government—the presidency, the legislature, and the judiciary. This balance of power is consistent with the pluralist image of democracy in the United States. But political systems, like all other humanly created systems, do not always work exactly as planned. In recent years several views of the American presidency have been expressed, especially views on the power that the holder of that office can wield.

Since the presidency of Franklin D. Roosevelt in the 1930s, the power of the president has been widely perceived to have increased, especially relative to the Congress and the judiciary. This presumed power has seemed to decline only during terms of office when the president did not want to exercise it. Dwight Eisenhower, for example, is generally viewed as a president who did not strive to demonstrate or expand the power of the presidency. Among more recent presidents, Gerald Ford and Jimmy Carter are also seen as relatively passive.

However, the presidents who occupied the White House between Eisenhower and Ford are viewed as active. John Kennedy, Lyndon Johnson, and Richard Nixon are regarded as presidents who tried and succeeded in various ways to exercise and strengthen the power of their office. Ronald Reagan was likewise considered a strong leader who increased the power of the presidency. George Bush has continued the tradition of strong presidents, at least in the realm of foreign policy (see below).

Among the many indications of the growth of presidential power in the United States in the last 50 years, the single most visible sign is the power to involve the nation in wars, military actions, and foreign adventures. According to the Constitution, the power to declare war is expressly given to Congress. But presidents can and often have taken actions leading to war or the equivalent of war (even though undeclared). Since World War II the United States has been involved in numerous military actions around the world, but in no instance has Congress declared war.

Although presidential power may rise and decline with the incumbent of the office, the underlying question still remains of how much basic power resides in the presidency. The answer may be seen best by dividing presidential power into different spheres: foreign-policy power, domestic-policy power, and "personal power."

Foreign-Policy Power

Aaron Wildavsky (1969) has noted that, in general, American presidents have had much greater success in controlling the nation's military and foreign policies than in dominating its domestic policies (Fleisher and Bond, 1988). The president, as commander-in-chief of the armed forces, can engage in many foreign-policy actions without the consent of the Congress or the people (Prados, 1986).

The most striking example of presidential power in the area of foreign policy occurred in the 1991 war with Iraq (Operation Desert Storm). In his book *The Commanders* dealing, in large part, with the decisionmaking leading up to the war, Bob Woodward (1991) makes it clear that it was George Bush who wanted the war and it was he who made the decisions leading to war. Although Bush ultimately did seek and obtain Congressional approval to use force (but even here Congress did not officially declare war), he had made all of the basic decisions about war without Congressional involvement. In fact, he was advised that legally he did not need Congressional approval, and he sought it only in order to present a united image to the world.

Operation Desert Storm also demonstrates the president's power over the military. Contrary to what one might have expected, U.S. military leaders were less willing than Bush to go to war and, in some cases, quite resistant to it. Bush repeatedly made decisions and public pronouncements that pushed the United States closer and closer to war with Iraq, and the military had no alternative but to try to implement the President's decisions by making sure that sufficient troops and materiel were in place.

A good example of this occurred when General Colin Powell, Chairman of the Joint Chiefs of Staff, was watching Cable News Network one day during the crisis. Decisions had already been made to send troops to the Persian Gulf to prevent Iraq from going beyond its capture of Kuwait and moving into Saudi Arabia. The president was talking to reporters and he was pressed on whether the United States was going to move militarily against Iraq. Bush said, "Just wait. Watch and learn . . . I view very seriously our determination to *reverse* (italics added) out this aggression against Kuwait" (Woodward, 1991, p. 260). This constituted a major escalation to not only defend Saudi Arabia, but also to push the Iraqis out of Kuwait. What was surprising here was that this all came as a great surprise to Powell, who had not been consulted about the decision nor informed that it had been made. Powell had grave reservations about such a course of action, and it appeared to him that "the President had six-shooters in both hands and he was blazing away" (Woodward, 1991, p. 261). It was the military man Powell who favored restraint and peace while the civilian president was pushing for war. As the commander-in-chief, it was the president's view that prevailed.

Even the hero of Operation Desert Storm, General Norman Schwarz-kopf, was far more dovish than the president. In an interview in *Life* magazine Schwarzkopf said: "In a lot of ways I am a pacifist—though that might be too strong a word. But I know what war is. I am certainly anti-war. But I also believe that there are things worth fighting for" (Woodward, 1991, p. 310). In a conversation with Powell, Schwarzkopf said that he was not convinced of the need for an offensive operation. He felt that such an operation would create lots of casualties and many difficulties. He wondered whether the president and his advisors were aware of the costs and dangers associated with such an operation. In a later interview, Schwarzkopf favored the continuation of sanctions against Iraq rather than an offensive operation. Of the idea posed by some that we get on with the war and kill lots of people, he said, "That's crazy. That's crazy" (Woodward, 1991, p. 313). Schwarzkopf concluded: "War is a profanity because, let's face it, you've got two opposing sides trying to settle their differences by killing as many of each other as they can" (Woodward, 1991, p. 313). Thus, in Woodward's view the war with Iraq illustrates that the president of the United States can unilaterally undertake a major war on his own without consulting with Congress and leading military advisors and can even act against their advice and wishes.

Domestic-Policy Power

Recent presidents have often found it difficult to extend their power to domestic issues. Even presidents who have been perceived as most powerful have often failed to attain their objectives in the realm of domestic policy. In a short period after John Kennedy's assassination, Lyndon Johnson was remarkably successful in getting several significant pieces of domestic legislation through the Congress. Among others, the Economic Opportunity Act (the War on Poverty program), Medicare, the Civil Rights Act of 1964, and the Voting Rights Act of 1965 were all passed during a two-year period. Several of these had been on the agenda for years but had previously failed to be enacted. Despite the dramatic success with domestic legislation early in his presidency, Johnson found it increasingly difficult to get domestic policies passed later in his tenure as president.

Richard Nixon and Jimmy Carter both faced serious political crises that weakened their support in Congress. The Watergate affair made it difficult for Nixon to get much of his domestic legislation through Congress during his last two years in office. Similarly, the capture of U.S. embassy personnel in Tehran, Iran, seriously weakened the Carter presidency, and portions of his domestic legislation failed to be passed by Congress. Especially during his first term, Ronald Reagan succeeded in getting much of his domestic legislation through Congress. As M.B. Oglesby, Jr., chief White House lobbyist, commented about 1984 congressional voting: "We won more than we lost" (*Congressional Quarterly Almanac*, 1985, p. 19-C). Reagan's fortunes with Congress declined, however, and in 1987 he lost far more votes than he won (*Congressional Quarterly Almanac*, 1987). George Bush has so far in his presidency been far less successful with his domestic policy than with his foreign policy.

The Iron Triangle.   Not only is the president often blocked by Congress but presidential policies (particularly at the domestic level) often are effectively blocked by what Hodgson (1980) calls the **Iron Triangle**—three points of power limiting presidential action. One point is the part of the existing bureaucracy that will be affected; the second is the interest group that has an economic stake in the outcome, and the third is the members of Congress who are on the relevant congressional committees and act on behalf of the special interest groups. Sometimes presidents discover that even the power of the White House cannot overcome the resistance of the Iron Triangle.

Personal Power

One of the most fascinating aspects of the power political leaders have is the control they exercise over the people around them in their everyday lives. This type of power is called *personal power*, and it allows presidents and other heads of state to command the people who serve them to do virtually anything. The memoranda of President Nixon reveal that he once asked his chief of staff to do something about the birds that were crashing into his oval office window at the White House (Oudes, 1988).

Often personal power is used for actions that are questionable and that border on being illegal. A retired director of the White House Military Office, Bill Gulley (1980), has described many of the things that he did at the request of four American presidents: Lyndon Johnson, Richard Nixon, Gerald Ford, and Jimmy Carter. Gulley says that the Military Office allows presidents the greatest freedom because the costs of things done under the cover of military secrecy can be hidden from public view. The amount of money available for such presidential projects seems unlimited; for example:

- Johnson had an airplane hangar on his ranch converted into a comfortable, completely air-conditioned movie theater. It was built ostensibly to show training films to "military personnel," but in fact only two Army baggage handlers were there periodically. Johnson's daughters did enjoy movies in the theater, however (Gulley, 1980, p. 92).

- Richard Nixon had millions spent on his two personal homes in Key

Biscayne, Florida, and San Clemente, California. Nixon also provided his millionaire friend Bebe Rebozo with a military phone system that gave him free world-wide phone service (Gulley, 1980, p. 158).

A mini-scandal that arose at both the beginning and end of the Reagan years involved the clothes and jewelry worn by the president's wife, Nancy Reagan. In 1981 Mrs. Reagan announced that she had been accepting clothing as loans (which she sometimes kept) from designers, including a $25,000 creation worn at the 1981 inauguration. Told that she must disclose such loans and gifts and that they might be taxable, Mrs. Reagan announced that she would no longer accept them. No such loans were disclosed, or appeared, on Reagan tax forms between 1982 and 1987. However, in 1988 it was disclosed that Mrs. Reagan had continued to borrow large numbers of expensive dresses (valued at well over $1 million) and jewelry during that period. One designer said that Mrs. Reagan had borrowed between 60 and 80 creations and had kept a large number of them. A jeweler told of loaning the First Lady "a pair of diamond earrings that are $800,000 with ten-carat drops" (Magnuson, 1988, p. 29). When it came to light that Mrs. Reagan had resumed the practice of borrowing clothes and jewelry, her press secretary dismissed the matter by saying, "She made a little rule, and she broke it."

Changes in American Politics

American politics has changed dramatically in recent years. These changes are especially clear in elections for the presidency and presidential politics, but some of the same changes have occurred at other political levels as well.

Money and Presidential Elections

One outcome of the Watergate scandal was the revelation that Richard Nixon, in his 1972 election campaign, had received huge, illegal, corporate contributions. In addition, large sums had come from individuals, some of whom were later rewarded with ambassadorships. The result was a 1974 law limiting individual and corporate contributions to presidential (and congressional) campaigns, and establishing public financing of presidential campaigns. Once nominated by his or her party, a candidate gets a set sum from the government and is not allowed to take private contributions. As a result of this dictum, the two parties waged the 1976 presidential campaign on roughly equal economic footing. A Commission on National Elections concluded that the reforms had worked and that public financing had "clearly proved its worth in opening up the process, reducing undue influence of individuals and groups and virtually ending corruption in presidential election finance" (Ignatius, 1988, p. D5). However, Congress soon made some changes in the law that subverted its effectiveness.

The 1979 changes to the law re-created the potential for imbalances in future elections. For example, state and local party organizations were allowed to spend unlimited sums for voter registration and efforts to get out the vote. An individual or corporation could give enormous sums (now called "soft money") to state or local drives aimed at helping elect a presidential candidate. In terms of its effect, this money worked in a way similar to giving it directly to the presidential candidates. Thus, the 1974 law was circumvented; huge contributions could again be made, albeit indirectly, to presidential campaigns (Drew, 1983).

That is, in fact, what occurred in the 1988 presidential election. Federal law allowed each party to spend $46.1 million in public funds and $8.3 million raised by the parties on the 1988 presidential race. But the election laws also allowed each party to raise an additional $50 million, much of it going directly or indirectly to the presidential election campaign. There were more $100,000 donors in 1988 than in 1972, when the excessive number of large contributions led to the 1974 law. Said the president of Common Cause, a public interest group: "We now face the potential of once again seeing the presidency out there on the auction block. It is incumbent on everyone to watch very closely any decisions made by the incoming Bush administration to give government benefits, appointments or financial advantage to these large donors" (Babcock, 1988, p. A20).

The Increasing Role of Television

Television is clearly playing a key role in politics, especially at the presidential level. The political candidate who controls the news broadcasts is almost certain to win the election. President Ronald Reagan was able to dominate the news media (Hertsgaard, 1988). Through television, Reagan overrode the stars of network news (Dan Rather, Tom Brokaw, etc.). "He stepped right past these stars and took his place alongside the Americans in their living rooms, and together they paid no great mind to what these media were saying" (Schram, 1987, p. 27). The key to Reagan's success was an emphasis on visual rather than verbal impact. Writer Martin Schram calls this "The Great American Video Game." Presidential advisers were able to create great visual scenes (e.g., Reagan with World War II veterans on the beach in Normandy) with the president in the forefront in order to manipulate the electronic media into building stories around the photo opportunities. Because television by its nature is a visual medium, the visual image tends to create a more powerful

Sociology in the News

The President's Chief of Staff Abuses His Power

The abuse of the personal power of presidents often extends to their top advisors. The most recent example involves President George Bush's chief of staff (and former Governor of New Hampshire), John H. Sununu. Sununu is known for his arrogance and abrasiveness, and he succeeded in alienating a number of top government officials with his high-handed manner. Sununu has refused to follow the usual procedure for presidential chiefs of staff of seeking to build relationships with powerful Washington groups. Instead, Sununu has often been contemptuous of all those who irritate him or get on his wrong side, whether they be members of Congress, publishers, friends of the president, or cabinet officers. As a result, Sununu has earned such nicknames as "Governor So-Know-It-All" and "The No-Neck Monster" (Randolph, 1990, pp. 16, 33).

One incident that illustrates why he earned such labels occurred during negotiations over the nation's budget when he described Senator Trent Lott of Mississippi as "an insignificant figure in this process." Asked if he would accept an apology from Sununu, Senator Lott said: "He is going to have to crawl over here and BEG for it . . . He just stuck the wrong pig" (Randolph, 1990, p. 16). To Representative Lindsay Thomas, Sununu said, "I don't care what you're saying. I'm not interested in anything you have to say" (Randolph, 1990, p. 35). Said Senator Robert Byrd (Democrat, West Virginia) of Sununu's behavior: "I have had 30 years in the U.S. Senate. I have never in my life observed such outrageous conduct . . . Your conduct is arrogant. It is rude. It is intolerant" (Randolph, 1990, p. 33). The events described below need to be seen in the context of Sununu's strained relationships with the Washington elite.

In May, 1991, it was discovered that Sununu was abusing his power by using military aircraft to take him on largely personal trips. Sununu made several visits to Colorado and New Hampshire, where he made speeches and went skiing. He also made two trips to Boston to see his dentist. On one occasion, Mr. Sununu flew from Key Largo, where President Bush was visiting, to West Palm Beach to see his parents. He paid $167 for the flight, meeting the policy that for such flights an official pay the normal coach fare plus $1. However, in this case, the plane had to be flown from Washington, D.C. to pick him up and then deliver him to West Palm Beach (from there he journeyed to other cities for apparently official business). While Sununu paid $167 for the personal part of the flight, the government estimated that the flight from Washington to Key Largo to West Palm Beach should have cost Sununu almost $12,000. Overall, Sununu's trips cost taxpayers over one-half million dollars, only a tiny fraction of which was reimbursed.

Many Washington insiders seemed to enjoy the discomfort that Sununu experienced as a result of the revelations about his personal trips. Because of all the ill will he had built up, Sununu found few defenders on the White House staff or on Capitol Hill.

As a result of the scandal, Sununu was forced to clear future trips with the White House counsel, and government aircraft could be used for personal trips only if there was "immediate and compelling need."

DOWD, MAUREEN. "White House Memo; Sununu: A Case Study of Flouting the Rules." *New York Times,* May 5, 1991, pp. 1, 34.
RANDOLPH, ELEANOR. "The Washington Chain-Saw Massacre." *Washington Post Magazine,* December 2, 1990, pp. W15ff.
ROSENTHAL, ANDREW. "White House Details Flights by Sununu." *New York Times,* April 24, 1991, p. A12.
Time, "Clipping John's Wings." May 20, 1991, p. 27.

impression than verbal communication. The candidate who can control visual imagery has the significant advantage in a campaign.

The 1988 Presidential Elections.   This emphasis on how the president, as well as candidates for the presidency, are covered by television news was particularly clear in the 1988 presidential elections. In fact, it has been claimed that "1988 is the year that television *was* the campaign" (L. Zuckerman, 1988, p. 66). As an example of the lengths to which politicians will go to manipulate television images, "one party, at its convention, deliberately muted the colors of the flag so they would televise better" (L. Zuckerman, 1988, p. 66).

Of central importance is how candidates are covered on the evening news broadcasts. Said one expert: "TV producers are like nymphomaniacs when it comes to visuals. . . . Television's insatiable need for pretty pictures has cheapened the campaign" (L. Zuckerman, 1988, p. 66). Said another: "Television news has been co-opted by the image makers and the media managers. . . . The manipulators learned that by controlling the pictures you end up controlling the content" (L. Zuckerman, 1988, p. 66). In the 1988 campaign George Bush stuck to choreographed scenes that played well on the news, while Michael Dukakis, following the older model, held almost daily news conferences. Although these press conferences were laudable in terms of Dukakis's accessibility to the press, they provided little in the way of visuals that could be used on the evening news. Bush's advisers didn't even mind when newscasters commented critically on the staged quality of Bush's appearances. Said one, "If we get the visual that we want . . . it doesn't matter as much what words the networks use in commenting on it" (L. Zuckerman, 1988, pp. 66, 71).

Increasing Attention to Campaign Advertising

Intimately related to the accelerating importance of television imagery is the increasing significance of campaign advertising, especially television ads, which, of course, depend heavily on their visual component (Jamieson, 1984). Television ads are important for several reasons. First, they build name recognition for the candidate. Second, they allow the candidates to frame precisely, in whatever way they want, the issues that they consider central to the election. Third, they allow the candidates to expose their temperaments and their talents in the most favorable light. Fourth, they are short (usually a minute) and therefore are in line with the limited attention devoted to such matters by most television viewers. (The 60-second spot ad has now replaced the 30-minute speech that was the norm in the 1952 presidential election.)

Many argue that television advertising played a central role in the victory of George Bush and the defeat of Michael Dukakis. On the one hand, Bush ran an aggressive—some said even vicious—television campaign in which he sought to tie the Massachusetts governor to pollution in Boston Harbor and the rape of a woman by a furloughed Massachusetts prisoner. Jamieson (1988a, p. C1), who saw the 1988 campaign as unprecedented in terms of fabrications, argues that Bush's (and to a lesser extent, Dukakis's) advertisements were sometimes outright lies. "Take, for example, this ad from the Bush campaign: The picture shows a pool of sludge and pollutants near a sign reading, 'Danger/Radiation Hazard/No Swimming.' The text indicts Dukakis for failing to clean up Boston Harbor. But the sign shown has, in fact, nothing to do with the Massachusetts governor or his record. Instead, it warns Navy personnel not to swim in waters that had once harbored nuclear submarines under repair." On the other hand, Dukakis failed to come up with either an adequate television response to such criticisms or a positive message of his own. In addition, some of his attempts at television imagery, such as a helmeted Dukakis riding in a tank, backfired as the public refused to accept the intellectual Dukakis in such a setting. Concern is increasing that the nature of television images, not ideas and issues, are decisive in presidential (and other) elections.

What is worrisome about the negative and distorted campaign advertisements is that they seemed to work (Edsall, 1988). Because of advertisements such as those mentioned above, many voters came to view Dukakis as weak on crime, ineffective in cleaning up the environment, unpatriotic, and left-wing, a politician who was out of step with the mainstream of the American electorate. In addition, advertisements focused public attention *away* from Bush's weaknesses. Bush was put on the offensive, which forced Dukakis into the position of responding to Bush's initiatives. The success of Bush's negative campaign makes it highly likely that we will see more of such campaigns in the future.

The Changing Nature of Political Speeches

In *Eloquence in an Electronic Age,* Kathleen Jamieson (1988b) has related the impact of television to the transformation of political speech-making. Jamieson writes that the increasing role of television is reducing the importance of memorable words and speeches. Instead, as mentioned earlier, the visual image matters most. "Television has changed public discourse dramatically. Increasingly, eloquence is visual, not verbal" (Jamieson, 1988b, p. 44). Even when television does report on the speeches themselves, the emphasis in newscasts is on the so-called "15-second sound bite." Jamieson (1988b, p. 9) reports a study that found that the average number of seconds a candidate for president was shown speaking on a network news segment in the 1984 campaign was slightly less than 15 seconds. By the 1988 campaign reports indicated that speaking time had been reduced to nine seconds (Kalb, 1988). Because political campaign speeches are tailored for television coverage and *not* the immediate audience, they have grown shorter, less than 20 minutes on the average, including time for applause. The focus in candidates' speeches and campaign appearances is on the limited, 15-second portion that is apt to be picked up by the national television networks. Since this 15 seconds will be seen by many times more than the number of people witnessing the speech or appearance, most of the attention of presidential advisors is lavished on producing just the right snippet for the TV news.

In addition to the decline of televised reports of speeches, televised speeches have undergone a similar decline. Prior to the advent of television, political speeches on radio were at first usually an hour in length, but by the 1940s the norm had dropped to 30 minutes. In the early years of television, speeches were that same length, but they rapidly decreased to five minutes, and by the 1970s the speech itself had been replaced by the 60-second advertisement. A tremendous decline in information transfer has occurred in this historical process, and complex ideas have given way to simple assertions. In addition, the brevity of contemporary speeches leads to increased use of hyperbole to catch the audience's attention.

Similar developments have affected debates between candidates for elected office. In contemporary televised debates, if they can really be called that, candidates have a minute or two to offer their position on a given issue. "By contrast, in each of their seven senatorial debates of 1858, Lincoln and Douglas spoke for ninety minutes each on a single topic: the future of slavery in the territories" (Jamieson, 1988b, p. 11).

Another development has been the increasing differentiation between speech writer and speech giver. Instead of writing their own speeches or daring to speak extemporaneously, today's politicians rely on texts written for them by professional speech writers. Hence, the successful modern politician needs to be good only at reading speeches and not at creating artful prose. In the political party conventions in 1988 it was generally agreed that both Bush and Dukakis gave extraordinary speeches. In both cases the speeches were written by batteries of speech writers.

The Rise of Political Consultants

Another reality of contemporary presidential politics is the increasing use of a wide array of political consultants. Several types of consultants are employed. Polling consultants are experts brought in to conduct various polls to tell the candidates how they are doing, what is working, what is not, how the opposition is doing, and so on (Barone, 1988). Media consultants are hired to help candidates get more media exposure and to be sure that the correct message comes across. The importance of media consultants was underscored when President-elect Jimmy Carter wrote to his media consultant, Gerald Rafshoon: "I'll always be grateful that I was able to contribute in a small way to the victory of the Rafshoon agency" (Sabato, 1981, p. 112). In addition, direct-mail fund-raising consultants are needed, whose expertise lies in the techniques necessary to raise the huge amount of money needed to finance a national political campaign. The danger in all these high-powered, high-priced consultants is that they are anxious to mold a candidate into an image that will win; the candidate may go along with these efforts, even if the image runs counter to who he/she "really" is (Sabato, 1981).

The Voters in Democratic Societies

The Apathy of Voters in the United States

As we noted at the beginning of this chapter, elections in the United States in the twentieth century have had relatively low voter turnouts. During the nineteenth century, American voter participation was much higher, with a peak of approximately 85 percent of those eligible to vote casting ballots during the presidential election of 1876. During the early years of the twentieth century, however, voter participation substantially declined: the rate of voter participation (43 percent) in 1920 was about half of what it had been in 1876. Since 1920, the high point of voter participation occurred in the Kennedy–Nixon contest of 1960, in which 63 percent of those eligible to vote cast ballots. Voter participation consistently declined until 1984, when the Reagan–Mondale contest attracted slightly more than half (53 percent) of those eligible to vote and ended a 20-year decline in the presidential-year voter-turnout rate (see table 16–1).

In the 1988 Bush–Dukakis election, the decline continued, and quite dramatically, as only 50.2 percent of eligible voters cast ballots (U.S. Bureau of the Census, 1988h). Furthermore, the total number of people voting was several million less than in 1984—the first time since 1944 that the total number of voters declined from one presidential election to the next.

This relatively low rate of voter participation contrasts sharply with the situation in other modern democracies. Since World War II, voter participation in Italy and Belgium has exceeded 90 percent. In Portugal, West Germany, and Norway, from 80 to 85 percent of those eligible actually vote, and from 70 to 80 percent of Canadians, Greeks, and Japanese vote (Glass, Squire, and Wolfinger, 1984). Overall, the average turnout in other industrialized countries is 80 percent of the eligible electorate (Powell, 1986, p. 16).

In contrast to the low voter turnout, however, there is one sense in which Americans appear to be more politically involved than the citizens of other democracies (Powell, 1986). In comparison with seven other industrial nations, U.S. citizens are most likely to feel that they have a say in what the government does, and that they have at least some interest in politics. These views of Americans are borne out by some of their political activities: Americans are most apt to discuss politics with others and to have worked for a party or candidate during an election. Thus, on a variety of attitudinal and behavioral measures, Americans are highly involved in the political process. If this is the case, then why the low voter turnout in U.S. elections?

Some important structural and institutional conditions in the United States make the average voter turnout relatively low. First, some industrialized nations invoke legal penalties if a citizen does not vote, but the United States does not mandate voter participation. Second, in many nations the government takes the initiative to get people to register to vote, but in the United States registration is left largely to the individual. Other aspects of the registration process inhibit voting in the United States such as the absence in most states of day-of-voting registration. Often it is inconvenient to get to registration sites during their hours of operation. If a person moves, he/she must reregister. Since almost half the population might move in a five-year period, a large portion of the electorate must make the *double effort* of registering *and* voting. In fact, a post-1988 election survey indicated that 37 percent of nonvoters did not vote because they were not registered. Two-thirds of these people indicated that they would have voted if they could simply have shown up on election day without prior registration. Three-quarters of these people think the elec-

Table 16-1. Percentage of Persons Eligible to Vote Who Voted in Presidential and Congressional Elections, 1920–1988

	Percentage of Those Eligible to Vote Who Voted	
Year	President	Representatives
1920	43	. . .
1922	. . .	32
1924	44	. . .
1926	. . .	30
1928	52	. . .
1930	. . .	34
1932	52	. . .
1934	. . .	41
1936	57	. . .
1938	. . .	44
1940	59	. . .
1942	. . .	33
1944	56	. . .
1946	. . .	37
1948	51	. . .
1950	. . .	41
1952	62	. . .
1954	. . .	42
1956	60	. . .
1958	. . .	43
1960	63	. . .
1962	. . .	45
1964	62	. . .
1966	. . .	45
1968	61	. . .
1970	. . .	44
1972	56	. . .
1974	. . .	36
1976	54	. . .
1978	. . .	35
1980	52.6	. . .
1982	. . .	38
1984	53.3	. . .
1986	. . .	33.4
1988	50.2	. . .
1990	. . .	33

Source: Data from U.S. Bureau of the Census, *Statistical Abstract of the United States,* 93rd ed. Washington, D.C.: U.S. Government Printing Office, 1972; and 105th ed. Washington, D.C.: U.S. Government Printing Office, 1985; 109th ed. Washington, D.C.: U.S. Government Printing Office, 1988h; 1990 data from *Congressional Quarterly Almanac,* vol. XLVI. Washington, D.C.: Congressional Quarterly Inc.: 901.

tion laws should be changed to allow easier registration (Dionne, 1988b). In recognition of the barrier to registration, efforts are under way in 1991 to pass a bill making it easier to register to vote (*Chicago Tribune,* 1991).

Another factor inhibiting voting in the United States is the electoral college system, which gives all of a state's votes to the winning candidate. With this system, neither political party will make an effort to get out the vote in states where the outcome appears to be a foregone conclusion.

Finally, voting in the United States is hampered by the fact that, unlike many European countries, there is no strong tie between belonging to certain groups (occupational, religious) and partisan political activity. Such a strong linkage between one's social group and one's political party seems to lead to a higher voter turnout.

Even in light of these structural and institutional barriers, a large number of U.S. citizens still choose not to vote in presidential and congressional elections. In contrast, there have been some state and local elections recently in which the turnout has been very high (Gans, C., 1988). Perhaps the issues of national elections are too remote for most people. Or it may be that citizens are "turned off" by excessively long political campaigns and the self-serving actions of the political candidates. With presidential campaigns now sometimes extending over a two-year or three-year period, many people often say that they are tired of the candidates' charges and counter-charges.

Beyond barriers to voting and legitimate reasons for not voting, people in a democratic society still have a responsibility to exercise their vote. Primarily through their votes they can shape and influence governmental policy and action. Yet substantial evidence shows that many people in the United States, particularly the young, simply do not care enough and are not interested enough to participate in elections.

War and Peace

As noted at the beginning of this chapter, the state not only has a monopoly of the use of physical force in a given territory but it also has the ability to declare war on other states (Weber, 1946). In the words of a famous military dictum, "War is the continuation of politics by different means." Our concerns about war (and peace) move us out of a discussion of politics within specific nations and into a discussion of political relationships between and among nations. We will return again to structural functionalism and conflict theory to demonstrate how these theoretical perspectives can help us to understand the global realm of war and peace.

The United States and the Soviet Union: The Cold War and Its Aftermath

The issue of war and peace at an international level has been dominated for several decades by the relationship between the United States and the

Soviet Union. Although these two nations did not directly enter into a shooting war with one another, they did engage in a "cold war" from the close of World War II to the end of the 1980s. During the cold war the Soviet Union was seen as expansionistic, seeking to pull more and more countries into the communist camp. From the Soviet Union's viewpoint, the United States was viewed as imperialistic, trying to make the world safe for capitalism. Thus, in a seemingly never-ending series of confrontations, the two nations squared off against each other in a number of different regions of the world. After World War II, for example, the Soviet Union actively supported East Germany while the United States allied itself with West Germany. More recently, the Soviet Union supported the *Sandinista* government in Nicaragua while the United States supported the rebels, the *Contras*. In these cases, and in innumerable others, the United States and the Soviet Union confronted each other in a non-shooting war, although fighting and dying did occur among the surrogates of the two countries (e.g., the *Sandinistas* and the *Contras*).

In addition to facing one another in a series of national showdowns, the United States and the Soviet Union sought superiority over one another in the realms of conventional and nuclear arms. The resulting arms race led to a buildup of military weapons on both sides that was extremely threatening. There was a constant danger that these weapcns, especially nuclear missiles, would be used by one side or the other, either by accident or as a first strike. Regardless of the reason for launching the first missiles, the other side was almost sure to make a massive retaliation. Thus, for several decades, the world was threatened with the possibility of destruction.

Conflict theory offers a useful sociological perspective on the cold war between the United States and the Soviet Union. An inherent conflict of interest prevailed between the two nations. The United States sought to protect and extend capitalist (or at least nonsocialist) economic systems around the world, while the Soviet Union held the view that socialist economic systems should be protected, and new socialist economies should be encouraged and supported. Each side had a corresponding ideology to support its actions. The ideologies differed in some respects, but both emphasized that their economic (and political) systems were in the best interests of the people of the world.

By the late 1980s, both the Soviet Union and the United States had experienced some setbacks in their efforts to protect and expand their interests. The United States had been unsuccessful in keeping Vietnam out of Communist control and had suffered a great deal of social upheaval in the process. The Soviet Union had engaged in a similar effort in Afghanistan and had also not achieved its goal. The Afghanistan experience may have caused a reassessment of what the best interests of the Soviet Union were. Thus, as the conflict of interest between the two countries became less severe, the cold war tensions also began to ease.

Among other things, in 1988, the Soviet Union and the United States negotiated a treaty eliminating intermediate nuclear weapons in Europe, and the Soviet Union unilaterally announced its intention to reduce its military force by half a million men, to make corresponding cuts in conventional arms, and to alter its military deployment patterns in Europe so that they were clearly in a defensive posture. Further cuts in nuclear weapons were made as a result of a treaty signed in mid-1991. Many say that the cold war has ended; the United States and the Soviet Union seem to have embarked on a course that, if it continues, could make the world a much safer and more harmonious place.

The change in the relationship between the United States and the Soviet Union is reflected in a decision made on May 28, 1991 to shift the focus of the North Atlantic Treaty Organization (NATO) (Smith, 1991). NATO was formed to oppose the Soviet Union and its Warsaw Pact allies and to prevent a massive invasion of Western Europe. However, with the easing of the cold war, the Warsaw Pact has largely ceased to exist. The Soviet Union is in the process of moving one-half million troops from Eastern Europe and is no longer seen as a significant threat to Western Europe. Thus, by 1994 NATO will cut back its troop strength and redefine its mission. NATO is to become more oriented to dealing with regional crises with small, rapid-deployment forces. However, NATO will still have the capacity to confront an invasion from the east, should the situation in the Soviet Union change. Furthermore, NATO is not (yet) surrendering its nuclear capacities in light of the fact that the Soviet Union retains its huge arsenal of nuclear weapons and that could once again constitute a threat if the Soviet Union were to dramatically alter its current policy (Montgomery, 1991).

This reduction of the possibility of war, and a corresponding increase in peace, was brought about under the leadership of Ronald Reagan in the United States (and continued under the presidency of George Bush) and Mikhail Gorbachev in the Soviet Union. Reagan's interest in reaching an accord with the Soviet Union was surprising given his reputation as a staunch anti-Communist and his well-known view that the Soviet Union was an "evil empire." However, it was probably this position that allowed him to reach a series of understandings with the Soviets. That is, because he was such a strong anti-Communist, the people in the United States trusted the fact that, if he were able to reach an understanding with the Soviet Union, it would be advantageous to the United States. To put it another way, a liberal Democratic president who was perceived to be "soft on Communism" would have had a much more difficult time gaining national political support for an agreement with the Soviets.

In his early years in office, Reagan found it difficult to deal with the Russians because of the instability in their leadership. Brezhnev had come to power in 1964, but by the early 1980s he was ill and enfeebled, and he died in late 1982. Andropov succeeded Brezhnev and, despite some promising beginnings, he, too, soon became ill and died in early 1984. His successor, Chernenko, was ill almost from the beginning, and he died in early 1985. Beginning in March, 1985, Reagan found himself faced with a relatively young and healthy Soviet leader, Mikhail Gorbachev, who was very different from his often belligerent predecessors. Gorbachev was a new kind of Soviet leader who was faced with a series of internal realities that required immediate and dramatic attention. His country's political and economic systems were not working well, and Gorbachev launched an effort to restructure Soviet society (*perestroika*). In order to create a climate for internal reform and to generate the money necessary for those reforms, Gorbachev needed to ease the tensions with the United States and to reduce nuclear and conventional military expenditures.

Gorbachev's efforts to ease the cold war can be analyzed from the point of view of structural functionalism. A major structure in the Soviet Union, the economic system, had not been functioning well and was rapidly deteriorating. Gorbachev needed to democratize the political structure and reduce the economic drain of the military in order to turn his attention to the faltering economy. Structural functionalism makes us aware of the interrelationship of societal structures; the recent history of the Soviet Union shows us that in order to change one structure (the economic system), other structures (political system, military) must also be transformed.

For decades, the success of the Soviet military had been tied to the weakness of the economy. As Bialer (1986, p. 280) puts it: "until recently the Soviet military sector could be modern precisely because the civilian economy remained backward. . . . simply put, the entire economy works for the military forces." The Soviet economy suffers, among other things, from extraordinary overcentralization, poor technology, declining production and productivity, and managers and workers who are unresponsive to the needs of the economy. The tangible results of these inadequacies include abominable service, waste, long lines, empty shelves, and goods of notoriously poor quality. In order to begin modernizing the economy, Gorbachev had to cut back the amount of his country's gross national product (GNP) devoted to military expenditures.

The money to be saved by military cutbacks, and the money to be gained from investments from the West, presumed because of the improved international climate, could help begin financing economic (and political) reforms at home. The view here, then, is that, in the last few years, the Soviet Union has led the way toward reducing the possibility of nuclear war and increasing the likelihood of long-term peace; its array of internal economic problems that required money and attention brought it to this point (Bialer, 1986; Galbraith and Menshikov, 1988; Hough, 1988; Frankland, 1987; Medvedev, 1986).

Summary

Political sociology is primarily concerned with the distribution and exercise of power, which is the ability to control other people's behavior and to carry out one's will. Legitimate power, or *authority*, involves acceptance of the exercise of power by members of a society or group, while illegitimate power, or *coercion*, is power that relies solely on force to achieve its objectives. The dominant political institution in modern societies is the state, which claims a monopoly over the legitimate use of force.

The United States is nominally a democracy, but three different views exist about the degree to which the nation is, in fact, democratic. The pluralist view emphasizes the existence of many competing interest groups. The give-and-take among these groups produces a relatively democratic system because no one group gains control. The neo-Marxist perspective stresses the way in which the dominant economic groups in the society hold the most political power. One major special interest group predominates in the U.S.: the military-industrial complex. This huge economic interest group can exert extraordinary influence on government policies. The dominance of this coalition supports a neo-Marxist view of political power in the United States. The elitist view also perceives that power is held by a relatively small group but sees this group as not limited to the economic elite.

The presidency is a key feature of the U.S. political system. Beginning in the 1930s, U.S. presidents started to increase their power relative to Congress and the judiciary. However, recent American presidents have had less power to define policy, especially in domestic affairs. Presidents retain considerable power in shaping foreign policy. Major political leaders in every society, including presidents of the United States, have great personal power, which is the control they exercise over the people around them and in their every-day lives.

Politics in the United States in general, and more specifically presidential politics, are changing dramatically. In spite of laws designed to limit individual contributions to presidential campaigns, ways have been found to funnel huge sums of money into them. This puts the presidency on the "auction block" and opens the possibility that huge contributors will be rewarded by the victor in various ways. Television news is playing an increasingly central role in presidential campaigns, with the emphasis more and more on visual images rather than substance. In a related area, advertising, especially on TV, is key to a presidential victory. Political speeches are growing shorter and less substantive, with emphasis shifting to the generation of the "correct" 10-second or 15-second "sound bite" for the evening news. Political consultants (e.g., media advisors) are more and more important to presidential campaigns. While evidence shows increasing voter apathy in presidential elections, Americans continue to be involved in various ways in political activities.

Concerns about war and peace dominate the international political scene. Conflicts of interest sparked the cold war between the Soviet Union and the United States for many decades, but these conflicts seem to have diminished somewhat, and tensions have decreased. Significant steps have been taken toward a more peaceful world.

CRITICAL THINKING

1. In what ways does a state wield power over its citizens? What means might be used to assure the continuation of power? What is the basis of governmental power in the United States?
2. Describe the three major forms of governments listed in the chapter and give a contemporary example of each.
3. What explanations would you offer for why the youngest voters in the United States have the lowest percentage voting in elections?
4. What is the military-industrial complex? In what ways does this interest group exert influence on government policy? What does this example teach you about the nature of power in our political system?
5. Is the U.S. political system truly democratic? Compare and contrast the three major sociological views of the U.S. political system: the pluralist, the neo-Marxist, and the elitist. What evidence can you muster to support each viewpoint?
6. In what ways has presidential power in the United States increased since the presidency of Franklin Roosevelt? How has the Iron Triangle limited presidential action? What role does personal power play in determining the effectiveness of a president?
7. Assess the impact of campaign finances, television, campaign advertising, political speeches, and PACS on presidential elections. Does the picture presented conform to society's notion of the ideal democracy?
8. Democracy in the United States is based on the notion that an informed electorate will participate in the selection of the nation's leaders. What evidence in this chapter contradicts this notion? What steps might be taken to make reality match the ideal? What might be the consequences of such action?
9. The United States is stereotyped as the greatest democracy in the world. How does U.S. voting behavior contradict this stereotype? Compare U.S. voting behavior with that in other Western democracies.

CONNECTIONS

Working Parents and Latchkey Children

Introduction

In a suburb of a large metropolitan city, 5-year-old Mark gets off his school bus and patiently waits on his doorstep for two hours until his mother gets home from work. "The child just started kindergarten this year," protested his teacher. "Beginning school is a big step in itself. But having to wait without adult supervision for such a long time puts even more stress and responsibility on this child that youngsters his age are not developmentally prepared to handle." (Robinson, Rowland, and Coleman, 1986)

Mark is a "latchkey" child, one of about 2.4 million children who are left unsupervised in their homes while their parents are working (Koblinsky and Todd, 1989). The heart-rending picture painted of Mark is similar to those routinely offered by the mass media—of children with their house keys hanging on dirty strings around their necks, going home to empty houses, where they are scared and lonely. Hardly a television station or a magazine hasn't devoted some time or space to the "problem" of latchkey children. Indeed, the mass media have played a significant part in making latchkey children a national *social problem*.

From a sociological perspective, as we have seen, social problems are best understood as phenomena that the people in a given society define as a problem at any given time. The "social problem" of latchkey children deserves a more careful and systematic examination. Here we will consider the issues associated with latchkey children from a sociological perspective.

Some Background Issues

Often the people who express concern about latchkey children imply that it is a very recent phenomenon. But latchkey children are not new in the United States. The term itself is derived from the eighteenth century, when doors were opened by lifting a latch. At the turn of this century, children who returned to unsupervised homes were called "dorks." This label was derived from the words *door key,* and should not be confused with the contemporary meaning and usage of "dork." During the Depression of the 1930s and during World War II, when fathers and mothers were either employed or at war, latchkey children were common.

Throughout our history a negative connotation has usually been associated with latchkey children; they have typically been viewed as neglected, as having to eat cold meals, and as not having their *mothers'* full-time attention and affection (Robinson, Rowland, and Coleman, 1986).

A common bias in discussions of latchkey children is to consider the employment of mothers as a primary cause of the problem. Yet most children have two parents, even when their parents are divorced, and thus an unsupervised child is one who has *neither* parent available for child care. The implicit assumption by those concerned about latchkey children, and one they often state explicitly, is that mothers have the primary responsibility for child care. This is, of course, a continuing reflection of the traditional gender role expectations for women, as discussed in chapter 10.

It is often taken for granted that there will be negative social and emotional consequences for children who are left alone and unsupervised. There are claims that these children will do poorly in school, have poor self-concepts, be more insecure, and be fearful. All of these claims or concerns about the negative consequences of unsupervised children can be called *latchkeyphobia.* But is latchkeyphobia based on fact or on stereotypes and myths? Do working parents inflict irreparable damage on their children by not being at home after school to offer chocolate chip cookies and milk? Was June Cleaver, of the 1950s' "Leave it to Beaver" show, a better mother than Roseanne, a current television working mother?

The answers to these questions are important because economic conditions in today's society often necessitate that both parents work. And in the case of single mothers, there may be no choice at all about working;

it is an absolute necessity. As a result, parents must make important decisions about how their children will be cared for when they are not at home. Therefore, the issues created by having children and holding jobs are likely to touch most families' lives. Two issues are of interest here: (1) What insights about latchkey children can be derived from the major sociological theories? (2) What research has been done (or should be done) to enhance our understanding of latchkey children? We will begin by seeing how the major sociological theories can add to our understanding of the issues.

Structural-Functional Theory

Writing in the 1950s, functionalist theorists, especially Talcott Parsons and his associates (Parsons and Bales, 1955), described a family system in which the roles of males and females (as well as children) were clearly defined and differentiated. This functional view was in conformity with the prevailing societal views of that time, which stressed that in the ideal family a woman should be in the home as a full-time homemaker to care for her family. If a woman were to be employed, her work should not interfere with her primary role responsibilities, especially the responsibility of caring for the children (Renzetti and Curran, 1989). Functional theory and popular opinion were in agreement—a woman who left her children unsupervised was neglecting her duty.

From the perspective of the 1950s' functionalists, the family as an institution functioned both as the primary socializing agent of children and as a stabilizing force for adults in the family setting. Family roles that were separate and distinct for males and females provided a balance and a stability that made the family a smoothly working social unit that contributed positively to the society.

Among sociologists today, this overly simple functional view of the family has very few, if any, supporters. The 1950s' functionalist view has been criticized on a number of grounds, but the most frequent complaint is that it gave a kind of scientific endorsement to the traditional gender roles of women and men that prevailed at the time. A closely related criticism is that this functional view of the family endorsed a particular family form as best for the participants and best for the society. As we have seen throughout the preceding chapters, both gender roles and family forms vary greatly from society to society and from one time to another. A scientific theory that simply supports one society's view at one time in its history is inadequate as a theory.

An equally important criticism of the traditional functional view of employed mothers is that it was inconsistent with the reality of the 1950s, because many mothers *were* employed, even then. The idea of mothers remaining in the home has grown increasingly out of touch with the contemporary reality of women and employment. Many mothers work because they are not in husband–wife households; they work because as single mothers they must. Even in households with both parents present, it is often necessary to have two earners. It is simply not possible today to describe the ideal family as one in which the husband is employed while the wife remains in the home to care for the children.

Contemporary functional theorists continue to be interested in the way societal structures influence the functioning of the society. With respect to the issue of work and the family, a functionalist today would focus on how the economic institution, or other institutions of the society, produce conditions to which the family must adapt and make adjustments. In the case of women and employment, the interest is likely to be on how being employed creates problems, stresses, and frictions in the family unit. The arrangements that parents have to make in caring for their children, including having children care for themselves when neither parent is available, is one such problem.

Conflict Theory

Conflict theory, because of its inherent concerns, seems to be even better suited than functional theory to the study of parents who, because of their work, may leave their children unsupervised in the home. Conflict theory emphasizes that conflict exists at all levels of social organization and in all social units. Conflict theorists at the macroscopic level expect to find conflict between social institutions, as, for example, conflict between the economy and the family. Conflict theorists at the microscopic level expect that there will be conflict in the family as a social unit. Conflict is expected and normal in social relationships. From a conflict perspective, for example, when parents work they will have to make decisions about child care that reveal competing or conflicting interests among family members.

Conflict theory, especially in its Marxian beginnings (chapters 1 and 13), emphasized how those who dominate the economic system will be in conflict with those who do the work. Furthermore, again as Marx emphasized, the capitalists will exploit the relative powerlessness of the workers in order to maximize their profits. One example of this conflict between workers and employers is in the area of child-care services for employees in the United States. Very few U.S. employers provide any kind of child-care services at the place of employment, or even make any accommodations to the child-care concerns of their employees. Employers resist because child-care services would be costly and would reduce their profits. Parents and single mothers have been unable to exert enough pressure on the government to provide child-care, again because dominant economic interests oppose the higher taxes (and thus lower profits) that would result.

Conflict theory sensitizes us to the conflict of interest between working parents and their employers. So far, parents, both married couples and single mothers, have proved to be relatively powerless in getting employers or the state to help them with their child-care needs. Since adequate and affordable child-care is often not available, many working parents, and especially single mothers, may leave their children unsupervised while the parents are at work (Mason, 1988).

Symbolic Interactionism

The sociological theory called *symbolic interactionism* offers another, and very different, view of latchkey children. This theory stresses the importance of symbols and their meanings. The meanings of symbols define situations for people and influence their responses to those situations. We saw earlier that the phrase *latchkey child* has a long and mostly negative history. When television, radio, and the print media consider the issue of working parents leaving their children without supervision, they invariably connect the label *latchkey children* to images of lonely, scared, and sometimes endangered youngsters. A more neutral, though still somewhat negative, label is *unsupervised children*. But some sociologists have pointed out that the term *self-care children* is even more neutral, and thus encourages a more objective approach (Cole and Rodman, 1987).

The major point to be made from a symbolic interaction viewpoint is that social problems are often created or diminished by the successful application of a label. Instead of thinking in terms of the negative images of latchkey children, if we were to think about self-care, the way would be opened to consider important questions in a more unemotional and objective way. For example, under what conditions is self-care by a child relatively safe and appropriate? At what age can a child be entrusted to care for himself or herself? In what kinds of communities, neighborhoods, and home settings is self-care more appropriate? At what time of the day, and for how much time, may children be left in a self-care situation? The main point from a symbolic interaction perspective is that the label we use to define a situation can strongly influence our response to it.

Social Exchange Theory

Since exchange theory focuses primarily on the interaction between individuals, we can expect it to be most important in the relationship between latchkey children and their parents. When parents ask children to care for themselves, they are asking their children to assume responsibility, but in return the parents are showing that they have trust and confidence in the child. Trust and confidence are likely to translate, in a general way, into more freedom for the child. This is consistent with social exchange theory, since the cost of more responsibility (as well as loneliness, and perhaps fear) is repaid with parental trust and greater personal freedom for the child.

This pattern of parent–child relations has been documented in the case of children who live with a single custodial parent after divorce. Such children are often given greater home and family responsibilities. Indeed, divorced mothers are often the parents who must ask their children to take care of themselves while they are at work. These children of divorce have been described as children who "grow up a little faster" (Weiss, 1979). In return these mothers often treat their children more as equals, rather than as subordinates. Again, this is an example of social exchange theory in action.

Looking at the Research

Definitions. Research on any subject requires precise and unambiguous definitions of key terms. While journalists and television broadcasters can use a term like *latchkey children* quite loosely, and thus imprecisely, a researcher cannot. To compare latchkey, or self-care, children with children who have adult care, a researcher must specify exactly what criteria must be met to qualify a child as a latchkey child. For example, does a latchkey child have to be the child of working parents? Not necessarily, since parents may be engaged in many different activities (shopping, recreation, medical appointments) that take them away from home, while their children are left to care for themselves (Cole and Rodman, 1987).

At what ages is an unsupervised child considered a latchkey child? Would a 15-year-old be considered a latchkey child? Generally an adolescent at this age is thought to be able to care for himself or herself. How young can a child be and still be thought of as a self-care child? Most people would agree that leaving a three- or four-year-old child alone would constitute a form of child neglect, and thus would be qualitatively different from self-care.

Other definitional questions deal with whether siblings are present in the home, and if so, what their ages are. An older sibling in the house, say a 19-year-old, can be seen as a surrogate parent for a younger child. But a younger sibling simply means more responsibility for the child. There is also the question of how much time the child spends alone, and how frequently. A child who must be at home five hours every day before a parent arrives home is in a different situation from the child who must occasionally wait alone for a half-hour because heavy traffic conditions detained a parent.

After considering all of these factors, one group of researchers concluded that a latchkey, or self-care, child should be defined as ". . . one between the ages of approximately 6 and 13 who spends time at home alone or with a younger sibling on a periodic basis" (Cole and Rodman, 1987, p. 93).

Studies. Even though the media have shown a flurry of interest in latchkey children, relatively few studies have been conducted by sociologists and other social scientists (Koblinsky and Todd, 1989). Cole and Rodman (1987) reviewed the studies that have been published, and found only five that studied the consequences of self-care for the functioning and development of children.

A study conducted by Rodman and his associates may be taken as an example of this research (Rodman, Pratto, and Nelson, 1985). In this study, 96 children in the fourth and seventh grades were studied; half were self-care children, and the other half had adult care. Pairs of these children (one self-care, the other adult care) were matched on age, sex, race, family composition, and family status. No statistically significant differences were found in their self-esteem, or in their feelings of having personal control over the events in their lives. Their teachers did not see significant differences between the self-care and adult-care children on social adjustment or interpersonal relations.

Some studies have found differences between self-care and adult-care children. For example, a study conducted in the 1970s found self-care girls to have some shortcomings in school social relations (Woods, 1972). Other studies, however, have found no differences between self-care and adult-care children. At best, the research results are mixed, but there is certainly no overwhelming evidence that children who care for themselves suffer serious negative consequences as a result of the experience (Cole and Rodman, 1987).

There is, however, some evidence that latchkey children show more independence, self-reliance, responsibility, resourcefulness, and maturity than their peers who are supervised. As Robinson, Rowland, and Coleman have concluded, "Whatever the reason, research to date suggests that many latchkey kids are doing well and appear to be growing and developing similarly to their nonlatchkey contemporaries" (1986, p. 33).

A need certainly exists for more research, especially research that asks more refined questions about the effects of self-care under different circumstances and varying conditions. But we already know that much of the sensationalism about latchkey children, and the more extreme examples of latchkeyphobia, is not supported by the available research.

In contrast to the pathetic description of the latchkey child Mark, waiting desolately on his front steps (one wonders why he didn't use his key), we have the case of Heather.

Ten-year-old Heather comes home from school, unlocks her front door, and secures it behind her. She calls her mother at work to inform her that she is home safe and sound and spends the next two hours completing homework until her mother gets home. "We have strict rules that Heather must follow when she's home alone," her mother says with ambivalence. "She knows that she is not to allow strangers or friends inside when I'm not home. She has a routine that she follows every afternoon so I feel pretty secure about that. I think being alone for a few hours a day makes her more self-reliant and responsible." (Robinson, Rowland, and Coleman, 1986)

But her mother then voices a concern that is apt to be expressed by all parents, whenever their children are not under their close supervision: "But I must admit that I worry about her constantly" (Robinson, Rowland, and Coleman, 1986). This parental attitude is apt to be a key distinguishing factor between self-care that is appropriate, perhaps even beneficial, and self-care that is inappropriate and potentially harmful to the child. Responsible parents must carefully consider the circumstances and conditions under which they ask their children to care for themselves.

References

COLE, CYNTHIA, and RODMAN, HYMAN. "When School-Age Children Care for Themselves: Issues for Family Life Educators and Parents." *Family Relations* 36, 1987.

KOBLINSKY, SALLY A., and TODD, CHRISTINE M. "Teaching Self-Care to Latchkey Children: A Review of Research." *Family Relations* 38, 1989.

MASON, MARY ANN. *The Equality Trap*. New York: Simon and Shuster, 1988.

PARSONS, TALCOTT, and BALES, ROBERT F. *Family, Socialization and Interaction Process*. New York: The Free Press, 1955.

RENZETTI, CLAIRE M., and CURRAN, DANIEL J. *Women, Men, and Society: The Sociology of Gender*. Boston: Allyn and Bacon, 1989.

ROBINSON, BRYAN E.; ROWLAND, BOBBIE A.; and COLEMAN, MICK. *Latchkey Kids: Unlocking Doors For Children and Their Families*. Lexington, Mass.: Lexington Books, 1986.

RODMAN, HYMAN. "Forget the Horror Stories About Latchkey Children." *Los Angeles Times*, September 5, 1985.

RODMAN, HYMAN; PRATTO, DAVID J.; and NELSON, ROSEMARY SMITH. "Child Care Arrangements and Children's Functioning: A Comparison of Self-Care and Adult-Care Children." *Developmental Psychology* 21, 1985.

WEISS, ROBERT S. *Going it Alone: The Family Life and Social Situation of the Single Parent*. New York: Basic Books, 1979.

WOODS, M.B. "The Unsupervised Child of the Working Mother." *Developmental Psychology* 6, 1972.

17 Population and Urbanization

- More people were *added to* the world's population in the last 12 years (1 billion) than existed in the entire world when the United States became a nation.

- This rapid growth in population is contributing to dramatic increases in the growth of the world's cities. In 1950 only 78 cities had more than a million residents. By the year 2010 over 500 cities will have a million or more residents.

Societies around the world have been deeply influenced, and continue to be shaped, by two unprecedented trends of the twentieth century: (1) population growth, in both individual societies and the world as a whole; (2) ever-increasing numbers of people living in urban rather than rural places.

The scientific study of population is called **demography.** Demographers study why and how populations grow and decline by examining the three basic processes that determine population size. The first process is **fertility,** a term used by demographers to indicate the actual childbearing behavior of people. The second is **mortality,** which refers to deaths and death rates of a specific population. The third is **migration,** which is the permanent (or semi-permanent) change of one's place of residence. In addition to studying these dynamic features of populations, demographers also consider the characteristics of the population (called **population composition**). The most frequently considered characteristics of a population are age and sex.

Fertility

Having children is fundamentally a social behavior since it is profoundly influenced by the social contexts in which people live. These contexts may be as large scale as the economic or political times or as small scale as the particular couples who are making decisions about whether to have a baby. Even if, as some people believe, there is a human "instinct" or genetic "drive" to have children, this explanation would not reveal why some people have many children, others have only a few, and some have none.

Just as individuals (or couples) vary greatly in the number of children they have, so do groups or categories of people. As an extreme example, the Hutterites, a fundamentalist religious group living in the plains states of the northern Midwest and southern Canada, have the record for the highest fertility ever reliably recorded for any population. As recently as the 1950s, Hutterite women had an *average* of nearly 11 children. The Hutterites oppose any methods of controlling childbearing, they marry in their late teens or early twenties, and they do not allow divorce. Among the Hutterites all property is owned in common and children are cared for communally. Because of these particular social arrangements and cultural values the Hutterites have what population scientists believe to be the maximum level of fertility (Stockwell and Groat, 1984). This maximum level of uncontrolled childbearing is called **natural fertility** (Bongaarts, 1987).

As an interesting contrast to the Hutterites, there were two U.S. religious groups of the nineteenth century for which fertility was almost nonexistent. The Shakers and the Rappites, both located in the eastern United States, prohibited sexual intercourse for most of their members. The only way these religious groups could grow in size was to recruit new members and to adopt children. Today the Rappites have completely disappeared, and only a handful of Shaker women survive (Kephart, 1976; Muncy, 1973).

The fertility extremes of the Hutterites on the one hand, and the Shakers and Rappites on the other, illustrate very well how social contexts influence childbearing. In contemporary American society differences in fertility still exist between some societal groups and categories, but the differences are not great, and they are less pronounced today than they were in the past. Some differences in fertility among religious, racial, and socioeconomic groups will be considered after we examine some general trends in fertility in the United States.

Childbearing in the United States today is at the lowest rate in history. At the time of the founding of the country the average woman had just under eight births. Today the number of births per woman is slightly less than two (1.9 average) (Ryder, 1990). The birth rate went down steadily through the entire nineteenth century and for nearly half of the twentieth. Then, after World War II, the birth rate went up substantially and remained high during the 1950s. This period between 1946 and 1960 is called the *baby boom.* By the late 1980s the birth rate had again fallen to a level that reflects the long, generally steady decline in childbearing in the United States (Westoff, 1986).

Since the baby-boom generation continues to affect the U.S. population and will continue to do so until past the middle of the twenty-first century, it qualifies as a demographic phenomenon of some importance. The "causes" of the baby boom are still not completely understood, but demographers do offer some explanations. Much of the increase in childbearing during the 1950s can be attributed to the high percentage of the U.S. population marrying (over 90 percent), and marrying at an early age. Throughout the entire twentieth century, Americans married youngest during the middle of the baby boom, in 1956. Although the ideal family size for many in the 1950s was three or four children, exceptionally large families did not produce the baby boom. Most of the increase in birth rates came from early and near-universal marriage, and rapid childbearing (Westoff, 1986).

The increase in birth rates during the baby-boom years came as a surprise to almost all demographers. The trend of declining childbearing had persisted for more than a century, and it was expected to continue. Since it did not, it raises the question of whether the birth rate could rise again, producing a new baby boom (Ryder, 1990). For the near future, that possibility appears unlikely, primarily because the trends for age of first marriage and age of having a first child have been going up for the last two decades. These trends are exactly the opposite of what occurred to produce the baby boom.

Social Factors Related to Fertility Rates

The influence of social factors on childbearing can be easily demonstrated by comparing the birth rates of various groups or categories in the society. For example, a century ago farm people in the United States had higher birth rates than the urban people. Today the differences in fertility between farm and urban people are not important, primarily because only 2 percent of the national population now lives on farms (U.S. Bureau of the Census, 1987). However, various religious, racial, and socioeconomic groups are of significant size in the U.S. population so their differences in fertility could be important.

Religion.   Because the Roman Catholic church disapproves of the use of mechanical and chemical methods of contraception (including sterilization), it might be assumed that the Catholic birth rate would be much higher than the birth rates of other religious groups. Such is not the case, however; for nearly two decades Catholic fertility has been almost the same, or only slightly higher than the fertility of non-Catholics (Westoff and Jones, 1979). One study during the 1980s, for example, found Protestant family size at 1.92 children and Catholic family size at 1.96 children (Westoff, 1986). In a recent study comparing Catholic and non-Catholic fertility in Rhode Island the number of children ever born was 2.29 for Catholic women and 2.07 for non-Catholic women (Williams and Zimmer, 1990). The higher fertility for Catholic women was produced entirely by the differences between Catholic and non-Catholic women who attended church weekly. For the women who attended church less frequently, the non-Catholic women actually had more children than the Catholic women (Williams and Zimmer, 1990).

With regard to contraception, Catholics in the United States use various birth control methods at about the same level as non-Catholics (Westoff, 1986). American Jewish women have somewhat lower fertility than either Protestants or Catholics (1.72 children), but the lowest levels of fertility are generally found among members of the population who claim no religion.

Race and Ethnicity.   Differences still exist in the fertility levels of different racial and ethnic groups in the United States. A comparison between whites and blacks finds that black women have, on average, about one-half child more than white women. Hispanic women in the United States have more children than either blacks or whites, although there are significant differences among Hispanics. Cubans have the lowest fertility among Hispanics, while Mexicans have the highest. Asian Americans generally have lower fertility than other Americans, although again there are important differences: Japanese Americans have lower fertility than whites, while Vietnamese in the United States have higher fertility than whites (Westoff, 1986).

Socioeconomic Status.   Most people accept the precept that socioeconomic status is related to fertility. In sociological terms, "lower socioeconomic status is associated with higher fertility." This is consistent with the old cliche that ends, ". . . and the poor get children." Although these statements are somewhat true, qualifications are necessary. For example, the opposite is the case in traditional peasant societies, where wealthier

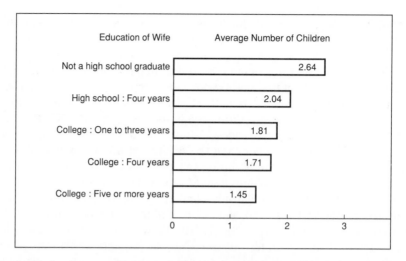

Figure 17–1.   Average Number of Children Born to Wives Aged 35–44 Years in Married-Couple Families, by Education of Wife, 1990. (*Source:* U.S. Bureau of Census, *Fertility of American Women: June 1990, Current Population Reports,* P-20, No. 454, Table 3, 1991).

land-owning couples may have more children than those less well off. Studies from India, Bangladesh, Iran, Nepal, the Philippines, and Thailand show some tendency for higher-status landowners to have higher fertility than other farm families. In these societies, owning land increases the demand for children and provides greater security for old age (World Bank, 1984).

In Western societies during the twentieth century, however, the relationship between socioeconomic status and fertility has usually been negative. But this negative relationship was strongest in the early part of the twentieth century, as the middle and upper middle classes started using family limitation methods that were not yet available to the lower classes.

In present-day American society, regardless of whether socioeconomic status is measured by educational level, occupational status, or income, higher-status women have fewer children. Of these three indicators of socioeconomic status, the educational attainment of a woman is the strongest variable. Among married women aged 25 to 34 years, those with less than a high school education have an average of 2.3 children, while women of the same age with four years of college have an average of 1.1 children. Of course, some of these college-educated women who are still in their twenties are likely to have more children before they complete childbearing years. Figure 17–1 shows the average number of children per woman aged 35 to 44 years (an age group that has probably completed most of its childbearing) at various educational levels. For this age group in 1990, there is still nearly a one-child difference between women who did not complete high school and women who completed college. Although this figure does show the expected relationship with socioeconomic status, the difference is less than one child between the lowest education group and college-educated women.

Mortality

Death is obviously a biological event, since every death is ultimately due to a biological cause. Nonetheless, social factors do contribute to differences in death rates among different groups and categories in society. Two distinctive aspects of social life are related to mortality differences: (1) the positions that people have in the social structure and (2) lifestyles.

Position in the social structure refers to the way some groups or categories have lower (or higher) places in some ranking system of the society. Life-style refers to the choices people make in the conduct of their daily lives. This includes how they eat, use alcohol or drugs, exercise, and so on. Life-style is not a precise scientific concept, but a number of causes of death are clearly associated with the choices people make about their lives. We begin our examination of the way in which these social factors influence mortality by considering some examples of how position in the social structure influences death rates and longevity.

Position in the Social Structure

In chapter 8 we saw how the position one has in the stratification structure of a society can influence length of life. People in the lower socioeconomic classes have higher death rates and a shorter life expectancy. As a general principle we may say that people who are in lower or disadvantaged positions in a society (or social structure) will have higher death rates and shorter lives.

This principle is also illustrated by comparing the life expectancies of black and white Americans. At birth a black female has a life expectancy that is five and one-half years less than a white female (black 73.4 years versus white 78.8 years). Black males are even more disadvantaged compared to white males since white males can expect to live seven and one-half years longer (National Center for Health Statistics, 1990). The difference between black and white life expectancy has been decreasing since the beginning of the twentieth century, when life expectancy for whites was about 16 years longer than for blacks (National Center for Health Statistics, 1988).

A distressing trend has occurred since 1985, however. Life expectancy has been declining among blacks, a trend that is especially pronounced among black males. In 1988 (the latest year for which data are available) the life expectancy for black males had dropped below 65 years. During these same years life expectancy among whites had been increasing. In the years when the life expectancy of black males was declining the life expectancy of white males increased by one-half year, up to 72.3 years.

During the twentieth century there has rarely been a year when life expectancy has declined, and when it did (as in 1979), the decline was related to a general cause of death (such as an influenza epidemic) that affected the death rates of all races. Several reasons are possible for the lowered life expectancy among African Americans in recent years, including increases in death rates due to homicide, accidents, tuberculosis, pneumonia, AIDS, and possibly to drug-related deaths (Hilts, 1988).

Gender Roles and Mortality. In chapter 10 we saw that the feminine gender role, especially in traditional, patriarchal societies, places women in subordinate positions to men. It follows, therefore, that females should have higher death rates or lower life expectancy than males. In fact, females in the contemporary world generally have a longer life expectancy than males, but that may be due to a biological advantage of females over males. We know, for example, that the death rate among male fetuses is higher than female fetuses during pregnancy, and that males have a higher death rate than females during the first four weeks of life. Both of these facts suggest that the female organism is more viable than the male organism, since social and cultural factors could not account for the lower death rates of females.

Yet societies do exist in which females do not survive as long as males, or they have only a slight advantage over males; these are often the same societies in which males have distinctly dominant positions in the social structure. For example, infanticide has been practiced in some societies, and in those cases, almost invariably, female infants are the ones who are killed or allowed to die. (See the Cross-Cultural Perspectives box: "Infanticide and the Preference for Male Children.") Today, for example, there are indications that some female infanticide is occurring in contemporary China as an outgrowth of the family limitation policies of the central government (Arnold and Zhaoxiang, 1986; Hull, 1990). In the Punjab state of India, where parents often do not want female children, the childhood mortality rate of females is twice as high as that of males (Das Gupta, 1987).

As another example of how women's subordinate status may affect their longevity, a World Bank report shows only three countries of the world (India, Pakistan, and Bhutan) in which female life expectancy is less than male life expectancy (World Bank, 1984). In the two large Asian countries, females generally hold a status subordinate to that of males (Miller, 1981; Preston, 1982).

Life-Styles and Mortality

Life-style, as we noted earlier, refers to the choices people make in the conduct of their daily lives. Today, in a country like the United States, heart disease, cancer, and accidents are major causes of death, and all appear to be greatly influenced by the choices we make in our daily lives. The significance of life-style choices on mortality is vividly illustrated by the use of tobacco and tobacco products. Most of the world lived without any knowledge and therefore use of tobacco until it was discovered by Columbus and his men in Cuba in 1492. Even then it took nearly 100 years before tobacco was successfully introduced to most Europeans (Ravenholt, 1990).

Since the latter part of the sixteenth century, however, human beings in great numbers around the world have chosen to smoke, sniff, and chew tobacco. The massive numbers of deaths produced by tobacco use has led one scholar to describe it as "Tobacco's Global Death March" (Ravenholt, 1990, p. 213). Worldwide, 5 trillion cigarettes are smoked annually and millions of tons of tobacco are consumed in other forms. The deaths resulting from the use of tobacco will rival those of the Black Death, smallpox, malaria, yellow fever, Asiatic cholera, and tuberculosis. The major difference between the deaths caused by tobacco and those caused by the other epidemics is that people choose to use tobacco. The worldwide death toll from tobacco use is estimated at 3 million annually. More than 50 million people will die during this century because of their choice to use tobacco (Ravenholt, 1990).

For specific examples of how the use of tobacco, along with other life-style choices, influence death rates we have the results of research on two religious groups in the United States: Mormons and Seventh-Day Adventists.

Mormons and Seventh-Day Adventists.   Both of these religions have doctrinal restrictions on the use of both tobacco products and alcohol. The Mormons also restrict the use of coffee, tea, and addictive drugs, while the Seventh-Day Adventists are urged to abstain from coffee, tea, other caffeine beverages, and meat (Enstrom, 1978; Phillips et al., 1980).

In an eight-year study of cancer death rates, Seventh-Day Adventists in California were compared with the general California population. With regard to cancers that are strongly related to smoking (such as cancer of the lungs, mouth, pharynx, and esophagus), the Seventh-Day Adventists had a risk of death that was only 20 to 30 percent of the general population of similar age and sex (Phillips et al., 1980). Even in the case of cancers that are not known to be smoking-related, the risk of death among Seventh-Day Adventists was only 65 to 75 percent of that for the general population (Phillips et al., 1980).

Cross-Cultural Perspectives

Infanticide and the Preference for Male Children

In societies around the world there is a preference for male babies over female babies. Parents in virtually every society candidly admit that they prefer their first child to be a male, and, in general, they prefer a larger number of sons than daughters (Williamson, 1978). This widespread cultural preference has often led to female infanticide, in which female babies are killed, or allowed to die, after they are born. While most examples of infanticide are historical, there is evidence that even in the contemporary world female babies are sometimes allowed to die because they are not wanted by their parents. Contemporary India, China, and Japan all provide illustrations of female infanticide.

In Japan the year 1966 was called the year of the Fiery Horse. According to traditional Japanese beliefs, a girl born in the year of the Fiery Horse was ill fated. Some Japanese parents apparently accepted this belief, because in 1966 a larger proportion of female babies died in the first month of life than would have been expected from the records of previous, or subsequent, years. While this could be a confirmation of the validity of the folklore, a more likely possibility is female infanticide (Kaku, 1975).

There is also much evidence of infanticide in India's history. Before the British outlawed the practice in 1870 with the passage of the Infanticide Act, female infanticide was openly practiced. In the nineteenth century the following dialogue occurred between a British official and an Indian landholder:

> 'It is the general belief among us, Sir, that those who preserve their daughters never prosper; and, that the families into which we marry them are equally unfortunate.'
>
> 'Then you think that it is a duty imposed upon you from above, to destroy your infant daughters; and that the neglect and disregard of that duty brings misfortunes upon you?'
>
> 'We think it must be so, Sir, with regard to our own families or clan!' (Miller, 1981).

In fact, the practice of female infanticide in some areas of India was so common that visitors noticed, and later censuses confirmed, that there was a shortage of females.

Why was female infanticide practiced so often in certain parts of India prior to 1870? Pride and money appear to be important factors. Fathers wanted to marry their daughters into families of equal or higher status, and a prestigious marriage required the payment of a large dowry. In addition, it was considered shameful to have unmarried daughters at home. Thus, if parents had many daughters or few resources, economics and pride would lead them to consider killing some as infants.

While open infanticide is no longer condoned in India, it may still be practiced in a more subtle manner. One researcher found that, in families where mothers expressed a preference for no more children, there was a higher rate of female infant deaths. Male infant deaths were also higher in such families, but not to the same degree as females (Simmons et al., 1982).

One observer of contemporary India has said:

> The actual murder of little girls has in great measure ceased, but it has been replaced . . . by a degree of carelessness hardly less criminal. (Miller, 1961)

In modern China, also, there is circumstantial evidence of some female infanticide. When China's one-child policy is rigidly enforced, a higher percentage of female first-children die than would normally occur (Hull, 1990).

Even in contemporary England, the fourth or fifth child of a family has a 25 percent greater chance of dying in infancy than a child who is the first born (Weeks, 1989). Although not indicating a preference for male children, or female infanticide, such evidence suggests that infanticide may be occurring, even in developed countries with modern medical systems.

HULL, TERRANCE H. "Recent Trends in Sex Ratios at Birth in China." *Population and Development Review* 16, 1990.
KAKU, KANAE. "Were Girl Babies Sacrificed to Folk Superstition in 1966 in Japan?" *Annals of Human Biology* 2, 1975.
MILLER, BARBARA D. *The Endangered Sex: Neglect of Female Children in Rural North India.* Ithaca, N.Y.: Cornell University Press, 1981.
SIMMONS, G.; SMUCKER, C.; BERNSTEIN, S.; and JENSEN, E. "Post-neonatal Mortality in Rural India: Implications of an Economic Model." *Demography* 19, 1982.
WEEKS, JOHN R. *Population: An Introduction to Concepts and Issues*, 4th ed. Belmont, CA.: Wadsworth Publishing Co., 1989.
WILLIAMSON, NANCY E. "Boys or Girls? Parents' Preferences and Sex Control." *Population Bulletin* 33, 1978.

Studies of Mormons in both California and Utah have shown similar results. In a study by Enstrom (1978), comparisons were made between Mormon males who were active in the church and U.S. males in general. The death rates for the Mormon men (aged 35–64) were only 35 percent of the death rates of U.S. white males of the same age category (Enstrom, 1978). Seen in a somewhat different way, active Mormon males at age 35 could expect to live about eight years longer than U.S. males as a whole at the same age.

Migration

Migration is the movement of individuals or groups from one place of residence to another when they have the intention of remaining in the new place for some substantial amount of time. By this definition it is not migration if someone simply travels someplace for a visit and returns. Even temporarily living in another place, as one might do at a summer vacation home, is not migration. The key to migration is that a new residence is being established. Sometimes that new residence may be a different house in the same neighborhood or community, but at the opposite extreme, the new residence may be in a different country. The term *immigration*, which we discussed in chapter 9, refers to migration from one nation or country to another.

Migration in the United States

Throughout the history of the United States, migration from one state, or one region, to another has been an important factor in determining the growth and development of the country. Historically the two major migration trends in the United States have been from rural to urban places, and from east to west. (Later in this chapter we will focus on migration from rural to urban places and, in particular, on the continuing growth of metropolitan areas.)

Migration to the Sun Belt. A general westward migration has characterized much of U.S. history, and it continues, but in recent decades that trend has been modified by a southward movement as well. The new migration pattern is toward the "Sun Belt"—the states in the southern and western parts of the United States that have mild climates. Although poorer economic conditions during the 1980s did slow migration to some of the oil-producing states on the Gulf Coast, Sun Belt states are still growing. In looking to the future, it is estimated that until the year 2010 the states of California, Texas, and Florida will experience more than half of the increases in the U.S. population. Some of that growth will be due to the migrants coming from other states, and another part will be due to immigration. Among these three states, Florida's growth will come primarily from internal migration, while Texas, and especially California, will add more population due to immigration (U.S. Bureau of the Census, 1988d).

Some states are expected to lose population in the next two decades, in part because of out-migration. These states are located primarily in the upper Midwest but also include some western, eastern, and border states. Specifically, the states expected to lose population in the next two decades include Montana, Wyoming, North Dakota, Nebraska, Iowa, Wisconsin, Illinois, Michigan, Indiana, Kentucky, Ohio, West Virginia, and Pennsylvania (U.S. Bureau of the Census, 1988d).

World Population Growth

The term **population explosion** has been widely used to describe the rapid growth of the world's population in the twentieth century. Although this is not a technical demographic term, it is an apt description of how much the population of the world has grown in the last 50 years. In comparison with the rest of human history, there has been an explosion in the number of the earth's inhabitants.

In the long history of human life on earth, which some archaeologists and anthropologists estimate to be as much as 2 million years, the human population did not grow very rapidly. It is estimated that even after the world was well into the Christian era, 1000 A.D., there were fewer than 300 million people (Durand, 1977). It took all the preceding thousands of years for the population of the earth to reach 300 million people, but in our time it takes less than four years to add that many people to the world's population.

In all likelihood, the world first achieved a population of 1 billion people in the early part of the 1800s. By 1930 the size of the population had reached 2 billion; the third billion was added in just 30 years, by 1960. The fourth billion was added in about 13 years, in 1973. Since then, the rate of growth has slowed down a little, but with a larger population base, it now takes only about 12 years to add a thousand-million people (a billion). Every four days a million more people are added to the earth's population.

Let us be clear on this point. A million people are added to the world's population every four days, despite the high death rates that prevail in many countries, despite high rates of infant mortality, despite deaths caused by wars, starvation, natural disasters, and disease. In other words, the number of births occurring each year exceeds the number of deaths, and thus the world's population grows by more than 85 million people each year.

Some people say that there is no population explosion, or that talk

Table 17–1. The Three Stages of the Modern Demographic Transition

Stage	Death Rate	Birth Rate	Population Growth Rate
1. Agricultural	High	High	Low
2. Transition	Low	High	High
3. Final	Low	Low	Low

about a population explosion is an exaggeration or scare tactic. Since the term has no precise definition, these charges are difficult to evaluate. However, two things can be said with certainty. First, the number of people being added to the earth's population each year is many times greater than ever before in human history. Second, since a 1.7 percent growth rate doubles the earth's population every 40 years, such growth cannot go on indefinitely. These facts have led most people to conclude that steps must be taken to slow down or stop the rate of population growth. As we will see below, not everyone agrees with this view, but in order to address the question of what should be done about world population growth, we must first understand why the earth's population, after hundreds of thousands of years of relative stability, started growing in the seventeenth century and has been growing especially fast in the last 50 years. It will help us if we first consider an important idea of demography called the Modern Demographic Transition.

The Modern Demographic Transition

The **Modern Demographic Transition** can be defined as a three-stage pattern of population change that occurs as a society is transformed from an agricultural to a fully industrialized, urban economy. The agricultural stage has a balanced population with a high death rate and a high birth rate. The transition stage has a growing population with a high birth rate and a decreasing death rate. And the final stage of the transition has a much lower population growth rate because the birth rate has dropped to a level roughly equal to that of the death rate. The three stages of the Modern Demographic Transition and the levels of population growth are shown in table 17–1.

Modern Demographic Transition theory helps to explain why the world's population is currently growing so fast. One point it makes clearly is that recent dramatic increases in population growth are caused by *changes in the death rate* and not by changes in the birth rate. Many people erroneously believe that the birth rate has been rising rapidly in many countries, thus producing rapid population growth. This is not true; the population has "exploded" because of the decline in the death rate.

The demographic transition occurred first in the countries of northern and western Europe. By the beginning of the eighteenth century, as the countries of this region began the process of modernizing and industrializing, their death rates started to decline. The birth rates in these countries, which had traditionally been high, remained at that level for some time. The result, of course, was population growth during the transition period. Although exceptions to this pattern were found in some European countries, they do not outweigh the far greater number of cases where mortality started declining at the beginnings of modernization, to be followed considerably later by declines in fertility (Beaver, 1975).

According to transition theory, modernization also brings about a decline in birth rates, but this decline comes much later than the decline in death rates. One reason why birth rates go down after death rates is that the characteristics of childbearing are very different from the characteristics of mortality. This is especially the case with respect to the positive value that most societies place on life (both producing it and keeping it going). Whereas lowering the death rate is completely consistent with the positive value placed on life, lowering the birth rate is not. Producing new life by having children, in society after society, is an act that is praised and greeted with joy. If fertility is to go down, it is necessary to some degree for individual couples to act contrary to this valued act. Even when it might be advantageous for an individual couple to refrain from having children, the prevailing values, supported by customs and norms, act as strong pressures for them to have children anyway.

Nonetheless, as the modernization process continues, and especially as societies become primarily urban instead of rural, the birth rates do go down. This is the final stage of the demographic transition, and usually means that population growth slows down greatly or stops completely. Today almost all European countries (as well as the United States, Canada, Australia, and New Zealand) have stopped growing at a rapid rate because their birth rates have declined to levels almost as low as their death rates. In some European countries, the birth rates are now equal to, or slightly lower than, the death rates, so their growth has stopped, at least for the moment. Currently, Denmark, Germany, and Hungary have birth rates as low as, or lower than, their death rates (Population Reference Bureau, 1991).

For European countries, the transition from high birth and death rates to low birth and death rates took about 200 years. The declines in the death rates came about because of changes and advances that evolved gradually. The entire demographic transition, as experienced in Europe, is shown in figure 17–2.

The demographic experience of the developing countries in the past 35 or 40 years has been similar to the European experiences in the transition stage, although one part of the process has been much more rapid. In the

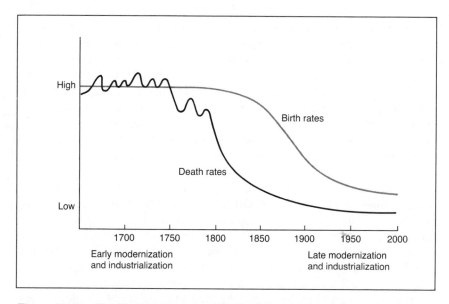

Figure 17–2.   The Modern Demographic Transition (as modeled on the Western European experience).

developing countries, representing 75 to 80 percent of the world's population, the decline in the death rate has been very fast. It has taken only a few decades for the death rates in these countries to drop because of the importation of medical, technical, and scientific advances from the developed countries. Since the birth rates have often remained high, the gap between births and deaths is great, and the resulting growth rate is extraordinary. In some areas of the world with huge populations, the birth rate remains very high, while the death rate is as low as that in the developed countries. For example, all of Latin America has a birth rate of 28 per 1000, while the death rate is seven per 1000. The growth rate for Latin America is 2.1 percent, which means that the present population of 451 million will double every 34 years if the current rate of growth continues (see figure 17–3).

The African continent, with a population of 677 million, has a growth rate even greater than that of Latin America (3.0 percent). However, in much of Africa the death rate is not as low, remaining at about 14 per 1000, while the birth rate is estimated at a very high 44 per 1000. Asia, with a population of 3.1 billion people, has a death rate of nine per 1000 and a birth rate of 27 per 1000, for a 1.8 percent increase per year (Population Reference Bureau, 1991).

Seen from the perspective of the Modern Demographic Transition, the current rate of world population growth is largely due to the fact that the

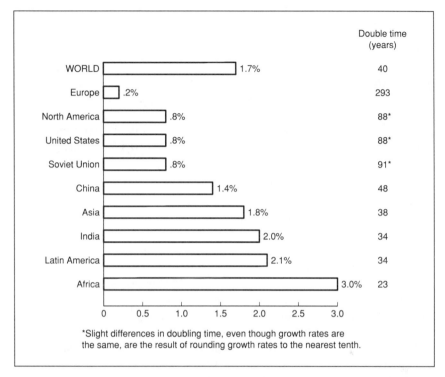

Figure 17–3. Growth Rates and Doubling Times for the World, the Five Continents, and Major Countries. (*Source:* Population Reference Bureau, 1991, *World Population Data Sheet* (Washington, D.C.: Population Reference Bureau, Inc. 1991).)

developing countries have reduced their death rates far more quickly than their birth rates. Birth rates remain high because of the value that societies place on producing life. Death rates have declined fairly quickly because people are likely to adopt the means for controlling death soon after they become available. Lowering birth rates, however, runs counter to the value placed on producing life, so methods of controlling birth are not so quickly adopted. Many, many individual couples have to modify their orientations toward childbearing before the birth rate begins to go down. Generally, this takes a considerable period of time, during which the population grows very rapidly.

This point raises the question about whether decreases in fertility can be brought about more quickly so that population growth will be less rapid. Much of the debate about population growth centers around the question of how fertility can be lowered in populations where it remains high. We consider some major points of view about this question next.

Approaches to Reducing Fertility

Some specialists on population have argued that it is not necessary to make any special efforts to lower fertility levels and slow population growth (Simon, 1981). However, this view is clearly in a minority; the broad consensus is that it would be better for individual countries and the world in general if the growth of population could be slowed. Three different views about reducing fertility can be identified: economic development, voluntary family-planning programs, and societal change.

Economic Development.   The following slogan is often heard from the advocates of this view: *Economic development is the best contraceptive.* The assumption is that developing countries, which are now experiencing the highest growth rates, will experience a lowering of fertility when their economies become more urban, industrialized, and modernized. Economic development in these countries is expected to have the same effects on fertility as it did in Europe, the United States, and other developed countries. This view reflects a faith that the modern demographic transition will take its course, just as it did in the societies that modernized in the nineteenth and early twentieth centuries.

Some advocates of the economic development view urge developing countries to adopt free-enterprise, capitalist economies as a way of hastening economic development. Others have taken a Marxist view and urge developing countries to adopt socialist economic principles as a way of achieving economic development. Both economic views, while otherwise diametrically opposed, believe that economic development is the easy way to bring fertility rates down and thus slow population growth. Critics of this view point out that economic development is impeded by high birth rates that produce large numbers of children who are not economically productive.

Voluntary Family Planning.   *Family-planning programs* have three basic elements: providing knowledge and information about reproductive physiology and contraceptive techniques; (2) providing contraceptive techniques; and (3) conducting a propaganda campaign that supports the small family ideal and the acceptability of contraception.

This approach is voluntary because the aim is not to coerce or force people to use contraception or limit their family size. In fact, in some countries, there is evidence that a substantial number of couples want fewer children than they have. There is evidence that with a well-run, comprehensive family-planning program, the reduction in fertility rates will come from fewer births of unwanted children (Freedman, 1990; Mauldin, 1983).

Societal Change. A number of demographers have pointed to the limitations of family-planning programs alone, arguing that without some basic societal changes, it will be difficult or impossible to reduce fertility. These advocates point out that most societies, especially many of the developing ones, have social institutions and cultural values that make large families both advantageous and desirable (Davis, 1967; Demerath, 1976).

The social institutions of many societies are arranged in such a way that children have economic value for parents. In many societies, even young children are able to contribute to the economic well-being of the family. This is especially true of children who live in rural areas who work in the fields, tend livestock, and take care of smaller children while their parents are working. Even in the urban areas of many Third World countries children begin working beside their parents at an early age. Later in life, children are economically beneficial because they will care for their elderly parents (Caldwell, 1982; Nugent, 1985).

Advocates of societal change argue that, in addition to family-planning programs, there must be reductions in these economic motivations for having children. For example, if compulsory education laws are passed, or if child-labor laws prohibit children from working, parents will have fewer economic motivations for large families. Similarly, if governments initiate some form of economic support in old age, such as a Social Security system, parents will be less motivated to have large families to care for them in old age.

Changes in the role of women in society can also be a factor that will reduce fertility levels. When women are isolated from participating in activities outside the home, their status (or worth) rests largely on their ability to bear and rear children. Under these societal and cultural conditions, where the primary role for women is motherhood, fertility is likely to remain high. To decrease fertility, societal changes can be made that will improve the status of women. Studies have shown that when women are given greater educational and employment opportunities, fertility declines (World Bank, 1984; Youssef, 1974).

Can Population Growth Be Slowed or Stopped?

Demographers have identified key ways of reducing fertility—through economic development, family-planning programs, and societal change—but the question still remains as to whether these solutions can be made to work in the real world. Many observers doubt that deeply embedded social institutions and cultural values can be changed among people who live in poverty, who are poorly educated, and who are bound by custom, superstition, and tradition. Although the efforts required to reduce fertility in many developing countries are difficult, accumulating evidence shows that when family-planning programs are combined with strategic societal changes, reduction can be accomplished.

Several countries that had high fertility rates 30 or 40 years ago, and were then considered less-developed countries, now have fertility levels similar to those of the United States and some European countries. Taiwan, South Korea, and Singapore are examples of countries that have lowered fertility through a combination of family-planning programs, some societal changes, and economic development. But the most important example is China, which, in the space of 40 years, has lowered its fertility to a level that would not have been anticipated in 1949. In 1984 and 1985 the crude birth rate of China (about 17.5) was at a level just slightly above that of the United States (16.0) (Hardee-Cleveland and Banister, 1988).

The Chinese reduction of fertility occurred, in part, because the government undertook extensive family-planning programs. The first program was started in 1954, and although it produced some decline in the birth rate, the most important family-planning program has been the well-publicized one-child program of the 1980s. But in addition, again going back to the 1950s, the Chinese made some societal changes that had the potential for reducing fertility (Greenhalgh, 1990). These included efforts to improve the status of women and laws to raise the age of marriage.

The one-child policy of China has often had a near-mandatory family-planning component, with close supervision of the contraceptive practices of couples and some penalties for disregarding the regulations. However, the one-child policy also includes some rewards, and these are consistent with what we have described as societal changes. Couples who agree to have only one child are given greater monthly stipends, better housing, preferred status for their children in schools, and supplemental pensions when parents reach old age (Chen and Kols, 1982). These rewards, in combination with the family-planning program, have been most effective in the major cities of China and somewhat less effective in the rural areas (Hardee-Cleveland and Banister, 1988; Whyte and Gu, 1987).

Since 1983 the Chinese government has sometimes modified its enforcement of the one-child program, but the government still has the aim of keeping its growth rate at less than 1.5 percent until at least the year 2000. The important point to be drawn from the Chinese experience is that fertility can be lowered to the levels of Western societies, even before a substantial amount of economic development has been achieved (Freedman, 1990; Greenhalgh, 1990; Whyte and Gu, 1987).

The Chinese experience, combined with those of a number of other developing countries, shows that the present rate of population growth in the world can be reduced in a relatively short period of time. But it can be done only with family-planning efforts, societal changes to reduce motivations for fertility, and, to the extent possible, economic development.

All of these efforts are most easily and successfully undertaken in cities and urban environments, as we have seen in the Chinese case. In the remainder of this chapter we examine the urbanization process, both in the United States and in other countries of the world.

Urbanization

The rise of cities has been one of the most dramatic and momentous developments in human history. Most of the classic European sociological theorists discussed in this book (Durkheim, Marx, Weber, Simmel, and others) focused much of their attention on efforts to understand the changes transforming Western civilization during the nineteenth and early twentieth centuries. One of the central concerns was to analyze the unprecedented social changes accompanying the process of urbanization.

Key Concepts in Urbanization

Several key terms and concepts help to develop a sociological understanding of our increasingly urban society. First, we need to identify what we mean by the term *urban.* Often people consider the adjective *urban* to carry the same meaning as the noun *city.* However, the two terms need to be distinguished. A **city** can be defined as a relatively large, permanent, and spatially concentrated human settlement with a population far more economically interdependent and occupationally diverse than in agriculturally oriented rural areas.

There are several bases for classifying a geographically defined area and its population as urban. The definitions developed by national census agencies generally focus solely on the numbers of persons living in a specified area. In the United States, any town, municipality, or other politically defined place with a population of 2500 or more residents is classified as **urban** by the U.S. Census Bureau. However, this number differs substantially in other nations. For example, in Greece only areas with populations exceeding 10,000 are defined as urban; in Denmark, villages with only 250 residents are defined as urban; in Canada, the official definition of an urban place is one with 1000 or more residents. In light of the confusion generated by such different standards, the United Nations has recommended a standard of 20,000 residents as the level of population necessary to characterize an area as urban. Sociologically this number makes sense, because an urban place is one that has a complex array of social, economic, political, and cultural characteristics that are unlikely to emerge in places with only a few hundred or few thousand residents.

A third concept—**urbanization**—refers primarily to the process by which an increasing percentage of a society's population comes to be located in urban areas. Thus, at any given time the extent of urbanization in a society is reflected by the proportion of the total population living in urban places. Urbanization occurs largely as a result of migration of formerly rural residents within a society to urban areas, or as a result of urban settlement patterns among immigrants from other societies. The resulting concentration of population in urban centers, in turn, contributes to an expansion of the scope of urban influence in modern societies. Indeed, the term *urbanization* is also used to refer to the concentration of economic activity, political administrative organization, communication networks, and political power in urban centers.

Urbanism refers to the "way of life" associated with urban residence. Much of the field of urban sociology has focused on ways in which living in urban places may affect the life-styles, attitudes, and social relationships exhibited by urban dwellers. As noted later in this chapter, sociologists continue to debate whether urban life is characterized by negative or positive features. However, there is little doubt that the unique experiences associated with the urban environment do contribute to ways of life that are very different from those in rural areas and small towns.

World Urbanization

The first cities appear to have been established during the period of 3000 to 5000 B.C. Until very recently, however, only a small proportion of the world's people were city dwellers. As late as 1850 only 2 percent of the world's population lived in cities of more than 100,000 persons. Today, about 40 percent of the world population resides in urban places, and that number is expected to increase to more than one-half by the year 2000 (Van der Tak, Haub, and Murphy, 1980).

The emergence of early urban settlement patterns seems to have depended upon two developments. The first was the existence of a surplus supply of food and other staples. The cultivation of grain, domestication of animals, and development of rudimentary agricultural technologies combined to create the **Agricultural Revolution.** These developments contributed to a shift from nomadic living patterns to residential stability, and allowed a family to produce more than it needed for its own survival. The second development, related to the first, was the emergence of forms of social organization other than those based solely on family and kinship ties.

Until recently, most cities were very small by modern standards. Cities of more than 100,000 people were extremely rare, although some, such as Rome in the second century A.D., were substantially larger.

A major factor underlying the development of an urban world occurred in the late 1700s and early 1800s with the Industrial Revolution. As we noted in chapter 13, the Industrial Revolution occurred when machines were substituted for hand tools, and when inanimate sources of energy (water, steam, coal, oil) were used for power instead of humans or animals. The development of machines for production and the use of new energy sources greatly increased productivity and gave rise to the factory system. Large numbers of workers were needed to work in the factories, as well as to distribute and sell the manufactured products. At the same time, improvements in agricultural technology made it possible for fewer farmers to supply the needs of an expanding population.

World urban growth has been especially rapid since World War II. The world's urban population grew from 724 million in 1950 to 1½ billion in 1975, and it is projected to exceed 3 billion by 2000. The number of cities with over 1 million inhabitants has tripled in the last 35 years; in 1950 only 78 urban centers had more than 1 million inhabitants, but by 1985 more than 258 metropolises exceeded this size (Dogan and Kasarda, 1988, p. 13). By 1980 there were 28 metropolitan areas in the world with over 5 million people; ten, with over 10 million; and three, with over 15 million (Hall, 1984, p. 3). Thus the last half of the twentieth century has witnessed "the greatest flowering of cities and urban life in world history" (Hall, 1984).

As table 17–2 shows, the world's largest cities are found today on every continent except Australia. They are located in both developed countries, such as the United States, France, and Japan, and in developing countries, such as Indonesia (Jakarta), India (Calcutta and Bombay), and Iraq (Baghdad). By the year 2000 two-thirds of the world's urban population will be located in developing countries (Dogan and Kasarda, 1988). Dramatic increases in growth are projected for Third World cities such as Mexico City; Sao Paulo and Rio de Janeiro, Brazil; Shanghai and Beijing, China; Bombay and Calcutta, India; Seoul, Korea; and Tehran, Iran (Hall, 1984) (See Table 17–2).

Urban Development in the United States

In 1790, when the first U.S. Census was taken, only one in 20 Americans (5 percent) was an urban resident. Since that time, the urban proportion of the population has increased in every decade except one (1810–1820). By 1980 nearly three-fourths (73.7 percent) of the U.S. population was urban (see figure 17–4). The U.S. population has become so concentrated that by 1980 the nation's urban residents occupied less than 2 percent of the land in the United States.

Preindustrial Cities

The urban proportion of the U.S. population remained quite low until well into the nineteenth century. Preindustrial cities were usually quite small, and they were predominantly commercial and shipping centers.

Table 17–2.　World's Ten Largest Urban Areas, 1990 and 2000

1990

Urban Area	Population (in millions)
Mexico City, Mexico	20.2
Tokyo-Yokohama, Japan	18.1
São Paulo, Brazil	17.4
New York, United States	16.2
Shanghai, China	13.4
Los Angeles, United States	11.9
Calcutta, India	11.8
Buenos Aires, Brazil	11.5
Bombay, India	11.2
Seoul, Republic of Korea	11.0

2000

Urban Area	Population (in millions)
Mexico City, Mexico	25.6
São Paulo, Brazil	22.1
Tokyo-Yokohama, Japan	19.0
Shanghai, China	17.0
New York, United States	16.8
Calcutta, India	15.7
Bombay, India	15.4
Beijing, China	14.0
Los Angeles, United States	13.9
Jakarta, Indonesia	13.7

Source: United Nations. *World Urbanization Prospects, 1990,* Sales No. E91. XIII. 11, p. 11, table 8.

The largest cities were East Coast seaports; Boston, for example, led the country in size and importance in 1743 with a population of slightly more than 16,000. In 1775, just before the American Revolution, Philadelphia's population of 40,000 made it the nation's largest city. In 1800, only six cities in the United States had more than 8,000 residents (Bridenbaugh, 1938; Gist and Fava, 1974, p. 63).

Industrial Cities

By the beginning of the twentieth century the United States had become the foremost industrial nation in the world, and the rapid urbanization of the country paralleled its increasing industrialization. The urban-industrial period between 1850 and 1920 marked the era of America's most dramatic urban growth. The urban portion of the total population rose from less than one-sixth (15 percent) in 1850 to over half (51.2 percent) by 1920. By 1920 New York City had more than 5.5 million inhabitants, and Philadelphia, nearly 2 million. Chicago grew from less than 4000 in 1830 to over 2 million in 1910.

Several factors contributed to this dramatic spurt in the urbanization of the United States. First, transportation improvements such as the construction of extensive inland canal systems and the building of transcontinental railroads made it easier to ship both raw materials and agricultural products. Second, manufacturing grew as the basis of urban economies. Unlike handicrafts and other home-based economic activities of the preindustrial city, manufacturing required the employment of large numbers of people in factories. The demand for unskilled factory labor attracted many residents from rural areas into the major industrial cities. By 1910 at least one-third of the total urban population consisted of native-born Americans who had migrated from rural areas.

As industrial growth continued, factory operators turned to European immigrants to provide an abundant and cheap labor supply. During the first decade of the twentieth century about 1 million immigrants entered the United States each year. The influx of foreign-born residents created in most U.S. cities a mosaic of immigrant neighborhoods, located in distinct areas where cheap housing was within walking distance of work.

Newcomers of each immigrant wave moved from one urban neighborhood to another as their social and economic status changed. Areas deserted by one ethnic group were often quickly taken over by members of another. For example, in the years following the Civil War, the Irish and Germans of New York moved from the Lower East Side to areas of north Manhattan and Brooklyn. Italians moved into the old Irish neighborhoods, while Russian and Polish Jews occupied the formerly German districts (Glaab and Brown, 1967, p. 139). **Invasion-succession** is the term used by sociologists to identify the process whereby one group moves to a different area and is replaced by another.

Although the immigrant neighborhoods usually contained a high proportion of one particular ethnic group, they were never entirely homogeneous. In contrast, urban black neighborhoods, which grew rapidly in the twentieth century, tended to be much more homogeneous and permanent. Social restrictions on geographical and social mobility for blacks contributed to the emergence of racially distinct cities within cities, where

Sociology in the News

Population, Progress, and Pollution in Mexico City—An "Ecological Disaster"

"Whether the weather is cold or hot, one thing is usually certain [in Mexico City]: it snows" (Uhlig, 1991, p. 1). "Snow" is the word for the fine white chemical powder that each morning covers everything in Mexico City and its vast, sprawling suburbs. The problems of air pollution that afflict Mexico City today illustrate those confronting most of the rapidly expanding urban areas in the developing world.

In 1950, Mexico City had a population of about 3 million, which grew to 15 million in 1980. It is estimated that its population will reach 26 million by 2000, making it the largest urban area in human history. As Mexico City approaches this position as the world's largest city, it has also acquired the dubious dictinction of having the most polluted air of any major metropolitan area in the world. The city's level of contaminants, said one of the country's leading environmentalists, is an "ecological disaster."

A combination of human waste, industrial emissions, smoke, and, especially, vehicle exhausts, the pollution in Mexico City exceeds by as much as four times the World Health Organization's maximum limits. These conditions have contributed to numerous illnesses, ranging from skin disorders, respiratory ailments, eye irritation, and increased susceptibility to heart attacks to infectious diseases such as salmonella and hepatitis. So severe are the health risks that officials at the American School, a prestigious preparatory school, cancelled all outdoor sports activities because they concluded that the harmful effects of vigorous exercise in Mexico City outweighed its benefits.

But it is not simply the dramatically increasing numbers of people living in Mexico City that has created this environmental crisis. First, Mexico City is located in a geological basin that traps pollutants and prevents winds from dispersing many of the contaminants, and its elevation—7280 feet—limits the oxygen needed for burning fuel. Equally important, however, is that the Mexican government's efforts to reduce pollution in Mexico City have been limited and ineffective. Few effective restrictions have been placed on emissions from vehicles and industries, which release 4.35 million tons of pollutants annually. Moreover, about 30 percent of the city's residents lack effective methods for disposing of human waste, which is carried both in the city's dust or is transported into the air as harmful gases. Increasingly, environmental crises such as that confronting Mexico City will represent major challenges to political leadership throughout the world; such challenges are likely to be especially acute as pressures for urban and economic growth increase in developing countries.

HALL, PETER. *The World Cities*, 3rd ed. London: Weidenfeld and Nicolson, 1984.
UHLIG, MARK A. "Mexico City: The World's Foulest Air Grows Worse." *New York Times*, May 12, 1991.

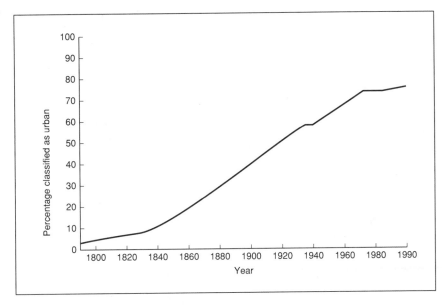

Figure 17–4. Urban Population of the United States: 1790–1980. (*Sources:* U.S. Bureau of the Census, *Statistical Abstract of the United States, 1961 and 1972,* pp. 14, 16; U.S. Bureau of the Census, *U.S. Commerce Dept. News,* Aug. 13, 1981.)

proportions of black population reached as high as 95 percent. By 1920 the enduring black ghetto had become firmly established in most U.S. cities.

Urban Differentiation. As cities grew in size and diversity, areas within them became increasingly specialized and differentiated. Rather than locating residential and commercial properties in the same neighborhood, cities came to be characterized by a distinct business district, a wholesale district, a manufacturing district, and so on.

During the first four decades of the twentieth century, numerous sociologists worked to develop general theories to explain the patterns of urban spatial differentiation. The **concentric zone model** (Park et al., 1925) suggested that urban differentiation occurred through the development of unique zones of land-use types, organized in successive rings around the city center. As indicated in figure 17–5, this approach identified a central business district at the core of the city, representing the economic center in which retail stores, theaters, hotels, banks, and office buildings were concentrated. Adjacent to this was the "zone of transition," an area of older warehouses, factories, and the deteriorating residential neighborhoods in which immigrant populations were initially concentrated. Next came the "zone of workingmen's homes," an area characterized by neigh-

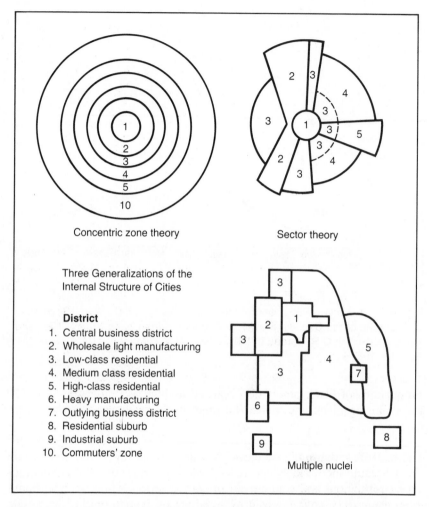

Figure 17–5. Patterns of Urban Spatial Differentiation. (*Source:* Chauncy Harris and Edward Ullman, "The Nature of Cities," *Annals of the American Academy of Political and Social Sciences* 242, November 1945, p. 13.)

borhoods often populated by second-generation and third-generation immigrant families. The fourth zone, called the "residential zone," was characterized primarily by middle-class residential neighborhoods. Finally, at the outer edge of the city were the upper-class residential areas and the "commuter zone," representing the earliest suburbs, in which upper-middle-class and upper-class populations resided.

Although the concentric zone model appeared to provide a fairly accurate depiction of urban differentiation in Chicago during the early twentieth century, sociologists who focused on other urban settings discovered that in many instances urban development patterns exhibited different characteristics. One attempt to account for such differences was the **sector model** (Hoyt, 1939), which focused on the importance of major transportation arteries such as streets and trolley lines as key determinants of development patterns, resulting in the appearance of wedge-shaped areas of unique land uses (see figure 17–5). A third approach, the **multiple nuclei model** (Harris and Ullman, 1945), suggested that in many cities a number of distinct centers of activity and land use may develop. As figure 17–5 illustrates, this approach focused on the importance of several different "nuclei" rather than one main urban core as the center for development patterns.

The Metropolis

As U.S. cities expanded and became differentiated, they also became increasingly intertwined with the outlying areas that surrounded them. In the process, urban areas became decentralized—that is, spread over a much broader geographic area. The **metropolis**—a large urban area containing a central city and surrounding communities that are economically and socially linked to the central city—is an urban form that has emerged in American society since approximately 1920. During the metropolitan period cities have been restructured and have become increasingly decentralized as both people and many of the cities' basic activities have been relocated.

Recognizing that many central cities and their adjacent communities have become integrated economically and socially, the United States Bureau of the Census has adopted a measure called a Metropolitan Statistical Area. A **Metropolitan Statistical Area (MSA)** is a geographic area (usually a county or series of counties) of at least 100,000 residents that includes a center city of 50,000 or more people. Presently, more than three-fourths (77 percent) of the United States' population lives in the nation's 283 MSAs (Frey, 1990, p. 5). Table 17–3 shows the 20 largest metropolitan areas in the United States.

In several parts of the country, MSAs have grown so large that the outer ring of one MSA area expands and ultimately overlaps with the outer ring of a neighboring one. The result is an unbroken chain of urban and suburban development, sometimes stretching for hundreds of miles. Urban scholars have referred to this continuous urban sprawl as a **megalopolis** (Gottman, 1961). As of 1986, the United States Bureau of the Census had identified 21 megalopolitan areas. The largest megalopolis in the United States today—familiarly known as the "Boston-Washington corridor"—stretches along the northeastern seaboard and encompasses more than 53,000 square miles from southern New Hampshire to northern Virginia. The trend toward contiguous urban development has also

Table 17–3. The 20 Largest Metropolitan Areas in the United States, 1988

Metropolitan Area	Size (millions)	Rank 1988	Rank 1970	Change
New York CMSA	18.1	1	1	—
Los Angeles CMSA	13.7	2	2	—
Chicago CMSA	8.1	3	3	—
San Francisco CMSA	6.0	4	6	+2
Philadelphia CMSA	5.9	5	4	−1
Detroit CMSA	4.6	6	5	−1
Boston CMSA	4.1	7	7	—
Dallas CMSA	3.7	8	12	+4
Washington, D.C. MSA	3.7	9	8	−1
Houston CMSA	3.6	10	13	+3
Miami CMSA	3.0	11	16	+5
Cleveland CMSA	2.7	12	9	−3
Atlanta MSA	2.7	13	18	+5
St. Louis MSA	2.4	14	11	−3
Seattle CMSA	2.4	15	17	+2
Minneapolis-St. Paul MSA	2.3	16	15	−1
San Diego MSA	2.3	17	22	+5
Baltimore MSA	2.3	18	14	−4
Pittsburgh CMSA	2.2	19	10	−9
Phoenix MSA	2.0	20	34	+14

Source: William H. Frey, "Metropolitan America: Beyond the Transition." *Population Bulletin* 45:2, July 1990, p. 18. Based on data from U. S. Bureau of the Census, 1970 Population Census and county estimates for 1988 prepared by the Population Division.

been pronounced near the Pacific and Atlantic coasts (Frey, 1990) and, to a lesser degree, around the Great Lakes. Although sociologists or urban planners find it difficult to predict accurately future urban patterns, they have projected that by the year 2000, the United States will have at least 25 megalopolitan areas (see figure 17–6).

Suburbanization and Its Consequences

Decentralization—of population, business, and industry—has, therefore, been the distinguishing feature of metropolitan America. This decentralization has usually been associated with the growth of **suburbs,** which are the urban areas adjacent to, but beyond, the political boundaries of a city. Although suburbs began to emerge in some areas before the turn of

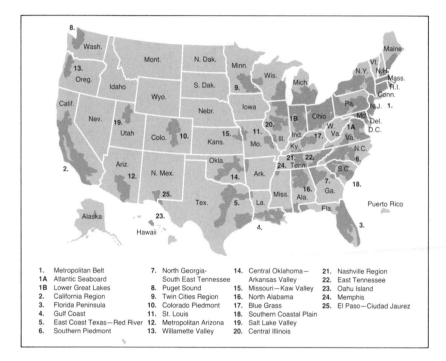

1.	Metropolitan Belt	7.	North Georgia–
1A	Atlantic Seaboard		South East Tennessee
1B	Lower Great Lakes	8.	Puget Sound
2.	California Region	9.	Twin Cities Region
3.	Florida Peninsula	10.	Colorado Piedmont
4.	Gulf Coast	11.	St. Louis
5.	East Coast Texas–Red River	12.	Metropolitan Arizona
6.	Southern Piedmont	13.	Willamette Valley

14.	Central Oklahoma–Arkansas Valley	21.	Nashville Region
15.	Missouri–Kaw Valley	22.	East Tennessee
16.	North Alabama	23.	Oahu Island
17.	Blue Grass	24.	Memphis
18.	Southern Coastal Plain	25.	El Paso–Ciudad Jaurez
19.	Salt Lake Valley		
20.	Central Illinois		

Figure 17–6. Megalopolis in the Year 2000. (*Source:* Presidential Commission on Population Growth and the American Future. *Population Growth and the American Future* (Washington, D.C.: United States Government Printing Office, 1972), p. 33.)

the twentieth century, suburban growth has been most pronounced since World War II. Since then the suburban population has grown much more rapidly than the population of central cities. In 1940 only about 17 percent of Americans lived in suburbs; by 1980 almost one-half (46 percent) of the U.S. population resided in suburban areas.

A prominent feature of the residential expansion into areas formerly at the periphery of central cities has been the selectivity of the suburbanization process: it has been primarily a middle-class phenomenon. Prompted by problems of urban decay and pollution, increasing concern over urban violence, and conflicts and tensions between minority groups and the white majority, many urban dwellers have fled to suburbia in search of cleaner air, lower crime rates, better schools, and affordable single-family housing (Fischer, 1984).

However, the rapid post-World War II suburbanization of the United States was greatly aided by both private enterprise and government programs. For example, use of the automobile, which sparked the suburbanization of modern America, as the primary means of transportation (instead of mass transit systems) reflected the impact of certain interest groups on public policy (Gottdiener and Feagin, 1988, p. 181). Other factors influencing metropolitan expansion included cheap energy, the investments of billions of federal dollars in massive urban expressways and interstate highway systems, and the provision of federally supported, low-interest mortgage programs that encouraged new suburban housing developments.

Policies that facilitated suburbanization also increased racial and class polarization. As a result of "white flight" from the central cities, suburbs have generally been overwhelmingly white and middle-class, while the central cities have increasingly been left to racial and ethnic minorities— blacks, Hispanics, and, recently, Asians. Moreover, the poor among these populations have been increasingly concentrated in central cities, especially in the nation's largest metropolitan areas (Sassen, 1990, p. 481). This poverty concentration, especially of blacks, has resulted from several factors, foremost among which has been racial segregation (Massey, 1990). Despite laws that should ensure fair housing practices, blacks have been prevented from entering the suburbs by deliberate exclusionary housing practices, exclusionary zoning ordinances, and the persistence of a stratification system that has blocked their social mobility. In 1980 about 75 percent of African Americans lived in urban central city areas. In contrast, only 25 percent of white Americans lived in the central cities. However, during the 1980s many central cities became racially and ethnically more diverse, as immigrants often made up for the continuing loss of the white population (Sassen, 1990; Frey, 1990, pp. 32–34). New York City, for example, experienced an overall population increase during the 1980s of 3.5 percent, despite a 10.9 percent decline in whites. Between 1980 and 1989 New York took in 854,000 immigrants, mainly from Asia, the Caribbean, and Latin America (Fiske, 1991, p. A18).

Although suburbs have frequently been portrayed simply as places where people live, business and industry have also moved out of the central city. This trend was a crucial aspect of the restructuring of the U.S. economy (Sassen, 1990). Although the movement of jobs from central cities to the suburbs had begun prior to 1970, it was especially pronounced during the economic restructuring of the U.S. city that occurred during the 1970s and 1980s. Deindustrialization and the exodus of jobs to the suburbs led to the decline of numerous central-city manufacturing, retail, and wholesale enterprises, especially in cities in the Northeast and Midwest.

Because of the loss of manufacturing jobs, many central-city manufacturing districts have become virtual wastelands of empty buildings and closed stores. Moreover, as we discussed in chapters 8 and 9, the loss of manufacturing jobs has greatly increased central-city unemployment and contributed to the increasing concentration of poverty and its related social dislocations—increased crime, welfare dependency, and family disruption.

Today the majority of people who live in suburbs also work there. Facilitated especially by interlocking expressways and advances in communications technology, twice as many workers in 1982 commuted *between* suburbs than commuted from suburbs to central cities (Leinberger and Lockwood, 1986). Industrial parks, real estate developments, shopping malls, and business offices have spread over the landscape of suburban and even outlying nonmetropolitan areas.

Some of the decentralization of urban populations has seen residents moving into small towns beyond metropolitan areas. This occurred especially during the 1970s, when areas outside of existing metropolitan areas grew more rapidly than either central cities or suburbs; those metropolitan areas that did grow during the 1970s were relatively small (under 250,000) and were located primarily in the South and the West (Frey, 1990, pp. 8–9). However, during the 1980s the growth of metropolitan areas once again exceeded that of nonmetropolitan areas. Nevertheless, most rural workers are employed in urban-type occupations. Indeed, agricultural employment today represents less than 10 percent of all nonmetropolitan jobs (Frisbee and Kasarda, 1988).

Recent Counter-Trends. As manufacturing has fled the central city, however, a recent counter-trend of growth has developed in highly skilled, managerial, professional, and technical information-processing occupations. The result has been the transformation of many cities from goods-producing and -processing centers to information-producing and -processing centers. As a result, while blue-color and relatively unskilled jobs have declined significantly, white-collar, information-processing jobs requiring substantial education have increased. For example, by 1980 the cities of New York and Boston had more people employed in knowledge-intensive, information-processing occupations than in manufacturing, construction, retail, and wholesale industries combined, a dramatic change from 30 years earlier, when the traditional urban industries outnumbered information-processing occupations by three to one (Kasarda, 1985). Most clearly exemplifying this trend have been "global" or "world" cities, such as New York, Los Angeles, Chicago, and San Francisco, which have become financial and trading centers in the international economy. Together with cities such as Tokyo, London, and Frankfurt, it is probable that, as the global economy becomes increasingly interdependent, such global cities "will become even more dominant as centers of international finance, headquarters for multinational corporations, and major exporters of advanced services" (Frey, 1990, p. 21).

Some observers interpret these trends as indications that the fortunes of the city will soon improve. Massive urban redevelopment projects, including large hotels, offices, civic centers, entertainment areas, restaurants, and retail shopping areas, sometimes within one "megastructure," have appeared in a number of cities. Boston's Quincy Market, Baltimore's Inner Harbor, San Francisco's Ghirardelli Square, Detroit's Renaissance Center, and Chicago's Water Tower Palace illustrate such urban revitalization.

The growth of high-rise administrative buildings constructed during the 1970s and 1980s symbolizes the recent growth in information-processing service occupations. Manufacturing, wholesale trade, and retail activities, which provided the economic base for cities in an earlier period, required large areas for the work of their employees. These space requirements could be met only with buildings spread horizontally over large areas. Information-processing enterprises, on the other hand, can be carried out efficiently in small spaces. "Thus people who process information can be stacked, layer after layer, in downtown office towers with resulting proximity actually increasing the productivity of those whose activities require an extensive amount of nonroutine, face-to-face interaction" (Frisbee and Kasarda, 1988, p. 636).

In addition to the development of some massive urban commercial complexes, other factors have contributed to changes in the social composition of American cities. First, the social composition of the suburbs is changing. The most rapid period of suburban development coincided with the post-World War II baby boom. Young couples moved to the suburbs to raise their children in a more "wholesome" and socially homogeneous environment. Moreover, the suburban life-style strongly emphasized traditional male and female gender roles. Today, however, more young women are rejecting the traditional role of housewife in favor of white-collar and professional occupations. Declines in the birth rate and in household size make large suburban homes both impractical and unattractive for many people. Increasing numbers of young adults are choosing to live in high-density settings such as condominiums and central city apartments, rather than in single-family dwellings.

People working in professional, managerial, administrative, and information-processing jobs in central city office complexes often seek housing close to their work. Moreover, such people are particularly attracted to the way of life offered by the city. The amenities of urban life, including its restaurants, clubs, parks, zoos, theaters, cultural activities, and sporting events, provide a stimulating and exciting range of opportunities often unavailable in the suburbs. Seeking to capitalize on these amenities, an "urban gentry" of young, affluent, business and professional people have, in some instances, moved into declining urban neighborhoods and restored their deteriorating stock of housing. This process of urban residential revitalization of older neighborhoods is known as **gentrification** (Zukin, 1987).

However, many central city residents, especially minorities, have not benefited from these changes in U.S. cities. First, although service sector jobs have grown, many central city residents lack the educational qualifications to take advantage of them. Instead, a mismatch has developed between the educational qualifications required for the knowledge-intensive jobs being created in the service sector and the educational skills of the minorities who make up an increasing proportion of the population of central cities. The situation in today's central cities is much different from that in central cities in the industrial period when widespread opportunities existed for those with little education and few skills. This mismatch between increasing educational requirements for urban employment and the educational attainments of central city residents represents one of the major dilemmas for urban social policy today (Kasarda, 1989).

Second, despite highly publicized revitalization efforts, the prospects for an urban renaissance are at best uncertain. Between 1968 and 1979 gentrification affected only a small fraction—less than 1 percent—of central city housing units. Nearly three-fourths of those who moved into restored housing units were intracity movers, not suburbanites who had moved to the city (Kasarda, 1980).

Third, urban redevelopment efforts, including the creation of urban megastructures and gentrification, have contributed to the displacement of substantial numbers of urban elderly and low-income residents (LeGates and Murphy, 1984; LeGates and Hartman, 1986; Sassen, 1990). The result has been the disruption of long-established and socially integrated neighborhoods, forcing many residents to experience financial distress as they look for new homes in housing markets characterized by an increasingly short supply of low-income housing (Hopkins, 1985; Sassen, 1990). In a study of the effects of gentrification in ten major U.S. cities, Nelson (1988) found that in most cities poor residents were displaced from gentrifying areas into lower-class areas, contributing to new concentrations of poverty.

The preceding discussion of the historic patterns of urban growth and development in the United States has focused primarily on patterns of population and economic growth and change and has ignored the crucial element of social conflict. However, Anthony Orum (1991) maintains that American cities, from their very beginnings, have *always* been involved in political and social struggles with other cities for domination and control of resources and they have *always* been the loci for conflicts among numerous competing interests seeking to assert their interests within cities. The study of the American city, Orum argues, must focus on "how it has developed into a sovereign territory, how it struggles continuously with other sovereign territories, and how battles animate its everyday life, particularly in the late twentieth century" (Orum, 1991, p. 605).

The Impact of Urban Life

Negative Views

Earlier we discussed the changes accompanying the rapid urbanization of Western society, in particular of the United States during the late nineteenth and early twentieth centuries. We noted that modern sociology emerged from the work of people who tried to understand and explain these changes. Most sociologists who considered the impact of increasing urbanization did not respond to it merely as disinterested social scientists. They themselves were products of societies being rapidly transformed, and in many instances they tended to view the passing of traditional society with nostalgia. The negative view of urban life, which for many years dominated sociological perspectives on the city, reflected in many respects the preference for a rural society that the early sociologists saw being undermined by the forces of modernization—by industrialization, bureaucratization, and urbanization.

As we noted in chapter 4, Ferdinand Toennies used the terms *gemeinschaft* and *gesellschaft* to distinguish the social relations characteristic of rural, traditional societies and modern, urban societies. *Gemeinschaft* communities are characterized by personalized, face-to-face relationships such as those in the family, the rural village, and the small town. *Gesellschaft* societies, in contrast, are associated with impersonal and distant relationships, the kind we associate with urban life. In *gemeinschaft* communities, social relationships are valued as ends in themselves. In *gesellschaft* communities, social relationships are little more than means to other ends; e.g., people associate only with those who reward them with money, goods, or services (Toennies, 1857/1957).

One of the earliest and most influential sociological analyses of the city was made by the German sociologist Georg Simmel (1903/1971). Primarily concerned with the psychological effects of urban society on individuals, Simmel observed that life in cities (as contrasted with life in small towns and rural areas) exposes people to a greater variety and intensity of stimuli. He argued that the more hectic pace and intensity of city life produce more psychological stress than the slower, less hectic, and more relaxed pace of rural life.

Simmel concluded that the greater psychic stress of urban life affects the emotional and intellectual character of urban residents. In attempting to adapt to and protect themselves from stresses created by the profusion of people and environmental stimuli about them, urban residents may suppress their emotions and follow only their intellect in deciding how to act. As a consequence, urban dwellers develop an emotional restraint or insensitivity in their dealings with others. They develop rational standards of calculation, punctuality, and exactness so that some semblance of order can be maintained within a chaotic array of events and social contacts. In Simmel's view, the more leisurely pace and more intimate nature of social life in rural areas enable people to be more spontaneous and less calculating in their personal relations than is characteristic of urbanites. Moreover, as urbanites are subjected to a barrage of stimuli, events, and individual differences, they become less likely to be shocked or excited by new, unusual, and bizarre events.

Simmel also recognized that cities allow a greater expression of personal freedom than do rural communities. Rural communities are apt to have restrictive social norms and conservative attitudes about social diversity, may severely restrict the expression of individual differences, and insure that those people who do not conform to the norms will feel social isolation from those who do. However, Simmel did not feel that this increased freedom necessarily enhanced the quality of human life. On the contrary, he contended that increased individual freedom tends to heighten the urbanite's feelings of social isolation and loneliness in the midst of a social milieu characterized by impersonality and anonymity, rather than intimacy and primary group ties.

Challenges to the Negative View

Simmel's negative perspective of urban life has been shared by several prominent American sociologists. In recent years, however, an increasing number of sociologists have argued for a more balanced assessment of the effects of urban life. Two closely related perspectives—the compositional and the subcultural approaches to urbanism—have challenged the idea that cities inevitably produce psychological distress and other dehumanizing effects (Fischer, 1984).

The **compositional theory of urbanism** emphasizes the positive aspects of the cosmopolitanism and diversity that characterize city life. Compositionalists view the city as a mosaic of different social worlds based on kinship, neighborhood, ethnicity, occupation, common interests, and lifestyle. The presence of these social worlds allows intimate, primary group relations to exist independently of the broader urban environment, affording protection against the city's anonymity and the psychological stresses emphasized by Simmel.

From the compositional perspective, behaviors and experiences of urbanites are shaped not so much by the size, density, or social diversity of the urban population as by the characteristics—including social class position, stage in the life cycle, and ethnic identity—of those who live there.

Even in the largest cities people create and live within communities— "urban villages"—that prevent them from feeling socially isolated. The traditional negative perspective of urbanism fails to distinguish how people act in public settings and how they act in more private contexts. Claude Fischer (1981) has suggested that in the "public world," urbanites are confronted by numerous others who are strangers and who are often perceived as "strange" because of the cultural diversity of the urban milieu. Therefore, in public contexts, most urban dwellers do tend to feel and act like anonymous, detached individuals.

In the "private world" of interactions among family and friends, however, social relations characterized by primary associations and mutual support and assistance tend to flourish. Indeed, the "personal communities" provided by the networks of association among urban dwellers appear to provide a majority of urbanites with greater opportunities for social attachments than may exist among small-town and rural dwellers (Fischer, 1982; Wellman, 1979).

The **subcultural theory of urbanism** argues that a city's size, density, and diversity do affect the urban experience, but in a positive way. Intimate social worlds are *created* and *enhanced* in an urban milieu, not broken down, as the critics of urban life argue. The urban environment provides opportunities to create a variety of meaningful subcultures (for example, ethnic, artistic, religious, gay/lesbian, literary, intellectual) that could not develop in smaller communities because there would not be a sufficient number—a critical mass—of similarly interested individuals. Urbanism can thus foster unconventional and deviant behavior, not because an impersonal city produces anomie and undermines social control but because it provides an environment in which subcultures identified as deviant by the larger society can be created and thrive. The subcultural and compositional perspectives differ slightly in their focus, but both demonstrate ways in which personal relationships are sustained and fostered in an urban environment.

In conclusion, the negative view of the city reflects a general tendency among both the American public and social scientists to exaggerate and romanticize the virtues of a rural existence, to which cities are often contrasted. Urban life certainly has its problems, but so do suburban and rural life. To assess accurately the effects of urbanism, we must examine them carefully and systematically.

Summary

Demography is the scientific study of population. The three basic processes of population are fertility (childbearing), mortality (death), and migration (change of residence). Age and sex are the two major demographic characteristics of population.

Fertility is a socially motivated behavior, as the extremes in childbearing behavior (the Hutterites, the Shakers, and the Rappites) illustrate. Childbearing in the United States today is at its lowest rate in history. Differences in fertility can still be found between religious, racial, ethnic, and socioeconomic status groups.

Mortality is influenced by one's social position and personal life-style. Migration shapes the growth and development of different parts of the country, and has generally been from rural to urban places, and from east to west in the United States.

The most far-reaching population issue today is the rapid growth of the world's population. The "population explosion" is a recent phenomenon in demographic history, having begun with the modernization and industrialization of various European states in the seventeenth and eighteenth centuries and accelerated greatly in the twentieth century. The theory of the Modern Demographic Transition holds that populations grow rapidly during the early stages of modernization because the death rate declines while the birth rate remains high. The rapid rate of the world's population growth today stems from the fact that the death rates in many of the developing countries have dropped while the birth rates remain high or very high.

Responses to the rapid growth of the world's population are varied. One view is that "economic development is the best contraceptive," so emphasis should be placed on development, and fertility declines will follow. A second view is the family-planning approach, which emphasizes contraception, education, and propaganda as ways of reducing fertility. A third view would combine the family-planning approach with societal changes to reduce motivations for childbearing. Contemporary China is an exemplar of the latter approach to reducing fertility.

Cities are a relatively recent form of human organization, although some did appear soon after the Agricultural Revolution. In more recent times the Industrial Revolution sparked the growth of cities. The pace of urban growth has been especially pronounced since World War II. Recent urban growth has been most rapid in Third World countries.

In the United States, industrialization in the nineteenth and early twentieth centuries led to urbanization. The process of suburbanization has seen the growth of primarily white suburbs and the abandonment of the central cities to minority residents and the poor. Business and industry have also been part of the flight to the suburbs, creating severe economic problems for the central cities. As suburban metropolitan fringes have moved farther away from central cities, they have overlapped with the fringes of other metropolitan areas, creating a continuous metropolitan complex known as a *megalopolis*.

Recently, counter-trends to the decentralization of American urban areas have been noted. Urban redevelopment projects in many cities have produced massive office buildings in which to conduct the growing number of central-city service jobs. Some cities have also experienced gentrification, but this process has not benefited all city residents, especially minorities and the poor.

The long-standing negative perception of urban life is being challenged today. Sociologists who emphasize a more balanced portrait of the city argue that the city's anonymity has not led to social anarchy and personal isolation. Instead, the city offers a "mosaic of social worlds," opportunities for the creation of intimate associations and communities based on kinship, neighborhood, ethnicity, occupation, or life-style.

CRITICAL THINKING

1. Explain how a demographic phenomenon, such as the baby boom, can have an effect on a variety of factors in a society.
2. What general trends in fertility are evident in the United States? The developed world? The developing world?
3. What factors might influence the rate of fertility in a given society? Give examples to support your ideas.
4. What three basic processes determine population size? Explain how each is affected by social factors.
5. What is the population explosion? Explain how this phenomenon is unprecedented in human history. Why should it concern you?
6. Speculate on the social effect of population measures such as the one-child policy in China. How would such measures affect social institutions, such as the family, education, and the economy?
7. Distinguish among the terms *urban, urbanization,* and *urbanism.*
8. Why is the Industrial Revolution considered to be a major factor in the development of urbanization?
9. Where are the ten largest urban areas in the world concentrated? In your opinion, is this a positive or negative phenomenon?
10. Describe the general history of urbanization in the United States. What general theories exist to explain the patterns of urban spatial differentiation? Which best describes the urban area closest to you?

18 Social Change, Collective Behavior, and Social Movements

"You can't teach an old dog new tricks." "Can a leopard change its spots?" "The more things change, the more they stay the same." Such folk sayings suggest that change is difficult and relatively rare. But, as we have seen throughout this book, change is pervasive. Indeed, our experience of the world teaches us that we live in the midst of ongoing change.

We have only to ask our parents or grandparents to describe life when they were growing up. Their descriptions of work, education, entertainment, and technology are apt to be very different from what we experience today. We can also compare a current map of Africa with one published in 1950, where we will see that many of today's countries were not in existence 40 years ago. As we saw in chapter 16, relations between the United States and the Soviet Union have undergone dramatic changes in the last decade. Some observers are even saying that the cold war, which has threatened our existence over the last 40 years, is over. The pace of change in East–West relations is, at the moment, almost dizzying (Goldman, 1987). Rather than living in a relatively changeless world, it appears at times that we live in an age in which everything that had been nailed down is coming loose.

In this chapter—building on prior discussions of social theory, bureaucracy, and culture—we look more closely at the nature of social change, at social movements, and at people's experiences of change.

The Meaning of Change

Social Change Defined

We define **social change** as variations over time in the relationships among individuals, groups, cultures, and societies. Social change is pervasive; all "of social life is continually changing" (Lauer, 1982, p. 4; Harper, 1989). In the family, for example, recent changes include the surge of married women and mothers into the labor force, and the increasing proportion of nontraditional living arrangements (such as an unmarried couple's living together). At the societal level, crime rates, population statistics, distribution of income, and level of technological development register measurable shifts. At the global level, trade patterns, political alliances, and the distribution of wealth take new shapes over time.

Patterns of Change

Change is not a purely haphazard process, but rarely are its patterns represented by smooth lines or curves. Patterns of change fall into three broad categories: a general trend (upward or downward), cyclic variations, and irregular or random variations. A general trend designates a long-term tendency to increase or decrease. Cyclic variations may occur around seasons or over periods of years or even centuries. Irregular variations are often tied to particular events, such as natural disasters, wars, or inventions. The U.S. economy, for example, has grown over the past century (an upward trend), has had a series of booms and recessions (cyclic variations), and has also had some short-term reversals and sudden surges (irregular and random variations).

At every level of human life (family, society, and the world), then, trends, cycles, and variations help us to identify changes that have occurred, changes that are currently occurring, and changes likely to occur in the future. Change is pervasive.

Theories of Change

In Aldous Huxley's *Brave New World*, one of the leaders of the Western world calls change a "menace." In the novel, the rulers of the society did not want any change. Wary of any invention or innovation, they cherished stability above all else. They believed that maintaining the social order as it was would keep them secure and happy. Had Huxley's characters understood history, they would have known that they could never bring human society into a state of changeless stability. Societies change as inexorably as the ocean tide comes in.

How do we account for the multitude of changes at the various levels of social life? Sociologists as well as other social scientists try to answer this question. Economists, political scientists, anthropologists, and psychologists tend to focus on a particular segment of society—the economy, political institutions, culture, or individual personalities. Sociologists try to understand the totality—how the social structure and culture change over time. They tend to look at change in terms of the social factors involved. They explore such factors as internal systemic strains and contradictions, interpersonal and intergroup processes such as conflict, technological developments, and institutional arrangements.

To begin to understand social change, some theorists have looked at the broad sweep of history. Others have focused on structure and process in the social order. In chapter 1 we discussed the Marxist perspective that identifies inherent conflicts in the social order as the driving mechanism of change throughout human history. We also looked at structural-functionalism, which posited more stability than change in social systems. Functionalists acknowledge that social systems change, but generally they argue that the forces tending toward stability are stronger than the forces tending toward change. In addition to these two perspectives, three other theories of change have been influential in sociology—cyclic theory, evolutionary theory, and conflict theory. We examine each type through a representative theorist.

Cyclic Theory

Cyclic theory conceptualizes change as an ongoing series of cycles rather than as a process with some kind of direction. The Greeks, Romans, and Chinese, among others, viewed history in terms of great cycles rather than in terms of progress or decline.

Pitirim Sorokin, a sociologist who formulated a cyclic theory of change, investigated the whole field of human culture, including art, science, literature, technology, philosophy, and law. He concluded that culture is composed of a series of parts that are unified around a fundamental principle and a basic value (Sorokin, 1941, p. 17). In any given age, more than one society can exhibit the same principle or basic value. The United States, Canada, and Western Europe could be one "culture" in Sorokin's terms because all of these societies are essentially materialistic. In a materialistic culture, science, art, literature, and all other cultural areas will be materialistic. Sorokin called the materialistic culture *sensate*. A **sensate culture** is one pervaded by the principle that the material or sensory world is the true reality and value. A second type is the **ideational culture,** pervaded by the principle that a supersensory or nonmaterial world is the true reality and the highest value. The third type, the **idealistic culture,** combines the other two in an integrated blend of the supersensory and the sensory (nonmaterial and material). Sorokin argued that medieval Europe, with its belief that the sensory world is only a transitional step on the way to the eternal City of God, typified an ideational culture, while the modern West typifies the sensate culture.

All of history, according to Sorokin, is a cyclic variation among the three types of cultures. Cultures grow and decline, and give way to one of the other types of culture. Our own Western system, he insisted, is not only sensate but an "overripe" sensate culture, ready to give way to an ideational or idealistic type. In the late 1930s, Sorokin (1957, pp. 699–701) forecast a number of dire developments that would signal the downfall of our sensate culture. Among them were an increasing loss of moral sensitivity, a mechanistic view of humans, the use of force and deception to maintain social order, the disintegration of the family, an obsession with quantity rather than quality, and an increase in such things as suicide, mental illness, and crime. In his analysis, these lamentable developments do not mean the demise of civilization but merely the transition to an ideational or idealistic culture, and a new period of growth and development in a more spiritual world.

Cyclic theory contributes to our understanding of change by identifying one important pattern of change in social life. Cyclic variations occur at every level of life, from the individual to the global. At the individual level, for example, cyclic variations appear in physiological functions, such as diurnal variations in body temperature and blood pressure. A great variety of social phenomena have been charted and shown to vary cyclically over time, including wars, crime, marriage and birth rates, and religious and scientific activity.

Cyclic theory, however, does not account for all of the important factors in change. Sorokin, in particular, fails to consider social-psychological factors. His theory casts people as virtual pawns of the massive sociocultural cycles in human history. Moreover, broad descriptions of cycles in social life fail to capture qualitative differences in different phases of the cycles. For example, to describe both the modern West and the Greco-Roman world at the birth of Christ as sensate cultures may be accurate, but it does not illuminate essential differences in the two cultures. There is more to change than cyclic variations.

Evolutionary Theory

In contrast to the cyclic theory, **evolutionary theory** gives direction to change. Gerhard and Jean Lenski (1982) have developed one of the more influential discussions of evolutionary change. Not all change, they argue, is evolutionary; some is cyclic, and some is unpatterned and random. But evolutionary change is the predominant pattern and differs from the others because it is a "process of cumulative change" (Lenski and Lenski, 1982, p. 56). Organic and sociocultural evolution are similar in some ways, including the fundamental fact that both are cumulative change based on systems of encoded information. Organic evolution is based in part on the information encoded in the DNA molecule. Sociocultural evolution is based on symbol systems, or language.

Thus, the Lenskis define sociocultural evolution as "the process of change and development in human societies that results from cumulative change in their stores of cultural information" (Lenski and Lenski, 1982, p. 60). Cumulative change occurs through the twin processes of innovation and selection. Innovation produces new variations, and selection produces decisions about which variations to retain and which to reject.

Inventions, discoveries, alterations of existing cultural elements, and diffusion from one society to another constitute the basic forms of innovation. More than anything else, however, technological developments provide the driving mechanism of change. New technologies help satisfy human needs more completely or more efficiently. Needs here refer to socially and culturally derived needs as well as to subsistence needs. We *need* to have esthetic satisfaction and to find self-fulfillment as well as to obtain food, clothing, and shelter. In the course of seeking satisfaction of such needs, people continually develop new technologies. Those technologies, in turn, alter social life by opening up new options for people. The dramatic changes in the shifts from simple hunting-and-gathering societies through agricultural and industrial societies to today's world highlight the impact of technological developments upon the social order. The store of cultural information in a computer society is vastly different from that in the stone-tool, plow, or steam-engine societies.

According to the Lenskis, the processes of innovation and selection occur at two different levels: in individual societies and in the world system. At the level of the individual society, the variations produced are cultural elements, some of which are retained while others are rejected. Those retained shape the character of the evolving social order. At the level of the world system, the variations produce entire societies. Those with the greater amount of technological information will survive and shape the character of the evolving world system. The world system has evolved from one in which the dominant social order was hunting and gathering, through systems dominated by the horticultural and the agrarian society, to a system dominated by an industrial society.

And where is evolution leading us? The Lenskis assert that human culture has been highly successful as an adaptive mechanism, for the human race has not only survived but has flourished in terms of sheer numbers. If we go beyond numbers and ask about progress toward such values as freedom, justice, and happiness, however, we find a complex situation. Technological developments have certainly raised the upper level of freedom, in the sense that those in the upper strata in industrial societies have a far greater range of options than those who had the most options in agrarian societies. The freedom of the average person is more debatable; industrial societies offer fewer physical and biological restraints but more social restraints. People in advanced societies today, for example, have far fewer problems with health than in former years, but they have more governmental restrictions.

Dealing with justice, the Lenskis point out that the amount of inequality in societies changes as we move from one type of society to another. Inequality increases in the shift from a hunting-and-gathering to a horticultural and agrarian society. The surplus of goods increases, but that surplus is invariably distributed unequally among the population. Industrial societies initially maintain this trend toward increasing inequality, but the trend finally reverses as industrialization continues.

The Lenskis raise important issues about equality, justice, and happiness that we cannot resolve here. Generally, they portray the course of evolution as one of progress for the human race. Evolutionary theory also underscores the fact that certain factors, such as technology, are far more crucial to the process of change than other factors. On the other hand, although evolutionary theory may be useful in explaining large-scale, long-term trends, it is not useful in accounting for the smaller-scale, shorter-term alterations in social life, such as alterations in social institutions or public attitudes. Nor is evolutionary theory useful for explaining the significant differences in societies at the same level of evolutionary development. In fact, some older evolutionists argued that the process of evolution demands that all societies evolve along the same lines toward the same kind of social order. Clearly, that has not happened. What else, then, is going on in social life that is crucial to our understanding of social change? For some theorists, the answer is conflict.

Conflict Theory

Conflict theory of change, as we have seen throughout, views change as the inevitable result of inherent conflicts between groups with diverse interests. In a statement representative of conflict theory, Dahrendorf (1959, p. 208) comments: "I would suggest . . . that all that is creativity, innovation, and development in the life of the individual, his group, and his society is due, to no small extent, to the operation of conflicts between group and group, individual and individual, emotion and emotion within one individual." The origin of social conflict, according to Dahrendorf, is the dominance relations that prevail in societies. Conflict is generally a struggle over the legitimacy of authority relations (Collins, 1990).

Dahrendorf develops four propositions to highlight the nature of conflict and its role in social change:

1. Every society is at every point subject to processes of change; social change is ubiquitous.

2. Every society displays at every point dissensus and conflict; social conflict is ubiquitous.

3. Every element in a society renders a contribution to its disintegration and change.

4. Every society is based on the coercion of some of its members by others (Dahrendorf, 1959, p. 162).

Change is inevitable because authority relationships are pervasive, and there will always be conflict over authority relationships.

The analysis of bureaucracy (chapter 4) provided specific illustrations of conflict as a force for change in industrial organizations. Many case studies have documented struggles between employees and management. In Dahrendorf's analysis, conflict will occur regardless of the nature of management, whether management is composed of owners, stockholders, or the government. Whether managers try to fashion a participatory system or a restrictive bureaucracy, conflict will still exist because it is rooted in the contradictory interests embedded in authority relationships. Conflict and its outcome—social change—are inevitable.

Conflict, like technology, is an important part of social change. Nevertheless, conflict does not explain all change, and it can sometimes impede change. In some Third World nations, such as Burma and the Sudan, intergroup conflict has been so intense that progress toward a modern, constitutional state has been stifled. Furthermore, some change occurs without conflict. As James G. March (1981, p. 563) points out, organizations may change "routinely, easily, and responsively." Many businesses have changed their internal structure and processes in an effort to enhance productivity or to adapt to a changed environment, and they have implemented the changes without conflict.

Conflict and Terrorism. In contemporary world conflicts, we find many militant groups that engage in terrorism. **Terrorism** can take many forms, but it can be defined as the systematic or threatened use of murder, injury, or destruction in order to achieve some political end (Laqueur, 1987, p. 72). By their actions, terrorists seek to create tensions that can ultimately lead to the changes they desire.

Over the years we have all heard of terrorist acts committed by such groups as the Irish Republican Army (IRA), Fatah, the major terrorist group within the Palestinian Liberation Organization (PLO), the Red Brigades (Italy), and others. Terrorists engage in a wide range of activities, including plane hijacking, kidnapping, embassy bombings, car bombings, and other violent acts.

Terrorists do not always achieve their aims. The objective of the IRA, for instance, is to free Northern Ireland from British control. As of this writing, however, Northern Ireland continues under British domination, and there is little sign that control will be relinquished in the near future. Changes have not occurred in spite of many terrorist activities undertaken by the IRA over a period of many years. The high point for IRA activities was 1972, when 467 people were killed, including 103 members of the British military. Occasionally, the IRA has taken even more extreme steps, such as their effort in the early 1980s to assassinate Prime Minister Thatcher when she attended a political convention in the resort city of Brighton, England. Despite these extreme steps, IRA actions have failed to bring about the desired changes.

The same could be said about Fatah and the Palestine Liberation Organization. This organization has sought to regain land from the Israelis in order to create a Palestinian homeland and, if possible, to eliminate Israel completely. Although conflict has certainly existed between the PLO and Israel, Israel remains firmly in place, and there is little immediate prospect of a homeland for Palestinians.

In spite of the failures of the IRA and the Fatah/PLO, it would be wrong to conclude that terrorist groups inevitably fail. For example, in the 1940s, terrorist groups like Irgun and the Stern Gang contributed to the ouster of the British from Palestine. Even in this case, however, the activities of the terrorists were not the decisive factor in achieving the desired objective. In summary, terrorism is a reflection of conflict and is being used as an instrument of conflicting groups, but its successes in bringing about social change have been limited.

Although all the types of theory are useful, no one adequately explains all change. Perhaps a future theorist will utilize elements of the various theories to fashion a more complete explanation of social change than is now available.

Sources of Change

Various change theories stress differing sources of change. Sorokin saw change as a normal outcome of the functioning of the social system. Marx pointed to inherent contradictions in the larger society, while conflict theorists stress the role of the struggle between groups with opposed interests. Functionalists identify many sources of change, both internal (such as strain in the system) and external (such as changes in the physical environment or war with another society). The functionalists correctly point out the multiple sources of change. All of the factors noted by the theorists, in fact, are part of the process of social change. We now discuss three of the more important factors: technology, ideologies, and competition/conflict.

Technology

Our earlier discussion of culture pointed to the importance of technology (Wallace, 1989)—materials, tools, machines, skills, and procedures—in a society. An examination of Ogburn's (1964) view of *cultural lag* established that change occurs first in material culture and that rapid technological change causes maladjustment because the old norms, roles, and, in some cases, values no longer seem to apply to the situation created by the new technology. The maladjustment, in turn, stimulates people to address the resulting problems. Thus change is ongoing as people must continually seek to adapt their nonmaterial culture to the material.

As an example of cultural lag, the development of nuclear armaments has made it irrational for nations to wage wars with these weapons in order to achieve political goals. And yet national leaders often talk about potential wars, or they even threaten wars, as if we were in a prenuclear-missile age.

How Technology Causes Change. Ogburn identified one of the ways in which technology causes change—by creating social problems that require people's action. But technology also leads to change in a second way—by increasing our alternatives. Consider, for example, the options opened up by the computer (Turkle, 1984). In many cases, the computer has radically altered the nature of the workplace (Zubuff, 1988), changing the kind and number of workers needed and the kind and amount of information that can be kept and used. The computerization of an office may mean that fewer workers are required, and that those who are needed will have to possess different skills (e.g., the ability to work at the computer terminal) than those who previously worked there. On the other hand, that office force can handle much more information (facts about inventory, production and clients, and forecasts about the future) than could the noncomputerized group. Largely because of the computer, the number of workers in the information field—those engaged in collecting and analyzing various kinds of data pertinent to an operation—has dramatically increased in modern nations. The computer's impact can be seen in virtually every human endeavor. New methods of education, such as computer-assisted instruction, are available. Health care can be individualized in a way not possible before; a hospital patient can be hooked up to a computer that will continually monitor his or her physical status or make analyses to facilitate an accurate diagnosis and treatment. Computers allow people to shop from their homes. Of course, the options are not all desirable. Computers can also be used to commit crime and to wage war. Criminals have learned to use the computer to "break in" to the operations of a company and steal information or materials. The military has used the computer to create frightening new weapons that can kill more people with greater accuracy at longer distances. The options opened up by the computer are enormously varied, but not all are conducive to human well-being.

The third way in which technology leads to change is by altering interaction patterns—new technologies frequently lead to new interaction patterns. For instance, one study has shown that a robot installed in a machine plant drastically altered the workplace (Goleman, 1983, pp. 40–41). In essence, the robot did the work previously done by a human, and the human ran the robot. Workers agreed that the robot had eliminated physical stress, but they noted other stresses that were added because the robot required the full attention of the worker. The joking and bantering of prerobot days were gone. As one worker put it, "I don't have time to talk with anyone. I don't want them breaking my concentration." The robot changed interaction patterns in the factory. In other cases, a new technology does not demand, but may result in, changed patterns. The automobile and television are examples of technologies that an individual can use to change his or her interaction patterns, though neither requires those changes. That is, one need not break off friendships or cut down on interaction with family members in order to use an automobile or television. In fact, the automobile can help one to maintain existing interaction patterns even after a move to a different location; television can be a shared experience with friends or family members. Most technologies do not require us to alter interaction patterns, but they give us the option to do so.

Ideology: Impediment or Facilitator of Change?

As we saw in chapter 8 on stratification, an *ideology* is a set of ideas that explains reality, provides directives for behavior, and expresses the interests of particular groups. An ideology may be elaborate, such as the ideologies of Marxism, capitalism, or Catholicism. Or the ideology may be focused on a specific issue, such as the ideologies of the prochoice and antiabortion groups. In either case, the ideologies fulfill several functions. For instance, groups in this controversy each have an ideology that explains their position on abortion; among other things, the ideologies take a position on whether the fetus is a living human. Antiabortionists argue that the fertilized egg is a human. From a biological point of view, they say, the fertilized egg is a unique, genetic entity. The Catholic church agrees, and adds that the fertilized egg must be considered a human because it has human potential, because "if you are conceived by human parents, you are human" (*Time*, 1981, p. 23). On the other hand, those who favor a woman's right to abortion argue that human life does not technically begin until some time after conception. For example, one biologist argues that fertilization is not the beginning of human life, but a "highly significant step in its continuity," since the egg and sperm are both living human cells. The fertilized egg lacks some of the important characteristics we attribute to people, including a nervous system and the ability to respond to stimuli. One may also consider a human as someone with self-awareness. But during the first three months, the fetus "lacks an adequate neural foundation for minimal subjective experience, let alone self-awareness" (Grobstein, 1982, p. 14).

For those opposed to abortion, however, the act is one of killing a human being, regardless of how soon the abortion occurs after conception. As a legislative aide put it, "We must do everything we can under our constitutional system to stop the killing of unborn children. We're talking about life and death" (*Time*, 1981, p. 20). For those who favor women's choice in the matter, the issue is one of a woman's right to have control of her body and her general well-being. A woman's right to self-determination is threatened, they say, by antiabortion efforts.

These ideologies also provide directives for behavior; each group actively lobbies and propagandizes in an effort to win public and governmental support. Each group tries to marshal support for political candidates who support their position. Antiabortionists mobilize supporters to picket (or disrupt) abortion clinics. And the ideologies clearly reflect the interests of the two groups; those who argue for choice in the matter feel that such choice is important to maintain the rights of women, while those who argue against abortion feel that the sanctity of human life generally, and of their quality of life in particular, is being threatened. In addition to serving the various functions for groups holding them, ideologies affect change in a number of ways.

Ideology as an Impediment to Change.   Although change is inevitable, some people who benefit enough from the existing order will always vigorously resist change. In some cases, people use ideologies to impede or block change. During the Middle Ages, the clergy used religious ideology to gain more power for themselves and to impede certain economic developments. For instance, they inhibited the development of economic surplus by defining usury as sinful. They diverted whatever surplus wealth there was from economic enterprises by stressing the insignificance of worldly gain and the crucial importance of spiritual works. Consequently, people tended to use their energies and resources to build religious monuments and secure greater favor with God. The large number of religious holidays and festivals similarly consumed people's time and energies, and diverted them from such things as economic development.

Nonreligious ideologies can also inhibit change. In the United States, people have used the ideology of equality of opportunity to resist changes that would benefit minorities. After all, they argue, if every person in the

United States truly has the same opportunity as every other person, why do we need such things as affirmative action laws?

The ideology of equal opportunity also inhibits the development of class consciousness and class antagonisms. Even the poorer among us may accept the ideology. In a survey of 105 rural people of Appalachia, 71 percent agreed with the statement: "Regardless of social class, anyone willing and able to work has an equal chance to earn a good income in this country" (Smith and Bylund, 1983, p. 259). To the extent that people accept the ideology, they will attribute their success or blame their failure on their own efforts and abilities rather than on the social structure in which they function. As a garbage man put it: "Look, I know it's nobody's fault but mine that I got stuck here where I am. . . . if I'd applied myself, I know I got it in me to be different, can't say anyone did it to me" (Sennett and Cobb, 1972, p. 96).

Ideology as a Facilitator of Change.   If ideology impedes change, it can also be used to facilitate change. Many changes in the U.S. are related to the ideology that technology will resolve all of our problems. For example, some people hold to the idea that we can resolve the problem of war by developing a superior military technology. In particular, in 1983 President Reagan proposed a system of defense that would defend against the missiles of any enemy. The system—dubbed "Star Wars"—would use laser beams and other technology to destroy incoming enemy missiles from space stations. "Let's use the wonders of technology not to make war, but to protect the peace" was President Reagan's argument (*San Diego Tribune*, 1986, p. A3). Of course, experts disagree about the feasibility and effectiveness of a Star Wars system. Some agreed with the President that such a system would be not only practical but effective in preventing war. Others, such as Nobel-Prize-winning physicist Hans Bethe (1985, p. 83), argue that the system is impractical "until there are technical breakthroughs that have not yet been conceived of." Other critics have argued that if a system such as this were to be developed, it would increase, not decrease, the likelihood of nuclear war.

Ideology has also facilitated action in social movements. In the women's movement, the ideology of female/male equality has led to the demand for female participation in areas formerly believed to be appropriate only for males. Women have entered the military academies, become a part of construction crews, and opted for careers in engineering—all considered unsuitable for women only a few years ago. Similarly, homosexuals have "come out" in large numbers and have begun to win such rights as marriage and adoption of children in some states. The pursuit of these rights was stimulated by the ideology that gays and lesbians are as normal as anyone else and deserve, therefore, the same rights as heterosexuals.

The Role of Competition and Conflict in Change

Competition and conflict have stimulated so much change that some sociologists would argue that all change is the result of these two forms of interaction. Although this view overstates the case, it is true that they are fundamental and pervasive aspects of social change.

Competition.   The importance of competition in change is well illustrated by the progress of science. While science is supposed to be governed by the norms of sharing, cooperation, and openness, in reality, fierce competition is more typical. For instance, three researchers won the 1977 Nobel Prize in Physiology or Medicine for their research on the role of hormones in the chemistry of the body. Two of the men—Roger Guillemin and Andrew Schally—were bitter enemies (Wade, 1981). At one time they were colleagues, but each formed his own team and set out to win the prize. In the course of the race, the two scientists often ignored the norms that supposedly govern science. For instance, they tried to avoid acknowledging each other's work. Guillemin left out Schally's work when he wrote review articles. Schally told members of his team not to talk to "the enemy." The two researchers even refused to report some of their advances at scientific meetings for fear that the other might pick up on the information and jump ahead in the race. Ultimately, they had to share the prize for discovering and characterizing the hormones that the brain uses to control various bodily functions. Their rivalry was intense, leading them to work fiercely toward the goal. For our analysis, the important point is that the goal was achieved, and that the competition facilitated the achievement by impelling the scientists to intensive work.

Conflict.   Conflict is a potent factor in change at all levels of life, including in organizations, communities, and whole societies. The conflict between workers and management, between ideological factions in communities and the nation, between individuals who dislike each other in an organization, between representatives of various social institutions such as religion and government—all are examples of the multitude of different conflicts that pervade societies.

The changes resulting from the conflict between students and college and university administrators in the 1960s illustrates the kind of shifts that can occur in organizations as a result of conflict (Kriesberg, 1982, pp. 248–249). The conflicts were ideologically based and centered on diverse goals. One conflict, for instance, focused on the role of the schools in national and local matters. Liberal and left-wing students protested such things as the contribution of university research to war generally and to the war in Vietnam in particular; the investments made by colleges and universities in corporations that students defined as exploiting the poor or contributing to international tensions and exploitation of Third World nations; and the expansion of school property that resulted in a displacement of the poor. Students and administrators also had conflict over such academic matters as the relevance of certain subjects for study and over such practical matters as dormitory rules.

The conflicts produced significant changes in a number of areas of college life. Rules about dormitory living were liberalized throughout the country, including the broadening or elimination of rules about curfews, drinking, and entertaining members of the opposite sex in dormitory rooms. There were curriculum changes, with many schools instituting programs of black studies and women's studies. Grade inflation occurred, and many schools gave students more pass/fail options for courses in lieu of grades. Some schools even ended their research affiliation with the military. Finally, as noted above, administrators in many schools agreed to student participation in the decision-making process. By the end of the 1970s, a survey of colleges and universities showed that students participated on the boards of trustees for 20 percent of the schools, and on faculty curriculum committees in 58 percent of the schools (Kriesberg, 1982, pp. 248).

Many of those changes have been reversed as a new generation of students showed less interest in participating in the administration of their schools, and administrators did nothing to encourage continued participation. By the late 1980s, students may have realized what they had lost, for conflict re-emerged as students on campuses around the nation sought to convince their trustees and administrators to withdraw investments in South African enterprises (Hirsch, 1990). Many students felt morally outraged by the fact that they attended schools that supported apartheid through investments, but they often discovered that they had little or no official influence.

In many instances, conflict and change become a self-sustaining process as the conflict leads to change that generates more conflict, leading to still more change. For example, the "green revolution" in India involved the use of new grains, irrigation, fertilizer, and pesticides (Lauer, 1982). Double and even triple crop yields resulted. The result was supposed to be an alleviation of the ever-critical food shortage in the nation as well as a boon to the financial well-being of small farmers. But because the new methods required substantial investment, large farmers benefited more than the small farmers. The investment was more than repaid in profits from the increased yields, but small farmers lacked the resources to make such investments. Moreover, many small tenant farmers found their rent raised as large land owners attempted to capitalize on the increased value of the land by forcing the tenant farmers off and using their own workers. Eventually, a number of land reform movements arose, as small farmers demanded consideration for their plight. The land reform movements have resulted in some gains for the small farmers in the form of redistribution of land, but the inequality and the conflict continue, which means that the pressure for change continues. The initial change generated conflict that created pressure for a different kind of change.

Collective Behavior and Social Change

Collective behavior is behavior expressed as part of a collectivity (such as a crowd), focused on a particular phenomenon or event (such as a concert or fight), in a situation of relative change, conflict, or uncertainty. Below we look at four types of collective behavior—crowds, rumors, disasters, and social movements.

Crowds

Turner and Killian (1972) distinguish among acting, expressive, diffuse, and conventionalized crowds. An **acting crowd** is a large number of people who are attempting to change something in their environment. A riot is an example. In 1991, a riot broke out in Washington, D.C. when a citizen was wounded by a police officer. The riot was attributed to the fact that the Hispanic community felt it did not have a say in the largely black D.C. government. In 1980, blacks in Miami rioted for three days after an all-white jury acquitted four white policemen in the beating death of a black businessman (Ladner, Schwartz, Roker, and Titterud, 1981). Over two-thirds of the participants who were surveyed said that they believed the riots would get people to pay more attention to the needs of the black community, and nearly half said that the riots would somehow make things better for the community. The rioters hoped to change their economic and political situation by dramatizing the extent of their grievances.

An **expressive crowd** is one in which there are intense displays of feelings and emotions, often accompanied by some kind of exuberant physical behavior. A religious revival meeting may become an expressive crowd when the members of a congregation engage in spontaneous singing, shouting, speaking in tongues, waving arms, and moving the body rhythmically. The fans at concerts often become expressive crowds when the music brings them to their feet in a frenzy of dancing, clapping, and singing.

A **diffuse crowd** is composed of dispersed individuals who follow a particular kind of behavior or experience a particular sentiment. Fads and crazes are forms of the diffuse crowd. Numerous fads and crazes of all kinds dot U.S. history, including an infatuation with certain games (Trivial Pursuit), with celebrities (the "mania" over the Beatles and some contemporary rock stars such as Michael Jackson and Madonna), with physical activities (piano-wrecking or running), with magical schemes (chain letters), and with daredevil activities (skateboarding). Fads occur in the arts and sciences as well as in everyday affairs. Experts in child-rearing at times have extolled the virtues of breastfeeding infants and at other times have lauded the superiority of bottle-feeding.

Finally, the **conventionalized crowd** is a collectivity gathered for a particular purpose and acting in accord with established norms. The people in the conventionalized crowd expect to experience mutual influence; they are not merely an assemblage of isolated individuals. A theater audience and fans at a sporting event are examples of conventionalized crowds. The fact that they are not merely a gathering of isolated individuals is underscored by such things as rhythmic clapping and chanting.

Emergent norm theory suggests that, when collective behavior such as crowds occurs, new norms, social relationships, communications patterns, and values often emerge, especially in response to unforeseen events. In other words, collective behavior is not just random, uncontrolled behavior; instead, it has some degree of social organization (Aguirre, Quarantelli, and Mendoza, 1988).

One tragedy involving a conventionalized crowd that panicked provides support for the emergent norm theory. In 1979, 11 people were killed as they tried to enter a rock concert. The British rock group The Who was scheduled to perform at a stadium in Cincinnati. As crowds massed outside the gates, attempting entry, many people closest to the entry points were crushed. In contrast to widespread interpretations by the mass media that this event was the result of unregulated, callous competition by young "barbarians" for good seats, Johnson (1987a, 1987b) found little evidence to support this interpretation. Instead, Johnson's study found many reports of people trying to help others endangered by the crush. They were not indifferent; they were physically unable to help. In addition, the study found that traditional gender-role behavior remained in effect as men took the lead in trying to help those in danger. Johnson's study also found that most members of the crowd were part of small, primary groups following established norms and values. Thus, Johnson concludes that, as emergent norm theory suggests, the social structure did not break down in Cincinnati.

Rumor

A **rumor** is unverified information that diffuses through a collectivity as a result of people's attempts to understand something. People need to make sense of their world. But many aspects of life are ambiguous, and the evidence is not clearly available for a meaningful interpretation. Rumors provide the information necessary for understanding. Thus, a rumor is a form of problem solving.

Rumors are likely to appear, then, whenever people lack the information necessary to make sense out of something. For instance, why would a young man not be interested in dating? If nothing about him suggests an answer, a rumor could solve the problem—he is gay. Why does a young woman at work suddenly appear so cheerful? If nothing about her life circumstances suggests an answer, a rumor could resolve the issue—she knows that she is getting the job for which two other people in the office have applied. Or, to take an incident from the news, what is the meaning of the well-known Procter & Gamble logo, the human face in the quarter moon looking out at 13 stars? Why would a soap company select such a logo? In 1980, a rumor began to circulate that answered the question—the symbol is satanic. Moreover, the rumor claimed that Procter & Gamble executives had admitted on television programs that they supported devil worship. Fundamentalist religious groups began to call for a boycott of all Procter & Gamble products. The company took the rumor and the boycott threats seriously, publicly denying any connection with Satan worship and filing defamation suits against three people known to have helped spread the rumor. Actually, there never were any executives on television discussing the logo, and the logo itself dates back to 1852. The 13 stars symbolized the original 13 colonies, and the face in the moon was simply a popular image at the time. Lacking such information, many people accepted the rumor as truth.

Thus, one of the important functions of a rumor is to reduce ambiguity, to make sense out of the world or some part of the world. As such, rumors can reduce anxiety because a world that cannot be understood is a threatening world. Rumors also legitimate and motivate certain kinds of behavior. The Procter & Gamble rumor led some fundamentalists to boycott the products. Race riots in the United States have frequently crystallized around, or been fanned by, rumors (Rosnow and Fine, 1976). When leaders of a movement are jailed, rumors of mistreatment may lead people to take action of various kinds. In an organization, rumors may circulate of an impending "shake-up," leading people to act to protect their own positions. Such rumors may be true or false. In either case, they help people make sense out of their situation and lead them to act accordingly.

Disasters

Much of the research on collective behavior in recent decades has focused on disasters (Kreps, 1989). A disaster may be a natural phenomenon, such as a flood or earthquake, or the result of human action and activity, such as a fire or an airplane crash. Research has shown that there are some common misconceptions about disasters (Wenger, Dykes, Sebok, and Neff, 1975). First, many people believe that disasters almost always create panic and flight. Actually, such behavior is rare. Disasters are more likely to involve convergence behavior—people converge toward the disaster. Some are residents who fled when the disaster first occurred, some are anxious friends or relatives, some are curious or desirous of helping, and some want to exploit the situation.

A second false belief is that looting typically occurs. Frequently rumors of looting spread widely, and police and national guard often are called on to prevent looting (again, the rumor leads to the behavior). But verified cases of actual looting are limited.

Third, most people believe that citizens will readily evacuate an area when warned about an impending disaster (such as a flood or hurricane). The people most likely to leave, however, are transients and visitors. Residents tend to stay, and some refuse to leave until they are forced by authorities.

Finally, most people believe that victims are in a state of shock, unable to fend for themselves immediately after the disaster occurs. But with a few exceptions, various needs are cared for and services provided by the victims themselves with some assistance from others in the immediate vicinity. Overall, people are more likely to deal with disasters rationally than irrationally (Kreps, 1984).

What are the consequences of disasters? They may bring about both short-term and long-term change. The short-term change is likely to be disruption of various kinds. Long-term consequences may be either positive or negative. Research into the effects of a 1974 tornado that killed 33 and injured 1200 in Xenia, Ohio, reported that some of the survivors discovered that they had more internal resources than they realized (Taylor, 1977). They handled the crisis well, and their self-esteem was enhanced. On the other hand, a study of those caught in a 1972 flood in a Pennsylvania town showed that after five years the disaster victims, compared to people in nearby towns that had not flooded, had a greater incidence of various kinds of physical illness and more problems of emotional health (Logue, Hansen, and Struening, 1981).

Social Movements

Social movements are a key type of collective behavior. By definition, they are integrally tied to change because they are collective efforts to resist or to bring about some kind of change. We focus here on the way social movements intersect with social change.

Why are social movements important? As individuals, we are limited in our ability to make the societal changes we would like. There are massive social forces that make change difficult; these forces include the government, large and powerful organizations, and the prevailing values, norms, and attitudes. As individuals going to the voting booth, we have minimal power. As individuals protesting to officials, we have minimal

Sociology in the News

Cyclone in Bangladesh

The world is accustomed to enormous disasters, but one of the greatest disasters in recent years was the cyclone that hit Bangladesh on April 30, 1991. While an exact death count is impossible, most estimates put the death toll well in excess of 100,000 people. It is estimated that 10 million people were left homeless. The cyclone hit with winds of 145 miles per hour and waves were as high as 18 feet. An aid worker for CARE described the scene:

> It's as though the whole country was a sandcastle and a huge wave just washed it away . . . Whole villages are gone. Bridges are wiped out. Bodies are everywhere . . . Islands that used to be inhabited are now devoid of life . . . They're just under water. (Drogin, 1991, p. A1)

Clearly, disasters such as this one are not preventable. However, the degree of devastation in Bangladesh is affected by a number of geographic and sociological factors. For one thing, the country is very small, only about the size of the state of Wisconsin. About 110 million people live in this small area, with the result that disasters like this one affect large numbers of people. For another, the country is largely an enormous river delta and is barely above sea level. It lies "at the head of a natural funnel formed by the Bay of Bengal" (Drogin, 1991, p. A29). These geographical facts serve to magnify the impact of a natural disaster such as a cyclone. As a result, Bangladesh has been devastated by six major cyclones in the last three decades. In fact, the 1991 cyclone is far from the worst. The 1970 cyclone, the deadliest of the twentieth century, killed approximately 300,000 people.

The problems caused by the cyclone are magnified by the poverty of the nation. For example, Bangladesh has only six functioning helicopters, and this deficiency greatly hampered the relief efforts. People living on the economic margins are less likely to survive such disasters. Furthermore, the cyclone is likely to lead to further hardship and impoverishment. Epidemics of communicable diseases such as cholera and dysentery are likely. Thousands of acres of rice crops that were ready for harvesting were destroyed. Thus, hunger, starvation, and perhaps death are in store for many victims of the storm. Further down the road are the consequences of the fact that land flooded with salt water may be unworkable for two or three years. The lack of crops will further impoverish the population. Other aspects of the economy were also hurt by the cyclone. For example, shrimp farms and fishing fleets, which provided needed employment (and food), have been destroyed. Homes, schools, and hospitals were demolished, leaving large numbers of people vulnerable to the elements in a country noted for its hot and humid climate.

Thus, while a cyclone like this one would have had devastating consequences anywhere in the world, the social and geographical characteristics of Bangladesh magnify its effects enormously.

CROSSETTE, BARBARA. "Bangladesh Reports Toll from Storm Near 40,000; Says it May Exceed 100,000." *New York Times,* May 3, 1991, pp. A1ff.
DROGIN, BOB. "New Storms Slow Aid to Bangladesh." *Los Angeles Times,* May 4, 1991, pp. A1ff.

power. As individuals standing against the tide of public opinion, we have little hope of exerting influence. As individuals confronting a corporate structure, we are doomed to frustration and failure. But if we combine with others who share our convictions, organize ourselves, and map out a course of action, we may be able to bring about numerous and significant changes in the social order. Through participation in a social movement, we can break through the social constraints that overwhelm us as individuals.

Types of Social Movements. Sociologists have classified four different types of social movements according to their relationship to social change: *revolutionary, regressive, reform,* and *expressive* (Rush and Denisoff, 1971). **A revolutionary movement** is an attempt to create a new social order. It aims at radical change, though not always by radical methods. Some Marxist groups see the violent overthrow of the government as the only realistic way to bring about the changes they desire. Libertarians in the United States, on the other hand, advocate laissez-faire capitalism and stress the efficacy of educating people to accept their ideology. Once the ideology is accepted, they argue, people will act on it to change the society accordingly (Lauer, 1976). In any case, a revolutionary movement always seeks to alter the power structure of the society.

Many examples of revolutionary movements exist, but one of the most recent took place in the Philippines in the early and middle 1980s. The Philippines had been led for almost two decades by the dictator Ferdinand Marcos. The immediate precipitant of the revolution was the assassination, probably planned by Marcos supporters, of opposition leader Benigno Aquino when he returned from exile in 1983. His funeral procession turned into a demonstration—the first of many demonstrations, some peaceful, some violent. In 1984 Marcos decided to call for a quick election which, because of its short lead-time, would give him an enormous advantage over any opposition candidates. However, the key opposition candidate turned out to be Corazon Aquino, the wife of Benigno Aquino. Corazon Aquino proved to be a very popular candidate, but she lost the election amid charges that the vote had been rigged by Marcos.

In the ensuing days and weeks, there were acts of civil disobedience as well as boycotts against businesses owned by Marcos's cronies. A coup attempt soon followed, and the people rallied around the dissident military officers leading the coup. Hordes of people positioned themselves between the rebel soldiers and troops loyal to Marcos, preventing the latter from attacking the rebels. Soon government soldiers began defecting to the side of the rebels. Not long after, Marcos fled the country in an aircraft provided by the United States, and Corazon Aquino became president of the Philippines (Simons, 1987).

Why do people get involved in revolutionary activities? On the surface, it would appear more rational for people to sit on the sidelines, to be "free riders," and wait to see how the revolution comes out. An individual who takes this position stands to gain the collective benefits of a revolution without incurring the private costs (e.g., risking injury or death). However, history shows that people do get involved in revolutions, often in large numbers. Such people might appear to be behaving irrationally, deviating from their personal interests. Although this may be true, individuals also adopt a collectively rational point of view, realizing that without their participation in revolutionary activities, revolutions will fail. Thus, some individuals are willing to risk the private costs, accepting the fact that their individual effect on the revolution will be minimal, in order to aid the collectivity (Muller and Opp, 1986).

A **regressive movement** attempts to restore a past or passing social order on the grounds that the past order is preferable to any other. For example, the long-standing battle over the teaching of evolution in the schools took on new intensity in the 1980s. The battle arrays those who stand for "scientific creationism" against those who affirm evolution. The former argue that the Book of Genesis gives an adequate account of the beginning of the world, that the universe is no more than roughly 7000 to 10,000 years old, and that the action of God rather than some impersonal evolutionary process is responsible for the existence of the world as we know it. Those who support current evolutionary theory, itself diverse, accept the idea of a slow process of change requiring billions of years for the world to reach its present stage. The evolutionary process involved the gradual emergence of humans from lower forms of life. Creationists want textbooks to reflect their view, or at least to give it equal weight with evolutionary theory.

In 1980, creationists were able to influence 11 state legislatures to consider bills that would require the teaching of scientific creationism in any biology class where evolution was taught. Texas had already established laws in 1974 that set guidelines for the content of textbooks, which made the teaching of evolution difficult. In 1981, Arkansas passed a law that required equal time for the two perspectives. Creationists also were able to persuade some textbook publishers to modify the way their books treated evolution and the age of the earth. But a series of court cases defeated the antievolutionists. A 1981 California court ruling held that the teaching of evolution without giving any attention to creationism did not infringe on the right of freedom of religion. The Arkansas law was ruled unconstitutional in 1982. In 1984, Texas repealed its antievolution textbook selection rules. In 1985, an appeals court upheld a ruling against Louisiana's "balanced treatment" approach to the issue. The creationist movement has been soundly defeated, but its members will undoubtedly continue their efforts to bring back a past social order.

Reform movements aim at alterations in the existing order to make it more acceptable. Typically, reform movements seek to make the existing order more effective or more equitable for more people. That may mean extending certain rights to people for whom they have been denied (such as occupational opportunities for women or equal housing and job opportunities for minorities). New legislation, rather than a radically altered power structure, may suffice to bring about such changes.

Expressive movements seek to change individuals, who will then either change the social order or adapt better to the existing order. Religious movements exemplify the expressive social movement. One of the most rapidly growing movements of recent decades is the charismatic or pentecostal movement, stressing the experience of "speaking in tongues." Those who have the experience, according to the ideology or the movement, have a supreme spiritual experience as well as concrete evidence of the presence of the Holy Spirit. The movement tends to operate independently of established churches, but has secured the commitment of many members of those churches.

Movements and Mobilization of Resources. Although there are various theoretical perspectives on collective behavior generally and social movements in particular, the newest approach to understanding movements uses the concept of resource mobilization (Jenkins, 1983). **Resource mobilization** refers to the idea that protest movements form not so much because of deprivation among people as in response to available resources and the effective mobilization of those resources. The level of grievances and extent of deprivation in a society are generally sufficient among some groups to justify protest. However, for a movement to arise, adequate resources must be available, as well as an organization and leadership to exploit those resources.

Three resources are particularly worthy of note—*members*, a *communication network*, and *leaders* (McAdam, McCarthy, and Zald, 1988). All social movements need members and usually recruit them through established lines of interaction. Second, social movements need a communication network to succeed. For example, the women's movement was aided by a communication network consisting of women involved in the Presidential and State Commissions on the Status of Women, established un-

Cross-National Perspectives

Self-Immolation as Protest in South Korea and India

Political protests reached something of a new height in the 1990s with the strategic use of self-immolation in both South Korea and India. Self-immolation is certainly not a new technique in political protests. It was employed by monks during the Vietnam War, and in South Korea there were three cases of self-immolation in political protests during 1986 (Sanger, 1991, p. A1).

The rash of self-immolations in South Korea in 1991 was part of long-running political protests against the government. In fact, protests led to promises of reform when Roh Tae Woo became president in 1988 (Jameson, 1988). However, the promises were not enough, and protests have become an annual event in South Korea. The outbreak of self-immolations in 1991 began when police beat a young protester to death during a demonstration over campus tuition increases. Shortly thereafter, a young woman sat down on a sidewalk and set herself on fire. Some students leapt from buildings in flames. On May 10, 1991 a Chonman University student, Yun Yong Soo, poured paint thinner over his body. He then set himself on fire and ran through a crowded hallway shouting "Down with the Roh Tae Woo regime!" (Reid, 1991, p. A16). On May 17, three protestors set themselves ablaze, including a 39-year-old woman who, after setting herself on fire, jumped from a railway bridge in front of thousands of people viewing a funeral procession for the protester beaten to death by the police (Bulman, 1991, p.A23). This was the eighth such incident in a three-week period.

These self-immolations reflect a view that more extreme measures are needed to bring about change in the Korean government. Said one student leader: "Rational methods don't work anymore" (Sanger, 1991, p. A3). By martyring themselves, students seem to believe that they will draw attention to their cause and help bring about a more meaningful change in the political system. Specifically, the students hope to draw, as they did in earlier protests, large numbers of middle-class Koreans into the streets to join the protest.

President Roh seemed unmoved by the self-immolations: "Engaging in illegal acts and even self-immolation is truly going against democracy . . . Radical rallies, no matter how small, will not be allowed because they are against the law and they make citizens nervous" (Reid, 1991, p. A16).

The protests, at least until recently, had a rather ritualized quality. For example, during one protest involving 10,000 students, a telephone worker quietly wended his way through the crowd, putting a new coat of paint on each of the telephone booths in the area. In general, the students and police stay about 50 yards apart. The students do deem it acceptable to throw stones and firebombs at police vehicles. However, they will not loot or damage homes, cars, or businesses in the area of the demonstration. For their part, the police will block off streets and lob tear gas canisters at the students, but they will not use guns against the protesters. However, in the recent protests, police squadrons, which have come to be called "white skeletons," have escalated the level of violence, and it is this that resulted in the beating death of the student mentioned above.

In India, while the government is involved in the protests and self-immolations, the main source of the problem is the conflict between upper and lower castes. The government headed by Prime Minister V. P. Singh created the problem through the creation of an affirmative action plan that would aid the lower- and lower-middle castes by setting aside about half of all public jobs for them (Coll, 1990a). Members of the upper castes oppose the plan because it will cost them jobs and, more important, because they feel threatened by the impetus such a program is likely to give to the lower castes. Said one upper-caste school principal, "because of [affirmative action], the backward classes want to finish the forward castes" (Coll, 1990a, p. A1). In fact, a lower-caste militia attacked a train and the upper castes have formed their own private armies. "I think there will be a civil war," said the school principal (Coll, 1990a, p. A1). Caste violence stemming from the government proposal resulted in approximately 100 deaths. Because of the protests, India's Supreme Court temporarily suspended the affirmative action plan.

During the protests, there were as many as two or three attempts at self-immolation per day by upper-caste students, some of whom were no more than 12 or 13 years old. For example, antique dealer Gulshan Chadha was attending a peaceful rally against the affirmative action proposal. In the midst of a discussion of the rash of self-immolations, the crowd noticed flames on the balcony of Chadha's building and realized that his 19-year old daughter had set herself on fire. They ran back to the building and doused the flames, but not before 90 percent of her body was covered with burns. Before she lapsed into a coma, she reportedly shouted "Death to V. P. Singh" (Coll, 1990b, p. A37).

The upper castes oppose the affirmative action plan on various grounds. First, they believe that it will prevent economic progress.

Second, they believe that it will reward people on the basis of birth rather than merit. One upper-caste prince, a former ambassador to the United States, links these two factors: "How are we going to break the shackles of poverty, ignorance and disease if we are going to institutionalize mediocrity?" (Coll, 1990a, p. A36). Third, it is believed that the plan will further bloat the already inefficient and corrupt public sector. Finally, such a quota system will discourage free enterprise and lead to incompetence throughout the occupational hierarchy.

For their part, the members of the lower castes argue for the new quota system on a variety of grounds. First, it will help eliminate discrimination against them. Second, it will reduce the indignities they suffer in India's highly stratified society. Third, better jobs will allow them to improve in a tangible fashion the quality of their lives. That such improvement is needed is reflected in the case of Om Prakash and his family. They have lived for *20 years* in a garbage dump, surviving on what they find amid the garbage to eat, use, or sell. Said Mr. Prokash, "This is the place for us. We can't get out of here . . . There's always hope, but we never reach anything. I'm sure my grandfather hoped, too" (Coll, 1990a, p. A36).

BULMAN, ROBIN. "Demonstrations by 200,000 Turn Violent in South Korea." *Washington Post*, May 19, 1991, p. A23.
COLL, STEVE. "Castes Conflict in India: Affirmative Action Ignites Protest, Suicide." *Washington Post*, October 18, 1990a, pp. A1ff.
COLL, STEVE. "Students' Suicides Shock India's Upper Classes." *Washington Post*, October 18, 1990, p. A37.
REID, T. R. "Korean Burns Himself Critically in Protest." *Washington Post*, May 11, 1991, p. A16.
SANGER, DAVID E. "Suicides by Korean Protesters Stir Unease and Fear of a Plot." *New York Times*, May 17, 1991, pp. A1ff,

der President John F. Kennedy, and feminists working within the Equal Employment Opportunity Commission (Freeman, 1983). Well aware of the inequities that they and other women faced, these women had contact with each other through their participation in the governmental organizations. Third, the leaders are usually drawn from preexisting groups. Other resources may also be important, such as support from well-to-do people, and institutional resources obtained from government agencies, private foundations, the mass media, and corporations (McCarthy and Zald, 1977). Resources may also be mobilized through the actions of professionals who, as part of their mobilization efforts, may aim to raise the consciousness of people to develop a clientele. The environmental and consumer rights movements, for example, were developed largely by professional organizers who educated people on the necessity of the movements.

Organizations are usually treated as entities that help people involved in a social movement attain their objectives. That is, preexisting organizations provide those involved with needed resources and solidarity. However, Conell and Voss (1990) have shown that a preexisting organization can also serve as an impediment to the achievement of the goals of a social movement. For example, a preexisting organization could serve to reinforce old identities while the existing situation requires that those involved develop new identities. More generally, organizations and other social phenomena that might be resources in one context can turn out to be impediments to a social movement in another context.

A Successful Social Movement: The 1985 Columbia University Divestment Protest In 1985, several hundred Columbia University and Barnard College students staged a demonstration in front of the university's main administration building. Their goal was to force Columbia to divest itself of stock held in companies that did business in South Africa and its apartheid regime. Five months later, the university capitulated and divested. Hirsch (1990) has studied how the protest group was able to get students to sacrifice their personal welfare for this collective cause. He found that four group processes created such a willingness on the part of students.

The first process is *consciousness raising.* It is through group discussions that students develop an ideological commitment to the group and the sense that its goals can be achieved only by using noninstitutional means. The second is *collective empowerment,* which often occurs at the protest site. If the participants see that many others are involved, they are likely to come to the view that the group is likely to achieve its goals. In other words, the existence of many other protesters creates a kind of "bandwagon effect." Third, *polarization* can lead members of the social movement to react to the other side (in this case, Columbia University) as a powerful and angry group. Polarization can lead to a heightened commitment to the group and to increased hostility to the opposition. Finally, *collective decision making* involves the members in all phases of the decision-making process, thereby heightening their commitment to whatever decisions are made. Even those who prefer a different course of action are likely to follow the group if they have been involved in the decision-making process. Hirsch found that all of these group processes were involved in the Columbia University divestment protest and helped explain its success. More generally, such group processes are likely to be central to most successful social movements.

Modernization and Development

Over the years sociologists have devoted much attention to the issue of the changing nature of developing countries (LDCs). For a time, that work was dominated by modernization theory. **Modernization** essentially meant the degree to which developing countries followed the model of the West—the degree to which they "Westernized." This mainly translated into economic growth, primarily the degree of industrialization (especially growth in manufacturing), but it also meant adopting Western social and cultural developments (Harper, 1989). In recent years, modernization theory has come under attack, primarily because of its ethnocentric bias that Western practices ought to be followed by the rest of the world.

Modernization theory has generally been replaced by development theory. **Development** may be defined as a general process of economic growth (in production, consumption, per capita income, etc.), but it does not necessarily mean that manufacturing industries must be emphasized. Economic development can be spearheaded by advances in mining, fishing, or agriculture. Emphasis lies not just on improvement in material well-being but also in the quality of people's lives. Societies can grow larger and more complex without copying the Western model. Saudi Arabia is a good example of a country that has developed substantially *without* following the West.

Among the earliest critics of modernization theory were those who accepted dependency theory (Frank, 1969). According to **dependency theory,** the developed countries did not represent the salvation of developing countries but were instead the *cause* of their underdevelopment. The West had grown rich on the basis of its exploitation of poor nations; its development required the underdevelopment of other nations. Modernization theory led developing countries to seek internal changes (e.g., develop manufacturing), but the real changes, according to dependency theory, had to be made in the relationships between developing and developed nations. Dependency theory was a forerunner to an orientation that has come to be the dominant approach to understanding development—world-system theory.

The World-System Approach to Development

World-system theory is an attempt to comprehend contemporary processes of development and underdevelopment (Wallerstein, 1974, 1979, 1980, 1989). Using the entire world as the unit of analysis, the **world-system theory** stresses the economic and power inequalities of the present international order. The world is viewed as a stratified system shaped by the world economy. In a geographical division of labor within the world economy, certain nations exploit the labor of others. In the core (richer) nations, free labor engages largely in skilled labor. In the peripheral (poorer) nations, there exists a preponderance of coerced and unskilled labor. Since the core nations are the major benefactors of the cheap goods and materials produced by the laborers in the poor nations, the situation is essentially one of exploitation.

World-system theorists argue that the gap between the rich and the poor nations is growing. A minority of the world's people are living well at the expense of the majority. How can such a system be maintained? Wallerstein identifies three mechanisms. The superior military power of the core nations minimizes the probability of a forceful alteration of the system by the poorer nations. Moreover, leaders of both rich and poor nations have an ideological commitment to the system; most leaders try to convince their people that progress can be made by working within the system rather than by rebelling against it and trying to establish a different system. Finally, a group of nations is midway in terms of affluence between the core and the periphery—the semi-periphery. The semi-periphery has a function similar to the middle class within a nation—symbolizing to the poorer nations the possibility of progress. It appears to demonstrate that the world situation is not simply one of an impervious core and a relatively powerless and exploited periphery. The existence of such a middle group, therefore, keeps the world from being polarized into two camps which could, ultimately, lead to the rebellion of the periphery and a worldwide war that would force alterations in the system.

A substantial amount of research supports world-system theory. The research underscores the significance of such things as world trade patterns and multinational corporations in constraining the development of the poorer nations. Essentially, the development of the poorer nations is tied up with processes in advanced capitalist societies. Changes have occurred in the economies of the developing nations like Venezuela over time, but those changes can be understood only in terms of the nation's linkage with the world capitalist economy (Roseberry, 1983).

Not only are the economies of the poorer nations dependent upon policies and practices of the rich nations, but the latter frequently work to the detriment of the former. For example, one factor that inhibits development in poorer countries is overurbanization—too heavy a concentration of the population in the urban areas and too much employment in service rather than manufacturing occupations. Both agriculture and industry suffer when there is overurbanization. Studies of the problem suggest that overurbanization is not simply the outcome of internal processes of a nation but is related to the nation's dependence on foreign capital (Timberlake and Kentor, 1983). The more a nation's economy depends on foreign capital, the more the nation tends to suffer from overurbanization. And as overurbanization increases, per capita economic growth tends to decline.

Even foreign aid has done little to change the advantage of the developed nations. In fact, both investments and aid have frequently resulted in worsening some aspects of the situation in developing nations. Bornschier et. al. (1978, p. 652) summarized the results of a number of studies based on data from 1950 to 1970 by saying, "foreign investment and aid have the long-term effect of decreasing the rate of economic growth and of increasing inequality."

World-system theory has recently been used to help explain the decline of the U.S. economy on the world scene. The world system has two long-term characteristics. First, periods of economic boom are followed by periods of economic stagnation. Second, a cycle of the rise and fall of a core nation comes to dominate the world system. From this point of view, the problems of the U.S. economy are traceable to the fact that these two cycles are currently intersecting. That is, the world economy is stagnating *and* the United States is simultaneously losing its dominant position in the world economy to Japan and other nations (Boswell and Bergeson, 1987).

World-system theory is derived from Marxian theory, but it has been criticized by Marxists for failing to emphasize the importance of social classes. To most Marxists the key issue is not the relationship between the core and the periphery but rather the relationship between social classes within given societies. A compromise position would be that *both* relationships between core and periphery *and* class relationships within society are of great importance (Bergeson, 1984). Others have criticized world-system theory for its oversimplification: reducing a complex world into a simplistic core/semi-periphery/periphery model.

The Paths to Development

Developing nations tend to follow some similar and some divergent paths as they develop. Among other things, the population tends to grow, the middle class expands, status depends more upon achievement than upon ascription, nationalism (as opposed to localism) is emphasized, functions of the state are expanded, emphasis on universal education is increased, and some functions of the family (such as education and health care) are lost. In the occupational structure, a shift is seen toward the white-collar and more skilled kinds of jobs. Other similarities include the tendencies toward urbanization, secularization, and bureaucratization. All three processes can facilitate the development process. Urbanization can provide a nation with centralized political control, opportunities for education, and coordination of activities, and can help break down the local loyalties that may impede national development. Secularization frequently involves not the demise of religion, but a change of religion and a new emphasis on reason, a prime requisite of a modern nation. Bureaucratization can give a nation the organizational structure necessary for efficient development.

On the other hand, the similarities do not mean that all developing nations become alike. Even in the same country, two urban areas or two bureaucratic organizations can be quite different from each other. To say that the developing nations are becoming urbanized, secularized, and bureaucratic, therefore, is not to say that they are becoming exactly like the West. Two important reasons account for the differences. The first is the point mentioned above—the different context in which nations develop today. And second, what a nation becomes depends in part upon the traditions on which it builds. Development does not obliterate all traditions; it modifies some, and builds on some.

India offers a good example of the importance of tradition. In the city of Madras, a process of adaptation between traditions and development exists (Singer, 1972). Many scholars have argued that the Hindu religion has impeded change in India because of its emphasis on such things as otherworldliness. They based their arguments, however, largely on teachings in Hindu scriptures rather than on the actual practice of religion in India. When orthodox Hindus learned of the Western interpretation of their religion, they were astounded and asked how India could have achieved so much historically if Hinduism precluded rational action, as Westerners claimed. In fact, Singer found that about half of the industrial leaders in Madras were Brahmans, high-caste Hindus who would be the most careful of all Hindus to observe the religious traditions. The leaders did not find an inherent conflict of interest between their faith and their careers. Rather, they adapted each to the other. For example, Westerners read the Hindu scriptures and looked at traditional practices and believed that members of different castes should not eat together under any circumstances. While at their businesses, leaders would work and eat with members of other castes, although they would not do so outside the business settings. The leaders did not define this act as a violation of their devout commitment to Hinduism. Furthermore, rather than giving four to six hours a day to rituals, in accord with orthodox teaching, the Hindu leaders would take 15 to 30 minutes. Some performed their rituals early in the morning, others prayed while they shaved and washed, and still others said they would perform their obligations when they were older. Thus, the Indian business leaders retained a modified form of their traditional practices while engaging in the process of development.

The flexibility of tradition has also been shown in a study of the kinship structure (the *Hamula*) in an Arab community in Israel (Al-Haj, 1988). Although some changes in attitudes in response to development were found, actual behavior did not change in a parallel fashion. The traditional kinship structure did not break down in the face of development.

It retained much of its customary form, but it also reorganized in an effective manner and became well integrated into the modern system. Thus Westernization is *not* the inevitable result of development.

The Consequences of Change

The consequences of change include those defined by people as both desirable and undesirable. Any particular change can have manifold consequences for human life, but not all of those consequences will be welcome to people.

Negative Consequences

Some observers argue that rapid change is always a traumatic experience for humans. For instance, Toffler's (1970) "future shock" thesis asserts that rapid change overwhelms the individual's capacity for adaptation, resulting in physical and psychological distress. According to Toffler, modern society is changing rapidly in every area—norms, values, institutions, and technology. An individual might handle rapid change in one area as long as he or she has stable anchors elsewhere. When we are forced to confront a world that requires us to continually adapt and readapt in all areas of our lives, our capacity for adaptation simply cannot handle the challenge, and we fall prey to various physical and mental problems.

But despite the pervasiveness of change, the future shock thesis overstates the case. People who perceive the world to be changing very rapidly around them do have higher levels of stress than others, but the stress is moderated if they define the changes as desirable (Lauer, 1974). In other words, the same change can have very different impacts upon people depending upon whether they define the change as desirable or undesirable. For one person, the computerization of the workplace poses a threat, while another finds it an exciting challenge. For one person, a new housing code causes financial strain, while another finds it desirable because it enhances property values. Any change will be defined as desirable by some and as undesirable by others; the consequences for physical and emotional well-being will therefore also differ.

Changes associated with development also have a number of deleterious effects on individuals. Industrialization and modernization tend to bring an increase in certain diseases or higher rates of illness generally (such as higher rates of tuberculosis in nations during the early stages of industrialization, and an increased incidence of diarrhea, ulcerative colitis, and asthma among Westernized people). High rates of tuberculosis during early industrialization result from lack of sanitation and crowding in growing urban areas. The rate of diabetes in urbanized areas of Africa and Asia increased in part because of increased sugar consumption and lower expenditure of energy (Eaton, 1977). Development also tends to break down traditional interpersonal ties. Many people in developing nations feel isolated after they migrate to the cities. The consequences might be a variety of psychosomatic complaints. Finally, as a result of the various strains and stresses associated with the changes in the developing society, some increase in mental illness, anxiety, alcohol consumption, and crime and violence is also noted (Lauer, 1982).

In addition, development can ravage and deplete the natural environment, which could eventually lead to declines in a country's economic development. For example, it is argued that the deforestation of the Amazon has had negative economic effects on Brazil (Bunker, 1984; Katzman, 1987). Technological advances in communication (e.g., television) can adversely affect the culture and make political repression more possible. Involvement in the international market by less developed countries may lead them to export workers to more developed countries, thereby weakening their internal labor force (Evans and Stephens, 1988).

Thus, although development continues to have allure for many developing countries, those nations are increasingly sensitive to the problems involved in development as well.

Positive Consequences

If change brings about a certain amount of trauma, it also yields much that is desired. Many things that we value—affluence, enhanced health, opportunities for advancement, diminished inequality—have come (for developed countries) through the changing of old sociocultural systems. With all of the problems attendant upon modern civilization, few people would care to lead a regressive movement and return to a premodern form of life.

Some positive consequences of change appear in development. The people of such recently developed countries as Japan and Korea have clearly enjoyed unprecedented leaps in their standard of living. Many people in these countries, as well as in still-developing nations, not only are better off economically but experience a life of greater happiness with fewer physical and mental ailments. Those who benefit financially and interpersonally from development report a deeper satisfaction with life. However, we should remember that not all nations, or all people in those nations, benefit from development. Some people remain impoverished while others are succeeding; some endure severed relationships while others are building new, more meaningful ties (Assael and German, 1970).

The East Asian Success Story.   Economic development in East Asia in recent years has been remarkable (Balassa, 1988). Everyone is familiar with the startling growth in the Japanese economy, but in many ways more startling has been the development of the "Four Tigers"—Hong Kong, South Korea, Singapore, and Taiwan. Even less developed East Asian countries like Thailand and the Philippines have demonstrated strong growth, stronger than a nation like India. How do we account for this remarkable set of success stories?

The key factor in the development of these countries appears to be their active involvement in the export of an array of products including electronics of varying types, clothing, and—in the case of South Korea— automobiles. Exports fuel economic expansion for several reasons. First, exports lead countries to invest in industries that make use of a given nation's specific advantages (e.g., natural resources, personnel). Second, these countries are able to overcome the limitations of their domestic markets, which may be too poor and or too small to fuel economic expansion. Large export markets allow them to take advantage of economies of scale (e.g., mass production). Third, export competition among companies leads them to refine their organizations, develop new technologies, and so on. Fourth, the governments of these nations have tended to modernize (e.g., develop up-to-date communications facilities), to create stable systems of economic exchange, and to create a government bureaucracy that will help rather than hinder exports. In other parts of the world, government bureaucracies have developed regulations and controls that have stifled economic development. Thus, a variety of factors help us to understand economic development in East Asia and its positive consequences.

The Domino Effect

The **domino effect** refers to the tendency for any technological development to set off a chain of other developments. As a result, the process of change is self-perpetuating. The effect occurs, in part, because any particular innovation tends to have a variety of applications—a "technological convergence" (Rosenberg, 1976). For example, there was no machine-tool or machinery-producing sector of the U.S. economy in the first part of the nineteenth century. Factories produced their own machines for their own use. Between 1840 and 1880, however, some firms began manufacturing machinery for the use of other firms. Although at first a factory would make a particular kind of machine for a particular use, firms found that the skills needed for any particular machine could be applied to making others. Thus, firms that initially made only machines for textile factories began to make locomotives; the technology for making firearms was used to make sewing machines; and skills used for producing sewing machines and bicycles were applied later to the manufacture of automobiles.

A second reason for the domino effect is **serendipity,** the accidental discovery of something while looking for something else. Here "looking for something else" means looking for a different solution or working on a different problem. Numerous incidents of serendipity mark the history of science and technology, including Galvani's discovery of electric current, Roentgen's discovery of x-rays, Fleming's discovery of the antibiotic effect of penicillin, and Goodyear's discovery of the vulcanization of rubber. Researchers frequently find not only what they are directly looking for but other things as well—so the process of technological change is self-perpetuating.

Summary

Social change refers to variations over time in the relationships among individuals, groups, cultures, and societies. Because social change is patterned, we can distinguish trends, cyclic variations, and irregular or random variations.

A variety of theories attempt to explain change. Cyclic theorists, exemplified by Sorokin, view change as an ongoing series of cycles rather than as a process with direction. Evolutionary theorists view change as a directional process; Lenski and Lenski, key exponents of this approach, see technological developments as the major determinant of change. Conflict theorists, exemplified by Dahrendorf, view change as the inevitable result of inherent conflicts between groups with diverse interests.

Technology, one of the most important sources of change, brings about change by increasing our alternatives, altering interaction patterns, and generating social problems. Ideologies affect change in diverse ways, sometimes acting as impediments or barriers, sometimes as facilitators. Competition and conflict have stimulated much change, especially in scientific developments.

Collective behavior frequently arises from change, or it may produce change. Crowds may have the specific purpose of bringing about some kind of change in their immediate environment. Rumors help people resolve ambiguity in their situations and may be used to legitimate certain behavior, such as rioting. Disasters may result in both short-term and long-term changes.

Social movements, collective efforts to promote or resist change, can be classified as revolutionary, regressive, reform, or expressive. One explanation for movements is the resource mobilization perspective, which stresses the importance of mobilizing sufficient resources to redress the grievances always present in a population.

Modernization and development are general processes that include economic growth in less developed countries. Although development is a pervasive pattern in the contemporary world, influences such as world trade patterns and multinational corporations make the process very different from that experienced earlier by the West. Development generally includes urbanization, secularization, bureaucratization, and a changed stratification system, but the process does not necessarily obliterate all traditions.

Change has both positive and negative consequences, and any particular instance has both gainers and losers. Technological change tends to set off a domino effect, a chain of other developments that make the process self-perpetuating.

CRITICAL THINKING

1. In general, how successful is terrorism in promoting social change? Think of recent examples of terrorist incidents described in the newspapers or on television. To what degree were these efforts at change successful?
2. How do sociologists account for the multitude of changes at various levels of life? Give a brief explanation of the perspectives of the following schools of thought: cyclic, evolutionary, and conflict theory. Compare and contrast the theories in terms of their usefulness in explaining various types of social change.
3. In what ways does the introduction of new technology in society cause change? Are these changes positive or negative? What happens when a society's old norms, roles, or values no longer apply to the situation created by new technology?
4. In what ways does ideology facilitate or impede change in society? Give specific examples to support your ideas.
5. Many people view conflict in a negative light. In what ways is conflict useful in promoting social change? In what ways has competition been useful in promoting social change?
6. What stereotypes exist about people's behavior during disasters? Are these stereotypes supported by the evidence presented in this chapter?
7. Compare and contrast the different types of social movements presented in the chapter. Which have been evident in U.S. history? How important is resource mobilization in determining the success of a social movement?
8. Compare and contrast modernization and development theory. Why has development theory proved to be more useful in explaining changes in less developed countries? What are the advantages and disadvantages of development? Is Westernization an unavoidable aspect of development?
9. Describe the world-system theory of development. What evidence supports this viewpoint?

CONNECTIONS

Reproductive Technology

Introduction

For $10,000, Anna Johnson, age 29, agreed to have an embryo implanted in her uterus and act as a surrogate mother for Mark and Crispina Calvert. The Calverts provided the ovum and the sperm, which were joined in a laboratory petri dish before being transferred to Johnson's womb. Even though Johnson initially agreed to give possession of the baby to the Calverts, she changed her mind when she came to believe that the Calverts had lost interest in her pregnancy. Johnson now claims the baby is hers because she established biological and maternal bonds with the fetus. In her words, "The baby, while it is growing inside me, has my cells and my blood nurturing this child, maintaining its life" (*Washington Post*, 1990, p. A9).

The case of Anna Johnson raises yet another issue in the perplexing social, legal, and ethical questions that have resulted from modern reproductive technologies (Fromer, 1983). Johnson claimed that she had rights to the child because she carried and nurtured the fetus and gave birth to the baby. Her claim, she believed, overrode the claims of the Calverts, who actually produced the ovum and sperm. The court eventually ruled against Ms. Johnson, denying her parental or even visitation rights to the baby she had become emotionally attached to during her pregnancy (Walker, 1990).

The dispute between Anna Johnson and the Calverts is similar to the more famous Baby M case, which we will discuss below. Both cases reflect some of the major issues that grow out of modern reproductive technologies. We will be using a sociological perspective to consider some of these issues.

Major Reproductive Technologies

Most of the major methods of reproductive technology involve couples or individuals who cannot have children because of physical or medical problems. For married couples who have experienced infertility, there are now procedures that allow them options other than adoption. Of course, reasons other than infertility cause some couples, or individuals, to use the new reproductive technology. The major kinds of reproductive technology in use today are:

1. *Artificial insemination and sperm banks.* Artificial insemination involves the implantation of sperm into a woman's uterus. This method is often used by couples when the man is sterile and sperm are taken from a donor. But, of course, this method can be used by any woman who wishes to become pregnant, whether she is married or not. Sperm banks now exist in which donor sperm are stored in a frozen state. There are even some specialized sperm banks for those who are selective about the donor. The most well-publicized is located in California and is popularly called the "Nobel sperm bank." This enterprise specializes in storing the sperm of famous and successful scientists, including three who are Nobel prize winners (Matthews, 1982).

2. *Test-tube babies or in vitro fertilization.* A test-tube baby, or the use of in vitro fertilization, is different from artificial insemination because an ovum is taken from a woman and combined with sperm from a husband or a donor, then fertilized in a laboratory. The baby does not actually grow inside a glass test tube, but the egg and sperm are brought together in a special medium that has been placed in a glass dish. The resultant fertilized egg is later implanted into the woman's uterus (Hartley, 1981; Zimmerman, 1982).

3. *Surrogate motherhood.* Surrogate mothers are childbearing women used by other women who are physiologically incapable of carrying a baby to full term. In this type of reproductive technology the

husband's sperm are generally used to impregnate the surrogate mother who has agreed, through legal contract, to give the baby to the couple at the time of birth (Volpe, 1987).

4. *Gender selection.* At the present time there is only one certain way of selecting the gender of one's child before birth, but there are a number of techniques that purport to change the probability of having a male or female baby. The only certain way is by combining a technique called amniocentesis with abortion. Amniocentesis involves withdrawing and analyzing a small amount of amniotic fluid from the uterus of a pregnant woman. This method is used most commonly to determine if there are any fetal abnormalities (such as Down's syndrome), but it can also be used to determine the gender of the fetus. Thus, it is possible to abort the pregnancy if the fetus is not of the desired gender.

Obviously, many people object to gender selection simply because it involves abortion, since they object to abortion for any reason. However, abortion is not the issue here, for gender selection is likely to be possible by other means. Gender selection is now accomplished in farm animals by separating sperm bearing the (XY) chromosome (male) from those bearing the (XX) chromosome (female). Then through artificial insemination the gender of choice can be produced. In the future, there are apt to be other technologies that will allow gender selection without either abortion or artificial insemination. The interesting sociological question is whether couples and individuals will select the gender of their children, and what the social implications will be if they do.

All of these types of reproductive technology are so recent that it is difficult to see all their social ramifications. In the remainder of this discussion we will see how sociological theories and research can help us to understand the implications of these technological innovations in reproduction. We will begin by seeing what some of the major sociological theories can add to our understanding of the issues.

Structural-Functional Theory

Structural-functional theory focuses attention on the functions or purposes of social structures, including the institutions of a society. In chapter 11 we saw that the family institution normally carries out a number of crucial functions that aid in the survival of a society. Among those functions, and especially important for our consideration of reproductive technology, are *reproduction* and the *regulation of sexual behavior*. The new reproductive technologies are generally consistent with the reproductive function of the family. It is now possible for virtually all married couples to have children, if they are willing, and have the economic resources, to use the methods of artificial insemination, in vitro fertilization, or, in some cases, surrogate mothering. By using these methods, couples who would otherwise be childless can now have children, thus continuing the family lineage, and supplying new members for the society.

The family function of controlling sexual behavior is, however, differently affected by the new reproductive technologies. Societies often control sexual behavior through the institution of marriage. This is illustrated most vividly in the case of lesbian or gay couples, who have often been deprived of having children because of their sexual preferences. These restrictions acted as a societal control on individuals whose sexual preferences did not accord with those of the majority. Individuals who insisted on homosexual relationships were deprived of children and families. It is still not possible for gay or lesbian couples to marry in the United States, but by using the new reproductive technology they are having children. Today, many lesbian couples are using artificial insemination, often with a male friend as a donor, to have children of their own. From this example we see that the new reproductive technologies are changing the way in which the family system has traditionally functioned to control sexual behavior.

Conflict Theory

We have seen throughout this book that conflict theorists, and particularly followers of Marx, often focus on the economic inequalities that exist in societies. Some people simply have greater access to the goods, services, and benefits of the society than others do. Indeed, people at the bottom of the socioeconomic structure may be exploited so that those at the top may enjoy the greater benefits.

Two of the new reproductive technologies illustrate vividly how benefits are unequally accessible, and may be exploitative of the poor. Both in vitro fertilization and surrogate mothering are very costly and thus are practically available only to the relatively well-off. In vitro fertilization is extremely expensive—each fertilization attempt may cost up to $7000 (Lemonick, 1989). Since not every attempt will be successful, the total cost is prohibitive for couples or individuals with modest or low incomes. Even more costly is the expense associated with surrogate mothering. In most cases the woman who becomes impregnated and carries the baby to the time of its birth is paid between $10,000 and $15,000 (*The Kansas City Times*, 1989). In addition, the hospital delivery costs, associated medical bills, legal fees, and a variety of incidental costs are paid by the couple receiving the baby. All told, the cost of having a baby through a surrogate mother is likely to run into tens of thousands of dollars. Obviously, only the highest socioeconomic-status couples will be able to spend this amount of money.

Conflict theorists emphasize that in addition to economic inequalities in the availability of reproductive technology, there is also frequently exploitation of the poorer classes. While $10,000 to $15,000 may be a considerable expense for a couple "purchasing" a baby, it is not an exceptionally large amount to pay a woman who agrees to use her body to produce a baby. In general, women who agree to be surrogate mothers are apt to be lower income women.

The most famous surrogate mother case—the "Baby M" case—is a prime illustration of the inequities and exploitation that can often be found when women agree to produce a baby for money. In this case, William and Elizabeth Stern, both professionals, contracted with Mary Beth Whitehead to bear a baby for them. Ms. Whitehead was not employed, and her husband at the time was a garbage collector. This case gained national notoriety when Ms. Whitehead decided late in the pregnancy that she wanted to keep the baby. In this case she was the biological mother because she both provided the ovum and carried the baby to the time of its birth. Mr. Stern was the biological father because his sperm was used to impregnate Ms. Whitehead. The two sides fought for the custody of the child and, after a long and unpleasant legal battle, the Sterns won. Ms. Whitehead was, however, granted limited visitation rights.

Many observers of this case believe that the decision reflected the unequal economic (and social) positions of the two opposing sides. While it is true that Ms. Whitehead had made a contractual agreement to turn the baby over to the Sterns, it is also true that part of the court's decision was based on the Sterns' ability to provide Baby M with more economic advantages. This case is consistent with what conflict theory would predict—namely, that people in higher economic positions will be able to win out over, and even exploit, people with lower economic positions.

Symbolic Interactionism

As we have seen throughout this text, symbolic interactionists believe the development of a child's self-concept is a crucial aspect of the socialization process. Through the early years of their lives, children begin to see themselves as distinct from others, but their views about themselves are received from significant others, especially parents. They look toward parents for judgments about their own behaviors.

When parents use various forms of reproductive technology, they may have to use very different ways of explaining to their children the circumstances of their births. This raises some serious symbolic interactionist questions about how such explanations will affect the self-esteem of children who were conceived and brought to life by unconventional means. What will it mean to the children of surrogates who are told that their birth mothers gave them up at birth for a large fee?

We noted in chapter 3 that in the United States, as well as many other societies, a great significance is attached to the concept of *biological father*. The same is, of course, true for the biological mother. Will the children of surrogate mothers experience the same problems as adopted children, some of whom feel a need to learn the identity of their biological parents? Symbolic interactionists would predict that in the U.S. they would.

Social Exchange Theory

Social exchange theorists, as we have seen, are concerned with the rewards and costs that people experience in their interaction with others. This theory, then, will direct our attention to the costs and rewards involved in the new reproductive technologies we have been discussing. Furthermore, the theory emphasizes that costs and rewards must be balanced, or reciprocal.

In the case of surrogate mothering, and specifically the Baby M case that we have just considered, the contractual arrangement made between the Sterns and Mary Beth Whitehead was obviously an attempt at reciprocity. The Sterns agreed to pay Ms. Whitehead a specified amount of money, for which she agreed to bear a child and turn it over to them. As Ms. Whitehead neared the end of her pregnancy, however, she decided that the costs of losing the baby were no longer reasonable for the rewards ($10,000) she was to receive. This example also reminds us that exchange theory is not limited to issues of money, but can involve the exchange of anything of value. There have been some surrogate mothers who have reported that part of their reward, in addition to the money they received, was the satisfaction they received from providing a baby for a couple that would not otherwise be able to have a child of their own.

Artificial insemination involves a different set of costs and rewards. When a sperm bank is used, the costs and rewards are again primarily economic. Donors of sperm are usually paid for their sperm, and the recipients pay a fee for the sperm and the service. Often donors are medical students who earn extra money (about $30) for contributing to the sperm bank, an action which for them is a straightforward economic reward. Many lesbian couples report that they receive sperm from a male friend, rather than the more impersonal sperm bank. In these cases the male donors apparently receive as their reward the friendship of the couple, since they almost never expect any rights to the child.

Looking at the Research

Since the reproductive technology we have been discussing is so new, relatively little research has been completed (McKinney, 1989). Yet, the use of reproductive technology is increasing. The first "test-tube" baby was born in 1978, and now there are 138 medical centers that do in vitro fertilization, and many couples are on their waiting lists (*American Demographics*, 1987). Over 500 babies have been born to surrogate mothers (Leslie and Korman, 1989). Artificial insemination has been much more widely used, with more than 250,000 babies conceived in this way. Gender selection has been used in an indeterminate number of cases, but it is not likely that many couples have aborted their pregnancies in order to have a child of a selected gender. This judgment is based on the research that has been done on how Americans feel about selecting the gender of their children—by any means.

National surveys of the U.S. adult population have shown that a little over one-third of adult women approved of the idea of being able to predetermine the sex of their children, and a substantial majority (59.1 percent) disapproved (Pebley and Westoff, 1982). The question asked in this survey was general and abstract, since no method was identified and no conditions were specified. In a different survey, many more people approved when they were asked about selecting the gender of a child if it were used to avoid a gender-linked hereditary defect (Chico and Hartley, 1981). There was also greater approval for gender selection in the case of a couple who already had two or more children of the same sex and wanted their last child to be of the opposite sex.

One of the outcomes of gender selection that has frequently been predicted is an excess of males in the resulting population if couples could (and would) easily choose the gender of their children (Etzioni, 1973; Williamson, 1978). If U.S. women who have not yet had children were to satisfy their gender preferences, among their firstborn they would have 189 boys for every 100 girls (Williamson, 1976a). The preference for boys over girls is worldwide, found in almost every country. Only five societies have been found that preferred girls over boys. All were very small, and only two still exist as they were described in the anthropological literature (Williamson, 1976b). With these minor exceptions, it can be said that the vast populations of the world—India, China, the Middle East, Latin America, and Africa, as well as Europeans and North Americans,—all have a strong preference for males.

Some interesting additional evidence for male preference is found in the folk-sayings of widely different cultures:

A German adage goes: "A house full of daughters is like a cellar full of sour beer."

A Chinese proverb: "Eighteen goddesslike daughters are not equal to one son with a hump."

The Talmud states: "When a girl is born, the walls are crying" (Corea, 1985, p. 190).

Since most methods of reproductive technology are such recent innovations, we have only begun to see the societal and cultural changes that may occur as they are used more extensively. For it is almost certain that these and other reproductive technologies will be used increasingly in the future, and will provide countless exciting opportunities for sociological analysis and research.

References

American Demographics 9, 1987.

CHICO, NAN PAULSEN, and HARTLEY, SHIRLEY FOSTER. "Widening Choices of Motherhood of the Future." *Psychology of Women Quarterly,* 1981.

COREA, GENA. *The Mother Machine: Reproductive Technologies from Artificial Insemination to Artificial Wombs.* New York: Harper and Row, 1985.

ETZIONI, AMATAI. *Genetic Fix.* New York: Macmillan, 1973.

FROMER, MARGOT J. *Ethical Issues in Sexuality and Reproduction.* St. Louis: The C.V. Mosby Co., 1983.

HARTLEY, SHIRLEY FOSTER. "Attitudes Toward Reproductive Engineering: An Overview." *Journal of Family Issues* 2, 1981.

LEMONICK, MICHAEL D. "Trying to Fool the Infertile." *Time,* March 13, 1989.

LESLIE, GERALD R., and KORMAN, SHEILA K. *The Family in Social Context,* 7th ed. New York: Oxford University Press, 1989.

MATTHEWS, JAY. "Surrogate Motherhood Becoming an American Growth Industry." *Washington Post,* January 25, 1983.

MCKINNEY, KATHLEEN. *Human Sexuality: The Societal and Interpersonal Context of Reproduction.* Norwood, N.J.: Ablex, 1989.

PEBLEY, ANNE R., and WESTOFF, CHARLES F. "Sex Preferences in the United States: 1970 to 1975." *Demography* 19, 1982.

ROWLAND, ROBYN. "Technology and Motherhood: Reproductive Choice Reconsidered." *Signs: Journal of Women in Culture and Society* 12, 1987.

The Kansas City Times. "New Issues Surround Test-Tube Surrogacy," April 8, 1989.

VOLPE, E. PETER. *Test-Tube Conception: A Blend of Love and Science.* Macon, Ga.: Mercer University Press, 1987.

WALKER, JILL. "Genetic Parents Win Custody of Baby." *The Washington Post,* October 23, 1990.

Washington Post. "Surrogate's Lawsuit May Redefine Parenthood," August 15, 1990, p. A9.

WILLIAMSON, NANCY E. "Sex Preferences, Sex Control, and the Status of Women." *Signs: Journal of Women in Culture and Society* 1, 1976a.

WILLIAMSON, NANCY E. *Sons or Daughters: A Cross-Cultural Survey of Parental Preferences,* Vol. 31. Sage Library of Social Research. Beverly Hills: Sage, 1976b.

WILLIAMSON, NANCY E. "Boys or Girls? Parents' Preferences and Sex Control." *Population Bulletin,* 1978.

ZIMMERMAN, SHIRLEY L. "Alternatives in Human Reproduction for Involuntary Childless Couples." *Family Relations* 31, 1982.

GLOSSARY

Acculturation *See* Cultural assimilation.

Achieved status A status that people acquire through their own efforts.

Acting crowd A large number of people trying to change some aspect of their immediate environment.

Adult socialization Those occasions in life when adults learn the new behaviors expected of them as they enter new occupations, professions, work settings, institutions, or life stages.

Agricultural revolution The shift from hunting-and-gathering subsistence patterns to the cultivation of grains and domestication of animals.

Alienation Breakdown of the natural connections between people and their work, other people, and the natural world.

Anglo-conformity The American concept of assimilation that assumes that minorities should adopt traits of the dominant group.

Anomie A state of normlessness; situations in which individuals are uncertain about the norms and values of society.

Anticipatory socialization The process of learning what will be expected of one in a status before entering that status.

Apartheid The South African legal system of "separate development" that perpetuates white power and privilege.

Apostates People who early in their lives have a religious identity but later come to renounce or reject it.

Applied research Research designed and conducted to answer a specific practical question or solve a particular social problem.

Ascribed status A status into which individuals move, or are placed, irrespective of their efforts or capacities.

Assimilation The integration or incorporation of a minority into the mainstream of a society.

Attitudinal discrimination Discrimination that stems from prejudicial attitudes and usually involves direct and overt forms of behavior.

Attitudinal objectivity Scientists maintaining an attitude of fairness and honesty when planning and conducting their research.

Authority Legitimate power; the exercise of power that is accepted by those over whom it is exerted.

Autocracy A form of government in which ultimate authority is vested in a single person.

Basic research Research designed and conducted to test hypotheses derived from theories.

Bureaucracy An organization that has a division of labor, hierarchical authority, rules and procedures, impersonality in relations among members, and selection and promotion based on competence and expertise.

Bureaucratic personality The tendency of bureaucrats to conform slavishly to organizational rules, with the result that the rules are more important than the task or objective of the organization.

Capitalism Economic system that emphasizes the private ownership of property and the means of production (raw materials, factories, machines, and equipment).

Capitalists Marx's term for the owners of the means of production in a capitalist economic system.

Caste system The most rigid and closed of stratification systems in which one's status is inherited and fixed, and people are prohibited from marrying members of other strata.

Catch-22 A situation in which the rules of a bureaucracy are in conflict in such a way as to block action.

Charisma Extraordinary qualities, often believed to be supernatural, that give a leader authority over others.

Church A large, socially acceptable, institutionalized religious group.

City A relatively large, densely populated, and diverse settlement of people.

Civil religion The system of symbols, beliefs, values, and practices that have sacred meaning for a nation and a people.

Class Social ranking in a stratification system based on one's relationship to the means of production; more commonly, social ranking based on economic factors such as income and wealth.

Closed class system A system of stratification in which people's positions are fixed and there is little possibility of social mobility.

Coercion Power that is based on the threat or use of force and is therefore considered illegitimate by the people who are forced to do what they do not wish to do.

Coercive organization An organization that uses force to control those at the bottom of the structure.

Collective behavior Behavior that is expressed as part of a collectivity, focused on a particular phenomenon or event, involves a situation of change, conflict, uncertainty, or ambiguity, and is relatively unconstrained by well-established social patterns.

Communicable disease Disease that can be transmitted to people in a variety of ways, including other people, animals, other organisms, food, and water.

Competitive capitalism Capitalist system in which no one capitalist, or small group of capitalists, can gain complete or uncontested control over the market.

Compositional theory of urbanism A model of urban life that emphasizes the importance of social class, ethnicity, and life-cycle stage in determining urban social relationships.

Computer abuse Unauthorized entry into someone else's computer data and altering, stealing, or sabotaging it.

Concentric zone model A model of urban development emphasizing differences in urban land use involving a series of successive rings surrounding a central business district.

Concept A word or phrase that summarizes some meaningful part of the social world.

Conflict theory A view of society as constantly in a state of imbalance and conflict, in which social groups or societies are composed of units that are often engaged in a struggle for power.

Conflict theory of change Change seen as a result of conflicting interests between groups.

Conformists People who accept cultural goals and conventional means to them.

Conspicuous consumption   Acquiring things simply to display them and to show that one can afford them.

Control group   Subjects in an experiment who are not exposed to the experimental variable.

Convenience sample   Research subjects who are conveniently available to complete questionnaires or to be interviewed.

Conventionalized crowd   A collectivity gathered for a particular purpose and acting in accord with established norms.

Correlation   A measure of how much two variables are co-related or associated; indicated by a correlation coefficient, expressed as a decimal fraction from -1.00 to $+1.00$, that summarizes the degree and direction of the relationship between the variables.

Counterculture   A societal group that is consciously in opposition to the widely held norms and values of the dominant culture.

Crime   Deviant behavior that violates the law and is subject to formally sanctioned punishment by the larger society.

Crimes against people (violent crime)   Crimes involving the threat of injury, or threat (or use) of force, against victims.

Criminology   The subfield of sociology devoted to the study of crime, criminal behavior, and the treatment of criminals.

Cross-cultural studies   Often anthropological reports and descriptions of other (often small) nonliterate societies and their cultures.

Cross-national research   The collection of similar types of data in two or more societies so that results can be compared.

Cult   A small, voluntary, and exclusive religious group that has created a new religious system.

Cultural assimilation   A process by which members of subcultures and minorities acquire cultural characteristics (including values, beliefs, language, and behaviors) of the dominant group.

Cultural diffusion   The spread of a cultural trait from one society to another.

Cultural lag   Social and cultural practices that are no longer appropriate when technological change occurs faster than social systems can adapt.

Cultural relativism   An approach that evaluates the behavior of the people of other societies, not on the basis of the evaluator's own culture, but in terms of the culture under consideration.

Cultural values   A key component of culture, the standards of desirability, of rightness, and of importance in a society.

Culture   The entire complex of ideas and material objects that people of a society (or group) have created and adopted for carrying out the necessary tasks of collective life.

Cyclic theory   The theory of social change in which change is seen as an ongoing series of recurring cultural emphases rather than as a process with some kind of direction.

Deindustrialization   The decline of U.S. industry through plant shutdowns, layoffs, and downsizing.

Delabeling   A process by which a deviant label is shed and replaced by a socially acceptable label.

Democracy A form of government in which there are periodic opportunities for the people being governed to retain or replace governing officials.

Denominational pluralism A situation in which different religious groups coexist in a society, with no single group dominating.

Dependency theory A theory that argues that the developed countries are not the salvation of developing countries, but the cause of their underdevelopment.

Dependent variable A variable that is changed or influenced by an independent variable.

Descriptive statistics Statistics used to communicate information about numerical data.

Descriptive survey A survey designed to obtain some basic information about a population, e.g., surveys of attitudes and behavior, opinion polls, and market surveys.

Development The general process of economic growth, not necessarily emphasizing manufacturing.

Deviance Any behavior that most members of a society or social group consider a violation of group norms.

Differential association theory A sociological theory that sees deviance as learned by individuals being socialized by a group of people who engage in and accept deviant behavior.

Diffuse crowd A large number of dispersed individuals who follow particular kinds of behavior or who experience a particular sentiment, e.g., fads and crazes.

Direct expulsion Use of laws and government policies to expel minorities.

Discreditable stigma A negative characteristic of a person that is neither known about by those present, nor immediately perceived by them.

Discredited stigma A negative characteristic of a person that is known about already or is evident to any observer.

Discrimination Unfavorable treatment of people because of their group membership.

Dominant group *See* Majority group.

Domino effect The tendency of any technological development to set off a chain of other developments.

Dramaturgy Performances by individuals aimed at manipulating situations in ways favorable to themselves.

Dyad Two people engaged in interaction.

Dysfunction The detrimental consequence for a society of some social structure.

Economy The social institution involved in the production and exchange of a wide range of goods and services.

Elite deviance Deviant or criminal acts committed by the wealthy and powerful members of society.

Elite A small group of people who come to power and dominate the population.

Emergent norm theory In collective behavior, a theory that emphasizes the similarity between collective behavior and institutionalized social life. When some form of collective behavior is occurring, new norms, social relationships, communication patterns, and values emerge.

Empiricism The act of experiencing something with one's senses, in contrast to imagination and speculation.

Ethnic group A group that is socially defined on the basis of its cultural characteristics. Members of an ethnic group consider themselves, and are considered by others, to be part of a distinct culture or subculture.

Ethnicity   The sense of belonging to and identifying with a particular ethnic group.

Ethnocentrism   The view held by the people of a society that they are of central importance in the universe and therefore their ways of doing things are the right ways.

Evolutionary theory   A theory of social change in which change is seen as directional, a process of cumulative change.

Exclusion   Policies and practices that seek to maintain a society's cultural homogeneity by refusing to admit culturally different groups.

Experimental treatment   Exposure to the independent variable in an experiment.

Experimental group   Subjects in an experiment who are exposed to the experimental variable.

Experiments   Research method in which the independent variable is under the control of the researcher so that its impact on a dependent variable can be observed directly.

Explanatory surveys   Surveys attempting to find independent variables that relate to or account for differences in behaviors or attitudes.

Expressive crowd   A group of people displaying intense feelings, emotions, and exuberant physical behavior.

Expressive movements   A social movement aimed at changing individuals, who will then either change the social order or adapt better to the existing order.

Expulsion   Practices and policies that seek to move minorities from areas controlled by the dominant group.

Extermination   Practices and policies that seek to reduce, destroy, or eliminate a minority population.

Felonies   Serious crimes, punishable by a year or more in prison.

Feral children   Wild children—children who have allegedly been reared in the wild by animals.

Field experiments   Experiments conducted in settings that are natural and involve activities that are relatively normal.

Folkways   Rules that generally govern everyday conduct, such as the rules for eating.

Function   According to structural-functional theory, a positive purpose or consequence necessary for the continued existence of a society (or some other social system).

Functional theory   *See* Structural-functionalism.

Functional theory of stratification   An application of structural-functional theory stressing how social inequality and differential rewards are necessary to motivate the most able people to fill a society's most important tasks; the stratification system is seen as beneficial to the individual and the society.

Game stage   Mead's final stage of a child's social development in which the child simultaneously assumes the roles of a number of other people and responds to the expectations made of them by these people.

***Gemeinschaft* societies**   Toennies's term for societies characterized by personal, face-to-face relationships, such as those in families, rural villages, and perhaps small towns.

General deterrence The threat of punishment having the intention that people will not commit crimes because they fear they will be caught and punished.

Generalized other The internalization of the norms of the larger social group or society by an individual.

Genocide *See* Extermination.

Gentrification The process in which affluent people move into and restore previously declining older urban neighborhoods.

Gesellschaft **societies** Toennies's term for a society characterized by impersonal and distant social relationships; people interact with each other, but in very limited ways, and for what the relationship may provide in terms of calculated self-interest. Associated with urban life.

Group A relatively small number of people who interact with one another over time and thereby establish patterns of interaction, group identity, and rules or norms governing behavior.

Heterodox revelation A religious experience or doctrine that is critical and disruptive of the existing religious and social order.

Historical-comparative method The examination and comparison of the events and histories of whole societies, or of the events and histories of major components of societies (e.g., religious systems).

Horizontal mobility Movement from one social position to another of equal rank.

Hypothesis A statement about how various phenomena are expected to be related to each other.

Ideal culture Values and norms that most people are aware of and accept, but do not necessarily live up to.

Ideal type A logical, exaggerated, and "pure" model of some phenomenon one is studying or wishes to analyze.

Idealistic culture Culture that blends the supersensory and sensory (nonmaterial and material) worlds.

Ideational culture Culture dominated by the principle that a supersensory or nonmaterial world is the only true reality and the highest value.

Ideology A set of ideas used to legitimate and justify the existing social order; also a set of ideas that explains reality, provides directives for behavior, and expresses the interests of particular groups.

In-group A group with whom members are involved and with whom they identify.

Income The economic resources that people receive or obtain during a specified period of time.

Income sufficiency The amount of money needed to purchase the basic necessities of life.

Independent variable A variable that is thought to produce a change in some other variable.

Index offenses (street crimes) Crimes against people and property crimes.

Indicators Observable phenomena that indicate the presence or absence, or level, of a concept.

Indirect expulsion Use of harassment, discrimination, and persecution to force minorities to leave an area or nation.

Individualism The importance placed on the rights, freedoms, and responsibilities of every person.

Industrial Revolution   In the nineteenth century, a rapid major social and economic change marked by the use of power-driven machinery; the rise of the factory system.

Inferential statistics   Techniques that assist in making statements about a population from a sample.

Innovators   People who accept cultural goals but reject conventional means.

Institution   A set of groups and organizations, with norms and values, that attend to the basic needs of a society.

Institutional discrimination   Practices or policies that appear to be neutral but have the effect of excluding minorities from positions of power and prestige.

Intergenerational mobility   Differences between the social-class position of children and the social-class position of their parents.

Intersender role conflict   Situation in which two or more people have conflicting expectations of a person in a given role.

Interrole conflict   Situation in which expectations attached to one role are in conflict with expectations of another role.

Interview   Questions asked by an interviewer or researcher, in person or by telephone.

Intragenerational (or career) mobility   Movement in the class structure by individuals during their lifetimes.

Invasion-succession   The process whereby one identifiable group moves to a different part of an urban area and is replaced by another group.

Iron Triangle   Three points of power in the government—bureaucracy, interest groups, and Congress—that limit presidential action.

Isolation   A condition resulting from a feeling of not belonging to one's workplace or other settings; a dimension of alienation.

Juvenile delinquency   Illegal or antisocial behavior on the part of a minor.

Knowledge and beliefs   A body of information created and accepted by the people of a society that influences their behavior.

Labeling theory   A sociological theory that focuses on the process by which some people in society are able to label other individuals as deviant.

Laboratory experiments   Experiments conducted in specially designed rooms that are equipped with one-way mirrors, audio systems, and video recording equipment.

Latent function   A less obvious, unanticipated, or unexpected consequence of a social structure.

Laws   The norms that are written and enforced by the government.

Liberation theology   A contemporary Christian religious doctrine emphasizing social justice for the poor and dispossessed.

Life expectancy   The average number of years that people in a social or demographic category will live.

Life chances   The likelihood of realizing a certain standard of living or quality of life as it is affected by one's position in a stratification system.

Looking-glass self   The image of oneself that is a reflection of how others respond to one.

Macroscopic sociology   The sociological study of the larger social units—groups, organizations, cultures, and societies.

Majority group   A group that occupies a position of superior power, prestige, and privilege, and is able to realize its goals and interests even in the face of resistance.

Mana The force or power believed to be inherent in a sacred object.

Manifest function The intended and well-recognized purpose or consequence of a social structure.

Mass production Production system in which products are standardized, parts are interchangeable, the production process yields high volume, the flow of materials is synchronized, and the entire process is as continuous as possible.

Master status A position so important that it dominates or overrides all other statuses, both for the person and for all other people.

Material culture The artifacts, objects, and tools used by the members of a particular society.

Materialism A preoccupation with acquiring more and more possessions and property.

Mean A numerical average of a set of numbers, obtained by adding all the numbers in a set and dividing the sum by the total number of cases in the set; a measure of central tendency.

Meaninglessness A condition in which one cannot see one's place and significance in the broader scheme of things; a dimension of alienation.

Median The middle number of a distribution of numbers arranged from lowest to highest; a measure of central tendency.

Medicalization of society The tendency to exaggerate the importance of medicine and to call something an illness that was not previously thought of in this way.

Megalopolis An area of continuous urban and suburban settlement formed when the outer rings of adjacent metropolitan areas merge.

Melting pot A description of assimilation as many different ethnic groups contribute to the creation of a new and different culture.

Meritocracy An ideology that justifies social inequality by emphasizing equality of opportunity.

Metropolis A large urban area containing a central city and the surrounding communities that are economically and politically linked to the central city.

Metropolitan Statistical Area (MSA) A term used by the United States Census Bureau to refer to a geographic area (usually a county or series of counties) of at least 100,000 residents that includes a center city of at least 50,000 inhabitants.

Microscopic sociology The sociological study of the smallest social units—individuals, their thoughts, and actions.

Military-industrial complex The informal but closely knit cooperation between military and industrial sectors that tends to foster the mutual interests of each.

Minority group A group that occupies an inferior or subordinate position of prestige, power, and privilege; is excluded from full participation in the life of the society; and is the object of discrimination by the majority group.

Misdemeanors Minor crimes punishable by less than a year in prison.

Mode The most frequently observed number in a set of numbers; a measure of central tendency.

Modern Demographic Transition A three-stage pattern of population change occurring as societies industrialize and urbanize.

Modernization The degree to which less developed countries follow the model of the developed countries of the West.

Monopoly capitalism Modern capitalist system in which one or a few capitalists control a given sector of the economy.

Mores Rules relating to serious behaviors and moral standards, such as stealing, robbing, killing, espionage.

Multiple nuclei model A model of urban development emphasizing that cities have several distinct centers of activity.

Myth A sacred story that communicates the moral prescriptions of divine beings and binds believers into a community and a belief system.

Nation-state A state that has power over people living in a distinct geographical area known as a nation.

Natural selection A theory that states that the fittest members of any species will be allowed to survive and to spread their traits throughout the population.

Neo-Marxian theory A sociological theory in which legal and political systems are seen as being built upon, and are a reflection of, a society's economic base.

Net financial assets Household wealth after equity in homes and vehicles has been deducted.

Net worth Household wealth based on the difference between assets and liabilities.

New class The stratum of managers, executives, scientists, intellectuals, and other professionals who have gained positions of power in bureaucratically dominated societies.

"New" immigration Immigrants of the late nineteenth and early twentieth century who were drawn primarily from southern and eastern Europe (e.g., Poland, Italy, Greece, Russia).

Nonverbal symbol A physical display that has social meaning.

Norm of reciprocity A standard that calls for two interacting people to give one another things of equal or almost equal value.

Normative, *or* **voluntary, organization** An organization that controls participants by its norms and values.

Norms Rules for what should and should not be done in given situations.

Objectivity In science, conducting research in a way that personal, subjective views do not influence research results.

"Old" immigration The wave of immigrants from northern and western Europe (e.g., Great Britain, Germany, Ireland, and Scandinavia) who immigrated to the United States primarily between 1820 and 1895.

Oligarchy A small, powerful, controlling group at the top of an organization having almost all of the control and power.

Open class system A system of stratification in which there are few obstacles to people's moving up or down in the system.

Organization A deliberately constituted collectivity aimed at achieving specified goals, with clearly delineated statuses, roles, and rules.

Organized crime Self-perpetuating, structured, and disciplined associations in which profits are obtained wholly or in part through illegal means.

Orthodox revelation A religious experience or doctrine that supports the existing religious and social order.

Out-group From the point of view of in-group members, a group to which outsiders belong.

Participant observation A research method that typically involves the researcher directly in the lives and events of the people being studied; the researcher is both a participant and an observer.

Personal control The idea that individuals cannot be made to do things that they do not want to do by social, political, or economic forces.

Personal values The values individuals use to make decisions about their personal lives and how they will respond to public issues.

Play stage Mead's second stage of a child's social development in which the child evaluates himself or herself from the point of view of significant others.

Pluralism (1) A system in which different ethnic or racial groups can coexist equally and be preserved. (2) A political situation in which a number of competing interest groups exert power, with no single group able to control all situations.

Political crime Misconduct and crime committed within or against a political system.

Postindustrial society A society that was formerly industrial, but is now primarily producing services and information, rather than manufactured goods.

Posttest measurement Measurement of the dependent variable after the experimental treatment has been introduced.

Poverty index The federal government's estimate of the annual income necessary to meet minimal living costs in the United States.

Poverty rate The percentage of the population below the poverty line.

Power The ability of an individual or group to realize its interests and to impose its will upon others, despite resistance.

Power elite Small group of nationally influential persons who occupy key positions in large corporations, the executive branch of government, and the military.

Powerlessness A condition of being dominated by another individual or by circumstance; a dimension of alienation.

Prejudice A set of rigidly held negative attitudes, beliefs, and feelings toward members of another group.

Preparatory stage Mead's first stage of a child's social development in which the young child engages in imitation of those around him or her.

Prestige The esteem, honor, and social approval accorded to an individual or a social status.

Pretest measurement Measurement of the dependent variable before the introduction of the experimental variable.

Primary deviance Early, nonpatterned acts of deviance.

Primary socialization Socialization by parents (or caregivers) that lays the foundation for personality development.

Primary groups Groups characterized by intimate face-to-face association and cooperation, typically small and close-knit.

Procedural objectivity Performing and reporting all research tasks so that any interested person will know how the research was conducted.

Profane Those things socially defined as everyday, commonplace, utilitarian, and ordinary; contrasts with the sacred.

Proletariat As used by Marx, the masses of workers, the subordinate, propertyless members of a capitalist society who must sell their labor to capitalists in order to survive.

Property crime Crimes aimed at gaining or destroying property unlawfully.

Prophetic function Those circumstances in which religion provides standards for critically examining, challenging, and changing the existing social order.

Protestant ethic A system of beliefs and actions involving a moral commitment to hard work, frugality, self-denial, acquisitiveness, and systematic calculation.

Qualitative research Sociological studies that use verbal descriptions and analysis, often done by those who claim that the subject matter of sociology cannot be reduced to mathematical formulae and statistical techniques.

Quantitative research Sociological studies that use numerical measurement and statistical analysis as a way of conducting research.

Questionnaire Written set of self-administered questions delivered to respondents by hand or mail.

Race A group that is socially defined on the basis of physical characteristics.

Racism Belief in the inherent superiority of one racial group and the inherent inferiority of others.

Random sample A sampling procedure giving every person in a population an equal chance of being selected in the sample.

Rational-legal authority Legitimization of authority by the rule of law; authority derived from the rules and regulations of the system rather than from personal qualities of individuals or tradition.

Rationality A form of human action based primarily on efficiency; goals and objectives set and achieved in the most efficient way possible.

Real culture The everyday conduct of people, which may differ from the ideal culture.

Rebels People who reject both cultural goals and means and substitute new goals and means.

Recidivism Reimprisonment for new crimes committed after having previously served time in prison.

Reciprocity The socially accepted idea that if you give something to someone, he or she must give you something of equal or near equal value in return.

Reference groups Groups that a person takes into account when evaluating his or her actions or characteristics.

Reform movement A social movement aimed at altering the existing social order to make it more acceptable.

Regressive movement A social movement aimed at restoring a past or a passing social order on the grounds that the past order is preferable to any other.

Religion An institutionalized system of symbols, beliefs, values, and practices dealing with those things believed to be sacred and with questions of ultimate meaning.

Resocialization The process of unlearning old norms, roles, and values, and learning new ones required by a new social environment.

Resource mobilization The idea that protest movements arise as a result of the existence of available resources and the effective mobilization of those resources.

Retreatists People who reject both cultural goals and conventional means of conduct.

Reverse socialization When people who are normally the ones being socialized are instead doing the socializing.

Revolutionary movement A social movement aimed at creating a new social order.

Ritual Complex, communally shared, ceremonial expressions of religious experience that have become institutionalized.

Ritualists People who cannot achieve cultural goals but continue to adhere strictly to conventional means of conduct.

Role Behavior generally expected of one who occupies a particular status.

Role conflict Situation in which a person who holds a position is confronted with conflicting or contrary expectations so that compliance to one makes compliance to the other difficult.

Role making The ability of individuals to modify their roles, at least to some degree.

Role orientation An individual's emphasis on specific aspects of a role.

Role overload Situation in which an individual in a role is confronted with a large number of expectations and finds it difficult, if not impossible, to satisfy all of them in a given time period.

Routinization of charisma The process of passing on the qualities associated with an individual leader and incorporating them into the characteristics of a group or organization.

Rule creators Those who devise society's rules, norms, and laws.

Rule enforcers Those who attempt to maintain social control and order through the threat or actual application of undesirable labels.

Rumor Unverified information that diffuses through a collectivity as a result of people's attempting to understand something.

Sanctions Punishments for violation of mores.

Sapir–Whorf hypothesis The idea that perceptions of reality are shaped by words and language.

Secondary analysis The reanalysis of survey data sets collected by other researchers.

Secondary deviance Forms of deviance that persist in individuals and that cause them to organize their lives and personal identities around their deviant status.

Secondary groups Groups that are typically large and impersonal; members do not know each other as intimately or completely as do the members of a primary group.

Sect A small, voluntary, and exclusive religious group that has broken away from an existing religious organization.

Sector model A model of urban development that emphasizes the influence of transportation paths (waterways, railways, and highways) in determining patterns of urban land use.

Secularization A decline in the authority of religious beliefs, values, and practices.

Self-concept An individual's thoughts about and evaluations of himself or herself.

Self-esteem The degree to which people have positive views of themselves.

Self-estrangement A condition of not being able to express one's abilities, potentialities, and personality in one's work or other settings; a dimension of alienation.

Sensate culture Culture dominated by the principle that the sensory or material world is the only true reality and the highest value.

Separatism A system in which minorities choose to be isolated from the majority group.

Serendipity The accidental discovery of something while looking for something else.

Sexual coercion Sex through force or rape.

Sick role The role of sick people in society with respect to how they are supposed to act when ill.

Significant other People close to an individual whose views shape an individual's self and provide definitions of other social objects; most common examples are parents, family members, friends, marriage partners, fellow workers, etc.

Social change Variations over time in the relationships among individuals, groups, cultures, and societies.

Social control Process by which a group or society enforces conformity to its demands and expectations.

Social epidemiology The study of the frequency and pattern of a disease within a particular population.

Social exchange theory A theory emphasizing that motivations for human behavior are found in its costs and rewards; that a person will repeat behaviors that have been rewarded and will stop behaviors that have been costly.

Social integration Belonging to, or being part of, social groups or society.

Social mobility Movement of people from one position in a system of stratification to another.

Social movements Collective efforts to resist or bring about some kind of social change.

Social stratification The hierarchical structure of social inequalities that are institutionalized; the manner in which scarce resources and social rewards are distributed among different social categories.

Social structure A regular pattern of social interaction and persistent social relationships, e.g., the socioeconomic status system.

Social survey Collecting information from a sample of people through questionnaires or interviews.

Socialism Economic system in which the means of producing goods and services are publicly or collectively owned.

Socialization The process by which a person learns and generally accepts the ways of a particular social group or society.

Society A population of people living in a given territory, who share a culture and have a system of patterned interaction—a social structure.

Sociobiology A theory that posits that human behavior reflects genetically inherited traits that have been acquired through the evolutionary process of natural selection.

Sociological theories Theories that explain a wide range of human behavior and a variety of social and societal events.

Sociology of religion The study of the social manifestations of religions, including experiences, behaviors, beliefs, social roles, and organizational structures.

Specific deterrence The threat of an actual punishment of an individual is supposed to deter him/her from committing other crimes in the future.

State The dominant political institution in modern societies and the sole source of legitimate physical force.

State capitalism Capitalist system in which capitalist enterprises continue to exist, but where there are also state-owned enterprises and the state regulates and manages the economy.

Statistics Techniques used to process numbers produced by research and measurement.

Status A position or place within a set of social relationships; also used in stratification to denote social ranking on the basis of prestige.

Strain theory A sociological theory that sees deviance as being caused by lack of congruence between institutional means and cultural goals.

Structural assimilation The integration of minorities into primary and secondary social relations with the dominant group.

Structural-functional theory A theory emphasizing that every societal pattern (structure) makes some positive or negative contribution to the society.

Structural mobility Social mobility resulting from changes in a society's occupational structure.

Subcultural groups (*or* subcultures) Societal groups that differ significantly from the dominant culture.

Subcultural theory A sociological theory that sees deviant behavior as conformity to the norms and values of a subculture that are different from those of the larger society.

Subcultural theory of urbanism An interpretation of urban life that emphasizes how the city's size, density, and diversity create a variety of subcultures that provide meaningful social settings for its inhabitants.

Subordinate group *See* Minority group.

Suburbs Urban areas adjacent to but beyond the political boundaries of a city.

Symbolic interactionism A theory that views social phenomena primarily through interaction among individuals at the symbolic level.

Symbols Words, gestures, and objects that communicate meaning because people agree on and recognize what they represent.

Taboo A religious proscription against physical contact with objects.

Technology The complex interplay of machines, equipment, tools, skills, and procedures for carrying out tasks.

Terrorism Systematic, or threatened, use of murder, injury, or destruction in order to achieve some political end.

Theology The rational and logical development of religious belief systems.

Theory A set of ideas that provide explanations for a broad range of phenomena.

Total institution A closed organization that is set apart from the rest of society, forms an all-encompassing social environment, and serves as the only source of meeting the needs of its members.

Totalitarianism A form of government involving state control and regulation of all major institutions in a society.

Tradition The ways things have been done for a long time in a society or social group; as a source of authority it comes primarily from the position into which one is born.

Triad Three people engaged in interaction.

Underclass The most impoverished segment of American society for whom poverty is relatively permanent.

Urban A place in which population exceeds a specific number of residents. The United States Bureau of the Census identifies as urban all towns and municipalities having more than 2500 residents.

Urbanism The ways of life characteristic of urban residents.

Urbanization The process by which the population of a society becomes concentrated in cities; also refers to the concentration of economic activity, political-administrative organization, communication networks, and political power in urban centers.

Utilitarian organization An organization that uses money to control those at the bottom of the structure.

Variables Objects or phenomena that can change from one size, state, or degree to another.

Verbal symbols Verbal utterances that are part of the spoken or written language of a society.

Vertical mobility Movement upward or downward in social rank.

Veto group A special interest group that attempts to defend itself by blocking the actions of other groups.

Victimless crime Crimes in which it is difficult to identify a victim; participants choose to be involved in the activities.

Wealth The accumulated economic resources that people possess or have acquired over time.

White ethnics Contemporary descendants of the "new" immigrants.

White-collar crime Crime committed by upper-status people in the course of their occupations.

Working poor Working people whose incomes fall below the poverty line.

World-system theory A theory that stresses the economic and power inequalities of the present international order.

REFERENCES

ABBOTT, ANDREW. *The System of Professions: An Essay on the Division of Expert Labor.* Chicago: University of Chicago Press, 1988.

ABRAHAMSON, MARK. *Functionalism.* Englewood Cliffs, N.J.: Prentice-Hall, 1978.

ABRAMOWITZ, MICHAEL. "Primary Health Care Lacking for D.C.'s Poor, Study Shows." *Washington Post,* August 3, 1988.

ACKER, JOAN R. "Women and Stratification: A Review of the Literature." *Contemporary Sociology* 9, 1980.

ADAMS, PATRICIA F., and HARDY, ANN M. "AIDS Knowledge and Attitudes for July–September 1990: Provisional Data from the National Health Interview Survey." Washington, D.C.: Vital and Health Statistics of the National Center for Health Statistics, April 1991.

AGUIRRE, B.E., QUARANTELLI, E.L., and MENDOZA, JORGE L. "The Collective Behavior of Fads: The Characteristics, Effects, and Career of Streaking." *American Sociological Review* 53, 1988.

AHRONS, CONSTANCE R. "The Continuing Coparental Relationship Between Divorced Spouses." *American Journal of Orthopsychiatry* 51, 1981.

AHRONS, CONSTANCE R., and RODGERS, ROY H. *Divorced Families: A Multidisciplinary Development View.* New York: W.W. Norton & Company, 1987.

AKERS, RONALD L., and COCHRAN, JOHN K. "Adolescent Marijuana Use: A Test of Three Theories of Deviant Behavior." *Deviant Behavior* 6, 1985.

ALDOUS, JOAN. "Birth Control Socialization: How to Avoid Discussing the Subject." *Population and Environment* 6, 1983.

ALEXANDER, JEFFREY C., and COLOMY, PAUL. "Neofunctionalism Today: Reconstructing a Theoretical Tradition." In George Ritzer (ed.), *Frontiers of Social Theory.* New York: Columbia University Press, 1990.

ALEXANDER, KARL L., ENTWISLE, DORIS R., CADIGAN, DORIS, and PALLAS, AARON. "Getting Ready for First Grade: Standards of Deportment in Home and School." *Social Forces* 66, 1987a.

ALEXANDER, KARL L., ENTWISLE, DORIS R., and THOMPSON, MAXINE S. "School Performance, Status Relations, and the Structure of Sentiment: Bringing the Teacher Back In." *American Sociological Review* 52, 1987b.

AL-HAJ, MAJID. "The Changing Arab Kinship Structure: The Effect of Modernization in an Urban Community." *Economic Development and Cultural Change* 36, 1988.

ALLEN, CRAIG M. "On the Validity of Relative Validity Studies of 'Final Say' Measures of Marital Power." *Journal of Marriage and the Family* 46, 1984.

ALIC, JOHN A., and JONES, MARTHA CALDWELL. "Employment Lessons from the Electronics Industry." *Monthly Labor Review,* 109, 1986.

ALWIN, DUANE F. "College Effects on Educational and Occupational Attainments." *American Sociological Review* 39, 1974.

AMERICAN COUNCIL ON EDUCATION. *One Third of a Nation.* Washington, D.C.: American Council on Education, 1988.

AMSDEN, ALICE H. *Asia's Next Giant: South Korea and Late Industrialization.* New York: Oxford, 1989.

ANDERSON, BARBARA GALLATIN. *First Fieldwork: The Misadventures of an Anthropologist.* Prospect Heights, Ill.: Waveland Press, 1990.

ANDERSON, STEPHEN A., RUSSELL, CANDYCE S., and SCHUMM, WALTER R. "Perceived Marital Quality and Family Life Cycle Categories: A Further Analysis." *Journal of Marriage and the Family* 45, 1983.

ANTONOVSKY, AARON. "Social Class, Life Expectancy and Overall Mortality." *Milbank Memorial Fund Quarterly* 45, 1967.

APGAR, WILLIAM C., JR., and BROWN, H. JAMES. *The State of the Nation's Housing.* Cambridge, Mass.: Joint Center for Housing Studies of Harvard University, 1988.

APPLE, MICHAEL W. *Teachers and Texts: A Political Economy of Class and Gender Relations in Education.* New York: Routledge & Kegan Paul, 1986.

ARENDELL, TERRY J. "Women and the Economics of Divorce in the Contemporary United States." *Signs* 13, 1987.

ARIÉS, PHILLIPE. *Centuries of Childhood.* New York: Random House, 1962.

ARLUKE, ARNOLD, KENNEDY, LOUANNE, and KESSLER, RONALD C. "Reexamining the Sick-Role Concept: An Empirical Assessment." *Journal of Health and Social Behavior* 20, 1979.

ARNEY, WILLIAM RAY. *Power and the Profession of Obstetrics.* Chicago: University of Chicago Press, 1982.

ARNOLD, FRED, and ZHAOXIANG, LIU. "Sex Preference, Fertility, and Family Planning in China." *Population and Development Review* 12, 1986.

ASCH, SOLOMON. *Social Psychology.* Englewood Cliffs, N.J.: Prentice-Hall, 1952.

ASSAEL, M., and GERMAN, G.A. "Changing Society and Mental Health in Eastern Africa." *The Israel Annals of Psychiatry and Related Disciplines* 8, 1970.

AUERBACH, STUART. "New Index Shows U.S. Losing Ground." *Washington Post,* June 3, 1988.

AVERY, ROBERT B., and ELLIEHAUSEN, GREGORY E. "Financial Characteristics of High-Income Families." *Federal Reserve Bulletin* 72, 1986.

AWN, PETER J. "Sufism." In Mircea Eliade (ed.), *The Encyclopedia of Religion.* New York: Macmillan, 1987.

BABCOCK, CHARLES R. "Big Donations Again a Campaign Staple." *Washington Post,* November 17, 1988.

BACHMAN, JERALD G., JOHNSTON, LLOYD D., and O'MALLEY, PATRICK M. *Monitoring the Future: Questionnaire Responses from the Nation's High School Seniors 1986.* Ann Arbor: University of Michigan Press, 1987.

BACHMAN, JERALD G., WALLACE, JOHN M., O'MALLEY, PATRICK M., JOHNSTON, LLOYD D., KURTH, CANDACE L., and NEIGHBORS, HAROLD W. "Racial/Ethnic Differences in Smoking, Drinking, and Illicit Drug Use among American High School Seniors, 1976–89." *American Journal of Public Health* 81, 1991.

BACHMAN, JERALD G., JOHNSTON, LLOYD D., O'MALLEY, PATRICK M., and HUMPHREY, RONALD H. "Explaining the Recent Decline in Marijuana Use: Differentiating the Effects of Perceived Risks, Disapproval, and General Lifestyle Factors." *Journal of Health and Social Behavior* 29, 1988.

BAHR, STEPHEN J. "Marital Dissolution Laws: Impact of Recent Changes for Women." *Journal of Family Issues* 4, 1983.

BAKER, RAY STANNARD. *Following the Color Line: American Negro Citizenship in the Progressive Era.* New York: Harper Torchbooks, 1964.

BALASSA, BELA. "The Lessons of East Asian Development: An Overview." *Economic Development and Cultural Change* 36, 1988.

BARAN, PAUL A., and SWEEZY, PAUL M. *Monopoly Capital: An Essay on the American Economic and Social Order.* New York: Modern Reader Paperbacks, 1966.

BARKER-BENFIELD, G.J. *The Horrors of the Half-Known Life: Male Attitudes Toward Women and Sexuality in Nineteenth-Century America.* New York: Harper & Row, 1976.

BARKER, IRWIN R., and CURRIE, RAYMOND F. "Do Converts Always Make the Most Committed Christians?" *Journal for the Scientific Study of Religion* 24, 1985.

BARNETT, ROSALIND C., and BARUCH, GRACE K. "Determinants of Fathers' Participation in Family Work." *Journal of Marriage and the Family* 49, 1987.

BARON, JAMES N., and BIELBY, WILLIAM T. "Organizational Barriers to Gender Equality: Sex Segregation of Jobs and Opportunities." In Alice S. Rossi (ed.), *Gender and the Life Course.* New York: Aldine, 1985.

BARON, JAMES N., MITTMAN, BRIAN S., and NEWMAN, ANDREW E. "Targets of Opportunity: Organizational and Environmental Determinants of Gender Integration within the California Civil Service, 1979–1985." *American Journal of Sociology* 96, 1991.

BARONE, MICHAEL. "The Power of the President's Pollsters." *Public Opinion,* September/October, 1988.

BARRETT, DAVID B. "Adherents of All Religions by Eight Continental Areas, mid-1990." *1991 Britannica Book of the Year.* Chicago: Encyclopaedia Britannica, 1991.

BARRINGER, FELICITY. "Census Shows Profound Change in Racial Makeup of the Nation." *New York Times,* March 11, 1991.

BAZEMORE, GORDON. "Delinquent Reform and the Labeling Perspective." *Criminal Justice and Behavior* 12, 1985.

BEACH, FRANK A., ed. *Human Sexuality in Four Perspectives.* Baltimore: The Johns Hopkins University Press, 1977.

BEAVER, STEVEN E. *Demographic Transition Theory Reinterpreted.* Lexington, Mass.: Lexington Books, 1975.

BECKER, HOWARD S. *Outsiders: Studies in the Sociology of Deviance.* New York: The Free Press, 1963.

BECKWITH, CAROL. "Niger's Wodaabe: People of the Taboo." *National Geographic,* October 1983.

BELL, DANIEL. *The Coming of the Post-Industrial Society: A Venture in Social Forecasting.* New York: Basic Books, 1973.

BELLAH, ROBERT N. "Civil Religion in America." *Daedalus,* Winter, 1967.

BELLAH, ROBERT N., and HAMMOND, PHILLIP E., eds. *Varieties of Civil Religion*. New York: Harper & Row, 1980.

BELLAH, ROBERT, MADSEN, RICHARD, SULLIVAN, WILLIAM M., SWIDLER, ANNE, and TIPTON, STEVEN M. *Habits of the Heart*. New York: Harper & Row, 1985.

BENEDICT, RUTH. "The Vision in Plains Culture." *American Anthropologist* 24, 1922.

BENET, SULA. *Abkhasians: The Long Living People of the Caucasus*. New York: Holt, Rinehart & Winston, 1974.

BERGER, ARTHUR A. "Introduction." In Arthur A. Berger (ed.), *Television in Society*. New Brunswick, N.J.: Transaction Books, 1987.

BERGER, JOSEPH. "Being Catholic in America." *New York Times Magazine*, August 23, 1987.

BERGER, PETER. *The Sacred Canopy: Elements of a Sociological Theory of Religion*. Garden City, N.Y.: Doubleday, 1967.

BERGER, PETER, and LUCKMANN, THOMAS. *The Social Construction of Reality*. Garden City, N.Y.: Anchor Books, 1967.

BERGESON, ALBERT. "The Critique of World-System Theory: Class Relations or Division of Labor?" In Randall Collins (ed.) *Sociological Theory—1984*. San Francisco: Jossey-Bass, 1984.

BERK, RICHARD A., LENIHAN, KENNETH J., and ROSSI, PETER H. "Crime and Poverty: Some Experimental Evidence from Ex-Offenders." *American Sociological Review* 45, 1980.

BERKE, RICHARD L. "PAC's Hear, and Make, Calls for Their Abolition." *New York Times*, November 21, 1988a.

BERKE, RICHARD L. "Experts Say Low 1988 Turnout May be Repeated." *New York Times*, November 13, 1988b.

BERNARD, H. RUSSELL. *Research Methods in Cultural Anthropology*. Newbury Park, Cal.: Sage Publications, 1988.

BERNARD, JESSIE. *The Female World from a Global Perspective*. Bloomington, Ind.: Indiana University Press, 1987.

BERRYMAN, PHILLIP. *The Religious Roots of Rebellion: Christians in Central American Revolutions*. Maryknoll, New York: Orbis Books, 1984.

BETHE, HANS A. "Can Star Wars Make Us Safe?" *Science Digest*, September, 1985.

BETTELHEIM, BRUNO. "Punishment vs. Discipline." *The Atlantic* 256, 1985.

BIALER, SEWERYN. *The Soviet Paradox*. New York: Knopf, 1986.

BIDWELL, CHARLES E., and FRIEDKIN, NOAH E. "The Sociology of Education." In Neil J. Smelser (ed.), *Handbook of Sociology*. New York: Sage, 1988.

BIELBY, WILLIAM T., and BARON, JAMES N. "Men and Women at Work: Sex Segregation and Statistical Discrimination." *American Journal of Sociology* 91, 1986.

BIGGART, NICOLE. *Charismatic Capitalism: Direct Selling Organizations*. Chicago: University of Chicago Press, 1989.

BILLY, JOHN O.G., and UDRY, J. RICHARD. "The Influence of Male and Female Best Friends on Adolescent Sexual Behavior." *Adolescence* 20, 1985.

BILLY, JOHN O.G., LANDALE, NANCY S., and McLAUGHLIN, STEVEN D. "The Effect of Marital Status at First Birth on Marital Dissolution Among Adolescent Mothers." *Demography* 23, 1986.

BIRD, GLORIA W., BIRD, GERALD A., and SCRUGGS, MARGUERITE. "Determinants of Family Task Sharing: A Study of Husbands and Wives." *Journal of Marriage and the Family* 46, 1984.

BIRENBAUM, ARNOLD, and SAGARIN, EDWARD. *Norms and Human Behavior*. New York: Praeger, 1976.

BLACK, MERLE, and REED, JOHN SHELTON. "Perspectives on the American South." In *Annual Review of Society, Politics and Culture* 2. New York: Gordon & Breach, Science Publishers, 1984.

BLANCHARD, FLETCHER A., LILLY, TERI, and VAUGHN, LEIGH ANN. "Reducing the Expression of Racial Prejudice." *Psychological Science* 2, 1991.

BLAU, PETER. *The Dynamics of Bureaucracy*. Chicago: University of Chicago Press, 1963.

BLAU, PETER. *Exchange and Power in Social Life*. New York: John Wiley, 1964.

BLAU, PETER M., and MEYER, MARSHALL W. *Bureaucracy in Modern Society*, 3d ed. New York: Random House, 1987.

BLAUNER, ROBERT. *Alienation and Freedom*. Chicago: University of Chicago Press, 1964.

BLOOD, ROBERT O., JR. *Love Match and Arranged Marriage*. New York: Free Press, 1967.

BLOOD, ROBERT O., and WOLFE, DONALD M. *Husbands and Wives: The Dynamics of Married Living*. New York: The Free Press, 1960.

BLUESTONE, BARRY, and HARRISON, BENNETT. *The Deindustrialization of America*. New York: Basic Books, 1982.

BLUESTONE, BARRY, and HARRISON, BENNETT. "The Great American Job Machine: The Proliferation of Low Wage Employment in the U.S. Economy." Study Prepared for the Joint Economic Committee of the Congress. Washington, D.C., 1986.

BLUM, LINDA, and SMITH, VICKI. "Women's Mobility in the Corporation: A Critique of the Politics of Optimism." *Gender and Society* 13, 1988.

BLUMBERG, ARTHUR, and BLUMBERG, PHYLLIS. *The School Superintendent: Living with Conflict.* New York: Teachers College Press, 1985.

BLUMBERG, RAE LESSER. "A General Theory of Gender Stratification." In Randall Collins (ed.), *Sociological Theory—1984.* San Francisco: Jossey-Bass, 1984.

BLUMBERG, RAE LESSER. "Introduction: The Triple Overlap of Gender Stratification, Economy, and the Family." In Rae Lesser Blumberg (ed.), *Gender, Family, and Economy.* Newbury Park, Calif.: Sage Publications, 1990.

BOAS, FRANZ. *Handbook of American Indian Languages.* Washington, D.C.: U.S. Government Printing Office, 1911.

BOCK, E. WILBUR, BEEGHLEY, LEONARD, and MIXON, ANTHONY J. "Religion, Socioeconomic Status, and Sexual Morality: An Application of Reference Group Theory." *The Sociological Quarterly* 24, 1983.

BOCK, KENNETH. *Human Nature and History: A Response to Sociobiology.* New York: Columbia University Press, 1980.

BOHANNAN, PAUL. "The Six Stations of Divorce." In Paul Bohannan (ed.), *Divorce and After.* New York: Doubleday, 1970.

BOLTON, CHARLES D., and KAMMEYER, KENNETH C.W. *The University Student.* New Haven, Conn.: College & University Press, 1967.

BONACICH, EDNA. "A Theory of Ethnic Antagonism: The Split Labor Market." *American Sociological Review* 37, 1972.

Bondweek. "Control U.S. Takeovers by Foreign Multi-National Firms, Says EPI." May 15, 1989.

BONGAARTS, JOHN. "Why High Birth Rates Are So Low." In Scott W. Menard and Elizabeth W. Moen (eds.), *Perspectives on Population: An Introduction to Concepts and Issues.* New York: Oxford University Press, 1987.

BOOCOCK, SARANE SPENCE. *Sociology of Education,* 2d ed. Boston: Houghton Mifflin, 1980.

BOONE, LOUIS E., KURTZ, DAVID L., and FLEENOR, C. PATRICK. "The Road to the Top." *American Demographics* 10, 1988.

BOOTH, ALAN, and EDWARDS, JOHN N. "Age at Marriage and Marital Stability." *Journal of Marriage and the Family* 47, 1985.

BORDEWICH, FERGUS M. "Colorado's Thriving Cults." *New York Times Magazine,* May 1, 1988.

BORJAS, GEORGE J. *Friends or Strangers: The Impact of Immigrants on the U.S.* New York: Basic Books, 1990.

BORNSCHIER, VOLKER, CHASE-DUNN, CHRISTOPHER, and RUBINSON, RICHARD. "Cross-National Evidence of the Effects of Foreign Investment and Aid on Economic Growth and Inequality: A Survey of Findings and a Reanalysis." *American Journal of Sociology* 84, 1978.

BOSE, CHRISTINE E., and ROSSI, PETER H. "Gender and Jobs: Prestige Standings of Occupations as Affected by Gender." *American Sociological Review* 48, 1983.

BOSK, CHARLES L. *Forgive and Remember: Managing Medical Failure.* Chicago: University of Chicago Press, 1979.

BOSWELL, TERRY, and BERGESON, ALBERT. "American Prospects in a Period of Hegemonic Decline and Economic Crisis." In Terry Boswell and Albert Bergeson (eds.), *America's Changing Role in the World-System.* New York: Praeger, 1987.

BOTTOMORE, T.B. *Classes in Modern Society.* New York: Pantheon Books, 1966.

BOULTON, MARY, et al. "Social Class and General Practice Consultation." *Sociology of Health and Illness* 8, 1986.

BOUVIER, LEON F. "Immigration at the Crossroads." *American Demographics* 3, 1981.

BOUVIER, LEON F., and GARDNER, ROBERT W. "Immigration to the U.S.: The Unfinished Story." *Population Bulletin* 41, 1986.

BOWLES, SAMUEL, and GINTIS, HERBERT. *Schooling in Capitalist America: Educational Reform and the Contradictions of Economic Life.* New York: Basic Books, 1976.

BREAULT, K.D. "Suicide in America: A Test of Durkheim's Theory of Religious and Family Integration, 1933–1980." *American Journal of Sociology* 92, 1986.

BRAITHWAITE, JOHN. "The Myth of Social Class and Criminality Reconsidered." *American Sociological Review* 46, 1981.

BRAITHWAITE, JOHN. "White Collar Crime." In Ralph H. Turner and James F. Short, Jr. (eds.), *Annual Review of Sociology.* 11. Palo Alto, Calif.: Annual Reviews, Inc., 1985.

BRAVERMAN, HARRY. *Labor and Monopoly Capital: The Degradation of Work in the Twentieth Century.* New York: Monthly Review Press, 1974.

BRIDENBAUGH, CARL. *Cities in the Wilderness: The First Century of Urban Life in America.* New York: Ronald Press, 1938.

BRODERICK, CARLFRED B. "How to Rewrite Your Marriage Script So It Works." *Redbook*, February 1979.

BRODERICK, CARLFRED B. *Marriage and the Family*, 3d ed. Englewood Cliffs, N.J.: Prentice Hall, 1989.

BROMLEY, DAVID G. *Falling From the Earth: Causes and Consequences of Religious Apostasy.* Beverly Hills, Calif.: Sage, 1988.

BROWN, ROBERT MCAFEE. "Recent Titles in Liberation Theology." *Quarterly Review* 159, 1986.

BROWNING, GENIA K. *Women and Politics in the USSR: Consciousness Raising and Soviet Women's Groups.* New York: St. Martin's Press, 1987.

BROWNMILLER, SUSAN. *Against Our Will: Men, Women and Rape.* New York: Simon and Schuster, 1975.

BRUBAKER, ROGERS. *The Limits of Rationality: An Essay on the Social and Moral Thought of Max Weber.* London: George Allen & Unwin, 1984.

BRUSH, LISA D. "Violent Acts and Injurious Outcomes in Married Couples: Methodological Issues in the National Survey of Families and Households." *Gender and Society* 4, 1990.

BRYANT, CLIFTON D. *Sexual Deviancy and Social Proscription: The Social Context of Carnal Behavior.* New York: Human Sciences Press, 1982.

BUMPASS, LARRY L., SWEET, JAMES, and MARTIN, TERESA CASTRO. "Changing Patterns of Remarriage." *Journal of Marriage and the Family* 52, 1990.

BUMPASS, LARRY L., and SWEET, JAMES A. "National Estimates of Cohabitation." *Demography* 26, 1989.

BUNKER, STEPHEN G. *Underdeveloping the Amazon: Extraction, Unequal Exchange, and the Failure of the Modern State.* Urbana: University of Illinois Press, 1984.

BURGESS, JOHN. "Study Says U.S. May be Behind Japan in Commercializing Superconductors." *Washington Post*, June 29, 1988.

BURGESS, JOHN. "Television Takeover." *Washington Post-Business*, May 26, 1991.

BURGESS, ROBERT G. *In the Field: An Introduction to Field Research.* London: George Allen & Unwin, 1984.

BURMAN, PATRICK. *Killing Time, Losing Ground: Experiences of Unemployment.* Toronto: Wall and Thompson, 1988.

BURRIDGE, KENELM O.L. "A Tangu Game." *Man*, 1957.

Business Week. "Delivering What Makeup Only Promises." February 8, 1988.

BUSH, DIANE MITSCH, and SIMMONS, ROBERTA G. "Socialization Processes Over the Life Course." In Morris Rosenberg and Ralph H. Turner (eds.), *Social Psychology: Sociological Perspectives*, new ed. New Brunswick, N.J.: Transaction, 1990.

CAHAN, ABRAHAM. *The Rise of David Levinsky.* New York: Harper Torchbooks. 1966. Originally published 1917.

CALDWELL, JOHN C. *Theory of Fertility Decline.* New York: Academic Press, 1982.

CALIFORNIA ASSEMBLY OFFICE OF RESEARCH. *California 2000: A People in Transition.* Sacramento: Assembly Office of Research, 1986.

CALHOUN, A.W. *A Social History of the American Family.* 3 vols. New York: Barnes & Noble Books, 1945.

CAMPBELL, ANNE. "Self Definition by Rejection: The Case of Gang Girls." *Social Problems* 34, 1987.

CAMPBELL, ANNE, and MUNCER, STEVEN. "Them and Us: A Comparison of the Cultural Context of American Gangs and British Subcultures." *Deviant Behavior* 10, 1989.

CAMPBELL, ERNEST Q. *Socialization: Culture and Personality.* Dubuque, Iowa: William C. Brown, 1975.

CAPLOW, TED. "Contrasting Trends in European and American Religion." *Sociological Analysis* 46, 1985.

CARLSON, BONNIE E. "Wife Battering: A Social Deviance Analysis." In Josefina Figueira-McDonough and Rosemary Sarri (eds.), *The Trapped Woman: Catch-22 in Deviance and Control.* Beverly Hills, Calif.: Sage, 1987.

CARLSON, PETER. "Leader of the Snack PAC." *Washington Post Magazine*, November 13, 1988.

CARTER, BILL. "Children's TV, Where Boys Are King." *New York Times*, May 1, 1991.

CARTER, DEBORAH J., and WILSON, REGINALD. *Ninth Annual Status Report: Minorities in Higher Education.* Washington, D.C.: American Council on Education, 1991.

CHAGNON, NAPOLEON A. *Yanomamo: The Fierce People.* New York: Holt, Rinehart & Winston, 1968.

CHAGNON, NAPOLEON A. "Life Histories, Blood Revenge, and Warfare in a Tribal Population." *Science* 239, 1988.

CHAMBLISS, WILLIAM J. "A Sociological Analysis of the Law of Vagrancy." *Social Problems*, 1964, *12*.

CHARON, JOEL M. *Symbolic Interactionism: An Introduction, An Interpretation, An Integration*, 3d ed. Englewood Cliffs, N.J.: Prentice Hall, 1988.

CHEN, P.C., and KOLS, A. "Population and Birth Planning in the People's Republic of China." *Population Reports*, Series J, No. 25. Baltimore, Md.: Johns Hopkins University, 1982.

CHERLIN, ANDREW J. "Remarriage as an Incomplete Institution." *American Journal of Sociology* 84, 1978.

CHERLIN, ANDREW J., and McCARTHY, JAMES. "Remarried Couple Households: Data from the June 1980 Current Population Survey." *Journal of Marriage and the Family* 47, 1985.

Chicago Tribune. "Problems Persist in Voter Bill." May 21, 1991.

CHIROT, DANIEL. "The Rise of the West." *American Sociological Review* 50, 1985.

CHRISTIE, ROBERT. *Empire in Wood*. Ithaca: New York State School of Industrial and Labor Relations, 1956.

CHRONICLE OF HIGHER EDUCATION. *The Almanac of Higher Education, 1991*. Chicago: The University of Chicago Press, 1991.

CIARDI, JOHN. *A Browser's Dictionary and Native's Guide to the Unknown American Language*. New York: Harper & Row, 1980.

CLARK, JOHN. "Presidential Address on the Importance of Our Understanding of Organizational Conflict." *The Sociological Quarterly* 29, 1988.

CLINES, FRANCIS X. "On the Streets, A Shrug at a Falling Star." *New York Times*, Aug. 25, 1991.

CLOWARD, RICHARD, and OHLIN, LLOYD. *Delinquency and Opportunity: A Theory of Delinquent Gangs*. New York: The Free Press, 1960.

COCHRAN, JOHN K., BEEGHLEY, LEONARD, and BOCK, E. WILBUR. "Religiosity and Alcohol Behavior: An Exploration of Reference Group Theory." *Sociological Forum* 3, 1988.

COCKERHAM, WILLIAM C. *Medical Sociology*, 3d ed. Englewood Cliffs, N.J.: Prentice-Hall, 1986.

COCKERHAM, WILLIAM C. *This Aging Society*. Englewood Cliffs, N.J.: Prentice-Hall, 1991.

COCKERHAM, WILLIAM, et al. "Social Stratification and Self-Management of Health." *Journal of Health and Social Behavior* 27, 1986.

COHEN, ALBERT K. *Delinquent Boys: The Culture of the Gang*. Glencoe, Ill.: The Free Press, 1955.

COHEN, ARTHUR M., and BRAWER, FLORENCE. *The American Community College*. San Francisco: Jossey-Bass, 1982.

COHEN, ROBIN. *Endgame in South Africa?* Paris: Unesco Press, 1986.

COLBURN, DON. "Medicine, Losing Its Appeal." *Washington Post-Health*, August 30, 1988.

COLE, STEWART G., and COLE, MILDRED WISE. *Minorities and the American Promise*. New York: Harper & Row, 1954.

COLESANTO, DIANE, and DeSTEFANO, LINDA. "Public Image of TV Evangelists Deteriorates." *The Gallup Report*, 288. 1989.

COLLINS, RANDALL. "A Conflict Theory of Sexual Stratification." *Social Problems* 19, 1971.

COLLINS, RANDALL. *The Credential Society: An Historical Sociology of Education and Stratification*. New York: Academic Press, 1979.

COLLINS, RANDALL. *Sociology of Marriage and the Family: Gender, Home and Property*, 2d ed. Chicago: Nelson-Hall, 1988.

COLLINS, RANDALL. "Conflict Theory and the Advance of Macro-Historical Sociology." In George Ritzer (ed.), *Frontiers of Social Theory*. New York: Columbia University Press, 1990.

CONCONI, CHUCK. "Personalities." *Washington Post*, March 27, 1991.

CONELL, CAROL, and VOSS, KIM. "Formal Organization and the Fate of Social Movements: Craft Association and Class Alliance in the Knights of Labor." *American Sociological Review* 55, 1990.

CONGRESSIONAL BUDGET OFFICE. *The Changing Distribution of Federal Taxes: 1975–1990*. Washington, D.C., 1987.

Congressional Quarterly Almanac, vol. XL, 19-C. Washington, D.C.: Congressional Quarterly Press, 1985.

Congressional Quarterly Almanac. "Reagan Took a Beating on Key Votes in 1987." Washington, D.C.: Congressional Quarterly, Inc., 1987.

CONRAD, PETER. "The Discovery of Hyperkinesis: Notes on the Medicalization of Deviant Behavior." *Social Problems* 23, 1975.

CONRAD, PETER. "Problems in Health Care." In George Ritzer (ed.), *Social Problems*, 2nd ed. New York: Random House, 1986.

CONRAD, PETER, and SCHNEIDER, JOSEPH W. *Deviance and Medicalization: From Badness to Sickness*. St. Louis: Mosby, 1980.

CONVERSE, JEAN M., and PRESSER, STANLEY. *Survey Questions: Handcrafting the Standardized Questionnaire.* Beverly Hills, Calif.: Sage Publications, 1986.

COOK, KAREN S., O'BRIEN, JODI, and KOLLOCK, PETER. "Exchange Theory: A Blueprint for Structure and Process." In George Ritzer (ed.), *Frontiers of Social Theory.* New York: Columbia University Press, 1990.

COOK, T.D., and CAMPBELL, D.T. *Quasi-Experimentation: Design and Analysis Issues for Field Settings.* Chicago: Rand-McNally, 1979.

COOLEY, CHARLES HORTON. *Human Nature and the Social Order.* New York: Charles Scribner's, 1902.

COOLEY, CHARLES HORTON. *Social Organization: A Study of the Larger Mind.* New York: Charles Scribner's, 1909.

COOPER, KENNETH J. "SAT Scores Drop Fourth Straight Year." *Washington Post,* August 27, 1991.

CORNFIELD, DANIEL. "Union Decline and the Political Demands of Organized Labor." *Work and Occupations* 16, 1989.

COSER, LEWIS A. *The Functions of Social Conflict.* Glencoe, Ill.: The Free Press, 1956.

COX, GARY W. "Closeness and Turnout: A Methodological Note." *Journal of Politics* 50, 1988.

CRAWFORD, CHRISTINE. *Mommie Dearest.* New York: William Morrow, 1978.

CRIPPEN, TIMOTHY. "Old and New Gods in the Modern World: Toward a Theory of Religious Transformation." *Social Forces* 67, 1988.

CROSSETTE, BARBARA. "India's Descent." *New York Times Magazine,* May 19, 1991.

CROUSE, JAMES, and TRUSHEIM, DALE. *The Case Against the SAT.* Chicago: The University of Chicago Press, 1988.

CURRIE, ELLIOTT, DUNN, ROBERT, and FOGARTY, DAVID. "The Fading Dream: Economic Crisis and the New Inequality." In Jerome H. Skolnick and Elliott Currie (eds.), *Crisis in American Institutions.* Glenview, Ill.: Scott Foresman and Company, 1988.

CURTISS, SUSAN. *Genie: A Psycholinguistic Study of a Modern-Day "Wild Child."* New York: Academic Press, 1977.

DAHL, ROBERT. *Pluralist Democracy in the United States: Conflict and Consent.* Chicago: Rand McNally, 1967.

DAHRENDORF, RALF. *Class and Class Conflict in Industrial Society.* Stanford, Calif.: Stanford University Press, 1959.

DAS GUPTA, MONICA. "Selective Discrimination Against Female Children in Rural Punjab, India." *Population and Development Review* 13, 1987.

DAUNER, JOHN T. "Man Gets Prison for Racial Attack." *Kansas City Times,* February 3, 1987.

DAVENPORT, WILLIAM H. "Sex in Cross-Cultural Perspective." In Frank A. Beach (ed.), *Human Sexuality in Four Perspectives.* Baltimore: The Johns Hopkins University Press, 1977.

DAVIS, KAREN, and ROWLAND, DIANE. "Uninsured and Underserved: Inequities in Health Care in the United States." In Peter Conrad and Rochelle Kern (eds.), *The Sociology of Health and Illness: Critical Perspectives 1986.* New York: St. Martin's Press, 1986.

DAVIS, KINGSLEY. "Extreme Isolation of a Child." *American Journal of Sociology* 45, 1940.

DAVIS, KINGSLEY. "Final Note on a Case of Extreme Isolation." *American Journal of Sociology* 50, 1947.

DAVIS, KINGSLEY. "Population Policy: Will Current Programs Succeed?" *Science* 158, 1967.

DAVIS, KINGSLEY. "Wives and Work: Consequences of the Sex Revolution." *Population and Development Review* 10, 1984.

DAVIS, KINGSLEY, and MOORE, WILBERT E. "Some Principles of Stratification." *American Sociological Review* 10, 1945.

DAVIS, SHELLEY J. "The 1990–1991 Job Outlook in Brief." *Occupational Outlook Quarterly* 34.

DEBUONO, BARBARA A., SINNER, STEPHEN H., DAAMEN, MAXIM, and McCORMACK, WILLIAM M. "Sexual Behavior of College Women in 1975, 1986, and 1989." *The New England Journal of Medicine* 322, 1990.

DE CREVECOEUR, J. HECTOR ST. JOHN. *Letters from an American Farmer.* New York: Penguin Books, 1782/1981.

DEDMAN, BILL. "Blacks Turned Down for Home Loans from S&Ls Twice as Often as Whites." *Atlanta Constitution,* January 22, 1989.

DeLAMATER, JOHN, and MacCORQUODALE, PATRICIA. *Premarital Sexuality.* Madison, Wisc.: University of Wisconsin Press, 1979.

deMAUSE, LLOYD, ed. *The History of Childhood.* New York: The Psychohistory Press, 1974.

DEMERATH, NICHOLAS J. *Birth Control and Foreign Policy: The Alternatives to Family Planning.* New York: Harper & Row, 1976.

DEMERATH, N.J., III, and WILLIAMS, RHYS H. "Civil Religion in an Uncivil Society." *The Annals of the American Academy of Political and Social Science* 480, 1985.

D'EMILIO, JOHN, and FREEDMAN, ESTELLE B. *Intimate Matters: A History of Sexuality in America.* New York: Harper & Row, Publishers, 1988.

DEMO, DAVID H., and ACOCK, ALAN C. "The Impact of Divorce on Children." *Journal of Marriage and the Family* 50, 1988.

DENTLER, ROBERT A., and ERIKSON, KAI T. "The Functions of Deviance in Groups," *Social Problems* 7, 1959.

DENZIN, NORMAN K. *The Recovering Alcoholic.* Beverly Hills, Calif.: Sage, 1986.

DENZIN, NORMAN K. *The Alcoholic Self.* Beverly Hills, Calif.: Sage, 1987.

DeSTEFANO, LINDA. "Church/Synagogue Membership and Attendance Levels Remain Stable." *The Gallup Poll Monthly* 292, 1990.

DE TOCQUEVILLE, ALEXIS. *Democracy in America*, Vols. 1 and 2. New York: Schocken Books, 1961.

DICKENSON, JAMES R. "Reagan: AIDS is 'Health Enemy No. 1' " *Washington Post*, April 2, 1987.

DINGES, WILLIAM D. "Catholic Traditionalism." In Joseph H. Fichter (ed.), *Alternatives to American Mainline Churches.* New York: Rose of Sharon Press, 1983.

DINGES, WILLIAM D. "Quo Vadis, Lefebvre?" *America*, June 18, 1988.

DINNERSTEIN, LEONARD, and REIMERS, DAVID M. *Ethnic Americans: A History of Immigration and Assimilation.* 3rd edition. New York: Harper & Row, 1987.

DIONNE, E.J., JR. " 'Solid South' Again, but Republican." *New York Times*, November 13, 1988a.

DIONNE, E.J., JR. "If Nonvoters Had Voted: Same Winner, but Bigger." *New York Times*, November 21, 1988b.

DiPRETE, THOMAS A., and SOULE, WHITMAN T. "Gender and Promotion in Segmented Job Ladder Systems." *American Sociological Review* 53, 1988.

DOBSON, RICHARD B. "Mobility and Stratification in the Soviet Union." In Alex Inkeles, James Coleman, and Neil Smelser (eds.), *Annual Review of Sociology*, 3. Palo Alto, Calif.: Annual Reviews, Inc., 1977.

DOGAN, MATTEI, and KASARDA, JOHN D. *The Metropolis Era.* Newberry Park, Calif.: Sage, 1988.

DOMHOFF, G. WILLIAM. *Who Rules America Now?* Englewood Cliffs, N.J.: Prentice-Hall, 1983.

DORRIS, MICHAEL A. "The Grass Still Grows, the Rivers Still Flow: Contemporary Native Americans." *Daedalus* 110, 1981.

DOTTER, DANIEL L., and ROEBUCK, JULIAN B. "The Labeling Approach Re-examined: Interactionism and the Components of Deviance." *Deviant Behavior* 9, 1988.

DRAPER, PATRICIA. "!Kung Women: Contrasts in Sexual Egalitarianism in Foraging and Sedentary Contexts." In R. Reiter (ed.), *Toward an Anthropology of Women.* New York: Monthly Review Press, 1975.

DREW, ELIZABETH. *Politics and Money: The New Road to Corruption.* New York: Macmillan, 1983.

DUBERMAN, LUCILE. *The Reconstituted Family: A Study of Remarried Couples and Their Children.* Chicago: Nelson-Hall, 1975.

DUFF, JOHN B. *The Irish in the United States.* Belmont, Calif.: Wadsworth, 1971.

DUKE, BENJAMIN. *The Japanese School: Lessons for Industrial America.* New York: Praeger, 1986.

DUNCAN, GREG, J., et al. *Years of Poverty, Years of Plenty: The Changing Economic Fortunes of American Workers and Families.* Ann Arbor, Mich.: Institute for Social Research, 1984.

DUNNING, ERIC; MURPHY, PATRICK; and WILLIAMS, JOHN. "Spectator Violence at Football Matches: Towards a Sociological Explanation." *The British Journal of Sociology* 37, 1986.

DURAND, JOHN D. "Historical Estimates of World Population." *Population and Development Review* 3, 1977.

DURKHEIM, EMILE. *Suicide.* New York: The Free Press, 1951. Originally published 1897.

DURKHEIM, EMILE. *The Division of Labor in Society.* New York: The Free Press, 1964. Originally published 1895.

DURKHEIM, EMILE. *The Elementary Forms of Religious Life.* New York: The Free Press, 1965. Originally published 1912.

DUTTON, DIANA B. "Explaining the Low Use of Health Services by the Poor: Costs, Attitudes, or Delivery Systems." *American Sociological Review* 43, 1978.

DWORKIN, ANDREA. *Intercourse.* New York: The Free Press, 1987.

DWORKIN, ANTHONY GARY. *Teacher Burnout in Public Schools*. Albany, N.Y.: State University of New York Press, 1987.

DYE, THOMAS R. *Who's Running America? The Reagan Years*, 3d ed. Englewood Cliffs, N.J.: Prentice-Hall, 1983.

EATON, CYNTHIA. "Diabetes, Culture Change, and Acculturation: A Biocultural Analysis." *Medical Anthropology* 1, 1977.

Economic Report of the President. Washington, D.C.: U.S. Government Printing Office, 1983.

The Economist. May 13, 1985.

EDER, DONNA. "Ability Grouping as a Self-Fulfilling Prophecy: A Micro-Analysis of Teacher–Student Interaction." *Sociology of Education* 54, 1981.

EDSALL, THOMAS B. "Poll Shows GOP Attacks Worked Against Dukakis." *Washington Post*, November 16, 1988.

EDWARDS, RICHARD. *Contested Terrain: The Transformation of the Workplace in the Twentieth Century*. New York: Basic Books, 1979.

EDWARDS, RICHARD C., REICH, MICHAEL, and WEISSKOPF, THOMAS. *The Capitalist System*, 3d ed. Englewood Cliffs, N.J.: Prentice-Hall, 1986.

EHRLICH, HOWARD J. *Campus Ethnoviolence and Policy Options*. Baltimore: National Institute Against Prejudice and Violence, 1990.

EISENHOWER, DWIGHT D. "Liberty Is at Stake." In Herbert I. Schiller and Joseph D. Phillips (eds.), *Super-State: Readings in the Military-Industrial Complex*. Urbana: University of Illinois Press, 1972.

EKEH, PETER. *Social Exchange Theory: The Two Traditions*. Cambridge, Mass.: Harvard University Press, 1974.

ELASHOFF, J.D., and SNOW, R.E. *Pygmalion Reconsidered*. Worthington, Ohio: Charles A. Jones, 1971.

ENGELS, FRIEDRICH. *The Origin of the Family, Private Property and the State*. New York: International Publishers, 1972. Originally published 1884.

ENGLAND, PAULA, and McCREARY, LORI. "Gender Inequality in Paid Employment." In Beth B. Hess and Myra Marx Ferree (eds.), *Analyzing Gender: A Handbook of Social Science Research*. Beverly Hills, Calif.: Sage, 1987.

ENGLAND, PAULA, FARKAS, GEORGE, KILBOURNE, BARBARA, and DOU, THOMAS. "Explaining Occupational Sex Segregation and Wages: Findings from a Model with Fixed Effects." *American Sociological Review* 53, 1988.

ENSTROM, JAMES E. "Cancer and Total Mortality Among Active Mormons." *Cancer* 42, 1978.

ENTWISLE, DORIS R., and HAYDUK, LESLIE ALEC. "Lasting Effects of Elementary School." *Sociology of Education* 61, 1988.

ERDRICH, LOUISE, and DORRIS, MICHAEL. "Who Owns the Land?" *New York Times Magazine*, September 4, 1988.

ERIKSON, KAI. "Notes on the Sociology of Deviance." In Howard S. Becker (ed.), *The Other Side: Perspectives on Deviance*. New York: The Free Press, 1964.

ESCOBAR, GABRIEL. "Washington Area's 703 Homicides in 1990 Set Record." *Washington Post*, January 2, 1991.

ETZIONI, AMITAI. *A Comparative Analysis of Complex Organizations*. New York: The Free Press, 1961.

EVANS, PETER B., and STEPHENS, JOHN D. "Development and the World Economy." In Neil Smelser (ed.), *Handbook of Sociology*. Newbury Park, Calif.: Sage, 1988.

EVANS-PRICHARD, E.E. "Sexual Inversion Among the Azande." *American Anthropologist* 72, 1970.

FACELIERE, R. *Love in Ancient Greece*. Translated by James Cleugh. New York: Crown, 1962.

FANTE, JOHN. "The Odyssey of a Wop." In Oscar Handlin (ed.), *Children of the Uprooted*. New York: George Braziller, 1966.

FARLEY, REYNOLDS, and ALLEN, WALTER R. *The Color Line and the Quality of Life in America*. New York: Russell Sage Foundation, 1987.

FARNSWORTH, MARGARET, and LEIBER, MICHAEL J. "Strain Theory Revisited: Economic Goals, Educational Means, and Delinquency." *American Sociological Review* 54, 1989.

FARSON, RICHARD. *Birthrights*. New York: Macmillan, 1974.

FAUPEL, CHARLES E. "Heroin Use, Street Crime, and the 'Main Hustle': Implications for the Validity of Official Crime Data." *Deviant Behavior* 7, 1986.

FEAGIN, JOE C. "The Continuing Significance of Race: Antiblack Discrimination in Public Places." *American Sociological Review* 56, 1991.

FEIN, ESTER B. "Glasnost Is Opening the Door on Poverty." *New York Times*, January 29, 1989.

FELMLEE, DIANE, and EDER, DONNA. "Contextual Effects in the Classroom: The Impact of Ability Groups on Student Attention." *Sociology of Education* 56, 1983.

FERNANDEZ, JOHN P. *Child Care and Corporate Productivity: Resolving Family/Work Conflicts.* Lexington, Mass.: Lexington Books, 1986.

FERREE, MYRA MARX. "The View from Below: Women's Employment and Gender Equality in Working Class Families." *Marriage and Family Review* 7, 1984.

FERREE, MYRA MARX. "She Works Hard for a Living: Gender and Class on the Job." In Beth B. Hess and Myra Marx Ferree (eds.), *Analyzing Gender: A Handbook of Social Science Research.* Beverly Hills, Calif.: Sage, 1987.

FIELDS, GEORGE. *From Bonsai to Levi's: When West Meets East: An Insider's Surprising Account of How the Japanese Live.* New York: Macmillan, 1983.

FINE, GARY A. "Symbolic Interactionism in the Post-Blumerian Age." In George Ritzer (ed.), *Frontiers of Social Theory.* New York: Columbia University Press, 1990.

FINE, GARY A. *With the Boys: Little League Baseball and Preadolescent Culture.* Chicago: University of Chicago Press, 1987.

FINEBERG, HARVEY V. "The Social Dimensions of AIDS." *Scientific American* 259, 1988.

FINKELHOR, DAVID. *Sexually Victimized Children.* New York: The Free Press, 1979.

FINLEY, MERRILEE K. "Teachers and Tracking in a Comprehensive High School." *Sociology of Education* 57, 1984.

FIREBAUGH, GLENN, and DAVIS, KENNETH E. "Trends Antiblack Prejudice 1972–1984: Region and Cohort Effects." *American Journal of Sociology* 94, 1988.

FISCHER, CLAUDE S. "The Public and Private Worlds of City Life." *American Sociological Review* 46, 1981.

FISCHER, CLAUDE S. *To Dwell Among Friends: Personal Networks in Town and City.* Chicago: University of Chicago Press, 1982.

FISCHER, CLAUDE S. *The Urban Experience*, 2nd ed. New York: Harcourt Brace Jovanovich, 1984.

FISHER, SUE. "Doctor–Patient Communication: A Social and Micro-Political Performance." *Sociology of Health and Illness* 6, 1984.

FISHER, SUE, and GROCE, STEPHEN B. "Doctor–Patient Negotiation of Cultural Assumptions." *Sociology of Health and Illness* 7, 1985.

FISKE, EDWARD B. "New York City's Population Gain Attributed to Immigrant Tide." *New York Times*, February 22, 1991.

FLAIM, PAUL O. "New Data on Union Members and Their Earnings." *Employment and Earnings* 32, 1985.

FLAIM, PAUL O. "Population Changes, the Baby Boom, and Unemployment," *Monthly Labor Review* 113, 1990.

FLEISHER, RICHARD, and BOND, JON R. "Are There Two Presidencies? Yes, But Only for Republicans." *Journal of Politics* 50, 1988.

FORD, DANIEL. "Rebirth of a Nation." *The New Yorker*, March 28, 1988.

FORISHA, BARBARA LUSK. *Sex Roles and Personal Awareness.* Glenview, Ill.: Scott, Foresman, 1978

FORREST, JACQUELINE DARROCH, and SINGH, SUSHEELA. "The Sexual and Reproductive Behavior of American Women, 1982–1988." *Family Planning Perspectives* 22, 1990.

FORSYTH, CRAIG J., and BENOIT, GENEVIEVE M. " 'Rare, Ole, Dirty Snacks': Some Research Notes on Dirt Eating." *Deviant Behavior* 10, 1989.

Fortune. "The Downside of Downsizing." May 23, 1988a.

Fortune. "The Soviet Economy." April 9, 1988b.

Fortune. "America's Competitive Revival." January 4, 1988c.

Fortune. "Genentech Has a Golden Goose." May 9, 1988d.

Fortune. "The Global 500: The World's Biggest Industrial Corporations." July 30, 1990.

FOX, A.J., and ADELSTEIN, A.M. "Occupational Mortality: Work or Way of Life." *Journal of Epidemiology and Community Health* 32, 1978.

FOX, GREER LITTON. "The Mother–Adolescent Daughter Relationship as a Sexual Socialization Structure: A Research Review." *Family Relations* 29, 1980.

FOX, GREER LITTON, and INAZU, JUDITH K. "Patterns and Outcomes of Mother–Daughter Communications About Sexuality." *Journal of Social Issues* 36, 1980.

FRANCE, ANATOLE. *Crainqueville.* Freeport, N.Y.: Books for Libraries, 1922.

FRANK, ANDRE GUNDER. *Capitalism and Underdevelopment in Latin America: Historical Studies of Chile and Brazil.* New York: Monthly Labor Review Press, 1969.

FRANKL, RAZELLE. *Televangelism: The Marketing of Popular Religion.* Carbondale and Edwardsville: Southern Illinois University Press, 1987.

FRANKLAND, MARK. *The Sixth Continent: Mikhail Gorbachev and the Soviet Union.* New York: Harper and Row, 1987.

FREEDMAN, RONALD. "Family Planning Programs in the Third World." *Annals of the American Academy of Political and Social Science* 510, 1990.

FREEMAN, Jo. "On the Origins of Social Movements." In Jo Freeman (ed.), *Social Movements of the Sixties and Seventies*. New York: Longman, 1983.

FREEMAN, RICHARD B., and MEDOFF, JAMES L. *What Do Unions Do?* New York: Basic Books, 1984.

FREIDSON, ELIOT. *Profession of Medicine*. New York: Dodd, Mead, 1970.

FREIDSON, ELIOT. *Doctoring Together*. New York: Elsevier, 1975.

FREY, WILLIAM H. "Metropolitan America: Beyond the Transition." *Population Bulletin* 45, 1990.

FRIEDMAN, EMILY. "The Uninsured: From Dilemma to Crisis." *Journal of the American Medical Association* 265, 1991.

FRIEDMAN, THOMAS L. "Kahane Appeal to Oust Arabs Gains in Israel." *New York Times*, August 5, 1985.

FRIEDRICH, CARL J., and BRZEZINSKI, ZBIGNIEW. *Totalitarian Dictatorship and Autocracy*, vol. 2. Cambridge, Mass.: Harvard University Press, 1965.

FRISBIE, W. PARKER, and KASARDA, JOHN D. "Spatial Processes." In Neil J. Smelser (ed.), *Handbook of Sociology*. Beverly Hills, Calif.: Sage, 1988.

FURSTENBERG, FRANK F., JR. *Unplanned Parenthood: The Social Consequences of Teenage Childbearing*. New York: The Free Press, 1976.

FURSTENBERG, FRANK F., JR. "Premarital Pregnancy and Marital Instability." In George Levinger and Oliver C. Moles (eds.), *Divorce and Separation: Context, Causes, and Consequences*. New York: Basic Books, 1979.

FURSTENBERG, FRANK F., JR. "The Social Consequences of Teenage Parenthood." In Frank F. Furstenberg, Jr., Richard Lincoln, and Jane Menken (eds.), *Teenage Sexuality, Pregnancy and Childbearing*. Philadelphia: University of Pennsylvania Press, 1981.

FURSTENBERG, FRANK F., JR., MORGAN, S. PHILIP, MOORE, KRISTIN A., and PETERSON, JAMES L. "Race Differences in the Timing of Adolescent Intercourse." *American Sociological Review* 52, 1987.

GALBRAITH, JOHN KENNETH, and MENSHIKOV, STANISLAV. *Capitalism, Communism and Co-existence*. Boston: Houghton Mifflin, 1988.

The Gallup Report. "Religion in America." Report No. 259, 1987.

GALLUP, GEORGE, JR., and HUGICK, LARRY. "Racial Tolerance Grows, Progress on Racial Equality Less Evident." *Gallup Poll Monthly* 297, 1990.

GALLUP, GEORGE, JR., and NEWPORT, FRANK. "More Americans Now Believe in a Power Outside Themselves." *Gallup Poll Monthly* 297, 1990.

GAMSON, WILLIAM A. *The Strategy of Social Protest*. Homewood, Ill.: The Dorsey Press, 1975.

GANS, CURTIS. "No Wonder Turnout Was Low." *Washington Post*, November 11, 1988.

GANS, HERBERT J. *Middle American Individualism*, New York: The Free Press, 1988.

GANS, HERBERT J. "Deconstructing the Underclass." *Journal of the American Planning Association* 56, 1990.

GARBARINO, JAMES, and SHERMAN, DEBORAH. "High-Risk Neighborhoods and High-Risk Families: The Human Ecology of Child Maltreatment." *Child Development* 51, 1980.

GECAS, VIKTOR. "The Influence of Social Class on Socialization." In Wesley R. Burr, Reuben Hill, F. Ivan Nye, and Ira L. Reiss (eds.), *Contemporary Theories About the Family: Research-based Theories*, Vol. I. New York: The Free Press, 1979.

GECAS, VIKTOR. "Contexts of Socialization." In Morris Rosenberg and Ralph Turner (eds.), *Sociological Perspectives in Social Psychology*. New Brunswick, N.J.: Transaction Books, 1990.

GECAS, VIKTOR, and SCHWALBE, MICHAEL L. "Beyond the Looking-Glass Self: Social Structure and Efficacy-Based Self-Esteem." *Social Psychology Quarterly* 46, 1983.

GECAS, VIKTOR. "Contexts of Socialization." In Morris Rosenberg and Ralph H. Turner (eds.), *Social Psychology: Sociological Perspectives*, new edition. New Brunswick, N.J.: Transaction, 1990.

GEHRIG, GAIL. *American Civil Religion: An Assessment*. Monograph Series, 3. Storrs, Conn.: Society for the Scientific Study of Religion, 1979.

GELLES, RICHARD J. *Family Violence*, 2nd ed. Beverly Hills, Calif.: Sage, 1987.

GELLES, RICHARD J., and CORNELL, CLAIRE PEDRICK. *Intimate Violence in Families*, 2nd ed. Newbury Park, Calif.: Sage Publications, 1990.

GERBER, JURG, and SHORT, JAMES F., JR. "Publicity and the Control of Corporate Behavior: The Case of Infant Formula." *Deviant Behavior* 7, 1986.

GERSHUNY, JONATHAN, and ROBINSON, JOHN P. "Historical Changes in the Household Division of Labor." *Demography* 25, 1988.

GERTH, HANS, and MILLS, C. WRIGHT, eds. *From Max Weber: Essays in Sociology*. New York: Oxford University Press, 1958.

GIALLOMBARDO, ROSE. *The Social World of Imprisoned Girls: A Comparative Study of Institutions for Juvenile Delinquents*. New York: John Wiley, 1974.

GIBNEY, FRANK. "The Strange Ways of Staphorst." *Life*, September 27, 1948.

GIELE, JANET Z. "Introduction: The Status of Women in Comparative Perspective." In Janet Z. Giele and A.C. Smock (eds.), *Women: Roles and Status in Eight Countries.* New York: Wiley-Interscience, 1977.

GIELE, JANET Z. "Gender and Sex Roles." In Neil J. Smelser (ed.), *Handbook of Sociology.* Beverly Hills, Calif.: Sage, 1988.

GIST, NOEL P., and FAVA, SYLVIA FLEIS. *Urban Society,* 6th ed. New York: Thomas Y. Crowell, 1974.

GLAAB, CHARLES N., and BROWN, THEODORE A. *A History of Urban America.* New York: Macmillan, 1967.

GLADWELL, MALCOLM. "City, Suburbs Battle for Scanning Device." *Washington Post-Health,* August 23, 1988.

GLASS, DAVID, SQUIRE, PEVEREILL, and WOLFINGER, RAYMOND. "Voter Turnout: An International Comparison." *Public Opinion,* December/January 1984.

GLAZER, NATHAN, and MOYNIHAN, DANIEL P. *Beyond the Melting Pot: The Negroes, Puerto Ricans, Jews, Italians, and Irish of New York City.* Cambridge, Mass.: The MIT Press, 1963.

GLENN, NORVAL D., and KRAMER, KATHRYN B. "The Marriage and Divorces of the Children of Divorce." *Journal of Marriage and the Family* 49, 1987.

GLENN, NORVAL D., and SHELTON, BETH ANN. "Regional Differences in Divorce in the United States." *Journal of Marriage and the Family* 47, 1985.

GLENN, NORVAL D., and SUPANCIC, MICHAEL. "The Social and Demographic Correlates of Divorce and Separation in the United States: An Update and Reconsideration." *Journal of Marriage and the Family* 46, 1984.

GLICK, PAUL, and LIN, SUNG-LING. "Recent Changes in Divorce and Remarriage." *Journal of Marriage and the Family* 48, 1986.

GLOCK, CHARLES V., and STARK, RODNEY. *Religion and Society in Tension.* Chicago: Rand McNally, 1965.

GOFFMAN, ERVING. "The Moral Career of the Mental Patient." *Psychiatry* 22, 1959a.

GOFFMAN, ERVING. *The Presentation of Self in Everyday Life.* Garden City, N.Y.: Anchor Books, 1959b.

GOFFMAN, ERVING. *Asylums: Essays on the Social Situation of Mental Patients and Other Inmates.* Garden City, N.Y.: Anchor Books, 1961.

GOFFMAN, ERVING. *Stigma: Notes on the Management of Spoiled Identity.* Englewood Cliffs, N.J.: Prentice-Hall, 1963.

GOLDBERG, STEVEN. *The Inevitability of Patriarchy.* New York: William Morrow, 1973.

GOLDFIELD, MICHAEL. *The Decline of Organized Labor.* Chicago: University of Chicago Press, 1987.

GOLDMAN, MARSHALL I. *Gorbachev's Challenge: Economic Reform in the Age of High Technology.* New York: W.W. Norton and Co., 1987.

GOLEMAN, DANIEL. "The Electronic Rorschach." *Psychology Today,* February 1983.

GONZALEZ, DAVID. "Hispanic Voters Struggle to Find the Strength in Their Numbers." *New York Times,* May 26, 1991.

GOODE, ERICH, ed. *Marijuana.* Chicago: Aldine, 1969.

GOODE, WILLIAM J. "The Theoretical Importance of Love." *American Sociological Review* 24, 1959.

GOODE, WILLIAM J. "Why Men Resist." In Barrie Thorne, with Marilyn Yalom (eds.), *Rethinking the Family: Some Feminist Questions.* New York: Longman, 1982.

GORDON, DAVID M. "Class and Economics of Crime." *Review of Radical Political Economies* 3, 1981.

GORDON, MICHAEL, and SHANKWEILER, PENELOPE. "Different Equals Less: Female Sexuality in Recent Marriage Manuals." *Journal of Marriage and the Family* 33, 1971.

GORDON, MILTON M. *Assimilation in American Life: The Role of Race, Religion and National Origins.* New York: Oxford University Press, 1964.

GOTTDIENER, M., and FEAGIN, JOE R. "The Paradigm Shift in Urban Sociology." *Urban Affairs Quarterly* 24, 1988.

GOTTMAN, JEAN. *Megalopolis: The Urbanized Northeastern Seaboard of the United States.* New York: Twentieth Century Fund, 1961.

GOULDNER, ALVIN W. *Patterns of Industrial Democracy.* Glencoe, Ill.: The Free Press, 1954.

GOULDNER, ALVIN W. "The Norm of Reciprocity." *American Sociological Review* 25, 1960.

GOUGH, E. KATHLEEN. "The Nayars and the Definition of Marriage." *The Journal of the Royal Anthropological Institute of Great Britain* 89, 1959.

GOUGH, KATHLEEN E. "Is the Family Universal: The Nayar Case." In Norman Bell and Ezra Vogel (eds.), *A Modern Introduction to the Family.* New York: The Free Press, 1960.

GOULD, STEPHEN JAY. *Ever Since Darwin.* New York: W.W. Norton & Co., 1977.

GOVE, WALTER, ed. *The Labelling of Deviance: Evaluating a Perspective,* 2nd ed. Beverly Hills, Calif.: Sage, 1980.

GRACEY, HAROLD. "Learning the Student Role: Kindergarten as Academic Boot Camp." In Dennis Wrong and Harold Gracey (eds.), *Readings in Introductory Sociology.* New York: Macmillan, 1967.

GREELEY, ANDREW M. *Ethnicity in the United States: A Preliminary Reconnaissance.* New York: John Wiley, 1974.

GREELEY, ANDREW M. "The Ethnic Miracle." *The Public Interest* 45, 1976.

GREENBERG, DANIEL S. "Finding Time to Produce." *Washington Post,* March 6, 1979.

GRELLA, CHRISTINE E. "Irreconcilable Differences: Women Defining Class After Divorce and Downward Mobility." *Gender & Society* 4, 1990.

GROBSTEIN, CLIFFORD. "When Does Human Life Begin?" *Science* 82, 1982.

GRUSKY, DAVID B., and HAUSER, ROBERT M. "Comparative Social Mobility Revisited: Models of Convergence and Divergence in 16 Countries." *American Sociological Review* 49, 1984.

GULLEY, BILL (WITH REESE, MARY ELLEN). *Breaking Cover.* New York: Simon and Schuster, 1980.

GUNTER, B. G., and GUNTER, NANCY C. "Leisure Styles: A Conceptual Framework for Modern Leisure." *Sociological Quarterly* 21, 1980.

GUSFIELD, JOSEPH R., and MICHALOWICZ, JERZY. "Secular Symbolism: Studies of Ritual, Ceremony, and the Symbolic Order of Modern Life." In Ralph H. Turner and James F. Short, Jr. (eds.), *Annual Review of Sociology* 10. Palo Alto, Calif.: Annual Reviews, 1984.

GUTTMAN, ALLEN. *From Ritual to Record: The Nature of Modern Sports.* New York: Columbia University Press, 1978.

HABERMAN, CLYDE. "Flow of Turks Leaving Bulgaria Swells to Hundreds of Thousands." *New York Times,* August 15, 1989.

HABERMAN, CLYDE. "Turks Say Hussein Plotted to Drive Out the Kurds." *New York Times,* April 12, 1991.

HADAWAY, C. KIRK, and ROOF, WADE CLARK. "Apostasy in American Churches: Evidence From National Survey Data." In David G. Bromley (ed.), *Falling From the Faith.* Beverly Hills, Calif.: Sage, 1988.

HADDEN, JEFFREY K., and SHUPE, ANSON. *Televangelism: Power and Politics on God's Frontier.* New York: Henry Holt & Company, 1988.

HAGE, JERALD (ed.). *Futures of Organizations: Innovating to Adapt Strategy and Human Resources to Rapid Technological Change.* Lexington, Mass.: Lexington Books, 1988.

HALBERSTAM, DAVID. *The Reckoning.* New York: William Morrow and Co., 1986.

HALL, PETER. *The World Cities,* 3d ed. London: Weidenfeld and Nicolson, 1984.

HALLORAN, RICHARD. "Notes of a Sumo Wrestling Fan." *New York Times,* January 6, 1974.

HALPERN, SYDNEY. *American Pediatrics: The Social Dynamics of Professionalism, 1880–1980.* Berkeley: University of California Press, 1988.

HAMILL, PETE. "Facing Up to Drugs: Is Legalization the Solution?" *New York,* August 15, 1988.

HAMMOND, JUDITH. "Biography Building to Insure the Future: Women's Negotiation of Gender Relevancy in Medical School." *Symbolic Interaction* 3, 1980.

HARDEE-CLEVELAND, KAREN, and BANISTER, JUDITH. "Fertility Policy and Implementation in China, 1986–88." *Population and Development Review* 14, 1988.

HARPER, CHARLES L. *Exploring Social Change.* Englewood Cliffs, N.J.: Prentice Hall, 1989.

HARPER, DOUGLAS. *Good Company,* abridged edition. Chicago: University of Chicago Press, 1989.

HARRINGTON, MICHAEL. *The New American Poverty.* New York: Penguin Books, 1984.

HARRIS, CHAUNCEY, and ULLMAN, EDWARD. "The Nature of Cities." *Annals of the American Academy of Political and Social Science* 242, 1945.

HARRIS, JEAN. *Stranger in Two Worlds.* New York: Macmillan Publishing Company, 1986.

HARRIS, LIS. "Holy Days—I." *The New Yorker,* September 16, 1985.

HARRIS, LIS. *Holy Days: The World of a Hasidic Family.* New York: Summit, 1986.

HARRIS, MARVIN. *Cows, Pigs, Wars, and Witches: The Riddles of Culture.* New York: Vintage Books, 1974.

HARRIS, MARVIN. *America Now: The Anthropology of A Changing Culture.* New York: Simon and Schuster, 1981.

HARTWIG, M.C. "Aborigines and Racism: An Historical Perspective." In F.S. Stevens (ed.), *Racism: The Australian Experience,* vol. 2. New York: Taplinger, 1972.

HAUG, MARIE R., and FOLMAR, STEVEN J. "Longevity, Gender and Life Quality." *Journal of Health and Social Behavior* 27, 1986.

HAUGHEN, STEVEN E., and MEISENHEIMER, JOSEPH R., II. "U.S. Labor Market Weakened in 1990." *Monthly Labor Review* 114, 1991.

HAY, DAVID. "Religious Experience Amongst a Group of Post-Graduate Students—A Qualitative Study." *Journal for the Scientific Study of Religion* 18, 1979.

HAYGHE, HOWARD. "Rise in Mothers Labor Force Activity Includes Those with Infants." *Monthly Labor Review* 109, 1986.

HAYNES, SUZANNE C., and FEINLEIB, MANNING. "Women, Work and Coronary Disease: Prospective Findings From the Framingham Heart Study." *American Journal of Public Health* 70, 1980.

HAZANI, MOSHE. "A Path to Deviance: A Multi-Stage Process." *Deviant Behavior* 7, 1986.

HEARN, FRANK (ed.). *The Transformation of Industrial Organization*. Belmont, Calif.: Wadsworth, 1988.

HEFFERNAN, ESTHER. *Making It in Prison: The Square, the Cool, and the Life*. New York: Wiley-Interscience, 1972.

HELLER, JOSEPH. *Catch-22*. New York: Dell, 1955.

HENLEY, NANCY M. *Body Politics: Power, Sex and Non-Verbal Communication*. Englewood Cliffs, N.J.: Prentice-Hall, 1977.

HENLEY, NANCY M., and THORNE, BARRIE. "Womanspeak and Manspeak: Sex Differences and Sexism in Communications, Verbal and Nonverbal." In Alice G. Sargent (ed.), *Beyond Sex Roles*. St. Paul, Minn.: West, 1977.

HENSHAW, STANLEY K., KOONIN, LISA M., and SMITH, JACK C. "Characteristics of U.S. Women Having Abortions, 1987." *Family Planning Perspectives* 23, 1991.

HERBERG, WILL. *Protestant, Catholic, and Jew*. Garden City, N.Y.: Anchor Books, 1955.

HERTSGAARD, MARK. *On Bended Knee: The Press and the Reagan Presidency*. New York: Farrar Straus Giroux, 1988.

HESS, BETH B., and FERREE, MYRA MARX. "Introduction." In Beth B. Hess and Myra Marx Ferree (eds.), *Analyzing Gender: A Handbook of Social Science Research*. Beverly Hills, Calif.: Sage, 1987.

HESS STEPHEN. "Why Great Men Are Not Chosen Presidents." *Society*, July/August 1988.

HETHERINGTON, MAVIS E., COX, MARTHA, and COX, ROGER. "The Aftermath of Divorce." In J.H. Stevens, Jr., and M. Matthew (eds.), *Mother–Child, Father–Child Relations*. Washington, D.C.: National Association for the Education of Young Children, 1978.

HEWITT, JOHN P. *Self and Society: A Symbolic Interactionist Social Psychology*, 3d ed. Boston: Allyn and Bacon, 1984.

HEYDEBRAND, WOLF V. "New Organizational Forms." *Work and Occupations* 16, 1989.

HILTS, PHILIP J. "Blacks' Life Expectancy Drops." *Washington Post*, December 15, 1988.

HIRSCH, ERIC L. "Sacrifice for the Cause: Group Processes, Recruitment, and Commitment in a Student Social Movement." *American Sociological Review* 55, 1990.

HIRSCHMAN, CHARLES, and WONG, MORRISON G. "Trends in Socioeconomic Achievement Among Immigrant and Native-Born Asian-Americans, 1960–1976." *Sociological Quarterly* 22, 1981.

HIRSCHMAN, CHARLES, and WONG, MORRISON G. "The Extraordinary Educational Attainment of Asian-Americans: A Search for Historical Evidence and Explanations." *Social Forces* 65, 1986.

History of the Church of Latter-Day Saints. Salt Lake City: Deseret News Press, 1902.

HOCHSCHILD, ARLIE R. *The Managed Heart: Commercialization of Human Feeling*. Berkeley: University of California Press, 1983.

HODGKINSON, HAROLD L., with OUTTZ, JANICE HAMILTON and OBARAKPOR, ANITA M. *The Demographics of American Indians: One Percent of the People; Fifty Percent of the Diversity*. Washington, D.C.: Center for Demographic Policy, 1990.

HODGKINSON, VIRGINIA A., WEITZMAN, MURRAY S., and KIRSCH, ARTHUR D. "From Commitment to Action: How Religious Involvement Affects Giving and Volunteering." In Robert Wuthnow, Virginia A. Hodgkinson, and associates, *Exploring the Role of Religion in America's Voluntary Sector*. San Francisco: Jossey-Bass, 1990.

HODGSON, GODFREY. *All Things to All Men*. New York: Simon and Schuster, 1980.

HODSON, RANDY, and ENGLAND, PAULA. "Industrial Structure and Sex Differences in Earnings." *Industrial Relations* 25, 1986.

HOFFMAN, SAUL D., and DUNCAN, GREG J. "What *Are* the Economic Consequences of Divorce?" *Demography* 25, 1988.

HOFFMAN, SHIRL J. "Evangelicalism and the Revitalization of Religious Ritual in Sport." *Arete* 2, 1985.

HOGE, DEAN R., and ROOZEN, DAVID A. *Understanding Church Growth and Decline: 1950–1978*. New York: Pilgrim Press, 1979.

HOLLINGER, RICHARD C., and LANZA-KADUCE, LONN. "The Process of Criminalization: The Case of Computer Crime Laws." *Criminology* 26, 1988.

HOLLINGSHEAD, AUGUST B., and REDLICH, FREDERICK C. *Social Class and Mental Illness.* New York: John Wiley, 1958.

HOMANS, GEORGE. *Social Behavior: Its Elementary Forms*, 2d ed. New York: Harcourt Brace Jovanovich, 1973.

HOOYMAN, NANCY R., and KIYAK, H. ASUMAN. *Social Gerontology: A Multidisciplinary Perspective.* Boston: Allyn and Bacon, 1988.

HOPKINS, ELLEN. "The Dispossessed." *New York*, May 13, 1985.

HOPKINS, KEITH. "Brother–Sister Marriage in Roman Egypt." *Journal for Comparative Study of Society and History* 22, 1980.

HOUBOLT, JAN. "An Empirical Critique of Blauner's Concept of Powerlessness on the Automobile Assembly Line." Paper presented at the 53rd Annual Meeting of the Eastern Sociological Society, Philadelphia, Pa., 1982.

HOUGH, JERRY. *Russia and the West: Gorbachev and the Politics of Reform.* New York: Simon and Schuster, 1988.

HOUT, MICHAEL. "More Universalism, Less Structural Mobility: The American Occupational Structure in the 1980s." *American Journal of Sociology* 93, 1988.

HOUT, MICHAEL, and GREELEY, ANDREW M. "The Center Doesn't Hold: Church Attendance in the United States, 1940–1984." *American Sociological Review* 52, 1987.

HOYT, HOMER. *The Structure and Growth of Residential Neighborhoods in American Cities.* U.S. Federal Housing Administration. Washington, D.C.: U.S. Government Printing Office, 1939.

HUBER, JOAN. "Trends in Gender Stratification, 1970–1985." *Sociological Forum* 1, 1986.

HUBER, JOAN, and FORM, WILLIAM H. *Income and Ideology.* New York: The Free Press, 1973.

HUDSON, WINTHROP. *Religion in America.* New York: Charles Scribner's, 1973.

HUGHES, CHARLES C., ed. *Custom-Made: Introductory Readings for Cultural Anthropology.* Chicago: Rand McNally, 1976.

HUGHES, DAVID. "When Nurse Knows Best: Some Aspects of Nurse/Doctor Interaction in a Casualty Department." *Sociology of Health and Illness* 10, 1988.

HUMMEL, RALPH P. *The Bureaucratic Experience.* New York: St. Martin's Press, 1977.

HUMMEL, RALPH P. *The Bureaucratic Experience*, 3d ed. New York: St. Martin's Press, 1987.

HUMPHREYS, LAUD. *Tearoom Trade: Impersonal Sex in Public Places*, enlarged ed. Chicago: Aldine, 1975.

HUNT, JENNIFER. "The Development of Rapport through the Negotiation of Gender in Field Work Among Police." *Human Organization* 43, 1984.

HUNT, JENNIFER. "Police Accounts of Normal Force." *Urban Life* 13, 1985.

HURYN, JEAN SCHERZ. "Giftedness as Deviance: A Test of Interaction Theories." *Deviant Behavior* 7, 1986.

HYER, MARJORIE. "'Sin' of Gender Discrimination Denounced." *Washington Post*, December 8, 1985.

IGNATIUS, DAVID. "What's Left of Big Steel?" *Washington Post-Outlook*, March 20, 1988a.

IGNATIUS, DAVID. "Return of the 'Fat Cats.'" *Washington Post-Outlook*, November 20, 1988b.

INKELES, ALEX. "Social Stratification and Mobility in the Soviet Union." In Reinhard Bendix and Seymour Martin Lipset (eds.), *Class, Status, and Power.* Glencoe, Ill.: The Free Press, 1968.

JACKALL, ROBERT. *Moral Mazes: The World of Corporate Managers.* New York: Oxford University Press, 1988.

JACQUET, CONSTANT H., JR. *Women Ministers in 1986 and 1977: A Ten Year View.* New York: National Council of Churches, 1988.

JACQUET, CONSTANT H., JR., ed. *Yearbook of American and Canadian Churches, 1990.* Nashville: Abington Press, 1990.

JAMESON, SAM. "Roh Takes Over, Vows End to Repression in S. Korea." *Los Angeles Times*, February 25, 1988.

JAMIESON, KATHLEEN HALL. *Packaging the Presidency: A History of Presidential Campaign Advertising.* New York: Oxford University Press, 1984.

JAMIESON, KATHLEEN HALL. "For Televised Mendacity: This Year is the Worst Ever." *Washington Post-Outlook*, October 30, 1988a.

JAMIESON, KATHLEEN HALL. *Eloquence in an Electronic Age: The Transformation of Political Speechmaking.* New York: Oxford University Press, 1988b.

JAYNES, GERALD DAVID, and WILLIAMS, ROBIN M., JR. *A Common Destiny: Blacks and American Society.* Washington, D.C.: National Academy Press, 1989.

JEFFRIES, VINCENT, and RANSFORD, EDWARD. *Social Stratification: A Multiple Hierarchy Approach.* Boston: Allyn and Bacon, 1980.

JENCKS, CHRISTOPHER. "Is the American Underclass Growing?" In Christopher Jencks and Paul E. Peterson, eds. *The Urban Underclass*. Washington, D.C.: The Brookings Institution, 1991.

JENCKS, CHRISTOPHER, and PETERSON, PAUL E., eds. *The Urban Underclass*. Washington, D.C.: The Brookings Institution, 1991.

JENKINS, C. DAVID. "Social Environment and Cancer Mortality in Men." *New England Journal of Medicine* 308, 1983.

JENSEN, GARY F. "Functional Research on Deviance: A Critical Analysis and Guide for the Future." *Deviant Behavior* 9, 1988.

JOHNSON, CLIFFORD M., MIRANDA, LETICIA, SHERMAN, ARLOC, and WEILL, JAMES D. *Child Poverty in America*. Washington, D.C.: Children's Defense Fund, 1991.

JOHNSON, JEFFREY C. *Selecting Ethnographic Informants*. Newbury Park, Calif.: Sage Publications, 1990.

JOHNSON, NORRIS R. "Panic at 'The Who Concert Stampede': An Empirical Assessment." *Social Problems* 34, 1987a.

JOHNSON, NORRIS R. "Panic and the Breakdown of Social Order: Popular Myth, Social Theory, Empirical Evidence." *Sociological Focus* 20, 1987b.

JOHNSTON, LLOYD D., O'MALLEY, PATRICK M., BACHMAN, JERALD G. *Drug Use, Drinking, and Smoking: National Survey Results From High School, College, and Young Adults Population, 1975–1988*. Rockville, Md.: National Institute on Drug Abuse, 1989.

JOINT ECONOMIC COMMITTEE OF THE CONGRESS OF THE UNITED STATES. "Poverty, Income Distribution, The Family and Public Policy." 99th Congress, 2nd Session. Washington, D.C.: U.S. Government Printing Office, 1986.

JONES, A.E., and PLACEK, PAUL. "Teenage Women in the USA: Sex, Contraception, Pregnancy, Fertility and Maternal and Infant Health." In Theodora Ooms (ed.), *Teenage Pregnancy and Family Impact: New Perspectives on Policy*. Philadelphia: Temple University Press, 1981.

JONES, FAUSTINE C. "External Crosscurrents and Internal Diversity: An Assessment of Black Progress, 1960–1980." *Daedalus* 110, 1981.

JOSEPH, NATHAN. *Uniforms and Nonuniforms: Communication Through Clothing*. Westport, Conn.: Greenwood Press, 1986.

JOY, LESLEY A., KIMBALL, MEREDITH M., and ZABRACK, MERLE L. "Television and Children's Aggressive Behavior." In T.M. Williams (ed.), *The Impact of Television: A Natural Experiment in Three Communities*. Orlando, Fla.: Academic Press, 1986.

KAHN, ROBERT L., WOLFE, DONALD M., QUINN, ROBERT P., SNOEK, J. DIEDRICK, in collaboration with ROSENTHAL, ROBERT A. *Organizational Stress: Studies in Role Conflict and Ambiguity*. New York: John Wiley, 1964.

KALB, MARVIN. "TV, Election Spoiler." *New York Times*, November 28, 1988.

KALBERG, STEPHEN. "Max Weber's Types of Rationality: Cornerstones for the Analysis of Rationalization Processes in History." *American Journal of Sociology* 85, 1980.

KAMMEYER, KENNETH C.W. "The Feminine Role: An Analysis of Attitude Consistency." *Journal of Marriage and the Family* 26, 1964.

KAMMEYER, KENNETH C.W. "The Dynamics of Population." In Harold Orel (ed.), *Irish History and Culture: Aspects of a People's Heritage*. Lawrence, Kans.: The University of Kansas Press, 1976.

KAMMEYER, KENNETH C.W. "The Decline of Divorce in America." Paper presented at the annual meeting of the Midwest Sociological Society, Minneapolis, Minn., 1981.

KAMMEYER, KENNETH C.W. *Marriage and Family: A Foundation for Personal Decisions*. Boston: Allyn and Bacon, 1987.

KAMMEYER, KENNETH C.W., and GINN, HELEN L. *An Introduction to Population*. Chicago: The Dorsey Press, 1986.

KANDO, THOMAS M. *Leisure and Popular Culture in Transition*, 2d ed. St. Louis: C.V. Mosby, 1980.

Kansas City Star. "Infant Mortality Rate Leveling Off." October 18, 1984.

KAPLAN, FRED. "A Post-Gulf Look at Military Costs." *Boston Globe*, September 9, 1990.

KASARDA, JOHN D. "The Implications of Contemporary Distribution Trends for National Urban Policy." *Social Science Quarterly* 61, 1980.

KASARDA, JOHN D. "Urban Change and Minority Opportunities." In P. Peterson (ed.), *The New Urban Realities*. Washington, D.C.: Brookings Institution, 1985.

KASARDA, JOHN D. "Urban Industrial Transition and the Underclass." *Annals of the American Academy of Political and Social Science* 501, 1989.

KATZ, HARRY C. *Shifting Gears: Changing Labor Relations in the U.S. Automobile Industry*. Cambridge, Mass.: The MIT Press, 1985.

KATZ, MICHAEL B. *The Irony of Early School Reform*. Cambridge, Mass.: Harvard University Press, 1968.

KATZ, MICHAEL B. *Class, Bureaucracy and Schools: The Illusion of Educational Change in America.* New York: Praeger, 1971.

KATZ, MICHAEL B. *Reconstructing American Education.* Cambridge, Mass.: Harvard University Press, 1987.

KATZMAN, MARTIN T. "Ecology, Natural Resources, and Economic Growth: Underdeveloping the Amazon." *Economic Development and Cultural Change* 35, 1987.

KEITH, VERNA M., and FINLAY, BARBARA. "The Impact of Parental Divorce on Children's Educational Attainment, Marital Timing, and the Likelihood of Divorce." *Journal of Marriage and the Family* 50, 1988.

KELLY, DEAN M. *Why Conservative Churches Are Growing.* New York: Harper & Row, 1972.

KEMPTON, MURRAY. "Quality of Milken Mercy." *Newsday,* September 27, 1990.

KEPHART, WILLIAM M. *Extraordinary Groups: The Sociology of Unconventional Life-Styles.* New York: St. Martin's Press, 1976.

KEPHART, WILLIAM M. *The Family, Society and the Individual,* 5th ed. Boston: Houghton Mifflin, 1981.

KERBO, HAROLD R. *Social Stratification and Inequality.* New York: McGraw-Hill, 1983.

KERCKHOFF, ALAN C. "Effects of Ability Grouping in British Secondary Schools." *American Sociological Review* 51, 1986.

KERCKHOFF, ALAN C., CAMPBELL, RICHARD T., and WINFIELD-LAIRD, IDEE. "Social Mobility in Great Britain and the United States." *American Journal of Sociology* 91, 1985.

KHOO, SIEW-EAN. "Living Together as Married: A Profile of De Facto Couples in Australia." *Journal of Marriage and the Family* 49, 1987.

KILGORE, SALLY B. "The Organizational Context of Tracking in Schools." *American Sociological Review* 56, 1991.

KIMBALL, MEREDITH M. "Television and Sex-Role Attitudes." In Tannis M. Williams (ed.), *The Impact of Television: A Natural Experiment in Three Communities.* Orlando, Fla.: Academic Press, 1986.

KINARD, E. MILLING, and REINHERZ, HELEN. "Effects of Marital Disruption on Children's School Aptitude and Achievement." *Journal of Marriage and the Family* 48, 1986.

KING, MARTIN LUTHER, JR. *Why We Can't Wait.* New York: Harper & Row, 1963.

KINGSNORTH, RODNEY, and JUNGSTEN, MICHAEL. "Driving Under the Influence: The Impact of Legislative Reform on Court Sentencing Practices." *Crime and Delinquency* 34, 1988.

KINSEY, ALFRED C., POMEROY, WARDELL B., and MARTIN, CLYDE E. *Sexual Behavior in the Human Male.* Philadelphia: W.B. Saunders, 1948.

KINSEY, ALFRED C., POMEROY, WARDELL B., MARTIN, CLYDE E., and GEBHARD, PAUL H. *Sexual Behavior in the Human Female.* Philadelphia: W.B. Saunders, 1953.

KITAGAWA, EVELYN, and HAUSER, PHILIP M. "Education Differentials in Mortality by Cause of Death, United States 1960." *Demography* 5, 1968.

KITSON, GAY C., and MORGAN, LESLIE A. "The Multiple Consequences of Divorce: A Decade Review." *Journal of Marriage and the Family* 52, 1990.

KLEIN, MALCOLM W. "Labeling Theory and Delinquency Policy: An Experimental Test." *Criminal Justice and Behavior* 13, 1986.

KLINE, MARSHA, JOHNSTON, JANET R., and TSCHANN, JEANNE M. "The Long Shadow of Marital Conflict: A Model of Children's Postdivorce Adjustment." *Journal of Marriage and the Family* 53, 1991.

KOHLBERG, L. "A Cognitive-Development Analysis of Sex-Role Concepts and Attitudes." In Eleanor Maccoby (ed.), *The Development of Sex Differences.* Stanford, Calif.: Stanford University Press, 1966.

KOHN, MELVIN L. *Class and Conformity: A Study of Values,* 2d ed., with a reassessment. Chicago: University of Chicago Press, 1977.

KOHN, MELVIN L. "Cross-National Research as an Analytic Strategy." *American Sociological Review* 52, 1987.

KOHN, MELVIN L., with MILLER, JOANNE, MILLER, KAREN A., SCHOENBACH, CARRIE, and SCHOENBERG, RONALD. *Work and Personality: An Inquiry into the Impact of Social Stratification.* Norwood, N.J., Ablex, 1983.

KOHN, MELVIN L., ed. *Cross-National Research in Sociology.* Newbury Park, Calif.: Sage Publications, 1989a.

KOHN, MELVIN L. "Cross-National Research as an Analytic Strategy." In Melvin L. Kohn (ed.), *Cross-National Research in Sociology.* Newbury Park, Calif.: Sage Publications, 1989b.

KOHN, MELVIN L., and SCHOOLER, CARMI. "Occupational Experience and Psychological Functioning." *American Sociological Review* 38, 1973.

KOMAROVSKY, MIRRA. *Dilemmas of Masculinity: A Study of College Youth.* New York: W.W. Norton, 1976.

Kosmin, Barry A., and Lachman, Seymour P. "The National Survey of Religious Identification, 1989–90." Research Report. New York: The Graduate School and University Center of the City University of New York, 1991.

Kreps, Gary A. "Sociological Inquiry and Disaster Research." *Annual Review of Sociology* 10, 1984.

Kreps, Gary A. "Future Directions in Disaster Research: The Role of Taxonomy." *International Journal of Mass Emergencies and Disasters* 7, 1989.

Kriesberg, Louis. *Social Conflicts*, 2d ed. Englewood Cliffs, N.J.: Prentice-Hall, 1982.

Kulka, R.A., and Weingarten, H. "The Long-Term Effects of Parental Divorce in Childhood on Adult Adjustment." *Journal of Social Issues* 35, 1979.

Kurdek, L.A., Blisk, D., and Siesky, A.E. "Correlates of Children's Long-Term Adjustment to Their Parents' Divorce." *Developmental Psychology* 17, 1981.

Kurtz, Howard. "Media Notes." *Washington Post*, May 27, 1991.

Kutner, Nancy G. "Issues in the Application of High Cost Medical Technology: The Case of Organ Transplantation." *Journal of Health and Social Behavior* 28, 1987.

Kutscher, Ronald E. "Overview and Implications of the Projections to 2000." *Monthly Labor Review* 110, 1987.

Ladner, Robert A., Schwartz, Barry J., Roker, Sandra J., and Titterud, Loretta S. "The Miami Riots of 1980: Antecedent Conditions, Community Responses and Participant Characteristics." In L. Kriesberg (ed.), *Research in Social Movements, Conflicts and Change*, vol. 4. Greenwich, Conn.: JAI Press, 1981.

Laqueur, Walter. *The Age of Terrorism*. Boston: Little, Brown, 1987.

LaRossa, Ralph. "And We Haven't Had Any Problems Since: Conjugal Violence and the Politics of Marriage." In Murray A. Straus and Gerald T. Hotaling (eds.), *The Social Causes of Husband–Wife Violence*. Minneapolis: University of Minnesota Press, 1980.

LaRossa, Ralph. "The Transition to Parenthood and the Social Reality of Time." *Journal of Marriage and the Family* 45, 1983.

Lauer, Robert H. "Ideology and Strategies of Change: The Case of American Libertarians." In Robert H. Lauer (ed.), *Social Movements and Social Change*. Carbondale: Southern Illinois University Press, 1976.

Lauer, Robert H. *Perspectives On Social Change*, 3d ed. Boston: Allyn and Bacon, 1982.

Lawler, John J., and West, Robin. "Impact of Union-Avoidance Strategy in Representation Elections." *Industrial Relations* 24, 1985.

Lazarsfeld, Paul. "Notes on the History of Quantification in Sociology—Trends, Sources, and Problems." In Harry Woolf (ed.), *Quantification: A History of the Meaning of Measurement in the Natural and Social Sciences*. New York: Bobbs-Merrill, 1961.

LeGates, Richard T., and Hartman, Chester. "The Anatomy of Displacement in the United States." In Neil Smith and Peter Williams (eds.), *Gentrification of the City*. Boston: George Allen & Unwin, 1986.

LeGates, Richard T., and Murphy, Karen. "Austerity, Shelter, and Social Conflict in the United States." In William K. Tabb and Larry Sawers (eds.), *Marxism and the Metropolis*. New York: Oxford University Press, 1984.

Lehman, Edward W. "The Theory of the State Versus the State of Theory." *American Sociological Review* 53, 1988.

Leinberger, Christopher B., and Lockwood, Charles. "How Business is Reshaping America." *The Atlantic Monthly*, October, 1986.

Lemert, Edwin. *Human Deviance, Social Problems, and Social Control*. Englewood Cliffs, N.J.: Prentice-Hall, 1967.

Lemert, Edwin. *Human Deviance, Social Problems, and Social Control*, 2d ed. Englewood Cliffs, N.J.: Prentice-Hall, 1972.

Lenski, Gerhard. "Marxist Experiments in Destratification: An Appraisal." *Social Forces* 57, 1978.

Lenski, Gerhard, and Lenski, Jean. *Human Societies*, 4th ed. New York: McGraw-Hill, 1982.

Lerner, Gerda. "The Lady and the Mill Girl: Changes in the Status of Women in the Age of Jackson." *Midcontinent American Studies Journal*, Spring 1969.

Levine, Barry B., ed. *The Caribbean Exodus*. New York: Praeger, 1987.

Levy, Frank. *Dollars and Dreams: The Changing American Income Distribution*. New York: Russell Sage Foundation, 1987.

Lewis, Neil A. "Police Brutality Under Wide Review by Police Department." *New York Times*, March 15, 1991.

Lewis, Robert A., ed. *Men in Difficult Times: Masculinity Today and Tomorrow*. Englewood Cliffs, N.J.: Prentice-Hall, 1981.

Liebman, Robert C., and Wuthnow, Robert. *The New Christian Right*. New York: Aldine, 1983.

LIEBERT, ROBERT M., and SPRAFKIN, JOYCE. *The Early Window: Effects of Television on Children and Youth*, 3rd ed. New York: Pergamon Press, 1988.

LIN, NAN, and XIE, WEN. "Occupational Prestige in Urban China." *American Journal of Sociology*, 1988.

LINK, BRUCE G., CULLEN, FRANCES T., STRUENING, ELMER, and SHROUT, PATRICK E. "A Modified Labeling Theory Approach to Mental Disorders: An Empirical Assessment." *American Sociological Review* 54, 1989.

LINK, BRUCE. "Reward System of Psychotherapy: Implications for Inequities in Service Delivery." *Journal of Health and Social Behavior* 24, 1983.

LIPSET, SEYMOUR MARTIN. *The First New Nation*. New York: Basic Books, 1963.

LIPSET, SEYMOUR MARTIN. "Comparing Canadian and American Unions." *Society*, January/February 1987.

LIPSET, SEYMOUR MARTIN, TROW, MARTIN, and COLEMAN, JAMES. *Union Democracy*. Garden City, N.Y.: Anchor Books, 1962.

LITKE, JAMES. "Study Hits Federal Efforts on Work-Place Safety." *Washington Post*, July 16, 1988.

LITTLE, ROGER. "Buddy Relations and Combat Performance." In Oscar Grusky and George A. Miller (eds.), *The Sociology of Organizations*. New York: The Free Press, 1970.

LOCK, MARGARET. "Protests of Good Wife and Wise Mother." In Edward Norbeck and Margaret Lock (eds.), *Health, Illness, and Medical Care in Japan*. Honolulu: University of Hawaii Press, 1987.

LOGAN, JOHN R., and SCHNEIDER, MARK. "Racial Segregation and Racial Change in American Suburbs, 1970–1980." *American Journal of Sociology* 89, 1984.

LOGUE, JAMES N., HANSEN, HOLGER, and STRUENING, ELMER. "Some Indicators of the Long-Term Health Effects of a Natural Disaster." *Public Health Reports* 96, 1981.

LONGFELLOW, CYNTHIA. "Divorce in Context: Its Impact on Children." In George Levinger and Oliver C. Moles (eds.), *Divorce and Separation: Context, Causes, and Consequences*. New York: Basic Books, 1979.

LORBER, JUDITH. "Deviance as Performance: The Case of Illness." *Social Problems* 14, 1967.

LORBER, JUDITH. *Women Physicians*. New York: Tavistock, 1984.

LORD, WALTER. *A Night to Remember*. New York: Henry Holt, 1955.

LOSH-HESSELBART, SUSAN. "Development of Gender Roles." In Marvin B. Sussman and Suzanne K. Steinmetz (eds.), *Handbook of Marriage and the Family*. New York: Plenum Press, 1987.

LOWENSTEIN, DOUGLAS, and LOWENSTEIN, ROCHELLE. "The Baby and Us." *The Washington Post Magazine*, October 16, 1983.

LUEPNITZ, DEBORAH ANNA. *Child Custody*. Lexington, Mass.: D.C. Heath, 1982.

LUMSDEN, C.J., and WILSON, E.O. *Promethean Fire*. Cambridge, Mass.: Harvard University Press, 1983.

LUXENBERG, STAN. *Roadside Empires: How the Chains Franchised America*. New York: Viking, 1985.

LYON, DAVID. "From 'Post-Industrialism' to 'Information Society': A New Social Transformation?" *Sociology* 20, 1986.

MACCOBY, E.E., and JACKLIN, C.N. *The Psychology of Sex Differences*. Stanford, Calif.: Stanford University Press, 1974.

MAGNUSON, ED. "Why Mrs. Reagan Still Looks Like a Million." *Time*, October 24, 1988.

MALINOWSKI, BRONISLAW. *Magic, Science, and Religion and Other Essays*. New York: Anchor Books, 1955. Originally published 1925.

MALCOLM X. *The Autobiography of Malcolm X*. New York: Grove Press, 1966.

MANTON, KENNETH G., and MYERS, GEORGE C. "Recent Trends in Multiple-Caused Mortality, 1968–1982: Age and Cohort Comparisons." *Population Research and Policy Review* 6, 1987.

MARCH, JAMES G. "Footnotes to Organizational Change." *Administrative Science Quarterly* 26, 1981.

MARCUS, RUTH. "Supreme Court Approves Sobriety Checkpoints." *Washington Post*, June 15, 1990.

MARSHALL, VICTOR W. *Last Chances: A Sociology of Aging and Dying*. Monterey, Calif.: Brooks/Cole, 1980.

MARTIN, SUSAN EHRLICH. *Breaking and Entering: Policewomen on Patrol*. Berkeley: University of California Press, 1982.

MARTIN, TERESA CASTRO, and BUMPASS, LARRY L. "Recent Trends in Marital Disruption." *Demography* 26, 1989.

MARTY, MARTIN E. "Transpositions: American Religion in the 1980s." *The Annals of the American Academy of Political and Social Science* 480, 1985.

MARTY, MARTIN E. "Two Years That Shook the World." *1991 Brittanica Book of the Year*. Chicago: Encyclopaedia Brittanica, 1991.

MARX, KARL *The Economic and Philosophic Manuscripts of 1884*. Dirk J. Struik, ed. New York: International Publishers, 1964. Originally published 1932.

MARX, KARL. *Capital: A Critical Analysis of Capitalist Production*, vol. 1. New York: International Publishers, 1967. Originally published 1867.

MASON, KAREN OPPENHEIM, and LU, YU-HSIA. "Attitudes Toward Women's Familial Roles: Changes in the United States, 1977–1985." *Gender & Society* 2, 1988.

MASHETER, CAROL. "Postdivorce Relationships between Ex-spouses: The Roles of Attachment and Interpersonal Conflict." *Journal of Marriage and the Family* 53, 1991.

MASSEY, DOUGLAS S. "American Apartheid: Segregation and the Making of the Underclass." *American Journal of Sociology* 96, 1990.

MASSEY, DOUGLAS S., and DENTON, NANCY A. "Trends in the Residential Segregation of Blacks, Hispanics, and Asians: 1970–1980." *American Sociological Review* 52, 1987.

MASSEY, DOUGLAS S., and DENTON, NANCY A. "Suburbanization and Segregation in U.S. Metropolitan Areas." *American Journal of Sociology* 94, 1988.

MASSING, HERTA H. "Decoding 'Dallas': Comparing American and German Viewers." In Arthur A. Berger (ed.), *Television in Society*. New Brunswick, N.J.: Transaction Books, 1987.

MATHEWS, LINDA. "When Being Best Isn't Good Enough." *Los Angeles Times Magazine*, July 19, 1987.

MATTHEWS, MERVYN. *Privilege in the Soviet Union*. London: George Allen & Unwin, 1978.

MATTHEWS, MERVYN. *Poverty in the Soviet Union: The Life-Styles of the Underprivileged in Recent Years*. London: Cambridge University Press, 1986.

MAULDIN, W. PARKER. "Population Programs and Fertility Regulation." In Rodolfo A. Bulatao and Ronald D. Lee (eds.), *Determinants of Fertility in Developing Countries*, vol. 2. New York: Academic Press, 1983.

MAUSS, ARMAND L. "Sociological Perspectives on the Mormon Subculture." In Ralph H. Turner and James F. Short, Jr. (eds.), *Annual Review of Sociology*, 10. Palo Alto, Calif.: Annual Reviews, Inc., 1984.

MAYER, JOHN E., and ROSENBLATT, AARON. "Encounters with Danger: Social Workers in the Ghetto." *Sociology of Work and Occupations* 2, 1975.

MAYER, KURT B., and BUCKLEY, WALTER. *Class and Society*, 3d ed. New York: Random House, 1970.

McADAM, DOUG, McCARTHY, JOHN D., and ZALD, MAYER N. "Social Movements." In Neil J. Smelser (ed.), *Handbook of Sociology*. Beverly Hills, Calif.: Sage, 1988.

McCARTHY, JOHN D., and ZALD, MAYER N. "Resource Mobilization and Social Movements: A Partial Theory." *American Journal of Sociology* 82, 1977.

McCARTNEY, ROBERT J. "Milken Gets 10-Year Prison Sentence." *Washington Post*, November 22, 1990.

McCULLOCH, JOCK. *Asbestos: Its Human Cost*. St Lucia: University of Queensland Press, 1986.

McCURDY, DAVID W., and SPRADLEY, JAMES P., eds. *Issues in Cultural Anthropology: Selected Readings*. Boston: Little, Brown, 1979.

McGUIRE, JACQUELINE. "Gender Stereotypes of Parents with Two-Year-Olds and Beliefs about Gender Differences in Behavior." *Sex Roles* 19, 1988.

McKEOWN, THOMAS. "A Historical Appraisal of the Medical Task." In G. McLachlan and T. McKeown (eds.), *Medical History and Medical Care: A Symposium of Perspectives*. New York: Oxford University Press, 1971.

McKEOWN, THOMAS. *The Modern Rise in Population*. London: Edward Arnold, 1976.

McKEOWN, THOMAS. *The Role of Medicine: Dream, Mirage, or Nemesis?* Princeton, N.J.: Princeton University Press, 1979.

McKINLAY, JOHN, and McKINLAY, SONJA. "The Questionable Contribution of Medical Measures to the Decline of Mortality in the United States in the Twentieth Century." *Milbank Memorial Quarterly/Health and Society* 55, 1977.

McMILLEN, MARILYN M. "Differential Mortality by Sex in Fetal and Neonatal Deaths." *Science* 204, 1979.

McNEIL, LINDA M. *Contradictions of Control: School Structure and School Knowledge*. New York: Routledge & Kegan Paul, 1986.

MEAD, GEORGE H. *Mind, Self and Society*. Chicago: University of Chicago Press, 1962. Originally published 1934.

MEAD, MARGARET. *Sex and Temperament in Three Primitive Societies*. New York: Mentor Books, 1935.

MEAD, MARGARET. *Culture and Commitment: A Study of the Generation Gap*. Garden City, N.Y.: Natural History Press/Doubleday, 1970.

MEAD, MARGARET. *Blackberry Winter*. New York: William Morrow, 1972.

MEDVEDEV, ZHORES A. *Gorbachev*. New York: W.W. Norton, 1986.

MELLEN, S.L. *The Evolution of Love*. San Francisco: W.H. Freeman, 1981.

MELTON, J. GORDON. *The Encyclopedia of American Religions*, 2d ed. Detroit: Gale Research Company, 1987.

MELTZER, BERNARD N. "Mead's Social Psychology." In Jerome Manis and Bernard N. Meltzer (eds.), *Symbolic Interaction: A Reader in Social Psychology*, 3d ed. Boston: Allyn and Bacon, 1978.

MENNERICK, LEWIS A., and NAJAFIZADEH, MEHRANGIZ. "Observations on the Missing Linkage Between Theories of Historical Expansion of Schooling and Planning for Future Educational Development." *International Review of Education* 33, 1987.

MERNISSI, FATIMA. *Beyond the Veil: Male–Female Dynamics in Modern Muslim Society*. Bloomington, Ind.: Indiana University Press, 1987.

MERTON, ROBERT. "Social Structure and Anomie." *American Sociological Review* 3, 1938.

MERTON, ROBERT. *Social Theory and Social Structure*, rev. ed. New York: The Free Press, 1957.

MERTON, ROBERT. *Social Theory and Social Structure*, 3d ed. New York: The Free Press, 1968.

MEYER, LAWRENCE. *Israel Now: Portrait of a Troubled Land*. New York: Delacorte Press, 1982.

MEYER, MARSHALL W., STEVENSON, WILLIAM, and WEBSTER, STEPHEN. *Limits to Bureaucratic Growth*. New York: de Gruyter, 1985.

MICHELS, ROBERT. *Political Parties: A Sociological Study of the Oligarchical Tendencies of Modern Democracy*. New York: The Free Press, 1962. Originally published 1915.

MIDDLETON, RUSSELL. "Brother–Sister and Father–Daughter Marriage in Ancient Egypt." *American Sociological Review* 27, 1962.

MILGRAM, STANLEY. *Obedience to Authority*. New York: Harper & Row, 1974.

MILLER, B.D. *The Endangered Sex*. Ithaca, N.Y.: Cornell University Press, 1981.

MILLER, BRENT C., and BINGHAM, C. RAYMOND. "Family Configuration in Relation to the Sexual Behavior of Female Adolescents." *Journal of Marriage and the Family* 51, 1989.

MILLER, STEPHEN. "The Social Base of Sales Behavior." *Social Problems* 12, 1964.

MILLING, KINARD E., and REINHERZ, HELEN. "Effects of Marital Disruption on Children's School Aptitude and Achievement." *Journal of Marriage and the Family* 48, 1986.

MILLMAN, MARCIA. *The Unkindest Cut: Life in the Backrooms of Medicine*. New York: William Morrow, 1977.

MILLMAN, MARCIA. *Such a Pretty Face: Being Fat in America*. New York: W.W. Norton, 1980.

MILLS, C. WRIGHT. *The Power Elite*. New York: Oxford University Press, 1956.

MILLS, C. WRIGHT. *The Sociological Imagination*. New York: Oxford University Press, 1959.

MIRANDE, ALFREDO. *Gringo Justice*. South Bend, Ind.: Notre Dame University Press, 1987.

MIRANNE, ALFRED C., III, and GRAY, LOUIS N. "Deterrence: A Laboratory Experiment." *Deviant Behavior* 8, 1987.

MIROWSKY, JOHN, and ROSS, CATHERINE. "Belief in Innate Sex Roles: Sex Stratification Versus Interpersonal Influence in Marriage." *Journal of Marriage and the Family* 49, 1987.

MITOFSKY, WARREN J., and PLISSNER, MARTIN. "Low Voter Turnout? Don't Believe It." *New York Times*, November 10, 1988.

MITZMAN, ARTHUR. *The Iron Cage: An Historical Interpretation of Max Weber*. New York: Grosset & Dunlap, 1969.

MIYAHARA, KOJIRO. "Inter-College Stratification: The Case of Male College Graduates in Japan." *Sociological Forum* 3, 1988.

MOFFATT, MICHAEL. *Coming of Age in New Jersey*. New Brunswick, N.J.: Rutgers University Press, 1989.

MONK-TURNER, ELIZABETH. "The Occupational Achievements of Community and Four-Year College Entrants." *American Sociological Review* 55, 1990.

MONROE, PAUL. *Founding of the American Public School System*. New York: Macmillan, 1940.

MONTGOMERY, PAUL L. "NATO Is Planning to Cut U.S. Forces in Europe by 50%." *New York Times*, May 29, 1991.

Monthly Labor Review. "Labor Month in Review." 113, 1990.

Monthly Labor Review. "Labor Month in Review." 114, 1991.

MOONEY, ELIZABETH C. "A Widow's World: Growing Up Alone in Middle Age." *Washington Post*, July 26, 1981.

MOORE, CHARLES A. "Taming the Giant Corporation? Some Cautionary Remarks on the Deterrability of Corporate Crime." *Crime and Delinquency* 33, 1987.

MORGAN, EDMUND. *Visible Saints: The History of a Puritan Idea.* Ithaca, N.Y.: Cornell University Press, 1963.

MORGAN, S. PHILIP, LYE, DIANE N., and CONDRAN, GRETCHEN A. "Sons, Daughters, and the Risk of Marital Disruption." *American Journal of Sociology* 94, 1988.

MORGAN, S. PHILIP, and RINDFUSS, RONALD R. "Marital Disruption: Structural and Temporal Dimensions." *American Journal of Sociology* 90, 1985.

MOTT, FRANK L., and HAURIN, R. JEAN. "Linkages Between Sexual Activity and Alcohol Use Among American Adolescents." *Family Planning Perspectives* 20, 1988.

MULLER, EDWARD N., and OPP, KARL-DIETER. "Rational Choice and Rebellious Collective Action." *American Political Science Review* 80, 1986.

MUNCY, RAYMOND L. *Sex and Marriage in Utopian Communities: 19th Century America.* Bloomington, Ind.: University of Indiana Press, 1973.

MURDOCK, GEORGE P. "Comparative Data on the Division of Labor by Sex." *Social Forces* 15, 1937.

MURDOCK, GEORGE P., and PROVOST, CATRINA. "Factors in the Division of Labor by Sex: A Cross-Cultural Analysis." *Ethnology* 12, 1973.

MURPHY, CARYLE. "Former Executive, 2 Others in Defense Probe Plead Guilty." *Washington Post*, March 10, 1989.

MURRAY, CHARLES. *Losing Ground: American Social Policy 1950–1980.* New York: Basic Books, 1984.

NAJAFIZADEH, MEHRANGIZ, and MENNERICK, LEWIS A. "Worldwide Educational Expansion from 1950 to 1980: The Failure of the Expansion of Schooling in Developing Countries." *The Journal of Developing Areas* 22, 1988.

NAOI, ATSUSHI, and SCHOOLER, CARMI. "Occupational Conditions and Psychological Functioning in Japan." *American Journal of Sociology* 90, 1981.

A Nation at Risk: The Imperative for Educational Reform. Washington, D.C.: The National Commission on Excellence in Education, 1983.

NATIONAL CENTER FOR HEALTH STATISTICS. *Vital Statistics of the United States, 1986, Vol. II, Sec. 6, Life Tables.* Washington, D.C.: U.S. Government Printing Office, 1988.

NATIONAL CENTER FOR HEALTH STATISTICS. "Advance Report on Final Mortality Statistics, 1988." Monthly Vital Statistics Report, Vol. 39. Washington, D.C.: U.S. Government Printing Office, 1990.

NATIONAL CENTER FOR HEALTH STATISTICS. *Health, United States, 1989.* Washington, D.C.: U.S. Government Printing Office, 1990.

NATIONAL CENTER FOR HEALTH STATISTICS. *Health, United States, 1990.* Washington, D.C.: U.S. Government Printing Office, 1991.

NATIONAL COUNCIL OF CHURCHES. *An Inclusive Language Lectionary.* Philadelphia: Westminster Press, 1983.

NAUGHTON, JIM. "The Devil and Duffy Strode." *The Washington Post*, August 29, 1988.

NELSON, KATHRYN P. *Gentrification and Distressed Cities: An Assessment of Trends in Intrametropolitan Migration.* Madison, Wisc.: University of Wisconsin Press, 1988.

NELSON, LYNN D., and BROMLEY, DAVID G. "Another Look at Conversion and Defection in Conservative Churches." In David G. Bromley (ed.), *Falling From the Faith.* Beverly Hills, Calif.: Sage, 1988.

New York Times. "Life Term Is Upheld in Theft of $120.75." March 19, 1980.

New York Times, January 21, 1989.

NEW YORK TIMES/CBS NEWS POLL. "Portrait of the Electorate." *New York Times*, November 10, 1988.

NEWACHECK, PAUL W., et al., "Income and Illness." *Medical Care* 18, 1980.

NEWHOUSE, JOHN. "Profiles (Margaret Thatcher) The Gamefish." *The New Yorker*, February 10, 1986.

NEWMAN, WILLIAM M. *American Pluralism: A Study of Minority Groups and Social Theory.* New York: Harper & Row, 1973.

NEWTON, GERALD. *The Netherlands: A Historical and Cultural Analysis.* Boulder, Colo.: Westview, 1978.

NIEBUHR, H. RICHARD. *The Social Sources of Denominationalism.* New York: Henry Holt, 1929.

NIMMO, DAN. "Elections as Ritual Drama." *Society*, May/June 1985.

NOCK, STEVEN L., and KINGSTON, PAUL WILLIAM. "The Family Work Day." *Journal of Marriage and the Family* 46, 1984.

NORDOFF, CHARLES. *The Communistic Societies of the United States.* New York: Schocken Books, 1971. Originally published 1875.

NORTON, ROBERT. "Measuring Marital Quality: A Critical Look at the Dependent Variable." *Journal of Marriage and the Family* 45, 1983.

NOVAK, MICHAEL. *The Joy of Sports.* New York: Basic Books, 1976.

NUGENT, JEFFREY B. "The Old-age Security Motive For Fertility." *Population and Development Review* 13, 1985.

OAKES, GUY. *The Soul of the Salesman.* Atlantic Highlands, N.J.: Humanities Press International, 1990.

OAKES, JEANNIE. "Classroom Social Relationships: Exploring the Bowles and Gintis Hypothesis." *Sociology of Education* 55, 1982.

OAKES, JEANNIE. *Keeping Track: How Schools Structure Inequality.* New Haven, Conn.: Yale University Press, 1985.

O'BRIEN, WILLIAM V. "International Crimes." In David L. Sills (ed.), *International Encyclopedia of the Social Sciences.* New York: Macmillan, 1968.

O'DEA, THOMAS F., and AVIAD, JANET O'DEA. *The Sociology of Religion,* 2d ed. Englewood Cliffs, N.J.: Prentice-Hall, 1983.

OGBURN, WILLIAM F. *Social Change.* New York: The Viking Press, 1964. Originally published 1922.

OGLE, LAURENCE, and ALSALAM, NABEEL, eds. *The Condition of Education: 1990 Edition.* Washington, D.C.: U.S. Government Printing Office, 1990.

O'HARE, WILLIAM P. "Poverty in America: Trends and New Patterns." *Population Bulletin* 40, 1985.

O'HARE, WILLIAM P. "America's Welfare Population: Who Gets What?" *Population Trends and Public Policy.* Washington, D.C.: Population Reference Bureau, 1987.

O'HARE, WILLIAM P., and FELT, JUDY C. "Asian Americans: America's Fastest Growing Minority Group." *Population Trends and Public Policy.* Washington, D.C.: Population Reference Bureau, 1991.

OKIE, SUSAN. "South American Cholera Epidemic Among Worst." *Washington Post,* April 26, 1991.

OKONJO, KAMENE. "The Dual-Sex Political System in Operation: Igbo Women and Community Politics in Midwestern Nigeria." In N.J. Hafkin and E.G. Bay (eds.), *Women in Africa.* Stanford, Calif.: Stanford University Press, 1976.

OLIVER, MELVIN L., and SHAPIRO, THOMAS M. "Wealth of a Nation: A Reassessment of Asset Inequality in America." *American Journal of Economics and Sociology* 48, 1989.

OLSON, DAVID H., and CROMWELL, RONALD E., eds. *Power in Families.* New York: John Wiley, 1975.

OLSON, PHILIP. "Modernization in the People's Republic of China: The Politicization of the Elderly." *The Sociological Quarterly* 29, 1988.

OMANG, JOANNE. "A-Worker Exposure Soars, Group Says." *Washington Post,* September 5, 1981.

OMANG, JOANNE. "The Secret Handicap: Millions of American Adults Can't Read." *Washington Post,* November 25, 1982.

ORCUTT, JAMES D. "Differential Association and Marijuana Use: A Closer Look at Sutherland (With a Little Help from Becker)." *Criminology* 25, 1987.

ORTEGA Y GASSET, JOSÉ. *The Revolt of the Masses.* New York: W.W. Norton, 1932.

ORUM, ANTHONY M. "Apprehending the City: The View from Above, Below, and Behind." *Urban Affairs Quarterly* 26, 1991.

OUDES, BRUCE, ed. *From: The President Richard Nixon's Secret Files.* New York: Harper & Row, 1988.

OUTLER, ALBERT. *Library of Protestant Thought: John Wesley.* New York: Oxford University Press, 1964.

PAGET, MARIANNE A. *The Unity of Mistakes: A Phenomenological Interpretation of Medical Work.* Philadelphia: Temple University Press, 1988.

PARSONS, TALCOTT. *The Social System.* Glencoe, Ill.: The Free Press, 1951.

PARSONS, TALCOTT. "The School Class as a Social System: Some of Its Functions in American Society." *Harvard Educational Review* 29, 1959.

PARELIUS, ANN PARKER, and PARELIUS, ROBERT J. *The Sociology of Education.* Englewood Cliffs, N.J.: Prentice-Hall, 1978.

PARK, ROBERT E., BURGESS, E.W., and McKENZIE, RODERICK D., eds. *The City.* Chicago: University of Chicago Press, 1925.

PARKS, MICHAEL. "Gorbachev Plans Tough Steps to Rescue Economy." *Los Angeles Times,* April 10, 1991.

PATERNOSTER, RAYMOND. *Capital Punishment in America.* New York: Lexington Books, 1991.

PATTERSON, JAMES T. *The Dread Disease: Cancer and Modern American Culture.* Cambridge, Mass.: Harvard University Press, 1987.

PEAR, ROBERT. "Millions Bypassed as Economy Soars." *New York Times,* March 16, 1986.

PERL, PETER. "Lower Pay for Women Blamed on Job Barriers." *Washington Post,* December 15, 1985.

PERROW, CHARLES. *Complex Organizations: A Critical Essay*, 3d ed. New York: Random House, 1986.

PERRY, STEWART E. *San Francisco Scavengers: Dirty Work and the Pride of Ownership*. Berkeley: University of California Press, 1978.

PERSELL, CAROLINE HODGES. *Education and Inequality: A Theoretical and Empirical Synthesis*. New York: The Free Press, 1977.

PESCOSOLIDO, BERNICE A., and GEORGIANA, SHARON. "Durkheim, Suicide, and Religion: Toward a Network Theory of Suicide." *American Sociological Review* 54, 1989.

PETERS, JOHN F. "Adolescents as Socialization Agents to Parents." *Adolescence* 20, 1985.

PETERS, THOMAS J., and WATERMAN, ROBERT H. *In Search of Excellence: Lessons from America's Best-Run Companies*. New York: Harper & Row, 1982.

PETERSON, GARY W., and ROLLINS, BOYD C. "Parent–Child Socialization." In Marvin B. Sussman and Suzanne K. Steinmetz (eds.), *Handbook of Marriage and the Family*. New York: Plenum Press, 1987.

PETERSON, JAMES L., and ZILL, NICHOLAS. "Marital Disruption, Parent–Child Relationships, and Behavior Problems of Children." *Journal of Marriage and the Family* 48, 1986.

PETERSON, RICHARD A., SCHMIDMAN, JOHN T., and ELIFSON, KIRK W. "Entrepreneurship or Autonomy? Truckers and Cabbies." In Phyllis L. Stewart and Muriel G. Cantor (eds.), *Varieties of Work*. Beverly Hills, Calif.: Sage, 1982.

PETROW, STEVEN. *Dancing Against Darkness: A Journey Through America in the Age of AIDS*. Lexington, Mass.: Lexington Books, 1990.

PFEIFFER, JOHN. "Girl Talk—Boy Talk." *Science* 85 January/February, 1985.

PHILLIPS, KEVIN. *The Politics of Rich and Poor*. New York: Random House, 1990.

PHILLIPS, ROLAND L., KUZMA, J.W., BEESON, W. LAWRENCE, and LOTZ, TERRY. "Influence of Selection Versus Lifestyle on Risk of Fatal Cancer and Cardiovascular Disease Among Seventh-Day Adventists." *American Journal of Epidemiology* 112, 1980.

PIFER, ALAN, and BRONTE, D. LYDIA. "Introduction: Squaring the Pyramid." *Daedalus* 115, 1986.

PIKE, E. ROYSTON. "The Natural History of the Kiss." In Charles C. Hughes (ed.), *Custom-Made: Introductory Readings for Cultural Anthropology*, 2d ed. Chicago: Rand McNally, 1976.

PIOTRKOWSKI, CHAYA S., and GORNICK, L. "The Impact of Work-Related Separations on Children and Families." In J. Bloom-Feshbach and S. Bloom-Feshbach (eds.), *The Psychology of Separation*. San Francisco: Jossey-Bass, 1987.

PIOTRKOWSKI, CHAYA S., RAPOPORT, ROBERT N., and RAPOPORT, RHONA. "Families and Work." In Marvin B. Sussman and Suzanne K. Steinmetz (eds.), *Handbook of Marriage and the Family*. New York: Plenum Press, 1987, pp. 251–283.

PLECK, JOSEPH H., and SAWYER, JACK, eds. *Men and Masculinity*. Englewood Cliffs, N.J.: Prentice-Hall, 1974.

PLIVEN, FRANCES FOX, and CLOWARD, RICHARD. *Why Americans Don't Vote*. New York: Pantheon, 1988.

PLUNKERT, LOIS. "The 1980's: A Decade of Job Growth and Industry Shifts." *Monthly Labor Review* 113, 1990.

POLIT, DENISE F., and FALBO, TONI. "Only Children and Personality Development: A Quantitative Review." *Journal of Marriage and the Family* 49, 1987.

POLLACK, ANDREW. "Medical Technology 'Arms Race' Adds Billions to the Nation's Bills." *New York Times*, April 29, 1991.

POMERLEAU, ANDREE, BOLDUC, DANIEL, MALCUIT, GERARD, and COSSETTE, LOUISE. "Pink or Blue: Environmental Gender Stereotypes in the First Two Years of Life." *Sex Roles* 22, 1990.

POPE, LISTON. *Millhands and Preachers*. New Haven: Yale University Press, 1942.

POPENOE, DAVID. "Beyond the Nuclear Family: A Statistical Portrait of the Changing Family in Sweden." *Journal of Marriage and the Family* 49, 1987.

POPULATION REFERENCE BUREAU. "World Population Data Sheet, 1991." Washington, D.C.: Population Reference Bureau, 1991.

POULANTZAS, NICOS. *Political Power and Social Classes*. London: NLB and Sheed and Ward, 1973.

POUSSAINT, ALVIN F. "A Negro Psychiatrist Explains the Negro Psyche." In Norman R. Yetman and C. Hoy Steele. *Majority and Minority: The Dynamics of Racial and Ethnic Relations*. Boston: Allyn and Bacon, 1971.

POWELL, DAVID E. "Soviet Society Today." In Uri Ra'anan and Charles M. Perry (eds.), *The USSR Today and Tomorrow: Problems and Challenges*. Lexington, Mass.: Lexington Books, 1987.

POWELL, DOUGLAS H., and DRISCOLL, PAUL F. "Middle-Class Professionals Face Unemployment." In Peter I. Rose (ed.), *Socialization and the Life Cycle*. New York: St. Martin's Press, 1979.

POWELL, G. BINGHAM. "Voter Turnout in Comparative Perspective." *American Political Science Review* 80, 1986.

POWERS, WILLIAM K. "Indians of the Plains." In Mircea Eliade (ed.), *The Encyclopedia of Religion*. New York: MacMillan, 1987.

PRADOS, JOHN. *Presidents' Secret Wars*. New York: William Morrow, 1986.

PRATT, BETH. "Many Profess to Feel Holy Presence." *Lubbock Avalanche-Journal*, August 16, 1988.

PREBISH, C.S. "Heavenly Father, Divine Goalie. Sport and Religion." *Antioch Review* 42, 1984.

PRESSER, HARRIET B. "Shift Work and Child Care among Young Dual-Earner American Parents." *Journal of Marriage and the Family* 50, 1988.

PRESTHUS, ROBERT VANCE. *The Organizational Society*, rev. ed. New York: St. Martin's Press, 1978.

PRESTON, SAMUEL H. *Biological and Social Aspects of Mortality and the Length of Life*. Leige: Ordina, 1982.

PRESTON, SAMUEL H. "Children and the Elderly: Divergent Paths for America's Dependents." *Demography* 21, 1984.

PRINCETON RELIGIOUS RESEARCH CENTER. *The Unchurched American*. Princeton, N.J.: Princeton Religious Research Center and the Gallup Organization, 1978.

PRITCHARD, LINDA K. "Religious Change in Nineteenth-Century America." In Charles Y. Glock and Robert N. Bellah (eds.), *The New Religious Consciousness*. Berkeley: University of California Press, 1976.

PROSEN, ROSE MARY. "Looking Back." In Michael Novak (ed.), *Growing Up Slavic in America*. Bayville, N.Y.: EMPAC. 1976.

QUINN, JAMES F. "Sex Roles and Hedonism Among Members of 'Outlaw' Motorcycle Clubs." *Deviant Behavior* 8, 1987.

RADIN, PAUL, ed. *Crashing Thunder: The Autobiography of a Winnebago Indian*. New York: D. Appleton, 1926. Published in 1920 as Part 1 of the autobiography.

RAINES, HOWELL. *My Soul Is Rested*. New York: Bantam Books, 1978.

RAINWATER, LEE. "The Lower Class: Health, Illness and Medical Institutions." In Irwin Deutscher and Elizabeth J. Thompson (eds.), *Among the People: Encounters with the Poor*. New York: Basic Books, 1968.

RASCHKE, HELEN J. "Divorce." In Marvin B. Sussman and Suzanne K. Steinmetz (eds.), *Handbook of Marriage and the Family*. New York: Plenum Press, 1987.

RASOR, DINA. *The Pentagon Underground*. New York: Random House–Times Books, 1985.

RAVENHOLT, R.T. "Tobacco's Global Death March." *Population and Development Review* 16, 1990.

RAVITCH, DIANE. *The Schools We Deserve: Reflections on the Educational Crises of Our Time*. New York: Basic Books, 1985.

READ, KENNETH E. *The High Valley*. New York: Columbia University Press, 1980.

REED, EVELYN. "Is Biology Woman's Destiny?" *International Socialist Review*, 1971.

REEDER, LEO G. "The Patient-Client as a Consumer: Some Observations on the Changing Professional-Client Relationship." *Journal of Health and Social Behavior* 13, 1972.

REIMAN, JEFFREY H. *The Rich Get Richer and the Poor Get Prison*. New York: John Wiley, 1979.

REINHOLD, ROBERT. "In the Middle of L.A.'s Gang Warfare." *New York Times Magazine*, May 22, 1988.

REINHOLD, ROBERT. "Aloft Without Nicotine: Can Smokers Cope?" *New York Times*, February 26, 1990.

REISCHAUER, ROBERT D. "Immigration and the Underclass." *The Annals of the American Academy of Political and Social Science* 501, 1989.

REISS, IRA L. *Family Systems in America*. New York: Holt, Rinehart and Winston, 1980.

REISS, IRA L. *Journey into Sexuality: An Explanatory Voyage*. Englewood Cliffs, N.J.: Prentice-Hall, 1986.

REISS, IRA L., and LEE, GARY R. *Family Systems in America*, 4th ed. New York: Holt, Rinehart & Winston, Inc., 1988.

REMINI, ROBERT V. *Andrew Jackson and the Course of American Democracy, 1833–1845*. New York: Harper & Row, 1984.

RENSBERGER, BOYCE. "African Women Save Energy Using Head for Heavy Loads." *Washington Post*, February 23, 1986.

RENSBERGER, BOYCE. "Sexual Competition and Violence." *Washington Post*, February 29, 1988.

RESKIN, BARBARA F., and HARTMAN, HEIDI, eds. *Women's Work, Men's Work: Sex Segregation on the Job.* Washington, D.C.: National Academy Press, 1986.
RICH, SPENCER. "Nursing Shortage Called Widespread." *Washington Post*, July 17, 1988.
RICHARDSON, LAUREL. *The New Other Woman: Contemporary Single Women in Affairs with Married Men.* New York: The Free Press, 1985.
RICHEY, RUSSELL E., and JONES, DONALD G. *American Civil Religion.* New York: Harper & Row, 1974.
RIESMAN, DAVID. *The Lonely Crowd.* New Haven, Conn.: Yale University Press, 1961.
RILEY, MATILDA WHITE, FONER, ANNE, and WARING, JOAN. "Sociology of Aging." In Neil J. Smelser (ed.), *Handbook of Sociology.* Beverly Hills, Calif.: Sage, 1988.
RITZER, GEORGE. "The Permanently New Economy: The Case for Reviving Economic Sociology." *Work and Occupations* 16, 1989.
RITZER, GEORGE. *Metatheorizing in Sociology.* Lexington, Mass.: Lexington Books, 1991.
RITZER, GEORGE. *The Big Mac Attack: The McDonaldization of Society.* Forthcoming.
RITZER, GEORGE. *Classical Sociological Theory.* New York: McGraw-Hill, 1992a.
RITZER, GEORGE. *Sociological Theory*, 3rd ed. New York: McGraw-Hill, 1992b.
RITZER, GEORGE, and WALCZAK, DAVID. *Working: Conflict and Change*, 3d ed. Englewood Cliffs, N.J.: Prentice-Hall, 1986.
RITZER, GEORGE, and WALCZAK, DAVID. "Rationalization and the Deprofessionalization of Physicians." *Social Forces* 66, 1988.
ROBERTS, ELIZABETH, KLINE, DAVID, and GAGNON, JOHN. *Family Life and Sexual Learning: A Study of the Role of Parents in the Sexual Learning of Children.* Cambridge, Mass.: Population Education, 1978.
ROETHLISBERGER, FRITZ, and DICKSON, WILLIAM J. *Management and the Worker.* New York: John Wiley & Sons, 1964. Originally published in 1939.
ROHLEN, THOMAS P. *Japan's High Schools.* Berkeley: University of California Press, 1983.
ROLLINS, B.C., and GALLIGAN, R. "The Developing Child and Marital Satisfaction of Parents." In R.M. Lerner and G.B. Spanier (eds.), *Child Influences on Marital and Family Interaction.* New York: Academic Press, 1978.
ROMAN, MEL, and HADDAD, WILLIAM. *The Disposable Parent: The Case for Joint Custody.* New York: Penguin Books, 1978.
ROOF, WADE CLARK. "Return of the Baby Boomers to Organized Religion." In Constant H. Jacquet, Jr., ed., *Yearbook of American and Canadian Churches 1990.* Nashville: Abington Press, 1990.
ROOF, WADE CLARK, and HADAWAY, C. KIRK. "Denominational Switching in the Seventies: Going Beyond Stark and Glock." *Journal for the Scientific Study of Religion* 18, 1979.
ROOF, WADE CLARK, and MCKINNEY, WILLIAM. *American Mainline Religion: Its Changing Shape and Future.* New Brunswick, N.J.: Rutgers University Press, 1987.
ROOZEN, DAVID A., MCKINNEY, WILLIAM, and THOMPSON, WAYNE. "The 'Big Chill' Generation Warms to Worship: A Research Note." *Review of Religious Research* 31, 1990.
ROSE, ARNOLD. *The Power Structure.* New York: Oxford University Press, 1967.
ROSE, PETER I., ed. *Socialization and the Life Cycle.* New York: St. Martin's Press, 1979.
ROSEBERRY, WILLIAM. *Coffee and Capitalism in the Venezuelan Andes.* Austin: University of Texas Press, 1983.
ROSECRANCE, JOHN. "Compulsive Gambling and the Medicalization of Deviance." *Social Problems* 32, 1985.
ROSEN, SHERWIN, and TAUBMAN, PAUL. "Changes in the Impact of Education and Income on Mortality in the U.S." In Linda DelBene and Foritz Schueren (eds.), *Statistical Uses of Administrative Records with Emphasis on Mortality and Disability Research.* Washington, D.C.: U.S. Department of Health, Education and Welfare, 1979.
ROSENBAUM, EMILY, and KANDEL, DENISE B. "Early Onset of Adolescent Sexual Behavior and Drug Involvement." *Journal of Marriage and Family* 52, 1990.
ROSENBAUM, JAMES E. *Making Inequality: The Hidden Curriculum of High School Tracking.* New York: John Wiley, 1976.
ROSENBERG, MORRIS. *Conceiving the Self.* New York: Basic Books, 1979.
ROSENBERG, MORRIS, and TURNER, RALPH H. "Introduction to the Transaction Edition." In Morris Rosenberg and Ralph H. Turner (eds.), *Social Psychology: Sociological Perspectives*, new edition. New Brunswick, N.J.: Transaction, 1990.
ROSENBERG, MORRIS. "The Self Concept: Social Product and Social Force." In Morris Rosenberg and Ralph H. Turner (eds.) *Social Psychology: Sociological Perspectives*, new edition. New Brunswick, N.J.: Transaction, 1990.
ROSENBERG, NATHAN. *Perspectives on Technology.* New York: Cambridge University Press, 1976.
ROSENTHAL, ROBERT, and JACOBSON, LENORE. *Pygmalion in the Classroom.* New York: Holt, Rinehart & Winston, 1968.

ROSNOW, RALPH L., and FINE, GARY ALAN. *Rumor and Gossip.* New York: Elsevier, 1976.

ROSS, CATHERINE E., and DUFF, RAYMOND S. "Returning to the Doctor: The Effect of Client Characteristics, Type of Practice, and Experience with Care." *Health and Social Behavior* 23, 1982.

ROSS, CATHERINE E., MIROWSKY, JOHN, and HUBER, JOAN. "Dividing Work, Sharing Work, and In Between: Marriage Patterns and Depression." *American Sociological Review* 48, 1983.

ROTH, JULIUS A. *Timetables: Structuring the Passage of Time in Hospital Treatment and Other Careers.* Indianapolis: Bobbs-Merrill, 1963.

ROTH, JULIUS A. "Treatment of the Sick." In J. Kosa, Aaron Antonovsky, and Irving Kenneth Zola (eds.), *Poverty and Health.* Cambridge, Mass.: Harvard University Press, 1969.

ROTHMAN, DAVID. *The Discovery of the Asylum: Social Order and Disorder in the New Republic.* Boston: Little, Brown, 1971.

ROWAN, BRIAN, and MIRACLE, ANDREW W., JR. "Systems of Ability Grouping and the Stratification of Achievement in Elementary Schools." *Sociology of Education* 56, 1983.

ROWE, JAMES L., JR. "Insurance, Tobacco, Rail PACs Increased 1990 Contributions." *Washington Post*, May 3, 1991.

ROY, DONALD. "Efficiency and the 'Fix': Informal Intergroup Relations in a Piecework Machine Shop." *American Journal of Sociology* 60, 1954.

ROY, DONALD. "Banana Time: Job Satisfaction and Informal Interaction." *Human Organization* 18, 1959–1960.

RUBIN, LILLIAN BRESLOW. *Worlds of Pain: Life in the Working Class Family.* New York: Basic Books, 1976.

RUBIN, LILLIAN B. *Erotic Wars: What Happened to the Sexual Revolution?* New York: Farrar, Straus & Giroux, 1990.

RUBINSON, RICHARD, and RALPH, JOHN. "Technical Change and the Expansion of Schooling in the United States, 1890–1970." *Sociology of Education* 57, 1984.

RUDIN, A.J. "America's New Religion." *The Christian Century* 89, 1972.

RUNCIE, JOHN F. "By Days I Make the Cars." *Harvard Business Review*, May–June 1980.

RUNDALL, THOMAS G., and WHEELER, JOHN R.C. "The Effect of Income on Use of Preventive Care: An Evaluation of Alternative Explanations." *Journal of Health and Social Behavior* 20, 1979.

RUSH, GARY B., and DENISOFF, R. SERGE. *Social and Political Movements.* New York: Appleton-Century-Crofts, 1971.

RUSHING, WILLIAM A. "The Supply of Physicians and Expenditures for Health Services with Implications for the Coming Physician Surplus." *Journal of Health and Social Behavior* 26, 1985.

RUSSELL, CHRISTINE. "What Do You Know About AIDS?" *Washington Post Health*, February 5, 1991.

RYAN, WILLIAM. *Blaming the Victim.* New York: Pantheon Books, 1971.

RYDER, NORMAN R. "What Is Going to Happen to American Fertility?" *Population and Development Review* 16, 1990.

RYSCAVAGE, PAUL, and HENLE, PETER. "Earnings Inequality Accelerates in the 1980's." *Monthly Labor Review* 113, 1990.

SABATO, LARRY J. *The Rise of Political Consultants: New Ways of Winning Elections.* New York: Basic Books, 1981.

SACHAR, HOWARD M. *A History of Israel, Volume II, From the Aftermath of the Yom Kippur War.* New York: Oxford University Press, 1987.

SADKER, MYRA, and SADKER, DAVID. "Sexism in the Schoolroom of the '80s." *Psychology Today*, March, 1985.

SAFILIOS-ROTHSCHILD, C. "Study of Family Power Structure: 1960–1969." *Journal of Marriage and the Family* 32, 1970.

SANDAY, PEGGY REEVES. *Female Power and Male Dominance.* New York: Cambridge University Press, 1981.

SANDEFUR, GARY D., and TIENDA, MARTA. *Divided Opportunities: Minorities, Poverty, and Social Policy.* New York: Plenum Press, 1988.

San Diego Tribune. February 7, 1986.

SASSEN, SASKIA. "Economic Restructuring and the American City." *Annual Review of Sociology* 16, 1990.

SAUNDERS, DANIEL G. "When Battered Women Use Violence: Husband-Abuse or Self-Defense?" *Violence and Victims* 1, 1986.

SAVETH, EDWARD N. *American Historians and European Immigrants.* New York: Columbia University Press, 1948.

SAXE, LEONARD, and FINE, MICHELLE. *Social Experiments: Methods for Design and Evaluation.* Beverly Hills, Calif.: Sage, 1981.

SCANZONI, JOHN. *Sexual Bargaining: Power Politics in the American Marriage.* Englewood Cliffs, N.J.: Prentice-Hall, 1972.

SCANZONI, JOHN. "Social Processes and Power in Families." In Wesley R. Burr, Reuben Hill, F. Ivan Nye, and Ira L. Reiss (eds.), *Contemporary Theories About the Family: Research-Based Theories*, Vol. I. New York: The Free Press, 1979.

SCHAEFER, WALTER E., OLEXA, CAROL, and POLK, KENNETH. "Programmed for Social Class: Tracking in High School." *Trans-Action* 7, 1970.

SCHEFF, THOMAS J. *Being Mentally Ill.* Chicago: Aldine, 1966.

SCHRAM, MARTIN. *The Great American Video Game: Presidential Politics in the Television Age.* New York: William Morrow, 1987.

SCHULTZ, JAMES H., BOROWSKI, ALAN, and CROWN, WILLIAM H. *Economics of Population Aging: The "Graying" of Australia, Japan, and the United States.* New York: Auburn House, 1991.

SCHUMAN, HOWARD, STEEH, CHARLOTTE, and BOBO, LAWRENCE. *Racial Attitudes in America: Trends and Interpretations.* Cambridge, Mass.: Harvard University Press, 1985.

SCHUMM, WALTER R., and BUGAIGHIS, MARGARET A. "Marital Quality over the Marital Career: Alternative Explanations." *Journal of Marriage and the Family* 48, 1986.

SCHUR, EDWIN. *Crimes Without Victims: Deviant Behavior and Public Policy.* Englewood Cliffs, N.J.: Prentice-Hall, 1965.

SCHUR, EDWIN M. *The Americanization of Sex.* Philadelphia: Temple University Press, 1988.

SCHWALBE, MICHAEL L. *The Psychosocial Consequences of Natural and Alienated Labor.* Albany, N.Y.: State University of New York Press, 1986.

SCHWARTZ, HILLEL. *Never Satisfied: A Cultural History of Diets, Fantasies and Fat.* New York: The Free Press, 1986.

SCOTT, DANIEL T. *Technology and Union Survival: A Study of the Printing Industry.* New York: Praeger, 1987.

SEDLAK, MICHAEL W., WHEELER, CHRISTOPHER W., PULLIN, DIANA C., and CUSIK, PHILIP A. *Selling Students Short: Classroom Bargains and Academic Reform in the American High School.* New York: Teachers College Press, 1986.

SENNETT, RICHARD, and COBB, JONATHAN. *The Hidden Injuries of Class.* New York: Vintage Books, 1972.

SEWELL, WILLIAM H. "Inequality of Opportunity for Higher Education." *American Sociological Review* 36, 1971.

SHAIKEN, HARLEY. *Work Transformed: Automation and Labor in The Computer Age.* Lexington, Mass.: Lexington Books, 1986.

SHANK, SUSAN E. "Women and the Labor Market: The Link Grows Stronger." *Monthly Labor Review* 111, 1988.

SHANNON, LYLE W. "Assessing the Relationship of Adult Criminal Careers to Juvenile Careers." In C. Abt (ed.), *Problems in American Social Policy.* Cambridge, Mass.: Abt Books, 1980.

SHAPIRO, CONSTANCE H. "Sexual Learning: The Short-Changed Adolescent Male." *Social Work* 25, 1980.

SHAPIRO, MARGARET. "Saturday Night Fervor." *Washington Post*, April 11, 1988.

SHAVIT, YOSSI, and FEATHERMAN, DAVID L. "Schooling, Tracking, and Teenage Intelligence." *Sociology of Education* 61, 1988.

SHEFFIELD, CAROLE J. "Sexual Terrorism: The Social Control of Women." In Beth B. Hess and Myra Marx Ferree (eds.), *Analyzing Gender: A Handbook of Social Science Research.* Beverly Hills, Calif.: Sage, 1987.

SHELL, ELLEN RUPPEL. "The Getting of Respect." *The Atlantic*, February, 1988.

SHEPHERD, GORDON, and SHEPHERD, GARY. *A Kingdom Transformed: Themes in the Development of Mormonism.* Salt Lake City: University of Utah Press, 1984.

SHERIF, MUZAFER. "A Study of Some Social Factors in Perception." *Archives of Psychology* 27, 1935.

SHERIF, MUZAFER. *Groups in Harmony and Tension.* New York: Harper & Brothers, 1953.

SHERMAN, LAWRENCE W., and BERK, RICHARD A. "The Specific Deterrent Effects of Arrest for Domestic Assault." *American Sociological Review* 49, 1984.

SHERMAN, LAWRENCE W., and COHN, ELLEN G. "The Impact of Research on Legal Policy: A Case Study of the Minneapolis Domestic Violence Experiment." *Law and Society* 23, 1989.

SHORTER, EDWARD. *A History of Women's Bodies.* New York: Basic Books, 1982.

SIEGEL, JACOB S., and TAEUBER, CYNTHIA M. "Demographic Perspectives on the Long-Lived Society." *Daedalus* 115, 1986.

SILBERMAN, CHARLES E. *Crisis in the Classroom: The Remaking of American Education*. New York: Random House, 1970.

SILVER, MARC L. *Under Construction: Work and Alienation in the Building Trades*. Albany, N.Y.: State University of New York Press, 1986.

SILVESTRI, GEORGE T., and LUKASIEWICZ, JOHN M. "A Look at Occupational Employment Trends to the Year 2000." *Monthly Labor Review* 110, 1987.

SILVESTRI, GEORGE T., LUKASIEWICZ, JOHN M., and EINSTEIN, MARCUS E. "Occupational Employment Projections Through 1995." *Monthly Labor Review* 106, 1983.

SIMMEL, GEORG. "The Dyad and the Triad." In Kurt Wolf (ed.) *The Sociology of Georg Simmel*. Glencoe, Ill.: The Free Press, 1950.

SIMMEL, GEORG. "The Metropolis and Mental Life." In Donald Levine (ed.). *Georg Simmel: Individuality and Social Forms*. Chicago: University of Chicago Press, 1971. Originally published 1903.

SIMMONS, J.L. "Public Stereotypes of Deviants." *Social Problems* 13, 1965.

SIMMONS, J.L., and McCALL, GEORGE J. *Social Research: The Craft of Finding Out*. New York: Macmillan, 1985.

SIMON, JULIAN L. *The Ultimate Resource*. Princeton, N.J.: Princeton University Press, 1981.

SIMON, JULIAN L. *The Economic Consequences of Immigration*. Cambridge, Mass.: Basil Blackwell, 1989.

SIMON, RITA, and LANDIS, JEAN. *The Crimes Women Commit, The Punishments They Receive*. Lexington, Mass.: Lexington Books, 1991.

SIMONS, LEWIS M. *Worth Dying For*. New York: William Morrow and Co., 1987.

SIMPSON, GEORGE EATON, and YINGER, J. MILTON. *Racial and Cultural Minorities: An Analysis of Prejudice and Discrimination*, 5th ed. New York: Plenum, 1985.

SINGER, MILTON. *When a Great Tradition Modernizes*. New York: Praeger, 1972.

SINGH, J.A.L., and ZINGG, ROBERT M. *Wolf Children and Feral Man*. New York: Harper & Row, 1942.

SLOMCZYNSKI, KAZIMIERZ M., MILLER, JOANNE, and KOHN, MELVIN L. "Stratification, Work, and Values: A Polish–United States Comparison." *American Sociological Review* 46, 1981.

SMALL, STEPHEN A., and RILEY, DAVE. "Toward a Multidimensional Assessment of Work Spillover into Family Life." *Journal of Marriage and the Family* 52, 1990.

SMITH, ADAM. *The Wealth of Nations*. New York: The Modern Library, 1937.

SMITH, DANIEL S. "The Dating of the American Sexual Revolution." In Michael Gordon (ed.), *The American Family in Social Historical Perspective*, 2nd ed. New York: St. Martins Press, 1978.

SMITH, DOUGLAS A., and GARTIN, PATRICK R. "Specifying Specific Deterrence: The Influence of Arrest on Future Criminal Activity." *American Sociological Review* 54, 1989.

SMITH, HEDRICK. *The Russians*. New York: Quadrangle Books, 1976.

SMITH, JAMES D. "Trends in the Concentration of Personal Wealth in the United States, 1958 to 1976." *Review of Income and Wealth* 30, 1984.

SMITH, KEVIN B., and BYLUND, ROBERT A. "Cognitive Maps of Class, Racial, and Appalachian Inequalities Among Rural Appalachians." *Rural Sociology* 42, 1983.

SMITH, R. JEFFREY. "NATO Sets New Stance for New Era." *Washington Post*, May 29, 1991.

SNIPP, C. MATTHEW. "American Indians and Natural Resource Development." *American Journal of Economics and Sociology* 45, 1986.

SNYDER, THOMAS D. *Digest of Educational Statistics 1987*. Washington, D.C.: U.S. Government Printing Office, 1987.

SOLDO, BETH J., and AGREE, EMILY. "America's Elderly." *Population Bulletin* 43, 1988.

SOLLIE, D., and MILLER, B. "The Transition to Parenthood as a Critical Time for Building Family Strengths." In N. Stinnet and P. Knaub (eds.), *Family Strengths: Positive Models of Family Life*. Lincoln: University of Nebraska Press, 1980.

SOLZHENITSYN, ALEXANDER I. *The Gulag Archipelago*. New York: Harper & Row, 1973.

SOMMER, ROBERT, BURSTEIN, EMILY, and HOLMAN, SANDY. "Tolerance of Deviance as Affected by Label, Act, and Actor." *Deviant Behavior* 9, 1988.

SONENSTEIN, FREYA L., PLECK, JOSEPH H., and KU, LEIGHTON C. "Sexual Activity, Condom Use and AIDS Awareness Among Adolescent Males." *Family Planning Perspectives* 21, 1989.

SORENSEN, GLORIAN, et al. "Sex Differences in the Relationship Between Work and Health: The Minnesota Heart Survey." *Journal of Health and Social Behavior* 26, 1985.

SOROKIN, PITIRIM A. *The Crisis of Our Age*. New York: E.P. Dutton, 1941.

SOROKIN, PITIRIM A. *Social and Cultural Dynamics*. Boston: Porter Sargent, 1957.

SOUTH, SCOTT. "Economic Conditions and the Divorce Rate: A Time Series Analysis of the Postwar United States." *Journal of Marriage and the Family* 47, 1985.

SOUTH, SCOTT. "Sex Ratios, Economic Power, and Women's Roles: A Theoretical Extension and Empirical Test." *Journal of Marriage and the Family* 50, 1988.

SOUTHERN POVERTY LAW CENTER. "'Move-In' Violence: White Resistance to Neighborhood Integration in the 1980s." Montgomery, Ala.: Southern Poverty Law Center, 1987.

SPANIER, GRAHAM B. "Measuring Dyadic Adjustment: New Scales for Assessing the Quality of Marriage and Similar Dyads." *Journal of Marriage and the Family* 38, 1976.

SPANIER, GRAHAM B., and FURSTENBERG, FRANK F., JR. "Remarriage and Reconstituted Families." In Marvin B. Sussman and Suzanne K. Steinmetz (eds.), *Handbook of Marriage and the Family*. New York: Plenum Press, 1987.

SPECTOR, MALCOLM. "Legitimizing Homosexuality." *Society*, July/August 1977.

SPINDLER, GEORGE D., and SPINDLER, LOUISE. "Anthropologists View American Culture." *Annual Review of Anthropology* 12, Palo Alto, Calif.: Annual Reviews, Inc., 1983.

SPITZE, GLENNA. "Work and Family." *Journal of Marriage and the Family* 50, 1988.

SPITZER, CINDY. "The Invisible Toll on Rescue Workers." *Washington Post-Health*, May 10, 1988.

"The Sport of Religion: The Ritual Athletes of Iran." CBS television program, February 9, 1972.

SPRECHER, SUSAN, MCKINNEY, KATHLEEN, and ORBUCH, TERRI L. "Has the Double Standard Disappeared? An Experimental Test." *Social Psychology Quarterly* 50, 1987.

STACK, STEVEN. "The Effect of the Decline in Institutionalized Religion on Suicide, 1954–1978." *Journal for the Scientific Study of Religion* 22, 1983.

STACK, STEVEN. "New Micro-level Data on the Impact of Divorce on Suicide, 1959–1980: A Test of Two Theories." *Journal of Marriage and the Family* 52, 1990a.

STACK, STEVEN. "The Effect of Divorce on Suicide in Denmark, 1951–1980." *The Sociological Quarterly* 31, 1990b.

STAFFORD, MARK, and GIBBS, JACK. "A Major Problem with the Theory of Status Integration and Suicide." *Social Forces* 63, 1985.

STAFFORD, MARK, and GIBBS, JACK. "Change in the Relation Between Marital Integration and Suicide Rates." *Social Forces* 66, 1988.

STARK, RODNEY, and BAINBRIDGE, WILLIAM SIMS. "Of Churches, Sects, and Cults: Preliminary Concepts for a Theory of Religious Movements." *Journal for the Scientific Study of Religion* 18, 1979.

STARR, PAUL. *The Social Transformation of American Medicine*. New York: Basic Books, 1982.

STAUDOHAR, P., and BROWN, H. *Deindustrialization and Plant Closings*. Lexington, Mass.: D.C. Heath, 1987.

STEBBINS, ROBERT. "The Meaning of Academic Performance: How Teachers Define a Classroom Situation." In Peter Woods and Martyn Hammersley (eds.), *School Experience*. New York: St. Martin's Press, 1977.

STEEMI, FEHMIDA. "Higher Settlements in 1989 End Innovative Decade." *Monthly Labor Review* 113, 1990.

STEIN, LEONARD I. "Male and Female: The Doctor–Nurse Game." In James P. Spradley and David W. McCurdy (eds.), *Conformity and Conflict: Readings in Cultural Anthropology*, 2d ed. Boston: Little, Brown, 1974.

STEINBERG, LAURENCE, and SILVERBERG, SUSAN B. "Influences on Marital Satisfaction During the Middle Stages of the Family Life Cycle." *Journal of Marriage and the Family* 49, 1987.

STEINMETZ, SUZANNE K. "Family Violence." In Marvin B. Sussman and Suzanne K. Steinmetz (eds.), *Handbook of Marriage and the Family*. New York: Plenum Press, 1987.

STELLMAN, JEANNE, and DAUM, SUSAN M. *Work Is Dangerous to Your Health*. New York: Vintage Books, 1973.

STERN, PHILIP M. *The Best Congress Money Can Buy*. New York: Pantheon, 1988.

STEVENS, ROSEMARY. *American Medicine and the Public Interest*. New Haven, Conn.: Yale University Press, 1971.

STOCKWELL, EDWARD G., and GROAT, H. THEODORE. *World Population: An Introduction to Demography*. New York: Franklin Watts, 1984.

STRAUS, MURRAY A. "Victims and Aggressors in Marital Violence." *American Behavioral Scientist* 23, 1980.

STRAUS, MURRAY A., and GELLES, RICHARD J. "Societal Change and Change in Family Violence from 1975 to 1985 As Revealed by Two National Surveys." *Journal of Marriage and the Family* 48, 1986.

STRAUS, MURRAY A., GELLES, RICHARD J., and STEINMETZ, SUZANNE K. *Behind Closed Doors: Violence in the American Family*. Garden City, N.Y.: Anchor/Doubleday, 1980.

STRICKLAND, W.P., ed. *Autobiography of Peter Cartwright, The Backwoods Preacher*. New York: Carlton and Porter, 1856.

STROUSE, JEREMIAH, and FABES, RICHARD A. "Formal Versus Informal Sources of Sex Education: Competing Forces in the Sexual Socialization of Adolescents." *Adolescence* 20, 1985.

STRYKER, SHELDON. "Symbolic Interactionism: Themes and Variations." In Morris Rosenberg and Ralph H. Turner (eds.), *Social Psychology: Sociological Perspectives*, new edition. New Brunswick, N.J.: Transaction, 1990.

SUMNER, WILLIAM GRAHAM. *Folkways: A Study of the Sociological Importance of Usages, Manners, Customs, Mores, and Morals.* Boston: Ginn, 1906.

SUPLEE, CURT. "The Electronic Sweatshop." *Washington Post-Outlook*, January 3, 1988.

SURRA, CATHERINE A. "Research and Theory on Mate Selection and Premarital Relationships in the 1980s." *Journal of Marriage and the Family* 52, 1990.

SUSSER, MERVYN W., HOPPER, KIM, and RICHMAN, JUDITH. "Society, Culture, and Health." In D. Mechanic (ed.), *Handbook of Health, Health Care, and the Health Professions.* New York: The Free Press, 1983.

SUTHERLAND, EDWIN H. *Principles of Criminology*, 4th ed. Chicago: Lippincott, 1947.

SWAFFORD, MICHAEL. "Sex Differences in Soviet Earnings." *American Sociological Review* 43, 1978.

SYME, S. LEONARD, and BERKMAN, LISA F. "Social Class, Susceptibility, and Sickness." In Peter Conrad and Rochelle Kern (eds.), *The Sociology of Health and Illness.* New York: St. Martin's Press, 1981.

SZINOVACZ, MAXIMILIANE. "Family Power." In Marvin B. Sussman and Suzanne K. Steinmetz (eds.), *Handbook of Marriage and the Family.* New York: Plenum Press, 1987.

TALESE, GAY. *Thy Neighbor's Wife.* New York: Doubleday, 1980.

TANNER, NANCY. "Matrifocality in Indonesia and Africa and Among Black Americans." In M.Z. Rosaldo and L. Lamphere (eds.), *Women, Culture, and Society.* Stanford, Calif.: Stanford University Press, 1974.

TAYLOR, ELLA. *Prime Time Families: Television Culture in Postwar America.* Berkeley, Calif.: University of California Press, 1989.

TAYLOR, VERTA. "Good News About Disaster." *Psychology Today*, October 1977.

TEITELBAUM, MICHAEL S., and WINTER, JAY M. *The Fear of Population Decline.* New York: Academic Press, 1985.

TERKEL, STUDS. *Working.* New York: Pantheon Books, 1974.

THIO, ALEX. *Deviant Behavior.* Boston: Houghton Mifflin, 1978.

THOITS, PEGGY A. "Self-Labeling Processes in Mental Illness. The Role of Emotional Deviance." *American Journal of Sociology* 91, 1985.

THOMPSON, LARRY. "The AIDS Statistics: Despite Prevention Efforts, HIV Continues to Spread." *Washington Post Health*, April 3, 1990.

THOMPSON, SHARON. "Putting a Big Thing into a Little Hole: Teenage Girls' Accounts of Sexual Initiation." *The Journal of Sex Research*, 27, 1990.

THOREAU, HENRY D. *Walden: Or, Life in the Woods.* Boston: Ticknor and Fields, 1854.

THORNBERRY, TERENCE P., and FARNSWORTH, MARGARET. "Social Correlates of Criminal Involvement: Further Evidence on the Relationship Between Social Status and Criminal Behavior." *American Sociological Review* 47, 1982.

THORNTON, ARLAND. "Cohabitation and Marriage in the 1980s." *Demography* 25, 1988.

THORNTON, ARLAND, and FREEDMAN, DEBORAH. "The Changing American Family." *Population Bulletin*, 38 1983.

THORNTON, ARLAND, and CAMBURN, DONALD. "Religious Participation and Adolescent Sexual Behavior and Attitudes." *Journal of Marriage and the Family* 51, 1989.

THORNTON, RUSSELL. *American Indian Holocaust and Survival.* Norman: University of Oklahoma Press, 1987.

TIGER, LIONEL. *Men in Groups.* New York: Random House, 1969.

TIMBERLAKE, MICHAEL, ed. *Urbanization in the World-Economy.* New York: Academic Press, 1985.

TIMBERLAKE, MICHAEL, and KENTOR, JEFFREY. "Economic Dependence, Overurbanization, and Economic Growth: A Study of Less Developed Countries." *The Sociological Quarterly* 24, 1983.

Time. "The Battle over Abortion." April 6, 1981.

Time. "Racism on the Rise." February 2, 1987.

Time. "Fed Up, Fearful and Frazzled." March 14, 1988a.

Time. "A Move to the Right." November 14, 1988b.

TITTLE, C.R., VILLEMEZ, W.J., and SMITH, D.A. "The Myth of Social Class and Criminality: An Empirical Assessment of the Empirical Evidence." *American Sociological Review* 43, 1978.

TODD, ALEXANDRA DUNDAS. *Intimate Adversaries: Cultural Conflict between Doctors and Patients.* Philadelphia: University of Pennsylvania Press, 1989.

TOENNIES, FERDINAND. *Community and Society.* New York: Harper Torchbooks, 1957. Originally published 1887.

TOFFLER, ALVIN. *Future Shock.* New York: Random House, 1970.

TOREN, NINA. "The Bus Driver: A Study in Role Analysis. *Human Relations* 26, 1973.

TREIMAN, DONALD. *Occupational Prestige in Comparative Perspective.* New York: Academic Press, 1977.

TRICE, HARRISON M. "The Outsider's Role in Field Study." In William J. Filstead (ed.), *Qualitative Methodology: Firsthand Involvement with the Social World.* Chicago: Markham, 1970.

TRICE, HARRISON M., and ROMAN, PAUL. "Delabeling, Relabeling and Alcoholics Anonymous." *Social Problems* 17, 1970.

TRILLIN, CALVIN. "Black or White." *The New Yorker* 62, April 14, 1986.

TROELTSCH, ERNST. *The Social Teachings of the Christian Churches.* New York: Macmillan, 1931.

TROVATO, FRANK. "A Longitudinal Analysis of Divorce and Suicide in Canada." *Journal of Marriage and the Family* 49, 1987.

TSCHETTER, JOHN. "Producer Services Industries: Why Are They Growing So Rapidly." *Monthly Labor Review* 110, 1987.

TUMIN, MELVIN M. *Social Stratification,* 2d ed. Englewood Cliffs, N.J.: Prentice-Hall, 1985.

TURKLE, SHERRY. *The Second Self: Computers and the Human Spirit.* New York: Simon and Schuster, 1984.

TURNER, JONATHAN H., and MARYANSKI, ALEXANDRA. *Functionalism.* Menlo Park, Calif.: Benjamin/Cummings, 1979.

TURNER, JONATHAN H., SINGLETON, ROYCE, JR., and MUSICK, DAVID. *Oppression: A Socio-History of Black–White Relations in America.* Chicago: Nelson-Hall, 1984.

TURNER, MARGERY AUSTIN, FIX, MICHAEL, and STRUYK, RAYMOND J. "Opportunities Denied, Opportunities Diminished: Discrimination in Hiring." Washington, D.C.: The Urban Institute, 1991.

TURNER, RALPH H., and KILLIAN, LEWIS M. *Collective Behavior,* 2d ed. Englewood Cliffs, N.J.: Prentice-Hall, 1972.

UNITED NATIONS DEPARTMENT OF INTERNAL ECONOMIC AND SOCIAL AFFAIRS. "National Accounts Statistics: Compendium of Income Distribution Statistics." *Statistical Papers.* Series M. No. 79. New York: United Nations. 1985.

UNITED NATIONS. *World Population Trends and Policies, 1987 Monitoring Report.* Population Studies No. 103. New York: United Nations, 1987.

U.S. BUREAU OF JUSTICE STATISTICS. *Report to the Nation on Crime and Justice: The Data.* Washington, D.C.: U.S. Government Printing Office, 1983.

U.S. BUREAU OF JUSTICE STATISTICS. *Crime in the United States: 1987, Uniform Crime Reports for the United States.* Washington, D.C.: U.S. Government Printing Office, 1988a.

U.S. BUREAU OF JUSTICE STATISTICS. *Justice Expenditures and Employment Extracts: 1982 and 1983—Data from the Annual General Finance and Employment Surveys.* Washington, D.C.: U.S. Government Printing Office, 1988b.

U.S. BUREAU OF JUSTICE STATISTICS. *Prisoners in 1987.* Washington, D.C.: U.S. Government Printing Office, 1988c.

U.S. BUREAU OF JUSTICE STATISTICS. *Crime in the United States: 1989, Uniform Crime Reports for the United States.* Washington, D.C.: U.S. Government Printing Office, 1990.

U.S. BUREAU OF THE CENSUS. *Statistical Abstract of the United States, 1985.* Washington, D.C.: U.S. Government Printing Office, 1984.

U.S. BUREAU OF THE CENSUS. *Population, Part 1. U.S. Summary.* Washington, D.C.: U.S. Government Printing Office, 1984.

U.S. BUREAU OF THE CENSUS. "Rural and Urban Farm Population: 1987." *Current Population Reports.* Series P-27, No. 61. Washington, D.C.: U.S. Government Printing Office, 1987.

U.S. BUREAU OF THE CENSUS. "Educational Attainment in the United States: March 1987 and 1986." *Current Population Reports.* Series P-20, No. 428. Washington, D.C.: U.S. Government Printing Office, 1988a.

U.S. BUREAU OF THE CENSUS. "Money Income and Poverty Status in the United States: 1987." *Current Population Reports.* Series P-60, No. 161. Washington, D.C.: U.S. Government Printing Office, 1988b.

U.S. BUREAU OF THE CENSUS. "Poverty in the United States: 1986." *Current Population Reports.* Series P-60, No. 160. Washington, D.C.: U.S. Government Printing Office, 1988c.

U.S. BUREAU OF THE CENSUS. "Projections of the Population of States, by Age, Sex, and Race: 1988 to 2010." *Current Population Reports.* Series P-25, No. 1017. Washington, D.C.: U.S. Government Printing Office, 1988d.

U.S. BUREAU OF THE CENSUS. "School Enrollment—Social and Economic Characteristics of Students: October 1986." *Current Population Reports.* Series P-20, No. 429. Washington, D.C.: U.S. Government Printing Office, 1988e.

U.S. BUREAU OF THE CENSUS. "The Hispanic Population of the United States." *Current Population Reports*. Series P-20, No. 418. Washington, D.C.: U.S. Government Printing Office, 1988f.

U.S. BUREAU OF THE CENSUS. "Voting and Registration in the Election of November 1988." *Current Population Reports*. Series P-20, No. 435. Washington, D.C.: U.S. Government Printing Office, 1989.

U.S. BUREAU OF THE CENSUS. "Household Wealth and Asset Ownership: 1988." *Current Population Reports*. Series P-70, No. 22. Washington, D.C.: U.S. Government Printing Office, 1990a.

U.S. BUREAU OF THE CENSUS. "Money Income and Poverty Status in the United States: 1989." *Current Population Reports*, Series P-60, No. 168. Washington, D.C.: U.S. Government Printing Office, 1990b.

U.S. BUREAU OF THE CENSUS. *Statistical Abstract of the United States, 1990*. Washington, D.C.: U.S. Government Printing Office, 1990c.

U.S. BUREAU OF THE CENSUS. "The Hispanic Population of the United States: 1989." *Current Population Reports*, Series P-20, No. 449. Washington, D.C.: U.S. Government Printing Office, 1990d.

U.S. BUREAU OF THE CENSUS. "Census and You." Census Bureau Press Release. April 1991.

U.S. BUREAU OF THE CENSUS. "Fertility of American Women: June 1990." *Current Population Reports*. Series P-20, No. 454. Washington, D.C.: U.S. Government Printing Office, 1991.

U.S. BUREAU OF THE CENSUS. "Poverty in the United States: 1990." *Current Population Reports*, Series P-160, No. 175. Washington, D.C.: U.S. Government Printing Office, 1991a.

U.S. BUREAU OF THE CENSUS. "Money Income of Households, Families, and Persons in the United States: 1990." *Current Population Reports*, Series P-60, No. 174. Washington, D.C. U.S. Government Printing Office, 1991b.

U.S. CENTERS FOR DISEASE CONTROL. "Premature Mortality by Income Level—Multnomah County, Oregon, 1976–1984." *Morbidity and Mortality Weekly Report* 37(10), 1988.

U.S. CENTERS FOR DISEASE CONTROL. *HIV/AIDS Surveillance Report*, May 1991.

U.S. COMMISSION ON CIVIL RIGHTS. *The Economic Status of Americans of Asian Descent*. Washington, D.C.: U.S. Government Printing Office, 1988.

U.S. COMMISSION ON CIVIL RIGHTS. *Intimidation and Violence: Racial and Religious Bigotry in America*. Washington, D.C.: U.S. Government Printing Office, 1990.

U.S. DEPARTMENT OF AGRICULTURE. *Budget Estimates for the United States Department of Agriculture*. Washington, D.C.: U.S. Government Printing Office, 1986.

U.S. IMMIGRATION AND NATURALIZATION SERVICE. *Statistical Yearbook of the Immigration and Naturalization Service, 1989*. Washington, D.C.: U.S. Government Printing Office, 1990.

U.S. News and World Report. "When Blocks Battle to Stay Lily-White." December 9, 1985.

USEEM, ELIZABETH L. *Low Tech Education in a High Tech World: Corporations and Classrooms in the New Information Society*. New York: The Free Press, 1986.

USEEM, MICHAEL, and KARABEL, JEROME. "Pathways to Top Corporate Management." *American Sociological Review* 51, 1986.

VAN DER TAK, JEAN, HAUB, CARL, and MURPHY, ELAINE. "A New Look at the Population Problem." *The Futurist*, April 1980.

VEBLEN, THORSTEIN. *The Theory of the Leisure Class: An Economic Study of Institutions*. New York: Macmillan, 1899.

VERBRUGGE, LOIS M. "Females and Illness: Recent Trends in Sex Differences in the United States." *Journal of Health and Social Behavior* 17, 1976.

VERBRUGGE, LOIS M. "Gender and Health: An Update on Hypotheses and Evidence." *Journal of Health and Social Behavior* 26, 1985.

VOYDANOFF, PATRICIA. "Work Role Characteristics, Family Structure Demands, and Work/Family Conflict." *Journal of Marriage and the Family* 50, 1988.

WADE, NICHOLAS. *The Nobel Duel*. Garden City, N.Y.: Anchor Books, 1981.

WAITE, LINDA J., HAGGSTROM, GUS W., and KANOUSE, DAVID E. "The Consequences of Parenthood for the Marital Stability of Young Adults." *American Sociological Review* 50, 1985.

WAITZKIN, HOWARD. "Information Giving in Medical Care." *Journal of Health and Social Behavior* 26, 1985.

WALDO, GORDON, and GRISWOLD, DAVID. "Issues in the Measurement of Recidivism." In Lee Sechrest, Susan O. White, and Elizabeth D. Brown (eds.), *The Rehabilitation of Criminal Offenders*. Washington, D.C.: National Academy of Sciences, 1979.

WALDRON, INGRID. "Sex Differences in Illness Incidence, Prognosis and Mortality: Issues and Evidence." *Social Science & Medicine* 17, 1983.

WALLACE, ANTHONY F.C. *Religion: An Anthropological View*. New York: Random House, 1966.

WALLACE, ANTHONY F.C. *The Death and Rebirth of the Seneca*. New York: Vintage/ Random House, 1969.

WALLACE, MICHAEL. "Brave New Workplace: Technology and Work in the New Economy." *Work and Occupations* 16, 1989.

WALLERSTEIN, IMMANUEL. *The Modern World-System*. New York: Academic Press, 1974.

WALLERSTEIN, IMMANUEL. *The Capitalist World Economy*. Cambridge, England: Cambridge University Press, 1979.

WALLERSTEIN, IMMANUEL. *The Modern World-System II: Mercantilism and the Consolidation of the European World-Economy, 1600–1750*. New York: Academic Press, 1980.

WALLERSTEIN, IMMANUEL. *The Modern World-System III: The Second Era of Great Expansion of the Capitalist World-Economy, 1730–1840*. New York: Academic Press, 1988.

WALLERSTEIN, JAMES S., and WYLES, CLEMENT J. "Our Law-Abiding Law-Breakers." *Probation* 25, 1947.

WALLERSTEIN, JUDITH S., and KELLY, JOAN B. "The Effects of Parental Divorce: Experiences of the Preschool Child." *The Journal of the American Academy of Child Psychiatry* 14, 1975.

WALLERSTEIN, JUDITH S., and KELLY, JOAN B. "Effects of Parental Divorce: Experience of Children in Later Latency." *American Journal of Orthopsychiatry* 46, 1976.

WALSH, DIANA CHAPMAN. *Corporate Physicians: Between Medicine and Management*. New Haven: Yale University Press, 1987.

WALTERS, VIVIENNE. "Company Doctors' Perceptions of and Responses to Conflicting Pressures from Labor and Management." *Social Problems* 30, 1982.

WARNER, W. LLOYD, and LUNT, PAUL S. *The Social Life of a Modern Community*. New Haven, Conn.: Yale University Press, 1941.

WASBURN, PHILO C. *Political Sociology: Approaches, Concepts, Hypotheses*. Englewood Cliffs, N.J.: Prentice-Hall, 1982.

WASH, DARREL PATRICK, and BRAND, LESLIE E. "Child Day Care Services: An Industry at a Crossroads." *Monthly Labor Review* 113, 1990.

Washington Post. "Pope Emphasizes Motherhood Role." January 11, 1979.

Washington Post. "More Money for Male Doctors." February 16, 1988a.

Washington Post. "Why Nurses Quit: The Frustration Behind the Shortage." July 12, 1988b.

Washington Post. "Tuesday's Turnout." November 13, 1988c.

Washington Post. "For the Record." June 9, 1988.

WATSON, J. MARK. "Outlaw Motorcyclists: An Outgrowth of Lower Class Cultural Careers." *Deviant Behavior* 2, 1980.

WAX, ROSALIE. *Doing Field Work*. Chicago: University of Chicago Press, 1971.

WEBER, MAX. *From Max Weber: Essays in Sociology*. H.H. Gerth and C. Wright Mills (eds.). New York: Oxford University Press, 1946. Originally published 1918.

WEBER, MAX. *The Methodology of the Social Sciences*. New York: The Free Press, 1949. Originally published 1903–1917.

WEBER, MAX. *The Protestant Ethic and the Spirit of Capitalism* (Talcott Parsons, trans.). New York: Oxford University Press, 1958. Originally published 1904–1905.

WEBER, MAX. *Economy and Society: An Outline of Interpretive Sociology*, 3 vols. Guenther Roth and Claus Wittich (eds.). New York: Bedminster Press, 1968. Originally published 1921.

WEED, FRANK J. "Organizational Mortality in the Anti-Drunk-Driving Movement: Failure Among Local MADD Chapters." *Social Forces* 69, 1991.

WEED, JAMES A. "National Estimates of Marriage Dissolution and Survivorship." *Vital and Health Statistics*, Series 3, No. 19. Washington, D.C.: U.S. Government Printing Office, 1980.

WEGMANN, ROBERT. "Classroom Discipline: An Exercise in the Maintenance of Social Reality." *Sociology of Education* 49, 1976.

WEISMAN, STEVEN R. "Broken Marriage and Brawl Test a Cohesive Caste." *New York Times*, February 21, 1988.

WEISS, ROBERT S. *Marital Separation*. New York: Basic Books, 1975.

WEISS, ROBERT S. *Going It Alone: The Family Life and Social Situation of the Single Parent*. New York: Basic Books, 1979.

WEITZ, ROSE, and SULLIVAN, DEBORAH. "License Lay Midwifery and the Medical Model of Childbirth." *Sociology of Health and Illness* 7, 1985.

WEITZMAN, LENORE J. *Sex Role Socialization: A Focus on Women*. Palo Alto, Calif.: Mayfield, 1979.

WEITZMAN, LENORE J. *The Marriage Contract: Spouses, Lovers and the Law*. New York: The Free Press, 1981.

WEITZMAN, LENORE J. *The Divorce Revolution: The Unexpected Social and Economic Consequences for Women and Children in America*. New York: The Free Press, 1985.

WELLMAN, BARRY. "The Community Question: The Intimate Networks of East Yorkers." *American Journal of Sociology* 84, 1979.

WELTER, BARBARA. "The Cult of True Womanhood: 1820–1860." *American Quarterly*, Summer 1966.

WENGER, DENNIS E., DYKES, JAMES D., SEBOK, THOMAS D., and NEFF, JOAN L. "It's a Matter of Myths: An Empirical Examination of Individual Insight into Disaster Response." *Mass Emergencies* 1, 1975.

WERTZ, DOROTHY C., SORENSON, JAMES R., and HEEREN, TIMOTHY. "Can't Get No (Dis)-Satisfaction." *Work and Occupations* 15, 1988.

WERTZ, RICHARD W., and WERTZ, DOROTHY C. "Notes on the Decline of Midwives and the Rise of Medical Obstetricians." In Peter Conrad and Rochelle Kern (eds.), *The Sociology of Health and Illness: Critical Perspectives 1986*. New York: St. Martin's Press, 1986.

WEST, CANDACE. "Actions Speak Louder Than Words: Communicating Control in a Cross-Sex Conversation." Paper presented at the Annual Meeting of the Southern Sociological Society, New Orleans, 1978.

WEST, CANDACE. "When the Doctor Is a 'Lady': Power, Status, and Gender in Physician–Patient Encounters." *Symbolic Interaction* 7, 1984.

WESTOFF, C.F., and JONES, E.F. "The End of 'Catholic' Fertility." *Demography* 16, 1979.

WESTOFF, CHARLES F. "Fertility in the United States." *Science* 234, 1986.

WHITE, LYNN K., BOOTH, ALAN, and EDWARDS, JOHN. "Children and Marital Happiness: Why the Negative Correlation?" *Journal of Family Issues* 7, 1986.

WHITE, MERRY. *The Japanese Educational Experience: A Commitment to Children*. New York: The Free Press, 1987.

WHYTE, MARTIN KING, and GU, S.Z. "Popular Response to China's Fertility Transition." *Population Development and Review* 13, 1987.

WILCOX, CLYDE. "PACs and Pluralism: Interest Group Formation and Partisanship." *Polity* 21, 1988.

WILDAVSKY, AARON, ed. *The Presidency*. Boston: Little, Brown, 1969.

WILEY, NORBERT. "The Micro-Macro Problem in Social Theory." *Sociological Theory* 6, 1988.

WILLIAM T. GRANT FOUNDATION. *The Forgotten Half: Pathways to Success For America's Youth and Young Families*. Washington, D.C.: The W.T. Grant Commission Office, 1988.

WILLIAMS, LINDA B., and ZIMMER, BASIL G. "The Changing Influence of Religion on U.S. Fertility: Evidence from Rhode Island." *Demography* 27, 1990.

WILLIAMS, ROBIN M., JR. *American Society: A Sociological Interpretation*, 3rd ed. New York: Alfred A. Knopf, 1970.

WILLIAMS, TANNIS M., and BOYES, MICHAEL C. "Television-Viewing Patterns and Use of Other Media." In Tannis M. Williams (ed.), *The Impact of Television: A Natural Experiment in Three Communities*. Orlando, Fla.: Academic Press, 1986.

WILLIAMS, TANNIS M., ed. *The Impact of Television: A Natural Experiment in Three Communities*. Orlando, Fla.: Academic Press, 1986.

WILLIAMS, TERRY. "Exploring the Cocaine Culture." In Carolyn D. Smith and William Kornblum (eds.), *In the Field: Readings on the Field Research Experience*. New York: Praeger, 1989.

WILLIAMS, TERRY, and MAJOR, TED. *The Secret Language of Snow*. New York: Sierra Club/Pantheon Books, 1984.

WILLIAMSON, JEFFREY G., and LINDERT, PETER H. *American Inequality*. New York: Academic Press, 1980.

WILSON, WILLIAM JULIUS. *The Declining Significance of Race*. Chicago: University of Chicago Press, 1978.

WILSON, WILLIAM JULIUS. *The Truly Disadvantaged: The Inner City, the Underclass, and Public Policy*. Chicago: University of Chicago Press, 1987.

WILSON, WILLIAM JULIUS. "The Cost of Racial and Class Exclusion in the Inner City." *Annals of the American Academy of Political and Social Sciences*, 501, 1989a.

WILSON, WILLIAM JULIUS, ed., "The Ghetto Underclass: Social Science Perspectives." *The Annals of the American Academy of Political and Social Science* 501, 1989b.

WILSON, WILLIAM JULIUS. "Studying Inner-City Social Dislocations: The Challenge of Public Agenda Research." *American Sociological Review* 56, 1991.

WOLFE, TOM. "The 'Me' Decade and the Third Great Awakening." *New York*, August 23, 1976.

WOLFF, EDWARD N. "Estimates of Household Wealth Inequality in the United States, 1962–1983." *The Review of Income and Wealth* 33, 1987.

WOLINSKY, FREDRIC D. *The Sociology of Health: Principles, Practitioners, and Issues*, 2d ed. Belmont, Calif.: Wadsworth, 1988.

WOLINSKY, FREDRIC D., MOSELY, RAY R., II, and COE, RODNEY. "A Cohort Analysis of the Use of Health Services by Elderly Americans." *Journal of Health and Social Behavior* 27, 1986.

WOLINSKY, FREDRIC D., and WOLINSKY, SALLY R. "Expecting Sick-Role Legitimation and Getting It." *Journal of Health and Social Behavior* 22, 1981.

WOLPE, PAUL ROOT. "The Maintenance of Professional Authority: Acupuncture and the American Physician." *Social Problems* 32, 1985.

WOMACK, JAMES P., JONES, DANIEL T., and ROOS, DANIEL. *The Machine that Changed the World*. New York: Rawson Associates, 1990.

WOODWARD, BOB. *The Commanders*. New York: Simon and Schuster, 1991.

WORLD BANK. *World Development Report 1984*. New York: Oxford University Press, 1984.

WORLD BANK. *World Development Report 1988*. New York: Oxford University Press, 1988.

WRONG, DENNIS. "The Oversocialized Conception of Man in Modern Sociology." *American Sociological Review* 26, 1961.

WUTHNOW, ROBERT. "Sociology of Religion." In Neil J. Smelser (ed.), *Handbook of Sociology*. Beverly Hills, Calif.: Sage Publications, 1988a.

WUTHNOW, ROBERT. *The Restructuring of American Religion: Society and Faith Since World War II*. Princeton, N.J.: Princeton University Press, 1988b.

WYLE, FREDERICK S. " 'New World Order' is in a Tailspin." *San Francisco Chronicle* 5, February 6, 1991.

WYLIE, C. *Village in the Vaucluse*, 2d ed. Cambridge, Mass.: Harvard University Press, 1961.

XIAOHE, XU, and WHYTE, MARTIN KING. "Love Matches and Arranged Marriages: A Chinese Replication." *Journal of Marriage and the Family* 52, 1990.

YARROW, M.R., CLAUSEN, J.A., and ROBBINS, P.R. "The Social Meaning of Mental Illness." *Journal of Social Issues* 11, 1955.

YENCKEL, JAMES. "Smoke: In the Air and on the Ground." *Washington Post*, June 5, 1988.

YETMAN, NORMAN R. *Majority and Minority: The Dynamics of Race and Ethnicity in American Life*, 4th ed. Boston: Allyn and Bacon, 1985.

YETMAN, NORMAN R. *Majority and Minority: The Dynamics of Race and Ethnicity in American Life*, 5th ed. Boston: Allyn and Bacon, 1991.

YINGER, J. MILTON. "Contraculture and Subculture." *American Sociological Review* 25, 1960.

YOUSSEF, NADIA HAGGAG. *Women and Work in Developing Societies*. Westport, Conn.: Greenwood Press, 1974.

ZELNIK, MELVIN, and SHAH, FARIDA K. "First Intercourse Among Young Americans." *Family Planning Perspectives* 15, 1983.

ZIMDARS-SWARTZ, SANDRA L. "The Virgin Mary: Mother as Intercessor and Savior of Society." In Sharon S. Brehm (ed.), *Seeing Female: Social Roles and Personal Lives*. Westport, Conn.: Greenwood Press, 1988.

ZIMDARS-SWARTZ, SANDRA L. "Popular Devotion to the Virgin: The Marian Phenomena at Melleray, Republic of Ireland." *Archives de Sciences Sociales des Religions*, 1989a.

ZIMDARS-SWARTZ, SANDRA L. "Religious Experience and Public Cult: The Case of Mary Ann Hoof." *Journal of Religion and Health* 28, 1989b.

ZIMDARS-SWARTZ, SANDRA L. *Encountering Mary: From La Salette to Medjugorje*. Princeton: Princeton University Press, 1991a.

ZIMDARS-SWARTZ, SANDRA L. "Visions and Visionary Experience in Religion." *Religion*. 28, 1991b.

ZIMMERMAN, SHIRLEY. "The Welfare State and Family Breakup: The Mythical Connection." *Family Relations* 40, 1991.

ZORZA, VICTOR. "When Brothers Share Wives, Age Counts." *Washington Post*, May 2, 1982.

ZUBOFF, SHOSHANA. *In the Age of the Smart Machine: The Future of Work and Power*. New York: Basic Books, 1988.

ZUCKERMAN, EDWARD. *Almanac of Federal PACs*. Washington, D.C.: Amward Pubs. Inc., 1988.

ZUCKERMAN, LAURENCE. "The Made-for-TV Campaign." *Time*, November 14, 1988.

ZUKIN, SHARON. "Gentrification: Culture and Capital in the Urban Core." *Annual Review of Sociology* 13. Palo Alto, Calif.: Annual Reviews, Inc., 1987.

NAME INDEX

SUBJECT INDEX